THE BLAST

THE BLAST

Alexander Berkman, editor

Introduction by
Barry Pateman

AK
PRESS

EDINBURGH · OAKLAND · WEST VIRGINIA

The Blast
Edited by Alexander Berkman
with introduction by Barry Pateman
ISBN: 1-904859-08-9   ISBN13: 9781904859086
Copyright © 2005 AK Press

AK Press
PO Box 12766
Edinburgh
Scotland EH89YE
www.akuk.com
ak@akedin.demon.co.uk
(0131) 555.5165

AK Press
674A 23rd St.
Oakland, CA 94612
USA
www.akpress.org
akpress@akpress.org
(510) 208.1700

The addresses above would be delighted to provide you (for $1) with the latest complete AK catalog, featuring several thousand books, pamphlets, zines, audio products, video products and stylish apparel published and distributed by AK Press. Alternatively, visit our websites for the complete catalog, latest news and updates, events and secure ordering.

Library of Congress Control Number: 2004110809

Cover design: Jonathan BH Rowland

Layout and Restoration: Jonathan BH Rowland

Printed in Canada

CONTENTS

Introduction

In the late winter and early spring of 1914 waves of militancy surged through the city of New York, as unemployment grew. Clashes between police and demonstrators were brutal, and tension and anger festered on both sides. During that winter Alexander Berkman had been continually working with the unemployed movement in New York, supporting the occupation of churches by groups of the unemployed who demanded that the churches provide food and shelter for the cold and hungry, as well as attempting to bring the various organizations supporting and representing the unemployed together. Eight years out of prison his organizational skills were impressive; his commitment to anarchism as strong as ever and his influence on a new generation of young New York anarchists was present for all to see. Indeed his life had, much to his bemusement one senses, made him almost a mythic figure in the eyes of some.

Then on 20 April 1914 striking miners and family members were machine gunned, burnt and beaten in their tent colonies in Ludlow, Colorado by a detachment of the National Guard. Twenty-two people were killed. The strikers, on strike against the Colorado Fuel and Iron Company (controlled by John D. Rockefeller) won immediate support from militants across America. In New York Berkman announced the formation of the Anti-Militarist League to the press on 23 April. Based at the *Mother Earth* office, the League, with Berkman as its treasurer-secretary, urged "insurrection rather than war," and Berkman promised to raise funds to send "men, arms, and ammunition" to Colorado. The League was, he argued, not only dedicated to the fight against war and militarism, especially the impending threat of war with Mexico, but also to fomenting domestic insurrection.

At this same time, Rockefeller was living, (and seemingly refusing to express any words of regret) in his family's country estate in Tarrytown, 30 miles north of New York. Berkman, the Anti-Militarist League, Italian anarchist groups and other radicals took the fight to Rockefeller. Demonstration after demonstration took place, first outside Standard Oil in New York City, and later outside Rockefeller's residence in Tarrytown. Violence regularly broke out between demonstrators, police and Tarrytown residents — many of whom resented the presence of the demonstrators. The demonstration on 22 June was particularly violent with demonstrators being attacked both by residents and the police.

As demonstrations against Rockefeller continued, a bomb exploded at 1626 Lexington Avenue around 9am on 4 July. Three anarchists, Charles Berg, Arthur

Caron and Carl Hanson died in the blast. Their friend, Marie Chavez, was also killed. The three men had taken part in New York's unemployed movement, in the demonstrations at Tarrytown and were members of the Unemployed section of the IWW. Considerable evidence suggests that Berkman; the dead men and others had planned to plant the bomb near Rockefeller's house. Immediately the dead men were seen as heroes and martyrs. The July 1914 edition of *Mother Earth* carried on its front cover an illustration of a sculpture designed by Adolf Wolff with the names of the dead anarchists prominently displayed. Reports of the speeches at a huge memorial rally for the dead in Union Square filled the magazine. Some explicitly argued for violent reprisal and praised the use of dynamite. Emma Goldman, away on a speaking tour sent a telegram "we honor the memory of our dead comrades, the victims of the capitalist system and the martyrs of labor."

Meanwhile, in May 1914 the Mother Earth Publishing Association had published Voltairine de Cleyre's Selected Works, edited by Berkman, a project he had been working on throughout 1913. The book is a sensitive and telling introduction to de Cleyre's work and evidence of Berkman's understanding of, and respect for, the writer and the nuances of her thoughts and talents. However all this physical and intellectual work on Berkman's part could not hide the tensions that were building up in the community centered around Mother Earth magazine. Begun by Emma Goldman and Max Baginski in March 1906, Berkman had edited the magazine from March 1907. His name appears for the last time as editor in March 1915, although he had left the job some months before that. The causes of his departure appear to be the usual mix of the personal and the political that is such a regular feature of splits in the anarchist movement, although just what happened is still unclear. We do know that Emma Goldman appears to have been manifestly uneasy with the New York activities or at least Berkman's involvement in them. There appears to have been tensions in and around the Mother Earth household at 20 East 125th St where Berkman and others lived. We also know that in a September 1914 letter to Goldman couched in his typical style of cutting honesty and affection for her, he wrote, "Now as to ME — yes dear, we both feel a change must be made... the first thing needed is to get some one else as editor for ME." The two close comrades and friends had moved away from each other.

Publicly no mention of this political and personal split occurred. Instead in the October 1914 *Mother Earth* Berkman jokingly announced that in celebration of his first visit to Pittsburgh (and his attempt to kill Frick) in 1892 and in honor of his fourteen year stay in the Western Penitentiary there as a result of his actions, he planned a celebratory tour that would begin in this, for him, most symbolic of places. "Afterward I shall go further west." The November 1914 *Mother Earth* announced a string of cities where he would be throughout November and

December. His aims during this tour would be to "organize anti-militarist Leagues and to help strengthen and federate existing Anarchist groups." The January 1915 *Mother Earth* featured his first tour report, detailing his arrest in New York on the eve of his departure (after a farewell party there was a skirmish with the police!!) and the eventual commencement of his tour on 10 November. The next travel report ("An Innocent Abroad 2") in February 1915 *Mother Earth* is less upbeat. He finds Kansas City depressing and adds a postscript — a postscript that reflects the constant tension in Berkman during this period of his life. A tension between writing and action as to which was the best form of propaganda. "It is cold and snowing outside, scantily clad, weak figures shuffle past my window. If words could thaw out their frozen misery and send the burning love of their suffering flowing through the heart of a callous world — I would write and write…"

It is hard to determine quite what Berkman intended to do at the end of his tour. One senses it was brought about by a desire to get away rather than to arrive. Everything, though, changed for him in February 1915 with the arrest of the anarchists Mathew Schmidt and David Caplan for involvement in the bombing of the *Los Angeles Times* Building in October 1910. Both men had been living semi-underground since the explosion; Schmidt primarily in New York, Caplan in Bainbridge Island, near Seattle with friends and comrades supporting them. There was a bitter edge to their arrest for Goldman and Berkman. The two men had been betrayed by Donald Vose, who not only had been living in Goldman's house, but more painfully, was the son of anarchist Gertie Vose, a friend of Goldman's since 1899. Schmidt and Caplan were taken back to Los Angeles to stand trial.

Berkman had arrived in California in the spring of 1915 and had spoken both in Los Angeles and in San Francisco. Mathew Schmidt was the first one scheduled for trial and Berkman quickly became involved in his defense campaign. There appears to have been disagreements about how best to defend Schmidt. (Many of these disagreements stemmed from the earlier unsuccessful defense of the McNamera brothers for the bombing which had ended when the brothers surprisingly pleaded guilty, and sections of the labor movement felt betrayed, either for believing that the brothers were innocent, or because their guilty plea had hurt the cause of organized labor throughout the country.) Berkman argued for a nation wide campaign of agitation to save Schmidt and Caplan. After all they were prisoners in the social war. The two men's immediate defense teams appeared to favor a more moderate, legalistic approach. Some type of compromise appears to have been made. Berkman was given a roving brief which, conveniently moved the convicted anarchist and would be assassin away from the legal eye of the storm in Los Angeles. In the August 1915 *Mother Earth*, Berkman wrote, "I have been selected by the Caplan-Schmidt Defense League of Los Angeles to help organize the solidaric forces of all the elements friendly to this fight." Initially Berkman was wary of approaching labor unions. In a 30 June 1915 bulletin of the Caplan-Schmidt Defense League he claimed, "it is up to the true revolutionists to get out of the clutches of the enemy. It will not do to rely too much on trade union assistance. The conservatism of their leaders makes them lukewarm toward men with our ideas." Berkman crossed the country, Denver, Kansas City, Detroit, Pittsburgh, New York — retracing his earlier steps. Both he and Goldman spoke at a large meeting at New York's Harlem Casino on the 16 September 1916. Over this period of time, Berkman also found the militant labor unions, local branches, and local officials that would support the imprisoned men. Labor was awakening and would help energize and increase the social war.

It was from this mixture, then, of militant anarchist activity and labor organization that *The Blast* was born. To Berkman's mind the paper would be a mouthpiece for the "Social rebels" who are "tired of the endless fruitless discussion of theories and philosophies" and the rank of the workers that "chafes at the cushion and antiquated methods" ("An Intimate Word to the Social Rebels of America", *Mother Earth*, December 1915). The paper would close the gap between writing and action. It would, he argues in the same article, "gather together the forces of rebellion throughout the country, give the militant spirit clear expression and help it form itself into action." *The Blast* would be based in San Francisco.

All in all, *The Blast*, ran from 15 January 1916 – June 1917. Initially the paper was a weekly (its headed notepaper announced it was a "Revolutionary Labor Weekly"), it became semi-monthly in March 1916, more erratic from September 1916, moving to New York in May 1917. There were twenty-nine issues in total. It appeared when the war between capital and labor intensified, when the European war was slaughtering hundreds of thousands and preparation for war was sweeping America. Speakers and writers were imprisoned for advocating birth control, free speech was at a premium and a palpable sense of threat, of danger, was in the air. The first issue was put together by Berkman, Margaret Eleanor Fitzgerald ("Fitzie" Berkman's companion who had accompanied him from New York on his various tours) and Eric Morton, a San Francisco anarchist and labor organizer (who in 1899 had attempted to tunnel Berkman out of prison). This premiere issue of 15 January 1916 asserted its Bakunist legacy, "nothing is more important than to destroy. Thus will *The Blast* be destructive, thus will *The Blast* be constructive." A time of change was now possible, social rebels must give blind rebellion, "a spark of hope," a "light of vision." With Robert Minor's cover illustration of the fat capitalist gloating on the scales, balanced by the dead bodies of workers, this opening statement set the tone for the paper. It would be fierce, uncompromising and implacably at odds with capitalism in all its shades and structures. There could never be any compromise. Its title was deliberate.

There is, then, a sense of expectancy, of tension that runs through the paper. Partly because it reflected the many tensions in San Francisco (for Berkman centered around labor and capital) and partly because of Berkman and the editorial team's sense that some type of upheaval, some type of change was imminently possible. Yes there were defeats — Schmidt was sentenced to life imprisonment on 12 January 1916 — but some type of victory, some type of social change was tantalizingly near. Topics running through *The Blast* included Ireland, Mexico and the anarchist PLM, Birth Control, the situation in Russia, Indian Nationalism, Caplan and Schmidt, various labor disputes and the Anti-War movement (Berkman, Goldman and other American anarchists had signed the International Anarchist Manifesto On the War in 1915). The attempts of the Preparedness Movement (especially cultivated in the Hearst press and adopted enthusiastically by San Francisco's anti-union Chamber of Commerce) to improve the nation's defenses were a particular target of the papers wrath.

Contributors to the paper included Margaret Sanger, Charles Erskine Scott Wood, Sara Bard Field, Tom Mooney, and interesting reprints from Tolstoy, Josiah Warren and Nietzsche. Articles tended to be less reflective; it was after all an agitational paper. Those that were, Wood's early work on labor for instance, were very much grounded in experience. Running through each issue was a conscious note of defiance that became an in your face aggression often introduced by the viciously satirical cartoons that were on the front cover of most issues (many by Robert Minor) and continued by many of the articles that Berkman, especially, wrote. Attempts to censor the paper by halting its distribution in the mails were mocked and challenged. "We hereby declare our independence of the Autocrat of the Post Office and of his governmental and plutocratic chiefs...We defy them to do their worst" ("To Hell With Government", 1 May 1916). There is a sense in the paper that it has had enough of these old tired and corrupt values and will ignore them. *Anarchism has its own ideals and we will live by them* is the message clearly signaled in each issue. Goldman and Berkman had read Nietzsche avidly and he was a real presence here. Not just in the raffle of a set of his works to make money for the paper but also in its note of angry defiance and its willingness to challenge all values and what they represented.

This is not really the occasion to go over all the complexities, confusion, horror and nuances around the San Francisco Preparedness Day explosion. To summarize and explain the conflict between labor and capital in San Francisco, its history and personalities would take too long. All we can do is to present it from the perspective of those around *The Blast*. We do know that on the evening of 19 July, Warren Billings and Tom Mooney met at the office of the paper, allegedly to discuss a $5,000 bribe offered to Billings by corporate detective Martin Swanson to implicate Mooney in explosions carried out against United Railroads. Anti-Preparedness rallies and meetings took place the week before the Preparedness Day march and, as luck would have it, Emma Goldman was speaking in the city also, using her visit as an opportunity to build bridges with Berkman. The Parade took place on Saturday 22 July. As it wound down Market Street a bomb exploded on Steuart St., near its intersection with Market. Eight people died immediately and two more died during the subsequent months. Forty more were injured. By 1 August five people had been arrested and charged with murder—Tom and Rena Mooney, Warren Billings, Ed Nolan and Israel Weinberg. All were well-known labor supporters and radicals. The offices of *The Blast* were raided on 29th July without a search warrant. No evidence was collected, no arrests were made.

Reading the mainstream papers of the time gives us some clue to the anger, revulsion and fear that swept over the city. The defendants were presumed to be guilty and were abandoned by many of their former friends and acquaintances. Many simply lay low and said nothing. How remarkable then that in this atmosphere of fear and intimidation the 1 September issue of *The Blast* pledged unconditional support for the defendants, and linked their plight to the ongoing struggle of labor against capital. It requested that all money for their defense be sent to the newly organized International Workers Defense League in care of Robert Minor, secretary-treasurer. From this small beginning Berkman put all of his energies into their defense. Billings was sentenced to life imprisonment on 7 October, but by early November Berkman was in New York drumming up union support and talking to the large United Hebrew Trades. They pledged assistance. He spread the word wherever he went, argued, persuaded and cajoled union after union to support the men. He secured a good and thorough lawyer in W. Bourke Cockran to defend Mooney. On 31 December 1916 *The Blast* was raided again. Subscription lists and correspondence were taken. Still the paper came out; still it rallied around the prisoners, arguing their case, bringing those initially intimidated back into the fold.

By May of 1917, after appearing rather sporadically, *The Blast* had moved to New York. Its 1 May 1917 issue argued that although Billings and Mooney were imprisoned, other papers such as the San Francisco *Bulletin* were exposing the conspiracy against the men. "*The Blast* reserves for itself the right of being where there is the greatest need and the greatest danger. Therefore we came to New York to devote most of our time and energy to anti-militarist work." Only two issues were printed in New York. On 7 June *The Blast* was excluded from the mails. On 15 June Emma Goldman and Alexander Berkman were arrested, he in *The Blast's* office above the office of *Mother Earth*, she in the *Mother Earth* office, both hard at work. Both of them had fought vociferously against conscription and, with Fitzie and others, had helped form the No Conscription League. Both were charged with conspiracy to induce persons to refuse to register under the Draft Act (Selective Service Act). Found guilty on 9 July 1917 they were both sentenced to two years imprisonment and a fine. They began serving their sentences on 2 February 1918.

The publishers of this facsimile edition are to be congratulated on their efforts. If for nothing else they are giving us a chance to see what Berkman and others said, rather than what people tell us they said. All too often the history of anarchism has been based on clever interpretation rather than actual reality. It's a wonderful pleasure to have primary sources like this accessible. The paper shows us the power of visual imagery. It reminds us that agitational papers can have depth and ironic, wry humor. *The Blast* though refuses to preach to the converted. It tries to go beyond its natural community of social rebels and reach out in a clear, straightforward way to the unpolitical, the non-militant. Its use of clear and straightforward language, its consistency of tone are clear indications of that strategy. This is not a paper that rails angrily against the world like steam coming out of a safety valve. It's a paper that is angry and determined and urges its readers to think, and then fight back. For Berkman every day is an insurrection against the prevailing culture of capitalism. Fight back when you can and where you can. Never give up.

The publication of *The Blast* was in Berkman's eyes, the continuation of an intensified battle with the state. It reflected social war. A social war for Berkman, that temporarily ended only with Caplan and Schmidt, Tom Mooney and Warren Billings, and thousands of others languishing in American prisons. And for Emma Goldman and himself sailing out of New York harbor on the SS Buford during that cold, cold early morning on 21 December 1919 towards the Bolshevik Revolution and a life of permanent exile.

Barry Pateman

VOL. I　　　SAN FRANCISCO, SATURDAY, JANUARY 15, 1916　　　**No. 1**

THE GOLDEN RULE

THE GOLDEN RULE

Eric the Red

The Golden Rule has lived too long,
  A myth from days of old,
It tied the hands that, grim and strong,
  Might stay the rule of Gold.
Let now the shackles of the past
Be shatter'd by a Blast.

The Rule of Gold—and Steel as well—
  With aid of cant and creed,
Has made fair Earth a living Hell
  Where only thieves succeed.
The Golden Rule—Christ stands aghast—
  A leaf before the Blast.

While Labor bleeds, hyenas laugh;
  It thrills their putrid blood;
They dance around their golden calf,
  At peace with self and God.
But he laughs best who laugheth last:
Beware the final Blast!

✤ ✤ ✤

WHY THE BLAST?

DO you mean to destroy?

Do you mean to build?

These are the questions we have been asked from many quarters, by inquirers sympathetic and otherwise.

Our reply is frank and bold:

We mean both: to destroy *and* to build.

For, socially speaking, Destruction is the beginning of Construction.

Superficial minds speak sneeringly of destruction. O, it is easy to destroy—they say—but to build. to build, that's the important work

It's nonsense. No structure, social or otherwise, can endure if built on a foundation of lies.

Before the garden can bloom, the weeds must be uprooted. Nothing is therefore more important than to destroy. Nothing more necessary and difficult.

Take a man with an open mind, and you will have no great trouble in convincing him of the falsehood and rottenness of our social structure.

But when one is filled with superstition and prejudice, your strongest arguments will knock in vain against the barred doors of his bigotry and ignorance. For thousand-year-old superstition and tradition is stronger than truth and logic.

To destroy the Old and the False is the most vital work. We emphasize it: to blast the bulwarks of slavery and oppression is of primal necessity. It is the beginning of really lasting construction.

Thus will THE BLAST be destructive.

And THE BLAST will be constructive.

Too long have we been patient under the whip of brutality and degradation. Too long have we conformed to the Dominant, with an ineffective fist hidden in our pocket. Too long have we vented our depth of misery by endless discussion of the distant future. Too long have we been exhausting our efforts and energy by splitting hairs with each other.

It's time to act.

The time is NOW.

The breath of discontent is heavy upon this wide land. It permeates mill and mine, field and factory. Blind rebellion stalks upon highway and byway. To fire it with the spark of Hope, to kindle it with the light of Vision, and turn pale discontent into conscious social action—that is the crying problem of the hour. It is the great work calling to be done.

To work, then, and blasted be every obstacle in the way of the Regeneration.

A LESSON FROM THE WORLD WAR

Warren Van Valkenburgh

THE position of the holy men of Europe is not an enviable one these days. Between their allegiance to the Omnipotent and their allegiance to the rulers of the particular countries that they happen to abide in, the slumbers of these men of faith and learning must be anything but sound.

The King of the Vatican is in a particularly sorry plight. Since the loss of the Papal States in '70, the Pontifical throne has been gradually tottering. Now that Italy has joined the Allies and is fighting against Austria, the Pope is placed in the position of having "to whip the Devil around the stump." He must handle Italy with tenderness, even though the interests of the Catholic Church would be greatly jeopardized should the Central Powers be crushed. Italy cannot much longer remain the home of Peter's Rock. Gradually, but surely, the favor of the Vatican has been growing less and less in Unified Italy; and war or no war, the time is not far distant when a new home will have to be found for this remnant of the Inquisition. The one last place under the sun where the rule of the priest will be absolute and profitable is with the Hapsburgs. Some day in the early future the Pope and his minions will wearily wend their way to the Austrian graveyard.

Should Austria by any chance be bartered away by the Kaiser, or conquered and divided by the Allies, that day would be a sorry one for the Church of Rome. It is really a delicate position. If Austria loses, the House of Hapsburg will see the end of its bloody reign. If Italy loses, woe betide the fate of the Vice-Regent's headquarters. None but clever politicians could successfully weather such exasperating circumstances as those now being faced by the Mother Church of Christendom.

German Catholics curse the ground of Atheistic France. British Protestants behold the Kaiser as the Devil incarnate; while to the German Lutherans he is a wingless angel. The Catholic element of England professes outraged anguish at the sacking of Belgium, blind to the record of its own British lust that for over seven hundred years has dyed the soil of Ireland crimson with its native blood. The wisdom of the Pope in closing his eyes to the wanton massacres of Christian by the Turks now taking place, is comparable only to the unoffending attitude assumed by that gentleman at Belgium's ruin at the beginning of the war. Possibly the angelic history of Leopold's Catholic soldiers in the Congo was on his mind; more likely, though, the reason for the sycophantic position of the Catholic Church, through its supreme head, has to do with the future welfare of that God Trust, instead of with any consideration for its dupes who are now engaged in blowing one another into Mary's bosom under the various flags.

The Catholic Church has nothing in common with humanity; nor does any sensible person argue that it has.

After all is said and done, there is no use giving up one's flat till another one has been rented. The temporal end of the Vatican is taken care of by the Pope. The spiritual is left to the flock. However they dispose of it, matters not. It never *was* carried as an asset on the Papal balance sheet.

The Turk alone has reason to rejoice in the present carnage. He can get even with the Christian. All the other nations at war are calling on the self-same God to help their particular side win; but what benefits they will derive is not apparent. Obviously this God must be a Demon or a Fool. If he heeds the Germans, he is deaf to the British. If he listens to the prayers of the Moujik, where will the Turks come in at the finish? However is a real live God going to make so many different decisions satisfactorily?

Even the Pope, who is supposed to be on better terms with Jehovah than all the other inhabitants of the world, does not care to take a definite stand.

This great conflict would really be worth while if it were assured that despotism in every form should perish. But it won't. The Catholic and Protestant rulers will take care that their harvest of victims, stolen as they are from the cradle, shall not wane. The State will permit of any degree of moral elasticity—from polygamy to promiscuity—until a new crop of kids will have grown; and the churches of all denominations will graciously fall in line and sanctify the decision of the governments that make it.

There is one worse evil than the theological evil, and that is the patriotic evil. The Catholic Church is a big obstacle in progress' path, but her power is dwindling down. The institution of the soldier is a greater evil than all the mental chains that now exist, because the Church no longer wields the power of long ago, while the State does and it uses the soldier as an implement.

It is to be hoped that the war will not only tear the foundation from under the institutions of organized superstition of every denomination, but that it will teach the survivors of this frightful butchery that all tyranny rests finally upon force; moreover, that inasmuch as they, themselves, are the persons who really possess it, the retention of it from those who use it for their own ends would simply mean that the world will be theirs for the taking.

(By Wire)

BIRTHDAY greetings! Let THE BLAST re-echo from coast to coast, inspiring strength and courage in the disinherited, and striking terror into the hearts of the craven enemy, now that one more of our brothers has fallen a victim to the insatiable Moloch.

May THE BLAST tear up the solidified ignorance and cruelty of our social structure. Blast away! To the daring belongs the future.   —Emma Goldman.

THE BLAST

Revolutionary Labor Weekly
569 Dolores St., San Francisco, Cal.
Mail Address, Box 661   Phone, Park 499

Alexander Berkman, Editor and Publisher
E. B. Morton, Associate Editor   **M. E. Fitzgerald,** Manager

SUBSCRIPTION
$1.00 Yearly   60c Six Months   5c Copy
Bundle rates, 2½c per copy in bundles of ten.
Advertising rates on application.
Application for entry as second-class matter at the postoffice at
San Francisco pending.

COMMENTS

The Greatest Lie

MANY are the lies that pass for truths. But the greatest and most pernicious of them all is the cunning insistence on "harmony between capital and labor."

It is the "harmony" of inevitable, eternal discord, the symphony of master and slave, the love of the jackal for its prey. On this harmony capital battens, while labor grows anemic, in body and spirit.

* * *

The Greatest Truth

ALL the big volumes of accepted political economy have served only to obscure this the greatest of all truths:

All wealth is the result of human effort applied to natural resources.

In other words, labor is the sole producer of all wealth. It therefore logically follows that the creators of the wealth are the rightful owners of it.

They are. But the real owners are not in possession. Why not? Think it over.

* * *

The Great Problem

THE above problem is supposed to be the most perplexing problem of the world. It is hard to tell why. It can easily be solved by the most primitive intelligence.

If you cannot solve it, it is because you have studied political economy or heard somebody talk learnedly about it.

Thousands of volumes have been written to *explain away* the fact that if you are robbed you are robbed.

But the fact remains.

* * *

The Remedy

WHAT are you going to do about it?

THE BLAST will try honestly and fearlessly to point the way.

* * *

Our Platform

THAT is our platform. If you are interested, help along. There is no money back of this paper. There is only HOPE and DARING. We count on *you*, on you who read and understand these simple words.

Don't Be a Hypocrite, U. S.

IF Jack and Jim are shooting at each other, and you are supplying the ammunition, you are guilty of murder if any one is killed.

That's your own legal code.

Don't shed crocodile tears over the widows and orphans you are helping to make. It's disgusting hypocrisy to pass around the hat to buy bandages for the victims of your own murderous greed.

* * *

The Mathew A. Schmidt Case

THERE is too much beating about the bush in cases of this kind. We will be frank, no matter whom it hurts.

A terrible mess has been made of the Schmidt case. "Mat" and his chief advisers have absolutely failed to realize that his trial was but an incident in the great warfare of capital against labor: one chapter in the drama of the Merchants' & Manufacturers' Association's fight against militant unionism.

Would you stake your life when playing with a crooked gambler whose dice you know to be loaded?

The dice of the law are always loaded against the militant worker picked out for the masters' revenge.

This being the situation, Schmidt was convicted even before he entered the court room. For legal Justice is the eager bedpan bearer to King Mammon.

The question of technical guilt or innocence in such cases becomes a detail of no particular significance. Witness Patrick Quinlan, who was active in the Paterson Silk Weavers' strike, innocently serving seven years in the penitentiary. Witness also, on the other hand, the legally "guilty" labor men torn free from the clutches of the money beast.

The masters dare only what their slaves permit.

The Schmidt trial was conducted like an ordinary murder case. Attorney N. Coghlan, in charge of the defense, repeatedly emphasized that it was no labor trial.

With the inevitable tragic result.

How long is this to go on? How long are the militant workers of this country going to permit their best men to be thus sacrificed to the harlot of legality?

Joe Hill, a corpse; Ford and Suhr, Rangel and Cline, the McNamara Brothers and numerous other rebel workers rotting in the prisons. Now Schmidt joins them. Caplan is to come next, and then another and another—and it will never end till labor faces the situation boldly and throws its defi to the law-and-order cannibals:

To hell with the rules of *your* game! We'll play it our own way.

* * *

Judas Made Respectable   ... ...

JUDAS Iscariot delivered the Nazarene agitator into the hands of the Roman District Attorney. This base betrayal incensed the people against the mercenary stool-pigeon. Judas had enough decency to go and hang himself.

Has Donald Vose Meserve as much decency as Judas Iscariot? He seems to feel quite at home in the City of Otis, and as respected as the Judge, District Attorney and Wm. Burns.

* * *

State Ethics

WHEN an individual "prepares" to resist aggression by toting a gun, the State imprisons him on the theory that his preparedness might lead to aggression.

If the State possessed sincerity or brains, instead of mere brute force, it would apply the theory to itself.

* * *

The Worm Turns

GRIMY with toil and smoke, hollow cheeked and misery laden, they crawl from their dark hovels and holes. Their cries of rage and bitterness split the air. Terror stricken is the smug philistine.

Madly the gaunt figures tear through the streets, venting their fury with voice and deed. Fine silks and satins, diamonds and cut glass are torn and broken by the very hands that made them.

For the first time in their dull existence they feel the strength of a great passion, and lo! the beauty and power of Daring: the crawling slave is transformed into the Samson of the Temple.

It is Youngstown, Ohio.

FROM THE EARTH, A CRY

EMPERORS, stand to the bar! Chancellors, halt at the barracks!
Landlords and Lawlords and Tradelords, the spectres you conjured have risen—
Communists, Socialists, Nihilists, Rent-rebels, Strikers, behold!
They are the fruit of the seed you have sown—God has prospered your planting. They come
From the earth, like the army of death. You have sowed the teeth of the dragon!
Hark to the bay of the leader! You shall hear the roar of the pack
As sure as the stream goes seaward. The crust on the crater beneath you
Shall crack and crumble and sink, with your laws and rules
That breed the million to toil for the luxury of the ten—
That grind the rent from the tiller's blood for drones to spend—
That hold the teeming planet as a garden plot for a thousand—
That draw the crowds to the cities from the healthful fields and woods—
That copulate with greed and beget disease and crime.
                                        —John Boyle O'Reilly.

PREPAREDNESS
R. E. Bell

WITH subtle cunning this word is being dinned into the ears of the American worker.

Prepare to spend millions upon millions for machines and equipment to facilitate the murder of human beings!

Prepare to kill peaceful fellow workingmen from some other country who would never think of going to war, were they not—like ourselves—victims of the superstition that there is something sacred in the commands of rulers or governments.

No people in history has ever voted for war, though nations have often voted to pay for the blunders of rulers.

Still, it is not unthinkable that a people might vote so, considering that the means of education are in the hands of those who profit by war.

Every newspaper controlled by Big Business and opposed to Labor is in favor of a large Army and Navy. You will find nearly all of these papers opposed to the income tax, to the inheritance tax, to taxation of automobile oil, to the Seamen's Act, opposed to special taxes on war profits, opposed with might and main even to government manufacture of its own supplies. In short, they want the government to spend money without stint, but let the poor pay and they get the profit.

Preparedness? Yes, they were well prepared in Europe. All of them. And what have they got? The satisfaction that through thorough preparation they have succeeded in making more widows, more orphans, and spread more human corpses to manure the untilled fields than their most brutal and savage ancestors ever dreamed of.

Defend your home! Very well—but first let us get one. Let the Landlord and the Real Estate sharks defend their property. We need not go to foreign countries to grab homes from poor devils there, who at best possess very little There are plenty of homes here: but those who built them may not use them. In every city-block there are dozens of "For Rent" signs, and homeless people galore.

Prepare, you disinherited, to take possession of the homes right before your nose, and then defend them against any man who demands that you pay him tribute. The worker's enemy is not some one in a foreign land. It is the parasite upon his back right here at home.

Prepare not by making instruments to kill, but by refusing to make them.

Build no battleship, make neither gun nor bayonet; let the grass grow over the fortress, and let the General go to work. Turn no night-stick for the policeman, but give him a guide book instead. Tether the man-eating district attorneys with the cows in a peaceful pasture.

When that is done, open the jails; for then there will be no criminals, except perhaps a few harmless kings to be treated in an asylum.

THE ERECTORS' ASSOCIATION versus MATHEW A. SCHMIDT

IN the year 1906 the Erectors' Association, a subsidiary of the Steel Trust, passed a resolution at the behest of John Pierpont Morgan, forbidding any of its members to deal with organized labor. The penalty for non-compliance meant that to such a firm the Steel Trust refused to furnish steel.

Thus the gauntlet was thrown down and war declared upon the last remaining union in the steel industry.

To surrender meant less pay and longer hours for the workers; a lower standard of living; more deprivation of necessities; less opportunities for their children.

Poverty upsets the common rule of mathematics: the more people poverty is divided up among, the larger share each individual gets.

The human animal, like all others, will fight for its food.

In the grim struggle for existence the recently acquired "morality" of the human species goes for naught, be it in the trenches of Europe, or on the industrial battlefield of America. The Bridge and Structural Ironworkers' International organized a campaign of resistance.

Aside from the fact that they have maintained their organization and actually improved their condition, the direct testimony rendered by a flock of scab contractors in the recent trial of Mathew A. Schmidt, charged with having aided and abetted J. B. McNamara, is eloquent proof of the terrible efficiency of the Ironworkers' campaign.

As to the l-e-g-a-l guilt of Mathew A. Schmidt, THE BLAST considers it of no consequence, except as it affects Schmidt individually, his family and his friends.

Were he as innocent as driven snow, the fact that he was of, for and with aggressive militant labor, would be sufficient to convict him in Los Angeles before a jury of petrified scissor-bills with barely sufficient intellect to distinguish between a reasonable doubt and two dollars a day.

The one and only hope of penetrating the dense fog of village morality, which hangs like a pall over "the scabbiest town on earth," was by labor showing its teeth, ignoring the stupid rules of court procedure, and the thousand and one trivial objections of lawyers who seemed to be afraid that a ray of real information concerning labor should reach the jury.

Be it said to the everlasting credit of the late Judge Charles Fairall, then chief counsel for the defense, that he saw that the human rather than the legal side was of paramount importance, in a case where classes clash.

Though himself a law-sharp, through his association with men like Lincoln Steffens, Clarence Darrow and Fremont Older, he had reached the conclusion that, in cases of this kind, the creation of a sympathetic understanding in the minds of a jury of labor's struggles, trials and temptations, was worth volumes of legal arguments.

Mr. Fairall's sudden and mysterious death as a sad blow to the defense.

Through the influence of the conservative labor element, a conservative lawyer was engaged. Fairall's successor as chief counsel, Nathaniel Coghlan, is considered an excellent lawyer (whatever that means); but being an aristocrat by birth, training and association, he could not see that this was a LABOR case, and so declared. To him it was an ordinary murder case,—a mere incident in his legal career.

So when in his address to the jury he wound up his speech with remarks to the effect that he was as firmly convinced that they had the wrong man as he was convinced of the efficacy of prayer; aye, as sure of it as he was that the atheists had not as yet driven God out of Heaven, every juryman knew he was bluffing.

No lawyer believes in the efficacy of prayer. If he did, he would not study law but prayer books.

And as for atheists driving God out of Heaven, the old doggerel: "A mother was chasing her boy 'round the room, and while she was chasing her boy 'round the room, she was chasing her boy 'round the room" might have been quoted with as much aptitude.

God and the atheists are old-time sparring partners, giving weekly exhibitions before churches and liberal clubs.

But however sad the outcome, due credit must be given to Mr. Coghlan and his associates for bringing out a matter of paramount interest to labor: The bomb found at Zeehandelaar's house had been analyzed by the city chemist, Mr. Miller, who found it contained vaseline, sawdust and sodium nitrate. There was not an explosive element in it.

This fact was reported to the District Attorney. Yet that noble champion of the people, elected as a "friend of labor," carefully suppressed it in order to facilitate the hanging of labor men.

To further grease the skids under the judicial juggernaut, a training school for witnesses was very successfully conducted by a former lieutenant of the immaculate Mr. Burns.

There is, of course, no such thing as justice where all the money and machinery of law is on one side.

The prosecution had witnesses gathered from Japan to Canada, a squealer at $6.00 per day and free rent from Honduras, a stoolpigeon graduate of Mr. Burns' seminary for liars and a candidate for the fat rewards, ever written large across the heavenly firmament of the Judas Iscariots.

Questions and answers were carefully prepared and typewritten, so that witnesses might take them home for study. Every step of the prosecution showed the eagerness to win rather than a desire for justice.

Justice for labor begins where capitalism ends.

Who was indicted for the murder of working men, women and children at Ludlow?

Not one.

NOT GUILTY
Margaret H. Sanger

THERE seems to be considerable misapprehension among those who are interested in my coming trial. Many are under the impression that the indictments pending are for circulation of forbidden information. This, of course, is not true. I have been indicted under Section 211 of the Federal criminal code, for alleged obscenity. They were issued against me as editor and publisher of *The Woman Rebel*. My "crime" consists not in giving the information, but solely in the advocacy of birth control. There are three indictments, based on twelve articles, eleven of which are for *printing the words* "prevention of conception." To the elect of federal officialdom these words themselves are considered lewd, lascivious and obscene. In none of these articles is any information given,—simply discussions of the subject addressed to working women of this country.

Many "radical" advisers have assured me that the wisest course for me to follow in fighting the case would be to plead "guilty" to this "obscenity," and to throw myself upon the mercy of the court, which would mean, according to those familiar with the administration of "justice," a light sentence or a small fine.

It is unfortunate that so many radicals and so-called revolutionists have failed to understand that my object in this work has been to remove, or to try to remove, the term "prevention of conception" from this section of the penal code, where it has been labelled by our wise legislators as "filthy, vile and obscene," and to obtain deserved currency for this valuable idea and practice.

The problem of staying out of jail or getting put into jail is merely incidental in this fight. It is discouraging to find that advanced revolutionists of this country are frantically trying to save agitators from jail sentences and thereby losing sight of the real and crucial issues of the fights. If we could depend upon a strong and consistently revolutionary support in such battles, instead of weakened efforts to effect a compromise with the courts, there would be much greater stimulation for individuals to enter revolutionary activity.

To evade the issue in this case, as I have been advised to do upon the assumption that to keep out of prison were the sole aim and object of my birth control propaganda, would mean to leave matters as they have been since 1872. But it is time for the people of this country to find out if the United States mails are to be available for their use, as they in their adult intelligence desire, or if it is possible for the United States Postoffice to constitute itself an institution for the promulgation of stupidity and ignorance, instead of a mechanical convenience.

The first step in the birth control movement or any other propaganda requiring a free press, is to open the mails to the people of this country, *regardless of class*. Nothing can be accomplished without the free and open discussion of the subject.

These indictments have had the effect of opening the discussion of birth control in magazines and papers of the most conservative nature, whose editors would have been horrified at the subject—previous to my arrest.

When my case is called in the federal courts, probably next month, I shall enter a plea of "not guilty," in order to separate the idea of prevention of conception and birth control from the sphere of pornography, from the gutter of slime and filth where the lily-livered legislators have placed it under the direction of the late unlamented Anthony Comstock, and in which the forces of reaction are still attempting to hold it.

⚓ ⚓ ⚓

THE HUMAN MASS
Luke North

HENRY FORD'S discovery that the people themselves are to blame for the war in Europe instead of the munition manufacturers—if he is correctly reported in the daily press—is not very startling, or important, or true. Did he think the manufacturers were doing the fighting themselves? Most of us have known all along that the European shambles were being operated by just plain, common people, the workingmen, the masses; they always are. They go to the slaughter with a relish, unquestionably; they could not, en masse, be driven there—though some of them are.

But why do they go to war with a relish? Why do they go out and murder each other, in battalions—and at whose instigation? Maybe Mr. Ford is a good Christian and will answer, "Free Will—Original Sin"—and that will close the discussion, of course.

It is an easy and comforting thing for the tired business man to say, "O, the people themselves are to blame." It leaves more time for the enticements of whist or golf or philanthropy. And sometimes it is said by the weary or disheartened radical—for whose inspiritment these elementary considerations are offered:

People influence each other, consciously and unconsciously. The stronger influence the weaker, and the weaker the still weaker, while negatively even the weak influence the strong. Everybody is influenced all the time more or less, by every person and thing he contacts. The human mass is impressionable. It is instigated, influenced, to move this way or that way, do this or the other—not by blind circumstances, but by the conscious, purposeful united effort of human intelligences.

It is influenced toward war and slavery by the concepts of Christian theology. It is instigated to war and exploitation by the daily press which, in turn, is instigated by a bare ten thousand human intelligences strong of purpose, absolutely united therein, and animated by a monstrous, inhuman Greed.

The human mass is not inherently evil—it is only malleable, responsive to the strongest influence cast upon it. The actual number of those who are now designedly influencing it, is very small—but they are united, not as to details, but in purpose.

The human mass could be molded to its own unfoldment—swiftly, directly—were the influence of a united radicalism cast upon it. United not in details or doctrine, but upon a single line of concrete action. Can you doubt it?

PITTSBURGH
Jacob Margolis

AGAIN we are on the industrial map. Once more have we achieved the distinction of the workshop of the world. Unprecedented tonnage, enormous pay-rolls, universal employment, much business, sublime prosperity. Upon whom have the blessings of war been showered in such unstinted profusion? Twice blessed are we, and, in the spirit of the Yuletide, we give prayer and thanks for this our prosperity and plentiful work.

At last are the workers happy, for their hopes and aspirations have been answered. There is full time, and even that greater joy—overtime. Can you, in the darkest crannies of your memory, recall a worker who did not, upon meeting his fellow worker, ask him the all-absorbing and vital question, "Are you working?" Certainly have they transvalued all life in terms of work, and think of the joy that prevails when the chief hope in life, when the consummation of all desires is achieved, when all have work, gobs of work, much work, hard work, soul-destroying work, dirty work, killing work, in such abundance.

When the virtuous and righteous Allies chose America as the place to purchase all munitions of war, did they realize what happiness they were conferring upon the workers of Pittsburgh? What of those killed by the shells and guns and cannon made here? What if the flower of the manhood of France, Germany, England and Russia are being torn up and thrown to the winds? What of it all? We have work—intoxicating work.

Everybody is too busy working and reaping the whirlwind of prosperity to think of anything else. Ah, have you seen the monkey-wrench machinist, that artist of the lathe, in all his greasy, grimy glory, with that heroic gleam in his eye, as he wipes away the sweat with waste in one hand and an oil can in the other? He has worked a thirteen-hour night turn and has made $3.00. He has worked on shells; six-inch shells, eight-inch shells, ten-inch shells, and even larger ones, and he knows the joy of work well done. In their work-madness they are as men who have been starved and are suddenly confronted with quantities of delicious food. They gorge themselves and hoard what they cannot consume. They will take it with them and gloat over it, conceal it, bury it, but the experience has been too profound for reasonable action.

A thousand stacks vomiting fire and smoke, the hiss of molten metal, the whirr of the machines, the shriek of the locomotive, the bustle of the store, and above all, the shrill, penetrating whistle of the factory; all spell work, glorious work, joyous work, plentiful work; the music of the spheres, the symphony of joy, the choir celestial are all bound up in these joyous sounds.

I know not whether I like the worker gorged with work or the unemployed. In either case he is beastialized. How hideous is our system of exploitation and starvation, oscillating between no work and overwork, cowardice and swinishness! Man's madness to make a living has deprived him of the knowledge of life, and when he has already made a living, does he stop with one living and live? Not he. Rather make a hundred livings than live one life.

Sporadic outbreaks here and there; a moulders' strike for eight hours; incipient strikes at Westinghouse in several departments; a strike at the Pittsburgh Machine Tool Company; another at the MacClintock-Hemphill Company; some few have quietly and soberly asked for eight hours, but the demand is not at all insistent. More money and much work are the cries, and swinish capital grants both without a struggle, for cannot they well afford it? DEATH PAYS WELL.

The madness of prosperity and work is upon us, and until that passes away we are closed to all reason and life. The dominant note is work! work!! WORK!!! The workers, too, will be surfeited with it, and then perhaps some action, some struggle, some life.

❦ ❦ ❦

THE HOLY CITY
Birt Ely

THE main industry of Los Angeles, next to the gentle art of inducing tourists to support a large but hungry real estate population by investing in climate, is the manufacture of movies.

But the motion picture producers have failed to appreciate the utopian dream of General Hungry Growl Otis of doing business entirely without labor. Conducting a national and international business, with the bulk of the film patronage coming from the working class, the managers have realized that a truce with labor redounds to the benefit of their exchequer.

Hence the one oasis in the trade union desert of Los Angeles is the motion picture plant. They employ union labor, and thereby violate the particular ethics prevailing in Los Angeles. These erring sinners must be reformed, and naturally it is the preachers that are sicked on to them. They are guaranteed to suffocate anything that gives the least sign of real life. On the plea, therefore, that immorality exists among the movie actors and actorinos, the Moral Efficiency Squad of Los Angeles got busy.

But they struck a snag. Instead of the general fumigation expected, the managers got sore. They are threatening to move to sinful San Francisco, where a union card and the joy of sex may be acknowledged without social ostracism. And lo and behold! Already there are signs of the purity squad backing down.

Moral: *Purity is popular only when it pays.*

SUBSCRIPTION BLANK
THE BLAST, Box 661, San Francisco, Cal.

I enclose $................ for which send me THE BLAST

for.................... { Year
{ Months

Add balance to THE BLAST Sustaining Fund.

Name................

Address ....

VOL. I   SAN FRANCISCO, SATURDAY, JANUARY 22, 1916   No. 2

"THE COURT ORDERS——"

"THE COURT ORDERS——"

(Labor Limericks)

THE Court in its Majesty lifted its voice—
Safely surrounded, of course, by its boys.
    The Law was expounded,
    And Labor, dumbfounded,
Was wond'ring, Who's making that noise?

A thought, like a bolt from a summer-lit sky
Struck Labor's mind, brought a gleam to his eye.
    Uncover'd at last
    By Truth's fearful blast,
Stood naked the hideous Lie.

He saw the proud master with half-hidden sneer,
Ruling meek slaves by brute force or by fear.
    By dropping his hand
    The whole robber band
Was made in a moment to hear.

In anger he let out a stentorian cry,
Fright'ning the Court, so it never knew why.
    With yawps like a whelp,
    His "Honor" cried Help!
The coppers ne'er batted an eye.

In danger the watchdogs are always asleep.
Lift thy hands, Labor, and make a clean sweep.
    Be not a dull Giant,
    But Worker Defiant
Who wills that to toil is to reap.

ASPIRATIONS OF THE BLAST

THE BLAST is not a decent, respectable paper. Decency and Respectability—Mother Grundy's bastard twins—change, like the fashions, with age, country and climate, mostly without rhyme or reason.

If you are a sissified mollycoddle of the good old kind that would put draping around a piano leg and go to bed in a night cap, drop this paper right now. It will surely shock you: for the truth is stark naked.

It is said: "The truth shall make you free." So it shall. But the truth is not a nugget found by luck. He who diligently searches will find grains of it now and then. THE BLAST preaches no dogma. Its mission is more revolutionary: to arouse independence of feeling, thought and action, without which there is no road to human freedom.

Freedom is primarily a state of mind. It can neither be chained in a dungeon nor heralded from the throne. There is no royal road to it, though the pathways are many. THE BLAST proposes to discuss them.

Any man or movement enlisted in the battle for the right of the worker to the Earth and the fullness thereof, will find in THE BLAST a fighting friend, regardless of regimental insignia.

THE BLAST has no time to split hairs over policies.

If an institution has the elements of slavery within it, we shall grill it, no matter how respectably moss-grown it has become with age.

If THE BLAST can aid in sweeping away the cobwebs of tradition, and call to life the vision of a better, freer world, without oppression and legalized theft, without soldiers and bloodshed, without priests and superstitions, without politicians and graft, plutocrats and paupers, we shall not have worked in vain.

We know our limitations.

We are not profound philosophers. Hence we refuse to be slaves to consistency.

We are not learned scholars. Therefore faulty rhetoric will not freeze the blood in our veins.

We are free from the blight of professional journalism. We shall not worry ourselves to death about style.

We are but workers with a passion for Freedom and with the determination to express it in the face of all difficulty and danger.

If you are with us, *now* is the time to prove your interest and solidarity.

THE BLASTERS.

THE BLAST   Three

WHAT IS THE MATTER WITH LABOR?

LABOR lacks solidarity. Labor lacks any approach to solidarity. Labor lacks any vital idea which will lead to solidarity. Here, in my opinion, is the missionary work for true labor leaders,—to bring the masses of Labor to a conception of their strength in unity; the absolute necessity for a completely united labor.

Labor now thinks in terms of unions, and in spite of certain affiliations and amalgamations each union is a unit for itself. The more skilled trades and the more powerful unions form an aristocracy of labor, a perfectly foolish thought for any one in the ranks of Labor to entertain, no matter how high his salary and how great his skill. You might as well talk of aristocracy on a sinking ship, where every person must take his turn at the pumps or all must perish. The vital idea never to be dimmed is that there is but one cause, Labor's cause. But one oppression, the capitalistic system. Not capitalists. They are men. Often excellent men, and it is a great mistake to direct attention to individuals. Individuals die, but systems remain, and Labor's task is to abolish the system which automatically makes capitalists. To that task every soul in the ranks of Labor should be summoned, without distinction as to race, color, sex or skill. The troubles and oppressions of the dullest laborer handling pick and shovel are identically the troubles and oppressions of the Brotherhood of Engineers, or the Electrical Workers. There is only one cause—Labor's cause. All labor, without any distinction. Only one foe—the System which denies to Labor the fruit of its own toil. But now Labor thinks in terms of locality, as well as in terms of unions. The labor troubles of Los Angeles belong to Los Angeles. The labor troubles of Paterson belong to Paterson. Of course, sometimes the question is made a little more general and always there are a few individuals who see the necessity of the solidarity of labor on every question concerning labor, but as a rule Labor likes to limit the trouble—to isolate it—as if it were measles or smallpox. It is as if the artillery of an army looked some miles away and said, "Ah! Our infantry over there is being annihilated. Too bad!" And went on with its dinner.

Meat-cutters shiver on strike while every other trade in the butcher business goes contentedly on with its master's work. Carpenters walk out and painters, plasterers and plumbers remain on the job. Teamsters in Chicago may be starving on a strike, while teamsters in San Francisco and everywhere else go about their business.

I know the reasons given for this lack of cohesion, that the others who remain on the job may by their contributions aid the strikers, etc., etc., and I know the risks of striking with the risk of an empty bread-pan. Nevertheless, the plan has all the weakness of the bundle of sticks which could be easily broken separately but resisted all power when bound together. If Labor had absolute solidarity, no resistance to it could last three days, and it would only be a question of how intelligently Labor used its power. But I think we could safely trust the evolution of ideas to govern that.

What I think Labor has never perceived, because we have never seen it put into action, is that the cause of striking teamsters in Chicago is not only a cause for teamsters everywhere, but for all Labor everywhere. There is only one cause: Labor's cause.

Labor also now thinks in terms of wages and hours. It has no further vision; no deeper understanding; no higher hope. Its leaders are not teaching it to think in terms of revolution, but are quite content with spasmodic skirmishes over wages and hours and are hilariously jubilant if successful, without apparently the slightest idea that they have not touched the real issue at all. Labor leaders seem to me essentially as

conservative as preachers or capitalists. It never occurs to them to ask why Labor and why Capital! Why this dividing line, on one side of which are all the toilers, the creators of wealth, living from hand to mouth, and on the other side the few absorbers of wealth, dangerously rich? Labor rushes forward for remedial legislation and again is jubilant if it has scratched the surface, but I hear very few powerful voices teaching Labor that there is a force like gravity beyond the power of legislation, working night and day to automatically separate the people into the poor serf-toilers and the rich capitalistic overlords. It is the same power which made the aristocracy of Greece; the plutocracy of Rome; the feudal lords of the Middle Ages. The same power that is making our plutocracy today. It is the ability of a shrewd and privileged Few to control the planet on which we live and out of which by labor all things come. In other words, it is the ability to monopolize the earth and the choicest treasures thereof. This monopoly is not only made possible, but it is inevitable, so long as we have a system of land-holding which is in essence identically the feudal system, namely: a paper grant or deed from some grantor, giving to the grantee, by reason of the mere scrap of paper, absolute ownership of the land described, utterly regardless of any necessity, possession or use. This system has always, automatically, separated society economically into over-lords and serfs. It is this system which has permitted and stimulated a few persons or individuals to own all the iron-ore, anthracite coal, bituminous coal, timber and other valuable natural resources of this country. They own them absolutely and they warn all the world off as trespassers, regardless of whether they are putting them to use or not. It is the system which permits the shrewd speculator, who is first on the ground, to seize and hold the valuable portions of the earth, even the agricultural lands, and the after-born are left as serfs in the land of their birth, or may go out and starve upon the waste places.

Under such conditions, automatically created by such a system, what can Labor do but work for its master? From this land monopoly and the privileged class created by it come further powers and privileges created by such privileged class through the machine it has always controlled called Government. It is an absurdity to speak of any government as representative of the people. It always represents the great interests, the property class. This Government creates zones of privilege into which only the few may creep. Taxation power used as a privilege to create bonuses, directly or indirectly; banking powers and privileges. Inevitably, therefore, when the machine drove out the artisan (and art) these privileged capitalists naturally became the owners of the machines. The laborer himself became an appendage to the machine, or a serf to the soil, and in either case he must beg his job, hat in hand, from his master. What else can he do? Where can he go, and what other remedy is there than destroying this monopolistic system of privilege? And yet Labor continues to make a begging warfare for jobs, for hours, for wages.

It is true in this warfare Labor is often big-voiced, even truculent, but when its voice is biggest it secretly carries its hat in its hand, knowing instinctively that the overlords have the greater power, as things now are, for they own the earth, the machines, the jobs.

So, also, while its voice is loudest, Labor in its inner heart carries the fear that it and its women and children will starve unless the great masters allow it very soon to go to work again creating more wealth for confiscation by the master-class.

As I look over the world, nowhere has Labor had a clear idea that it need not starve. Always it is fettered by the idea of Law and vested rights; property rights. It does not seem to have got it into its brain and blood that it, itself, has created all the food and clothing in the warehouses and the stores; all the guns and ammunitions in the armories, and all it needs is to help itself according to its needs, for necessity knows no law.

It would seem as if Labor by some sort of instinct ought to grasp the idea that no capitalist or group of capitalists could make a machine, a bolt of cloth, or a barrel of flour, a gun, or a cartridge; yet the giant Labor sits naked, without bread, gun or ammunition, and is afraid to take what in reality is its own creation and only a false and vicious system declares to be the property of another.

Labor is, as a slave-class always is, pathetically law-abiding, and its leaders take great pride in the fact that they are law-abiding citizens and make it very plain that they will repudiate all who are not. They forget that the world moves only by some citizens becoming not law-abiding. The common people of England under Cromwell were distinctly not law-abiding when they cut off the head of Charles; nor were the people of the French Revolution law-abiding. They were law-breaking but also law-making citizens, for after all true law is the will of the people, not enactments by so-called representatives of the people who have never represented any but the property class, but enactments by the very body of the people themselves in action. John Brown was not a law-abiding citizen when he helped run-away slaves to freedom, and he was not ashamed of his unlawful acts.

What Labor needs, in my opinion, is a little more self-respect, not conceit; a little more boldness in action, not in talk, and, above all, an understanding grasp of the idea that the cause of Labor is really the cause of the race. That the salvation of the race and Labor is revolution, not petty tinkering, and that the revolution can only be brought about, whether by volcanic action or by slow evolution, by Labor's firm belief that the cause of the lowest is the cause of the highest; that there is but one cause,—Labor's cause, and it is the same, not only country-wide but world-wide.

This present war is a war between governments, not between peoples, and when I say it is a war between governments, that is the same thing as saying it is a war between the exploiting classes of each country, quarreling one with the other. The root of the quarrel is trade, territory, colonies, manufacture, bonds, investments; new regions and channels for exploitation. The people of each country have far more quarrel with their own masters and governors than they have with each other. Or, to put it better, each has more quarrel with the system in its own country which begets masters and governors. Indeed, the plain peoples have no quarrel with each other. They have nothing to gain but death and no hope but to return to their old jobs, burdened with added taxation. But they have a great quarrel with the system which creates exploiters and wars.

The industrial war, which is always smouldering in this country and in Europe, is part and parcel of the great international world war now going on. They rise from a common cause. In both lies this question: How long will Labor endure exploitation by a capitalistic class? Or, again, to put it more accurately, for we must not be misled into looking at individuals, how long will Labor endure this feudal system which automatically breeds an exploiting class of overlords at one end and a mass of serfs at the other?

Labor, the great Giant which rends mountains and turns aside rivers, must beg for the right to work because of its belly, and the highest vision it has is to mutter now and then about its wages and hours. No, it is not even a giant. It is a dismembered giant, with a leg lying here and an arm there; here a toe, there a finger; and a head nowhere. And the arms, legs, fingers and toes are each twitching a little bit trying to do something separately; the great toe secretly despising its little brother. Or, let us better say, it is not a dismembered giant, but one which has never yet been put together: no head has ever been placed upon the great powerful body. But when this happens, and the Giant acts with one body and speaks with one voice, it can, without force or violence, reform the world and bless mankind. But not till then.

CHARLES ERSKINE SCOTT WOOD

ψ ψ ψ

THE CAT IN THE BAG

"WE are not going to war just because we make an increase in our military equipment of from twenty-five to fifty per cent. We need an army for its moral influence, if for nothing else. In a nation of 100,000,000 there are liable to be riots, mobs and insurrections, which cannot be regulated except by the presence of an army."

—Ex-President Taft in *World's Chronicle.*

Right you are, Bill. But awful careless to let the cat out of the bag so soon.

It would not be safe if the workers of the country should see through the scheme.

From ancient autocracy to modern plutocracy the ruling families were strong for the trained cut-throat, the soldier.

The soldier protects the ruler from the righteous indignation of the mob.

The multimillionaire families (you will find their names in the World Almanac), ruling America by the grace of the Almighty Dollar, as much as any royal scamp that ever disgraced a throne by divine right, are a unit for a large army.

And who, may we ask, is the mob?

Who are the insurrectionists?

Why, it is the natural crowd, grown restless. Tired of being fleeced, tired of politicians' empty promises, tired of taking in the slack in the belt when hunger gnaws.

It is Labor straightening its back, stretching its mighty grip for the wealth it created.

It is "the starving and dangerous myriads, coming from mines and mills, pale-faced girls and women with hard-eyed children pouring from dens of filth and toil, out to the air of heaven, crying to Labor to rise, to be high as the highest that rules them, to own the Earth in their lifetime and hand it down to their children."

Therefore must our *business* men, preferably, be trained in the gentle art of killing and absolute *obedience;* for without *obedience* there would be neither hangman, nor soldier, neither master nor slave.

"Our Kings are the same as the Kings of old,
    But a Man stands up where there crouched a clown;
The Evil shall die when his hand grows bold
    And the fist of the People shall strike at the crown."

Bill Taft, a bum president, but a first-class announcer through the plutocratic megaphone, has shown the real reason for preparedness.

It is a challenge and a warning to Labor.

THE BLAST

Revolutionary Labor Weekly
569 Dolores St., San Francisco, Cal.

Mail Address, Box 661   Phone, Park 499

Alexander Berkman, Editor and Publisher
E. B. Morton, Associate Editor   **M. E. Fitzgerald,** Manager

SUBSCRIPTION
$1.00 Yearly   60c Six Months   5c Copy
Bundle rates, 2½c per copy in bundles of ten.
Advertising rates on application.
Application for entry as second-class matter at the postoffice at
San Francisco pending.

COMMENTS

British Conscription

THE power inherent in Labor has never been demonstrated more forcibly than by the stand of the Railway and Mine men of Great Britain against Conscription.

The mere threat of a general strike in the two industries was sufficient to force the powerful Government of His Majesty, King of Great Britain and Emperor of India, to back down in quick time. The Government lost no time in assuring these organizations that they would be exempt from the provisions of the Conscription Act.

The great governmental secret is that the authorities *knew* that the threat of the workers was backed by courage and determination to make good.

Question: If Labor in only two industries can thus force a strong government to its knees, is there anything that the solidaric attitude of the unified Labor of a given country could not accomplish?

Or the solidarity of the whole of International Labor?

What a lesson, especially to the timid Labor of our own land!

* * *

The A. F. of L. Convention

THE delegates to the recent A. F. of L. Convention, held at San Francisco, seem to have entirely failed to get the spirit of the speeches made by the fraternal delegates from Great Britain—C. G. Ammon and E. Bevan.

"The British workman," said Ammon in addressing the Convention, "is ready to give his life to the nation as soon as the capitalist and landlord are ready to give up their property to the nation."

The significance of these words fell, apparently, upon deaf ears. The Convention of the greatest organization of Labor in America failed to take a definite stand toward the most burning questions agitating the country today—questions upon the solution of which will vitally depend the fortunes of Labor in the coming years.

* * *

The Liberty and Peace of the Republic

ON the question of Preparedness, President Gompers had this to say to the Convention:

"I am against militarism. * * * We are living in a republic, but a republic does not assure protection and peace. The people who would not defend our institutions of liberty and peace, are not worth having a republic."

Labor enslaved, brutalized and humiliated. Unemployed tramping the streets, hungry and cold, in the vain search of a job. Workers by the thousand killed, maimed and crippled in mine, mill and factory. Strikers shot down in cold blood, the wives and children of dispossessed miners burned alive in their tents. Labor men filling the prisons and penitentiaries of the country.

Is this the "liberty and peace of the republic" you want to defend, good Mr. Gompers?

* * *

Preparedness

NO one has a more direct and vital interest in the question of Preparedness than the workers.

They will have to do the preparing.

They will build the factories and munition plants.

They will manufacture the guns, shells, powder and other death-dealing instruments of warfare.

They will do the transporting.

They will produce and supply the food for *themselves* while they are doing all this preparing.

They will be commanded to go to the front.

They will be the fodder for the cannon.

In *this* country.

And in all the other countries.

They—some of them—will remain corpses on the field of battle.

They will leave widows and orphans, in sorrow, misery and poverty.

They—some of them—will return home armless and legless, crippled and maimed for life, pitiful objects of charity.

They—most of them—will have to look for a job. Some will find it, many won't.

They will work in the shops and factories. The unemployed will wait outside to take their places at lower wages.

They will struggle and suffer and fight for a bare living and go out on strike.

They will be shot down by the guns and munitions they themselves had made.

And the Generals will be decorated, and the Masters will celebrate jubilantly, *"Our* country is saved!"

Why War?

* * *

THERE are many factors:

Commercial rivalry among the Big Business interests of the different countries;

The spirit of racial and national antagonisms cultivated by Christian "brotherhood" and capitalistic cannibalism;

The murderous superstition that civilization can be advanced by wholesale slaughter;

The village notion that you are better than the other fellow because you happen to be born *here;*

The fool idea that because people live across an imaginary border line they are essentially different from you, or worse;

The persecution mania of small minds that your village is always in danger from your neighbors;

The savage relic in our hearts that some one must be punished if something goes wrong;

The murderous insanity that national honor can be anything different than your own honor as a man;

The fiction that you have any cause to kill men whom you have never seen or heard of and against whom you have no grievance whatever;

The patriotic aberration that, though it is murder to kill when you are dressed in citizen's clothes, it is heroic and glorious to slaughter wholesale when you put on a soldier's uniform.

The idea that you are a free-born man, subject to no one's orders, and a Christian whom the Lord commanded, "Thou shalt not kill," but—that it is your sacred, patriotic and Christian duty to kill every one in sight when a man with more gold braid on his uniform than on yours orders you to shoot.

But the most gigantic idiocy of them all: that we, the workers, have anything to gain by slaughtering other workers.

* * *

Quite A Difference

THERE is much talk about the benefit and profit this country is deriving from the war in Europe.

It's a confusion of terms.

No benefit can accrue to anyone from the murder of millions of men, the devastation of whole countries, and the multiplication of cripples, widows and orphans.

War *benefits* no one, but there are *profits* in it, great profits—for the American munition manufacturers.

* * *

Slave Morality

THE *Labor Clarion,* the official journal of the California State Federation of Labor, as well as of the San Francisco Labor Council, in an editorial entitled "The Conviction of Schmidt," has the following to say:

> "No attempt is made to maintain that union men are never guilty of crime and if after a fair trial, free from bias and prejudice, guilt is established, organized labor will join the balance of society in condemnation, whether the crime is due to selfishness or is the action of an over-zealous fanatic."

Is the editor of the *Labor Clarion* really so naive as to believe that a labor man can secure "a fair trial free from bias and prejudice" in the courts of the enemy?

It is this kind of editorial piffle that keeps the workers from realizing the actual facts of the labor situation and dooms their struggles to defeat.

As to "organized labor joining the balance of society in condemnation,"—that's just the great tragedy of Labor. But too often it "joins in condemnation,"—even of its own brothers in the hands of the enemy.

We hope that the intelligent militant elements of California Labor will protest against the sentiments of the *Labor Clarion,* pretending to represent organized Labor. The eagerness to be "respectable" is what is keeping the workers in bondage. It is time they would emancipate themselves from their slave morality.

THE AWAKENING

"Rise like lions after slumber
In unvanquishable number,
Shake your chains to earth like dew
Which in sleep had fallen on you—
Ye are many,—they are few."
—Shelley.

THE poet's cry, after the broken slumber of a hundred years, rings out a message of hope to the workers and its threatened menace to the upper crust of society.

Out of the seemingly hopeless conflict of tactics and politics, out of the storm and stress of industrial warfare, like a mail-clad Pallas from the Jovian brow, springs Labor defiant, bidding the masters halt.

The "Empire Builders" of Great Britain bend their knees to the very class they have always so haughtily despised.

Suddenly they realize that neither King nor Parliament, neither Dukes, Lords nor anointed Bishops, neither Brewer-Baronets nor imported American dollar aristocrats, nay, not one in the whole crest-embroidered troop is worth a tinker's damn in the crisis that faces the "Empire."

The workers of England have at last realized that their boasted political liberty is but a sham as long as industrial slavery continues.

The masters have played their last trump.

Slimy parliamentarians, desperate at the workers' "unpatriotic" attitude in refusing to defend their imaginary homes, succeeded in passing the Munition Act, a law which rehabilitates slavery in England.

Recently twenty-eight strikers were fined for "unlawfully ceasing to work." The overlords were not satisfied. Relying upon the workers' superstitious reverence for legal enactments, they now propose to make the "unlawful" cessation of work a prison offense.

But the last poisoned straw, Conscription, did not break the patient camel's back. It stiffened its spine and aroused its temper.

Labor flung the gauntlet back in the masters' teeth. With conscious power and defiance rings the challenge of Labor. According to latest United Press dispatches—

> "The National Railway Men's Union, one of the strongest of Great Britain's labor organizations, today defied the government to enact its conscript bill. After introducing one of the most severe resolutions yet fostered by any union, the Executive Committee hinted at an immediate general strike on transportation lines if the measure passes.
>
> "'Unless the government is prepared to confiscate the wealth of the privileged classes,' said the resolution, 'for a more successful prosecution of the war, railroad workers will resist to the uttermost the confiscation of men whose only wealth is their labor power!'"

Oi, oi, what a language from a workingman to his "betters"! But it had the dangerous ring of sincerity in it, and a word to the wise ones seemed sufficient, for the dispatch adds:

> "This move, coupled with the anti-conscription resolutions adopted yesterday by representatives of

800,000 miners, gave the government considerable concern. Premier Asquith conferred informally with cabinet members, and it is rumored that, in view of the possibility of serious action from the railway and mine men, he was trying to amend the bill so as to eliminate these groups from its operation."

Of course, the bill will be amended so as to exempt the unions which show strength and spirit, in the hope that at least the weak and unorganized may submit.

Now is the crucial time for the organized workers of England to speak, not alone for themselves, but for all Labor.

Let no lure of group exemption undermine their solidarity.

Conscription is now advocated boldly and persistently by the plutocracy of America. Experience has taught them that it is difficult to get recruits for the army even at present. The much advertised "opportunity for travel at good pay" which flares from the recruiting office posters in peace, means rubbing, scrubbing and polishing hooks and brass buttons; in war, rotten meat, typhus, cannon food and—glory and promotion for the officers.

It is now up to American Labor to speak—to speak in unison with their British brothers. The hands of Time are moving.

THE BALLAD OF YOUNGSTOWN
Lydia Gibson Mestre

FOR weeks and weeks the strike had run, for hungry days and days;
And frozen was the winter sun, and hunger often slays;
For weeks and weeks we had held fast, just where we had begun;
We thought we had them there at last, such weeks the strike had run!

We thought, poor fools, we had them there; (three cents was the dispute—
Three measly cents to each man's share—and children starved to boot!)
So when the scabs began to work (God knows what sort of pay!)
We pulled together with a jerk to chase them out that day.

Scab-chasing is all very well, but it's evil-smelling quarry;
The boys all yell: "The scabs to hell—we're here now—we should worry!"
You've seen a bunch get going? Then you know how once they're started
They're off, ten or a thousand men, even the chicken-hearted.

They owned the town, the boys, that night, who knew not wealth nor glory;
The masters crouched at home in fright—say, isn't that some story?
The masters trembled in their shoes, their women shook with fear;
Those forty-hundred men let loose made noises weird to hear.

Those forty-hundred half-starved men looted and burned and slaked;
Years upon years of anger then out of their hearts were waked;
Years on years of humility, years upon years of toil,
Grim grey days of servility;—now they could have the spoil.

Years upon years they paid for it, they and their fathers, too;—
Work—(even work, they prayed for it!) toiled till all was blue!
Tonight gems hung in their grizzled ears; silk and lace for carousers—
Wine and food and hearty cheers, while the masters hide in the houses!

Fire and orgy and all excess—yes, we are "violent,' very—
That night was a long way from success, but for once the boys were merry!

A BLAST FROM YOUNGSTOWN

UP from the black hell-hole of Ohio, from Youngstown, comes the volcanic blast of revolt, revealing the smouldering fire that needs but a fanning to burst into the roaring flame of a full-fledged revolution.

Men, known by number like convicts, barefooted women and scantily-clad children got into action.

And lo! in one short night the smiles of smug satisfaction faded from the philistines' faces.

For the starveling crowd no more cringed meekly before the lash of Hunger. Diamonds and jewelry, clothing and food, drinks that brought joy for the moment—all were theirs for the taking.

"Thieves!"—you cry. Not so; not *they*. The thieves were the masters who stole the fruit of the workers' labor, allowing but 15 cents an hour for their toil at the fiery furnace.

And now after stealing the brawn of the men, the joy of the mothers and the hopes of the young, year after year, they squeal like cornered rats over the loss of a measly million, no dollar of which they themselves had created.

Save us, police! Send the militia! The State, its ear attuned to the call of capital, comes to the rescue.

Horrible news:

"Grimy hands stained with toil wearing diamond rings."

"Burly giants wrap themselves in silk."

"Gold watches flung like cigars into overall pockets."
Well,—why not?

Why not have the hard-working producer in possession of these things rather than the coupon-clipping parasites?

"The citizens arm against the horrible strikers."

"The citizens place dynamite under the bridge, ready to blow it up if the strikers attempt to cross."

But suppose the strikers planted dynamite under a bridge in order to blow up armed "citizens?"

The whole press would rend the air with shrieks of vengeance for such "dastardly deeds."

Who are the "citizens?"

And who are the strikers?

Let us take their own words for it: The citizens are two hundred specimens of the "better class." The "strikers are desperately poor."

Noble "citizens!"

AN OLD GHOST IN A NEW SHEET

SAN FRANCISCO real estate sharks, finding the market for suckers dull, have revived an old industry.

They have been selling "influence" with the City Fathers in the matter of garage permits. Two Hundred and Fifty Dollars seems to have been the scale.

If a garage owner wanted to prevent a competitor from getting a permit, he bought Two Hundred and Fifty Dollars worth of influence.

If a man wanted to start a garage, he invested Two Hundred and Fifty Dollars in influence.

Coming and going, the game worked like a charm.

We have the word of the City Fathers themselves that they knew nothing about it, and never got a whiff of the cash.

Stern logic forces us to the conclusion that there is no good reason why a Grand Jury should investigate this matter.

Priests have been selling influence with our Heavenly Father since time immemorial. They have sold indulgences for sins intended to be committed and absolution for sins already sinned, and no Grand Jury ever interfered.

To the credit of the City Fathers be it said that they protested against the practice as soon as they knew. Our Heavenly Father, who should have known all along, still remains silent.

VOL. I   SAN FRANCISCO, SATURDAY, JANUARY 29, 1916   No. 3

IF HE ONLY WOULD——

RESISTANCE TO OPPRESSION

LABOR, organized as well as unorganized, owes a debt to those within its ranks who have had the daring to resist the master class in defense of the working class.

It is tragic to see labor leaders and their editors repudiating the McNamaras, Ford and Suhr, Quinlan, Schmidt or Joe Hill on the plea that Organized Labor cannot "afford to encourage violence."

It is this cringing slave philosophy, this repudiation of the fighting spirit of Labor, which has given the employing class almost unlimited opportunity for violence by proxy; that is, through hired gunmen, police, the courts and similar agencies.

Ford and Suhr gave life and impetus to the California Commission on Housing and Immigration, and the Federal Commission on Industrial Relations was virtually created as a result of the McNamaras' war.

The report of the latter Commission contains a radical analysis of industrial conditions, the import of which Labor has not as yet fully digested.

From Chapter VIII we quote as follows:

"The general effect of the decisions of American courts, however, has been to restrict the activities of labor organizations and deprive them of their most effective weapons, namely, the boycott and the power of picketing, while on the other hand the weapons of employers, namely, the power of arbitrary discharge, of blacklisting, and of bringing in strikebreakers, have been maintained and legislative attempts to restrict the employers' powers have generally been declared unconstitutional by the courts. Furthermore, an additional weapon has been placed in the hands of the employers by many courts in the form of sweeping injunctions, which render punishable acts which would otherwise be legal, and also result in effect in depriving the workers of the right to jury trial."

After expressing grave doubts as to the efficacy of the Clayton Act, the report declares all efforts to restrict the rights and powers of the employers to correspond in substance with those allowed trade unions, have failed absolutely—not only on account of the intervention of the courts, but on account of the ineffectiveness of legislation against blacklisting and arbitrary discharge.

As Labor admittedly has all the worst of the law, and no possible redress through it, why in the name of common sense should Labor be law-abiding? On the subject of violence we quote from the Industrial Relations Commission report: "Violence is seldom, if ever, spontaneous, but arises from a conviction that fundamental rights are denied and that peaceful methods of adjustment cannot be used. * * * The arbitrary suppression of violence by force produces only resentment which will rekindle into greater violence when opportunity offers. Violence can be prevented only by *removing the cause of violence;* industrial peace can rest only upon industrial justice. * * * Throughout history where a people or a group have been arbitrarily denied rights which they conceived to be theirs, reaction has been inevitable."

"Violence is a natural form of protest against injustice."

"No strike can be won if the employer can operate his plant without difficulty."

"When governmental institutions are thus corrupted and used as instruments of oppression, men can only resist with such power as they have, not alone for the protection of themselves and their families but for the preservation of the fundamental rights of themselves and their fellow citizens."

The peaceable and orderly progress of civilization is a social myth. It was invented thousands of years ago by masters who had found that fooling the slaves involved less personal risk and strenuous effort than the application of the lash.

As faithfulness to the master class and conspicuous ability to subdue rebellious sentiment was the only condition upon which a slave overseer might be released from his own bondage in ancient times, so it is now.

The climbers within the ranks of Labor, provided the masters think them safe, sane and conservative, emancipate themselves from toil and generally graduate into political jobs. To them Labor is not Vision—it is a living.

✿　✿　✿

CAN YOU PROVE IT?

WE radicals are constantly being accused of making assertions without proof. For instance, if you should declare, with Dr. Chapman, that "Government is an organized system of exploitation within a given territory," you would instantly be challenged to prove your statement. "For *this* government is conceived in liberty," the infatuated patriot will say. Yet, in spite of that, you can prove your definition true even for this country. Or, rather, a university professor has already done it for you. Merely say: "Allow me to suggest, my friend, that you read a book by the eminent Prof. Charles A. Beard, of Columbia University, called 'An Economic Interpretation of the United States Constitution,' You will then be convinced that the 'fathers of the Constitution' established it mainly so that they themselves and others of similar interests could speculate in government securities, could collect high rates of interest from hard-working farmers, could gain fortunes by buying up Western lands which the work of other men would make valuable, and could exploit men and women in manufactures and commerce."

The same plan used to form a government in the interests of the moneyed class is being worked right now in their efforts to transform the school system of this country. Until within the last ten years little organized effort has been made to capture the schools. Locally, it is true, the "substantial citizens" were ele ted to serve on school boards and thus influenced the selection of teachers and, to a certain extent, the conduct of the schools. But the capitalists themselves were not well organized then; hence did not exercise this power effectively.

Now the situation has changed. Even a casual reader of the newspapers knows that something is happening to the schools. The masters are organized, and are out to capture the schools of this country. As I said before, the same general plan is used for this onslaught against liberty that the venerated fathers employed in framing the constitution which has so well served their class. One trivial example will illustrate, as a full explanation is not within the scope of this article.

"The national movement for the development of thrift was started by the American Society for the Development of Thrift, of which F. W. Strauss, banker, of Chicago, is the president and financial backer. The plan of the movement is to inculcate thrift in the American people. This organization was started about four years ago. It was through the influence of the Society of Thrift that the National Educational Association got behind the movement. The members of the committee appointed at Oakland, where the N. E. A. met last summer, are each to take up different phases of the subject, and will report at a gathering at Detroit, February 22, 1916. This will be held in conjunction with the National School Superintendents' convention at that time."

Among the subjects to be treated are the following: The Thrift Movement and Its Relation to Rural Life; Its Relation to Banking, Accounting, School Savings Banks and Similar Institutions; Relation to the Industries; Its Relation to Men's Organizations, such as Commercial Clubs and Labor Unions; Relation to Educational Movements. One means of arousing interest in thrift is the offering of attractive prizes in the national essay contest on thrift. The adult contest is open to all, and a first prize of $750, a second of $250 and a third of $100 is offered. In the school children's contest, $350 is offered in prizes.

Here, clearly outlined in a newspaper report, are the successive moves by which the bankers are trying to get their grip on the schools. Note: One man, a banker, organizes a local group; then makes it national. This body then sends representatives to the National Educational Association at its annual convention. There they gain a body of principals and superintendents to present their plans to a gathering of superintendents the following February. These worthy gentlemen, the autocrats of the school system, are ready listeners to bankers, manufacturers and all big business men. Have you ever noticed how royally these ruling schoolmen are wined and dined by commercial clubs, merchants' and manufacturers' associations, and their like, during all school conventions? Then they go home full of the advice they have received from their entertainers, call a meeting of their principals, and repeat the same to them. These, in turn, pass it on to the teachers under them, who have no choice but to carry it out on the children, whose habits and lives are thus shaped for them.

We sometimes speak of legislation as though it is the molding force in the community, and as though it is instigated by the people concerned, through their representatives. Here is legislation more vital than any lawmaking body ever enacted. It is originated in a banker's brain, passes on from the top of the school system down to the children, almost without sanction or approval from either the teachers, the pupils, or the parents themselves—if they will allow it.

But, you may say, it is good for little children to learn to save. That may or may not be so. But should the whole tremendous psychological force of the school system be brought to bear upon the child to teach him to save, for the reason that a banker in Chicago conceives it is healthy for the future banks to have a generation of savers? or because employers of all kinds realize that to reduce the standard of living in this country means an opportunity to hold down wages?

What have the parents to say?

Who rules our Schools?

AN UNDESIRABLE TEACHER.

MEXICO
Selig Schulberg

ALL wars of modern times have had their inception in commercial rivalry. The Mexican war was and is no exception to the rule. The Pearson Syndicate, an oil concern, a rival of the Standard Oil Company, had all the Governmental favors under President Diaz. When Madero challenged the Diaz administration, he did it with the support of the Standard Oil Company.

In the *Congressional Record* of the Sixty-third Congress will be found quotations read from the record by a Senator from Michigan with regard to the subject. It appears that at the outbreak of the Mexican revolution, headed by Francisco I. Madero, against President Diaz, the Eagle Oil Company, which includes the Aguila Oil Company, dealing in the refined products of oil, and the Pearson oil concessions, belonging to Lord Cowdray of England, producing crude oil, were doing their business in sharp rivalry with the Waters-Pierce Oil Company, a Missouri corporation operating in Mexico. The controlling interest and the stock of the Waters-Pierce Oil Company was owned by the Standard Oil Company.

The Rockefellers made the Mexican situation, and have fostered it. They have hired their Otises and Hearsts to bark for war, and all of the murder, rapine and sorrow can be placed at their door. If now they force intervention, the Standard Oil Company of America should be held responsible for every boy sacrificed on the altar of their greed.

While the Standard Oil Company is putting on a solemn face and dishing out a few dimes to the starving of Belgium, it is at the same time manipulating things to enhance the value of its vast holdings of oil and mineral lands.

Toilers of America, if the Hearsts, Otises and Rockefellers have property, for which they want protection, in Mexico, let *them* protect it!

Four   THE BLAST

THE BLAST

Revolutionary Labor Weekly
569 Dolores St., San Francisco, Cal.

Mail Address, Box 661   Phone, Park 499

Alexander Berkman, Editor and Publisher
E. B. Morton, Associate Editor   **M. E. Fitzgerald**, Manager

SUBSCRIPTION
$1.00 Yearly   60c Six Months   5c Copy
Bundle rates, 2½c per copy in bundles of ten.
Advertising rates on application.
Application for entry as second-class matter at the postoffice at
San Francisco pending.

COMMENTS

Labor Intervention

THE jingo press, inspired by Big Business interests, is howling for intervention in Mexico. The excuse offered is the recent killing of a score of Americans.

Statistics for the year just past show that during 1915 no less that 22,565 working men were killed in the factories of the *United States* (not in the Mexican Revolution), mostly by preventable accidents. This number does not include the many workers shot down in strikes and the thousands starved to death and driven to suicide in the orderly process of our peaceful civilization.

We haven't noticed any capitalistic papers calling for intervention in behalf of Labor to stop this Murder by Greed. Why should they? It is the source of their masters' profits. It is a safe bet that there will be no intervention in this until the workers take the matter into their own hands.

* * *

There's a Reason

SOME people think it rather strange that the preparationists are so strenuously opposing the proposal that the government manufacture its own munitions.

It isn't a bit strange. What's the use of advocating Preparedness if there are to be no profits in it for the big armament manufacturers?

* * *

The Balance of Power

FRANKLY, we prefer Kill-'em-all Teddy to the timid apologists for Preparedness for "adequate defense."

We would rather be told by a ruffian in the plainest Anglo Saxon to go to hell than to be unsuspectingly shoved down the stairs by the soft-gloved hands of a Judas.

The militarists of the Roosevelt type make no foul excuses. They want conscription and universal military service in order to be ready for the bloody struggle which they are determined to precipitate.

But the lady-like preparationists hide themselves behind "adequate defense," though every school boy knows that "adequateness" means keeping step with the almost unlimited and ever-increasing armaments of the great European powers. It means turning this country into a vast military camp like Russia or Germany.

But neither the blood-thirsty militarist nor the hypocritical preparationist is really dangerous. They will do nothing but shout.

The real danger is in Labor. What will Labor do? That is the *only* important question. The issue is in the hands of the workers, in theirs alone. They are the real power that will ultimately decide. Without them, not a wheel can be turned, not a bullet cast.

It's up to you, workers.

* * *

If He Only Would

DO you see the cartoon on our first page? Well, that's what you *could* do, if you only would.

You could make your bloodsuckers see stars, make them feel closer to heaven or hell than they ever dreamed of being in this life.

You could knock the stuffin' out of them, literally and figuratively. You could squeeze the very breath out of Capitalism, squeeze it out so hard that it should never come to again.

You *could* do it—aye, so easily, for "you are many, they are few," and the power of life and food is all in *your* hands. You could do it with one hand, with only your Left, while your Right would be free to create and to build, and to re-shape Life nearer to your heart's desire, for the well-being of all.

Well, why don't you? You have the power. You need only *to will*.

* * *

The Myth of Peace

THE Fords, the Bryans, the Jane Addams may be quite sincere. If so, they are blind leaders of the blind.

All their talk about international peace is an impossible dream as long as capitalism lasts.

The first requisite for International peace is National peace. National peace can not exist where there is no industrial peace. And there will be no industrial peace until the industrious man enjoys the fruit of his industry.

THE BLAST does not stand for "peace at any price." It is in favor of war—war to the bitter end of the combined workers of the world against their despoilers.

* * *

Sancta Simplicitas

THE Trades and Labor Assembly of Minneapolis, Minn., has evidently been encouraged by the action of the British Railway and Mine men in their determined stand against conscription.

The Minneapolis Assembly passed a resolution demanding the seizure of the property of the rich in the event of war to balance the sacrifice of workers' lives.

Splendid! we thought as we read the news. The brave example of the British workers is bearing good fruit.

With much joy we read the Resolutions of the Labor Assembly, till we reached the last passage, and then—then we realized the difference between the British toiler and the American Sovereign of Labor.

What did the British Railway and Mine men do? They threatened a general strike and forced the government to back down.

And the Minneapolis Trade and Labor Assembly? They "resolved that copies of their resolution be sent to the Union League Club, to Theodore Roosevelt and Woodrow Wilson *for their endorsement*."

Can you beat it?

The Necessity of Resistance

THE Executive Council of the A. F. of L. has issued a circular to all unions calling on the organized workers to contribute the wages of an hour's labor for the benefit of the Danbury Hatters.

It will be recalled that the long struggle of the Hatters' Union of Danbury, Conn., against the Anti-Boycott Association and the hat manufacturers, resulted in the courts fining the union $300,000. The bank deposits and homes of the hatters have now been attached to insure payment of the award.

January 27th has been selected as the date on which the workers should contribute an hour's wages to save the Hatters from their plight. There is no doubt that Labor will respond with funds. It always does in such matters, and to that extent it evidences a generous spirit of solidarity.

But we make bold to ask, "Why pay the award?" According to the circular of the Executive Council of the A. F. of L., the Danbury Hatters are *victims of greed and injustice.*

Do free and independent men meekly submit to greed and injustice? Are these the descendants of Patrick Henry who demanded "Give me liberty, or give me death!"?

Submission means increased and ever-increasing oppression and injustice. To hell with paying the awards of greed. If the Danbury Hatters have a spark of Patrick Henry's spirit, let them *resist the attachment* of their homes and let the two-million-headed American Federation of Labor prove its real solidarity by backing up the action of the victimized Hatters.

* * *

Labor Mollusks

LABOR leaders and almost every labor and "radical" publication have been straining hard to explain away the Youngstown riot. The strikers—they feverishly assure us—had no part in it. It was "outsiders," hired thugs from Pittsburgh, agents of Germany, visitors from the Moon, perhaps, but the workers—never!

Why all these protestations, gentlemen? Have the slaves of Youngstown not suffered enough to break out into a riot? Were they not oppressed and tyrannized over beyond the limit of even a slave's endurance? And when the mill guards shot into the defenseless strikers, wantonly killing several men, would you still have their fathers and mothers, brothers and sisters look on meekly and bow their backs in cowardly submission?

Verily, ye apologists for labor violence, ye are slimy mollusks. A man who had nothing to "defend," but who has backbone—Frank P. Walsh—had this to say in his report: *"Violence is a natural form of protest against injustice."*

A Labor Issue

SOME people—well meaning and otherwise—have advised us to ignore Religion and Church and deal only with Labor matters. We also notice that our friend Caroline Nelson, in her article in this issue, says in effect that people now-a-days do not fear the Church any more.

It's a grave mistake. Present-day wage slavery, like all slavery, is *not* the result of capitalism. The reverse is true. Capitalism is the result, not the cause. Capitalism could not continue another fortnight if the workers refused to support it.

The Church with its hoary superstitions is one of the great factors that keep the workers in obedience and submission.

Throughout history the priest—of all denominations—has always sided with King and Master. He has kept the eyes of the people riveted upon "heavenly things" while the exploiters were despoiling them of their earthly possessions.

The Church is the handmaiden of all Tyranny and Oppression.

* * *

This Is the Life

"LABOR is Life, not Vision," triumphantly concludes the editor of *Organized Labor,* after having editorially kicked the "dreamers and visionaries" off the map.

What a brilliant grasp of the situation, what profundity of thought!

The limits of our little Earth are all too inadequate for our editor to prove his erudite conclusion. He had to go outside of the earth, beyond the confines of this sphere, clear out into the Universe for an analogy of Labor's role in the scheme of things.

Says he: "Unyielding and irrevocable as the law of gravitation and the forces and powers which hold the planets and the stars and the orbits of the heavens immovable on their motion through the Universe."

Again, "The forces of the great Cosmos, which comprise the Universe, are always at work, gently, along the lines of least resistance towards the goal of their infinite, ultimate destiny."

The wind and the storm, the thunder and lightning, nature's ravages on land and sea, the death-dealing blizzard, cyclone and earthquake—do these not prove that Nature is at work—as the editor so truly remarks—*"gently,* along the lines of least resistance"?

His difficult premise thus proven, he proudly concludes, "Labor is life, not vision."

Can it be a typographical error? Didn't he mean, Labor is *a living?* For, in spite of all his rhetorical excursions into the Cosmos, his vision and aspirations for Labor must indeed be limited if he is satisfied to regard the miserable, degrading existence of the toilers as Life.

PREPAREDNESS IS HELL

L. E. Claypool

THE man who advocates "Preparedness" has no right to denounce a man who carries a gun in a peaceful community. A nation is nothing but an aggregation of human beings. The traits and propensities peculiar to a nation are the same as those peculiar to the constituent citizenry.

The excuse offered by the Militarists—for that is all these preparedness parties are—for large army and navy appropriations is that the other nations are armed, ready to fight. Very well; we have in this city perhaps 3,000 belligerent gents who secretly carry guns. They are armed, ready to fight. This being true, why may not you or I carry concealed weapons, that we may be prepared for these gents in the event they threaten us? O, the law will not let us. Who is this law, that can do something which the people who gave it existence cannot do? If the law won't let us carry guns, why does it let them?

I never carried a gun in my life, and I never expect to. For twenty-eight years nobody has threatened my life. I am not "prepared," and yet I do not worry about the gunmen of the city. I do not worry for the simple reason that I don't give the gunmen any incentive to gun me. I insist that if the United States would quit doing things to other nations to make them want to fight, said United States would never have to fight. Take our Monroe Doctrine. It is an obsolete prohibition. It is silly for this country, when it can't take care of its own internal injustices, to issue notice to the world that it will not tolerate colonization in South America. South America is able to take care of herself. And where do we get the right, anyhow, to say this or that piece of land shall not be settled upon, when the land lies outside our own jurisdiction? We ought to let South America alone. She resents our attitude, and just to show that she does she buys nearly all her goods from Europe when it would be even cheaper to get them here. She does it because our capitalists and officials have been so arrogant and patronizing.

We will not let other nations outrage South America, but we do not hesitate to do it ourselves. Take Columbia. I'll bet there are not ten men in this city who know the truth about our relations with this benighted southern republic. If they do know it, their patriotism or their shame keeps them from admitting the knowledge. Well, the truth is that we stole the country called Panama from Columbia and built a canal through it. To be sure we stole it legitimately, just like a monopolist steals money, or some of our big real estate men steal land. But we stole it just the same. We did it by inciting sedition in Panama and making the inhabitants believe they were imposed on by Columbia. Says the U. S.: "Panama, strike for your liberty; we will back you." Glittering inducements were offered to Panama, and she seceded. The U. S. fleet stood lazily nearby for the purpose of putting the fear of God in the hearts of the Columbians, whose navy consisted of three rowboats, and whose army is smaller than the police force of New York City. Some of our latter day diplomats have had trouble with their consciences, and the United States recently apologized to Columbia and gave her $25,000,000. You may have noticed, though, that we did not give Panama back to Columbia. It is just as if I would come and steal a cow from you and then give you $1.50 twenty-five years after I stole the cow and beg your pardon. This Panama cow has given birth to a billion dollars calf in the meantime.

In our dealings with Mexico we have done little better. In 1845 we stole a piece of territory from Mexico as big as the State of Missouri. Any historian who is proficient in his profession will admit this. At the time the Department of State tried to salve it over with the conscientious folks of the country by calling it "Manifest Destiny." Up to the time Huerta became president of Mexico we had robbed Mexico of an average of $150,000,000 a year. Go to the local stockholders in the Lucky Tiger mine. Go to the owners of the Orient Railroad. Go to the Archbold (Rockefeller) oil and sulphur interests, and ask how much they paid the Mexican Government for the right to exploit —rather for the privileges of exploiting. Ask them how much they paid Mexican labor. Ask them how much they exacted from the various Mexican State Governments as the price of those improvements the Americans promised to make but never made? Just ask them and see what they say.

In this city lives a man who spent years in Mexico hiring peons. He hired them as do all Americans. Two dozen or so peons are engaged to work at a small sum daily. They are hired while they are under the influence of the most vicious intoxicant known. It is made by distilling the juice of the century plant. In this state of mind the poor Indian will agree to anything. He is given some money to work in advance, and then must work until he pays that back, for under the laws of Mexico a laborer can't quit as long as he is in debt to the employer. By keeping them constantly in debt the Americans make slaves out of the peons; hence—peonage.

All this is not said for the mere novelty of running down America. This is a good country, but it has been in the hands of bad managers. The people have not been to blame. It has been the bodymasters of the nation. From the time we began to violate treaties made with the Indians up to the time we stole the Philippines from Spain, the managers of the Government have gyped and gouged. You can't gyp and gouge without making enemies. Enemies will seek revenge. I don't know but what they are entitled to it. But a country that behaves itself has no worries. Sweden and Holland are not prepared when compared with Germany and France. Yet they are not being molested. Ah, but you say, "What about Belgium?" After all of your other arguments have failed you shout, "What about Belgium?"

Most of you gents that yell never heard of Belgium until this war broke out. A lot of you probably don't know yet that the language of the Belgians is French. Further, you don't know that Belgium had a treaty with England and France which placed the little nation in the war before the German invasion. You may not know that French and English engineers and military experts had surveyed the land and were preparing to make it a battle ground long before Germany actually did so. It is too bad that innocent Belgians were killed. It is an outrage. But it is as much the fault of the rulers of Belgium as it is of the rulers of Germany. Belgium was "prepared," from a military standpoint, and she is paying the price today. Sweden and Holland are not "prepared," and are peaceful.

To be prepared means that you are ready to fight. It means that you expect a fight. And nothing in the history of the world was ever gained by a fight except honor and bruises, and neither one is worth a damn. The element that wants preparedness is the silk stocking gang. They do not expect to do any fighting themselves—war or no war—but they do expect the sucker to do it in order that they of the silken hosiery may linger languorously amid their present luxuries.   —*The Hammer.*

✦ ✦ ✦

A LETTER FROM TOM MANN

MANCHESTER, ENGLAND, January 4, 1916.
Dear Friend Aleck:

I am much interested in your bringing out a new weekly. I certainly think there is room for it, and a fine chance for educational work; and you are wise not to be tied to any "ism." I only received your letter yesterday, and hasten to send a few words of congratulation and encouragement. I feel sure you have well gauged the mental attitude of the people of the U. S. A., in your exceptional activities of the last two years; and you should be equal to commanding the co-operation of fellow workers in the Labor movement.

As you are aware, I lay especial stress upon the Industrial Organization. The longer I live, and the more experience I get, the greater importance I attach to organization. Of course I know how reactionary some organizations are, and how sadly the best of them need a proper appreciation of the Ideal; but I can recall no effort that has been put forth within my experience, no matter how self-sacrificing it may have been, or lofty in aim and aspiration that has really benefited the worker in any direct way except through the agency of organization.

So if I may venture to say so, I hope THE BLAST will stand definitely for industrial organization, for each and every section of the workers; and while advocating the highest ideals, will always favor the practical application of the principle of betterment, and do something of value in raising the standard of life of the workers by hand and brain.

Here in England, in the eighteenth month of the war, the changing psychology of the workers is in a plastic con-

dition. Special efforts are being made to enroll in the army all of a military age; already there are four and a half millions in the British army, and over two millions on munition work, and in connection with the efforts of the conscriptionists and the opponents thereto, there is many a lively tussle taking place. Many workmen are under the impression that it is the intention of the conscriptionists to apply the compulsory principle to the industrial workers, and therefore they are very hostile. In this connection comes along the right relationship of the workers, individually and collectively, to the State, and especially as regards what shall be attempted after the war.

It is not easy to learn with correctness what is going on in the workers' ranks in Germany, but having regard for the large percentage which undoubtedly desired to see drastic social and economic changes before the war, it must surely be the case that most of them or all of them equally desire such change brought about as speedily as possible. Europe is certainly in the melting pot, and what will be the outcome is difficult to forecast, but I fail to see any force in the arguments of those who contend that the United States ought to take part in the war.

Russia alone could provide another fifteen million soldiers, as far as man power goes, if necessary. As regards the fleet, the combined navies of the Allies are on such a scale that another dozen or so of battleships is of little account.

I am not disposed to attempt a discussion of what might happen if America sided with Germany, Austria and Turkey. (As you know, all letters to and from the U. S. A. are dealt with by the censor; therefore the usual freedom of expression is somewhat limited.) * * * * I am primarily concerned to see the Unions putting in a claim, and backing it effectively, for some substantial measure of control in the workshops, as a practical step towards controlling the economic situation at the close of the war, and after.

When the workers appreciate the importance of actually controlling the conditions under which they work, and use the readiest and most effective means by which to do this, the trade unions will become the reconstructive agencies through which the workers will function as producers and consumers. The form the changes will take are likely to be changes in the working hours, regulated so that every one will have an opportunity of participating in useful work, and enjoying the results. I believe this to be worthy of systematic attention in your columns.

                                        TOM MANN.

NOTICE

READERS OF THE BLAST and all other friends and sympathizers are cordially invited to attend

THE OPENING
of the
CURRENT EVENTS CLUB

FRIDAY, February 4th, 8 P. M. sharp, at AVERILL HALL, Market and Ninth Streets.

No lectures. Discussion of the important events of the week, in the political, industrial, social, educational and literary life.
-:-   Introducing the discussion, February 4th, ALEXANDER BERKMAN   -:-

THE GREAT GAME

A. B.

Dramatis Personae:

I—Manufacturers and Capitalists.

You—The Workers.

BLACK FIGURE.

(Curtain rises.)

I: Go down into the bowels of the earth. Bring forth the coal and gold, the iron, silver and precious stones.

You: It is done.

I: Build factories, fashion tools and shape the world into joy and beauty.

You: It is done.

I: Good, my men. Glorious! What wealth, what riches are mine!

A FEW VOICES: Yours? Why, WE created it all!

(Commotion on the stage.)

MORE VOICES (*angrily*): It's ours! *We* made it.

I: Silence! Didn't I *order* it done?

VOICES: But it's ours. We made it.

I: Call in the Law!

(Enter Dark Figure, clad in Black, carrying Bible in one hand, naked sword in the other. Both hands mailed.)

(Solemn silence as the Law speaks.)

THE LAW: It is his. So it is decreed. The integrity of our just and free institutions must be maintained.

(All reverently kneel before the Dark Figure.)

Exit Law.

I (*proudly jubilant*): It is mine, by Law.

YOU: We are poor. Our wives need food, our children are hungry.

I: I will give you the things you need—

YOU: Give us! Give us!

I: In return for more work. I will sell the things you make and I will give you wages for it.

YOU: Wages! Good Wages?

I: Yes, a fair wage.

YOU: Here, here! A fair wage!

I: I will give you food and clothing in return for your wages.

YOU: Kind, kind Master! Here, take our wages.

(I takes the wages and portions out the scanty food.)

(You, having devoured the food, stands empty-handed, with satisfied mien.)

I (*with deep self-satisfaction*): Industry and thrift are the backbone of our great national prosperity.

YOU: But we have nothing left.

I: Elect me to office and I will pass a law to open free soup kitchens for those among you who are deserving of my bounty.

YOU: Hurrah! Hurrah! Our Candidate!

Torch-Light Procession. *Curtain falls slowly.*

LETTER BOX

A. C. For years the militants of this country have been lamenting the absence of a live revolutionary labor paper. It's here now. THE BLAST is at their service. There is no money back of this paper. It will be able to exist only with the co-operation of those who realize the great need of such a paper. It is therefore up to you and other good rebels to get on the job. Help spread THE BLAST. See to it that it gets into the unions of your city; get subscriptions; put it on the stands and cover the various meetings and lectures. Do it now.

SAM AND FRIENDS. The "Chain Gang" and other planned departments will materialize as soon as we can catch our breath. We, in the office here, are good union men, but just now we are working 18 hours every day, Sundays included. There's all kinds of editorial, managerial and clerical work to be done. Come and help.

"BILLY," Kansas City. We're waitin', waitin'. A word to the wise, you know.

S. L. The man who invented letter-writing was certainly a nuisance. Our days are too short for much personal correspondence. We'll speak through THE BLAST.

A. ROSENBERG, Phila. It is a fine thought on your part to make a house-to-house canvass for THE BLAST. Wish we had more like you in every city.

GROUP "VOLONTA" and OTHERS. Reports of meetings, lectures, etc., must be brief. Space in THE BLAST is very limited.

MEETINGS AND LECTURES
(Under this heading announcements will be made free of charge to Labor and Radical Organizations)

CURRENT EVENTS CLUB will meet every Friday, 8 P. M., **sharp**, at Averill Hall, 1256 Market Street near 9th. No lectures. Discussion of important events of the week. Everybody invited to the OPENING of the CLUB, Friday, February 4th. ALEXANDER BERKMAN will open the discussion.

* * *

GRAND BEAN SOCIAL, given by Dr. Bayo, Woodmen's Hall, 3345 Seventeenth Street, Saturday, January 29th, 8 p. m. Admission, 10 cents.

* * *

"VOLONTA," an anarchist propaganda group, will welcome visitors at its meeting place, 1602 Stockton Street, corner Union. Discussion in English and Italian, every Saturday evening.

* * *

THE INTERNATIONAL RADICAL LIBRARY of Chicago holds lectures every Saturday evening, in its club rooms at 712 S. Loomis Street. Friday evenings, discussions. Admission free.

VOL. 1   SAN FRANCISCO, SATURDAY, FEBRUARY 5, 1916   No. 4

FOUND——AND LOST

TO THE WORKERS

Frank A. Fearnley

Your kings and your countries need you,
    You, the sons of honest toil;
But your countries have been stolen,
    You're needed to guard the spoil.

Flower of the nations' manhood,
    They need you but a day;
Mayhap, the morning's sun will rise,
    On heaps of bleeding clay.

I see the bloody plains of war
    Swept clear with shot and shell;
Death's scythe is sweeping quick and fast,
    Gape wide the jaws of hell.

I hear the cannon's roar,
    The cry of souls in anguish;
And maimed and mangled, friend and foe,
    Are left to die and languish.

O men, where does the honor lie,
    In deeds of foulest murder;
To rob a mother of her son,
    Or children of their father.

You build the ships, the ships of war,
    To dominate the foam;
To guard the land you don't possess,
    And your hovel, called a home.

You build the lofty palace hall,
    You build the prison cell;
You forge the fetters of the chain,
    To bind yourselves in hell.

You toil and sweat, you spin and weave,
    You plow the fertile lands,
Yet in the fruitful summer time,
    You stand with empty hands.

Remember this, the great are great,
    Whilst you, on knee, are bended;
But stand and act and think like men,
    The tyrants' day is ended.

🙚 🙚 🙚

WHY REVOLUTIONARY?

MANY a gentle soul shrinks from the word revolution. They see in it naught but shedding of blood, and erroneously imagine the revolutionist a monster. Logically they might as well revile the surgeon whose operation, bloody though it be, relieves human suffering, or the gardener with his pruning hook who lops off superfluous branches that the tree may grow.

It is their very love of humanity or their hatred of tyranny which makes revolutionists in every land sacrifice social standing, liberty, life itself for the cause of human freedom.

Revolutionists are the milestones on the road of progress.

The nice, good, law-abiding muttonhead rapturously listens to the screech of the eagle on Fourth of July and cracks his elbow waving a piece of bunting on a stick, shouting "Hurrah, hurrah, for the flag that makes us free!" Next morning, likely as not, his freedom has a kink in it, and he dog-trots around from one shop to another begging the masters of the bread, "Please, mister, give me a job!"

As for the flag making him free, he might as well have a rabbit's foot in his pocket or a ring in his nose, for all the good it does him.

The same with other nations. The Britisher swells with pride over the Magna Charta and over Cromwell's revolution; the French celebrate the fall of the Bastile; the Italians jubilate over Garibaldi the Liberator and his red-shirted revolutionists.

Revolutions are celebrated in every land by the most respectable conservatives as a matter of mere stupid tradition. Their historical interpretation is left to the social outlaw, the revolutionist of today.

George Washington would have been hanged as a traitor had the British gotten hold of him. John Brown was hanged as traitor; still, his soul goes marching on. Not one American in a thousand knows the names of his judges. Cromwell and Garibaldi would have met John Brown's fate had they failed.

But what of those that have not succeeded?

There are none:

"They never die who fall
    In a great cause. The block may soak their gore,
    Their heads may rotten in the sun; their limbs
    Be strung to city gates and castle walls.
    But still their spirit walks abroad. Though years
    Elapse and others share as dark a doom,
    They but augment the deep and sweeping thought
    Which overpowers all others and turns the world
    At last to freedom."

In all history the ruling classes never surrendered an iota of their power except through force or fear. Nor did the masters ever cease encroaching upon the liberties of the people until the people revolted in self-defense. In self-defense the power over work or idleness (which means practically the power over life and death), now possessed by the employing class, must be broken by Labor. This requires preparation through revolutionary education and organization.

The clash on the barricades may be a long way off. It may never come if Labor musters enough solidarity to accomplish the General Strike, the revolution of the coming days. Again, if Labor does not in time awaken to the dangers of militarism, the gatling guns may win temporary victory for the master class. But even a revolution unaccomplished is not a failure. As well talk of the failure of the human hand because on first attempts it fails to accomplish tasks requiring skill and practice. The revolutionary ideas which prompt resistance cannot be stayed by machine guns.

The men and women, forgotten and unsung though they be, who have helped spread revolutionary ideas, are the true makers of history, in comparison to whom the leaders made conspicuous by time and circumstance are mere figureheads.

In this there is work for all. Are you doing your share? You can, by aiding THE BLAST.

The basest of all slaves is he who glories in the clanking of his chains. Don't be one of them.

We met a proud patriot the other day and stuck a BLAST before his bewildered eyes. As he did not resist, we took a dollar from him for a subscription. But when we asked him to give a few copies to the boys in the shop, he refused to do it for fear of losing his job. Still he thought this was a free country and he was horrified at the word revolution, till we told him that since the revolution in Mexico the bosses down there have had to give three months' notice before they could fire a low-down peon.

Then he liked it.

There are millions of the same kind running wild. Go after them.

THE BLASTERS.

❦ ❦ ❦

LIFE IS VISION

My Dear Berkman:—

Thank you for the January 22d issue of *Organised Labor*, with the editorial "Labor is Life—Not Vision." I am not sure I understand it. The writer gives a high place to the visionaries (dreamers), and yet the general tenor seems to be the uselessness of vision for any practical purpose or to change the inevitable curse of Labor.

Of course, if Labor's present curse be inevitable, nothing will change it; but I believe nothing is inevitable in life but death, and death is the gateway through which a new life continually comes, pushing away the old as an obstruction. As individuals we rebel against death, but if we only knew it, death is the most vital force there is.

I infer the writer contrasts Labor as a hard, stern, eternal fact with Vision—as dreams, soothing but deceiving, because he says in effect "Artists, dreamers, poets, philosophers are often inclined to complain that Labor has no vision. They burn and yearn for a change of conditions which will bring with it relief and more general happiness. Yet in their hopes and aspirations they overlook the fact that Labor is Life and not Vision. It is stern reality. Momentary exultation results from Vision, etc."

Now, as I view it, Labor is no more Life than Leisure. The Labor class has no more Life than the Capitalistic class, or the Idle Rich, or the Idle Poor. All humanity is Life. Life is Vision. Without Vision life is mere existence. Perhaps the clam dreams of a perfect beach and a perfect tide, and none to molest or destroy; or even pictures the day when he will clasp the fingers of the exploiter in a clammy grasp and drag him down to destruction. But so far as we know, the clam has no vision—it merely exists.

Shall Labor be the same? The slaves of Rome dreamed of Leisure and Freedom, and rebelled and lost. Still they did dream, they did rebel, and were happier in their rebellion. The peasants of Germany dreamed of Freedom and Leisure, and rebelled in the Peasants' War, and lost. Still they did dream, they did rebel. The Peasantry of England dreamed of Freedom and a democracy, and rebelled, and won,—and the march toward man's economic and political freedom began. The peasantry of France dreamed of a little more the life of a man and a little less the life of a hog, and rebelled, and won—and another small step toward human freedom was taken. The miner and the factory weaver of England had a vision of collective strength, asking a little more the life of a man and a little less the life of a brute, and won,—the step called Labor Unions. Watts saw the lid of a tea kettle lifting and had the vision of the giant Steam. Stephenson dreamed the railway locomotive. Franklin dreamed electricity and Morse the telegraph, and the world was changed.

Man's whole world rests upon vision. Not only Shakspeare and Milton glancing from heaven to earth, from earth to heaven, and, as imagination bodied forth the forms of things unknown, turning them to shapes and giving to airy nothing a local habitation and a name.

Not only Homer, Goethe, Beethoven, Moliere, Villon, Dante, Cervantes, but Archimedes, Von Humboldt, Karl Marx, Danton, Pasteur, Proudhon, Tolstoy, Kropotkin, Galileo, Bruno, Ferrer, Darwin, Arkwright, Tom Paine, Jefferson, Lincoln, Bell, Edison, Mergenthaler. Everything which marks man apart from the unprogressive clam is Vision. And shall Labor, which is Life and which is the builder of all, be denied Vision?

Vision is no empty dream, no floating cobweb. It is man's vital force. The only vital force save the mere existence of the idiot. It is very definite in its terms— sometimes it murders, sometimes it dynamites.

Labor's ceaseless and endless struggle for a little more leisure, a little more freedom—a little more the life of a man and a little less the life of a brute—is but the dynamic life-force shaking off the clogs and endeavoring to realize its vision of a day when work shall be for uses and not exploitation. When the laborer, though he earn his bread by the sweat of his face, shall also sit with his children in the shade of his vine and fig tree and have leisure to enjoy his own soul and be free.

The Persians say leisure is one of the gateways to heaven. I know freedom is the very instinct of the soul. And, above all, shall not the laborer have a vision of that day when he shall not be classed apart as the "laboring class," but he and his shall in all things be respected according to his own deserts; himself serene in a natural self respect, not the false boasting of one who feels he boasts a lie. Has Labor no vision of a city without slums? A factory without hovels? A mine without slaves?

Unless Labor has these visions, they will never materialize—and Labor will never be free. But they will come, for Labor truly is Life and Life is Vision.

If the Labor leaders have not vision, or having it do not dare, others will be thrown up from that seething mass below whose ferment is Vision.

Vision is Life. It is all there is save mere sodden, contented, fixed, brutish existence. And the greatest Vision for Labor today is Solidarity. That is practical enough. That goes down to the very root of Labor's Life—and that is Vision. Let me repeat: If Labor be Life, as indeed it is, then Labor is Vision, for the Essence of Life is Vision.

CHARLES ERSKINE WOOD SCOTT.

THE POWER OF THE PRESS
Caroline Nelson

IN ancient times the Church ruled the world with an iron rod. Before mankind could make the slightest progress, that power had to be curbed. The Church and its hierarchy are now driven into the field of defense. Its power to form and shape the opinion of the public, particularly of that portion which belongs to the working class, is weak. No intelligent men really fear the Church today.

But they do fear the press. The press has absorbed the arrogant power that the Church used to have, and it uses it just as ruthlessly. The press has the power to silence any voice and to bury any cause in the grave of oblivion, and it does not hesitate to use it. It is the most powerful ally of the ruling power. Like the Church of old, it pretends that it has an undying affection for the poor. It begs for them for Christmas, and prepares festivities and presents for the outcasts and poverty-stricken. In a certain large city on the coast several papers that were particularly active in helping the poor this year, dug into the pockets of the newsboys, and charged them twenty-five cents more for a hundred papers than they had paid previously. The news sellers had to foot the bill of the Christmas glories graciously handed out by those papers. They not only have to foot it for Christmas, but all the year round; thus paying for it over and over again. But the news sellers are helpless; they have no voice. Therefore why not charge the bill up to their account in a nice legitimate way? That is the same old game that the Church used to play, perhaps a little less brazenly.

This power of the press must be curbed before the working class can make any headway in modern times. Men and women with brains and the courage of their convictions must rise up and smite that power. They must unmask its dark and evil methods of creating public opinion, and its diabolical way of serving the powers that be and the public at the same time.

That is why the workers must create a press for themselves. A press that should be a great deal more than merely a feeble voice of the workers' own feeble desires. It must be a press that can destroy the Old and lead the way to the New. It should possess some of the daredevil spirit of a Voltaire and the deep insight and fearlessness of a Thomas Paine. It should steer clear of economic dogmatism and sociological infallibilities which have been so fatal to it in the past. It should not make a mountain out of a mole-hill, or feed its readers on small talk and sensationalism about victories that are doubtful; for that is only playing the game of the capitalist press, which can't be beaten by a little sheet in the labor world. The workers are constantly crying, "Show us the way out!"

Nor is it enough to point out that all slavery is based on industrial bondage; for on the foundation of industrial serfdom has been reared a whole social structure that shields and guards this foundation to such an extent that it is almost impossible to touch it. There is, for instance, THE SCHOOL that moulds the child's mind to fit the System, and shapes the young into narrow little patriots, eager to protect the Existing with their own lives, if need be. This must obviously be changed if the workers are to make any real progress on the road to industrial freedom.

The toilers must have something more to fight with than their pennies and high-sounding phraseology. They must have an ever-increasing intelligence and an ever-decreasing competition among themselves, built on greater solidarity and smaller families.

With these remarks I hope that THE BLAST will go out into the world full of courage, to make friends—not out of charity, but because of genuine admiration.

JUSTICE DEFINED

IT is dangerous to tell the people that laws are not just; for they obey only for the reason that they think them just. Hence they must be told at the same time that they must obey them because they are laws, as they must obey superiors, not because they are just, but because they are superiors. All sedition is prevented, then, if we can make this understood and it is, properly speaking, the definition of justice.—PASCAL.

THE POOR MAN'S TAXI

NO better illustration of the impotence of politics, as an instrument for social betterment, can be had than the treatment accorded the jitneys. With the advent of the poor man's taxi, the practice, not tolerated in any European country, of slamming passengers into a street car like mud into a scow, was on the point of being abolished. The emancipation of the straphangers seemed near.

But as Mr. Yerkes, of Chicago, now happily dead, once remarked: "The dividends are in the straps."

In order to provide dividends for millionaire street car magnates rather than comfort for the public, the lowly jitney bus has practically been legislated out of existence in every city where it had a foothold, under the pretense of "protecting the public."

The dear public never had a look in.

The sacred and supposedly omnipotent ballot gets a bad attack of paralysis every time it runs up against submarine dollar diplomacy.

NONE are more hopelessly enslaved than those who falsely believe they are free.—GOETHE.

THE human race is in the best condition when it has the greatest degree of liberty.—DANTE.

THE BLAST   Five

THE BLAST
Revolutionary Labor Weekly
569 Dolores St., San Francisco, Cal.
Mail Address, Box 661   Phone, Park 499

Alexander Berkman, Editor and Publisher
E. B. Morton, Associate Editor   M. E. Fitzgerald, Manager

SUBSCRIPTION
$1.00 Yearly   60c Six Months   5c Copy
Bundle rates, 2½c per copy in bundles of ten.
Advertising rates on application.
Application for entry as second-class matter at the postoffice at San Francisco pending.

COMMENTS

Promises and Performance

THE British Conscription Bill is expected to become a law this month. The government promised the workers that the law will not be used against Labor.

Verily, it is to laugh. Unfortunately, there are still too many who have faith in governmental promises.

It reminds us that when the State Constabulary was created in Pennsylvania, the government solemnly assured the workers that the new police would do only patrol duty in the outlying districts. But no sooner was the Constabulary organized than it was let loose upon striking workingmen. The fiendish brutality of this State police has been so terrible that its members are now universally known among the workers of Pennsylvania as the Cossacks.

Beware of your masters' promises.

It seems, however, that not all the workers of Great Britain can be so easily fooled. In the recent Labor Congress a very strong minority of the Labor delegates voted against the infamous bill. May the workers of America take notice.

* * *

At Home

THE American jingoes now demand universal conscription in this country. That means forcible service. But surely the people of the United States have sense enough to defend themselves when in danger. Why, then, must they be forced to it?

The militarists are letting the cat out of the bag. Their arguments prove that the workers really have no reason to defend the country of their masters. That's why they want to force them to it.

* * *

Defending Your Robbers

LET'S talk it over, Henry Dubbs. There is vast wealth in this country of yours: plenty of gold and silver, precious stones, gigantic warehouses where good things are stored, palaces and fine buildings worth millions of dollars, billions of bank deposits and many other fine things.

All that wealth needs defending. But let us ask you, Mr. Worker, what share of all this wealth do you own? Or your wife and your children? Or your fellow-worker on the bench next to you?

You don't own any of it, you say? Well, now, that's strange. Didn't you and the others like you build and create all those things? Still you insist that you don't own anything of it?

Then why th' hell do they want *you* to protect it?

Tell us, please.

Labor Goes A-Begging

THE Brotherhood of Locomotive Engineers, Brotherhood of Locomotive Firemen, the Order of Railway Conductors and Brotherhood of Railway Trainmen are considering a demand for an 8-hour day. It is very questionable whether the Kings of the iron steed will grant the request, which means a strike of 400,000 men.

It is as if an audience of 5000 people were to beg permission of the Chairman of the meeting to please let them leave the hall when they got tired holding down their seats. Suppose the Chairman refused? Well, wouldn't they get up and just walk out?

Those 400,000 men are the actual power that keeps the railroads going. Without them not a car could be moved or an engine fired. The whole railroad industry is in their hands, absolutely. And they—they ask permission of the Chairman to please let them leave the hall.

Stupid, isn't it? Suppose these 400,000 men just decided to *leave* after 8 hours' work, or after 6, or 4 hours? What could the Masters do about it? Why, just nothing. The railroads must be run; the Rockefellers, Harrimans and other kid-gloved ones can't run them themselves. They would simply submit.

Ah, but that means Solidarity and spunk. The Labor leaders would be the first to object to such an un-slavish proceeding.

* * *

Investigation Dope

NO less than four separate Commissions are now "investigating" the Youngstown strike. If you watch them carefully some of them may actually report that "conditions in the mills could be improved."

It's an easy game for the bosses. If their slaves are dissatisfied and show signs of rebellion, all that's necessary is to appoint a commission, or several, to "investigate." That ends the trouble, the "hands" go back to work, and the satisfied coupon clipper says with a sigh of relief, "Thank goodness, it's settled now."

That is just the tragedy. It's too easily "settled," always to the satisfaction and profit of the boss.

* * *

Resistance to Political and Industrial Tyranny

WE are glad the Department of Labor finally decided to permit Emmeline Pankhurst, the English suffragette, to enter this country. It is stupid, of course, to have such questions come up at all. Why shouldn't any one enter this country? Are the great people of the United States afraid to hear any one's views?

But the admission of Mrs. Pankhurst has special significance. The Department decided to let her in on the ground that her offenses were political. In other words, her many acts of violence—for which she was repeatedly convicted and imprisoned—do not constitute, in the stilted language of officialdom, "moral turpitude." In plain English it means that violence committed by political offenders is not to be considered criminal.

Very likely the action of the Labor Department was merely a sop thrown to American suffragists. This is election year, you know, and the administration needs support, especially of those women who have the vote in this country. It may also be, of course, that the liberal decision of the Department is partly due to the progressive ideas of Commissioner Louis F. Post, the Single Taxer.

However, whatever the real cause of the decision, the logic on which it was officially based is good: acts of violence committed by political offenders cannot be considered proof of moral turpitude or as being criminal. With equal logic we go further. We hold that violence committed by soldiers of the industrial war—not only in England but right here in our own country—is equally justifiable with acts of violence by political offenders. Both are fighting against tyranny, and—if anything—industrial tyranny over men in America is greater than the political tyranny of Great Britain over its women. Therefore resistance more necessary.

* * *

Electing the Boss's Wife

SPEAKING of suffragettes, English or American, it is understood of course that we do not oppose woman suffrage. The vote will do working *women* no more good than it does working *men*. Woman, like man, is entitled to no less than she can take.

But what we mean to point out is this: Some people imagine that the suffragists and suffragettes are inspired by a new passion for liberty. That's a mistake. What inspires them is the *passion to govern*.

It is not woman, as a sex, that is the victim of existing conditions. It is only the *working* woman—exactly as is the working man.

Will the working woman gain anything by electing her boss's wife to office?

* * *

Defiance of Authority

THE Margaret Sanger mass meeting proved a great success. The Chief of Police of San Francisco warned the meeting not to circulate any family limitation literature. But the spirit of the gathering was such that not only were the forbidden pamphlets circulated in the audience, but one of the speakers handed them out direct from the platform.

Oi, what a defiance of holy authority!

But it is this kind of defiance, open and unafraid, that defeats prohibition and oppression. It was the courageous stand of Margaret Sanger in defying the law against advocating family limitation that roused thousands of people to the need of such work—people who are now also ready to defy the law.

We need more of this kind of resistance in our submissive, timid American life. Especially do the workers need it.

* * *

A Good Example

JUDGES are known to be good stickers. They never quit their fat jobs voluntarily. Only death can take them off the bench.

But the exceptional does happen occasionally, and it certainly deserves a comment. John H. Stevenson, Municipal Judge of Portland, Oregon, actually quit his position of his own free will. It was a fine thing to do. Still finer

are the reasons given by him for his action: "If I could help the people who come before me, I might remain. But I cannot help them, and I am constantly called upon to penalize them. I have been doing this daily now for more than two years and I cannot longer continue."

No stronger indictment could be brought against our criminal society that dooms thousands to misery and hopeless punishment in order to enable the few to roll in luxury. Think of the thousands who daily face the Judges in our police courts—year in and year out—just to be penalized without being helped.

If those judges had the least spark of manhood or decency they would follow the example of the Portland Justice.

* * *

Moulding Slaves

AMERICAN professors, like Scott Nearing and others, have for years been promptly kicked out from the high seats of "learning," when they dared express opinions contrary to the masters' teachings. Now it is the turn of the pupils. Harold B. Matson, a senior in the San Francisco High School, has been peremptorily dismissed (half a term before graduation) for expressing himself against military training in the school. Matson had issued a pamphlet announcing the advent of the *Scholastic Rebel*, a school paper opposed to militarism.

Fie on the carping critics who charge our educational institutions with being incubators of obedient slaves. Our schools are designed to develop manhood, independence of thought and self-reliance in the pupils. The Matson case proves it, does it not? And it is only one out of many.

THE SCHMIDT CASE—AND BEFORE
Ed Gammons

WHEN the McNamara boys were sentenced in Los Angeles four years ago by Judge Bordwell, for complicity in the *Times* explosion, the era of industrial peace came into existence. To quell the intensive feeling of labor unionism against the vile subterranean tactics of the Merchants' & Manufacturers' Association, well-meaning sociologists established a truce with the main condition that no more prosecutions would be instituted in connection with the McNamara case. This institution of the industrial Golden Rule in Los Angeles was heralded near and far. We were told that the capitalist class was experiencing a radical change of heart, that the philosophy of Jesus of Nazareth was entering into their business conduct, and that in view of this astounding development the industrial struggle would inevitably lose its aggressive demeanor in favor of a conciliatory spirit.

Years went by. The organization of the Los Angeles workers proceeded slowly, but William J. Burns was relentlessly hunting for Caplan and Schmidt, with ten thousand dollars of blood-money constantly in view. Finally the "great American sleuth" located his victims, in September, 1914. Were they hurried to Los Angeles? No. On the witness stand, a couple of weeks ago, Burns explained that he wanted to bag both his victims at one shot, and that though he located Schmidt in September, 1914, he was not quite sure about the whereabouts of Caplan. A very important fact in connection with this delay was that John D. Fredericks, District Attorney, who prosecuted the Mc-Namaras and who was a party to the "Golden Rule" truce, did not vacate office till the 1st of January, 1915. He was succeeded by Thomas Lee Woolwine, who was elected solely by the labor vote. In his pre-election campaign this legal star was marvelously profuse in declaring that the Steel Trust, or any other corporation, would not be allowed to prostitute the office which he aspired to, in any campaign against labor. To the editor of the local newspaper he solemnly declared that he would never indict a single soul in connection with the *Times* case, and that no power on earth could compel him to reopen it. He wished he could "take his heart out of his breast and give it as a hostage for his honest intentions."

By the middle of February the Labor-loving, altruistic Woolwine was complaisant, and Burns paraded his victims into Los Angeles. The Golden Rule was an abortion only—it never lived. The mask was off, and we heard Los Angeles ring with the demand for the blood of Caplan and Schmidt. They had millions to convict. They dragged in Noel, of Indianapolis, as a sure convictor; Clarke, the Cincinnati felon and perjurer; Davis, debonair would-be murderer and felon; McManigal, the arch-traitor; and, lastly, Donald Vose Meserve, the most contemptible of them all, who betrayed his friends for a few dollars, whose most daring deed was that of dipping into his room-mate's pocket in Seattle, and who is now a lonely outcast without shame or friends. This was the hell-crew which for three months yelped at Mathew A. Schmidt, a man whom only one of them had ever seen—and that in New York—and who towered above them all in every manly virtue and honest trait.

Thus Mathew A. Schmidt joins the McNamaras, Ford, Suhr, Quinlan, Lawson and our other comrades who are held by the enemy. Once a revolutionary is enmeshed in the law—the "rule-ridden game," as Melville Davisson Post calls it—the chances are all against him; the dice are loaded.

As the struggle goes on and on, the need for action on the industrial field is apparent. The courts are courts of *law*—not of *justice*. The workers must realize the power they have in their hands, the power which determines whether our railroads will run tomorrow, whether our factories will cloud the blue sky with the smoke of industry, whether the humming wires will carry the news of the East to the West, aye, whether our masters of industry shall eat their breakfasts. Education of the working class is our crying need. Tell them the story of Lawrence and Ludlow; tell them how sixty-five per cent. of the Belgian working class won their demands by a general strike; let them know what the Federal Commission on Industrial Relations reported after they reviewed the industrial battle ground. It is not a time for personalities and isms; the working class must be educated to the point of bitter re-

sistance. And when the spirit of utter discontent stalks, North and South, East and West, the awakened workers will not be long in changing from the slough of despondency and misery to the bright new era of industrial freedom.

🌱 🌱 🌱

THE HUMAN MASS
Luke North

BLASTING is a good and surely a necessary task, but I submit that radicalism needs it more than does the mass. Radicalism's brain is in a rut. It is thinking, talking, writing, about as it did thirty years ago—it is still blasting and hammering at the unthinking mass. It should be welding the mass and leading it toward construction. It is still yelling, "Stupid, blind, slavish people, wake up and throw off your chains!" The mass is not aroused that way, not even to the Christian trenches and death machines. Nor is it led by teaching it economics. Those who expect to save the world by educating it in the mysteries, or even the essentials, of the various economic creeds, are still blinder than those who think to blast it out of God's and Mammon's strangle hold.

"God and my country!" led the masses to the European shambles. It is a stronger urge than all the common sense, rationalistic shibboleths of radicalism. Why? Because it holds high an Ideal—a false ideal as we know, but that is no matter. It is a very exalted ideal, entirely removed from any sort of immediate personal advantage. It is an exalted and untainted ideal (however damfoolish we know it to be). There is no cheap dross on it, no mud of the market or the bank. It stirs the deepest recesses of human nature.

At heart the human mass is neither mechanistic nor materialistic—it is spiritual, in the highest, deepest value of that much-abused word. At heart the mass is not a gluttonous, sensual brute to be lured by food. It was not so lured or led by the priesthoods. Radicalism, if it really cares to do anything, might well sit at the feet of Catholicism and learn how the mass is molded, led (to its own doom); it will be led to its own unfoldment in much the same manner, or it will wait the toilsome centuries' unfoldment from within.

It is radicalism's task to give the mass an unsullied ideal, free of personal interest. . . .

I trust THE BLAST will be turned not on the mass, but on its natural leaders, the Intelligent Minority—radicalism. The mass is as it is. It is not now amenable to logic or to dynamite—perhaps it will be some day, if radicalism learns how to lead it.

PRELIMINARY NOTICE
Labor Bodies and other friendly organizations are hereby requested to co-operate with us on the
INTERNATIONAL COMMUNE FESTIVAL
in Commemoration of the 45th Anniversary of the Paris Commune of 1871, SATURDAY, MARCH 18th, 8 P. M., Averill Hall, 1254 Market Street, opposite City Hall.

Excellent music program and addresses.

THE COMMITTEE.

FOR YOUNG FOLKS

THE other day I dropped in to visit a friend. As I opened the door, I heard excited voices inside. I knew that Tommy was again getting a scolding. Tommy, you must know, is my friend's youngest son, a boy of about twelve years.

"Why can't I have it?" I heard Tommy ask.

"I told you, you can't," his father answered angrily.

"But I want to know why I can't," cried Tommy.

"You can't, that's all. Shut up now."

I didn't stay long there. I don't like to be where people are quarreling. But I wanted to know what they were quarreling about. So when I was ready to go I called to Tommy:

"Say, Tom, let's go down to the park, will you?"

"You betcher," said Tom.

Tom and I are old friends, so I made no bones about wanting to know why his father scolded him.

"Well, you see," he said, "my pants are all torn and I asked father to buy me a new pair. He said I couldn't have it. I asked him why and he told me to shut up."

I could see that Tom felt very hurt. At first I thought it was because he couldn't have new pants, but after awhile he said:

"It's always 'shut up!' It makes me sick. Father never tells me why. 'You can't, that's all'," Tommy tried to mimic his father's voice.

I saw that Tommy was a fine, proud lad. Why shouldn't he know, I asked myself. I was thinking hard over it as I walked with the boy, when he broke out again.

"I ain't no kid any more," he said angrily. "Father don't know that."

"You know what, Tom," I said, "if your father doesn't answer your questions, *I'll* try to answer them."

"Will you?" he cried joyfully.

But the next minute he said, "No, you can't."

"Why?" I asked, a little hurt. "Try me; perhaps I can."

"No, it ain't that," he answered. "There's many things I want to know, oh, ever so many questions I can ask. And if you ain't around, how am I going to remember them all?"

Here was a hard one. I was anxious to know what questions Tom would ask me, and I wanted to help him to an answer. But he was right. I am a busy man and I couldn't see him often. What could be done?

I looked at Tommy as we were walking along. His fine young face seemed troubled. I could see he was thinking hard. All of a sudden he stopped.

"Say, I got it," he cried. "I'll write it out."

"What do you mean, Tommy?"

"Well, every time I think of something to ask you, I'll write it down, and then when I see you, I'll ask you all the questions at once."

"It's a fine idea, Tom," I said. But as I was speaking, another thought struck me. Perhaps I would have never thought of it if it were not for Tom.

"It's a fine idea, Tom," I said again, "but what do you say to this: you write down your questions and bring them to me. You know I publish a paper. Well, I'll answer your questions in the paper."

"You'll put my name in, too?" he asked bashfully.

"Yes, if you want it."

"Do I? But—" he stopped as if ashamed.

"But what, Tom?"

"People will read it and think my questions foolish."

"Oh, no, don't worry about that, Tom. Questions are never foolish when you really want to know."

"Honest, now?"

"Honest."

And that's how Tom and I made the bargain. He said he'll bring me his questions, but he was afraid there will be too many. But when I told him that it will be all right, he said he would tell the other fellows to send in their questions, too. They all had questions, he said; the boys and the girls also. And I'll bet that you boys and girls, who read this, have some questions, too. Send them in to me. And next week I am going to answer Tom's first question, the one that his father wouldn't answer. ALECK.

MEETINGS AND LECTURES

(Under this heading announcements will be made free of charge to Labor and Radical Organizations)

CURRENT EVENTS CLUB will meet every Friday, 8 P. M., sharp, at Averill Hall, 1256 Market Street near 9th. No lectures. Discussion of important events of the week.

* * *

Saturday, February 12th, 8 p. m., Union of Russian Workers will produce Gogol's play "Marriage." American Film Hall, 425 Hoffman Avenue. Admission, 25c.

* * *

ARTHUR SWAN will speak at the Solidarity Club, Sunday, February 6th, 8 p. m., on "The Revolution in Mexico." Woodmen's Hall, 3345 Seventeenth Street.

VOL. 1   SAN FRANCISCO, SATURDAY, FEBRUARY 12, 1916   No. 5

The Boss's wife can buy information to limit her family.

The Boss can buy your children to supply his factories with cheap labor.

THE STATE AND THE PEOPLE

Voltairine de Cleyre

What have you done, O State,
    That the toilers should shout your ways;
Should light up the fires of their hate
    If a "traitor" should dare dispraise?

What do you mean when you say
    "The home of the free and brave"?
How free are your people, pray?
    Have you no such thing as a slave?

What are the lauded "rights,"
    Broad-sealed, by your Sovereign Grace?
What are the love-feeding sights
    You yield to your subject race?

The rights! Ah! the right to toil,
    That another, idle, may reap;
The right to make fruitful the soil
    And a meagre pittance to keep!

The right of a woman to own
    Her body, spotlessly pure,
And starve in the street—alone!
    The right of the wronged—to endure!

The right of the slave—to his yoke!
    The right of the hungry—to pray!
The right of the toiler—to vote
    For the master who buys his day!

You have sold the sun and the air!
    You have dealt in the price of blood!
You have taken the lion's share
    While the lion is fierce for food!

You have laid the load of the strong
    On the helpless, the young, the weak!
You have trod out the purple of wrong;—
    Beware when their wrath shall wreak!

🕮   🕮   🕮

THE MEANING OF MARGARET SANGER'S STAND

Reb Raney

I see a scale as I begin to write: On one side is Hearst, Roosevelt, et al., laden with gas bombs and tools made for slaughter. They appear to ascend, for they are held aloft by the inanimate wings of a powerful aeroplane labeled Fear; on the other side of the scale is Margaret Sanger, descending sufficiently to touch the form of a bent, very weary little creature, who plainly is Woman. As she touches the dejected figure, it looks toward the other side of the scale, hesitates for just a moment, and then, without removing its gaze from the terrifying thing above, smiles very faintly but perceptibly. You can see this picture yourself, if you close your eyes and think a moment. It isn't a fancy. It's real.

As to how Margaret Sanger was able to do this thing, with the entire weight of institutional decay against her; and notwithstanding her words that "if we could depend upon a strong and consistently revolutionary support in such battles, instead of weakened efforts to effect a compromise with the courts, there would be much greater stimulation for individuals to enter revolutionary activity": Margaret Sanger herself has proved that "support" is secondary and not primal. She has illustrated that when a man or a woman goes armed with a Purpose, with utter faith in him or herself, and with that sublime indifference which reckons personal safety a matter of no consequence, the result cannot be other than an indentation which is both luminous and lasting. It never occurred to this daring soul to inquire if anyone would stand by her. Her "revolutionary activity" was not the fruit of assurances of support from liberal-minded discerners. No, it was the product of her own discernment, and woe be to the set, immobile thing which collides with the seeing eye that isn't afraid.

Oh, you labor leaders, and would-be saviors, and argumentative theorists, mark you well the clause, "which reckons personal safety a matter of no consequence." The fact that Margaret Sanger never for a moment cared what be-

came of *her,* is why she was able to open the door to a new, freer, wider, loftier sphere for herself and the rest of her statute-bruised sisterhood. If any fault can be found with labor men who have been on trial, it is that they shrink back and sit in silence while professional fakirs deny that Labor itself is On Trial. It is this cringing timidity that invites buckshot in law courts as well as out of them. Support is a thing which responds to Fearlessness. Let the man or woman who *acts* stand up and face dissension, and dissension—which is as fickle as a Fifth Avenue baby—will resolve itself into the kind of acclaim that moves jurists to listen.

Too long has woman moistened the world with blood gifts wrung from her unwilling frame by her color-blind sons. She has received, sustained, brought forth endlessly, for what? For "the new crop," as Bismarck called the new edition of infant soldiers-to-be, after the Franco-Prussian war. And this because the printed words "prevention of conception" have been labeled unspeakably vile by the very ones who trade on the workability of the process! Fie, on the whole hypocritical job-lot of phrase-building nincompoops! Man, with all his intellect and sagacity, has chiefly succeeded in marring the very coating of the earth with the bleached corpuscles of his own sons. Nor has he stopped. But Woman has. And surely the birds in the belfries of heaven will concur in saying it was time that a victim should step forth and say: You shall drain us no longer!

The particular point of interest in this case is Mrs. Sanger's purpose "to separate the idea of prevention of conception and birth control from the sphere of pornography." She shows the keenness of her mind by realizing that this is the vulnerable point of the "nasty" theory argument. Who has not from childhood been told that the sex union is a kaleidoscopic affair—holier than heaven if done by script, but baser than hell if done otherwise. Just so, do the decreers tell us in one breath that woman is the holiest thing the Great Builder ever chiseled, while with pen and paper they write it as their opinion that the same charming creature is only good in spots, and that that person who would save her from having an additional spot should be castigated penally forevermore. As if it is not the same woman and the same acts which have given them the stature and temerity to assail the thing they do not even faintly comprehend!

So all because a single woman stood up and refuted the idea that there was anything "nasty" about *any* woman, we ladies are hereafter to derive the benefits of sex preparedness. Where are you, Editors, you sleepy absorbers of Annielaurieism? Flick the clots from your worn-out quill pens and speak for that which has come about in spite of you. Never mind your military preparedness or your anti-military preparedness. Here is something moving in your midst, which is going to rust every hole in your cannon belchers and muffle your powder in an eternity of sleep.

🙣 🙣 🙣

THE WOMAN REBEL

I, a woman, am first a human being.

I know now that I am no longer a mystery. I am one of a species, possessing certain characteristics in common with all members of my species, male and female. I possess a body; I require food, shelter and raiment. I possess the power of locomotion. I possess the power of conscious and sub-conscious mental action. I possess of myself five senses. I can see, feel, hear, taste and smell. I, a woman, can do these things of myself. I am also an individual detached from all others, but united to my kind by a community of common interests.

I possess the power of self-development, which is my most sacred right. I possess, also, the power of self-education, to appropriate to my own needs that knowledge which I desire and which I believe to be to my interest to possess, for I possess the power of free-thought.

I possess the power to reject, for myself, all teaching, dogma and tradition which conflict with my sense of personal liberty, for I possess my own spirit.

I also possess the power of co-operation with my fellows and the power of mutual aid, which I count among my joys and evidence to myself of my own development.

I possess the power to give and receive love, for I possess my own emotions and the intelligence to distinguish between emotion and sensation.

I possess the appreciation of beauty: in nature, the arts and in sympathetic companionship with my fellows, and the power to appropriate these according to my own needs.

I possess the function of motherhood and the power to exercise it or reject it, according to the dictates of my conscience and desire, for I possess my own body. I possess the power of reproduction, but I am more than a biological specimen—I am a human spirit.

I am The Interpreter of Life. Not for others, but in terms of my own needs.

NELLIE TERRY CRAIG.

FORBIDDEN KNOWLEDGE

IN the United States in this "enlightened" year of our Lord, 1916, Margaret Sanger, of New York, stands accused of disseminating scientific knowledge regarding the limitation of offspring. This knowledge, which any wealthy woman may buy from her physician, is withheld from the poor that they may by prolific breeding furnish a plentiful and cheap labor supply.

The denial by the State of a woman's right over her own body constitutes slavery, and teaching slaves was ever a crime.

"A little knowledge is a dangerous thing"—to the master when the slave gets it. Let the women rebel. Our readers may see history repeating itself by looking backward a hundred years:

"Any person that teaches any person of color, slave or free, to read or write, or causes such persons to be so taught, is subject to a fine of thirty dollars for each offense; and every person of color who shall keep a school to teach reading or writing is subject to a fine of thirty dollars, or to be imprisoned ten days, and whipped thirty-nine lashes." (City Ordinance, Savannah, Ga., 1818.)

"The reason for this law is that teaching slaves to read and write tends to dissatisfaction in their minds, and to produce insurrection and rebellion." (American Slave Code, p. 321.)

🙣 🙣 🙣

SAVE THE CRACK

THE Boston Massacre of March 5, 1770, may be regarded as the first act in the drama of the American revolution. "From that moment," said Daniel Webster, "we may date the severance of the British Empire."

The presence of British soldiers in King Street, Boston, excited the indignation of the people. Led by Crispus Attucks, a mulatto slave, they attacked the main guard, with more valor than discretion, and were fired upon by Captain Preston's company. Crispus Attucks was the first to fall. In November, 1855, Boston erected a monument to the negro slave who started the American Revolution. That was a long time before the Liberty Bell was ever heard of, and long before it got cracked.

It is recorded in modern history, however, that when this "sacred emblem of American liberty" was returning through darkest Texas from the San Francisco Fair, to its resting place in Sleepy Hollow, Pa., an enraged crowd of citizens (not a mob) sought to attack the Liberty Bell party because a member of the party lifted a negro girl to the car and let her kiss the relic.

The recent lynching of five negroes in Georgia is another instance of the "peaceful and orderly progress of our civilization."

Not even the most law-abiding association of white wage slaves has raised its voice in protest.

Our boasted "equality before the law" becomes a dead letter if the other fellow's skin is darker than ours.

Why bemoan the crack in the Liberty Bell? That crack is truly emblematic of American liberty. In fact, we might sell the Bell as junk, and just save the crack.

A WORD TO YOU

YOU say you are a radical. Perhaps even a revolutionist. You belong to this or that school of social philosophy. You believe that present conditions are wrong; that they create misery and poverty, crime and degradation. You long for a saner and happier life.

What are you doing to help bring it about? You know that things don't change of themselves. You admit that effort is needed. You realize that it is necessary to get more people to think as you do, to make them dissatisfied with what Is, and to inspire them with the passion and courage to strive for the Better.

How is that to be done? Discussion alone won't do it. Making programs for future generations will not change the present.

You know that it is not enough to curse the capitalist, to rave at the intellectual, or to sneer at the masses. That may be good to relieve your feelings. But it does not get you anywhere. Nor is it enough to say, what's the use. When you are hungry, you don't satisfy yourself that way. You have to do something to get a meal. And generally you get it; if you didn't, you wouldn't be here now. Not that it would matter, but the fact is, you *are* here. You usually get the thing you go after, if you go after it hard enough.

That's how things are gotten. We'll get a better world if we want it hard enough. A great thinker once said, "We could have an ideal society tomorrow if enough people would imagine it." If we would imagine and want a thing hard enough, we'd do something to get it. What are *you* doing about it?

What's to be done? you ask. The very first step is to make people dissatisfied with the THINGS THAT ARE. Conscious discontent is the beginning of Change. The second step is to rouse the hope of Something Better and the determination to achieve it.

THE BLAST is trying to do this. Never mind theoretical differences of opinion. We all agree that it is necessary to wake the sleeping, to rouse the slave to a passionate hatred of his chains, to point the way of liberty

and progress, and inspire the courage and will to assert his manhood.

That is the work of THE BLAST. Are you willing to help? We can't do this work alone. We need your co-operation. Help gather the Voice of Discontent. It's everywhere, in every "brow that boldly thinks, in every hut that harbors grief, in every bosom that pants and struggles for relief." Its combined volume has power enough to shake the very foundations of our rotten social structure.

Come, help us gather the hosts of discontent and imbue them with conscious purpose. Their irresistible march will sweep off the earth all that is false, decayed and rotten.

Not in the next century or in the next decade is this to be done. It must be done now. It *can* be done—with your help.

Will you help?

We are waiting to hear from you.

THE BLASTERS.

THE MADNESS OF JINGOISM

WORSE than all the bloodshed of war is the madness and murderous insanity with which Jingoism fills the heart and mind. Think of Rudyard Kipling now demanding that "all the Teutons be exterminated." He emphasizes this good Christian advice by adding, "The Teutons must be killed in retail if they cannot be killed in wholesale." Nor is Kipling the exception. Most of the great writers, poets and artists of the Allies, as well as of Germany and Austria, speak in similar terms.

Shall we of the United States invite this terrible madness? Let those who still remain sane lose no time in stemming the onrushing tide of bloodthirsty Jingoism in this country.

PREPARE! PREPARE!!

YOU, rebel workers, radicals and revolutionists of whatever persuasion—wake up before it is too late! Do you want this country to become a military camp like Prussia or an armed barracks like Russia?

That is just what will happen if you continue to sit idly by while mad Jingoes and munitions manufacturers frighten the popular mind with the fear of imaginary external enemies

and inflame it with murderous patriotism.

Prepare, workers, rebels, revolutionists, to be treated in times of peace as your rebel brothers are treated in Russia. Remember Black Friday—and the Ludlow massacre. It is not such a far cry from Colorado, Michigan, Paterson and Lawrence to Moscow and Petrograd.

Are you going to permit militarism to get the upper hand in this country?

TO WORK, REBELS!

GET on the job, you militant workers. Forget your pet schemes for a while. A great menace is facing you. It is gaining momentum with every passing day. Your inactivity lends it courage and strength.

O that I might paint for you the monster of militarism, to show you its true face in all its horrible nakedness. To picture to you the thousands upon thousands of dead, the numberless widows and orphans, the millions of maimed and crippled, the wretched remnants of what once were healthy, strong human beings, the hopeless misery and woe. To show you your chains riveted tenfold stronger than they are even now, your slavery more galling and degrading.

Will you keep silent while all this is coming about? Rouse yourselves! Raise your voice from the Pacific to the Atlantic. Let it resound in every village, city and State till it circles this wide land, East and West, North and South, carrying terror into the hearts of the enemies of Man, the craven politician and the profit greedy masters that fatten on your brawn and blood.

To work, then! Organize mass meetings, speak from street corners, send your agitators through the length and breadth of the land. Let your motto be, Not a man for militarism; our lives for Liberty!

Young Folks

Sorry that your column had to be left out this week. We are awfully crowded for space. Have patience till next week. Meanwhile write to me.

ALECK.

THE BLAST

Revolutionary Labor Weekly
569 Dolores St., San Francisco, Cal.

Mail Address, Box 661   Phone, Park 499

Alexander Berkman, Editor and Publisher
E. B. Morton, Associate Editor   **M. E. Fitzgerald,** Manager

SUBSCRIPTION
$1.00 Yearly   60c Six Months   5c Copy
Bundle rates, 2½c per copy in bundles of ten.
Advertising rates on application.

Entered as second-class matter at the postoffice at San Francisco,
Cal., January 14, 1916, under the Act of March 3, 1879.

HOW ABOUT OURSELVES?

Warren Van Valkenburgh

FOR nineteen centuries the Caucasian minority of the human race has presumed to monopolize civilization, and claim for itself all the laurels for whatever questionable progress has been made during that time.

The current events taking place in Europe are fairly indicative of the height above the beast to which this pale-faced Arrogance has elevated mankind.

Looking out upon the wake of our course through the ages, one might be excused for inquiring in just what degree of development we today stand superior to any stage of human conduct prevailing during the pre-Christian period.

We prate of the inventive genius that has conquered the elements and made them the servants of man; we boast of mechanical achievements capable of lightening the burdens of labor; of the scientific discoveries that have laid bare the mysteries of Nature; of the revelations whereby through the concentration of known forces, hitherto undreamed of, projects are being daily engineered.

Yet with all the accomplishments that investigation and experience have rendered possible, the welfare of the people is gradually and surely being gathered into the hands of the few who rule and dominate the earth and its inhabitants.

The invention of the printing press far outshines any other single step toward the intellectual emancipation of the masses.

It made men's minds neighbors.

It made possible the interchanging of ideas.

It dethroned the handful of learned ones and gave to man that essential of life which distinguishes him from the brute. By means of the printed page, dormant passivity was generated into healthy discontent.

But with its virtues it also brought vices.

Given an inkling of the luxuries awaiting the unscrupulous, few are the men who can forego the temptation of selling their consciences for the gift we moderns call "success"; and what is more, those few cannot be trusted.

With the broadening of education, made possible by the printing press, the many were taught traits that previously were known to but the privileged few. That the crowning crime of the printing press is the cultivation of soulless deceit, a glimpse into the past unfolds before us.

Hence, instead of the ancestral traditions being handed down to us by word of mouth—which taught the Jews and Hindoos to think—the people now accept the predigested dogmas of teachers' mush as the swine receive their swill.

Why should we wonder, then, that the Powers of Privilege divide the Gods in as many parts as there are nations and churches, and inspire the people to destroy *themselves,* instead of their festering plagues called authorities.

The thrones of the mighty are immediately responsible for the miseries of men, but the primary seat of the power they wield comes from the source upon which it finally lands.

Not the rulers alone are to blame for the crimes they continually commit: the people must recognize the joint conspiracy.

When they are frank enough to admit this, and cease to deal in lies when the truth would serve them better, Justice will arouse from her eternal slumber and a Better Day shall dawn.

THE ALLIES

FROM darkest New Jersey comes the cheerful news (see front page Hearst papers) that the modest William R. is highly praised for his fight against Demon Rum by no less a personage than Billy Sunday, the painless extractor of pennies. Somehow we always had a feeling that this peerless pair would come together, like the proverbial birds of a feather.

With Willie making war and peace, according to the wind that blows the most nickels, and Billy passing the hat among the fans attending the perpetual fight between God and the Devil, we are sure our country is safe.

But Hell is going to hell sure. For Billy says that with Willie's aid "the rum traffic is doomed to hell where it belongs." We lift our voice in protest. It is unconstitutional,—rank heresy. Hell is a dry place, absolutely.

* * *

Causes of War

WHEN the workers become too restless under the lash of commercialism, the word is passed along that some other country is ruining "our markets," or "insulting our flag" to the everlasting detriment of our "national honor."

And our national honor is generally well hidden in the capitalist's pocket.

* * *

Labor's Friends

A recent banquet tendered by E. H. Gary, head of the Steel Trust, in "honor" of Theodore Roosevelt, was attended by seventeen men who own or control 10% of the wealth of the United States.

Gary knew what he was doing.

It is also stated on good authority that a certain labor politician in San Francisco spent $2500 entertaining a number of delegates to the late A. F. of L. Convention at a private banquet, where the bubbling juice flowed like water. A blind ruler of the blind—drunk with power.

Both live on the back of Labor, but Gary at least does not make any hypocritical pretense of friendship.

DIRECT ACTION VS. RESPECTABILITY

IN striking contrast to the "We didn't do it" attitude of the respectable labor leaders and organizers of the A. F. of L., is the report of George P. West, acting on behalf of the Industrial Relations Commission, relative to the Youngstown riot.

The lesson of Youngstown as we glean it from the report is this:

The wage policy of two so-called "independent" concerns, the Republic Iron & Steel Co. and the Youngstown Sheet & Tube Co. was determined by that of the Steel Corporation, substantially the same conditions of employment prevailing. When the strike started on December 29th, the officers of the steel companies sought the opinion of Judge Gary, president of the Steel Trust, who advised them to resist an advance in wages.

The strike culminated in the rebellion of January 7, 1916, when East Youngstown was sacked and a million dollars worth of property, accumulated from underpaid toil, destroyed.

"The strike," says the report, "was the natural outgrowth of a spontaneous, unorganized rebellion against an economic and industrial regime so oppressive and brutalizing as to overshadow the immediate provocation and render it comparatively insignificant . . . Not only is there likelihood of a repetition of the Youngstown strike at any one of the large steel plants, that altogether employ nearly 300,000 men, but investigation discloses that even such a disaster, shocking as it is, must be regarded as trifling when compared with the heavy toll of death and suffering that has been exacted day after day and year after year by what have come to be regarded as normal conditions in the steel industry."

In 330 typical cases investigated, the heads of the families earned an average of $440 a year. Forty per cent of them earned less than $400, and fourteen per cent less than $200 a year. During the past 8 years the mills have given employment to workmen for only 3 to 5 days a week. In these plants, which since 1913 have earned 12 per cent on common stock, the privilege of working 3 days a week during slack times was doled out as charity, after properly investigating that the man's family was really in need. To keep them alive, baskets of food were occasionally distributed to the most starved families, the cost of which was later deducted from the men's wages.

Summing up the strike the report says: "Your investigator finds that the strike at the Republic Iron & Steel and the Youngstown Sheet & Tube plant won a ten per cent increase in wages, not only for 14,500 strikers, but for all of the employees of the steel corporation, so that it will eventually benefit directly nearly 300,000 men . . . Prosecuting Attorney Henderson declared publicly after his investigation that organized labor had nothing to do with the strike and riot at this plant, although its representatives tried in vain to reach the strikers with restraining influence."

The eternal shame of it!

The slow plodding tactics of the Federation are so hopelessly ineffective that an unorganized mob with a little direct action accomplishes more for 300,000 men in a few days than the A. F. of L. has done in ten years. And when the slaves spontaneously rebel, the official labor leaders try to "reach the strikers with their restraining influence." By sitting on the lid they earn even the approbation of a prosecuting attorney.

The workers have no more insidious enemy than the chicken-hearted labor leader who advises them to be patient and respectable. An ounce of direct action is worth more than tons of paid advice of labor politicians.

THE AMALAGAMTED CLOTHING WORKERS OF AMERICA AND THE CHICAGO STRIKE

THE Amalgamated Clothing Workers of America is the youngest International Organization in this country. It came to life just fifteen months ago out of the ashes of the old Garment Workers' Union.

It happened at the seventeenth biennial convention in Nashville. Officialdom, feeling its throne tottering, resorted to a disguised pretence to refuse to seat the delegates from all the clothing centers. The unseated delegates adjourned to another hotel, where the formation of a revolutionary trade union based on the principle of industrial unionism, took place. In the course of its short existence the Amalgamated has made itself felt all over the country. It has become the expression of true unionism, the nucleus of the revolutionary clothing workers.

The urge that comes with a purposeful ideal inspired its members to make the seemingly impossible possible, to awaken the neglected, sleeping tailor.

No sooner did the delegates return from the historic Nashville convention when a strike broke out in Baltimore, against the firm of Sonneborn & Co. It was the Tailor System against human conditions, the machine versus man, and man won. Then came a prolonged strike in Boston. There the remnants of the old Garment Workers, the bona fide organization recognized by the A. F. of L., were openly scabbing, as they did in Chicago. The strike was lost, but not as in the olden days was it declared off by the General President, issuing orders from his hotel. The members themselves decided to retreat, only to come back at a more opportune time. Next came the New York situation where a strike was averted by a mere mobilization. Recently there were threats of another outbreak, but our forces again got in line ready to fight, and again the manufacturers heeded our demands. They did not dare to fight the fighting A. C. W. of A. The result was full recognition of the Amalgamated and of the principle of the union shop.

For many years Chicago has been the scene of labor struggles, but never before in its history did Chicago witness a strike of the nature the Amalgamated waged. Long will it remain in the memory of the revolutionary movement as one of the bitterest struggles the workers have ever fought.

As in other strikes, the police lined up with the bosses. Vain were the attempts made to stop their brutality against the strikers. It will be remembered that during this struggle two strikers lost their lives, several were injured, and nearly two thousand were arrested; and finally five leaders were indicted on charges of conspiracy and inciting to riot. The indictments were found by a jury composed of business men and bankers, with James Forgan, president of the First National Bank, as its foreman. At the hearing of this grand jury it was proven that the clothing manufacturers employed sluggers who beat up and maimed strikers, and that the Chicago police assisted them at so much per day. Yet it was not "sufficient evidence" to indict any of the manufacturers.

The Chicago strike demonstrated that the Amalgamated is able to take care of its fights. It is admitted by all who are acquainted with the situation that the strikers did not suffer so much starvation, privation, and want as they did in 1910 under the old regime. At that time a bona fide International, twenty years in existence, could not donate more than four thousand dollars, while the International Office of the Amalgamated, less than one year in existence, raised thirty thousand dollars for the Chicago strike.

The Chicago strike typifies the character of the Amalgamated, with its sacrifices and its hardships and the perseverance and courage of the rank and file. It has inspired and revolutionized the tailor; it has made him conscious and aggressive. That is the lesson of a revolutionary labor body.

JACOB POTOFSKY.

INJUNCTIONS

The Hon. Peter Grosskopf, Peace of Justice, Grants a Few to the Employers

Seldom Good

IN the case of the Coal Operators, et al, versus the Coal Miners, et al., in which the Operators is praying dot ve should give them some injunctions which is restraining the working peoples from striking, this Honorable Court vill now hand him down his opinions und decidings.

In the very commencing of the beginning of our Honorable discourse ve wish to say dot, it has been brought to the notice of this Court dot some peoples is of the opinion dot ve can't restrain the striking peoples from striking or nothing else.

Such a talking like dot is for sure a jackass talk for ve is the only Honorable Peace of Justice vot has been able to keep anybody und everybody from striking: when ve is in the humor to do it.

If it should be deemed advisable to do so ve would issue some injunctions restraining the clocks from striking und ve would like to see them violate our Honorable decree.

The controlling question in this case is, can the working peoples be restrained?

It is the decidings of this Peace of Justice dot they can.

Well, if they can be restrained, who is better qualified to do the job than ve is?

For instance: Who will be silly enough to say dot this Honorable Court cannot strain milk?

Well, if ve can strain milk, who will say dot ve can't take dot same milk vot ve have just strained und restrain him?

Any person vot is saying something like dot is for sure a dumb-head.

The logic of our reasoning being admitted ve vill now proceeding mit our decidings.

Some careful examination of the case vill show even the most superficial persons dot the whole question hinges on the words STRAIN und RESTRAIN.

Now, vot is the facts in the case at bar?

The working peoples is dissatisfied mit the wages und conditions which the employers is giving them.

Being dissatisfied, as aforesaid, their relations is strained.

If their relations is strained, then, like milk, they can be restrained.

If the relations of the Working Peoples can be strained und restrained then ve hold, as a logical sequence, dot the Working Peoples themselves can be strained und restrained; to decide otherwise would be to decide in favor of class legislation.

Wherefore, whereas, whereupon und right away our decidings is dot, the aforesaid und aforementioned und specified Working Peoples is hereby und now restrained und during the continuance of our Honorable In-

junction they must not even allow their clocks to strike.

You is liking dot kind of a decidings? So? Vot?

CHICKENS COMING HOME TO ROOST

SOME Americans have been killed by "bandits" in Mexico, and as a consequence the American press, capitalistically owned and controlled, is howling for blood.

For the blood of the "bandits" particularly, and if that is not forthcoming, then the blood of any old Mexicans, through armed intervention.

The dear Christian brethren have forgotten all about the doctrine of turning the other cheek. Even the Mosaic law of an eye for an eye and a tooth for a tooth is too mild for most of them. Nothing but a wholesale killing of Mexicans will do.

It is the primal savage code of holding the family, the tribe or nation responsible for the act of any of its members.

It is the spirit behind war.

In his blind and unreasoning desire for revenge, the jingo with patriotism oozing from every pore, never asks the reason why.

The type of Americans who for years have infested Mexico, are the industrial and commercial pirates. Land grabbers, mine grabbers, and oil grabbers, and their managers, superintendents and foremen exploiting the cheap labor of the poor to the last drop of blood. Their only reason for being in Mexico was that legalized plunder was made easy and very profitable.

Then came the revolution and thieving by government assistance was no longer safe. The Rockefeller, Otis and Hearst interests howled long and piteously for the suppression of the revolution. Without peons to work, a million acre ranch was as worthless as a square foot of desert.

The Federal Government repeatedly issued warnings to Americans to get out of Mexico. Through the lust for dollars, these warnings frequently were unheeded. Yet men like Lincoln Steffens, John Turner and John Murra travelled with perfect safety. Why? Because they came to learn—not to exploit. And American workmen earning their bread in the sweat of their brow, were safer in revolutionary Mexico than among the Cossack constabulary in Pennsylvania, the militia of Colorado or the gunmen of Bayonne.

A revolution takes no cognizance of the laws of property.

For a revolution is in itself an assertion of the rights of man versus property and privilege.

The jails along our southern border, from California to Texas, are filled with Mexicans—not of the upper crust, but by workmen—guilty of being poor, jobless and lacking understanding of our benevolent vagrancy laws, which provide nice soft rock piles for the unemployed.

The murder of foreign workmen, not by fellow workers of the United States, but by the hired assassins of Capitalism, is an everyday occurrence.

Why did not some foreign government intervene in Colorado in behalf of the workers?

For the reason that governments operate only in the interests of the ruling class. Those murdered in Colorado were *only workers*.

Capitalism means profit versus human life.

THE PSYCHOLOGY OF WAR

THE fundamental cause of all wars is undoubtedly to be found in the military organization of society. The formation of an army is always prompted by the intention of an aggressive or a defensive war. To be a real military man one has to give up every ideal of human right, and have no other goal than the duty of authority. The primary condition for the strength and efficiency of an army is discipline, by which is meant the absolute submission of the individual will to the order of a leader. In other words, the man becoming a soldier ceases to be a man, and becomes a machine.

But human personality cannot be destroyed altogether, especially in the partly civilized epoch in which we are living. If you take away from the individual the spiritual force that underlies every deep human emotion, you must give him some other basis for his activity. For this purpose, the evil genius of despotism has invented for the soldier the glory and the honor of the flag. With that, it satisfies the idealism that grows in every heart. This gives a noble and holy glamor to the sacrifice which is demanded from the soldier, and at the same time forges the strongest link in the long chain by which despotism holds the nation in slavery.

The monotonous life in the barracks doesn't fulfil this purpose. It therefore becomes necessary to stimulate the courage and ambition of the soldiers by inspiring the hope of great battles and wonderful victories over the enemy. When the defender of the home country is thus excited to the proper patriotic pitch, thinking and dreaming only of murder, blood and violence, in order to win a medal or a title, it merely remains to cry: "Down with the Prussians!" "Down with the French!" These wild mottoes are repeated everywhere by peoples who—far from having any cause for mutual destruction—in reality have every reason to love each other. Instead, their passion of hatred is aroused by telling them that one nation has injured the honor and glory of some other.

Periodic wars are therefore primarily the product and forced result of military organization.

VOL. 1   SAN FRANCISCO, SATURDAY, FEBRUARY 19, 1916   No. 6

The Red Feast

AYE, fight, you fools—you workers torn with strife,
   And spill your steaming entrails on the field;
   Serve well in death the men you served in life,
So that their wide dominions may not yield.

Serve well that flag—the lie that still allures;
   Lay down your lives for. land you do not own.
And give unto a war that is not yours
   Your glory tithe of mangled flesh and bone.

Ah, slaves, you fight your master's battles well,
   The reek of rotting carnage fills the air;
Your trampled bodies give forth fetid smell—
   Sweet incense to the ghouls who sent you there—

A bloody mass of high heaped human woe
   For hungry vultures hovering on high . . . .
Black dogs, red muzzled, through the trenches go,
   Where your wan, pallid features face the sky.

Go, stagger, back, you stupid slaves who've "won,"
   Back to your stricken towns to toil anew,
For there your dismal tasks are still undone,
   And grim starvation gropes again for you!

What matters now your flag, your race, the skill
   Of scattered legions—were they not in vain,—
Once more beneath the lash you must distil
   Your lives to glut a glory wrought of pain.

In peace they ever lash you to your toil,
   In war they drive you to the teeth of death,
And even when your life-blood soaks the soil
   They give you lies to choke your dying breath.

So will they smite your blind eyes till you see,
   And lash your naked backs until you know
That wasted blood can never make you free
   From utter thralldom to the common foe . . .

Then you will find that "nation" is a name,
   And boundaries are things that don't exist;
That workers' interests, world-wide, are the same,
   And ONE the ENEMY they must resist!

The Rabbits and the Goats

ONCE there was a great clover meadow divided into two equal parts by a clear river which ran between. One field was the home of the grey rabbits, the other of the white rabbits. Each one had enough; none had too much, and all were happy.

One day four white goats came to the field of the white rabbits and four black goats to the field of the grey rabbits, and the goats said to the rabbits: "This field is ours. Do not touch a stalk of clover." "Who gave you the land?" asked the rabbits. "Our God and yours. The Man who lives on the Hill," answered the goats. "Oh!" said the rabbits.

Presently some of the older rabbits got together and, with noses twitching, nervously asked the goats: "Where shall we go and how shall we live?" "You cannot go anywhere," said the goats, "and if you will cut clover for us we will give you enough to keep you alive, unless you are greedy. The greedy must die." "Oh!" said the rabbits.

So the four white goats divided one field into quarters, each taking one as its own, and the four black goats divided the other field in the same way, and for a long time the rabbits brought the goats the hay which the goats sold to the pigs who lived on an island in the river. The goats became very fat and prosperous, but the rabbits had hardly enough to eat. The rabbits continued to have large families and grew more and more numerous, so that the clover allowed by the goats was not enough and the rabbits were starving. Some of the rabbits then said: "Brethren, four goats cannot harvest this clover. We do all the work. Let us stand together and refuse to labor unless we get more clover and shorter hours."

So the rabbits formed a hundred and thirty-seven unions, so that each rabbit could find a union for its kind. There was a union for rabbits with a spot on the right fore-foot, and a union for rabbits with a spot on the left fore-foot, and so on, for all manner of rabbits, including lop-eared rabbits and blind rabbits. Sometimes the rabbits with a spot on the left fore-foot would walk out and sit by the edge of the field and look at the clover and refuse to work unless given more clover and shorter hours. This action was called "a squat." Sometimes the rabbits with a spot on the right fore-foot would walk out on a squat. Sometimes it would be the lop-eared rabbits, or the three-toed rabbits, or the blind rabbits, or whichever was hungriest, and the others would do the work for the goats till those out on a squat would get so hungry looking at the clover they would, one by one, slip back into the field and go to work, and sometimes, if the crop was very big

and the pigs were squealing for clover, and business was good, the goats would give the squatting rabbits a little more to eat and shorter hours.

But when the rabbits had bred to such a multitude that there were more rabbits than were needed for the work, poor, hungry, mangy or scabby rabbits would offer to work for less clover, and then the whole thing would be in a dreadful uproar; the union rabbits would squeal "Scab!" at the poor mangy rabbits, and the goats would bleat: "Let them alone. We have a God-given right to have them work for us for less clover." And all the other union rabbits, left-foots, right-foots, fore-foots, hind-foots, lop-ears and so on—all except the ones who were squatting—would go on harvesting the goats' clover for them, but crying continually: "Scab! Scab! Scab!"

Things went on this way for a long time, the white rabbits and the grey rabbits getting poorer and poorer, and the white goats and black goats getting fatter and fatter. But presently the black goats and the white goats quarreled over which should furnish clover to the pigs. The black goats declared war on the white goats, and each shouted to their own rabbits: "Quit working for us now for a while and come fight for us"; so the white rabbits rushed at the grey rabbits and the grey rabbits rushed at the white rabbits and they killed each other, squealing strange squeals: "Patriotism!" "Fatherland!" "Our Country!" "Our Flag!" "The Goats forever!" "God bless our Goats!'"

The goats wept and gave a little clover to the orphan rabbits, and hung small yellow bells on the two-legged and three-legged rabbits who had lost legs in the war, so these rabbits sat all day tinkling their bells and were fed by the other rabbits and were greatly venerated for their intelligence.

During the war the white goats sent for white foxes to fight for them, and the black goats sent for black foxes to fight for them, and the rabbits were glad and said: "We will feed the foxes who fight for us."

After a long and bitter war, and the killing of many rabbits, peace was declared between the black goats and the white goats and they divided the Pigs' Island between them by a solemn treaty, and were fatter than ever. So the rabbits, white and grey, went back to their fields to work, only each had to labor harder because there were so many crippled rabbits and so many foxes to support. The rabbits were thus harder worked and poorer than ever, but every time they grumbled or one of their unions squatted the goats set the foxes on them and drove them back to work.

Things became so unbearable that an old grey rabbit called all the rabbits together, white and grey, and said to them: "Are we not all rabbits? Are we not all brothers? Are we not all enslaved? Our mistake was in admitting the right of the goats to own the land, because that has enslaved us. We must live from the land. Without it we die. Our remedy is to undo this error and to assert that not even our God, the Man on the Hill, can give away the ownership of the fields. They must be as before, open and free to whomsoever will use them. If the goats want clover, let them get what they can use, and no more. The same with the pigs, and the same with rabbits; and as for rabbits killing each other, it is worse than wicked—it is foolish." "But," said a large white rabbit, "what will become of the foxes?" "Let them die," said the grey rabbit. "But they won't die. They will eat us," said the white rabbit. "No," said the grey rabbit, "there are many more of us, and we can kick powerfully if we want to. Moreover, unless we work for the goats, how can they buy the chickens they feed to the foxes? Foxes cannot eat clover." "But how are we to do this? The goats are larger than we are," said the white rabbit. "Easily," replied the grey rabbit; "let us unite in one great brotherhood. Not lop-eared or blind rabbits, but just rabbits, all rabbits, in one common band. Then let us say to the goats: 'We will harvest no more clover for you. Work yourselves, or starve. We deny your ownership of the fields. We will help ourselves.' Oh, my brothers," he added, "see this mutilated ear which was chewed by a white rabbit while each of us was fighting for the goats, he for the white goats, I for the black. Let it be so no more. Let us all get together as one band of brothers. Let us break this ownership of our fields by the goats, and then no more shall our little ones starve in meadows of abundance." "Very fine words," said the white rabbit, "but only words. Do not listen to him. He is a visionary. A dreamer. Labor is not vision. Labor is life. Life is labor. Let us all go back to our jobs. That is life. We can from time to time squat and kick as before, separately and independently, for more clover and shorter hours. That also is life. Anything beyond a little more clover or shorter hours is vision, and sensible rabbits will not bother with it."

So the rabbits all returned to labor for the goats, while the foxes watched them from the shade.

—CHARLES ERSKINE SCOTT WOOD

The Meaning of War

WHAT, speaking in quite unofficial language, is the net purport and upshot of war? To my own knowledge, for example, there dwell and toil in the British village of Dumdrudge usually some five hundred souls. From these, by certain "natural enemies" of the French, there are successively selected, during the French war, say thirty able-bodied men. Dumdrudge, at her own expense, has suckled and nursed them; she has, not without difficulty and sorrow, fed them up to manhood, and even trained them to crafts, so that one can weave, another build, another hammer, and the weakest can stand under thirty stone avoirdupois. Nevertheless, amid much weeping and swearing, they are selected; all dressed in red; and shipped away at the public charges, some two thousand miles, or say only to the south of Spain, and fed there till wanted.

And now to that same spot, in the south of Spain, are thirty similar French artisans, from a French Dumdrudge, in like manner wending; till at length, after infinite effort, the two parties come into actual juxtaposition; and Thirty stands fronting Thirty, each with gun in his hand. Straightway the word "Fire!" is given; and they blow the souls out of one another; and in place of sixty brisk, useful craftsmen the world has sixty dead carcasses, which it must bury, and anew shed tears for.

Had these men any quarrel? Busy as the devil is, not the smallest! They lived far enough apart; were the entirest strangers; nay, in so wide a Universe, there was even, unconsciously, by Commerce, some mutual helpfulness between them. How, then? Simpleton! Their Governors had fallen out; and, instead of shooting one another, had the cunning to make these poor blockheads shoot.

—THOMAS CARLYLE

Only Labor Can Abolish War

PEACE congresses will not abolish war, nor is it the sincere wish of those who patronize them that war should be abolished. They are instituted mainly by those whose millions come from the manufacture of war munitions, or from land titles to barren acres which are only validated by armies and navies.

War will be abolished when the artisans and craftsmen cease to manufacture war implements—which are made solely for the purpose of keeping in subjection those by whose toil and skill they are fabricated. Kings and rulers seldom kill each other, but they always unite to kill workingmen—they are so united now.

How much will Carnegie subscribe for an educational campaign to teach workingmen not to make war implements? Not a penny. But he will give millions, if need be, to pay for shooting down men who should strike against work on battleships and cannon and refuse to permit others to take their jobs. Such is the sincerity of those who pray and pay for peace.

Peace congresses are fads of the foolish or crafty rich.

War will not be abolished by those interested in its loot. There is no hope for man at the top of the human heap. Only as the mass grows more intelligent and intolerant of slavery will conditions become more human. Wholesale murder will only cease when workingmen refuse to manufacture its implements.

—LUKE NORTH

Take Notice, Friends! About to go to press, we received the following wire from New York: "Arrested birth control charge. Under five hundred bond. Got postponement until twenty-eighth. Will try to get another extension. I want to prepare case thoroughly. Can you arrange protest meeting and make appeal? Will need money for publicity. Have written you at length. Send protests to City Attorney Edward Swann.—EMMA GOLDMAN."

THE BLAST

Revolutionary Labor Weekly
569 Dolores St., San Francisco, Cal.
Mail Address, Box 661   Phone, Park 499

Alexander Berkman, Editor and Publisher
E. B. Morton, Associate Editor   **M. E. Fitzgerald**, Manager

SUBSCRIPTION
$1.00 Yearly   60c Six Months   5c Copy
Bundle rates 2½c per copy in bundles of ten.
Advertising rates on application.
Entered as second-class matter at the postoffice at San Francisco,
Cal., January 14, 1916, under the Act of March 3, 1879.

Reflections

EDUCATION, education! is the cry on everyone's lips. "Knowledge will make you free." Is it really true? Will education *alone* make the people free?

As a matter of fact, the "educated" ones, with but few exceptions, are the strongest upholders of capitalism. Learned professors, scientists and similar intellectual rabble are almost always in the camp of the enemy, making use of every known device of science to perpetuate human slavery.

The same is generally true of the proletarian whose sole ambition is to become "educated." He learns enough to emancipate himself from the shop or the factory, and secures a well-paying position. The social question is then solved—so far as he is concerned.

And the thousands of radicals who have an education—what of them? Their usefulness in the revolutionary movement is nil. They know it all, you know. The sum total of all their argument is "What's the use, anyway?" Or, "The stupid workers don't deserve any better." They become either exploiters or scoffers.

* * *

THIS is not an argument against education. It is an argument for education PLUS.

"The workers—ah, they are so ignorant, you know," is the cry of the scientific ones. It's a lie. The workers know enough to make this world beautiful—for others. To create comfort, wealth and luxury—for others. They know enough to build palaces, produce gold and silver, shape rare gems, and fill the earth with all that is necessary to make life a song and a joy. They circle the earth with iron and steel, annihilate space and bring distant climes in closer touch; they build powerful engines that subdue and harness the forces of nature; they turn the wilderness into blooming gardens, level towering mountains, bridge rivers and seas; they chain the Niagara and conquer the very air.

They know, they know how to create wealth, and luxury and joy—all for others.

It isn't knowledge the workers lack. What they need is the courage and will to use their knowledge, their strength and skill in their own interest. They need backbone and the *will to be free.*

To develop this *will* is the real work of those who have the welfare of humanity at heart. The will to do and dare, the will *not* to be slaves. Knowledge alone keeps the world in bondage. Knowledge *plus* backbone will break every link of human slavery.

* * *

THE corrupting influence of politics has never been demonstrated more strikingly than in the case of Meyer London, the present Socialist representative in Congress.

I know Meyer London personally. He is a decent chap: in private life intelligent, sincere and devoted. But even a decent man is not immune from the poison of the political swamp. The stink of the legislative atmosphere has infected London the moment he entered Congress. He, the stanch internationalist, equipped with thorough knowledge, failed the moment his courage was put to the test. He did not dare beard the lion in his den.

Oh, London knows—he has plenty of education. His mind is thoroughly disciplined by long years of legal study; he is well versed in all the intricacies of scientific Socialism—he knows, he knows. Only one thing his knowledge did not give him: strength to retain his manhood and loyalty to his convictions in the face of the enemy. Asked on the floor of the Congress what the Socialists would do in case the United States were invaded, Meyer London replied emphatically that "the Socialists, like everybody else, would defend the country."

I am afraid that what London said is true. In spite of their education and thorough knowledge of things, in spite even of the Socialists' complete familiarity with the scientific analysis of everything under the sun, London and his followers lack backbone.

They haven't the courage to fly in the face of public prejudice, or defy popular sentiment. They are too cowardly to stand by an unpopular conviction. They mouth internationalism and the solidarity of the workers of *all* countries, but put them to the test, and they "will defend their country." That is to say, they will obey the command to slaughter the workers of other countries.

This is true not only of the Socialists but of most radicals, and even of some who call themselves revolutionists and Anarchists. Yes, strange as it may seem, there are even Anarchists who would defend *their* country, though an Anarchist knows that he has no country.

* * *

THAT is the great tragedy of our time. That is what paralyzes the revolutionary movement. We *know* many things, except how to be true to ourselves, to be *real men* and *women.* We are constantly calling on the workers to be solidaric, to make common cause with the toilers everywhere, together to deliver the fatal blow to their oppressors. But how many of us—militant workers, rebels, revolutionists—whatever our ism—are ready to stand up for our convictions when the test comes? It is easy to talk or write rebellion and revolution when we know we are safe. But look into your own heart and confess to yourself whether you have the strength to live up to your ideas and ideals when it is dangerous to do so.

And unless there be some of us who have this strength, all our propaganda is worthless. Because *example* is the most powerful means of agitation; it alone helps to change the world.

* * *

LET it be clearly understood: the danger of invasion is a nightmare of the jingo imagination. It is a mannikin dangled before the eyes of the American people by those who are hungry for graft, emoluments and profit. But if the war maniacs and profit mongers should actually succeed in forcing this country into war, let us at least remain true to ourselves, true to our sense of human brotherhood and labor solidarity, true to our ideal of the revolution of the masses against the war of their exploiters.

It makes no difference how many or how few are with us. There must always be a beginning, and it is up to every true revolutionist, in everything, to make the beginning with himself. As for me, I recognize neither flag nor country. I know only one invader: the government which robs me of liberty and forces me to do things against my will. I have but one enemy: the master who steals the fruit of my toil. I have nothing to defend in this or any other country. I have only my own interests to defend—the interests of my oppressed fellow-men throughout the world. I will not defend rulers or masters in any country. I will shoot the first recruiting officer rather than harm my brother proletarian, wherever he may come from.

—A. B.

The Great Art

I WENT last Monday to the shop of my bookseller, whose warehouses, with all their variety, often afford me nothing to read. "I have got today," said he, "by good luck, a new work, necessary to the happiness of mankind, and as full of instruction as delight. No one ought to neglect the perusal of this performance. The destiny of all depends upon it. Let me send it to you. It is entitled '*Tactics.*'"

"*Tactics!*" said I. "Alas! to this day I have been ignorant of the meaning of this learned noun."

"It is a word," answered my bookseller, "that is descended to us from the Greeks. It signifies the great art, or *the* ART by way of eminence; that of arrangement or order. The sanguine wishes of the most daring genius find themselves here fully gratified."

I bought his "*Tactics*" and rejoiced in the purchase. I hoped to find in this divine work the art of lengthening my life; of surmounting the miseries with which it is infested; of cultivating my taste; of subduing my passions; of subjecting my desires to the yoke of reason; of being just towards all men, without ever being their dupe. I shut myself up in my study; I read, I devour, I digest every word of so admirable a work. Great God! the object of this art was to instruct men to cut each others' throats.

I learned that formerly, in Germany, a guileless monk, to amuse his leisure, invented a certain composition of brimstone and saltpetre; that a large leaden ball, thrown out with a terrible report, ought to be directed to a certain height in order to descend to a certain level: and that this rule being attended to, death infallibly flies out from a brass cylinder in a certain curve called a parabola, and overturns a hundred blue automata standing all in a row. In a word, musket, dagger, sword with a sharp edge or a sharp point, are all good, all worthy of honor, provided that they kill.

In another chapter, the author describes a set of highwaymen prepared for nightly depredation, who, having taken their stand in a hollow way, and being properly furnished with sabres and scaling ladders proceed, in the first place, without sound of trumpet or drum, to the assassination of five or six sentinels. Afterwards, having dexterously climbed the walls of a city, while each honest trader was sleeping securely in his bed, they spread, from street to street, fire and sword; stab the men; ravish their wives; knock out the brains of the young children; and finally, exhausted with so many efforts, carouse in the midst of the bleeding bodies. The next morning they proceed, as in duty bound, to return thanks to God for their heroical enterprise; to tell him in Latin, with a nasal twang, that he alone is their protector; that, while the town was in flames, they could do nothing without him; that one can neither rob nor ravish to one's heart's content, nor massacre the defenceless, without God to second the undertaking.

Surprised as I was at the discovery of the boasted art, I hastened once more to my bookseller, out of breath with horror and amazement; returned to him his volume, and exclaimed, my eyes flashing with rage:

"Begone! Accursed bookseller of Beelzebub! Carry your '*Tactics*' to the Chevalier de Tot. He teaches the Turks to march in the name of the Lord. He instructs unbelievers to cover the Dardanelles with their cannon, and kill the inhabitants of the Christian world. Begone! Address yourself to the Court de Romanow; to the pitiless conqueror of Azof and Bender; but chiefly offer this admirable performance to the great Frederic. He knows more of this art than your author, and is upon more confidential terms with Lucifer. He is consummate master of this horrible science, more perfect in it than either Gustavus or Eugene. Begone! I will never believe that human nature came out—God knows when!—from the hands of its creator, thus to insult its omnipotent benefactor, to be guilty of so much extravagance, and so much insanity. Man, with his ten fingers, unarmed either for attack or defence, was never formed violently to abridge a life which necessity has already rendered so short. The gout with its chalkstones, and the hardened slime which forms itself into pebbles at the bottom of the bladder, the fever, the catarrh, and a hundred diseases more dreadful; a hundred mountebanks in ermine, still more the foes of our peace, would have been sufficient to render this globe a valley of tears, without its being necessary to invent this sublime art of war."

—Voltaire

The Growth of Revolution In India

MEN from England's vast dependency in India are fighting for her in Europe, and it is said that the Indians are helping England in every way, which she interprets to the world as proof of devotion and stanch loyalty on the part of India to English rule. She flings these "incontestible" facts in the face of those who claim that India is hostile to British rule and that her sons will revolt at the first opportunity.

It is true that some Indians are fighting in the British army and a few have volunteered their services. But who are they? They are the Indian soldiers who are part of the British-Indian army in India, whom poverty has driven to enlist under the British flag. And as professional soldiers, whose interest lies in pay only, they are required to go and fight whenever wanted. Hence when this great European war broke out, a large number of the Indian soldiers were shipped to Europe who were completely unaware of their proper destination! Some of them thought that they were to be shipped from one Indian port to another, while others believed that they were sailing for Africa! The truth of this statement can be substantiated by the Indians fighting in France and in Egypt, and by those who have been made prisoners by the Germans.

As regards the rest—who are, by the way, few in number—they are mostly adventurers and place-seekers. Those few Indian princes who are hanging around the British camps in France, those "bejeweled" rajahs who are subscribing to the British war-relief fund and aiding in other ways, who are they and what are they? Always lying in the clutches of the tyrannical British, always compelled by brute force to follow at the beck and call of the British, subservient to British caprice and practically prisoners in their own palaces, these Indian princes have been compelled to unloosen the strings of their purses to help—what the Imperial mandate called—a "holy cause for humanity"! Being always watched and suspected and never trusted by the British government, and politically absolutely impotent to have any independent will of their own, these maharajas are doing what they are ordered to do, directly or indirectly. If the sons of a few of these bejeweled farcical "chiefs" are hanging around the British army as "aides-de-camp," it is because once their ancestors were warriors to whom fighting was a profession, and whose degenerate descendants want to satisfy the hereditary instincts by hearing the trampling of a cavalcade or the roar of cannon! To these princes loyalty means self-preservation, and that loyalty is extracted through fear! It is only by means of this cloak of hypocrisy that these pampered rajahs can retain the luxury of a throne, however small and impotent it may be. As for the less favored ones—they are aiming at higher titles and more orders of distinction, and some are mere place-seekers.

But so far as *the masses* of India are concerned, they are inimical to British rule. The Indians have never taken kindly to the English who are aliens to them in color, speech, manners and religion. The English rule in India, founded by treachery, forgery, perjury, and kept by brute force, has always been hated. Whenever any opportunity has arisen, the Indians individually and collectively have shown their hostility to the alien domination. They have not forgotten the revolution of 1857, which they call the "first war of Indian independence," nor will they be slow in taking advantage of any opportunity, as soon as it presents itself. This dumb multitude is gradually giving expression to its feelings by diverse channels. They are boycotting British-made goods and patronizing the home-made articles, upholding their own institutions and are trying to build up national solidarity in various ways.

The English, with their characteristic love of "justice and fair play," and their "love of liberty," are doing their utmost to crush these patriotic aspirations. They hunt down the rebels, they hang and transport them, they sentence them to hard labor, they flog the boys; from time to time they start "pogroms" on the defenseless people, they gag the press and enact restrictive laws; they terrorize the people by every means. But what has been the effect? These persecutions have spread the revolutionary propaganda. The fierce desire for emancipation, which has struck deep roots in the hearts of the people, not finding any external outlet, is running underground. Their race-consciousness has been awakened and various methods of revolutionary propaganda are afoot to bring about national regeneration.

To the globetrotter and to the casual visitor, this part of the Indian national life is a sealed book. India seems to him to gloat over the chains forged for her! But far away from the glamor of the viceregal court life, far away from the official sunshine, far away from anglosthan, far away from the contact of the gaudy, bejeweled, imbecile maharajas and the henchmen of the British, only in the heart of Hindusthan you will find the true feelings. The sullen discontent that has always existed, the fierce hatred against the feringee and his ways, and the stern determination for emancipation, are coming to a head. Hence in India we see the phenomenon of the rapid rise and growth of the revolutionary movement. It is not the noisy demagogue quoting Burke and Queen Victoria's proclamation, and the Indian dummies put in the legislative councils that are the spokesmen of the dumb millions; but the martyrs that are dying by the hangman's noose, the men transported for life, sentenced to jail—they are the exponents of the new revolutionary gospel. These active workers may be in minority today, but the future of the country lies in their hands.

British rule in India today is shakier than ever; the present world war and England's troubles with Turkey have made it worse. India is now like a volcano which may burst out at any moment, at the first opportunity; and then British rule, founded by blood, will die in blood.   —*The Indian National Party.*

Be Content

DON'T ever be guilty of wanting anything, working-men. It is true that you build the palaces, manufacture the finest of shoes and clothing, raise the best of foods, and make the earth a paradise for the few wealthy. But you shouldn't want anything for yourselves.

Of course it is plain that you don't. I only mention it for fear that you might get it into your head that since you created all these things you are entitled to something more than the refuge and shanty shelter. That would be Anarchy, and I wish to warn you not only against Anarchy but against all agitators. Agitators are dangerous and are likely to get you into a worse fix than you are now in.

Of course, you haven't anything to lose, but don't worry about that. Work and be content, for over there the master prepares a house not built with hands, where you can go after you are dead—maybe. There is some little doubt about it, of course, but you should work and hope.

Don't ever read or think, gent. It wasn't intended that you should, and, as a rule, you are doing just what it was intended that you should. Always be a working mule—it's so much fun to pile up wealth all one's life for someone else to enjoy, and then when one dies get one of those half-cent burials, which the undertakers furnish paupers.

—EMANUEL JULIUS

Involuntary Servitude: A Step Toward Conscription

TWENTY-ONE postal clerks in West Virginia, who were indicted last November for conspiracy because they had the manhood to quit their jobs rather than submit to injustice, have been found guilty and fined a total amount of $1400.00.

The government attorneys and postoffice officials are reported to be highly elated at the outcome of the court proceedings; especially because this case, being the first of its kind, establishes a precedent for the future.

Instead of raising a howl of publicity to rally to their assistance the forces of Labor and every red-blooded lover of liberty, the defendants relied solely on legal talent. Of course, they were promptly handed the customary judicial package that Labor gets in the courts.

A legal fight between the U. S. government, with its unlimited resources, and a handful of working men is about as fair as a fight between a pigmy and a giant. The lawyer in the case knew it perfectly well, for he entered a plea of *nolo contendere* (I will not contest). In other words, he took the money and threw up the sponge, which is a perfectly respectable thing for a lawyer to do, though it would be disgraceful for a prizefighter.

In effect the decision is even more vicious and far-reaching than the Danbury Hatters' case. It is the first step toward conscription.

Roosevelt inaugurated the system of muzzling insubordinates, denying free speech and political expression to those working for the government in minor positions. It has remained for a liberal democratic administration to establish involuntary servitude among government employees. Considering that the government attorneys and postoffice officials are so triumphant over the decision, it is evident that they intend to extend the practice. From compelling men to work against their will is but a short step to forcing them to kill and be killed. *That is what conscription means.*

Same Old Fake

NO one will dream of charging police authorities with originality. But the methods of the Chicago department are really too stale. Evidently the police of that city feel that it is necessary to distract public attention from the fast accumulating charges of corruption and graft among the guardians of law and disorder. But is there no one in the department with enough brains to invent a more plausible diversion for the public than the threadbare old story of a "world-wide plan of destruction by an anarchistic organization of tremendous power, with headquarters in Rome and with a membership of fifteen in Chicago?"

What a powerful world-wide organization that has only fifteen members in the great city of Chicago! I can assure that great authority on Anarchists, Chief Shuettler, of Chicago, that I personally know several hundred Anarchists in his city.

I often wish that these "world-wide conspiracies" were real: that the rebels actually had a powerful organization to put the fear of god or devil into the hearts of those who batten on the blood and marrow of labor; to strike them with such terror that they should be eager to release their strangle-hold on humanity. But unfortunately there is no such organization, and there will be none till the down-trodden and disinherited take the matter into their own hands and wipe the bloodsuckers off the face of the earth, together with all their devices for enslaving man.

But the "great conspiracy" fake of the Chicago police is perhaps good enough to frighten the timid citizen into giving more police jobs to Irish patriots in Chicago. Incidentally, it may serve to create an "argument" for a stronger army against the internal enemy. After all, it is this enemy—discontent and rebellion at home—that our rulers fear a thousand times more than any external "invader."

—A. B.

The Parable of Another Samaritan

I STOOD on the bank of a swiftly running river whose turgid bosom was white with the broken bodies of men, women and children:—the industrial derelict, crippled, aged and shriveled with toil; the white slave, early old and robbed of beauty; the factory child with hollow socketed eyeballs and shrunken belly. Many were dead, some were dying, and others there were, not yet despairing, but from whose lips there came an anguished cry.

I reached into the waters and saved many, and back of me I heard the pulpit and the press of the unjust man acclaiming loudly that I was a philanthropist and a redeemer of men. And I was pleased with his fulsome plaudit, not seeing that those I saved passed by the unjust man and came down again to choke my torrent of sorrows.

And so it came that men called my name blessed, but the number of the miserable ever grew, when a loud voice rudely broke upon the satisfied tenor of my consciousness. saying, "Look above you. Go forth to the source of this wretched river to where the unjust man has his great machines." In great haste I went as the voice had spoken, and I said to the unjust man and his wolfish mercenaries, "You shall not longer grind the laughing-eyed innocents into your fearful mills, nor shall you starve them when the pearly breasts of earth swell and pain with abundant suck for them all, and you, sir, shall not feed the beautiful maidens into the scarlet maw of vice; and you shall no longer bruise and beat and break and kill the bodies of those who do the useful and the beautiful work of the world."

I looked again toward the press and the pulpit of the unjust man and saw them herding a mob which they set upon me, crying, "He preaches a strange doctrine."

—BRUCE ROGERS

The Young Folks

II

"WELL, now, how about my question?" Tom asked when we met again.

"We'll discuss it now, Tom."

"Discuss it? What do you mean?"

"We'll talk it over," I explained.

"Why, I thought you were to answer my questions."

"We'll answer them together. You will help me, Tom."

"But I don't know how."

"Well, let's see. You said you had asked your father to buy you a new suit—"

"No; a new pair of pants," Tom corrected me.

"Oh, yes, pants; and your father told you that you couldn't have them. You wanted to know why, and he wouldn't tell you."

"Yes. Now you tell me why he wouldn't buy them for me."

"All right. But first tell me, Tom, what is your father's business?"

"Why, don't you know? He works in Jones' factory. They make there the finest furniture in the city."

"I didn't see any of it in your house, Tom."

"Of course not; it's too expensive."

"But you say that your father makes it. Why doesn't he bring some of it home?"

"How you talk! It's Jones' factory, and everything made there belongs to him, and he sells it. Father can't afford to buy such dear furniture."

"But tell me, Tom, who makes all the furniture that Jones sells?"

"The men in the factory, of course."

"Does Jones himself make any of it?"

"You make me laugh. Jones is rich; he doesn't have to work."

"Let's look into this, Tom. You say that Jones himself doesn't make any of the furniture that he sells, so I suppose his workers make it?"

"Yes, of course."

"All of it?"

"Sure."

"Then if the men make it all, they can take some of it home when they need it."

"No, they can't. It don't belong to them. It belongs to Jones."

"How so, Tom?"

"Well, the factory is his, and all the tools and machinery, too."

"You mean that Jones built the factory, and made the tools and machinery—Jones himself?"

"No, no, he didn't. I saw some new machines taken into the factory last week. There was a sign on them that said they were made in Pittsburg."

"Who do you think made those machines in Pittsburg?"

"The machinists, of course."

"Well, then, if Jones himself didn't make the machinery, then perhaps he built the factory?"

"No, no, he didn't. It was workingmen who built the factory."

"Well, then, Tom, it seems that Jones didn't help much, so far. He didn't build the factory, nor the machinery, and he is not working on the furniture, either. Why does it all belong to Jones, then?"

"I—don't see why."

"There are many grown-ups can't see it, either. But it is not really hard to understand. The truth is, Tom, a factory couldn't belong to only *one* man. Why? Because one man couldn't build it. It takes many to do it. It takes bricklayers and masons, carpenters and plumbers, ironworkers and locksmiths, and many other workingmen to build a factory or a house. Even a common kitchen chair couldn't be made by one man working all alone. He would need a hammer and nails, or glue, and even before he could use these, he must get the lumber. He would need an axe and a saw. And somebody would have to give him food while he is making all these things. So you see that he would need the help of many other people even to make a chair. Everything that we have today is made by the work of many people, each doing some part of the work. We all live together, we work together, and the things we have should belong to all people together. That's why Jones' factory is not his at all. It really should belong to all the people who helped to build it."

"But perhaps Jones paid for it," Tom said.

"Perhaps he did. That means we must find out where Jones got the money. And, by the way, Tom, do you know what money really is?"

"Why, of course; it's cash."

"Well, we'd better talk this over next time. It's late now."

"But how about the pants that father wouldn't buy?"

"That belongs to the money question, Tom."

VOL. 1   SAN FRANCISCO, SATURDAY, FEBRUARY 26, 1916   No. 7

Behold the Enemy!   Prepare!

Patriotism
Dyer D. Lum

LOVE for home, for the spot around which cluster tender reminiscences of youth, where childhood's happy years were passed and with which we associate memories of loved ones now gone from us, is one of the most sacred sentiments. In the extension of that sentiment to the larger home, to the association of those speaking a common language, having common interests and wants, and sharing the same joys and sorrows, where race and language united and government did not oppress, love for fatherland also naturally followed. The national was an extension of the home idea; it carried with it the same careful protection, the same sense of dependence, the same guidance of wayward feet and solicitude for personal welfare.

But the "children of larger growth" look back with different emotions upon their life course. Children are growing to maturity whose tenderest years were associated with want; where home was a tenement in which discord and penury ruled; where early years were associated with factory life; where a father's love and a mother's smile were overcast by care, scrimping anxiety and nervous exhaustion; where want overlaid sentiment with the sordid veneering of selfishness, and physical exhaustion but led to moral deterioration.

The genius of fatherland became transformed into a driving, relentless task-master, with strong arms to lay burdens, not to caress; with a purpose foreign to that of parental guidance, a purpose to which their lives were subservient, a purpose to which their days became a weary round of exhaustive and ill-requited toil and their nights alone a period of relief; where blessing came in forgetfulness and despair with the return of wakefulness.

Our patrios today is capital; beneath his guidance we learn to direct our feeble steps in infancy, employ our hands in youth, drag our wearied limbs in middle life, and bend our aching backs in age. The god of birth, it welcomes us as a unit in the supply of labor; the god of marriage, it presides over the law of supply and demand and counts on prospective gain through increased competition; as god of old age, it provides us with a work-house or a pauper burial.

The transformation is complete. Uncle Sam has doffed his blue swallow-tail for broadcloth. Grown paunch-bellied, his nether garments are cut to measure and we make them. His genial face is pinched by avarice, the idyllic love becomes insatiate greed, and his task-masters' stripes, red with our blood, become the "flaunting lie" of civilization.

Awakened at last we refuse further obeisance to the American fetich—a striped rag!

Don't Become a Murderer!

YOUNG MAN! You whom the government is trying to entice into the army and navy, beware! Bethink yourself before taking the step. Consider what you are about to do, and the purpose you are to serve. Ask yourself the meaning of military service and of war. Do you want to prepare for murder? Do you want to be trained for wholesale slaughter and, when ordered, to kill your fellow-men, men like yourself, whom you have never even seen and who never did you any harm? Think of it, and if there is a spark of manhood in your heart, you will be filled with horror and disgust at the very thought of military service.

You may be one of the unemployed, without money or friends. But better a hundred times to suffer need and hunger than to don the uniform that stands for cowardly obedience and the murder of your brothers. Consider that it is this military power which you are asked to join, that is upholding the conditions which are keeping you and thousands of others in starvation and misery. If you put on the uniform, you help to strengthen and perpetuate this power and you become the blind tool of the class that robs and kills under the guise of patriotism. It pays them well. They even instill the little school-children with the spirit of boastful jingoism and murderous hatred, because patriotism enlarges profits and increases dividends. Do you want to help them?

It is unworthy of a thinking man to be a blind, obedient tool. But still more unworthy it is to train oneself for the purpose and to subject oneself to humiliation and inhuman treatment in order to learn how to kill and murder.

Young Man! You are a poor man, a child of the poor. It is a terrible and shameful spectacle that in every land the sons of the workingmen constitute the army whose purpose it is to perpetuate the slavery of labor. Can you complain of oppression and exploitation if you lend yourself to uphold the system of economic robbery, if you take up arms to defend it? As long as there are enough young men who permit themselves to be driven to slaughter like a herd of sheep and who are willing to participate in expeditions of robbery and murder (for that's what war really is), just so long the possessing classes will continue to rob and to murder, to slaughter by the wholesale and exterminate whole countries. You, the sons of the people, you young workingmen of the land, you alone can put an end to these terrible things and their frightful consequences, by refusing to join the army and navy, by refusing to be used as hangmen, manhunters and watchdogs.

Already "great" generals and other well-paid patriots speak of conscription. They want to introduce forced military service in this country, as has been done by the tyrannies of Europe. It is time to show them that the people see through their infamous schemes. Let the young generation remain away from the recruiting offices and refuse to be used as food for cannon.

The mission of the soldier is no different from that of the professional cutthroat who kills a man to order, except that the soldier receives less pay for his services, though he must be prepared not only for one murder but for wholesale killing. In bitter irony of his position, he is even commanded to sing the praises of the Lord who is supposed to be love and justice personified, and who is said to have commanded, "Thou shalt not kill."

The military uniform that seems so gay holds nothing but subjection and humiliation for the common soldier, and only a very meagre existence. He gets the mere crumbs when the glory and the profits of the bloody game of war are distributed. For the glory is all for the generals, the diplomats and statesmen, and the dollars are pocketed by the swindling suppliers of provisions, the cannon makers and manufacturers of arms, the ship builders and steel trust magnates. Young man, can you not understand why all these people with their hired slave drivers and paid newspaper writers are so patriotic? They are at all times ready to sacrifice the lives of poor devils for "the honor of the country." It means profit for them, and for that they cheerfully send to slaughter thousands who have been careless enough to fall into the net spread by the gaily decked agents of hell.

Beware of their traps! Too late will be regret when you are already caught. According to statistics about five per cent. of the men desert from the United States Army. It is a striking proof that the fine promises of the merry and happy life of military service are nothing but a lie and a snare. Don't be duped, young man. Your true interest lies with the great body of the toilers, in solidaric effort with the producers to possess themselves of the land and tools of production for the use and benefit of all.

Down with the slaughter of mankind!

Long live humanity!

Two Spirits

MILITARISM

SON of Mars! tempestuous spirit,
    Cursed in every thought and deed!
Men from thee all power inherit,
    Labor loses half its merit,
        Serving as the tool of greed.
Thou gives force to human passion,
    Animates the brute in self,
Making avarice the fashion,
    Crushing love in greed for pelf.

In thy steps comes deprivation
    From the land whereon we tread,
Thou gives landlords their vocation,
To place rent against starvation,
    Or a grave for loved ones dead.
Turning men to rapine's measures
    Wrangling christians interest seek,
And derive their greatest pleasures
    Squeezing profits from the weak.

INDUSTRIALISM

Son of Pax! From tumult turning,
    Healing on thy wings is brought;
Scenes of strife and carnage spurning,
On thy altar love's light burning,
    Flowery paths by thee are sought;
Waking sympathetic feeling,
    In the rugged breast of man,
Doom of all coercion sealing
    Where thy banner heads the van.

Ever onward still advancing,
    Commerce yet will yield the place
Where war's offspring now is prancing,
Force and greed and lust enhancing,
    And in equity find grace.
Step by step in man's progression
    Has been heard thy quiet voice,
Bidding Labor take possession—
    In fraternity rejoice.

Peace by Force

IT is a long time since we heard of any king killed in war. Nor have any prime ministers or millionaires been mentioned among the dead heroes. The generals are at the front, sure enough—when their armies retreat.

None of the Rothschilds have as yet coveted the Iron Cross, or the Victoria Cross, or the Legion of Honor. And none of the Krupps, the Creusots, the McVickers or the Duponts have had their precious skins scratched.

The United States is about to follow in Europe's footsteps.

The Carnegie Peace Foundation cost Andy about $10,-000,000. Yet now come Andy's most intimate friends and propose to spend $500,000,000 at a lick and upset his beautiful dream of peace, and Andy never lifts his brogue in protest. Jingoes everywhere argue that the first, last and only requisite for international peace is to increase the army and navy. "Statesmen" in other countries have the same insane notion that the possession of a fancy assortment of murder machines leads to peace. But THE BLAST utterly fails to see the logic of preparedness. If we prepare, some other nation will prepare a little bit more, and we logically have to go them one better. Carried to its bitter end, the maintenance of peace through increase of armament means the creation of a military caste maintained in idleness, and a ruinous industrial policy of manufacturing engines of destruction that become obsolete as soon as they are finished.

There is a real peace movement going on. Its leaders are not eulogized by a sycophantic press. Quite a few of them are in jail. They are the men in every country who openly advocate anti-militarism—the men who have the courage and honesty to tell the world to disarm—the men who are trying to open the eyes of workers of one country to the utter folly and brutality of killing workers of another country, whom they have never seen and against whom they have no grievance whatever, for the sole purpose of providing a market for capitalistic "over-production."

If universal peace is to come, it will not be through the lords above but through the workers below.

True, the advocates of anti-militarism have built no peace palaces at The Hague and do not try to create peace tribunals where lawyers can wrangle learnedly to their hearts' content. They act more wisely. They know that men trained for war are ultimately going to pursue their calling. They also know that a body of men skilled in the art of killing will invariably prove itself an instrument of tyranny.

Even George Washington, who as the Second Reader tells us, was an exemplary boy, could not resist the temptation to use his talent, where he "hadn't ought to." And we have no assurance that the breed of statesmen has improved since George's time.

As a matter of economy in blood and treasure, we suggest to those who wish to maintain peace by force, that instead of squandering $500,000,000 for armies and navies to kill millions of innocents, they appropriate, say one million, for the killing of those responsible for war.

We agree with President Wilson that the European war "was brought on by rulers, not by the peoples." A miscellaneous assortment of a hundred kings, diplomats, statesmen, financiers and generals decorating lamp posts in Berlin, Petrograd, London and Paris would soon end the slaughter in Europe.

The Spirit of Commercialism

"Build a lie;—yes, build a lie,
A large one—be not over tender;
Give it a form and raise it high
That all the world may see its splendor.
Then launch it like a mighty ship
On the restless sea of men's opinion,
And the ship shall sail before the gale
Imbued with motion and dominion.
Give it but size and the worst of lies
Shall float about the world forever."

HISTORY past and present proves the poet true. And we may add that even little, petty lies keep afloat a remarkably long time. Their form may change, but their essence remains the same.

In the Dark Ages when the Pope, acting as business agent for Lord Almighty, set the fashion in "morals," every social climber simulated piety in order to meet with approval.

In the days of Louis XIV, when the monarch was the "fountain of honor," the courtier type was in vogue. Dukes and princelings hung about the stairs of the king's mistresses with smirking obeisance, in order to curry favor with his majesty.

Every type or trait that for the time being met with social approval has had in its wake an army of miserable cheats trying to filch a little prestige.

Today Commercialism is the fountain source of lies. Men have ceased to produce for themselves; they produce to sell to others. Salesmanship is lauded as a "science." Anybody can sell to people who really want to buy; salesmanship is fooling people into buying. In the rivalry to unearth new strata of suckers to sell to, every possible form of lying is resorted to. "Tricks of trade," business "shrewdness," sensationalism, adulterating and misbranding of goods, counterfeit trademarks, forged or paid-for testimonials from celebrities, sale of diplomas and medals, "ads" masquerading as news dispatches or editorials.— lies and lies without end, just to sell. Lying by suggestion or association of ideas: a "Quaker" this or a "Royal" that, to suggest integrity, excellence, or purity. Every newspaper, magazine or street car fairly sizzles with lying ads promising anything from the abolition of pimples through the use of some perfumed grease named after the first lady in a leg-show, to the acquisition of near-immortality through drinking malt-whiskey.

The curse of commercialism runs through politics from the White House to the ward heeler. It sets a premium on chicanery, perfidy and all that is low and vulgar. Anything to stay in office; political color changes like a chameleon. Commercialism drives the fearless thinker and teacher out of our colleges and welcomes athletes posing as students. Professionals hungry for prizes pretend enthusiasm for physical culture. Writers dress their dish to the reader's taste, and the thick hide of the editor becomes tender and touchy under the lash of the cash register.

The courtroom is the home of perjury. Experts on handwriting, insanity, poisons or explosives render testimony favorable to the side that hires them. Lawyers plead, not for truth, but for cash. Judges—well, the less said the better: it would be unfit to print and unmailable under our postal laws.

Commercialism is responsible for the smooth-water labor leader who dares not attack fundamental evils or risk a battle with the masters for fear of losing prestige. With lofty patrician disdain he sneers at the storm-and-stress man and refers to him as an "irresponsible agitator." In which attitude he is heartily applauded by the master class who occasionally reward him with a crumb from the political table.

In the name of science, quacks, ambulance chasers, astrologers, healers by prayer and healers by magnetism, "Swamis" and "professors" do a flourishing commercial business. Preachers, pretended followers of the Prince of Peace, pray for more murder machines. Killing men pays better than saving souls. Our Christianity, our "culture," our whole civilization is one monumental fraud.

Nothing short of a revolution can make a thorough change. A revolution whose first step will be the taking over and direct management of the industries by the industrious, the producers. But a revolution presages a new era. And whatever is new lacks prestige, and is consequently scorned by impostors. That is why the greatest integrity of purpose is found in a movement's infancy.

Those who despise labor and seek to live by simulating usefulness are not going to support anything revolutionary. THE BLAST hopes to be a thorn in their flesh. Come on, friends, join us.   —THE BLASTERS

THE BLAST

Revolutionary Labor Weekly
569 Dolores St., San Francisco, Cal.
Mail Address, Box 661   Phone, Park 499

Alexander Berkman, Editor and Publisher
E. B. Morten, Associate Editor   M. E. Fitzgerald, Manager

SUBSCRIPTION
$1.00 Yearly   60c Six Months   5c Copy
Bundle rates 2½c per copy in bundles of ten.
Advertising rates on application.
Entered as second-class matter at the postoffice at San Francisco,
Cal., January 14, 1916, under the Act of March 3, 1879.

Muzzling Discontent

IT looks like an organized effort on the part of the Federal Government to silence the voice of protest and revolt in this country.

The press informs us that "Washington is taking a hand in investigating the Chicago poisoning case, with a view of suppressing Anarchist publications and *other obnoxious* agitation." On the heels of this announcement comes the news of the raiding of the office of the *Alarm,* the new Anarchist monthly published in Chicago, the arrest of Emma Goldman in New York, and the arrest of Ricardo and Enrique Flores Magon in Los Angeles, as well as threats of numerous other arrests and the suppression of all revolutionary publications.

Evidently Wilson & Co. consider these tactics a necessary step toward Preparedness. They are eager to discredit the anti-militarist movement, and thus gain an additional argument for strengthening the hands of the government. The pressure of the overlords on the White House professor must be pretty strong to make him forget his history. We want to remind him that, in the long run, suppression has never suppressed. People have a way of objecting to stink. Such objection may be very unpleasant to those who deal in the article, but you can't prevent people from smelling bad odors, unless you abolish the swamp that breeds them.

Preparedness may well serve to muzzle the people—for a while, but the Federal power isn't big enough to suppress discontent and revolt, or stifle the voice of the social rebel, for even in prison—aye, in the very grave—his silence speaks loud.

A Menace to Profit

FOR several years past Emma Goldman has been lecturing, among other subjects, on "Limitation of Family" and advising the workers why and how not to have many children. Now Comrade Goldman is facing trial for propagating superior quality in human stock as against inferior quantity.

The manufacturer needs "hands" for his factories. The State needs cannon fodder to protect the manufacturer, its partner. Together they share the profits.

Where do the workers come in? Well, they supply the "hands." Their women folk must also supply the bodies.

Every boss needs cheap labor. When the supply is plentiful, things are *cheap.* Therefore the boss is strong for large workingmen families. (His own is generally small).

The State needs soldiers. Therefore every ruler and governor wants the "common people" to breed and multiply.

Hence the arrest of such women as Margaret Sanger and Emma Goldman. Their agitation is a menace to profit.

Press Fakes

AN "enterprising" Associate Press man sent out the report the other day that he interviewed me in New York in re Jean Crones. According to that report, I condemned Crones in unmeasured terms and denied that he is an Anarchist.

The reporter seems not to have been troubled in the least by the irrelevant little circumstance that I happen to be in San Francisco and have been here for months. The story, more stupid than amusing, was of course purely a fake. But it is characteristic of the daily press: it is the stuff the good reading public is fed on regularly.

Jean Crones

BUT who is Jean Crones? Is he an Anarchist? Why did he try to poison the prelates of Church and State?

I have been asked these questions by many people, friends and otherwise.

I don't know Jean Crones. He may be an Anarchist or he may not. He may have tried to "clean up house," or the whole story may be a police fabrication to hide a common case of ptomaine poisoning. Even the best restaurants dish up adulterated rotten stuff tastily prepared and nicely served. Incidentally, it is always *apropos* to start a man-hunt against Anarchists. It diverts public attention from police corruption and even gives the "guardians" added prestige and importance. Above all, it serves to "discredit" the revolutionists.

Of course, it is possible that some one, says Crones, tried to kill the Archbishop and the Governor. Well, what of it? He may have seen in those two men the representatives of two institutions in society—Church and State—inimical to the best interests of the people. Did he think that he would abolish these evil institutions by killing their chief representatives? Hardly. But he may have wanted thus to express the protest of a sensitive, tortured soul against our social injustice, stupidity and superstition. Perhaps he wanted forcibly to call the attention of the country to the official follower of the lowly Nazarene sumptuously dining while thousands of men, "images of their Maker," are dying of starvation.

May be that some one or all of these motives actuated Crones. If so, he succeeded: his purpose is accomplished.

Philosophically speaking, it is well for the stupefiers and oppressors of man to realize, now and then, that tyranny breeds tyrannicide. It is a hopeful symptom for humanity.

Legal Murderers

JOE HILL, the I. W. W. poet, was recently murdered by the governor of Utah. The murderer went scot free.

Roy J. Horton, another I. W. W. speaker, was shot to death on the streets of Salt Lake City by Major H. P. Myton, a local political bully. There was no provocation. The murderer was acquitted.

And still some people wonder why there are Jean Crones. The wonder is that there are not more of them.

Wilson the Lackey of Carranza

ON February 18 agents of the Federal Government forced their way into the office of *Regeneracion*, the revolutionary weekly of the Mexican Liberal Party, published in Los Angeles, and brutally beat up and arrested the editors of the paper, Ricardo and Enrique Flores Magon.

I know Ricardo and Enrique, and I am proud to call them my comrades and friends. They are men of that rare type seldom produced outside of Russia and Mexico: men who have sacrificed social position, comfort and personal safety for the cause of the people. Men big enough to live in direst poverty in order to devote their time, ability and means to further revolution and liberty. Present-day America has failed to evolve such superior types of social consciousness. Indeed, it has not even learned to appreciate them. Their fate is misunderstanding, persecution and prison.

In spite of tremendous obstacles the Magons and their co-workers have for years been carrying on their great work. A double task faced them: to educate and organize the Mexican people into an effective weapon of revolution and, still more important—and more difficult—to enlighten the American people to the real issues involved in the Mexican uprising. It is due to a great extent to the efforts of *Regeneracion* and the Mexican Liberal Party in this country that Roosevelt and his presidential successors did not dare to interfere in Mexico.

No wonder that the activity of the Brothers Magon has proven a thorn in the flesh of the American exploiters and native oppressors of Mexico. The cry of Land and Liberty has been finding a thousand-fold echo in the bleeding hearts of the peons. Now Carranza and his henchmen have determined to stifle this rebel voice.

Repeatedly the bloodsuckers of Mexico have attempted to suppress our brave comrades. Roosevelt, then President of these free United States, used the whole power of the Federal Government to aid Perfidious Diaz in stamping out the revolutionary agitation of the Mexican Liberal Junta. Many of our brave Mexican comrades were railroaded to prison.

And now it is the learned academician in the White House who is hastening to the aid of Carranza and Wall street, to suppress the work of *Regeneracion*. They will again try to send the Magons to the penitentiary. We call on all rebels and fair-minded people not to permit this outrage.

A LETTER FROM MARIA MAGON.

Los Angeles, February 20, 1916.

Dear Comrade Berkman:

I wired you that Ricardo and Enrique Flores Magon were arrested and Enrique badly beaten. Your most welcome telegram was received after considerable delay. Owing to our somewhat remote location, the messenger failed to find our place yesterday. * * * Your interest in the case of our comrades and your recommendation of bondmen are most welcome and heartily appreciated.

I want to give you some of the details of the events attending the arrest. The violence spoken of in the papers was, needless to say, started by the bulls, as usual. While in the office the minions of the law became excited by Enrique asking some one to get his hat and coat. They began to abuse and manhandle him, and when he resented their abuse, they pounced upon him and beat him on the head with the butt of their guns, inflicting such serious wounds that it was necessary for him to be taken to the emergency hospital. The office and shop resembled a besieged fort after the fracas started, for the gang had so adroitly set the scenes that while they had watched the place all day, or in fact for several days, we never noticed them until they appeared at the office. Our place is surrounded by trees, and the lackeys made their appearance about 4 o'clock. They very "courteously" served the warrant on Ricardo, who was in the office, and the trouble started a few minutes later when Enrique was called in from the house and assaulted by the bulls.

The lackeys that entered the office were five or six in number and the men in the shop were helpless onlookers while the scuffle went on, as their slightest move was met with a gun pressed to their ribs, no one being able to raise a hand, contrary to what the papers say. Ricardo and Enrique were literally dragged to a waiting auto, a block away, Enrique bleeding profusely from head to foot.

The comrades were called yesterday for preliminary hearing, but not being yet represented by a lawyer, they refused to plead. Their bond originally set at $3000, has been raised to $7500 on some flimsy excuse. No one has been able to see them except a lawyer. We expect to engage Harriman to defend them. We received a very encouraging message from Emma also.

Yours for the Cause,
MARIA MAGON.

P. O. Box 1236, Los Angeles, Cal.

P. S.—I forgot to mention that as soon as the trouble had started, a swarm of armed bulls who had been concealed in the surrounding shrubbery, sprang from every direction, rifles in hand, making threats and ready for any excuse to fire.

M. M.

Blessed Georgia

SPEAKING in opposition to the Keating-Owen child labor bill, that eminent Christian congressman, W. J. Adamson, of Georgia, the champion of the poor, downtrodden millowners of the South and of the Constitutional right of children to work themselves to death, delivered himself as follows:

"Conditions of factory life and labor in Georgia are ideal. The factory communities are model villages. They have schools, churches and libraries, all liquor, gambling and vice being strictly and effectively prohibited. We teach the children of Georgia to work because an idle brain is the devil's workshop, idle hands the devil's instrument."

Virtuous prohibition State with its little Mary Phagans, its lynchings, and child labor! The Beveridge report on conditions under which women and children slave in the cotton mill district of Georgia was so shocking that senators from the chivalrous South argued it was unfit to print or to be circulated through the mails.

The National Security League
ALDEN WARD

"WHY don't you get in touch with The National Security League?" said my friends, when they understood I was out of organized journalism into the freer field of a freelance. "I will," I said. And I did.

When I had heard the case for The National Security League, Inc., I agreed to "write it up." When they asked me "Where?" I said: "Oh, in some weekly newspaper-magazine, I suppose."

And now I am keeping my promise. Not in the way they will like, though.

When I went to look up The National Security League, I asked as to the form and purpose and nature of the organization. I had previously formed an opinion from what I had read in the New York *Times*, but I wanted to be as fair as I could under the circumstances.

The reply was evasive. But I had confirmation of my opinion, all right. The National Security League, Incorporated, is a corporation engaged in the business of scaring the American people into creating a military Frankenstein of such proportions as to make further colonial conquests an imminent reality, and the further exploitation of "foreign fields" even more profitable than navalized England and prussianized Germany have found them to be. It is as much a corporation as the General Electric Company or the Pennsylvania Railroad Company. Its stock in trade is the credulity of yourself and your neighbors; its operations are based on the gullibility of the American people, on our ancient habit of letting other people do our thinking: editors and orators, and the like.

I inquired as to the personnel of the organization. "Who is back of this thing?" is the way I put it.

The first name mentioned was that of that arch-reprobate and imperialist, the character who became President of the United States by reason of the demise of William McKinley and who, being in the manger, remained there for seven and one-half years and found the job so congenial that he has been trying to get back ever since. I won't flatter him by naming him. Every person recognizes him even at this distance. He is the man who is always in the center of all talk and fuss about the army and navy and our foreign policy and our domestic policy and race suicide and—well, most everything. His name is synonymous with the expression Big Stick.

His comrades, or fellow conspirators, include such charming characters as James M. Beck, who, having been attorney general and profited accordingly, is now engaged in the equally profitable business of Anti-Germanism; A. J. Drexel Biddle, of Philadelphia, he of the Sabbath School-Boxing Ring fame; Charles J. Bonaparte, ex-secretary of the navy; Jacob M. Dickinson, ex-secretary of War; Myron T. Herrick, ex-governor of Ohio; John Grier Hibben, president of Princeton University; Philander C. Knox, ex-secretary of State; George Von L. Meyer; William Fellowes Morgan, of New York; Henry L. Stimson, ex-secretary of war; Oscar S. Straus, of New York; and David Jayne Hill. These ex-cabinet appointees, together with a scattering of flattered governors of Western states, form a National Committee whose main usefulness consists in the weight of their names, the actual fussing being left to Joseph H. Choate, who having been our alleged representative at the so-called Court of St. James, and having been delightfully spoofed by our English cousins, is now more English than American, and Alton B. Parker, formerly associated with William Jennings Bryan in chasing the Presidential bee, who are respectively Honorary President and Honorary Vice-President of the corporation. To a lesser degree Robert Bacon, as Chairman of the Board of Directors, and S. Stanwood Menken, as acting President, are engaged in this same delightful occupation, assisted by a Finance Committee of professional beggars whose business it is to raise Cain and millions for agitation and battle impedimenta. And back of these a staff of clerks and other sorts of slaves almost as imposing as that maintained by the National Association of Manufacturers. All as busy as mischief, all engaged in scaring us into a blue funk.

Money? They have gobs of it. Probably each member of the National Committee paid in several thousands of dollars for the privilege of being in on the fun.

Today there appears a significant large advertisement in the New York *Times*, etc., as follows:

MEN AND WOMEN OF AMERICA
YOU CAN HELP!

Prepare for defense without delay.

Help the campaign for National Preparedness by giving what you can to further the work of the National Security League.

We believe America's continued existence requires obligatory universal military training for our young men, and readiness for service by them for national defense.

The League needs funds to give one hundred million people all the facts.

Congress will act only when there is a positive demand from the people. To impress upon Congress the necessity of action, the League is organizing branches to widen its influence, and desires your membership.

Send your subscription at once to the National Security League, Inc., 31 Pine Street, New York City.

We need your help!

This is the sort of advertisement which the League can pay for. The sort of advertisement I am writing for them is the sort they cannot pay for. And they are going to get plenty of the latter kind.

The weakness of the League's case is shown in the last line of their paid space squeal. "We need your help!"

Certainly the League needs your help. Unless you help them at their contemptible work of intoxicating the masses into unconsciousness, they cannot ram the miserable plot they have hatched down our throats.

The League wants publicity. How many readers of THE BLAST will help me to advertise their work (!) by shouting their crime from street to street, from ear to ear, until the stupid and the blind and the meek shall all hear and rise up to throw their agitation into their faces, with the cry: "Prepare? Of course, prepare! Prepare against our real enemies, the traitorous murderers within our own borders—You!"?

※ ※ ※

THE convention of the United Mine Workers defeated a resolution to exclude National Guardsmen and State Constabulary from membership. Though every speaker denounced the use of the National Guard in strikes, the majority contended that it would be in violation of State and Federal law to deny them admission.

A striking example of licking the boot that kicks you. Miners on strike may have the satisfaction of being shot down by fellow miners, members of the militia.

If the law compels unions to admit to membership men whom they do not want, so much the worse for the law. It is time the workers would learn to put their own manhood and interests above the law of their masters.

* * *

WE sneer at the savage who worships some idol of his own making. The law-abiding citizen who bends in obedience to any fool thing printed in a statute-book has the savage backed off the boards as a victim of superstition.

An idol is at least perfectly harmless. That's more than can be said for most laws.

Open Forum

Such articles as "What Is the Matter With Labor?" by C. E. S. Wood, cannot fail to impress the progressive element of Labor. Some of the indictments apply also to the great majority in the so-called radical movements. As for instance: "When its voice is biggest, it secretly carries its hat in its hand," etc. Acts of violence are clamorously greeted, but as soon as the consequences of such deeds are to be taken, everybody runs to cover, and piles of money are spent to prove that the actors are law-abiding citizens, and did not commit the deed, instead of proclaiming to the enemies that Labor acted in self-defense and was justified in using the same means that the exploiters apply in dealing with the discontented workers. And if the radicals are encouraging such farce in the courts, is it any wonder when such ignoramuses as the editor of *The Labor Clarion* talk about the "guilt" and "crime" of Labor?

For many years I have been of the conviction that so long as we have not the courage to apply our ideas and ideals to life, whether friend or enemy, so long will we make but little headway in having our principles accepted and respected, even among the intelligent outsiders. I have no scruples about violence or any other means of self-defense (and there are not others when it comes to the deeds of the oppressed and exploited), but when such deeds are not backed up by a moral force —the courage of our convictions—the acts will do more harm than good toward the so much desired revolution.

To promote this spirit among Labor elements and radicals should be, in my humble opinion, the object of a radical paper.

Wishing you success in your hard task, I am, fraternally yours,
Lincoln, Cal.   —A. Isaac

How you ever got my name as a man so low in birth to be an anarchist I don't know. If any one gave you my name tell them that I am their friend no longer. I would be ashamed to let any of my friends or acquaintances know that an anarchist ever wrote me a letter. Hoping you or your confederates will never take the liberty to write my name again.
Everett, Wash.   —C. M. Robbins

You have sent me three issues of THE BLAST. Being well-supplied with reading stuff, I thought when I perused your first copy that it was not worth a dollar a year. I must re-inventorate, i. e., the first page of the three issues is worth the entire dollar.

Keep up the pace as set and within one year the entire capitalistic world will be throwing bricks your way. Enclosed find $1.00 and if possible begin me at your first issue.

Go after 'em. We can't all be pioneers, but we can help along a little in lesser ways. Your paper makes me young again. It has life. You are connected up with the universal dynamo. Don't let these wires rust out nor become loose in the tensions.
Janesville, Wis.   —Z. O. Bowen

Your request for a subscription to THE BLAST is noted, but in spite of all I know as to your past record, I must decline to appropriate any of my surplus to your cause.

In my opinion you have created more discontent than you have cured, and your disturbance of the peace of Pittsburg and New York City was not productive of any good for any person, except perhaps yourself, and even that is doubtful.

I am disposed to believe in your sincerity but your remedy for social disease does not seem to me worthy of confidence. After forty years of labor and self-denial I know no other cure for the ills of the world but industry, self-control and intelligent sympathy, service and sacrifice for others.
New York.   —Fred Gordon, Coffee Broker

The third issue of THE BLAST is so very good that I am sending an extra dollar for more copies. * * * I really believe the third BLAST is the best revolutionary paper I have ever seen—it is so solid with facts and lacking in bombast.

Yours for a better and saner world,
Tacoma, Wash.   —S. T. Hammersmarck

I thank you with my whole heart for THE BLAST. I confess that I have never read such deep philosophy put so plainly and simply. * * * The need of such a paper is great. The workers are beginning to realize the role they are called to play in the history of mankind. The blessed day will come. Grace to the forerunners like you and my most beloved comrade Goldman. * * * Fraternal greetings,
Hibbing, Minn.—George E. Andreytchine

BLAST *is* good. It's splendid—serious— and discusses things in a big way. People talk of it; remember what it says. BLAST is unique. Hope you'll keep it up and even grow.
Los Angeles.   —Luke North

VOL. 1   SAN FRANCISCO, SATURDAY, MARCH 4, 1916   **No. 8**

PARTNERS

Partners

I GLANCED casually out of my window. The little stretch of park facing my room looked like a living oasis of green bordered by dull cemented gray. The sun shone warm upon the turf, coaxing the women and children of the neighborhood into the open. Soon the grass was dotted with the young ones romping on the green. Their merry voices floated toward me, and my heart echoed their joy.

I was watching the kites gracefully swimming in the air, and the boys below shouting with glee as some ambitious kite would shoot like an arrow upward, outdistancing its competitors. Suddenly I noticed a commotion in the park. Men and boys were running toward the street, and in a moment a dense crowd blocked the traffic From the elevation of my window on the upper floor I could see an irregular opening in the center of the crowd and the figure of a man lying on his face. I rushed into the street. With some difficulty I forced my way through the constantly swelling crowd, till I reached the figure on the ground. I touched it, and the man slowly raised himself on his elbow. His hat had fallen from his head and the bright sun shone fully on his disheveled gray hair. His face was pinched with want and in his eyes I saw the hopeless look of misery.

I felt the crowd give about me. A policeman elbowed his way to the old man. "What's the matter?" he demanded, taking hold of the man's shoulder.

"I must have fainted," the man said weakly.

"Out of work?" some one in the crowd asked.

"Yes. Long time."

A young urchin handed the policeman an old weatherworn derby. "Here's his hat," he said sympathetically.

The officer placed it on the old man's head. "Where do you live?" he asked.

"I have no home."

The crowd became hushed. The policeman hesitated a moment. "Come with me, then," he said at last.

He assisted the old man to his feet. The crowd silently parted, making a narrow lane between two living walls. The officer, supporting his charge, stepped toward the street. But as the old man was crossing the curb he suddenly collapsed. His arm slipped from the policeman's grip and he fell in the street.

"Case of starvation," said some one in the crowd.

The policeman glanced around. There was no telephone station in sight. A look of worry crossed his face. "He may be croakin'," I heard him say under his breath.

The sound of an approaching automobile seemed to bring inspiration. The officer jumped into the street and halted the large shiny carriage. Edging my way closer, I caught a glimpse of a beautiful young woman in fashionable attire, accompanied by a gentleman of advanced age. I noticed his immaculate dress and superior manner as he stepped out of the machine. He spoke with irritation: "I am afraid we'll be late for luncheon, but if the man isn't drunk we'll take him to the hospital."

Several men meanwhile lifted the old fellow from the ground and were carrying him to the carriage. The girl raised herself from her seat as they were placing the unconscious form into the machine. Her bright eyes were eagerly following the scene. Suddenly she caught the rays of the sun playing on the waxlike features of the old man. "Oh, father!" she cried, "it's Jones—Jones, who worked in our mill!"

The crowd surged toward the carriage. "Stand back!" commanded the officer. He motioned to the chauffeur. "Charity Hospital! Quick!"

The Wailing of Wilson & Co.
Warren Van Valkenburgh

ANY person who is possessed of sufficient meanness to suspect the undertaker of praying for good business would probably be inconsiderate enough to infer that Hudson Maxim wrote "Defenseless America" for a similar motive; or that the House of Morgan is financially interested in the export of munitions; or that Woodrow Wilson meant German sympathizers in his "creatures of passion" speech. Who owns so warped an intellect as to conceive of such base designs is mentally derelict. He is worse. He is unpatriotic, and that is the crowning sin of all nations.

The American public is easily aroused by any means that do not require mental exertion. Thus while they attend the movies the politicians at Washington plan the bartering away of their destinies.

The prospect of an annual expenditure of five hundred million dollars will have little deterrent effect on that body of patriotic word mongers that the people have selected to guide the ship of State.

The recent amorous experience of the blushing old lover of the White House must surely have blinded him to the creed of neutrality which he so lately enunciated to his citizens, because in that memorable address to Congress he threw all discretion to the winds when he directed his venom toward those "who have uttered threats against our national peace * * * within our own borders." The professor wants adequate laws to crush those who dare assail "the honor and self-respect of the nation."

The time is coming when it won't be safe to have an appetite for frankfurters lest it be considered an evidence of disloyalty to an anti-German administration.

Aside from the suggestion to seal every lip that speaks in opposition to the party in power there is a very subtle and cleverly hidden cue that Congress get busy with a Defense of the Realm Act, made in America.

This hint is embodied in Wilson's reference to the transportation problem. If the suggested committee be appointed to ascertain the best means of obtaining Federal control of the railroads—and the best excuse for doing it—it will result in eventual dominance of railroad employees by the U. S. Government. This would place each man under federal jurisdiction; and, in time of stress render the railroad workers as much victims of State tyranny as ever the renegade Briand did in France during the C. G. T. strike a few years ago. The transportation workers could, were they willing to do it, so completely tie up the entire national commerce that military maneuvres would be impossible. Make a Federal case of it, and such an event as a strike would be considered as nothing less than *lèse majesté*. Such is the plan of Wilson to maintain the integrity of free institutions that exist only on paper.

The President should be given credit, however, for having been frank enough to tell the truth as to why he wants a citizen army of four hundred thousand men. It is not because of the fear of invasion by a foreign foe bent on destroying the glorious liberties of America. It is to protect the business men's interests, and Mr. Wilson says so. For that reason he calls upon the employers to make it desirable for their employees to join this citizen army. This is an admission that should accrue to Wilson many congratulations from those in whose defense he pleads.

Wilson and the other champions of preparedness have at last let out the public secret that Germany is jealous of our lordship over South America and that Japan wants the Philippines. Moreover, they hint that England, too, would bear watching. They have turned over some pages that any casual acquaintance with history knows by heart and bared the chameleon-like Nationalism of all the great powers that fought against each other at one time and with each other at another. This in itself should shed some light on the patriotic prevarication of one country being better than another, for if all wars are defensive—which they are to each individual country involved—then such a thing as an aggressive war cannot be and no nation should prepare for defense. A nation cannot defend itself if it is not attacked; therefore if none are aggressive there can be no war. There is not a country in Europe today that will admit that it is waging an aggressive struggle. And yet the war goes on.

But the militarists give us an idea of why we must prepare for trouble. It is because of our commercial dominance of the American continent. We must increase our armaments to protect the South American markets from German competition. Hundreds of young fools must accept the yoke of American militarism so that our business men may expand their trade and exclude all others from doing the same thing.

All the Congressional debates in the world will not mitigate the war peril, for no nation is yet ready for arbitration nor is there any likelihood that any nation ever will be. No nation, then, can lay claim to civilization, for civilized people are willing to discuss dissensions. The germ of civilization lies not in the ranks of the rulers. It lies in the palms of the people.

The workers can have no interest in the present war propaganda other than so far as they are personally concerned. The countries belong to the masters of wealth and position, and they alone should defend them. But of course they won't as long as the people can be reached by such empty appeals as those now being made in Washington and being circulated in censored shape for public consideration, and the worst of it all is that whether they approve of the stupendous expense of increasing the national defenses or not, they must pay the fiddler anyway.

It would seem that the most effective way to end any objectionable war and at the same time put fear in the hearts of the tyrants on high is to follow the advice of the clever critic who recently said, "Shoot the officers and go on home." It's worth trying, anyway.

The Ass and His Master

Fredericke Madsen

SERENE and calm he toils on terror's brink,
His lightning-brain and steel-nerve never shrink;
Creating ALL—yet—stalked by want and dread
He thanks YOU meekly for his crust of bread.

YOU feed upon his woe, his shame, his need,
As vultures 'pon a scarce-dead carcass feed;
And heap with taunts and insults rare and new
This million-headed ass who toils for YOU.

And yet he hopes for JUSTICE thru YOUR law,—
A lamb might find that in a tiger's claw.
The State and Court, from judge to spying tool,
All damn him as a weak and vicious fool.

Yet sometimes—from this stupid, slavish pack,
A HERO-SOUL dares fling YOUR violence back;
YOU quake—and rend him with YOUR law and lies
Seeking to kill *that* which all death defies.

The Vice of Moderation

I AM aware that many object to the severity of my language; but is there not cause for severity? I will be as harsh as Truth, and as uncompromising as Justice. On this subject I do not wish to think, or speak, or write, with moderation. No! No! Tell a man whose house is on fire to give a moderate alarm; tell him to moderately rescue his wife from the hands of the ravisher; tell the mother to gradually extricate her babe from the fire into which it has fallen—but urge me not to use moderation in a cause like the present. I am in earnest—I will not equivocate—I will not excuse—I will not retreat a single inch—and I will be heard. The apathy of the people is enough to make every statue leap from its pedestal and hasten the resurrection of the dead.   —William Lloyd Garrison

Man vs. State

AS there is no social sensorium, it results that the welfare of the aggregate, considered apart from that of the units, is not an end to be sought. The society exists for the benefit of its members; not its members for the benefit of the society. It has ever to be remembered that, great as may be the efforts made for the prosperity of the body politic, yet the claims of the body politic are nothing in themselves and become something only in so far as they embody the claims of its component individuals.

—Herbert Spencer

THE BLAST

Revolutionary Labor Weekly
569 Dolores St., San Francisco, Cal.
Mail Address, Box 661   Phone, Park 499

Alexander Berkman, Editor and Publisher
E. B. Morton, Associate Editor   M. E. Fitzgerald, Manager

SUBSCRIPTION
$1.00 Yearly   60c Six Months   5c Copy
Bundle rates 2½c per copy in bundles of ten.
Advertising rates on application.
Entered as second-class matter at the postoffice at San Francisco,
Cal., January 14, 1916, under the Act of March 3, 1879.

Comments

To Our Friends

THE ALARM, of Chicago, and the REVOLT, of New York, have been suppressed. Do you want THE BLAST to continue to exist? If you think this paper worth while, it's up to you to support it. We can't do it alone. Your letters of praise are very encouraging, but they will not pay the printer's bills. Assistance is needed at once. Don't put this aside and forget all about it. Show your interest and appreciation by your immediate response.

It Hurts

THE BLAST is making 'em real mad. The printer who did the first issues of this paper has refused to continue. He told us quite plainly that his "Catholic and other customers wouldn't stand for it." We had to find another printer.

In this connection it is significant that the two official labor papers of San Francisco have refused us the customary courtesy of exchanging copies with THE BLAST. Incidentally, one of these papers is published at our former printer's.

Wouldn't it be funny if THE BLAST's bitterest enemies were found, not among the capitalists, but in the ranks of labor?

If the crooked labor politicians feel hurt, THE BLAST is striking in the right spot.

Inviting Violence

THE Federal government has suppressed *The Alarm*, of Chicago, and the *Revolt*, of New York. We are not going to say that it is an outrage. Why should the government not commit outrages? Invasion of personal liberty, suppression of free speech and free press, silencing non-conformists and protestants, shooting down rebellious workers —all this is of the very essence of government.

We don't complain. We understand Wilson's position. He must do his master's bidding. This is the "sane policy." But we want to warn the weather cock in the White House that it may not prove *safe*. Suppression of the voice of discontent leads to assassination. *Vide* Russia.

Golden Rule Mush

A CORRESPONDENT writes: "Why not agitate *loving* each other into goodness instead of kicking each other into it?" This with reference to capital and labor.

The Golden Rule again. Turn the other cheek. Lick the hand that smites you. Tell the dispossessed widow, groveling in the street there with her half dozen starving kids, to love her landlord.

That's the morality that is making slaves of us. It is breeding weaklings, mollycoddles, too spineless to resist.

There is too much of this mushy talk, especially among so-called radicals. Not greater love but more hate we need. A strong, red-blooded hatred of everything that makes for injustice and oppression. Hatred of every factor, social and human, that upholds and perpetuates the love of slavery and chains.

"Ah, but we hate conditions, not persons," the goody-goody people tell us. Rot! You can't divorce conditions from the persons who support them and profit by them.

I hate them both.

Good Slaves

THE manufacturers of the South love the children of their employees. They are exerting every effort to give the little kids a chance to work in the factories.

They also know that their employees love their bosses. So they have been circulating a petition among the workers protesting against the Keating-Owen child labor bill now before Congress. And a good many of the miserable wretches have actually signed the petition.

Darling slaves. How they love their masters. Their just reward is awaiting them in Heaven.

Resistance Tempers Tyranny

THE Federal government at last dismissed the charges against Margaret Sanger. "Margaret Sanger is victorious!" writes our New York correspondent; "the right of woman to own and control her own body has been established."

We do not share our friend's optimism. It was publicity—the numerous protests written and wired to the authorities—that forced the government to "have another think." All government is cowardly. It possesses only the courage of the bully to intimidate the weak. If you realize your strength and have the courage to manifest it, the government bully will slink away. *Resistance tempers tyranny*.

That the *cause* of Margaret Sanger is not victorious is shown by the arrest of Emma Goldman in New York, on the charge of spreading Birth Control information. Very likely the authorities think that her case will give them less trouble. She is an Anarchist, and they figure that her persecution will not arouse as much public protest as the attempted suppression of Margaret Sanger.

The same agitation and protest that forced the government to dismiss the Sanger charges must be repeated in the case of Comrade Goldman. Realize the importance of this suggestion. Act accordingly and at once. Start a campaign of publicity. Hold mass meetings and wire protests, collective and individual, to Emma Goldman, care District Attorney, New York City.

We strongly urge the same mode of action in the case of Enrico and Ricardo Flores Magon, now in the Los Angeles jail. It is action that is needed, now. Never mind waiting for the trial. Trial means conviction: there is no more justice for the modern rebel in the courts of capital than there was for the Nazarene in the court of Pilate.

THE BLAST   Five

Life Is Vision and Vision Is Life

Harry Kelly

THE article by C. E. S. Wood in a recent issue of THE BLAST on "Life is Vision," and the editorial in *Organized Labor* on "Labor is Life—Not Vision," were thought-provoking and well worth while. They voice the eternal conflict between the ideal and the reality; each point of view is true and, taken together, represent the whole truth—at least it seems so to me.

In a discussion of social questions the welfare of particular individuals becomes of very minor importance, but to discuss social questions without having regard for particular individuals is to fall into the fatal error of discussing the whole without reference to its constituent parts. To tell "labor" it must organize and stand solid if it would emancipate itself from the domination of the parasitic class, is to make a statement that is absolutely incontrovertible. When we analyze this statement, however, we find that "labor" is a mass of units with individual interests, standards of living and even different attitudes toward the whole of which they are a part. In discussing the relation of capital and labor the sociologist speaks of the two as if they were separate organisms or different species with aims diametrically opposed to each other: capital's aim to prey upon labor and labor's aim to emancipate itself from the domination of capital. The status of labor and capital may be fixed, but the status of the laborer and capitalist fluctuates; within the space of one's own life-time the individual can belong to both camps. It is this mass of conflicting interests, standards of living and general culture that makes it impossible for "labor" ever to stand together in the sense that we generally use that term.

Twenty years ago the writer knew men who believed in the solidarity of labor in the personal sense; that is, they believed the day of awakening was at hand and "labor" was about to rise, overthrow the capitalist and take possession of the land and means of life. These individuals had various theories of social reconstruction, ranging from State Socialism to Individualist Anarchism, but all believed in according to the laborer the full fruits of his or her toil. Who does not remember those ardent believers in the coming of "The Day" when the social revolution would break out and "labor" come into its own? Some remember our calm, logical Individualist Anarchists who became so enthusiastic over the Bryan movement of 1896, as to vote for "16 to 1." Not that they believed the latter would bring any particular benefit, but they thought the campaign would have a tremendous educational value and "the next big battle would be over Mutual Banking or Free Money."

Twenty-five years have passed, the social revolution has not come and "Mutual Banking" is as dead as the roses of last summer, at least so far as it enters into the calculation of reformers, revolutionists or "labor." Men and women once active in the reform and revolutionary movements believe as ardently now as then that "labor" could, if it stood shoulder to shoulder, establish any form of social relationship it desired. Nevertheless they have dropped out of the movement and now attend to their own private affairs. This does not mean recantation or a repudiation of former ideals. It does, in some cases of course; but not in all. In fact, it is fairly safe to say that an uprising that had even a remote chance of success would bring to its support many thousands of those now living in retirement. We can call them cowards some other time, but just now let us devote ourselves to discussing them as social factors. Without losing faith in the ideal of a free humanity or the potentiality of "labor," they have come to realize that exploitation in some form or other has existed for a great many centuries and in all probability would not be abolished in their time.

Participation in the revolutionary movement does not, as a rule, increase individual incomes. But the holding of higher ideals often brings with it a desire for better food, clothes and houses and artistic desires which mean increased expenditure; and this makes the struggle to live harder than ever. It is this struggle between the ideal of a free humanity and the desire to live and enjoy life *now* that saps the vitality and soothes the emotions until they slacken, and in many cases causes them to die away entirely.

To urge men and women to enter the ranks of the revolutionists and emancipate themselves, by telling them "labor" can establish any form of social relation they wish if laborers only practice solidarity, is to convey the idea that if the individual addressed acts in a given manner the rest of "labor" would act likewise. It is on a par with the Socialists telling men to "vote for socialism and vote for a job." Men may, and have, voted for socialism for twenty or thirty years—so I am told—without getting a job as a result of that practice, and men and women can and do work for the social revolution all their lives and remain economic slaves to the end. "Labor" has as many conceptions of freedom as man has fancies, and to speak of what it can do if it acted as one man is to overlook the fact that it represents every reactionary idea and superstition extant as well as every ideal and noble impulse. Political Socialists and Social Revolutionists are fond of saying "the working class must emancipate itself," and nine times out of ten they select members of the bourgeois class, or educated proletarians inoculated with bourgeois conceptions and instincts, to represent them inside and outside of parliament or legislature. This may be good as a battle cry, but very few people seriously believe the working class will emancipate itself by itself. "Labor" as labor will probably never act as one man on any subject; its impulses and actions are and will be determined by small groups of idealists *inside* and *outside* the labor movement—this notwithstanding that the soldiers of the revolution, i. e., the units that compose the army, will consist of individuals acting from different impulses, inspired by different motives. Some will be inspired by the ideal of a free humanity, others by the desire to improve their own standard of comfort and to get some of the good things of life now denied them. The idealist is necessary because he has social consciousness and uplifts the revolution; his faith in man is a powerful factor toward progress. The realist soldier who struggles to obtain his own, furnishes the necessary bitterness to tear down outworn systems, destroy idols and root out superstitions. To urge men to work for the emancipation of "labor" is to ask them to work for an ideal, and while working for an ideal furnishes emotional satisfaction; more than that is necessary for people to live. To urge them to work solely for their material benefit is to rob them of the ideal without which man can not exist. Without labor life is impossible; thus Life is Labor. But without Vision life is equally impossible; therefore, to me, "Life is Labor and Labor is Vision."

"THIS war was brought on by rulers, not by peoples, and I thank God that there is no man in America who has the authority to bring war on without the consent of the people." —PRESIDENT WILSON

If, as Wilson says, this wholesale murder called war was brought on by rulers, rulers ought to be abolished.

No people ever gave their express consent to a war.

Here in the United States, as elsewhere, the people are systematically miseducated by prostitute editors, and smug statesmen controlled by high finance are the real rulers of the nation. Here, too, our rulers are preparing to lead us like sheep to slaughter.

If Romans had not been sheep, Caesar would not have been a wolf.

The Real Labor Problem

THIS is a conservative article inspired by an eminently conservative and deadly respectable journal, the *British Review*. The *B. R.* is shy on editors, two of them holding commissions in His Majesty's Army. (Being of the "upper clawsses" entitles a man to a commission, though he couldn't fight a sick butterfly.)

So the *British Review* advertises for an editor of the following attainments:

1. Intelligent sympathy with the traditions of Christian Civilization in Europe. (Christian Civilization is doing fine in Europe just now.)

2. Good knowledge of continental movements and affairs, a qualification rare in itself and rarer still in an Englishman of a conservative temperament. (Knowledge of Great Britain seems unnecessary.)

3. High standard of English scholarship coupled with that degree of familiarity with Latin and Greek classics which distinguishes the educated from the uneducated. (Latin makes a gentleman.)

We mention this because the *British Review* has an article entitled "The Real Labor Problem," which shows that a man with a little knowledge of home affairs, particularly as regards Labor, might not be out of place on its editorial staff.

Since the attitude of Labor in Great Britain on several occasions has threatened to upset the traditions the bourgeoisie loves so much, even high-brow papers like the *B. R.* condescend to discuss such vulgar topics as Labor. The writer in the *British Review*, E. T. Good, who confesses to having labored in days of yore, says that the "real labor problem is to make the average workman reasonably contented with his lot."

It sounds like a dairy advertisement of "milk from contented cows." It is the capitalist's viewpoint to a dot. Discontent interferes with production and, therefore, with profit. Seventy million individual working days were lost in England through strikes during the five years preceding the war. Seventy million days the cows did not produce.

The *British Review* divides laboring men into three classes: the low and inefficient type which needs stern discipline and compulsion; the intellectuals who because of "their large ideas and ready tongue are unsuitable for the workshops and no good for religion" and therefore should be suppressed by the government; and the ordinary man who "if well treated and not misled would cause no trouble." How to keep that ordinary animal from jumping the fence and breaking into the clover-patch—that's the problem.

Great Britain began speeding up in the nineties to meet the competition from the more submissive industrial slaves of the United States and Germany. Furnaces grew bigger and hotter; machines ran faster; material was made harder; appliances needed more strength and nerve for manipulation. Rest times were knocked off. Supervision was stricter. Still, with work intensified, food prices rose more rapidly than wages.

Labor politicians got into office on extravagant promises and could not make good. Whatever legislation was enacted did not pan out as expected. The Workmen's Compensation Act, providing the same insurance for the old and weak as for the young and strong, resulted in the old men being turned adrift and the younger ones speeded up. With the rush came more accidents. Accidents in shops doubled. The Minimum Wage Act resulted in a slave-driving supervision that went beyond human endurance.

No wonder labor grew turbulent, and the agitator went on agitating. Those that could not be destroyed frequently had the sting taken out of them by being elected to Parliament. Some of them became cabinet ministers dancing attendance upon the King, in black silk-knee breeches. Rubbing shoulders with "their betters," they became tarred with the same stick of conservatism. But in spite of their leaders, 200,000 miners struck in Wales, from where the navy gets its coal. Strikes in munition factories took place in spite of every effort of elected persons to keep the workers "contented."

Therefore the *British Review* reaches the conclusion that the first duty of statesmanship should be to enlist the power and influence of the British Unions. (We recommend the conclusion to the Los Angeles *Times*. Otis will throw a fit.) But Labor will not be placated even that way. The great fact that stares the British workmen in the face is that a few thousand men have an income of 1200 million pounds a year, while the sum total of wages doled out to the millions of workers amounts only to 600 million pounds.

The social economist of the *British Review* explains this condition by saying that "the foundation of great fortunes was gotten from the losses of unsuccessful capitalists and not from labor." How the unsuccessful capitalist had anything to lose that was not produced by labor, still remains a profound mystery to the *British Review*.

Until the workers in Great Britain and elsewhere abolish such conditions, the real labor problem is to make the toilers discontented with their lot.

Trapping Labor

IN THE EAST, the National Security League. In the West, the Pacific Coast Defense League. Back of both the munition manufacturers.

Between them they will squeeze the country for profits.

But without organized Labor they can't carry out their scheme. (If Labor only took the hint!) Therefore they are appealing to the trade unions to help.

The Pacific Coast Defense now comes to the rescue of organized Labor on this Coast. In its cabinet are high politicians, Governors, priests and sundry others,—all honorable gentlemen. There is power behind the scenes, for in a few short months they have succeeded in having all the Governors of the Western States, except Colorado, agree to make laws to prohibit the militia from shooting strikers during industrial struggles.

They want organized Labor to give the National Guard a clean bill of health, join them and be good patriots. In return they will get—a LAW.

Andrew J. Gallagher, a supervisor and prominent labor man in San Francisco, is also a "cabinet officer." He introduced the Pacific Coast Defense League to the regular meeting of the San Francisco Labor Council and spoke in favor of Labor co-operating to get this good law.

Paul Scharrenberg, a sailor, Secretary of the State Federation of Labor, said that he never had the nerve to introduce a proposition before a labor council that was so vague and indefinite.

Gallagher read letters from the President of the Pacific Coast Defense League—a Mr. Hanlon—whom nobody seems to know hereabouts; also from a number of Governors—all making generous promises. It was clear that all of a sudden, over night, as it were, the higherups feel awful about the way the militia has treated the poor working man in the past. Now once again the "Golden Rule" is here, they say, and they are sure the lion will lie down with the lamb.

Sad to relate, there seemed to be quite a number of delegates that fell for the plutes' war bunk. A few waxed warm and patriotic over the necessity for preparing to die for the bosses' land and country.

Of course, the *proposed* law already provides certain "exceptions" in which the militia may be used, as heretofore. Namely, in "race riots," against "sympathetic mobs," etc. Does any sensible worker doubt that when a real strike is on, when the strikers are burning down some obstruction or driving away rats and detectives, the government will not step in to "protect property" and use the loopholes of the proposed law to shoot down the workers and break the strike?

John O. Walsh, a molder, expressed in the Labor Council a sentiment that is growing among the workers. "If Labor must be prepared," he said, "let us form our own independent companies to defend ourselves against outsiders as well as against the militia."

A splendid suggestion. Let Labor take possession of the arms and ammunition they have produced. Let them form their own companies for their own protection. Then reconnoiter the vulnerable points of industry and transportation. Take charge of the mines and factories, and carry on production and distribution for the welfare of all instead of for the profit of the land barons and munition trusts.

Then, and not till then, will Labor deserve and command respect. That is the mission and dignity of Labor.

▨   ▨   ▨

THE BLAST is the friend of labor, the friend of organized labor. But a satisfied silence is the bar to all progress, and THE BLAST intends, as a friend of labor, always to say exactly what it thinks, and it thinks there is not enough solidarity among labor.

A Troubled Moralist

ELLA WHEELER WILCOX, one of the guardians and purveyors of Hearst-made morality, has unburdened her god-fearing soul in "poetry" and prose over one of those dainty news morsels whereby William the Panderer caters to the degenerate taste of sensationalism. The case of Mrs. Mohr (accused of having hired two negroes to kill her husband, a physician who had made nearly a million as an abortionist for the society ladies of Newport and Providence) inspired Ella to bestride her Pegasus and ride over considerable territory, such as the earth, the universe, a couple of astral planes and other places inhabited by God and the Revealing Angels, whoever they are.

On a classy excursion of this kind Ella naturally picks up a little astronomy. She informs us that "Our earth is making a circuitous journey toward a higher cycle, and just now it is passing through a zone of hate."

How delightfully simple! Here we have been getting grey-haired trying to place the blame for the row over in Europe. Statesmen have been publishing Blue Books, Green Books, and Books of every color of the rainbow, to assure us that their particular governments were as innocent as driven snow and that the guilt is on the other side. Now comes Ella and clears it all up. Kaisers, Czars, Kings and Capitalists, you are all absolved: the earth is in a hate-zone, a kind of fog-belt, as the lady-astronomer explains it.

Who steered the earth into this fog-belt, anyhow? Ella says "God is the captain of the ship." What's the use of blaming the crew, then?

Listen to further wisdom: "Unconsciously to themselves, no doubt, the hate-vibrations in the air had their effect upon the minds of all those involved in the Mohr tragedy." We most respectfully submit that such being the case, the two poor and friendless negroes should go free as well as the wealthy white lady. If their act was due to hate-vibrations in the air unconsciously received, it is absurd to punish them. Might as well hang a man for catching cold. "The murderous work," says the Hearstian soothsayer, "of Dr. Mohr put him in perfect accord with the hate-vibrations from the war-zone."

Our feeble intellect halts right here.

When a doctor has made nearly a million helping society ladies to maintain their shape, and has extended these operations for nearly a generation, these hate-vibrations from the war-zone seem somewhat belated, not to say entirely out-of-date.

The war is responsible for a lot of damphool things, but hardly for abortions in Newport.

Ella assures us in "poetry":

"All other sins may be condoned, forgiven,
"All other sinners may be cleaned and shriven;
"Not these, not these."

Now, that is really interesting. Such being the case, we suggest that Mrs. Wilcox stop this pernicious custom by acquainting her readers with Margaret Sanger.

"An ounce of prevention * * *"

Virtue Under Wagedom

J. K. Apelleby.

EVEN a Roman Lucretia would hardly be able to preserve her virtue in the conditions which compel so many American girls to shiver as they toil. Job would utterly lose his patience if he were compelled to enter the labor market and compete with the labor thieves in jail. The angel Gabriel would lose his angelhood in a month if he were compelled to live in an unventilated, fever-haunted tenement house, and had to keep himself, Mrs. Gabriel and half a dozen little Gabriels on 75 cents a day.

Overseas

Eastbourne, England,
February 5th, 1916.

THE event of the hour in the labor movement here in England is undoubtedly the Bristol Conference which has taken place during the last week of January. The most important feature of that conference is, beyond question, the twin resolutions which were proposed and adopted at one of its sittings.

The main business of the Conference was to discuss the Compulsion Bill. It did discuss it. And after a number of speeches delivered simultaneously from chairs, tables and platform, a resolution against the Bill was submitted to the delegates, and was carried by a majority of eight to one. Another resolution, asking the conference not to agitate for its repeal in case it becomes a law, was similarly carried although not by an equally large majority.

You think it queer, I suppose, and will probably wonder whether deciding not to agitate against a certain measure is really the best way of giving effect to your opposition to it. Perhaps not, from your point of view. But you Americans are living under happy, normal conditions. You are being oppressed and exploited as usual; your best friends and leaders, your Joe Hills and Schmidts and Caplans are torn away from you as usual; are persecuted, shot and imprisoned in quite the usual way, just as in the good old days of '87—everything proceeds with you as usual. But here conditions are different, certainly not *quite* normal. And under abnormal conditions all sorts of things will and are expected to happen.

* * *

Besides, it is important to remember that this is essentially a war against militarism. But you cannot combat any evil without knowing the nature of that evil. So, in order that the people should thoroughly understand (and feel) what the cursed system they are sent abroad to destroy really is, those that have the interests of the country close at heart have decided that they could not do better than to have the same system firmly established at home.

This explains the meaning of the second note at the Bristol Conference. For so simple and logical is this expedient that even those that are against compulsion in principle have decided to do nothing that may hinder its being put into practice.

The government, needless to say, promptly availed themselves of the hint, and the Bill became an Act.

* * *

Of course, there are many who refuse to see the wisdom of such proceedings. The I. L. P., for instance, is carrying on a vigorous agitation against the Act, and indeed against any form of compulsion whatever. There is also dissatisfaction and unrest among the organized workers, particularly in South Wales and on the Clyde. These simple people, who apparently cannot appreciate the good that is being done for them, have even threatened with strikes and strongly worded resolutions. Such unheard of ingratitude! Something will have to be done to silence them. And the best means whereby to obtain the necessary silence would certainly seem to be to make the military service Act applicable to industry. In other words, to introduce industrial conscription.

At any rate, that is the opinion of a very great and devoted friend of the people—Lloyd George. As one who has always entertained a true love for the workers, and is anxiously concerned about their happiness and well being, he is very much afraid that as long as there will remain to them a vestige of trade union rights and privileges, there will be strikes and threats of strikes, and the process of the dilution of labor by which he proposes to bring about "a future which has been the dream of many a great leader" will continually be hampered. Therefore by placing the worker on an equal footing and under the same obligations with the soldier, all these difficulties will be smothered out, and liberty and civilization forever secured.

It is doubtful, however, if the workers—ungrateful creatures that they are!—will ever appreciate such unselfish action on their behalf.   —S. D.

* * *

Carlton, Victoria, Australia,
January 24th, 1916.

Dear Comrade Berkman:—

I am sending a letter as I have not the time for an article by this mail. Propaganda here is very difficult owing to the War Precautions Act. The country is blood-mad. The frenzy of war is upon the people. The military is supreme and brutal to the last degree. The other day soldiers tarred and feathered a man who moved a resolution asking union men to ignore the recruiting card issued by the Labor Government. Recently I addressed an out-of-door meeting. There were present about ten thousand people. You can see by the enclosed newspaper clippings how brutally the soldiers attacked me, smashed the platform, burned the red flag and injured my back. Still I continued to speak until a sergeant of the army began to address the crowd, drowning my voice and compelling me to stop. I have been arrested, but the charges have been withdrawn by the police. I was speaking about recruiting. * * * As this letter may be opened and read. I cannot explain the facts without being arrested again.

Miss Adela Pankhurst was to speak at a meeting at the Bijou Theatre, but the soldiers rushed the platform and prevented the meeting being held.

The Labor Prime Minister advocates that force should be used against everybody who opposes militarism. A reign of terror exists at present. * * *

—J. W. Fleming

An Event in San Francisco

VOL. 1   SAN FRANCISCO, MARCH 15, 1916   No. 9

THE MASK OF PATRIOTISM

Villa or Wilson—Which Is the Bandit?

VILLA

PANCHO VILLA is the descendant of a long line of peons whose lives were spent in hard toil, cultivating the soil of Mexico and helping to produce foodstuffs for their fellow countrymen and profits for their exploiters.

Villa followed the same calling. His childhood was dark and dreary. The son of a peon, he passed his early youth in hard farm work, helping to support his family. The hand of greed lay heavy upon the people of Mexico. The hardest toil barely sufficed to keep the Villa family alive.

As a young man, Pancho saw an opportunity to improve his condition by securing work in a neighboring town. He took his widowed mother and younger children with him, he the chief support of the family. It was a garrison town, and one day Pancho learned that his oldest sister, a beautiful girl of 15, was seduced by an army officer. Pancho set out to find the man. He demanded that he make amends. The officer scorned the low peon, and young Villa shot and killed him.

The authorities ordered the arrest of Villa. Pancho knew that he, a despised peon, could expect no justice at the hands of the masters. He fled to the mountains. The government set a price on his head and declared him an outlaw.

But the townspeople knew Villa and the story of his wrongs. They admired him for challenging the right of an officer to violate the daughter of a peon. They aided Pancho and by their help he was able to avoid arrest. He gathered around him a circle of other peons embittered by the injustice and oppression they suffered. From time to time they made excursions to neighboring estates, expropriating rich land sharks and sharing the spoils of victory with the needy peons. He was an outlaw, but the people loved him and blessed his name.

When the Revolution broke out, Villa joined forces with the peons fighting for a chance to live, for a little land and liberty. He has kept up the fight against tremendous odds. Nor has Wall Street been able to corrupt him and buy him off, as they did with Carranza.

WILSON

Unlike Villa and his hard-working progenitors, Wilson comes from a long line of exploiters. His forefathers did neither spin nor sow. Yet, they always enjoyed the good things of life, parasites on the back of labor. Wilson himself, unlike Villa, has never tilled the ground nor worked in mine or factory. He has not helped in any productive or otherwise useful work. On the contrary, as teacher and college professor, he used every effort to poison the young minds with the dogmas and dominant views that support present institutions and make more secure the bondage of the people. As President, he has proved himself a menace to the welfare and peace of the country, a weather cock constantly swayed by the breezes from Wall Street. A puppet of the money magnates, his attitude on important issues has been dictated by Big Business. Preaching peace and sanity a few months ago, he has suddenly veered into the camp of mad militarism. The compelling hand of the munition and steel trust is dictating his policies. And now he cries loudest for the biggest navy of the world. The priests of Mammon got him, body and soul.

At this very moment Wilson is preparing to invade Mexico—poor, bleeding Mexico, for years torn by inner strife and weakened by the long struggle. He has ordered a "punitive expedition" against Villa. It is no secret that back of this outcry for the punishment of Villa are the American political and commercial pirates eager for the invasion of Mexico in the holy name of greater profits.

Villa killed a Mexican officer to avenge the ruin of his sister. Wilson is preparing to kill thousands of Mexicans on the pretext of avenging the death of some Americans. Which is the greater bandit—Villa or Wilson?

There is only this difference between them: Villa had the courage to do his own vengeance, taking the risks and profiting nothing himself.

Wilson sits safely in the White House and orders others to do the dirty work.

Labor Preparedness

PREPAREDNESS is surely a worthy aim. But you can't prepare unless you know what you are preparing for, or against what. To serve its purpose and to be effective, preparedness must have some definite object.

What, then, are the workers to prepare for? Military preparedness is either for the defense of your own country, or for attack upon another country, or for both purposes. What do we want to attack? Have the workers of America an interest in attacking some foreign country? No sane man will claim that they have. We can therefore dismiss this phase of the subject.

There remains preparedness for defense. It is important to know clearly just *what* the workers of this country are expected to defend. Supposedly they are to defend "the country". But what is "the country"? It consists of vast acres of land, rich natural deposits in gold mines, coal, silver and copper mines; great wealth representing accumulated products of toil, big industries, railroads, real estate values, etc. All this the workers are asked to defend. But do they own the broad acres, the gold, coal and silver mines, the railroads, the great industrial establishments, the mills and factories, or the other accumulated wealth of the Nation? They do not. What, then, is Labor to defend?

For years the workers have been involved in a struggle with the masters of the country—the possessors of all this wealth—to wrench from their grasp a greater share for the producers. Are the toilers suddenly to abandon their long struggle and rush to the rescue of their despoilers when their profits in some foreign market are threatened?

It is an encouraging sign of intelligence that the workers are awakening to the hard facts of the situation. The patriots for revenue—known in the East as the National Security League, and in the West as the Pacific Coast Defense League—have failed to enthuse the unions for the defense of the masters' wealth and country. Thus, the Butchers' Union of San Francisco, as well as the Riggers and Stevedores and other labor bodies, have declined to play the fly on the Bosses' hook. They have condemned the attempt to enlist union men in the militia. Some Labor organizations in the East and in the Middle West have even gone further. They are considering a plan of *Labor preparedness:* to prepare the workers against their real and only enemy: the capitalist vampire that lives on their blood and marrow; to prepare to defend Labor against the constantly growing rapacity and greed of the employer; to prepare to free Labor entirely from the bond of wage slavery.

That is the Preparedness this country needs, that Labor needs. The first step toward it is a country-wide organization of the Labor sentiment against militarism that is to increase the legal violence at the command of the bosses. We urge labor unions to take this step at once: to send anti-militarist speakers to every union in the country and to flood the land with anti-militarist leaflets.

That's to begin with. The next step is for Labor to take charge of the industries, abolish manufacture for profit, and establish an industrial democracy based on the full enjoyment of life for every person in return for useful effort.

This is the Preparedness that Labor needs. Preparedness to become truly human, self-respecting and independent men and women, who know their worth, the purpose of life, and the power of Labor united in solidarity.

This is the right kind of Labor Preparedness. This and nothing else.

The Rabbits and the Goats
Charles Erskine Scott Wood
II.

THE white rabbits and the grey rabbits increased so rapidly that presently there were many more rabbits than were needed to cut the clover, and in the struggle to get jobs the rabbits consented to take less and less clover for their work. Then the different unions passed laws that only so many rabbits would be allowed to learn the trade of their fathers, and all others must either find another trade and another union or join the "Scabs." But this did not help any. It increased the scabs and made trouble all along the line. And the rabbits continued to increase and the clover wages to decrease in nourishing power. Finally it was unbearable—rabbits, rabbits everywhere and no jobs. Then a very fat and meditative white rabbit called a meeting of all the rabbits, grey and white, and addressed them:

"Fellow rabbits, ladies and gentlemen: The trouble is there are too many rabbits for the job of cutting our masters' clover. We have agreed that to dispute our masters' right is visionary and unprofitable; therefore, the only other course is to reduce the number of rabbits. We can do this either by killing the young as they are born—"

At this loud squeals of horror went up from the mother rabbits. "Nevertheless, this is a practice," continued the orator, "which is sanctioned in some communities. But I suggest that a better plan is to take steps by some harmless method to prevent conception by the—"

"What steps?" interrupted a very thin, worn rabbit, the mother already of thirty-eight children.

"That I cannot say," replied the orator. "I am only announcing a theory."

"But," retorted the sad thin mother, "it is a condition, not a theory, that confronts us."

"I know," said the orator, "it is a very serious condition, but I am not a medical man. Now, there is the Welsh Rabbit, who is a doctor and conjurer. Let us hear from him."

The Welsh Rabbit coughed and began: "Multiplication is—"

"We don't want anything about arithmetic," interrupted the sad mother. "We—"

"I was not talking arithmetic," said the Welsh Rabbit. "I was talking Birth Control, and I was about to say when interrupted that multiplication is a mere blind instinct of nature. The clover has thousands of seeds. The rabbit numerous young. Each would be better if fewer. And we have as much right to regulate one as the other. The rabbit intellect was given to control Nature, not to be a slave to Nature's blindness."

"But how? How?" cried the mother almost weeping.

"Yes, how? How?" said many voices.

"I will tell you," replied Dr. Welsh Rabbit.

But at this moment a huge crow flew down and said: "The Man on the Hill has heard you and he says your talk is wicked. You must not in any way try to control Nature. And as rabbits breed like rabbits, you must let them forever breed like rabbits."

And a great many said loudly, "Yes, we must listen to the crow. He knows the will of the Man on the Hill. The crow is his messenger."

Just then the foxes rushed in and scattered the crowd and ate the Welsh Rabbit and the orator, because they were blasphemous and obscene and were trying to limit the labor market. The rest of the crowd said: "We have been very wicked to refuse to increase and multiply as the Man on the Hill has ordered. And we have been very obscene to try to lessen the labor supply for our lords, the goats. Let us go out on the squat for more clover and shorter hours. All else is vision and useless."

"Who shall go out on squat?" asked a one-eyed old white rabbit. Then it was voted that the one-eyed rabbits should squat. And they did so, and all the others went back to work and cut the clover for the goats, while the one-eyed squatted and starved and the scabs rushed in and the goats, the foxes and the crows loafed in the shade and laughed.

The foxes whispered to the crows: "Your idea about the Man on the Hill was a good stunt. Very clever!" and they all laughed some more. But the dear, soft, gentle rabbits met under the moonlight and Resolved, that the rabbits did not receive their full share of the product of their toil. Then all went home to bed so as to be up early for their work in the morning.

The Labor Market
T. H. Potter

THE monopolist said: "If we can only cut the workingman off from the land, we can then employ him at our own price.

And they did so.

Then they said: "If we can get his young son to work for us, the increased amount of labor on the market will enable us to get the two for about the price of one."

And they did so.

Then they said: "Now for his little girl; all three will only earn what the father did at one time."

And they did so.

And then they said: "Now reach for the mother." "But she has to take care of the baby." "Oh, we will pay one woman to take charge of twenty babies and scoop the nineteen."

And they did so.

Then they said:: "We won't pay that one woman. Appeal to the public—'tis so charitable."

And they are doing so.

Then the foxy one lay awake nights to think of something the babies could work at, that he might coin a few pennies off the kids.

Make the Nursery self-supporting. You know it would be "so independent."

And they will do it.

A Rare Nugget

THE welfare of the aggregate, considered apart from that of the units, is not an end to be sought. Society exists for the benefit of its members; not its members for the benefit of society. It has ever to be remembered that, great as may be the efforts made for the prosperity of the body politic, yet the claims of the body politic are nothing in themselves and become something only in so far as they embody the claims of its competent individuals.

—HERBERT SPENCER

DO not waste your time on Social Questions. What is the matter with the poor is Poverty; what is the matter with the rich is Uselessness.

Brave Voices From Prison

A MASSMEETING was held in San Francisco March 8th, in behalf of Ricardo and Enrique Flores Magon, now in the Los Angeles Jail. Our imprisoned comrades sent the following letter, to be read at the meeting. Unfortunately, it did not arrive in time. We urge our friends everywhere to take immediate action in this case.

Greetings, Comrades!

We have just learned of the massmeeting to take place in San Francisco to protest against the persecution to which the government is subjecting *Regeneracion* and ourselves, its writers.

We wish with all our hearts that we could be present with you at that meeting, but since it is impossible for us to be there in person, our thoughts will be with you instead. We heartily appreciate the solidarity of our brothers in San Francisco, to whom we send our fraternal sympathy and greetings.

Since February 18th we have been imprisoned and subjected to most brutal treatment. When we were arrested such violence was used by the minions that for awhile it looked as if they were intent upon assassinating us. Enrique was the victim of such a ferocious assault by one of the sleuths that he is still suffering from his wounds.

By the United States Marshal's orders, or rather by orders of the bandits of Wall Street, we are being kept in the strictest incommunicado. We are not allowed to see our friends, and even the members of our own families are barred from visiting us.

Our bonds have been set at $5000.00 each. As we are poor, this high bail is designed to keep us in jail until our case goes to trial. And meanwhile we are subject to the despotism of the Marshal, who inflicts punishment even before any judge imposes sentence.

Our crime? Our refusal to accept the authority of any Gods in heaven or on earth. "Neither God nor Master!" is our motto.

That is the doctrine we are teaching the Mexicans through *Regeneracion*. What the tyrants cannot forgive us is that we have advised our people—the Mexicans—to put this doctrine into practice, so as to build up a new social life in keeping with Justice and Freedom; a new system that will make it impossible for any man to profit by the sweat and misery of his fellowmen and that will not permit any one to climb on the backs of others by authority and obedience.

This is our crime. The government is trying to prevent us from continuing to commit this crime by locking up our voices in the dungeon. The proceedings of the Russian autocracy transplanted to free America! This is the boasted Democracy under whose cloak beats the heart of Torquemada. The Inquisition is not dead; we are living now in the Middle Age!

But let us not give ourselves up to sorrow. Courage, good comrades! The enemy stands unmasked. The government is proving by its own actions that Authority is not the alleged Guardian Angel of the weak to protect them against the aggressions of the strong. It proves itself to be the brutal hand that keeps us prostrate at the feet of our exploiters, so as to enable them with more ease and safety to press our brains and our blood into more profits.

Let us rejoice at this self-exposure of government. Tyranny holds its own undoing. The scorpion kills itself with its own poison.

From the depth of our dungeon we send our fraternal greetings to our brothers and comrades everywhere, upon whom we call to join in our cry, "Long live freedom of thought! More energy in the struggle for Land and Liberty!"

RICARDO FLORES MAGON,
ENRIQUE FLORES MAGON.

County Jail, Los Angeles, Cal., March 7th, 1916.

THE BLAST

Revolutionary Labor Paper
Published every 1st and 15th of the month
569 Dolores St., San Francisco, Cal.
Mall Address, Box 661   Phone, Park 499

Alexander Berkman, Editor and Publisher
E. B. Morton, Associate Editor   M. E. Fitzgerald, Manager

SUBSCRIPTION
$1.00 Yearly   60c Six Months   5c Copy
Bundle rates 2½c per copy in bundles of ten.
Advertising rates on application.
Entered as second-class matter at the postoffice at San Francisco,
Cal., January 14, 1916, under the Act of March 3, 1879.

Comments

Murder for Profit

THE Columbus (N. M.) incident, in which Villa men are supposed to have killed some Americans, is to be used as an excuse to invade Mexico. But suppose that some Canadian bandits had attacked a border camp and killed some Americans. Would Washington think of invading Canada?

Don't imagine for a moment that Wilson has ordered a military expedition into Mexico because he is so terribly outraged over the killing of Americans. Americans—American workers—are murdered every day in this country, and Wilson remains quite calm about it. Where was Wilson's indignation when unarmed strikers were shot down in East Youngstown? Did Washington send a military expedition to punish the murderers of the women and children in the tents of Ludlow, in Roosevelt, N. J., in McKees Rocks, in the Michigan Copper district? Did the Federal authorities or any State government *ever* send a punitive expedition to avenge the wholesale slaughter of workingmen, their wives and children in our own country?

Verily, Government, thy name is hypocrite and murderer. Wilson, as President, is forced to be the whore for American speculators with large interests in Mexico. For years they have been clamoring for the suppression of the Mexican revolution because it is interfering with the business of squeezing profits from the blood of the peon. Now they are jubilant. American bullets will soon restore "order" in Mexico, drive the peons back to work and secure the speculators in the undisputed possession of the land and natural resources they have stolen from the Mexican people. Let us hope they are reckoning without the host.

The Mask of Patriotism

INCIDENTALLY the "punishing of Villa" is to serve as an additional "argument" for a greater army The jingo press is doing its best to inflame the mob with the spirit of revenge against Mexico, on the one hand, and the menace of a "foreign invasion" on the other. And the good citizen readily falls for these hypocritical vaporings. Made stupid by his educators, he fails to see the mask of "patriotism" and "national defense" hiding the smirk of the fat land grabber, the munition and steel trust, the monopolist and manufacturer.

Systematically the public heart and mind are thus corrupted by the prostitute press, by our college professors, preachers and school teachers. The very youth of the country is being poisoned with the virus of national hatreds and racial antagonisms, and moulded into murderous tools in the name of a meaningless rag and a country owned by Rockefeller, Morgan & Co.

Menace to Labor

IN THIS insane preparation to turn the Republic into an armed camp, where are the forces to stem the tide of militarism? What are the radicals doing? And what is labor doing? For, after all, it is the workers that will ultimately be the chief victims of these imperialistic tendencies. Victims in a double sense. First, because labor will have to foot the bills for the enlarged militarism and navyism: labor which is the source of all wealth. And secondly, the military Frankenstein now being called into life will serve to crush rebellious workers whenever they demand better conditions and a greater share of their product.

It is therefore sickening to witness the apathy and indifference of the toilers to the preparedness that is ultimately designed to crush every aspiration of labor. Here and there a more intelligent union is awakening to the real meaning and purpose of a stronger army and navy. But the great bulk of organized labor is busy with stupid jurisdictional fights among themselves or wasting valuable time and energy in chasing ephemeral "labor laws" and growing enthusiastic over "reforms" of evils that are inherent in the very system of wage slavery. And all the while the bonds of subjection are being drawn tighter around the toilers.

Honest Idiocy

ANDREW FURUSETH, president of the International Seamen's Union, is no doubt an honest and sincere man. He is also supposed to be an able man. He is the author of the La Follette Seamen's Act. What wonderful things were promised the poor seamen if Congress could only be induced to make it a law. It would incalculably raise the standard of the seaman as man and worker; it would emancipate him from the autocracy of the ship masters; it would make him an independent and self respecting human being, a free man.

Well, Furuseth spent the better part of his life in convincing Congress that it would be a good thing to have this law. Incidentally also, thousands of dollars were spent from the funds of the union. At last the La Follette Seamen's Act became a law. And now comes Furuseth and complains that the law doesn't do the seamen any good at all. Why so, Andrew? Well, "this law is not being enforced," he says, "because the shipping interests have too much influence in Washington, and it is impossible to enforce the law."

It took our able Furuseth about twenty years to put

this law on the statute books and now he admits that it is impossible to enforce it. You poor simpleton! Did you really expect the ship magnates to enforce laws against their own interests? Have you lived fifty odd years and not found out that it is only the working boob who believes in enforcing laws against his own interests? Capitalists don't do that. Nor does the government, which is always the loyal servant of the capitalist.

It is men like Furuseth—honest and sincere idiots—who are the worst enemies of labor. They mislead the workers into believing that there is hope of bettering their condition by appealing to the lawmakers, instead of relying upon the invincible strength of their own economic power, backed by solidarity.

Wendell Phillips on Sabotage

TO ME, the Labor Movement means just this: It is the last noble protest of the American people against the power of incorporate wealth, seeking to do over again what the Whig Aristocracy of Great Britain has successfully done for 200 years. * * * We could discuss as well as you if you would only give us bread and houses, fair play and leisure, and opportunities to travel. We would sit and discuss the question for the next fifty years. It's a very easy thing to discuss for a gentleman in his study, with no anxiety about tomorrow. Why, the ladies and gentlemen of the reign of Louis XV and Louis XVI, in France, seated in gilded saloons and on Persian carpets, surrounded with luxury and the curious manufacture of ingenious Lyons and Rheims, discussed fine ideas and balanced them in dainty phrases, and expressed them in such quaint generalities that Thomas Jefferson borrowed the Declaration of Independence from their hands.

There they sat balancing and discussing sweetly, making out new theories and daily creating a splendid architecture of debates, till the angry crowd broke open the doors and ended the discussion in blood. They waited too long; they discussed about half a century too long. You see, discussion is very good when a man has bread to eat, and his children all portioned off and his daughters married and his house furnished and paid for, and his will made; but discussion is very bad when "Ye hear the children weeping, O my brothers, ere the sorrows come with years."

Discussion is bad when a class bends under actual oppression. *We want immediate action.* I know labor is narrow; I know she is aggressive; I know she arms herself with the best weapons that a corrupt civilization furnishes—all true. Where do we get these ideas? Borrowed them from capital, every one of them; and when you advance to the level of peace unarmed, we will meet you on the same. While you combine and plot and defend, so will we. * * * Labor comes up and says, "They have shotted their cannon to the lips; they have adopted every new method; they have invented every dangerous machine—and it is all planted like a great park of artillery against us. They have incorporate wealth; they have hidden behind banks; they have concealed themselves in currency; they have sheltered themselves in taxation; they have passed rules to govern us—and we will improve upon the lesson they have taught us. When they disarm, we will —not before. We will crumble up wealth by making it unprofitable to be rich.

PRISON MEMOIRS OF AN ANARCHIST
By Alexander Berkman

"One will search far before finding a more powerful picture of what deeds are perpetrated in the name of justice."
—San Francisco "Bulletin."

512 pages, illustrated. $1.15 postpaid.

To Our Friends

THE BLAST did not appear last week. Reason: lack of funds. It is not pleasant to repeat our call for aid. But if you think we need a revolutionary labor paper like THE BLAST, help to keep it alive. Every issue of THE BLAST costs $75.00. Our own resources are exhausted. We urge our friends to take action. Help us to get subscribers and readers. Talk the matter over with other comrades in your city and arrange a benefit for THE BLAST. Secure contributions to the Sustaining Fund. The need is urgent. Act at once if you want this paper to live.

THE BLASTERS.

Birth Control Propaganda

ONLY a few years ago the idea of Birth Control agitation was ridiculed even by most radicals. It wasn't necessary, they said; the time wasn't ripe for it, and it was forbidden by law, anyhow.

Today the subject of Birth Control is gaining ever wider recognition. Agitation in this matter has become an important factor in the labor movement; even the most timid radical now realizes the significance of this propaganda.

I do not share the view of some enthusiasts that Birth Control will make war impossible, solve the labor problem and liberate man and woman from bondage. It will do nothing of the kind; it will not solve any social problems. But it is bound to prove a vital factor in their solution.

Whether Birth Control is advisable or not, may be a debatable question. But the right to discuss it is not debatable. Discussion of every problem must be free, for only through such discussion can we ever arrive at a satisfactory, wholesome solution. In other words, I demand absolute free speech and absolute free press upon any subject that I am interested to discuss. If there are laws that prohibit such freedom, the worse for the laws.

This is the attitude taken by Margaret Sanger and Emma Goldman, as well as by many other progressive thinkers of America. Of course, the United States is the only semi-civilized country that has laws prohibiting the discussion of vital problems. But even in this benighted land we are making progress. A proof of it is to be found in the Federal authorities dismissing the eight charges against Margaret Sanger. The action of the government was due to its realization that the sentiment in favor of the free discussion of sex and family problems has grown in this country to an extent that makes existing laws against it inoperative. And by the way, that is the history of every law. It is operative only to the extent to which the people are willing to obey it.

But though the Federal government dismissed the case against Margaret Sanger, the New York authorities—more "moral" and evidently also denser than the Federal officers— have arrested Emma Goldman for advocating Birth Control.

The monster massmeeting recently held in Carnegie Hall, New York, in the matter of the arrest of Emma Goldman leaves no doubt as to the sentiments of the people of New York in this question. On March 10th a similar massmeeting took place in San Francisco. The keynote of the large assembly was the demand of absolute freedom of speech and press in discussing this vital subject, and the determination to nullify the law by supplying information concerning *Prevention of Conception* to those needing the same. Nor was this sentiment merely one of promise. It was proven an actual fact by the free distribution at the meeting of a special leaflet printed for the occasion giving the best preventives for women and men. The eagerness with which the large audience demanded copies of the leaflet was proof of its necessity, as well as of the changed sentiment.

To emphasize its sympathy with Birth Control agitation, the audience contributed toward a Fund to print a large quantity of these leaflets for house to house distribution in the city. Copies and bundles of these leaflets can be obtained free of charge at the Friday evening meetings of the Current Events Club, Averill Hall, 1260 Market Street, San Francisco; also through the office of THE BLAST.

The enthusiastic meeting closed with the unanimous decision to wire a telegram of protest to the authorities of New York.

STATEMENT OF BIRTH CONTROL MEETING—March 10, 1916.
Collection Birth Control Meeting..$53.65
Collection Current Events Club, March 3........................ 3.95
                                                                                        $57.60
Expenses—
Throwaways..$6.00
Stamps and envelopes.................................... 8.00
Hall rent.. 2.00
Telegram, New York.. 1.00
5000 "Preventives" Leaflet.......................... 9.50
                                                                                        26.50

Balance on hand...$31.10

Pernicious Tendencies

"THE pernicious tendency" of discontent is not a new discovery. A Roman tribune, L. Marcius Philippus, B. C. 104, stated that in the vast Roman Empire there were not 2,000 citizens who possessed any property. Cicero subsequently reproduced the statement to discourse on "the pernicious tendency of such talk," and that it leads toward schemes for the equalization of property; and, what greater mischief, he asks, can there be than this? The Roman republic fell from its own rottenness, and though its fall was slow and prolonged, we can draw no satisfaction from that fact.

Freedom was not then an inalienable inheritance as it is now assumed to be. Concentration of wealth now, as then, leads to prodigality and vice, but increased intelligence and freedom will not submit to the fate the spiritless Romans exhibited. Our plebeians stand in no awe of our patricians, nor will they be cajoled by them. American optimates may prate of "the pernicious tendency" of a knowledge of facts, but it will be in vain; the American populace, having tested freedom, will resist its restriction. They are quick to learn, and the object lessons of military drills and police brutality will not be lost if a modern Spartacus makes his camp in New York, Chicago or San Francisco.

Extract from a Private Letter

I HAVE often been asked if I believe in force. I reply it is a natural law. The most timid animals fight in defense of their natural rights. We are repeatedly told that resistance to tyrants is obedience to God, and that he who dares be free, himself must strike the blow. I do not claim to be like the cowardly cur who licks the foot that kicks it. Therefore I do believe that force should be resisted with force. But, no matter what I believe, it always will be. There is a strong sense of right and justice among all peoples throughout the world, which will eventually become crystallized, perhaps in the near future—who knows? When this happens they will ask what manner of men could they have been that allowed their best friends and unflinching champions to be hunted down and put to death, like wolves, by the merciless power of money.

Knights of the Double Cross

ANOTHER man of God, the Rev. Chas. E. Eaton, Rockefeller's pastor of the Madison Avenue Baptist Church, New York, has resigned to take up the cause of Preparedness.

The business of saving souls will be laid aside for a while in order that the business of killing may be given a boost.

Being a pious gentleman, the pastor is loath to call a spade a spade. Preparing to shoot people whom we have neither known nor seen nor have any quarrel with, he refers to as the "new Americanism, the new era of Christianity which must inevitably follow the European war." Slippery John, who has doubled the price of gasoline lately, could not express himself with more circumspection.

John D. himself is not making many speeches these days; he is too busy trying to earn an honest penny between prayers.

It will be noted that among other arrivals in Camp Preparedness are Mr. Vanderbilt and the Rev. Father Vaughn, whose special mission of a few years ago as annihilator of Socialism resulted entirely satisfactory to himself.

The tenacity of our "reverend" barnacles in attaching themselves to wealth is truly marvellous.

Sherman Was Wrong
Emanuel Julius

AN Amsterdam dispatch says the profits of the Krupp Steel Company during 1915 amounted to 86,000,000 marks ($21,-500,000), against 33,000,000 marks ($7,500,000), the preceding year, and that a dividend of 12 per cent was distributed. Sherman was wrong. War isn't hell—for some capitalistic plunderbunders. It's profitable. Patriotism pays.

Labor Omnia Vincit

THIS is Latin for "Labor conquers all." We say it in Latin because it isn't true in English. Labor has never conquered a right to its own productions.

E Pluribus Unum

THIS is Latin for "From many, one." It is the motto of this great republic. Originally this republic was a lot of sovereign States, just like a lot of trade unions which are sovereign in themselves. Then they made a confederation, but it wouldn't work; it was too loose-jointed. Too many sovereign States. Then they made this republic. In other words, all the little unions became one great union. We would like to see organized labor adopt the principle of this motto, an absolute solid one, from many.

WHAT is a capitalist?
One who has a capital time.
What is capital?
Stored-up labor.
How does the capitalist get the capital?
Labor hands it to him.

COME on, Mike, let's go to work.
I ain't working today. My union has ordered a strike.
Is that so? What for?
Ten cents a day increase.
Well, I wish you luck. The rest of us will go to work so we can pay our assessments and help you out. Ain't the bosses stupid? They don't see that it is their money that supports the strike.
That's so. There's nothing so stupid as a boss.
You know when the miners was on a strike in Colorado, the fellows in Wyoming and everywhere else kept on working and sent in assessments.
Yes, and coal. Ain't the bosses stupid?

Eight

THE BLAST

Correspondence

St. Louis, Mo., March 8, 1916.
Dear Comrades of THE BLAST:

I am enclosing Money Order for $25.50 derived from the entertainment given in this city for the benefit of THE BLAST.

After working hard for weeks to make this affair a success, this is all we realized. Talk about revolution, when the working class is so much behind the times. Here are the saloons and picture shows doing a flourishing business, while giving in return poisoned minds and bodies. And on the other hand there is a paper that is trying to develop minds and bodies, and yet so few come to its assistance. Unfortunately, this affair took place during the "Crone sensation." Many "sympathizers," who otherwise would have come, failed to show up. * * * While this affair was not much financially, we consider it a great moral success. For a long time we couldn't get the rebels of St. Louis together, in spite of all our efforts. And here at last we were again, the selected few, sitting all at one table.

Comrade J. M. Bluestone, who acted as toastmaster, after a very appropriate talk, opened the floor for discussion. Almost everyone had something to say for THE BLAST. There was old man Robinson (old in age, but young in spirit), followed by Nelson, Varney, McGrove, Schneider and many others, all enthusiastically agreeing that THE BLAST is the best revolutionary weekly we have at present in this country. The discussion, as usual, developed various suggestions how to help THE BLAST in its financial struggle. Some were in favor of giving a picnic on a larger scale early this summer for the benefit of THE BLAST. It is now under consideration. After recitations by the able rebel Gold, the crowd had what is called a "good time" until after midnight, when all went home, some happy and some "very happy." Fraternally yours,
—MAX COHEN
2732 Dayton St.

Chicago, March 7, 1916.

Comrades: When I received the last issue of THE BLAST (No. 8) I noticed the statement that *The Alarm* had been suppressed. I wish to inform you that such a thing did not happen, and I ask you to correct the error in your next issue. Fraternally yours,
—THEO. APPEL

(It gives me great pleasure to make this correction. Suppression of Anarchist publications is such a common occurrence that I naturally credited the report I received, especially because the March issue of *The Alarm*, long overdue, did not reach me until today.—ED.)

* * *

WHAT is a "martyr"?
A martyr is a savior who lost out.
What is an "Agitator"?
An Agitator is a fellow who cannot make a living.
What is a "Leader"?
A "Leader" is a fellow who can make a living.
What is a Dangerous Citizen?
One who thinks.
What is a Respectable Citizen?
A suit of clothes.

WHAT does Labor get out of War?
A job.
What job?
Making munitions.
What for?
To kill laborers.
Hurrah!

* * *

COMPETITION is the first Law of Trade.
Competition for Trade is the first Law of War.

* * *

OUR good friend, *Organized Labor*, says that the good hunter aims only at what is in sight.

But suppose he mistakes a fly on his gun barrel for an eagle, and doesn't see the bull moose beyond?

Poor Vision.

And what is in sight? What is in sight, for instance, for Caplan, Schmidt, John and Jim McNamara, Quinlan, Lawson, Ford and Suhr, Rangel and Cline, etc.?

And we wonder, what is in sight now for Joe Hillstrom.

What is in sight for those who dare death—for Labor's sake?

We know what is in sight for them from the exploiting overlords, but what has Labor in sight for them?

Is it to be forever Apology, Repudiation?

VOL. 1   SAN FRANCISCO, APRIL 1, 1916   No. 10

General $ in Command

General $ in Command

David Leigh

THE cartoon in this week's BLAST shows what General Dollar knows, what he will never forget, so long as people continue to worship his coat of arms. They call him "Revenge" in this Mexican instance, but that is only a nickname—one of half a dozen *noms de plume* which the old boy uses to avoid recognition. Sometimes he takes the name of "The Missionary Kid," "The Disinterested Developer," "The Slugger for Right," etc., etc., but it all amounts to the same thing. General Dollar himself is the head of the pseudonym array and his curves remain the same even though he ornament himself with a barrelful of terms.

And how he whines when the march begins! It is either "poor water," "poor air" or bunions on his "horses'" hoofs. He whimpers like a baby being broken of the sucking habit. And why? So that more "pacifiers" in the shape of human orderlies will be forthcoming. Yes, and he whines for nothing else. His pressmen whine for nothing else. They dread the day when the rattle shall be put out of reach—when they will have to drink plain milk unsugared—and have to *earn* the milk. Canny is General Dollar, far-seeing, calculating. He knows that Division follows such diversion even when the diversion is sham. He therefore makes it his business to take the minds of his minions off whatever pain they suffer while in his service by holding out the reward of—Thanks, in the form of a copper badge of honor!

And why does the old party decorate himself so extravagantly with misleading titles, with ornate reasons for his advance over feelings and hopes? Why does he do his person up like a Christmas tree when sallying forth to the echo of jangles? The reason is not cryptic. The old man has a horror of the nude. He has a horror of it because his own person unadorned is so repulsive. Fancy General Dollar showing himself without even the impress of a star on his breast! The idea is unthinkable. Any glass would crack if he stood up without furbelows in front of it.

And in the case of Mexico, what a spectacle we have of a sword-studded dinosaur in pursuit of one little frijole! And how edifying it is to see this armored brute chasing the husk of a single tamale on the pretext of avenging an insult to one of his extremities! For that matter, what kind of a yarn is it we are told, of how Villa with a handful of followers "invaded" a townful of cartridge-belted citizens with the result that seventy-one Mexicans were killed to seven slain innocents? Villa must have paraded up and down the main street of the village for the benefit of American sharpshooters, if the story be true. How else could the loss be such a one-sided affair? The tale is all very patriotic and vengeance-compelling, but it doesn't hang fire.

But a long tail needs but slight excuse to flap in the breeze. Our sensitive General has been pecked at (he says so) and a drop of blood shows on his vest front. Incidentally, he is the possessor of specially-constructed goggles which aid their owner to detect valuable oils and minerals; so Forward, boys, in the name of curves, cracks and cudgels! They're only Greasers anyhow. Instead of manufacturing tamales, let's put up the real thing—in cans.

There we have the General undraped but accurate. He lives off false faith, he feeds on abortive concepts, he waxes round and rosy when accoutered fools obey him in the name of outraged feelings he never at any time possessed.

It is the veriest rot to use the word "revenge" in the present connection. Why, if there is any revenge due, it is from the Mexicans for the depredations of the Gringoes on their land and life. Haven't the Pierces and the Waterses and the Rockefellers and the Hearsts for years been making meal of the bones and bodies of Mexicans, depriving them of food, depriving them of sleep, grinding the very marrow out of the heart and sinews of this people in order to make their already bloated profits bulge still further? It is the Mexicans who stand aggrieved. It is they who would be justified in putting to rout the whole flimflamming lot of greedy poachers who have squatted on their land.

Poor Mexico! Poor in one sense, yet in the face of what she has accomplished by way of breaking the yoke of oppression which for centuries has held her down, as a nation she makes the soft, satisfied, subservient American look like a pot of mucilage. The Mexicans are really fighting for something. They didn't confine their efforts to Words. They have sought things, taken them and *used* them. But the American? He still wants to be "represented" and he is—by the filchers. Spokesmen do it all for him. That is why nothing is ever done to benefit him.

But in the case of Mexico, part of the chain has been broken; not many links, but broken just the same. And when men have the force and courage to break a single link, they will re-break that chain even though it be soldered by the master tinsmith of all the world, General Dollar. You cannot put even a new baby back into the womb. Nature takes care of that. She contracts the orifice through which new life has emerged.

So with Mexico. General Dollar and all his tribe will find themselves unable to cram Emancipated men back into the slavish hole from which they have released themselves. And a cheer should go up from the heart of every Liberal that this is so. For the Mexican's fight is not a single fight. It is the fight of all those who are striving to throw off the stranglehold of mediaevalism, the scrawny clutch of a rapacity doomed finally to sink of its own over-weight.

Long life to the sons of Mexico who are making this fight! And a curse on the head of any and all who would attempt to block her in her glorious struggle for a free existence. May the clang of General Dollar's fall resound in her ears till her sleepiest children shall stand up and wonder why they have slept so long.

Our Task

SUCH equilibrium as our present world possesses is the precarious balancing of a pyramid of opposing selfishness upon an apex of wealth-begotten aristocracy. The science of this equilibrium is our orthodox political economy—the most dismal of sciences, with the most dismal of subjects. The human world will never stand solid until it rests upon the broad basis of simple humanity, whose apex is moral worth. So to place it is the task of our epoch.

David Caplan

THE TRIAL of David Caplan will open in Los Angeles on April 3d. He is charged with complicity in blowing up the *Times* Building, on October 1st, 1910. J. B. McNamara pleaded guilty to the charge and is now serving a life sentence in San Quentin. Mathew Schmidt was recently convicted in the same connection and sentenced to life imprisonment.

What is the outlook for David Caplan?

Let us look the situation square in the face.

The Merchants & Manufacturers' Association, the Otis interests, the Burns Detective Agency, the prosecution of Los Angeles County and the whole respectable, law-abiding citizenship of Los Angeles is and has been a solid unit for the conviction of Schmidt and Caplan. They have carried out the first part of their program to the extent of a life sentence for Schmidt. They will carry out the second part with the same precision. They may even carry out some other parts later on. It is no use fooling ourselves by hiding our heads, ostrich like, in the bushes and pretending not to see. No one else but ourselves are the sufferers from this kind of wilful blindness.

It is not a question of guilt or innocence. To Labor's enemies, the worker charged with active opposition to capital, is guilty even if innocent. To me, the worker at the bar of his enemies is innocent even if guilty. Innocent or guilty, Caplan is convicted beforehand in the courts owned by the masters. Caplan realizes this, as every intelligent worker must realize it. Therefore Caplan has decided, I understand, to cast the old tactics overboard. He knows he has nothing to hope from the legal line of defense followed in the Schmidt case. In that trial the labor and legal advisers of Schmidt took the stand that Mat could hope for a "fair trial" and "justice" at the hands of the Otises and their hired lackeys. If they honestly believed it, in spite of all past experience to the contrary, they were criminally stupid. If they merely pretended to believe such fairy tales, their sacrifice of Schmidt was the most damnable treachery.

I have been informed, on reliable authority, that Caplan refuses to be similarly sacrificed. He has nothing to hope from a legal defence on conservative lines. He has nothing to lose by taking the boldest stand. He has everything to gain—and first of all his self-respect—by facing his enemies as a man, a conscious worker and intelligent rebel against injustice and persecution.

It is therefore that I rejoice in the determination of Caplan to follow a new line of procedure in his trial. And with me, every true friend of labor must rejoice in the brave stand of David Caplan. Enough of the cowardice and hypocrisy imposed upon Labor's prisoners of war by pretended friends and spokesmen of Labor. Enough of the crawling, begging and pleading at the feet of the masters. Such an attitude leads only to the gallows and the penitentiary. The strong scorn the weaklings. And justly so. That's why no true man has any sympathy with cowardice and meekness. That's way Labor, the great

giant, is making itself the laughing stock in the eyes of the world by its eternal submission. It is time, high time, for the giant to straighten his bent back, look the world square in the face, and boldly proclaim: I can, because I will and dare!

Not till then will Labor have any real claim to respect, nor the power to achieve. It will be the proudest moment in the life of labor, its greatest red letter day, when at last the rebel shall arise out of the ranks and throw the challenge into the very face of the masters: YOU are the guilty, who feed on the blood of our children and devour the bodies of our people. *You* are the real murderers and enemies of man. I challenge your iniquitous justice, I defy your rules of the game!

The day will come when the rebel worker shall take this position. The day must come. And that day will carry joy and courage to the hearts of the disinherited and rally the best elements of labor around their *real* spokesmen.

The penitentiaries of this country are filled with Labor's prisoners of war. What power keeps them there? Surely not the handful of guards. Were Labor to make a determined demand for their release, no power would dare resist them. The unionists of San Francisco pride themselves, for instance, on their organized strength in this city and State. But what avails their strength if they lack the will, the intelligence or courage to use it for the benefit of the workers? San Quentin penitentiary is full of labor men. Why does Organized Labor on the Coast not demand the immediate release of the McNamaras, Albert Ryan, Ford and Suhr, Schmidt and Caplan? The Governor of the State is a "labor" man; the sheriff is a "labor" man; the warden of San Quentin a "labor" man—all put in office by the direct vote or consent of Labor. Organized Labor on the Coast has a great deal of influence, you know. But for what purpose are they using that influence? To give labor politicians fat jobs and a chance to betray the workers. If the unions of San Francisco would merely threaten a general strike the prison doors would quickly open to the McNamaras, the Schmidts and the Caplans.

Labor has the power. No one doubts it. The tragedy of it is, the labor politicians within the unions are the first to paralyze every effort of the workers to assert their power.

It is therefore that men like David Caplan must rely on their own strength and on the resources of the more revolutionary element among the workers. True, the unions now and then help with money. But it is not money that is of main importance in such cases. If the workers have to match dollars with the masters, the workers lose. The moral support of labor, boldly and publicly expressed, is of a thousandfold more effect than the treasury of the richest union. If the convention of the American Federation of Labor, recently held in San Francisco, had voiced a strong public protest in the case of Mathew Schmidt, then on trial, it would have accomplished a great deal more than the $3000 voted in secret session.

It is the moral support of all labor that David Caplan

demands, and has the right to demand. He demands it on the ground that when he faces the judge and jury in the Los Angeles courtroom, it will not be only David Caplan but *militant* Labor on trial. That being the situation, the case must be fought as a phase of the great labor struggle, a chapter in the social war.

To further this purpose, David Caplan has secured the services of Jacob Margolis, an attorney from Pittsburgh—a man of experience in the labor struggle, one with courage and ability to fight the case of Caplan on the basis of the larger issues involved, the issues of the class war.

Mr. Margolis will be assisted by other lawyers, but his instructions from Caplan himself are to ignore precedent and tradition, and to fight the case on revolutionary lines.

We urge our friends and comrades everywhere to rally to the aid of David Caplan. Make your voice resound throughout the country. Let us be done, once and for all, with legal respectability and conformity, so much prized by those who are anxious about their sinecures in the unions or their own precious skins. We have sacrificed enough rebels to the Moloch of legality and cowardice. Let us for once show that we are men, with the self-respect and spirit of manhood.

Alexander Berkman

In the Eyes of the Future

Charles Erskine Scott Wood

DAVID CAPLAN is to be tried April 3d. So many men are tried, hung and imprisoned that one more or less makes little difference. Suppose a thousand years from now some one digs up the fact that Caplan or Schmidt or McNamara was tried and imprisoned. It will look mighty small to the people of the distant future. But suppose a scholar writing the history of our times finds that we had a very curious civilization: Society divided into two classes, the one devouring the other and the two constantly at war in a never-ceasing struggle. That will certainly be interesting, even a thousand years from now. It will be a chapter in the life of the race—a mighty important chapter. Then our scholar of a thousand years hence will go on to show that the struggle was a life and death struggle. It meant life or death to the laboring masses. It meant life or death to society. It meant life or death to the race. For a race grows out of the mass, not from the few at the top. Nations perish when their masses become thin and weak. Our historian will record that the struggle to the death or life was a property struggle: a few men owning the earth and the social structure. These were called Capitalists, and they sought to continue the toilers in slavery and deny them their fair share of the wealth produced by their labor from the natural resources of the earth. Then this historian will show the terribly interesting fact—interesting even a thousand years from now—that the great mass of laborers were held in a bondage the cruelty of which was measured by what men, women and children of the wage slave class could exist on. Indeed, the children could not all exist, but enough survived to keep the mills, mines and factories

going. In the steel industry the average wage was about $475 a year, and about 35,000 men were killed every year in this industry. That the workers lived in squalor and starvation, the children born only into a life of grinding toil and degradation. That poverty compelled these slaves to set their children to work at the tender age of ten, or even at six and seven years. That from time to time the misery of the serfs forced a rebellion, in which the capitalists' government and hired professional slayers mercilessly shot, burned, jailed and hung the rebels. Then if it appears that in some such rebellion, or in a fury—not against miserable subordinates, but against the system and its maintainers—some men struck against the system and its maddening injustice or, if you please, against its supporters and profiters, it will be exceedingly interesting even a thousand years hence to read of these life grasping spasms, and then the names of the men who came out of the dull mass and sacrificed themselves in unequal combat against society and law will really be noteworthy. Just as Jack Cade's name is now noteworthy in English history. History is ceasing to see in him a rioter, rebel and destroyer of society, but rather one seeking to save. What he began, Cromwell continued. The end is afar off. Voltaire and Rousseau, the theorists, Danton and Mirabeau, the men of action, fought and destroyed "society," yet Carlyle says the French Revolution restored his faith in an overruling Providence.

It is not only the great revolutions that mark man's progress. John Brown, the one man, marks the abolition of slavery quite as well as the whole Civil War. All the men who lead in saving the race—that is, the common people—are law breakers, whether it be Cromwell or John Brown. So a thousand years hence the men accused of lawlessness—as David Caplan now is—may be judged as men aiming against a cancer in the social body.

It will be interesting to know what our scholar of a thousand years hence will say of Labor out of whose ranks these men came and for whose benefit they struck. I care as little as will our scholar of the future to discuss their wisdom. What concern is their wisdom, to the people for whom they sacrificed life and liberty? Will Labor disown and desert them? or secretly support and openly deny them? or wholly and as one man openly adopt and defend them? These will be interesting questions—even a thousand years hence.

*   *   *

PRESIDENT WILSON in a recent address said: "Law is a very complicated term. It includes many things that do not engage our affections."

Less scholastic, but more positively truthful, he might have said: "Law is a hell of a mess; it stifles human affections."

*   *   *

WAR is wrong in itself, even though a congress or a majority decide upon it. Let them who want war pay for all preparedness and do all the fighting—and there won't be any.

Past and Present

A. Mack

THE workers of early civilization were chattel slaves, not from choice, but from compulsion.

The workers of modern civilization are wage slaves, also not from choice, but from compulsion.

Chattel slaves worked hard, and received enough food and care to preserve their health and thus their power to labor; the death of a chattel slave was a distinct loss to the boss, as he had to buy or capture another to replace the lost one.

Wage slaves work harder, produce more, and receive of the wealth they produce just enough to enable them to replace their lost energy and to rear more wage slaves. The death of a wage slave is no loss to the boss; he does not have to buy or capture another—there are always plenty more in the industrial reserve army, and these hunger drives to the vacant job.

There appears some likeness between the positions of the workers at the two opposite ends of civilization, insomuch that they both are slaves, not from choice, but from compulsion. However, the compelling forces are not identical, as in early days it was the captor's lash, while today it is hunger's lash that is the driving power.

The early chattel slave was a free man before he was a slave, and lived a healthy, careless life among his natural surroundings in the bosom of his communal tribe. No inducements could entice him from his home of freedom to become the servant of any boss for any number of hours a day and a reward of a bare existence.

Direct action was necessary to force him into servitude. Before he would work for a master he had to be made a captive and driven by the overseer's whip to dispense with his laboring power. As he was ignorant he could not be expected to see that his interests and those of his master were identical, and as a consequence of his not comprehending this moral precept of the boss, and his respect for the masters' law and order being likewise imperfect, he was ever prone to the practice of Direct Action to liberate himself from his degrading drudgery.

We can thus see that the masters' dislike of Direct Action had its roots in the economic circumstances which piloted society through to modern capitalism. Is it any wonder that that early dislike has grown more fearful?

The modern wage slave, on the other hand, was born a slave; he never knew what freedom was; he has no chance of becoming a free man by running away from his master; if he runs away from one it is only to look for another—there is no escape for him, the relentless lash of hunger holds and drives him to the task. He and his class belong to the master class more securely than did the chattel slave. But the grinning tragedy of it all is that the average wage slave cannot realize it; he has become so thoroughly soaked with the master class ethics and education that he is now—according to the master—intelligent enough to recognize that his interests are wrapped up with those of the boss, and as a result he doesn't believe in using Direct Action to improve his position. Being also a fervent worshipper of the boss' law and order, and of his constitutional way of doing things, he entrusts his fate to the politician, who holds the power through the use of masters' law and order apparatus of *improving* (?) the workers' conditions without at the same time interfering with the profits of the boss. This method satisfies both the wage slave and the boss, and is known by the respectable name of political action. By the professional politician or by the aspiring politician it is reckoned far superior in effectiveness to *that damnable Direct Action,* because the latter vulgar method not only improves the workers' condition at the expense of the boss, but it removes the opportunity of the aspiring politician's reaping the glory and the graft. If there is one hopeful sign on the worker's horizon it is just this, that he appears to be shaking the stupor from his brain and commencing to see that his political flirting is useless, and that his only hope of emancipation is through the industrially organized might of the working class; for "the work of emancipating the workers must be the work of the workers themselves."

Labor and Song

Leah Lowensohn

FROM Langland's "Piers the Plowman" to this very day, a period of more than five hundred and fifty years, the same tale has been told, the same song has been sung, in literature, painting and sculpture, of the lives of those who labor. The condition of the worker has changed virtually very little during all these centuries. And this story has been so often told that when we hear it today, it fails to stir us to action. We have become so accustomed to the sound that it fails to make an impression. And yet the tale cannot be told too often.

It was Langland who first described, with an understanding that is born of sympathy, the misery, the sordidness, the wretchedness of the lives of the toilers. Later Thomas Hood reiterated the same story with poignant reality. Shelley, that buoyant and kindly spirit, struck a chord of defiance in behalf of his fellow men. He bid them wake to the consciousness of their strength. He bid

them use that strength in their own defense. And he held out to them the hope of victory. And again, William Morris hailed them with words of good cheer, of fellowship, of *camaraderie.* The lowly Millet pictured the peasant in the field with head low and shoulders bent. The mighty Meunier molded the miner in clay in the same attitude.

In our own time Arturo Giovannitti shoots his "Arrows in the Gale," and John Masefield consecrates his life to the song "of the maimed, of the halt and the blind in the rain and the cold." There is a gleam of beauty in all of these songs, but for the most part they are a record of the poverty, of the suffering, of the misery and the indignity of those who toil. The bent attitude of the worker, pre-eminently in Millet's portrayal of him, is symbolic of the humility and of the lack of dignity of Labor. Most of the songs of Labor have been cries of pain; shouts of rebellion, calls to arms. Never yet have they been songs of joy. When will they be that?

They will be that when laboring men and women throw off the yoke of humility and declare their right to the fruits of their toil. They will be songs of joy as soon as men and women reclaim the dignity of Labor, that dignity of which they were robbed not while they were asleep, but while they were hard at work; when work will have become an inward urge and not an outward force. And finally, they will be songs of joy, when men and women *take* that which is theirs by right, without asking nor even demanding it—for only those rights are ours which we are willing to *take* even at the risk of our lives. Then only will the singer be able to sing the song of joy, the true song of Labor! Then only will the last words of *The Voice of Toil* ring true:

"Come, shoulder to shoulder ere earth grows older!
The Cause spreads over land and sea;
How the world shaketh, and fear awaketh,
And joy at last for thee and me."

Prohibition : A Crime and a Menace

WHY do the opponents of prohibition always base their arguments on the claim that prohibition doesn't prohibit?

The claim is, of course, true; for prohibition under present conditions is a joke, and worse besides. But in making that fact their leading argument they beg the question at the start and play into the hands of the Bryans and other such "wise guys," and the asses who put up the coin for these.

For if the "Rum Demon" were one hundredth part the devouring monster that the fanatics claim, a way could be and ought to be found to end forever its career—in fact, would have been found long, long ere this.

If one-tenth of the nonsense and "statistics" talked by the prohibitionists were true, we should all be maniacs, imbeciles, degenerates and weaklings—such of us as might be left.

If one-tenth of the rubbish—so-called expert medical opinion —which is dinned into the ears of children in the public schools by the old maid teachers were really true, the "rumsoaked" Slavs, Teutons, Latins and Anglo-Saxons would necessarily have perished from the earth through physical and mental degeneracy.

If, as is taught, alcohol causes frightful diseases of the body and mind, which are passed on to the children by heredity; if the offspring of drunkards were imbeciles and dipsomaniacs and the like, then the Indo-European races never could have survived thousands of years of alcoholic indulgence. They necessarily would have become teetotalers or must have perished, and today all Europe and America would be inhabited by those prohibitionists par excellence, the engaging Turks, Kurds and Arabs.

Prohibition is a crime against the liberty of the individual and a menace to the nation. I oppose prohibition, not because it is difficult of enforcement, but because it would be dangerous to the progress and welfare of any people to enforce it.

I maintain that, instead of being a curse, alcohol is the handmaiden of intellectual and material progress, and that history abundantly proves it.

I contend that the races that have brought the world up from barbarism to civilization and lead the world today are "rumsoaked," as the prohibitionists are so fond of saying. Not only so, but races are vigorous in body and virile in mind almost in the ratio that they consume alcohol. Millions of the earth's inhabitants never touch alcohol, such as the great bulk of the Chinese, the East Indians, the Arabs and the Mohammedans of all kinds. Show me such and I will show you a people standing still or sliding backward in the evolution of humanity. All history teaches the same lesson.

Wine drinking Greece and Rome have left their imperishable imprint upon the thought, the art, the literature, the government, of all time as no other nations have ever done.

Later, when Europe had slumped backward into ignorance and superstition, came the wineless hosts of Mohammed and attempted to conquer the degraded, "rumsoaked" Europeans, constantly at war among themselves. Surely if total abstinence ever had a golden opportunity to show its vast superiority over drunkenness, that was the time. Yet the "rummies" of Charles Martel and Charlemagne drove back the water drinkers. When the roystering Spaniards landed in Mexico and Peru they met peoples well along in civilization for that period, but without, if I remember correctly, the alcohol drinking habit. Which proved the more virile, brave and intelligent? Ask history.

When the Mayflower landed at Plymouth Rock its pious travelers, carrying their bottle of booze ashore with their household effects, ran afoul of a husky, warlike red race of teetotalers. How long did the water drinkers keep their land from the Pilgrims, whose descendants were the guys who put "make" in Jamaica rum, and who at last accounts were still able to match muscles or wits with any total abstainers whatever at a ratio of about five to one?

The old South before the Civil War produced statesmen, thinkers, soldiers, men of learning and women of culture, courage and refinement. Physically and mentally the Southerners were unexcelled, whereas they should have been idiots and weaklings, according to the affecting philosophy taught in our public schools through the brow-beating of our pious prohibitionist, for was not a decanter on every sideboard, a "still" on nearly every farm, everybody drinking as a matter of course, and nearly everybody descended from the "souses" of Great Britain?

Whence came the bold and gallant rovers that built the British Empire; that found America and made it their own; that have girdled the earth and taken what they desired; that fought their way to the Poles?

Whence came the men who have led the world in science, in art, in government, in learning, for a thousand years—who tame the lightning and make it their servant, who talk across vast oceans, who fly like birds and travel under the sea?

Do these workers of wonders come from the water drinkers of the world? I trow not. Almost, if not quite, without exception they spring from nations "rumsoaked" for centuries.

Consider, if you please, the Germans—huge eaters and drinkers! Has anybody noticed any lack of physical or mental vigor after their age-old debauch as a race? I trow not.

Now, there must be a reason for all this. It could not be merely coincidental that all the arguments of the prohibitionists are made absurd and ridiculous by the facts of history.

I am far from saying that alcohol would make every race progressive. On the contrary, it probably hastens the extinction of a people incapable of development and progress—e. g., the American Indian and the Kongo savage. But the virile races need alcohol, and, needing it, they use it. If it were bad for them, these conquerors of the world and of the secrets of nature, the peoples who lead the world now and have led it in the past in progress and civilization, would either have discarded it long ago or it would have made them serfs and weaklings and degenerates instead of masters and conquerors.

PRISON MEMOIRS OF AN ANARCHIST
By Alexander Berkman

"One will search far before finding a more powerful picture of what deeds are perpetrated in the name of justice."
—San Francisco "Bulletin."

512 pages, illustrated. $1.15 postpaid.

THE BLAST

Revolutionary Labor Paper
Published every 1st and 15th of the month
569 Dolores St., San Francisco, Cal.
Mail Address, Box 661   Phone, Park 499

Alexander Berkman, Editor and Publisher
E. B. Morton, Associate Editor   M. E. Fitzgerald, Manager

SUBSCRIPTION
$1.00 Yearly   60c Six Months   5c Copy
Bundle rates 2½c per copy in bundles of ten.
Advertising rates on application.
Entered as second-class matter at the postoffice at San Francisco,
Cal., January 14, 1916, under the Act of March 3, 1879.

Will Organized Labor Help?

Tom Mooney

A NEW institution has sprung into activity. Its purpose is primarily the making of profits out of the war game, out of the wholesale slaughter of the workers by the workers, with the instruments of their own creation. But in order to have this war game carried out to the success of those who benefit from it, the opposing sides in the game must be somewhat equally matched, for duration, because the longer the game goes on the more profits the Steel Trust, the Standard Oil Company, the Du Pont Powder Company and the rest of their ilk, make out of the spilling of the workers' blood.

The Pacific Coast Defense League has a mission in this game. It plays the part of doctor, and it also has the aid of many specialists for the purpose of curing the sick and fast dying militia. Among them, and chief in importance, are two labor specialists: Andrew J. Gallagher, past president San Francisco Labor Council, and Tom Finn, Union Labor sheriff and member of the Stablemen's Union. The former is cabinet chairman of the League's labor committee; the latter, cabinet chairman of the publicity committee. These posts have been allotted to labor, as labor is the determining factor in this war business; it either makes it or breaks it. The next most important post in the cabinet is filled by E. W. Wilson, president of the International Banking Corporation. He is chairman of finance and the treasurer of the League. The International Banking Corporation, comparatively of recent origin, is one of the most gigantic financial combines ever formed in the world. It represents the Standard Oil, the Steel Trust, Morgan & Co., and all the other big international capitalist interests. This is fine companionship for two supposedly labor men in the business of giving the militia a clean bill of health.

I have in my possession a copy of the constitution of the League. To give an insight into the work of this organization, it is well to quote some of its purposes:

(Fourth) "It is also the object of the League to assist in bringing the National Guard of California, Oregon, Washington, Idaho, Montana, Nevada, Utah, Colorado, Arizona and New Mexico, to a higher degree of efficiency, as well as to a higher degree of popularity, with the great masses of our citizens in those Western States, and to that end to do all in its power to have the laws of those States so amended that the practice and duty on the part of the constituted authorities of calling the National Guard into service and action during industrial disputes and strikes be abolished; and to the end that the hostility that has heretofore arisen between labor and our National Guards may be eradicated, and to the further end that labor may unhesitatingly and with unhampered and unprejudiced patriotism join the ranks of these National Guards in times of peace, as well as in times of war, should war be forced upon us."

(Fifth). "It is also the object of said League to encourage and bring about in the schools and educational institutions of those Western States a healthy physical and military training of the male students, with a proper appropriation of funds therefor, so that with as little loss of time and inconvenience as possible they shall become bodily strong, robust and healthy, and at the same time become skilled and trained in military science,

and that the laws of said States governing the education of the young should be so moulded and amended as to bring about the results herein outlined. Also that laws be made to permit such male students to form, or join, cadet companies, composed of the students at the same educational institutions, and which shall provide for their equipment."

The "fifth object" of this League was forwarded to the San Francisco Board of Education, in the form of a resolution asking the board officially to approve by resolution the establishment of military training in *all* standard schools.

The Board of Education turned them down in no uncertain terms. Part of their resolution follows: "Resolved, That such establishment of cadet companies be entirely voluntary upon the part of the students and supplementary to their usual school exercises and outside of the usual school hours; that it in no respect take the place of the usual courses in physical training; and further resolved, That the secretary be instructed to send a copy of these resolutions to the committee on cadets and schools of the Pacific Defense League. Report approved and resolution adopted by unanimous vote."

One of the Board of Education's members in speaking on this matter said: "The schools are for the children to learn their lessons, and not to learn how to kill people." Now the question is, will the San Francisco Labor Council give this outfit a recommendation, or will it put a crimp in their rotten scheme? A. J. Gallagher is a representative labor leader; he has asked organized labor to consider this matter, and is urging favorable action upon it. He is a cabinet member of the League. He tried to get other labor men of prominence to act on the labor committee of the League, but after attending one meeting they refused to have anything more to do with it. The following unions have taken a stand against it: Waiters, barbers, butchers, riggers and stevedores, machinists and molders. Many other labor bodies are considering similar action.

It is the duty of every worker to have his union take a stand against the League, its aims and objects. The ten governors of the above mentioned States are respective numerical vice-presidents of the League. The cabinet has four capitalists, two lawyers, two labor men, one priest, one adjutant general, one legislative representative. These men constitute the respective chairmen of as many executive committees of the League; they can select as many in their given field as they want to. A great deal might be said about the motives of these men in this organization, but space will not permit it. It will suffice if I say that I agree with the sentiments of a worker in this community when he said that if they are not getting paid by labor's enemies they are scabbing on the job. This move of the League to trap the workers must be pushed back in the teeth of the labor crushers.

A Group That Does Things

Reb Raney

I N San Francisco there is an Italian group called Gruppo Anarchico. It appears to be made up of young men chiefly, though a few women attend its sessions. It holds forth in a dingy club room at 1602 Stockton street, where its members go to read revolutionary periodicals, hear red-blooded speakers and take active part in work which has intelligent resistance for its base. The work consists in *doing* things instead of talking about them; and that is why this particular circle has more meaning to it than twenty-seven hundred assortments of Socialistic confab.

On the window of the club room is a sign which reads: "GRUPPO ANARCHICO—VOLONTA." It is big, clear, done in red—and not a letter is missing. Worked in between the lines is a sketch of mountain peaks, with the flaming sun rising above them. Inside, the walls speak eloquently, with their picture of Montjuich, a print of the five Haymarket victims, pictures of Giordano Bruno and Francisco Ferrer, a number of revolutionary posters, and such inspiring placards as, "You aspire to liberty? Fools! Have the strength and liberty will come by itself." Numerous revolutionary booklets, newspapers, etc., are fastened on with clothes pins to a railing midway up the wall and are strung out the entire length of the hall, easily accessible to all who care to read them. A home-made desk-bookcase in the rear of the hall seems to be a sort of storehouse for excess literature.

I am told this group has no officers; that its members come and go as they please; that all contributions are voluntary, including the literature; that the door of the hall is *never* locked, notwithstanding the fact that the club room is on the ground floor; that *anybody* is welcome to come in and read to his heart's content; and that, most interesting of all, nobody even knows how many members this circle has. Each member stands responsible for his own acts, but cooperates with other members, all of whom are equally responsible. There isn't anything regular about this aggregation, as far as I can learn. It rests on a foundation of interest, intelligence, spontaneity and courage. Further than that, it just carries out its own wishes and never seems to think of asking leave of any official dignitary.

To illustrate: At the March 10 mass meeting, held in San Francisco to protest against Emma Goldman's arrest, free handbills were given out on which was printed information about preventives. It was simple information, plain enough for any man or woman to read and profit from. One of the Italian boys, interested in this circle, got one of the handbills and took it to his group's meeting place. The idea was instantly recognized as a good one, and one member of the circle forthwith offered to give $10 toward the printing of 20,000 of these bills in the Italian language, so that every man and woman in that district might *know* how to regulate the size of their families. More individuals came up with cash, and the result was that 20,000 leaflets were printed and passed out as freely as water. Then this happened:

One of those blue-birds known as policemen called at the club room and asked a member of the circle, Joseph Macario, who happened to be there, the what, how and why of the group's activity along birth control lines. Now Joseph Macario is beautiful to look at. There is nothing of the liar about him. He therefore didn't hedge, but answered in a way that earned for him an invitational command to call at the "Chief's" headquarters. Joseph went, not in the least ashamed for what he had done, but proud of the fact that he had done a good act, a helpful act, boldly, thoroughly and openly. The Chief looked him over, asked "why," and the boy answered this: "You know these things; you use them; why shouldn't I and the rest of us?" The Chief's answer was short and sweet. He used three words. He said to the key turner, "Lock him up." But there are bubbles in Italian blood. When you scratch it you are liable to get an effervescent reaction, which is just what happened in this case. An Italian attorney, Charles Sferlazzo, interested himself straightway, bailed the boy out, and now there promises to be a lively contest over the right of strangers, official or otherwise, to regulate bedroom affairs. The case is to come up this week, and the Italian boy is not going to be alone.

Another light on this case is this: Since the leaflets were printed priests have stopped to read those which were pasted up on the window of the club's quarters. By any chance can it be that the men in black recognized that such effrontery meant less births, less marriages, less funerals and therefore less fees, not to speak of the abatement of respect for mystery mongers, and decided for their own sakes that it would be well to stamp such efforts as "obscene" and thereby put an end to them? Just an idea, of course, but somehow it sticks.

The most important part about the work of these rebels is that they had the courage to stand back of their acts. They signed the name and address of their group on the leaflets they gave out, and they headed the leaflet with this significant announcement:

WORKERS! Procreate Only When You Like!
Numerous families increase the misery that is great already among the poor masses of workers. The capitalist vampires, by means of the priest, morally condemn the use of scientific means in order not to have children. This they do by threatening "hell" to those who intelligently refuse to put into the world numerous "unlucky"

(unfortunate) ones. And by means of politicians, judges and jailers they make laws, condemn and jail everybody —all those who try to diffuse among the people scientific knowledge. And indeed they tried, a short time ago, Margherita Sanger. They convicted Anderlini in the State of Illinois. A few days ago they arrested Emma Goldman in New York, and they threaten trouble to all those who have the courage to tell you the truth and let you know this practical means to prevent conception.

Joseph Macario stated that the information wasn't given out in the hope of solving the social question, but to protest against authority; "and by this to voice a stern protest against all limitations of free social development—on the part of consecrated authorities."

Last evening I went over to the club room of this circle to hear Alexander Berkman speak. We were a number, including Jake Margolis, the Pittsburgh attorney, who is to defend David Caplan in his coming trial. Both Berkman and Margolis talked to the crowd which filled the hall to overflowing. Everyone in the place listened with wrapt attention, including a number of gum-shoe tale bearers who took slurred notes in the rear of the the place. I can't begin to outline Berkman's talk here, but it was fine.

He told them intelligent resistance was the key to attainment under the present social system; that what was good for the crowd was good for the man; that anything, everything that served to make people discontented and actively and effectively resistant in their own defense was beneficial; that the man who ties a rope around your neck and accuses you of "disorder" if you attempt to undo the knot, is a bully and a faker and unworthy of the slightest consideration. Margolis, too, dwelt on the absolute necessity of throwing off imposed burdens, no matter in what form they present themselves. And at the finish both were roundly applauded. There were enough red bubbles in that hall to make a pudding that would reach to Mars.

After the meeting I learned that on the night before 6000 preventative leaflets had been placed in the mail boxes of as many citizens by the members of this group. They had confined their distribution to the Italian quarter and, of course, all the handbills were printed in Italian. Ten members had done the work, voluntarily, fearlessly, determinedly. Which only proves what Wendell Phillips said—that a dozen or so *determined* men can commit a revolution over night.

Fine examples are these youth, fiery, conscious, clear sighted. They know what ails them and they are not going to be over-delicate in putting an end to the nuisance. Which recalls the American brand of "bravery." What an invigorating sight it would be could we but see our native drudges take heart and emulate these dark-skinned defiers! Perhaps they will—when they see it is safe. More than one man has finally made his base by walking.

☒ ☒ ☒

Pierre Ramus Free!

I AM happy to be able to inform the American friends and comrades of Pierre Ramus (Rudolph Grossman) that *he is free.* I have just received this good news from him. The various reports about his sentence to 20 years' and life imprisonment, were exaggerated. Comrade Ramus writes me that he has just been released after serving three months for anti-militarist agitation in Austria.   A. B.

☒ ☒ ☒

THE BLAST PLEDGE FUND

Seattle, Wash., monthly pledge for six months:

S. Cohen	$5.00
A. Snellenberg	1.00
A. Halpern	1.00
Morris Greenberg	1.00
L. Berg	.50
H. Lerner	.50
Berkeley, Cal.:	
Stella Smith (weekly)	1.00
Collection, meeting, New York:	
Per R. Edelson	2.67

Young Folks
III.

"Isn't money everything?" cried **Tom**. "Why, if you have plenty of money, you, can get everything you want."

"That's a mistake, Tom. Suppose you are on board of ship, with plenty of money in your pockets. Now, suppose some accident happens and the ship is wrecked. Such things happen, you know. Perhaps you and a few other passengers are saved somehow and land on a desert island. You have money, but there is no food. Could you keep alive on the money, Tom?"

"No; of course not."

"Then you'd starve to death, in spite of all the money you might have. So you see, money is not everything. It is nothing at all unless there is something to be gotten for it."

"Then what good is money?"

"Money alone is of no use. It is only so much gold, silver and paper, and you can't live on that. You need food, clothing, houses and other such things to keep alive."

"Then we could do without money?"

"Of course we could. In old times people lived without money."

"Could we live now, too, without money?"

"To be sure. We would make the things we need, just as we do now, and then use them."

"Then we wouldn't have to buy them?"

"No. And therefore we wouldn't need money."

"So money is only to buy things with?"

"That's all. It's called exchange. Money is a means of exchange."

"I don't understand."

"Well, it's this way. Take your father, for instance. He's a carpenter and he's working in Jones' factory. Well, yesterday he made a table and he was paid $3.00 for it. That is, he traded or exchanged his day's work for $3.00. You told me that you wanted a pair of pants. Your father could use the $3.00 to buy you a pair. That means that he traded his day's work for $3.00 and then again traded the $3.00 for a pair of pants for you. That's exchange."

"So money is only to trade or exchange things?"

"That's all it is good for. You got to have things before you can exchange them. And if you haven't the things, money is of no use."

"But if we have the things, we could exchange them without money."

"Of course."

"Then why do we use money?"

"That's only to make a profit."

"What is profit?"

"Profit is what you get over and above what you really earn. Take Jones, for instance. Your father and other men work a whole week in the factory and make a lot of furniture. Say that altogether Jones' workers got paid $300.00 for the week's work. Besides their work, the cost of the lumber and running the factory (lighting, cleaning, keeping the machinery in repair, etc.), may amount, let us say, to $200.00. The furniture made that week, then, costs altogether $500.00. Now suppose I want to buy that furniture. Jones asks me $1,000 for it. The difference between what it cost to make the furniture—$500—and the price Jones gets for it—$1,000—will be profit."

"Then, I suppose, it is this profit that Jones keeps for himself?"

"Exactly. He profits by the work of your father and other workingmen."

"Then he must have bought his factory with such profits, and that's why you said his factory didn't really belong to him but to the workers who made it."

"I see you are beginning to understand."

"But that means that Jones is really robbing my father by making a profit on his work when Jones himself does nothing to earn it."

"Yes, it is robbery."

"Now I see. That's why father can't afford to buy me new clothes, or other things we need."

"Yes; Jones, as well as every employer, robs his workers of the greater part of what they produce."

"But why does father let him?"

"I suppose because he doesn't understand he is robbed."

"I'll tell father right away about it."

A.

WORKERS, this concerns YOU!

DAVID CAPLAN

There is a NOISY war in Europe. In this country a SILENT war is going on —the war between Labor and Capital. The victims of this war are all from the ranks of the workers. Your brothers fill the penitentiaries because they fought YOUR battles. Mathew Schmidt is the latest victim. Will you help save the next prey chosen by the bosses?

MATHEW SCHMIDT

DAVID CAPLAN
MASS MEETING

Carpenters' Hall, 112 Valencia St.
TUESDAY, APRIL 4th, 7.30 P. M.
(DOORS OPEN AT 7 P. M.)

Come to learn the important NEW developments in the case

ADMISSION FREE
SPEAKERS:

CHARLES ERSKINE SCOTT WOOD, of Portland, Poet, author
    and attorney.
WALTER M. HOLLOWAY, President Rationalist Ass'n of America
TOM MOONEY, Secretary International Workers Defense League
ED MORGAN, Poet and speaker
ALEXANDER BERKMAN, Author and lecturer
ED NOLAN, Machinist and organizer
WM. McDEVITT, Speaker and writer.
CARLO TRESCA, of New York, in Italian

Auspices International Workers Defense League of S. F., and Current Events Club

VOL. 1   SAN FRANCISCO, APRIL 15, 1916   No. 11

HIS BLOODHOUNDS

The Bloodhounds

THE bloodhounds of King Plute are on the trail of THE BLAST. Issue No. 10 has been excluded from the mails by order from Washington. The official objection is against the article, "A Group That Does Things," treating of Birth Control and mentioning the address of the Group. Orders had also been given to suppress the issue of March 15th (No. 9), though part of that issue had been mailed before the arrival of the governmental ukase.

The real reason for the suppression, however, is the fact that THE BLAST is "too strong," as one of the officials told us. "Too strong" for whom? For our readers or for the powers that rule? Have we come to this that any stupid Post Office clerk may decide what is or is not fit for the people to read? Who is this postal authority, anyhow, that presumes to censor our expressions and to dictate our mode of writing? To be sure, our writing may be strong: we write for redblooded men and women, not for the mollycoddles or corruptionists of the Post Office. And if our frank talk about Wilson and his lackeys, and their plutocratic employers, is not to their taste—so much the worse for them. They have the power—the passing power that rests on popular ignorance—to strangle THE BLAST and jail its editor. But they cannot put chains on thought, nor hold back the hands of Time. Our will is not to be subdued—in or out of prison we shall continue to voice the feelings and thoughts of the suppressed and down-trodden, all governmental censors notwithstanding.

*   *   *

Have we, or have we not, free speech and free press in this country? With Emma Goldman facing trial in New York for exercising the right of free speech; with the REVOLT, of New York, suppressed by the Post Office, and the Brothers Magon in jail because of their encouragement of the Mexican peons in their great struggle for Land and Liberty—to mention only a few recent cases—it seems to me that only the wilfully blind can persist in the belief that we have free speech or free press in this country.

These things are a myth. In America, as in the European monarchies, we enjoy only that modicum of freedom of speech and press which is palatable to the masters. There is free speech for those only who voice popular ideas—ideas approved of by the powers that be. But free speech has no significance whatever unless it means freedom to express unpopular ideas. The essence of progress consists in giving a hearing to the new and the unpopular. These, when approved and accepted, finally become popular. But before it has the opportunity to prove its worth, every untried idea is necessarily unpopular, because new. That is not saying that everything new is necessarily worthy and useful. But in order that we may separate the chaff from the wheat, every idea must be sure of a hearing. That is the meaning of free speech and free press: absolute freedom of expression.

It is in the interest of the lords of life to allow only as much, and the kind of, expression that does not militate against their power and influence. But where expression begins to undermine the foundations of that power, where it lays hold of the roots of the false ideas supporting our social structure of lies, robbery and murder, there permitted freedom ceases. When seriously threatened, the Beast of Privilege cries, "Halt! So far and no farther!"

But we are determined to ignore the Beast and its rules, its cries of rage and its cries of pain. We urge those who believe in real, unconditional freedom of speech and press to manifest their attitude by helping us in this important fight. Deprivation of postal service has put us to heavy expense. We ask our friends to co-operate with us and thus aid our determination to fight for uncensored freedom of expression.

Alexander Berkman

To the Enemies of Free Speech

Wm. Francis Barnard

AS WELL to lay your hands upon the Sun
And try with bonds to bind the morning light,
As well on the Four Winds to spend your might,
As well to strive against the Streams that run;
As well to bar the Seasons, bid be done
The Rain which falls; as well to blindly fight
Against the Air, and at your folly's height

Aspire to make all power that is, be none.
As well to do all this as to impeach
Man's tongue, and bid it answer to the schools;
As well to do all this, as give us rules,
And bid us hold our words within your reach;
As well all this, as try to chain man's speech.
So others learned before ye lived, O fools!

The Crimes of Governments

Josiah Warren

NOTHING is more common than the remarks that "no two persons are alike," that "circumstances alter cases," that "we must agree to disagree," etc.; and yet we are constantly forming institutions which require us to be alike, which make no allowance for the individuality of persons or of circumstances, and which render it necessary for us to agree, and leave us no liberty to differ from each other, nor to modify our conduct according to circumstances.

On what, then, rest all customs and institutions which demand conformity? They are all directly opposed to the individuality, and therefore false. Every one is by nature constituted to be his or her own government, his own law, his own church—each individual is a system within himself; and the great problem must be solved with the broadest admission of the inalienable right of supreme individuality, which forbids any attempt to govern each other, and confines all our legislation to the adjustment and regulations of our intercourse or commerce with each other.

To require uniformity in thought, feeling, or action, is a fundamental error in human legislation—a madness which would be equaled only by requiring all to possess the same countenance, the same voice, or the same stature.

Each individual should be at all times free to differ from every other in thought, feeling, word, and deed; and free to differ from himself, or to change from time to time; in other words, every one is constituted by nature to be, at all times, sovereign of himself, or herself, and of everything that constitutes a part of his or her individuality. Society, to be harmonious and successful, must be so constituted that there shall be no demand for an outward show of conformity or uniformity—that no person must have any power over the persons or interests of others; but that every one shall be, at all times, the supreme "law unto himself."

Theorists have told us that laws and governments are made for the security of person and property; but it must be evident to most minds that they never have, never will accomplish this professed object. Although they have had all the world at their control for thousands of years, they have brought it to a worse condition than that in which they found it, in spite of the immense improvements in mechanism, division of labor, and other elements of civilization. On the contrary, under the plausible pretext of securing person and property, they have spread wholesale destruction, famine, and wretchedness in every frightful form over all parts of the earth, where peace and security might otherwise have prevailed. They have shed more blood, committed more murders, tortures and other frightful crimes in the struggles against each other for the privilege of governing, than society ever would or could have suffered in the total absence of all governments whatever! It is impossible for any one who can read the history of governments, and the operations of laws, to feel secure in person or property under any form of government, or any code of laws whatever. They invade the private household, they impertinently meddle with, and in their blind and besotted wantonness presume to regulate, the most sacred individual feelings. No feelings of security, no happiness can exist in the governed under such circumstances. They set up rules or laws to which they require conformity, while conformity is impossible, and while neither rulers nor ruled can tell how the laws will be interpreted or administered till they have been repeatedly infringed, and punishment has been inflicted; under such circumstances no security for the governed can exist.

A citizen may be suddenly hurried away from his home and despairing family, shut up in a horrid prison, charged with a crime of which he is totally innocent; he may die in prison or on the gallows, and his family may die of mortification and broken hearts. No security can exist where this can happen; yet all these are the operations of laws and governments, which are professedly instituted for the "security of person and property."

Rulers claim a right to rise above, and control, the individual, his labor, his trade, his time, and his property, against his own judgment and inclination, while security of person and property cannot consist in anything less than having the supreme government of himself and all his own interests; therefore, security cannot exist under any government whatever.

They compel the individual to desert his family, and risk or lay down his life in wars in which he feels no wish to engage. They leave him no choice, no freedom of action upon those very points where his most vital interests, his deepest sympathies are at stake. He can feel no security under governments.

Great crimes are committed by the government of one nation against another, to gratify the ambition or lust of rulers; the people of both nations are thus set to destroy the persons and property of each other, and would be murdered as traitors if they refused. This is the "security of person and property" afforded by governments. With regard to security, we see that in the wide range of the world's bloody history there is not any one horrid feature so frightful, so appalling as the recklessness, the cold-blooded indifference with which laws and governments have sacrificed person and property in their wanton, their criminal career of self-aggrandisement, instead of protecting person and property.

The Modern Wage Slave

Hugh McGee

TODAY the man who works for wages, either by the hour, week or month, has no knowledge of the value of his work or the value of the product of his work. He is paid a wage which is only the amount necessary to provide him with food, clothing and shelter, so that he may continue working for his boss. The wages vary in different parts of the country only so much as living conditions are either higher or lower, and he must adapt himself to the fixed wage or starve.

The wage worker does not know why certain jobs pay 17 cents an hour and other jobs pay $100 a month. He only knows that for certain work a certain wage is paid in all parts of the civilized world. Being compelled to accept conditions as they are, he has never questioned the value of the product of his work. Wage slavery is a mystery. There is no apparent slavery to the man who can at any time quit his job and look for another master.

In the days of feudal slavery, when only the priest and noble had the advantages of a liberal education, the peasant or serf of the eighteenth century, though unable to read or write and whose world was limited to his master's field or estate, was still able to understand his position in society and there was no mystery about it.

He was given an acre or two of ground, which was his and his children's to enable them to supply the necessities of life. Its use was granted him so long as he worked for and supplied his feudal master with all his necessities and luxuries. He worked perhaps two hours to provide his own absolute needs and ten or twelve hours for his master. He could see the inequality of the arrangement, but resigned himself to the will of God as he was told by the priest, who acted as his master's representative.

Today the slave's material condition is better, though his position in society is that of servant or slave. No man is free whose right to work, so that he may live, depends on the interests of another man. Today the mastership is determined by the ownership and control of the land, the factories, the mines, the stores, the railroads and the immense and complicated tools that are now used. The slave condition is shown by the wage worker's dependence for even existence upon the master, who has the power to deny to the worker, at any time, an opportunity to work and thus deprive him of the only means to maintain his existence.

The State Superstition

ALONG with the tacit assumption that State authority over citizens has no assignable limits, which is an assumption proper to the militant type, there goes an unhesitating faith in State judgment, also proper to the militant type. Bodily welfare and mental welfare are consigned to it without the least doubt of its capacity. Having by struggles through centuries deposed a power which, for their alleged *eternal* good, forced on men its teachings, we invoke another power to force its teachings on men for their alleged *temporal* good. The compulsion once supposed to be justified in religious instruction by the infallible judgment of a pope is now supposed to be justified in secular instruction by the infallible judgment of a parliament; and thus, under penalty of imprisonment for resistance, there is established an education bad in matter, bad in manner, bad in order.

—HERBERT SPENCER

The Thieves' Convention

Ellis O. Jones

A NUMBER of thieves were conversing.

"I was not punished," said one; "I merely stole franchises, and they became vested rights before the people realized it."

"I was not punished," said another; "I was a public official and stole from the public. They only made me pay it back."

"They did not punish me," said a third; "I stole more than the people could count."

"I was not punished," said the banker; "I only stole from depositors. They have no rights which are bound to be respected."

"I was not punished," said the politician; "I stood in with the machine which could not afford to lose one of its trusted members."

"I was not punished," said the man of social prominence; "there were too many involved with me."

"I *was* punished," said the wage-worker; "I had no money, no friends and no job. I stole a loaf of bread to keep my family from starvation."

THE BLAST

Revolutionary Labor Paper
Published every 1st and 15th of the month
569 Dolores St., San Francisco, Cal.

Mail Address, Box 661   Phone, Park 499

Alexander Berkman, Editor and Publisher
E. B. Morton, Associate Editor   M. E. Fitzgerald, Manager

SUBSCRIPTION
$1.00 Yearly   60c Six Months   5c Copy
Bundle rates 2½c per copy in bundles of ten.
Advertising rates on application.
Entered as second-class matter at the postoffice at San Francisco,
Cal., January 14, 1916, under the Act of March 3, 1879.

Reflections

The Magon Case

IT IS sad and disgraceful that the militant elements of Los Angeles permit Ricardo and Enrique Flores Magon to remain so long in jail, for lack of bail. I personally know a number of radical men and women in that city who could, with a little effort, supply the required bond of $10,000 for the Magon Brothers. Why is it not done? Surely there is no one in the revolutionary movement deserving our active sympathy and aid more than these two men. They have given the best years of their lives to the cause of liberty; they have repeatedly suffered imprisonment for their loyalty to struggling Mexico, and now they are again in the hands of the enemy.

The charge against the Magons and Wm. C. Owen (editor of the English section of *Regeneracion*) primarily involves the freedom of press. There is undoubtedly a systematic attempt on the part of the Federal authorities to silence every voice that dares protest against tyranny at home and abroad, or to enlighten the public concerning the schemes of our political and commercial pirates. The *Revolt*, of New York, has been suppressed; two issues of THE BLAST have been excluded from the mails; Ricardo and Enrique Flores Magon are in jail for advising the peons to resist oppression, and now Washington is about to suppress *Regeneracion* by depriving it of second-class mail rights.

The workers, as a mass, do not yet realize that the persecution of such men as the Magons, or the suppression of fearless and outspoken voices, is the *direct concern of Labor*. Every unresisted act of tyranny strengthens the hands of the masters and rivets the stronger the chains of our dependence and obedience. To the shame of the labor movement of this country be it said, there has been hardly any mention of the Magon case in the official labor organs. The union politicians are too busy with "more vital issues"; namely, making more secure their own sinecures in the unions and preserving the good will and respect of the bosses. But the radical labor element knows that the suppression of the least among us is a blow to each and all of us. It is therefore a matter of self-defense on their part to bend all energies toward arousing public sentiment in behalf of the Magons and of all others threatened by the Masters' bloodhounds. Help us therefore to crystallize a strong sentiment that shall force the authorities to release their strangle-hold on those who, of stronger fiber than the average, dare to challenge the powers of darkness.

Courage vs. Meekness

ACCORDING to information sent out by the Transportation Brotherhoods' Bureau, of Cleveland, Ohio, the railway train crews and switchmen are making efforts to secure an 8-hour workday. The unit of wage payment is now based on the moving of rolling stock 100 miles at ten miles per hour. The men are asking for eight hours, or twelve and a half miles per hour; 100 miles in eight hours, and time and one-half for overtime after eight hours.

The conditions under which railway employees are now working are nothing short of slavery. Crews on dead freight service, or what is called "slop freight," are on the road 14 hours out of every 24. They spend an additional hour, after they get in, washing up and looking after the engine, and then, tired and sleepy, they are "free" to go home to wife and family. After eight hours they are given a two-hour call at the end of the rest period, to go on another fourteen or fifteen-hour trip. Thus these men have only 1½ waking hours at home—hardly enough time to get acquainted with their families.

Consider that the 309,177 men involved in this effort to secure better conditions belong to the most important industry of the country: without them all transportation would come to a standstill and thus all other industries immediately paralyzed. The official organ of these workers solemnly informs us that "their demands are just," and that, therefore, all right-thinking men should aid them. But in what manner can they be aided, except they help themselves? It is not outside aid they require. What they most need is the intelligence and determination to make good their demands by carrying them into action. They are not asking for a higher wage. They want shorter hours. Suppose these men agree *among themselves* to work 8 hours and *then quit*. Wouldn't that be more sensible and effective than begging the railroad magnates to please give them permission to do what they themselves have the power to accomplish?

A Pertinent Lesson

THE REAL purpose behind the demand for a large army has been made clear in Congress when the Hay army bill was passed by the lower house. Proposed amendments to prohibit the use of the National Guard for strike duty were promptly ruled out of order. Why should the militia *not* be used to suppress strikers? In truth, no good reason can be given. It would practically mean the abolition of the National Guard, since it has no other reason for existence. And surely no one dreams of even proposing such an unpatriotic thing.

We call the attention especially of the labor unions on the Coast to the stand Congress has taken in the matter. In view of the strenuous effort of certain "labor" leaders to spider-web the unions into the militia, the frank admission of our national legislators on this subject ought to pierce even the hard coco of the "practical" union man who eternally shouts for "harmony" between tiger and lamb.

The Spirit We Need

A LITTLE boy in Des Moines, Iowa, eleven years of age, refused to salute the American flag. To do so was against his convictions, he said. He remained steadfast even when threatened with prison. The boy, Hubert Eaves, is a Negro, which circumstance heightens our appreciation of his unusual manfulness and courage. Incidentally, it holds out the hope that not all of his race in this country have been demoralized by the Booker T. Washington ideal of becoming contented and obedient slaves.

A kindly Christian judge sentenced the boy to 9 years' prison. Now Hubert is in jail—over which proudly floats the Stars and Stripes, the emblem of freedom and liberty of conscience. But even in prison the young Negro is worth more than the flag.

Would we had more of his strength of purpose and character in the radical and labor ranks. This country would then be more fit for decent men and women to live in.

Effective Protest

THERE is no doubt that the Russian Revolution of 1906 had a powerful effect upon China. The efforts of the radical and revolutionary elements of that country, struggling for greater liberties for their people, were much stimulated by the example of the Russian people and the inspiration of Russian refugees in China. Their work finally culminated in the Chinese revolution of 1911.

The god-chosen emperor was irreligiously forced to abdicate, a constitution and parliament were established, with Yuan Shi Kai as president. So far as the welfare of the people is concerned, the change was merely nominal, as all political changes are. But the revolution destroyed the age-old popular awe of the "divine" emperor and fear of his authority. More than that, the dictatorship of the President did not long remain unchallenged by the people. The revolution continued, and the republican rulers of China were so hard pressed that they resorted to the extremity of converting the republic back into a monarchy, with Yuan Shi Kai as Emperor. But the clock of time cannot be turned backward. The people, having once tasted a little liberty, demanded more. Great Britain, Russia and Japan protested against the re-establishment of the monarchy. Yuan ignored the demands of those feared governments. The protest of the people, however, could not be ignored. The popular uprising against Emperor Yuan forced the government to submit, and now the republic has been restored in China, and all indications point to it that President Yuan will be forced to abdicate.

These events in China strikingly demonstrate the effectiveness of Direct Action. The voice of the people, expressed directly and firmly, is more potent and compelling than all the protests of the most powerful governments.

Forbidden Knowledge

THE CASE of Emma Goldman will be heard in the New York Courts on April 20th. She is charged with giving information on Birth Control: teaching the mothers of the poor how to have better and fewer children. It is a terrible crime to give knowledge to the people; that is, the kind of knowledge that may rob the masters of factory slaves and cannon fodder.

Emma Goldman is guilty; she has spent her whole life in giving the people forbidden knowledge. If the Courts convict her, it will be strictly according to law, which is there to protect the overlords against too much knowledge on the part of the masses. But she will *not* be convicted if the intelligent people, who realize the importance of Birth Control propaganda, will sound a warning, personal and collective, to the masters of life, as represented by the judges and prosecuting attorneys of the courts.

The Press Harlot

THE ECHO of the Crones newspaper poisoning has hardly died away, when another similar canard is let loose upon the gullible public. "A world-wide Anarchist conspiracy to do away with various royal heads in Europe and America." If the newspapers would give publicity to this idea as a suggestion for useful effort, the matter might

be worth considering. But to palm off a stale old lie as an actual fact is neither "news" nor original. It reminds one of a worn-out old prostitute protesting her virginity. I wonder in what besotted reporter brain this kind of "news" has its source. If such a performance at least had even the shadow of plausibility; but evidently our great news dispensers think any stale fake good enough for their readers.

Even "liberal" papers like the San Francisco *Bulletin* fill their columns with these disgusting drippings of the old press harlot. Thus the brain syphilis is spread among the people. No wonder things are rotten.

Who Is Manufacturing "News"?

A PRESS opinion from THE BLAST of San Francisco, reproduced on page 229 of *The Public*, attributed to "an enterprising Associated Press man" the sending out of a fake interview in regard to the alleged poisoner, Jean Crones, with Alexander Berkman in New York when he happened to be in San Francisco. The matter being brought to the attention of General Manager Melville E. Stone of the Associated Press by Mr. Oswald Garrison Villard of the New York *Evening Post* brought the following response:

I have your memorandum to Roy Martin transmitting copy of *The Public* with a clipping from THE BLAST at San Francisco, referring to an interview with Alexander Berkman, respecting Jean Crones. We have investigated the matter and find that we did not interview Berkman nor did we carry any story in relation to it.

The Associated Press is thus absolved of responsibility. But the fact remains that papers throughout the country did report a false interview of that kind in the form of a New York dispatch. These papers must know the agency from which they obtained it. Since this agency was not the Associated Press, it is the duty of the papers to expose the guilty one. The Chicago *Tribune* of February 20, for instance, had the following included in a long dispatch under a New York date line:

That Crones is a murderous maniac, following the impulses of his own disordered mentality is the belief not only of Emma Goldman, but also of Ben Reitman and Alexander Berkman.

Emma Goldman, as well as Berkman, has denied that such an interview took place. The incident, while in itself of little importance, shows how "news" is manufactured to suit the real or supposed prejudices of newspaper readers and publishers. Perhaps one of the papers which published this false dispatch may be public-spirited enough to name its source.

S. D. in *The Public*

The Power of the Plutocrat

I THINK that nowadays if—I do not say some prominent villain such as Nero, but—some most ordinary man of business wished to make a pond of human blood for diseased rich people to bathe in when ordered to do so by their learned medical advisers, he would not be prevented from arranging it, if only he observed the accepted and respectable forms; that is, did not use violence to make people shed their blood, but got them into such a position that they could not live without shedding it; and if, also, he engaged priests and scientists: the former to consecrate the new pond as they consecrate cannons, ironclads, prisons and gallows; and the latter to find proofs of the necessity for wars and bloodshed.

—LEO TOLSTOY

A Word to the Fearful

David Leigh

SOMETHING has happened in San Francisco. Something *always* happens when those who see, Act. In this case a youth has done the work, a mere boy who, by the strength of his simplicity and purpose, has stripped conventional power of its meaning.

Joseph Macario is the name of the defendant. He with others has broken the law, openly, defiantly, deliberately. He was charged with the offense of outraging "decency" by giving out information on methods of Birth Control. But Joseph Macario didn't cringe or hang his head when arraigned for his transgression. Instead, he stood up and faced his accusers like a man, knowing in his heart that pretense must fade when it is confronted by fearless reality.

This case came up in the police court. The judge, after a perfunctory hearing, pronounced sentence of six months against the accused, on the ground that the matter in question—leaflets containing information about preventives—was "indecent." Then Joseph was thrown in the cage and left to wrestle with the bugs which are bred from the monstrous thing we commonly designate "order." Apparently, the club of misrule had won the day, and the prisoner settled down to pay the price blind men exact as a tribute from those who see.

Only Joseph smiled as sentence was pronounced. He smiled as he entered the cage. He smiled after the Keeper had turned the key on him. But those who believed he had done right didn't smile. They glowered instead, and a glower from one who Feels has the power of hitting the mark before a blow is struck. This is the proof:

In that court room were Women, a number of them, women who were not tattered, who were not "poor," who had committed no crime but who had, upon seeing what happens to right when it collides with might, made up their minds that if "crime" must be committed in order to show club-men that they and their laws are in error, then "crime" they should have to the limit of woman's capacity. *The women who sat there in that court were going to break the law which keeps their sisters in pain, and break it so forcefully that it shattered pieces could never again take on form!*

The judge, however, had said that he would give answer the following day as to whether or not the boy should have a new trial. He might change his mind. Decreers do now and then. Meantime, the following letter was sent to him expressing the resentment and determination of these women; the letter was mailed in sufficient time for the judge to receive and read it before the opening of his court session:

1539 Clay Street, San Francisco,
March 30, 1916.

Judge Sullivan
Police Court
Hall of Justice
San Francisco

Sir: I was in your court room this morning to attend the hearing of Joseph Macario, the Italian boy whom you sentenced to serve six months in jail for the crime of imparting knowledge on methods of Birth Control. I wish to say here and now, in such a way that you cannot possibly misunderstand me, that I do not merely approve but enthusiastically commend such action as this boy and his fellow workers have taken. In my estimation no better work could possibly be done than that of informing poor, ignorant, misguided women how to lessen their own misery and that of their offspring. Any means which will make for the dissemination of knowledge calculated to stem needless pain, is in my judgment deserving of plaudits instead of censure. And this plainly is the purpose and accomplishment of the defendant in this case.

And let me say to you now that even if I had not been of this opinion prior to attending a single session of your court proceedings, one such ordeal would have been sufficient to convince me of the imperative need of spreading information of this character. Never in my life have I witnessed such scenes of degrading horror as I saw while sitting there in your official precinct, none of it chargeable to Birth Control—for Birth Control does not yet obtain. To me it was the epitome of all that lives by fear, brutality and leaden cowardice; and there was no mistaking the fact that the appalling result evidenced in your court was due to the very lack of intelligence you condone by passing judgment on this boy, Joseph Macario. How you or any other man could see those poverty-stricken women come in, babes in arms, and remain dumb to the fact that Birth Control enlightenment is what they need, is more than my mentality can fathom.

For your information I will state that I was a professional nurse for twelve years, during which time I came to know the torture and terror that poverty and ignorance inflict upon their victims. I know whereof I speak when I say that the greatest of all crimes is to wilfully withhold information from those who need it. There never was a greater impertinence than that of pseudo-superiority which arrogates to itself the right to impose its shallowness on those who are too weak to resist imposition.

As to your conclusion that the leaflet in question is "indecent": Intelligent opinion is not in accord with you. Scientists, men and women of culture and sympathy, all individuals who make a sincere claim to an understanding of life, unanimously concur in the belief that there is nothing "indecent" about *any* information which aims at improved conditions and better health for the community, individually and collectively. It is only the palsied superstition of unawakened conscience which still contends that knowledge, like the king's morsels, should be served on gold plates to those who have the price.

In conclusion, I repeat that you are representing the middle ages and not progress when you take the attitude you do in this case. Don't think for a moment that your little decree or any other little judge's decree is going to stop the free dissemination of necessary knowledge. All the judges, jailers and moralists on earth haven't the power to withstand the rising tide of certain betterment which is approaching on the crest of greater intelligence. Joseph Macario has paid in this instance. There will be plenty of others to pay as the battle for free speech and free press is waged and won. For myself, I would feel more honored in the company of this defendant than in that of any one or all of his judges.

Sincerely,
(Signed) REBEKAH E. RANEY.

The following day some, though not all, of the women were found again sitting there on the benches, before Joseph Macario's case was called. There is no anarchist on earth equal to a woman when she means business. The defendant's lawyer had a talk with the judge in his chambers. Two of the women, Mrs. Holloway and Mrs. Marron, told the jurist of the sentiment in this case. Then Joseph Macario was called to the bar. The judge told him there had been a "misunderstanding"; that he hadn t fully understood the case before; that as he now understood it, he saw no reason why information relating to methods of Birth Control should not be given out; and that he, Joseph Macario, guilty as charged, *was free to go and do his work as he saw fit!*

The judge even said to the boy, "If the anarchists have done this work, they have done good work."

And Joseph Macario—glory unto his soul!—answered, "The anarchists *always* do good work."

Should one use direct action or beg and sneak and slobber and crawl for the right to live and let others live? The answer is written in the court's action and the boy's liberation. We in San Francisco are free to give necessary information *in the open*, because courage combated cowardice and *took* its own instead of pleading for it!

Long live the Faith that flinches not at Fear!

The Blast Sustaining Fund

FOR APRIL

Lawrence Hazen, Custer, S. D., $3.00; M. Leites, Seattle, Wash., Land, S. F., $2.00 each; F. Huber, Rochester N. Y., O. Werner, Ocean Park, Calif., B. Axelrod, Lawrence, Mass., Morris Becker, N. Y., Fred Workman, S. F., Paul Saur, S. F., W. B. Murray, Berkeley, Calif., A. Bers, S. F., $1.00 each; H. J. Provost, Woodland, Calif., Gustavson, S. F., 50c each; John Braito, S. F., 40c.

Statement of the ownership, management, circulation, etc., required by the Act of Congress of August 24, 1912, of THE BLAST, published semi-monthly in San Francisco, Cal., for April 1, 1916: Publisher, Alexander Berkman, Box 661, San Francisco; Editor, Alexander Berkman, Box 661, San Francisco; Managing Editor, Alexander Berkman, Box 661, San Francisco; Business Manager, M. E. Fitzgerald, Box 661, San Francisco. Owner, Alexander Berkman, Box 661, San Francisco. Bondholders and security holders—none.

ALEXANDER BERKMAN, Publisher.
Sworn to and subscribed before me this 29th day of March, 1916.
GLORIA M. JONES.
Notary Public in and for the City and County of San Francisco, State of California.
(Seal)   (My commission expires Aug. 19, 1919.)

PRISON MEMOIRS OF AN ANARCHIST
By Alexander Berkman
"This is the only book that I know which goes deeply into the corrupting, demoralizing psychology of prison life."
—Hutchins Hapgood.
512 pages, illustrated. $1.15 postpaid.

"Our Business Is to Keep On Killing Germans" ---Father Vaughn

Horace Traubel

"OUR business is to keep on killing Germans." That's what the English Father Vaughn says. Do you know who he is? He's a follower of the meek and lowly Jesus. He's a braggart priest who dares between times to talk of the fatherhood of God and the brotherhood of man.

How these Christians love one another! How they fight one another! How they rob one another in peace and murder one another in war!

But we mustn't expect too much of an orthodox Christian. If he can worship a god who is capable of a hell hereafter, it's quite natural for him to believe in a man who's capable of a hell here.

No doubt there are just as good Christians in Germany today who are telling Germans that it's their business to keep on killing Englishmen.

Christians have no right to object when we tell on them.

We're not venomous. We don't subject them to our versions. We submit them to their own.

The best way to refute orthodox Christianity is to let it expose itself.

We may occasionally help it do that job. We may quote its masters as I do Vaughn. We may repeat back to it some of its own descriptions of itself.

Father Vaughn evidently feels that hell is so true it might as well begin here and now.

And so he wants to fire up the English hell for Germans at once. And in Germany similar gentle fathers want to fire up the German hell for Englishmen at once.

Christians give me a mixed conception of their theological preferences. They give me the impression of a god who raises hell in heaven and of a devil who raises heaven in hell.

As between this sort of a god and this sort of a devil, give me this sort of a devil. I could get on better with him. He seems to connect better with the sort of human nature I'm a part of and believe in.

I'd rather see the German Empire dead and Germans alive. I'd rather see the English Empire dead and Englishmen alive.

How long will it be the business of English Christians to keep on killing German Christians? How long will it be the business of German Christians to keep on killing English Christians?

Will they keep on killing Germans till there are no more to kill? Will they keep on killing Englishmen till there are no more Englishmen to kill?

Or are the English to keep on killing Germans until the English have killed all the English? Or are the Germans to keep on killing the English until the Germans have killed all the Germans?

For in this killing business the killer gets killed.

Killing may be a boomerang. It may become suicide instead of murder.

The Father doesn't say it's the business of English Christians and German Christians to get together and stop the war.

No.

He says it's their business to get as far apart as possible for loving and as near together as possible for hating.

But the Father should have given us some figures. He should have told us how many Germans he wants killed.

I suppose it's Christian to kill a certain number of Germans and perhaps not Christian to kill any Germans in excess of that certain number.

What is that certain number?

This Shylockian priest wants his pound of flesh.

Jesus forgave everybody. He forgave thieves, whores, plutocrats, liars, hypocrites and priests. Why, Jesus even forgave the virtuous. He even forgave the noble.

But the Father forgives nobody.

If Jesus was alive and was an Englishman I have no doubt he would forgive the Germans. And if He was alive and was a German I have no doubt He would forgive the English.

Maybe Jesus is alive and is in England. And maybe He's alive and is in Germany.

Open your eyes. Look for Him. But don't look for Him in the palaces. Look for Him in the jails.

Open your eyes. Look for Him. But don't look for Him among the so-called patriots. Look for Him among the so-called traitors.

The Father says: "Our business is to keep on killing Germans."

When I hear a frocked fraud talk like that I feel like retorting: "Our business is to keep on killing priests."

The New Doxology

PRAISE God from whom all cyclones blow;
Praise him when rivers overflow,
Praise him who whirls down house and
     steeple.
Who sinks the ship and drowns the people.
Praise God for dreadful Johnstown flood,
For scenes of famine, plagues and blood.
Praise him who men by thousands drowned,
But saved an image safe and sound;
Praise God when tidal waves do come,
Overwhelming stanch ships nearing home,
Praise him when fell tornadoes sweep
Their swift destruction o'er the deep.
Praise God for poor Dakota's drouth,
For fires and floods in west and south,
Praise him who sends the killing frost,
And Louisville's dread holocaust;
Praise God for the flood of eighty-four,
And the earthquake on the Pacific shore,
Praise God for sorrow, pain and woe,
For railroad wrecks, for storm and snow.
For parsons who, with hook and bell,
Demand your cash or threaten hell.
Praise God for war, for strife and pain,
For earthquake shocks, for tyrants' reign.
Praise him for rack and stake; and then
Let all men cry aloud, Amen.

Eight   THE BLAST

Young Folks

A True Tale

Charles—Pray, dear papa, let us have a very pretty story.

Father—With all my heart—what shall it be?

Charles—A bloody murder, papa!

Father—A bloody murder! Well, then—Once upon a time, some men dressed all alike . . . .

Charles—With black crapes over their faces?

Father—No; they had steel caps on:—having crossed a dark heath, wound cautiously along the skirts of a deep forest.

Charles—They were ill-looking fellows, I dare say.

Father—I cannot say so; on the contrary they were tall, presentable men:—leaving on their right hand an old ruined tower on the hill . . . .

Charles—At midnight, just as the clock struck twelve; was it not, papa?

Father—No, really; it was on a fine balmy summer's morning:—and moved forwards, one behind another . . . .

Charles—As still as death, creeping along under the hedges?

Father—On the contrary, they walked remarkably upright; and so far from endeavoring to be hushed and still, they made a loud noise as they came along, with several sorts of instruments.

Charles—But, papa, they would be found out immediately.

Father—They did not seem to wish to conceal themselves. On the contrary, they gloried in what they were about—they moved forwards, I say, to a large plain, where stood a pretty village, which they set on fire . . . .

Charles—Set a village on fire? Wicked wretches!

Father—And while it was burning, they murdered twenty thousand men.

Charles—O fie! papa! You do not in-tend I should believe this! I thought all along you were making up a tale, as you often do; but you shall not catch me this time. What! they lay still, I suppose, and let these fellows cut their throats!

Father—No, truly—they resisted as long as they could.

Charles—How should these men kill twenty thousand people, pray?

Father—Why not? The murderers were thirty thousand.

Charles—O, now I have found you out! You mean a BATTLE.

Father—Indeed I do. I do not know of any murders half so bloody.

* * *

CAPITAL "views with alarm"—what? Labor "points with pride"—to what?

PREMIUM

If you like THE BLAST, help us get subscribers. In appreciation of your efforts we will present you with a copy of PRISON MEMOIRS OF AN ANARCHIST for every 6 yearly subscriptions.

VOL. 1   SAN FRANCISCO, MAY 1, 1916   **No. 12**

THE "DIGNITY" OF LABOR

To Hell With the Government

THREE successive issues of THE BLAST have been vetoed by the Post Office censorship. The determination of the Washington authorities to suppress this publication is obvious. But the high muck-a-mucks of the government are too cowardly and hypocritical to inform us to that effect, honestly and frankly. That would not befit a "proud government." By the way, who was it that said that a government always represents the lowest social level? Evidently he knew. The methods used by the Federal government, the chambermaid of the money paunches, to suppress THE BLAST are beneath contempt. We were first informed by the local postal officials that issues 9 and 10 of our paper were prohibited to pass through the mails, by order from Washington. When No. 11 of THE BLAST appeared, it was again held up and we were informed that the Postmaster General had wired a SPECIAL ORDER to hold up EVERY issue of THE BLAST, and that our paper would not be permitted to pass through the mails until a copy of each issue had been forwarded to Washington, there to be passed upon its "fitness" to be circulated in this good and pious country. Accordingly, the first assistant Postmaster of this city, William Burke, informed us that he immediately forwarded a copy of No. 11 to Washington, and that he requested a reply by wire.

It would take five days, we were told, to receive the decision of the Postmaster General. At the end of that time we again got in touch with Mr. Burke. He expressed surprise that no reply had been received from Washington and promised to look into the matter. We waited a few more days and again sought information from the local postal officials. No reply had been received, we were informed, but Mr. Burke assured us that he would immediately telegraph to Washington to request the decision by wire.

We waited that day, and the next, and the next. Our repeated inquiries elicited no further information, except that a reply was being awaited. Our own urgent demand upon the Postmaster General to show cause why THE BLAST was being held up, and how long the embargo was to continue (as well as numerous other inquiries and protests from our friends and several radical organizations), remained unanswered. Meanwhile the paper was not permitted to pass through the San Francisco postoffice.

We waited another week, two weeks. Still no reply from Washington. In the absence of further instructions, the local postal authorities continued to apply the previous order excluding THE BLAST from the mails.

THE BLAST must have hit 'em pretty hard to make them so mad. But we are tired of awaiting the pleasure of His Majesty, Postmaster General Burleson, and his Comstockian censorship. Who the hell is Burleson, anyhow, to presume to dictate what is or is not "fit" to be read by the American public? As our friends, Douglas B. and Annie Bruce Carr Sterrett, of Washington, D. C., so well put it in their protest to Burleson, "The Post Office

was supposed to be mechanically efficient, and nothing beyond that. That it should now dictate on ethical questions is as absurd as if the railroads and street car companies were legally empowered to refuse to accept passengers whose ideas they did not like."

To the filthy mind, all things are filthy. The Postmaster General is evidently suffering from this Comstockian disease, but we have reason to believe that the suppression of THE BLAST is not so much due to the unfortunate mental condition of Burleson, as to the pressure from other quarters that have found our frank criticism "too strong" for their digestion, and very unpalatable to the powers that be. But whatever the reason or forces behind the suppression of THE BLAST, we are tired of the whole pestiferous gang and of the postal tyranny. We hereby declare our independence of the Autocrat of the Post Office and of his governmental and plutocratic chiefs. We are heartily sick of the whole canaille. We know that THE BLAST is a thorn in their side. We defy them to do their worst. We will continue to publish THE BLAST as long as we can find friends to support our resistance to this postal despotism. Rebels and liberty lovers, it is up to you to show if you are really sincere in your protestations. Help us to keep up THE BLAST. There is no greater menace to progress than the suppression of the radical press.

And let the overlords and their hirelings be warned that their craven and sneaky methods of stifling unpopular thought will but serve to drive our propaganda underground, *sub rosa* —as in Russia, for instance—and force it to assume more aggressive expression. In vain is the hope of the American governmental Black Hundred to suppress the Spirit of Revolt. In vain! For

Ye fools! Do I not live where ye have tried to pierce in vain?
Rests not a nook for me to dwell in every heart and every brain?
In every workshop breeding woe? in every hut that harbors grief?
Ha! Am I not the Breath of Life, that pants and struggles for relief?

'Tis therefore I will be—and lead the people yet your hosts to meet,
And on your necks, your heads, your crowns, will plant my strong, resistless feet!
It is no boast—it is no threat—thus history's iron law decrees—
The day grows hot, O Babylon! 'Tis cool beneath thy willow trees!

ALEXANDER BERKMAN

The First of May and the General Strike

THE MAY IDEA—in the relation of its revolutionary spirit to Labor struggles—first manifested itself in the economic battles of the Knights of Labor. The final theoretical aim of that organization—founded by Uriah S. Stephens and fellow workers in 1869, and bearing a pronounced radical character in the beginning of its history—was the emancipation of the working classes by means of direct economic action. Its first practical demand was the eight-hour day, and agitation to that end was an unusually strenuous one. Several strikes of the Knights of Labor were practically General Strikes. The various economic battles of that period, supported by the American Federation of Labor during its young days, culminated, on the first of May, 1886, in a great strike, which gradually assumed almost national proportions. The workingmen of a number of large cities, especially those of Chicago, ceased their work on that day and proclaimed a strike in favor of the eight-hour day. They thus served notice on their plutocratic masters that henceforth they will not be submissively exploited by the unlimited greed of the capitalists, who had appropriated the means of production created by many generations of Labor, thus usurping the position of masters—the good masters who kindly leave the workers the alternative of either prostituting their brawn or dying with their families of starvation.

The manly attitude of Labor in 1886 supported the resolution passed by the Labor Congress held at St. Louis, one year previously. Great demonstrations of a pronounced social revolutionary character took place all over the country, culminating in the strike of two hundred thousand workingmen, the majority of whom were successful in winning the eight-hour day.

But great principles of historic significance never triumph without a blood baptism. Such was also the case in 1886. The determination of the workingmen to decide for themselves how much of their time they were willing to sell to the purchasers of labor was looked upon by the exploiters as the height of assumption, and condemned accordingly. Individual capitalists, though unwilling, were nevertheless forced to submit to the demands of organized Labor; perceiving, however, in the self-respecting attitude of the working masses a peril threatening the very foundation of the capitalistic economic system, they thirsted for revenge. Nothing less would satisfy the cannibalistic master but human sacrifices: the most devoted and advanced representatives of the movement—Parsons, Spies, Engel, Fischer and Lingg—were the victims.

The names of our murdered brothers, sacrificed to propitiate an enraged Moloch, will always remain indivisibly linked with the idea of the First of May. Let it forever be remembered by the workers that it was the Anarchists who bore the brunt of those economic battles.

In vain, however, did organized capital hope to strangle the Labor movement on the scaffold. A bitter disappointment awaited the exploiters. True, the movement suffered an eclipse, but only a temporary one. Quickly rallying its forces, it grew with renewed vigor and energy.

In December, 1888, the American Federation of Labor decided to make another attempt to win the eight-hour day, and again by means of direct economic action. The strike was to be initiated by a gigantic demonstration on the First of May, 1890.

In the meantime there assembled at Paris (1889) an International Labor Congress. A resolution was offered to join the demonstration, and the day which three years previously initiated the eight-hour movement, became the slogan of the international proletariat, awakened to the realization of the revolutionary character of its final emancipation. Chicago was to serve as an example.

Unfortunately, however, the direction was not followed. The majority of the congress consisting of political parliamentarists, believers in indirect action, they purposely ignored the essential import of the First of May, so dearly bought on the battlefield; they decided that henceforth the First of May was to be "consecrated to the dignity of Labor," thus perverting the revolutionary significance of the great day into a mere appeal to the powers that be to grant the favor of an eight-hour day. By these means the parliamentarists degraded the noble meaning of the historic day.

The First of May "consecrated to the dignity of labor!" As if slavery could be dignified by anything save revolutionary action. As long as Labor remains mere prostitution, selling its producing power for money, and as long as the majority of mankind are excluded from the blessings of civilization, the First of May must remain the revolutionary battle cry of Labor's economic emancipation.

The effect of the Paris resolution soon manifested itself: the revolutionary energy of the masses became dormant; the wage slaves limited their activity to mere appeals to their masters for alleviation and to political action, either independent of, or in fusion with, middle-class parties. They quietly suffered their representatives in Parliament and Congress to defend and strengthen their enemy, the government. They remained passive while their alleged leaders made deals with the exploiters, hobnobbed with the bourgeois, and were banqueted by the exploiters, while oppression steadily grew in proportion and intensity, and all attempts of the wage slaves to throw off their yoke were suppressed in the most merciless manner.

But the disastrous defeats suffered by Labor on the field of parliamentarism and pure-and-simple unionism are radically changing the situation. Today we stand on the threshold of a new era in the emancipation of Labor: the dissatisfaction with the former tactics is constantly growing, and the demand is being voiced for the most effective weapon at the command of Labor —the General Strike.

It is quite explicable that the more progressive workingmen of the world should hail with enthusiasm the idea of the General Strike. The latter is the truest reflex of the crisis of economic contrasts and the most decisive expression of the intelligent dissatisfaction of the proletariat.

Bitter experience is gradually forcing upon organized Labor the realization that it is difficult, if not impossible, for isolated unions and trades to successfully wage war against organized capital; for capital is organized, into national as well as international bodies, cooperating in their exploitation and oppression of Labor. To be successful, therefore, modern strikes must constantly assume larger proportions, involving the solidaric cooperation of all the branches of an affected industry—an idea gradually gaining recognition in the trades unions. This explains the occurrence of sympathetic strikes, in which men in related industries cease work in brotherly cooperation with their striking brothers—evidences of solidarity so terrifying to the capitalistic class.

Solidaric strikes do not represent the battle of an isolated union or trade with an individual capitalist or group of capitalists. They are the war of the proletariat class with its organized enemy, the capitalist regime. The solidaric strike is the prologue of the General Strike.

The modern worker has ceased to be the slave of the individual capitalist; today, the capitalist class is his master. However great his occasional victories on the economic field, he still remains a wage slave. It is, therefore, not sufficient for Labor unions to strive to merely lessen the pressure of the capitalistic heel; progressive workingmen's organizations can have but one worthy object—to achieve their full economic stature by complete emancipation from wage slavery.

That is the true mission of Labor unions. They bear the germ of a potential social revolution; aye, more—they are the factors that will fashion the system of production and distribution in the coming free society.

The great giant of Labor must cease begging the master for a few more crumbs off the board of the wealthy. The supplicating posture of Labor, so strikingly illustrated in this issue by our gifted young artist Floyd Wilson, is the great shame and at the same time the terrible tragedy of Labor. May this giant soon learn to straighten his back, to look his masters straight in the face and realize the invincible economic power of united Labor to accomplish its great historic mission of abolishing wage slavery.

Then, only then, will the Dignity of Labor be vindicated and the true spirit and significance of the First of May translated into the actual emancipation of the working masses.

The Song of the Wage Slave
Ernest Jones

THE land it is the landlord's,
  The trader's is the sea,
The ore the usurer's coffer fills—
  But what remains for me?
The engine whirls for master's craft,
  The steel shines to defend,
With Labor's arms, what Labor raised,
  For Labor's foe to spend.
The camp, the pulpit, and the Law
  For rich men's sons are free;
Theirs, theirs the learning, art, and arms—
  But what remains for me?

  The coming hope, the future day,
    When wrong to right shall bow,
  And hearts that have the courage, man,
    To make that future NOW.

We bear the wrong in silence,
  We store it in our brain;
They think us dull, they think us dead,
  But we shall rise again:
A trumpet through the lands shall ring;
  A heaving through the mass;
A trampling through their palaces
  Until they break like glass:
We'll cease to weep by cherished graves,
  From lonely homes we'll flee;
And still, as rolls our million march,
  Its watchword brave shall be—

  The coming hope, the future day,
    When wrong to right shall bow,
  And hearts that have the courage, man,
    To make that future NOW.

A Voice of Protest

Alexander Berkman,
  San Francisco.

In reference to the suppression of your revolutionary paper, THE BLAST, we have some views to air. We have done so by writing to "the powers that be" regarding same.

We are living in an age of reason; and the theories of evolution and revolution have kept pace with time.

Prohibition of the use of the mails, as well as the suppression of freedom of thought and speech, proves conclusively to the workers of this land that they are living under the yoke of capitalism.

History and its traditions teach us that the struggle of the workers cannot be suppressed even by bloodshed.

From time immemorial the spirit of the toilers has not been trampled under without protest from all fair minded and intelligent people.

We, the workers of the world, ask not for favors. "Let all consult for all."

  Yours for freedom of thought and speech,
            Local 439, I. W. W.,
            Box 485, Brawley, Cal.

THE BLAST

Revolutionary Labor Paper
Published every 1st and 15th of the month
569 Dolores St., San Francisco, Cal.
Mail Address, Box 661   Phone, Park 499

Alexander Berkman, Editor and Publisher
E. B. Morton, Associate Editor   M. E. Fitzgerald, Manager

SUBSCRIPTION
$1.00 Yearly   60c Six Months   5c Copy
Bundle rates 2½c per copy in bundles of ten.
Advertising rates on application.
Entered as second-class matter at the postoffice at San Francisco,
Cal., January 14, 1916, under the Act of March 3, 1879.

Reflections

The Revolt in Ireland

REBELLION, individual or collective, is always good and justified. It is an indication that the spirit of resistance has not entirely been stifled. A very encouraging sign, for resistance to injustice and oppression is the cornerstone of true progress. Furthermore, rebellion is good practice. It strengthens the courage of the people and develops their defiance of authority and law. If successful, it imbues the rebels with greater confidence in the power of their will, as opposed to that of their masters and rulers: it tends to create more rebellion. If not successful, nothing is lost. For it is better and nobler to die on the barricades fighting the tyrant and his minions than to be killed in the factory slaving for the master.

Therefore I welcome the uprising in Ireland. Not that the Irish rebels really demand Land and Liberty, which alone spells freedom for the individual and well-being for the community. No. The present revolution in Ireland is of a Nationalist character. It demands "national independence," which is by no means synonymous with the liberty of the people, individually or collectively. National independence for Ireland, as for any other people, merely means substituting your "own" masters for those imposed on you. Nominally there is a difference; in reality there is none. The club of an Irish Republican policeman upon a Dublin citizen's head will hurt no less than the night stick of the English Bobby. It is not worth while shedding one's blood for a mere change of masters: that is, not worth while for a social revolutionist, for one who has looked *behind* the republican and democratic scenery and seen the same Master and Servant play going on, whatever the flag-rag sign on the billboards.

But the Irish Nationalist does not yet realize this. Therefore I'd rather see him rebel against England than remain passively submissive. But whether the uprising of Ireland is successful or not, the Irish people must learn sooner or later that their real struggle is not against England and its people, but against the lords of Land and Life who have enslaved the people of Great Britain no less than the Sons of Erin.

They will further have to learn that National independence is no cure for agrarian and industrial slavery, but that the salvation of the Irish people is to be found only in making common cause with the disinherited of all other countries, in a social revolution against the Universal Plunderbund whatever its national composition.

A Premium on Murder

TALK about the blessings of civilization! If absolute perversion of the human heart and mind constitutes progress, we have surely attained its apex. Apparently sane people, preachers and writers, are now strenuously championing the great revelation that a soldier killed in battle goes directly to Heaven, no matter how sinful his past.

They assure us that God will damn to eternal torture the man who, perhaps in the heat of passion, took the life of a fellow creature. But He will reward with extra generosity him who has systematically and with all due premeditation murdered great numbers of God's children.

This setting of a Christian premium on wholesale slaughter comes rather late in the day. The Mohammedans have beat them to it several centuries ago. But no monstrosity is too big for the good Christian to swallow. Behold the *greater* miracle of our modern civilization: Jonah swallowing the whale.

Direct Action

IT IS refreshing in these days of cowardly submission and fear for one's precious skin to find Emma Goldman refusing, on principle, to pay a fine and going to prison instead. She was sentenced to fifteen days in the Blackwell's Island Workhouse, but conditions on the Island are so rotten that the authorities did not dare send her there. I understand that Commissioner Lewis, of New York, said, "She is an intelligent woman and the conditions on the island are such, she would expose them after her release." As a result, Comrade Goldman is serving her sentence in Queen's County Jail, Long Island, presumably the cleanest prison that could be found for Emma Goldman.

The comparatively light sentence in this case and the recent dismissal of the Federal charges against Margaret Sanger are no doubt due to the pressure of public sentiment that is awakening to the need of Birth Control information. But neither of those cases really affects the law on the Federal and State statute books. The way to make the law inoperative is to *continue breaking it*. We are therefore glad to hear that at the monster Carnegie Hall mass-meeting arranged to greet the release of Comrade Goldman, on May 5th, a number of women are prepared to publicly and openly distribute the forbidden Birth Control leaflets, as we have recently done in San Francisco.

We commend this action to the women of other cities.

Speaking of breaking the law willfully and consciously, our readers will be interested in a bit of news that has been totally suppressed by the press as well as by the Federal government. On the very day of Emma Goldman's trial in New York, presiding Judge O'Keefe received a *special delivery letter* from San Francisco. The letter contained a very strongly-worded protest against the prosecution of Emma Goldman. It explained at length why and wherefore intelligent women favor Birth Control. As an evidence of good faith and determination, a *copy of the English leaflet describing methods of Birth Control* (recently published and distributed in San Francisco) together with a copy of the Italian translation *was enclosed in the letter to Judge O'Keefe.* FORTY women of San Francisco signed the protest, and thus made themselves legally liable to a term of five years in the penitentiary for sending the forbidden matter through the mails.

THE BLAST was suppressed for merely referring to that pamphlet. But the government dare not take action in the case of the women who actually sent the prohibited pamphlet by mail. It would never do to bring to trial *forty American women*—and the government quietly put its yellow tail between its legs.

Nay, more: they suppressed all information about it in the press, for the country would hold its sides with laughter when it learned that these San Francisco women actually made the Post Office take special pains in delivering to Judge O'Keefe, *quickly* and *safely*, the *pamphlet that must not pass through the mails.*

Ye gods, how Olympus must have roared.

David Caplan

IN REPLY to the numerous inquiries concerning the developments in David Caplan's case, I wish to say the following:

In the article, "David Caplan," in No. 10 of THE BLAST, I wrote that Caplan had finally decided—as I then believed—to have a revolutionary trial, and that for that purpose he had secured the services of Jacob Margolis, of Pittsburgh. Since those lines were written, the situation has changed. Caplan and Margolis could not agree upon the line of defense, and Margolis resigned and returned to Pittsburgh. The case has since been conducted by Nathan Coghlan and Edwin McKenzie, attorneys in the trial of Mathew Schmidt.

It is understood, of course, that every one has the exclusive right to decide on what lines his trial is to be conducted. Caplan has placed his fate in the hands of Coghlan, as his chief counsel—a lawyer without either sympathy for, or understanding of, the revolutionary labor movement. I regret the matter deeply and extend to David Caplan my sympathy.

※   ※   ※

IT is important to inquire whether it is not in the nature of uncontrolled power always to abuse itself. For my part, I have no doubt of it, and should as soon see the power that could arrest a stone in falling proceed from the stone itself as to trust force within any defined limits. I should like to be shown a country where slavery has been abolished by the voluntary action of the masters.

WAR is to kill the people and waste the land. Then settle around a table what could have been settled before.

HAVE two civilized peoples ever fought each other? If so, when? Name two peoples who, let alone by kings, dynasties, aristocracies and plutocracies ever fought each other. What did they have to fight for?

All Armor Plate—No Brains
B. C. Federationist

THE anti-preparedness movement has adopted a rather novel and effective method of putting a spoke in the wheel of the armor plate and munition boosters who are trying to coax, bully and frighten Uncle Sam into a huge military and naval "preparedness" obsession. They have built a huge model of the extinct "armored dinosaur," about fifteen feet in length and otherwise in proportion. This is mounted upon a truck and drawn through the streets, bearing upon one side the legend: "All armor plate—no brains," and upon the other, "This animal believed in preparedness; he is now extinct." It seems that this ancient dinosaur had no more intelligent way of overcoming the obstacles that confronted him along the pathway of his existence than that of continually putting on more armor in order to soften the effect of the bumps and jolts that he met with along the route. In consequence of this, he, in time, developed a body larger in proportion to the size of his brain than any other animal ever known, and became so weighted down with armor that he sank to extinction in the marsh lands of that age. His policy of life was truly the militaristic one of preparing to withstand the attack, instead of discovering and removing the cause which is responsible for it.

Possibly the Labor world might draw a valuable lesson from the life history of the dinosaur. For instance, let us suppose that the working class, or any section thereof, should refuse to extend its efforts beyond the mere setting up of defenses against the encroachments of capital upon the wages, working hours and other conditions of employment. This would be, in fact, equivalent to the continual addition of armor in order to soften the continually increasing blows. It would be following the route traveled by the dinosaur. By the same token it would result in extinction in the quagmire of oblivion. "All armor plate—no brains" would be the epitaph upon its tombstone. It may be that no section of the working class would ever follow so stupid a course. Then again it might be possible. We never can be quite sure as to what particular route will be taken by those whose horizon never extends beyond their jobs and whose ambitions never rise above a regular ration, of proportions most modest, indeed.

Once upon a time—well, let it go at that. It is a good story, and a true one, withal, because all true stories begin that way. It will be told at another time and many will marvel at the strange resemblance between the tale therein unfolded and the tale of the dinosaur's perambulations adown the boulevard of history. In the meantime let every workingman and woman set to work to study and understand the nature of that thing called capital that today rules the world, and against whose blows, encroachments and assaults the working class is forever trying to defend itself by adding to its armor plate. Perhaps the exercise of its brain power will disclose to the working class a more intelligent and effective means of escaping from the tyranny of capital than that of taking on scales of armor like a dinosaur.

The Basis of Modern Society

PRESENT society is based upon police, spies, and informers; the magistracy, the army, journalism, and cavil—deeply rooted and fatal elements—and I fear that their gangrene has so far eaten into the human mind, manners and customs that it will take a long time to eradicate it, for the police, spies and informers produce the abuse of confidence, calumny, denunciation, blackmail, suspicion and treachery.

The magistracy produces quarreling, suspicion, accusation, recrimination and base cowardice.

The army produces brutality, vanity, folly, rapine, barbarity, brigandage and assassination.

Journalism produces lying, jealousy, slander and defamation.

Courts of law produce equivocation, chicanery, insinuation, insincerity, double-dealing and dishonor.

So long as the people believe that they can obtain any benefit whatever by upholding these half-dozen demoralizing institutions, society will continue to be treacherous, cowardly, hypocritical, lying and barbarous.

A Case In Point

Alden Ward

THERE is probably no name more hated by American Labor than that of William J. Burns, the "hero" of the Los Angeles *Times* investigation, the man who brought "the dynamiters" to trial, the man who more than any other creature has had to do with the imprisonment of the McNamara brothers and Mathew Schmidt.

In another age, in another era, William J. Burns would be justly considered a criminal of the most dangerous sort. In our complex "civilization" he is lauded by press, pulpit and "public" as a great hero and scientist, a friend of "law and order." Still there are many who see William J. Burns as he really is. And hate him as a loathsome snake, fit only to be crushed beneath an iron heel.

But so far Burns has "gotten away with it." He is as yet unhung, and it is probable that he will continue to prosper and finally "pass away at his residence," a highly respected citizen.

In the meantime it is interesting to note that his friends and co-workers are getting into difficulties. Ever hear of Guy Biddinger? Well, he was once first lieutenant to William J. At this writing Governor Dunn of Illinois is wanting to see him on 51 charges. As the New York *Tribune* puts it: "He is wanted to face the ghost of an accusing past."

Biddinger was once a police sergeant in Chicago. Now he lives in New York, due to his association with the Val O'Farrell Detective Agency. It is from that city that Biddinger must go to call on Governor Dunn, and it is said to be practically decided that he will remain a guest of the State of Illinois for some time to come.

Among the reasons for Biddinger's trip to the Windy City are "an amazing series of crimes alleged to have been committed by Biddinger while a powerful member of the Chicago Police force," larceny, bribery, extortion, "assessment of graft and selling to prisoners their escapes." An interesting collection, indeed, with bail fixed at $80,000.

Let us remember that a man is known by the company he keeps, and that Biddinger and Burns were shoulder to shoulder during the period when Biddinger was achieving his present fame. It is in such hands as these that lies the fate of Labor's prisoners of war.

Incontestable Rights

A GENEALOGIST sets forth to a prince that he is descended in a direct line from a count, whose kindred, three or four hundred years ago, had made a family compact with a house, the memory of which is extinguished. That house had some distant claim to a province, the last proprietor of which died suddenly of apoplexy. The prince and his council instantly resolve that this province belongs to him of divine right. The province, which is some hundred miles from him, protests that it does not so much as know him; that it is not disposed to be governed by him; and, that, before prescribing laws for them, their consent at least is necessary. These allegations do not so much as reach the prince's ears. It is insisted that his right is incontestable. He instantly picks up a multitude, who have nothing to do and nothing to lose; clothes them with coarse blue cloth; puts on them hats bound with coarse white worsted; makes them turn to the right and left; and thus marches away with them to glory.

People at no small distance, on hearing that fighting is going on, and that, if they would join, there are five or six cents a day for them, immediately divide into two bands, like reapers, and go and sell their services to the best bidder.

These multitudes furiously butcher one another, not only without having any concern in the quarrel, but without so much as knowing what it is about.

Sometimes five or six powers are engaged, three against three, two against four, sometimes even one against five, all equally detesting one another, and friends and foes by turns, agreeing only in one thing, to do all the mischief possible.

A Timely Thought

THERE is double the pathos for us in the death of one little New York waif from hunger than there is in a million deaths from famine in China. It is not that distance glosses over the terrible picture of the Chinese horror, or that a feeling of national kinship with the waif impresses us the more sincerely with his plight. It is merely that the mind is unable to grasp suffering in the gross. Suffering is so intimately personal a thing that it must be explained through the personal equation, if at all.

For this reason there is grave danger of the very magnitude of the war hiding from us its real tragedy. We shall appreciate little the crime of a thousand deaths at the front unless we understand that each single one of these meant the tortures of hell for the man who died, a time of anguish for the kinsfolk, years of struggle for the widow whom the State will put off with a miserable pittance and a long, empty youth for the boys and girls over whom no parental care ever again will be extended.

To be found at the beginning of this conflict were many more tales than now of the individual horrors of the war, but these have simmered down to wholesale reports of casualties and destruction. The simmering down is part and parcel of a well-defined effort to keep the real facts from those who next will be at the front. But we, upon whom devolves the task of maintaining peace at least in our little portion of the globe, must not suppose that the terror of the war has decreased one whit simply because it is not being told.

Soldiers of War

René Benjamin

WHILE continuing to contemplate his feet in the water, moving them about to keep them from freezing, he said again and continually: "God Almighty!"

Bullets. Shells. Explosions. Crumbling. The quarters fell drop by drop, grain by grain in the desperate sandglass of this new, stupifying, horrifying life wherein men with vague minds and sore bodies waited in the fog, the cold, the mud, for Fate to show herself more compassionate. Confused images of home passed beneath their brows, but their flesh was frozen and numb under their stiffened cloaks; dull, awkward thoughts unfurled themselves within their minds, for they did not realize exactly why they suffered, cursing, swearing, freezing, dying, from discipline, from habit, like everybody. . . .

A foggy winter's day is in itself something so fatal that when night falls man is scarcely stirred by it. Gaspard put his wet rug over his head; and Mousse, trembling with cold, huddled up against him. The trench is as restless at night time as during the day. The men sleep, snore and moan, but they shiver and seek for comfort from each other. Seated or crouching, bunched up, their knees tight, their elbows well in as though to withhold the vanishing warmth, they crowd up against their neighbors with beseeching shoulders: physical brotherhood, moving and the most sincere.

The dawn, when it returns to these shiverings, is a wan, far more sinister hour than all the shadows of the night. To die then is no surprise, for it seems as though death's very shroud had grazed your eyes. With an empty stomach and chattering teeth you receive the command to keep ready for the attack and to fix the bayonet in the barrel of your rifle. The little click of weapons sends a shiver down your back. The weapons shine mournfully in the bleak light. And if your name is Mousse you remain silent, reflecting that a leap out of the trench means, no doubt, a leap into the other world. But if your name is Gaspard you simply wipe the hoar-frost off your moustache with the back of your hand and repeat your eternal "God Almighty!"

It's a refrain.

The trench, when you think you are living your last moment, is hard to climb. Then comes the surprise at being no longer buried; you seem to have grown; and, clenching hold of your rifle, you march gravely, your eyes searching for bullets. They come suddenly, sweeping the whole breadth of the atmosphere, and some men fall without a cry; but their fall face-forwards is interrupted by the weapon which slips and digs itself into the ground with the soldier hanging on it, stopped, impaled in a strange, frightful posture—dead and almost standing, half-slaughtered, horrible to see, like all corpses which do not seem at rest.

Mousse, as soon as the bullets began to whistle, said again to Gaspard:

"Eh, you won't forget my letter?"

And almost at once shells began to burst all around them. The enemy was three hundred metres away; they saw him grow out of the earth in little lumps of men which joined one another to form a moving wall. So they were to meet, to strike, to walk into each other. In spite of the bullets the French closed up.

The German wall became denser and approached nearer. A few holes lit it up: fallen men. The pointed helmets were now distinguishable. No one fired, and on each side the men marched on without a cry, gravely. But when the two troops were within fifty metres of each other they could be seen, as though someone from above directed them, inclined the one towards the right, the other towards the left, in a turning movement which seemed to have been agreed upon, or, rather, in a mutual terror to come into contact without having seen each other. They had to feel and look at each other, have time to hate; they were like dogs scenting and circling about one another before jumping at each other's throats.

But on this tragic calm new shells fell which tore, mutilated, and carried off pieces of the field and of the men.

One of them threw Gaspard and Mousse violently down.

When the thick, stinking cloud of its' smoke had vanished, Gaspard, stupefied, endeavored to rise. He fell again, saying:

"Oh, my leg! . . . God Almighty!"

His right leg was broken beneath the knee and hung limply, the trouser being torn and blood-drenched; and he stared in front of him, dulled, while his companions hurried on, head foremost, shoulder high, without taking notice.

He called in hollow tones: "Mousse . . . where are you?"

A voice answered:

"He's there, on the ground, his head opened, like a pie."

Gaspard jumped: "What? Is he done for?"

The voice answered, grumblingly: "More than likely."

Gaspard had not the strength to say any more. He was losing blood, and saw it flow and form a black spot on the ground. French and German were murdering each other; savage cries were heard. A new shell whistled by, fell, burst; the field opened, then rose, and an enormous wave of earth crumbled over Mousse's body. He was seen no more. The German guns had killed him: they buried him. The shell had made a hideous wound: it had at once dug his grave, laid him in it, and covered him. He returned to Earth without the aid of human hand. The war had struck him and kept him. Rest, following on death, at once. No fingering of the corpse, no pockets emptied, no groans, no words. Private Mousse: missing.

Gaspard began to moan.

"Ah! ah! William . . . if I could get at that pig."

Two stretcher-bearers approached who took him quickly, one under the back, the other by the arm-pits.

"Don't stiffen yourself. Allow yourself to be carried."

"Yes, yes; you're good coves; but if I held him, that pig!"

In spite of the shells bursting all around they rolled him on a wheeled stretcher as far as the road, where others undertook to take him to the ambulance. This had been fitted in a house in ruins, in a big cellar ripped open by shells. Gaspard, who was beginning to suffer and was suddenly raising himself on his stretcher, was laid down here.

Two surgeons approached. They said at once:

"My poor fellow, it'll have to be cut."

"Cut?" repeated Gaspard automatically.

"Yes, there," said the first surgeon.

"I don't think so: it had better be cut here," said the second surgeon. "Why there?" said the first. "Just as you like. Cut there," said the second. "No, no; I don't mind. We'll cut here," said the first surgeon.

Gaspard stared at them with his whole eyes, making an awful face and clenching his fists. Then he let his head drop and murmured once more: "God Almighty!"

His winter campaign has just lasted two-and-twenty hours.

※　※　※

HELPFUL PROTEST AGAINST THE POSTAL SUPPRESSION

M. I. Lerner, proceeds Los Angeles Picnic, $36.60;* Kitty Beck, Portland, Oregon, $15.00; Mr. and Mrs. M. Olson, Chicago, C. C. Everson, Palmyra, N. Y., $5.00; Amelia Fagerberg, Omaha, Neb., Charlie Tambrello, Cardiff, Ala., $2.50; Comrades of Albany, N. Y., per Rothberg, $3.50; Harry Schorr, St. Louis, Jennie Arnott, Palo Alto, Cal., Paul Munter, New York, Anna Bruce Sterrett, Washington, D. C., S. Cohen, Seattle, Wash., E. Belmont, Twin Falls, Idaho, J. L. Barker, Santa Barbara, Cal., $2.00; H. A. Erkelens, Seattle, Wash., A. Iglesias, Carmel, Cal., Fred Young, Springfield, Mo., Dr. Leo Kaplan, St. Louis, Mo., F. Rascher, St. Louis, Mo., Estelle M. Hughes, Eugene, Oregon, I. Mendelsohn, Allentown, Pa., John Chukan, Kenosha, Wis., M. Kisliuk, Washington. D. C., D. E. Wetzel, Denver, Colo., Dr. J. P. Pfeifer, Chicago, David Zimmerman, New York, A. Snellenberg, Seattle, La Claire, Seattle, D. Lorenzi, Gallatin, Pa., P. Cane, Brooklyn, Rose Stern, New York, John Snyder, Passaic, N. J., Wm. Shepps, Dover, N. J., $1.00; Karl Herlitz, Berkeley, Cal., 75 cents; C. Taraboi, Armo, Kansas, 60 cents; Gus Teltsch, Home, Wash., 50 cents; Jensen, Alameda, Cal., 25 cents; Picnic, Group Volonta, San Francisco, $37.00.

*The feat of Comrade Lerner who, *single handed,* arranged such a successful affair for the benefit of THE BLAST, is a striking demonstration what *one* man can accomplish, when willing and energetic, even in a graveyard like Los Angeles. Comrades in other cities will do well to follow the example of Lerner.

A. B.

Eight   THE BLAST

Young Folks

WHAT is Government?

Something that governs.

But what is it, a machine?

No, men.   Just men with power.

Has power of some men over all men ever been separated from tyranny?

Never.

Do the influential feel this tyranny?

Never.

Why not?

Because they make government.

Who are the influential?

The rich.

Who feel the tyranny?

The poor.

OH, papa! See the ragged man!

Yes, my son; that is a working man.

What is a working man?

A man who makes things; lots of things like clothes, houses, automobiles, furniture and good things to eat.

Then why does he look so ragged?

That's because he is a working man.

But don't working men make lots of things? Why don't they have something?

That, my son, is a deep subject. The working man hasn't got anything but his labor power. The capitalists own the machines.

Why, who made the machines, papa?

The working men.

Then why don't they own the machines, papa?

Because they don't want to.

Why, papa? Wouldn't that make things better?

Yes, but they seem to prefer to let the capitalists own the machines and the industries while they own nothing but the patches on their overalls.

Isn't that foolish, papa? I'd imagine they wouldn't like to have the capitalists take everything when they themselves can have lots of nice things by producing for themselves.

Yes, my son, you seem to understand sociology much better than the working people.—Ex.

| VOL. 1 | SAN FRANCISCO, MAY 15, 1916 | No. 13 |

THE CHAMPION OF FREEDOM AND DEMOCRACY

The Only Hope of Ireland

MOST Irishmen, in and out of Ireland, seem unanimous in condemning the brutality of the British government toward the leaders of the unsuccessful revolt.

There is no need to recite here the atrocious measures of repression practiced by England toward her subject races. The arrogant and irresponsible tyranny of the British government in this relation is a matter of history. The point of interest just now is, what did the Irish people, or at least the Sinn Feiners, expect England to do in the given circumstances?

I am not interested in the weak-kneed editors of Irish-American papers who bemoan, with all due decorum, Great Britain's "lack of generosity" in dealing with the captured Sinn Feiners, or who hide their cowardice by arguments about the "mistake" the British government has committed by its harsh methods.

It is disgusting to hear such rot. As a matter of fact, it is entirely in keeping with the character and traditions of the British government to show no quarter to rebels. Those familiar with the colonial history of Great Britain know that the English government and its representatives have systematically practised the most heinous brutality and repression to stifle the least sign of discontent, in Ireland, in India, Egypt, South Africa—wherever British rapacity found a source of aggrandizement. Burning villages, destroying whole districts, shooting rebels by the wholesale, aye, even resorting to the most inhuman torture of suspects, as in the Southwestern Punjab and other parts of India—these have always been the methods of the British government.

"The measures taken by us," said Sir Michael O'Dwyer, Governor of the province of Punjab, in his Budget speech in the Punjab Legislative Council, April 22, 1915, "have proven that the arm of the Sirkar (British government) is long enough to reach and strong enough to strike those who defy the law." The nature of this "long and strong arm" is clearly characterized by Lord James Bryce: "The English govern India on *absolute* principles. There is in British India no room for popular initiative or popular interference with the acts of the rulers, from the Viceroy down to the district official. Society in India is not an ordinary civil society. It is a military society, military first and foremost. The traveler feels himself, except perhaps in Bombay, surrounded by an atmosphere of gunpowder all the time he stays in India."

The Irish rebels and their sympathizers know all this. But what they don't know, or refuse to admit, is that these methods of suppressing discontent are not merely colonial policy. They have also been practiced by the English government at home, against its native sons, the English workers. Just now the iron hand of conscription is driving thousands of Great Britain's toilers into involuntary military servitude. Long terms of imprisonment are meted out to everyone having conscientious scruples against murder, to every anti-militarist protestant, and many have been driven to suicide rather than turn murderers of their fellowmen. The Irish people, like everyone else, ought to know that the claim of the English government of "protecting weaker nations and fighting for democracy" is the most disgusting hypocrisy ever dished up to a muttonhead public. Nor is the British government in this respect any better or worse than the governments of Kaiser, Czar or President. Government is but the shadow the ruling class of a country casts upon the political life of a given nation. And the priests of Mammon are always the ruling class, whatever the temporary label of the exploiters of the people.

We don't fool anyone by parroting that it was "a mistake" on the part of the British government to use the sternest methods against the Sinn Fein leaders. It was *not* a mistake. To the English government, to *any* government, the only safe rebel is a dead rebel. The ruthless shooting down of the insurrection leaders, the barbarous execution of James Connolly, who was severely wounded in the Dublin fighting and had to be propped with pillows that the soldiers could take good aim at him—all this may serve to embitter the Irish people. But unless that bitterness express itself in action, in reprisals—individual or collective—against the British government, the latter will have no cause to regret its severity. It is dangerous to let rebels live. If the Irish at home have no more spirit than the Irish in America, the English government has nothing to fear. The Irish-Americans are easily the most powerful influence in American political life. What have these Irish-Americans done to stop the atrocities of Great Britain? They have held a mass meeting here and there to "protest" against the continuing executions of the Sinn Feiners. They have sufficient political power in this country to cause President Wilson to call a halt to British atrocities, to force the English government to treat the Sinn Feiners as prisoners of war, which they are. But the Irish-American priests of Church and State would not dream of such drastic measures: politicians don't do that.

More effective yet it would have been if some member or members of the numerous Irish societies had captured a few representatives of the British government in this country, as hostages for the Irish rebels awaiting execution. A British Consul ornamenting a lamp post in San Francisco or New York would quickly secure the respectful attention of the British lion. The British Ambassador, in the hands of Washington Irishmen, would more effectively "petition" his Majesty, King Edward, for the lives of the Irish rebel leaders than all the resolutions passed at mass meetings.

After all, it is the Redmonds and the Carsons who are chiefly responsible for the failure of the rebellion in Ireland. They were the first to condemn the "rash step" of a people for centuries enslaved and oppressed to the verge of utter poverty and degradation. Thus they in the very beginning alienated the support that the uprising might have received in and out of Ireland. It was this treacherous and cowardly attitude of the Irish home-rule politicians that encouraged the English government to use the most drastic methods in suppressing the revolt.

May outraged Ireland soon learn that its official leaders are like unto all labor politicians: the lackeys of the rulers, and the very first to cry Crucify! when the people make the least motion to shake their masters off their backs.

The hope of Ireland lies not in home rule, nor in its leaders. It is not circumscribed by the boundaries of the Emerald isle. The precious blood shed in the unsuccessful revolution will not have been in vain if the tears of their great tragedy will clarify the vision of the sons and daughters of Erin and make them see beyond the empty shell of national aspirations toward the rising sun of the international brotherhood of the exploited in all countries and climes combined in a solidaric struggle for emancipation from every form of slavery, political *and* economic.

ALEXANDER BERKMAN

Revolution
Friedrich Nietzsche

There the gallows, rope and hooks,
   And the hangman's beard is red;
People 'round and poisoned looks,
   Nothing new and nothing dread!

Know it well—from fifty sources,
   Laughing in your face I cry:
Would you hang me? Save your forces!
   Why hang me who cannot die!

Beggars ye! who hate the tougher
   Man who holds the envied lot;
True I suffer, true I suffer—
   As to you—ye rot, ye rot!

I am breath, dew, all resources,
   After fifty hangings. Why!
Would you hang me? Save your forces!
   Would you kill me who cannot die!

Pro-Government Anarchists
Errico Malatesta

A MANIFESTO has just appeared, signed by Kropotkin, Grave, Malato, and a dozen other old comrades, in which, echoing the supporters of the Entente Governments who are demanding a fight to a finish and the crushing of Germany, they take their stand against any idea of "premature peace."

The capitalist Press publishes, with natural satisfaction, extracts from the manifesto, and announces it as the work of "leaders of the International Anarchist Movement."

Anarchists, almost all of whom have remained faithful to their convictions, owe it to themselves to protest against this attempt to implicate Anarchism in the continuance of a ferocious slaughter that has never held promise of any benefit to the cause of Justice and Liberty, and which now shows itself to be absolutely barren and resultless even from the standpoint of the rulers on either side.

The good faith and good intentions of those who have signed the manifesto are beyond all question. But, however painful it may be to disagree with old friends who have rendered so many services to that which in the past was our common cause, one cannot—having regard to sincerity, and in the interest of our movement for emancipation—fail to dissociate oneself from comrades who consider themselves able to reconcile Anarchist ideas and co-operation with the Governments and capitalist classes of certain countries in their strife against the capitalists and Governments of certain other countries.

During the present war we have seen Republicans placing themselves at the service of kings, Socialists making common cause with the ruling class, Laborists serving the interests of capitalists; but in reality all these people are, in varying degrees, Conservatives—believers in the mission of the State, and their hesitation can be understood when the only remedy lay in the destruction of every Governmental chain and the unloosing of the Social Revolution. But such hesitation is incomprehensible in the case of Anarchists.

We hold that the State is incapable of good. In the field of international as well as of individual relations it can only combat aggression by making itself the aggressor; it can only hinder crime by organizing and committing still greater crime.

Even on the supposition—which is far from being the truth —that Germany alone was responsible for the present war, it is proved that, as long as governmental methods are adhered to, Germany can only be resisted by suppressing all liberty and reviving the power of all the forces of reaction. Except the popular Revolution, there is no other way of resisting the menace of a disciplined Army but to try and have a stronger and more disciplined Army; so that the sternest anti-militarists, if they are not Anarchists, and if they are afraid of the destruction of the State, are inevitably led to become ardent militarists.

In fact, in the problematical hope of crushing Prussian Militarism, they have renounced all the spirit and all the traditions of Liberty; they have Prussianized England and France; they have submitted themselves to Tsarism; they have restored the prestige of the tottering throne of Italy.

Can Anarchists accept this state of things for a single moment without renouncing all right to call themselves Anarchists? To me, even foreign domination suffered by force and leading to revolt, is preferable to domestic oppression meekly, almost gratefully, accepted, in the belief that by this means we are preserved from a greater evil.

It is useless to say that this is a question of an exceptional time, and that after having contributed to the victory of the Entente in "this war," we shall return, each into his own camp, to the struggle for his own ideal.

If it is necessary today to work in harmony with the Government and the capitalist to defend ourselves against "the German menace," it will be necessary afterwards, as well as during the war.

However great may be the defeat of the German Army—if it is true that it will be defeated—it will never be possible to prevent the German patriots thinking of, and preparing for, revenge; and the patriots of the other countries, very reasonably from their own point of view, will want to hold themselves in readiness so that they may not again be taken unawares. This means that Prussian Militarism will become a permanent and regular institution in all countries.

What will then be said by the self-styled Anarchists who today desire the victory of one of the warring alliances? Will they go on calling themselves anti-militarists and preaching disarmament, refusal to do military service, and sabotage against National Defense, only to become, at the first threat of war, recruiting sergeants for the Governments that they have attempted to disarm and paralyze?

It will be said that these things will come to an end when the German people have rid themselves of their tyrants and ceased to be a menace to Europe by destroying militarism in their own country. But, if that is the case, the Germans who think, and rightly so, that English and French domination (to say nothing of Tsarist Russia) would be no more delightful to the Germans than German domination to the French and English, will desire first to wait for the Russians and the others to destroy their own militarism, and will meanwhile continue to increase their own country's Army.

And then, how long will the Revolution be delayed? How long Anarchy? Must we always wait for the others to begin?

The line of conduct for Anarchists is clearly marked out by the very logic of their aspirations.

The war ought to have been prevented by bringing about the Revolution, or at least by making the Governments afraid of the Revolution. Either the strength or the skill necessary for this has been lacking.

Peace ought to be imposed by bringing about the Revolution, or at least by threatening to do so. To the present time, the strength or the skill is wanting.

Well! there is only one remedy: to do better in future. More than ever we must avoid compromise; deepen the chasm between capitalists and wage-slaves, between rulers and ruled; preach expropriation of private property and the destruction of States as the only means of guaranteeing fraternity between the peoples and Justice and Liberty for all; and we must prepare to accomplish these things.

Meanwhile it seems to me that it is criminal to do anything that tends to prolong the war, that slaughters men, destroys wealth, and hinders all resumption of the struggle for emancipation. It appears to me that preaching "war to the end" is really playing the game of the German rulers, who are deceiving their subjects and inflaming their ardor for fighting by persuading them that their opponents desire to crush and enslave the German people.

Today, as ever, let this be our slogan: Down with Capitalists and Governments, all Capitalists and all Governments!

Long live the peoples, all the peoples!

☸   ☸   ☸

LET one imagine a number of men in chains, being beheaded every day in the sight of the others. Those who remain see their own condition in that of their fellows, and regarding each other with grief and without hope, await their turn. This is a picture of the condition of man.

—Pascal.

THE BLAST

Revolutionary Labor Paper
Published every 1st and 15th of the month
569 Dolores St., San Francisco, Cal.

Mail Address, Box 661   Phone, Park 499

Alexander Berkman, Editor and Publisher
M. E. Fitzgerald, Associate Worker   Carl Newlander, Assistant

SUBSCRIPTION
$1.00 Yearly   60c Six Months   5c Copy
Bundle rates 2½c per copy in bundles of ten.
Entered as second-class matter at the postoffice at San Francisco,
Cal., January 14, 1916, under the Act of March 3, 1879.

Reflections

Labor's Weapon

THE month of May, with its revolutionary traditions and aspirations, is indeed an inspiration to Labor. It may be aptly said that on the legalized September Labor Day the worker parades, but on May Day he takes stock of his wage slave condition.

Throughout the country the workers are stirring. Discontent at fighting pitch is manifest everywhere. Big strikes are taking place in most of the industrial centers of the country. Within the first week of May, according to figures compiled by the United Press, more than 800,000 workers received wage increases aggregating $75,000,000 annually.

When we consider that all this has been achieved by isolated strikes in separate industries, often even in the face of local and jurisdictional Labor fights, need we a better demonstration of the effectiveness of direct action on the economic field? Can anything gained by years of political begging compare with it? It is the most striking evidence of the power inherent in the solidarity of Labor. With that solidarity extended and grown more conscious, nothing within present society could resist the demands of the toilers.

Abolition the Cure

IT would be mistaken, however, to suppose that the increase in wages represents a *real* advance for Labor. It does not, if we consider the rise in the cost of living. The statistics compiled in the Public Health Bulletin No. 76, recently issued by the United States Public Health Service (working in co-operation with the Commission on Industrial Relations) shows that between 1900 and 1913 foodstuffs rose 60 per cent., while wages during the same period increased less than 30 per cent. The deficit between prices and wages has been even greater during the years 1914 and 1916. Thus the cost of commodities used as food advanced 106 per cent., while the increase in wages was about 25 per cent.

"If these facts are true," says Mr. Gompers, "then the entire Labor movement of the country has been a failure, and 50 years of my life and activity in that movement wasted."

The facts are indisputable. Statistical study of prices and wages proves it over and over, and these facts are quoted by officials of the American Federation of Labor in their demands for higher wages.

So far as actually—not seemingly only—raising wages is concerned, the Labor movement has certainly been a failure and Mr. Gompers' life entirely wasted. But the Labor movement has prevented the difference between prices and wages becoming even greater. Labor cannot rise above the level of its chains—*within* capitalism. It can rise only by breaking its chains, by abolishing the wage slavery of the capitalist regime.

Industrial Slaughter

THE losses on European battlefields, stupendous as they are, are less than the day-by-day slaughter wrought in times of "peace" by our industrial and economic conditions.

The United States is continually waging a bloody war within its own borders—a war in which the casualties sound more like the returns from the slaughter fields of Europe, but which in reality represent the numbers of workers killed and maimed in American industries and those reaped by the scythe of poverty, under-nourishment, occupational hazards and disease.

The report of the Commission on Industrial Relations shows that 250,000 adults are killed and 4,700,000 wounded each year by poverty and preventable disease, and that, furthermore, "each of the 30,000,000 workers in the United States loses on an average about nine days every year on account of sickness alone." These figures do not include the 100,000 American babies killed by poverty each year before they reach their first birthday. Such is the havoc that poverty, low wages and miserable conditions of existence play with the lives and health of the workers.

Fling these figures in the face of the political orator who mouths stale platitudes of the wonderful country you live in, with its freedom, prosperity and happiness.

Preparedness? Surely, we need preparedness for the worker against this terrible menace of capitalist aggression *at home*.

The Flag Superstition

JAMES A. MAURER, a Pennsylvania Labor union official and Socialist, in a recent speech in New York, quoted a military officer who had said "To hell with the Stars and Stripes" when strikers had carried an American flag at the head of their procession. The capitalist papers reported, with their usual honesty, that Maurer himself had said "To hell with the Stars and Stripes."

At this Maurer and the whole Socialist press have become much excited. They emphatically protest that Maurer was not and could not have been guilty of such a terrible crime.

Evidently the Stars and Stripes—the proud and glorious emblem of Ludlow, McKees Rocks, etc., is a sacred thing to the Socialists.

But not every one is a nationalist lickspittle. Professor William Lyons Phelps, who holds the chair of English literature at Yale, sees the glorious flag in a different light. In his recent lecture in Hartford, Conn., he said: "The flag and patriotism are but an illusion. It is not so much of a disgrace to spit upon the flag as to spill the blood of the nation upon it."

There is hope for a country that produces such men, even though he may soon learn, as did Professor Nearing, that fearless speech is not tolerated in an American university.

Prosperity—For Whom?

ACCORDING to their own statement, the *net* profits of the Steel Corporation for 1915 are $75,000,000.

The net war profits of the Duponts for 1915 are $57,890,758.

The annual report of the Bethlehem Steel Company shows net profits of $23,672,000 for 1915. It employs 22,064 people, all told. That is, the company "made" $1,077 per head for every employee.

This is called national prosperity. The workers, they that created this wealth—well, they are a negligible quantity. But there is good reason why the prosperous ones are strong for Preparedness.

Alarm Suppressed

PREVIOUS rumors concerning the suppression of the *Alarm*, of Chicago, were premature. But now word has reached us from Theodore Appel, the manager of the paper, that the *Alarm* has been forbidden the mails, definitely and absolutely.

With the *Alarm* silenced, the voice of the New York *Revolt* stifled, THE BLAST officially excommunicated, and *Regeneracion* threatened with the deprivation of second-class rights, the Post Office is doing rather brisk business in suppression.

No doubt it is a step in the direction of Preparedness. An *important* step. But the Federal authorities seem to forget that he who sits down on the lid of a boiling kettle may get a tender part of his anatomy badly burned.

Penalizing Education

SENDING Emma Goldman to prison for giving Birth Control information has not appeased the Beast of hypocritical morality. Now Dr. Ben Reitman has been sentenced to 60 days for a similar "crime."

The fighters for a better and happier childhood are able and willing to take the punishment that prostitute Justice visits upon them. But prison and jail will not silence the voice of the thousands of women crying for light and knowledge on a question most vital to them. The Birth Control propaganda must go on, will go on, till every home in this country is in possession of the forbidden knowledge.

THE BLAST is at all times ready to supply, on request, printed slips containing the necessary information.

Anti-Preparedness Demonstration

FROM reliable reports it is evident that great numbers of the workers of New York have been coerced into joining the Preparedness parade on May 13. That fact does not speak well for the courage and independence of the workers. But it also shows by what means the Preparedness mongers seek to manufacture public sentiment.

It is to be hoped that the Labor bodies of San Francisco will show different mettle. It is encouraging to note that representatives of several local unions emphatically repudiated any sympathy with the Preparedness demonstration planned for this city by the Coast Defense League. The suggestion that the Labor bodies of San Francisco organize an Anti-Preparedness parade is splendid, and should at once be acted upon. A Preparedness demonstration is the worst insult that can be offered Labor. It means to demonstrate their submission and servility to the munition grafters, and their willingness to slaughter at command their fellow workers equally submissive to their masters.

The workers of San Francisco have a rare opportunity to demonstrate their manhood and Labor-consciousness by organizing a monster parade and by declaring a boycott on the schemes of the patriots for revenue.

Trial of the Magons

THE trial of Enrique and Ricardo Flores Magon will begin in Los Angeles on May 31. Our readers know how intent the Federal government is on railroading our comrades to prison. Their intelligent and effective efforts in behalf of the peons have not been to the liking of the American exploiters any more than to the Mexican oppressors. Strong influences will be brought to bear to secure the conviction of the Brothers Magon. Technically they will be charged with having used the United States mails to spread "inflammatory appeals." But the real crime of our comrades was that they preached among the peons the great message of Land and Liberty, of emancipation from masters, both native and foreign. Their work interfered with the rich flow of profits into the coffers of the bloodsuckers, and that is the most unforgivable crime in the eyes of Wilson & Co. That's why the Brothers Magon will be made to suffer, but the rebels of this land can stay the hand of injustice by raising a country-wide movement, through their press and mass meetings, in behalf of our brave Comrades Enrique and Ricardo Flores Magon.

The Beast of Mammon

THE jury in the case of David Caplan brought in a verdict of disagreement. The Jungle Beast of Los Angeles is not appeased, however. It thirsts for more blood. In the Los Angeles *Times*, General Otis has already given the District Attorney the tip that Caplan must be forthwith brought to trial again.

There is no telling how a new trial may result. Besides, a new trial means another great expenditure of money from the meager funds of the workers. It would be much more economical, and more certain of result, if California Labor would serve notice on the Los Angeles authorities that the workers are opposed to a new trial and back up that notice by determination to call a General Strike on the Coast if their demand is not immediately complied with, and David Caplan, and Labor's other prisoners of war, released from the clutches of the enemy.

Should Labor Be Patriotic?

Lyov Tolstoy

TO keep the majority of men in submission, the minority in power employs the military caste.

Every government needs the army, first of all to keep its own subjects in submission, and secondly, to safeguard the exploitation of their Labor. But there is not only one government, there are many of them which all rule by violence and are ever ready to filch their neighbor's wealth created by subjects already reduced to slavery. That is why every government needs an army not only to keep in power at home, but also to defend its booty against greedy neighbors. The States are forced to compete in increasing their arms. The example set is contagious, as Montesquieu noticed 150 years ago.

Every increase in the fighting force by one State directed against its subjects causes uneasiness to the neighboring State and compels it to increase its army, too. If the armies today run into millions of men it is not only because of the fact that one State threatens another, it is also due above all to the desire to crush Labor unrest at home. One is the result of the others: the despotism of the governments grows with their power and their successes abroad, and their aggressive disposition keeps pace with their despotism at home.

This rivalry in armaments has brought the European governments to the necessity of establishing compulsory military service, which alone procures the greatest number of men with the least expenditure. Germany was the first to adopt conscription, and other nations followed suit. Thus all citizens have been called to arms to maintain the iniquities perpetrated upon themselves, so that *the citizens of a State have become the supporters of their tyrants.*

What is the motive power used by governments to induce peaceful nations to commit violence and murder? *It is called patriotism.* It is the art of proving that one group of population separated by a conditional imaginary line, called a frontier, is far superior and preferable in every way to another group of population which lives on the other side of this imaginary line. The most friendly relations, identity of religion, of language, of instruction, of common stock and most intimate friendship, do not prevent these two groups, at a given signal, from rushing at each other and cutting each other's throats, after the fashion of the most ferocious beasts. And the cause for this signal to kill is often a trifling misunderstanding on the part of the rulers of these two groups of people. These peaceful, good, friendly, laboring people throw themselves upon one another in such a case to destroy one another, invoking to their aid a God who, no doubt, must be a fierce Moloch, and both sides express the same blasphemies in the name of God and civilization!

Science: God's Mortal Terror

Friedrich Nietzsche

HAS the celebrated story been really understood which stands at the commencement of the Bible—the story of God's mortal terror of science? It has not been understood. This priest-book par excellence begins appropriately with the great inner difficulty of the priest: he has only one great danger, consequently "God" has only one great danger.

The old God, entire "spirit," entire high priest, entire perfection, promenades in his garden: he only wants pastime. Against tedium even Gods struggle in vain. What does he do? He contrives man: man is entertaining. But behold, man also wants pastime. The pity of God for the only distress which belongs to all paradises has no bounds: he forthwith created other animals besides. The *first* mistake of God: man did not find the animals entertaining. He ruled over them, but did not even want to be an "animal." God consequently created woman. And, in fact, there was now an end of tedium—but of other things also! Woman was the *second* mistake of God. "Woman is in her essence a serpent, Hera"—every priest knows that; "from woman comes *all* the mischief in the world"—every priest knows that likewise. Consequently, science also comes from her. Only through woman did man learn to taste of the tree of knowledge. What happened? The old God was seized with mortal terror. Man himself had become his *greatest* mistake; he had created a rival, for science makes godlike. It is at an end with priests and gods, if man becomes scientific! *Moral:* Science is the thing forbidden in itself; it alone is forbidden. Science is the *first* sin, the germ of all sin, *original* sin. This alone is morality. "Thou shalt *not* know." The rest follows therefrom.

By his mortal terror God was not prevented from being shrewd. How does one defend oneself against science? That was for a long time his main problem. Answer: Away with man, out of paradise! Happiness and leisure lead to thought—all thoughts are bad thoughts. Man *shall* not think—and the "priest in himself" contrives distress, death, the danger of life in pregnancy, every kind of misery, old age, weariness, and above all, sickness,—nothing but expedients in the struggle against science! Distress does not permit man to think. And, nevertheless, frightful! the edifice of knowledge towers aloft, heaven-storming, dawning on the Gods. What to do? The old God contrives *war:* he separates the peoples, he brings it about that men mutually annihilate one another (the priests have always had need of war). War, among other things, a great disturber of science. Incredible! Knowledge, the *emancipation from the priest,* augments even in spite of wars. And a final resolution is arrived at by the old God: "Man has become scientific. There is no help for it, *he must be drowned!*"

The beginning of the Bible contains the *entire* psychology of the priest. The priest knows only one great danger: that is science, the sound concept of cause and effect. But science flourishes on the whole only under favorable circumstances. One must have *superfluous* time, one must have superflous intellect in order to "perceive." Consequently man must be made unfortunate,—this has at all times been the logic of the priest. Only thereby, in accordance with this logic, come into the world "sin." The concepts of guilt and punishment, the whole "moral order of the world," have been devised *in opposition* to science,—in opposition to a severance of man from the priest. Man is not to look outwards, he is to look inwards into himself; he is not to look prudently and cautiously into things like a learner, he is not to look at all, he is to *suffer.* And he is so to suffer as to need the priest always. Away with physicians! *A Savior is needed.* The concepts of guilt and punishment, inclusive of the doctrines of "grace," of "salvation," and of "forgiveness"—*lies* through and through, and without any psychological reality —have been contrived to destroy the causal sense in man; they are an attack on the concepts of cause and effect. And not an attack with the fists, with the knife, with honesty in hate and love! But springing from the most cowardly, most deceitful, and most ignoble instincts. A priest's attack! A parasite's attack! A vampirism of pale, subterranean blood-suckers! When the natural consequences of a deed are no longer "natural," but are supposed to be brought about by the conceptual spectres of superstition, by "God," by "spirits," by "souls," as mere "moral" consequences, as reward, punishment, suggestion, or means of education, the pre-requisite of perception has been destroyed—*the greatest crime against mankind has been committed.* Sin, this form of human self-violation par excellence, has been invented for the purpose of making impossible science, culture, every kind of elevation and nobility of man. *The priest rules by the invention of sin.*

The Great Adventure

Herman Kuehn

THAT'S a great work undertaken by Luke North—"The Great Adventure." However much those of the insurgent temper may differ about doctrines and theories, "The Great Adventure" offers a rallying ground. As Luke North has said in *Everyman:* "'The Great Adventure' demands a free and open earth—and is more concerned to get it quickly than to prescribe the exact methods of achieving it."

Not much room here for politics, for theories or for sermonizings. Every intelligent man and woman knows instinctively that there's somewhat amiss with a social order in which idle land can be held from use. It requires no argument.

How to get rid of landlordism is the one great question. No matter what method is advised or proposed, all can gather under Luke North's banner and follow his leadership in "The Great Adventure." Tactics do not enter —they do not matter. Whatever your tactics, whatever your proposed policies, unless you are too proud to co-operate with others having an identical desire but preferring to pursue its gratification each in his own way, there is room for your energies in "The Great Adventure."

Whatever the appeal, be it to the spiritual and religious impulse, to the passion for humanity, to aspirations for freedom, for justice, for truth or any abstraction; be it for economic readjustments or the establishment of political ideals, all revolutionaires can adapt themselves to "The Great Adventure" and its purpose.

Socialists of both schools—the voluntarian and the compulsist—will find common ground in "The Great Adventure," for here, each augmented by the support of the other—they confront the common enemy. Singletaxers, to the extent that it is a free earth toward which they aspire and not merely the exaltation of a political plan, will not delay, but hasten, the opportunity to give practicality to their theory by joining in "The Great Adventure." Reformers of every school will find in "The Great Adventure" the help they crave for clearing of the ground.

Cheerfully I cast my lot with "The Great Adventure," —even so humble an academician as I may find a welcome in the ranks, although, according to the editor of THE BLAST I and "the thousands of radicals who have an education—what of them? Their usefulness in the revolutionary movement is nil."

Perhaps, despite that hasty verdict, some few of us despised "intellectuals" and "highbrows" may find, in "The Great Adventure," the opportunity of lifting their usefulness from the nil state—perhaps not to so exalted a level as is the usefulness of the more capable,—but at least enough to escape my comrade Berkman's impassioned condemnation.

EDITOR'S NOTE.—I love adventure. In fact, just now I am myself living through a very thrilling Adventure: the tenth anniversary of my resurrection from Pennsylvania. However, my friend Luke's "Great Adventure," and a reply to the several communications I have received regarding it, deserve more space than is at present at my disposal. In the next issue.

A Splendid Example

DEAR Comrade Berkman:
I am enclosing money order for seventy dollars, which was derived from a theatre performance arranged here for the benefit of THE BLAST, held on the 10th inst.

We were only two comrades when we first conceived of the idea of arranging a benefit—Meyer Adolf and myself, both practically unknown to the radical movement. Nevertheless, with an intense appreciation of the vital importance of a revolutionary "Blast" such as yours, we set to the task of making our affair a success—and this is the result achieved. Of course, this is a modest sum, but it shows what other comrades, better known to the movement, could accomplish toward insuring the future existence of THE BLAST. I feel sure that the lack of activity on the part of most comrades in this and other cities is not due to any indifference toward THE BLAST, but rather to the fact that they underestimate the amount of support which they are likely to receive. If they would only make an attempt, I feel confident that they would all be surprised at the readiness with which radicals generally would respond.

THE BLAST must survive in spite of all efforts of organized tyranny to suppress it! The fact that it is so distasteful to the enemy proves how vital its existence is to us and the revolutionary movements at large. Long Live THE BLAST!

Fraternally,
New York.   MORRIS BECKER.

Attention, Comrades of Chicago

IT is high time to stop theorizing as to the ways and means of bringing about the Social Revolution. *Start to act.*

THE BLAST and the *Revolt*, two revolutionary papers which proved a menace to the master class, have been suppressed by the postal authorities. THE BLAST is continuing to appear in spite of governmental prohibition. This paper is a splendid revolutionary publication, and you, Comrades, have the power to keep it going if you would only begin to act.

Send all possible financial help. Secure readers and subscribers, and spread THE BLAST in every part of Chicago. The suppression of the radical press is the greatest menace to the revolutionary movement. By supporting THE BLAST in its brave fight you can express your protest against the violation of the freedom of the press and further the revolutionary propaganda.
M. BURNSTEIN

1509 S. St. Louis Ave., Chicago, Ill.

Our Funny Column

"THE most bloody assault of the war is now taking place at Verdun. The Germans are utterly regardless of sacrifice. Whole units are being annihilated. At the proper moment a counter attack is expected to be delivered by the French, also without regard to cost of life or material."

German artisans, poets and artists destroying French artisans, poets and artists. Why? For what? For whom? Isn't it funny!

* * *

"The munition factories are working double shifts, night and day. Labor is getting its share of prosperity."

American wage slaves double shifting to slaughter European wage slaves. Isn't it funny!

* * *

"The step toward Preparedness is very well—but it ought to be understood as only a step. It will require far more to protect the American investments abroad, which are sure to follow."

And Samuel Gompers assures the President that "Labor" is with him in the policy of Preparedness. Isn't it funny!

* * *

We are to appropriate for Preparedness, as a beginning, half a billion dollars. There have been about a trillion minutes in the Christian era. The same amount of money would build hard surface trunk highways, developing the whole United States. It would endow half a dozen great universities. But it is to go into an army that won't be ready for four years—a navy that won't be ready for six years—and will be junk after it is ready. And Labor in some form finally pays all the taxes. Isn't it funny!

* * *

One war correspondent made a list of over eighteen hundred poets and artists killed—and then stopped. Think of the genius in art and science blotted out in this war. And for what? Isn't it funny!

* * *

And think of the hundreds of thousands, the millions of workers of the world blotted out who did not know they had a quarrel till their masters told them to kill each other. Isn't it funny!

* * *

And so Labor favors militarism if you call it "Preparedness." At least the leader of the A. F. of L. says so. Isn't it funny!

* * *

You women who are talking birth control, shut up! Didn't God say, "Increase and multiply"? Don't the employers need laborers? The more the cheaper. Aren't God and the Boss always on the same side? Birth Control! It's blasphemy against God and the employer. As for the babies, let them be born into hell. It's God's will. Isn't it funny!

FOR lack of space, account of "Helpful Protest" must be postponed till next issue.

PRISON MEMOIRS OF AN ANARCHIST
By Alexander Berkman
"This is the only book that I know which goes deeply into the corrupting, demoralizing psychology of prison life."
—Hutchins Hapgood.
512 pages, illustrated. $1.40 postpaid.

A B C Dialogue

A. Must not a poor working man wish himself at the devil, when he thinks how he is laboring hard all the day long, and gets so little, with scarcely a rag to cover his back, whilst so many thousand blue and red coats consume the fruits of his labor in vice and idleness?

B. Why do you complain of the blue and red coats? Is there not another vermin which consume our labor? I mean the black gowns!

A. The black gowns, my friend, are the supporters of religion.

B. The blue and red coats, my friend, are the supporters of the State.

A. Pray, sir, what is that which you call the State?

B. Pray, sir, tell me what do you call religion?

A. By religion I mean the archbishops, the bishops, the deans and prebendaries; their wives and mistresses, their legitimate and illegitimate children.

B. The State is the Queen's most gracious Majesty, her Ministers, her pensioners, their wives and mistresses, their legitimate and illegitimate children.

A. A most excellent State!

B. A most charming religion!

A. What you call the State I should call a corrupted government.

B. What you call religion I should call a corrupted church.

A. Our religion, sir, is founded upon the holy writings.

B. Our State, sir, is founded upon our most blessed constitution.

A. Say, rather, upon our blue and red coats.

B. Or, rather, upon the black and purple gowns.

A. But think for a moment of the eternal bliss which the church promises to the tithe and church ratepayers.

B. But reflect for a moment on the happiness which the government promises to its taxpaying, liege subjects.

A. Fudge!

B. Nonsense!

A. Sir, you are an infidel.

B. Sir, you are a Chartist.

A. Wretched citizens!

B. Miserable believers!

C. Tut, tut; hold your tongues, you fools, and listen to me: In a village in Hungary there lived two farmers—the drollest fellows under the sun. The one would not have destroyed one field mouse if you had given him a ton of gold, the other would not have allowed a slug to be destroyed if you had promised him the whole world, but the one who was fond of the mice saw perfectly the folly of his neighbor and laughed at him, and vice versa. Unhappily, the schoolmaster had not yet been abroad. Messrs. Martineau and Company's moral checks were unknown among the mice and the slugs, and they multiplied so fast that within a short time the labors of the farmers were entirely consumed by them.

A. Do you understand that?

B. Do you comprehend him?

A. Away with the slugs and the mice!

B. Away with the mice and the slugs!

C. Away with the vermin that consume in idleness the fruits of our industry!

A. B. C.—Amen!

—Scottish Chartist Circular, 1842

VOL. 1   SAN FRANCISCO, JUNE 1, 1916   No. 14

Ricardo and Enrique Flores Magon

JUSTICE and not bullets, is what ought to be meted out to the revolutionists of Texas; and from now on we should demand that the persecution of innocent Mexicans should cease. And as to the revolutionists, we should also demand that they be not executed.

"The ones who should be shot are the 'rangers' and the band of bandits who accompany them in their depredations.

"Enough of reforms! What we hungry people want is entire liberty based on economic independence. Down with the so-called rights of private property; and, as long as this evil 'right' continues to exist, we shall remain under arms. Enough of mockery!"

These utterances constitute the counts against the Magons. And for this they face from two to five years in the penitentiary!

Think of the Magons

Edgcumb Pinchon

TWO GRAND old veterans of the workers' fight are dying—in jail. One of them already has been removed to the county hospital; the other is still fighting death in the tank. They are awaiting trial on a grave charge—they mistrust politicians and have said so in plain print. In the columns of their paper they have advised the Mexican peons to stand guard over the land they have won—rifle in hand!

For this they have been beaten and tossed into the steel trap; their little hand-printed paper has been suppressed, and they themselves have been held incommunicado under an enormous bail.

These men were the first to face the monstrous Diaz. Driven from Mexico, they fled to the United States—only to meet persecution bitter and unrelenting. Five of the ten years they have passed in this country have been dragged out behind the Liberty Bell bars. And now they face another long term.

The names of Ricardo and Enrique Magon need no introduction where freedom is loved. As editors and publishers of *El Regeneracion*, issued in Los Angeles in the interests of free land and free men in Mexico and throughout the world, they have stamped strong memories on the hearts of the workers everywhere. For twenty years they have sacrificed health, ambition and wealth—for they are "hidalgos" by birth—and have risked death a thousand times in the service of their ideal—and ours.

The Workers' International Defense League of Los Angeles, organized "in the service of all those captured by the Enemy," is defending our old friends. At the time of writing the treasury is empty—and the trial is set for May 31!

Comrades, these men belong to you and you to them. Stand by them to the limit of your power. And if you care nothing for the individual victim where we all are victims, remember that the life of our press is at the hazard in this bold and impudent attack upon Ricardo and Enrique. Only by the most determined and unceasing resistance can we keep a breathing space about us.

Send all contributions to P. D. Noel, 621 American Bank Building.

Preparedness

I BELIEVE in a "Preparedness" of construction not of destruction.

I do not believe the way to prepare for peace is to prepare for war—the conflagration in Europe gives the lie to this. You get what you prepare for. They prepared for war and got it. I do not believe we need fear Europe in her exhaustion if we did not in her strength.

Does any one believe, seriously believe, the United States —the blood kin to all of Europe—need fear Japan? Japan is busy enough with Asia.

But if there be a risk, I think it better to take the chance, rather than the certainty of creating a military caste—a military spirit, a military standard of glory and patriotism in this country.

I know that "Preparedness" adds hundreds of millions to the tax burden (and the toilers finally pay the tax), but I see beyond this.

I know the battleship builders and munition makers will reap great profits, but I look beyond this.

I know the investors in foreign securities and in Mexican lands, mines and railways will feel they have an army to fight for them, but I look beyond that.

I see the children taught military ideals, blind obedience and an *unquestioning* "Patriotism" in the schools.

I see this young isolated country picking up the pestilence of feudal militarism just as Europe is burning it out.

I know there is not a French toiler, a German, Russian or Englishman who is really interested in this war. They turned in twenty-four hours from good will and intermarriages to a hate which is causing even the legless and armless wrecks in the trenches to tear each other like maniacs.

Why? What was their quarrel? What will they gain out of the final settlement? Are they acting by reason, or by passion inflamed by their rulers?

I see it as a war of "Preparedness" brought on by the masters, and fought for the masters.

I remember the words of Tolstoy which are indeed the words of history:

"To keep the majority in submission, the minority in power employs the military caste. Every government needs the army first of all to keep its own subjects in submission and make it safe to exploit labor."

I see that Preparedness means—we are setting our feet in that same path. Whether those now shouting for it know it or not, there are those who do know that in the future inevitable conflicts with Labor and the masses, a trained military caste will be valuable.

Labor will not be of that caste. Labor will have no arsenals, guns or ammunition of its own. The militia will be the middle class—the laboring class has no time. The middle class has always been the servants of the ruling class.

I do not fear a war from the outside, but I do fear one from the inside, if this "Preparedness" is carried into effect. For I believe it will make the peaceable solution of the economic social problem impossible.

I believe in another sort of preparedness. Prepare the children with ruddy cheeks and sturdy arms and legs. Prepare for them a happy childhood and schools which teach life, not only books. Be not afraid for truth, and broad toleration of every discussion. Prepare a government for the people, not the people for the government.

Prepare for liberty, not slavery.

Prepare a press which is for truth and not a prostitute for privilege. Prepare a pulpit which is for knowledge— lead where it may. Prepare courts which are for the Justice of Life, not of the law. Prepare a society in which there will be no unemployed in this undeveloped generous country. Prepare for the children a world where each may have his full share of life, love and happiness.

There is no preparation with force that will not end in force. No preparation to argue with bullets but the arguments will be with bullets. In "Preparedness" I foresee the forcible suppression of the struggling masses till it end in bloody revolution.

—CHARLES ERSKINE SCOTT WOOD

A Soldier's Song

Alden Ward

To be sung to the sound of drums, marching, at Labor's Anti-Preparedness Demonstrations

SUMMON me forth with trumpet and drum,
    I will come, I will come!
Summon me forth from my homely field,
Summon me forth from the harvest yield,
Summon me forth to my sword and shield!
    I will come, I will come!

Gather me in from hill and dale,
    I will come, I will come!
Gather me in to your flaunting flag,
Gather me in to the weary drag,
Gather me in to shoulder my Krag!
    I will come, I will come!

Order me down to the crimson trench,
    I will come, I will come!
Order me down to the cannon's breath,
Order me down to the flodden heath,
Order me down to a soldier's death!
    I will come, I will come!

Out of the Hell of a tortured soul,
    I will come, I will come!
Out of the Hell you have damned me to,
As you murdered me I shall murder you!
This is the cup that you would brew!
    I will come, I will come!

Shadows on Mist

Robert Morlett

SOMETIMES your heart becomes sick of the big important things of life. Your nature resents their attempted intrusion. Your brain seems to bend beneath the burden of them; and their imagined weight wearies your soul to death. Your mind becomes quite nauseated with the pride and honor of them. You feel tired; and you long passionately for some quick and sure escape from the enervating influence of the big important things that would swamp you.

After all, what are nobilities, and powers, and positions? Duty is only a slave-driver, and responsibility a sign of slavery. The majesty of endeavor falls on you. Righteousness feeds you up. Keeping the flag flying is a simile, or something like that, to turn down the corners of your mouth. The big important things, such as national soul, national need, national integrity, national indignation, and national all-pull-together-boys, serve but

to contract the lungs, and to shut out the sunrays. You soon begin to feel as if you were dying in a windowless and doorless cell. No wonder the heart sickens at big important things, and rushes to seek release in the trivial affairs of every day life.

And is any harm done? Hardly, for you escape to the open, the pure, the simple, and, it may be, the real. You leave the lies to grow gouty. You leave corruption to stew in its own juice. You leave national service to fatten and decay amidst its own filth. Behind you remain hypocrisy and clamor, suspicion, double-dealing, patriotic vice, and the tri-colored mammonism that takes its tints from the flag upon which it fawns. You shake off the parasites and trample upon the vermin. You dissever yourself from insanitary civilization; and, naturally enough, you approach nearer the heart of humanity.

Is it not true that the death of a son is more humanly interesting than the causes of the war? Is it not true that the suffering of someone near and dear to you affects you far more than the rights and wrongs of nations? Is it not true that the economic anxiety forced upon you by your brother patriots occasions you more worry and trouble than all the national needs put together?

Your heart bleeds painfully at the loss of your father. Compared to the torture of your lacerated love, the devastation of a whole nation is nothing. Yet the latter is a big important thing; and the former is a petty affair, easily to be overlooked, quickly to be forgotten, if we are to obey the appeals of the big important people, who are the priests of the shadows on the mists.

Thoroughly can you understand the lonely death of a son. Acutely can you grasp the affliction of a brother broken for life. Terribly can you realize the sordid misery of an incurable disease. Painfully can you comprehend the hopeless enmity between wages and foods. These are petty unimportant things, too trivial to offer opportunity for emphasis, too light and reasonless for consideration, too foolishly remote from the national conscience to petition attention.

Let us forget all the little affairs that make the fluid of life for us. Let us forget all the petty things of ordinary existence, the subdued, quiet, homely emotions, the goings and comings of life and love and death. Let us forget the commonplaces. Let us forget the social home life that we need and desire with all the inherited power of our natures. Let us forget everything we can realize; and let us remember the big important things we can only see as shadows on mist.

What does it matter if we can never hope to understand them? What does it matter if always they keep far apart from the progressive realities of our little lives? What does it even matter if we are inclined to be suspicious of them? It is our duty to conquer that mistrustfulness.

They are too big and important for our puny intellects. They are too big and important to harmonize with our life-needs. They are too big and important to be anything but unfriendly to our social welfare. Yes, perhaps; but we must have faith in these shadows on the mist; we must bow our heads to them in meek submission; we must worship, and, if necessary, immolate our lives and our life needs to them. We must forget the little unimportant things.

Ah! but we cannot. They come crowding around us. They take no denial. We must live, and we need them. If only we would learn the lesson they teach, it might be that amongst *the first things to disappear would be those terribly anti-social shadows on the mist.*

🏺 🏺 🏺

WE carry faithfully what we are given, on bruised shoulders, over rough mountains, and when perspiring, we are told: "Yea, life is hard to bear!" But man himself only is hard to bear. The reason is that he carries too many strange things on his shoulders. Like the camel, he kneels down and allows the heavy load to be put on his back.

—Nietzsche.

THE BLAST

Revolutionary Labor Paper
Published every 1st and 15th of the month
569 Dolores St., San Francisco, Cal.

Mail Address, Box 661   Phone, Park 499

Alexander Berkman, Editor and Publisher
M. E. Fitzgerald, Associate Worker   Carl Newlander, Assistant

SUBSCRIPTION
$1.00 Yearly   60c Six Months   5c Copy
Bundle rates 2½c per copy in bundles of ten.
Entered as second-class matter at the postoffice at San Francisco,
Cal., January 14, 1916, under the Act of March 3, 1879.

Reflections

Preparedness Psychology

THE advocates of preparedness parades are shrewd psychologists. They know, of course, that quantity, numbers prove nothing to the intelligent man. But they also know that the great voting herd is not made up of intelligently thinking beings. Size, large bulk, great numbers are imposing, convincing arguments to the average individual. Hence the idea of monster preparedness parades; the unthinking man is, like unto the Lord of Hosts, always on the side of the largest numbers. In this sense he may properly be said to be godlike.

Great pre-election parades and torchlight processions have latterly gone out of style. But two decades ago those were the chief argument of the politician to prove the justice of his cause and the undisputable fitness of his candidate. Candidates and platforms come and go, but the politician is always with us. His method is unchangeable; it is the unfailing appeal to the lowest intelligence and mob psychology.

To Abolish War

IT IS a promising sign that Labor bodies in various parts of the country are beginning to awaken to the heinous schemes of the militarists and their preparedness campaign. To offset the effect of the jingo parades it is well for the workers to organize anti-preparedness demonstrations in every large industrial center. Indifference of the toilers to this the greatest menace now facing them is a strong encouragement to the patriots for profit. It is therefore urgent upon the workers and all others opposed to militarism not only to boycott and remain away from the preparedness parades, but to more positively and aggressively crystallize and demonstrate their opposition to organized murder. Great anti-preparedness demonstrations are therefore of immediate necessity. That alone, however, will not do. At best such demonstrations, like all similar massings of people, are very negative in character; passive, I almost said. Something more positive, more active is needed.

Labor has been protesting and demonstrating for these many years but nothing has been or ever can be achieved by mere passive protest, be it at the ballot box or on the street. To be effective the voice of protest must be backed by determination to make good. Protest presupposes intelligent opposition to a certain condition or situation. But even the most intelligent opposition is ineffective if merely theoretic. There are thousands, aye millions of men all over the world strongly opposed to killing and murder, yet the European slaughter goes right on. Their opposition is theoretical, passive, not active. Aye, in the trenches there are at this very moment millions of soldiers conscientiously opposed to war and sick of bloodshed—and they keep right on loading their guns and shooting their fellow men, their brother workers, their "revolutionary" comrades even, who are equally opposed to war and as heartily sick of the whole business of murder.

No, such opposition won't do. It accomplishes nothing. It leaves things as they are. It finds superficial and purposeless satisfaction in protests and petitions, respectably ineffective demonstrations, and in the inane feeling of "conscious superiority."

I repeat: protest, intelligent opposition, must—to be effective—be backed by determination to act. The will to action is the vital need.

Today a great labor demonstration against war and preparedness. Tomorrow the very same workers hurrying back to the munition factories to continue the manufacture of the implements of human slaughter! Continuing to produce the very objects that make wars possible, even necessary.

Men of labor, brother workers—you, you alone have the power to call Halt! to war and make human slaughter forever impossible. You, the army of toilers, hold the key to the great problem of universal peace. In your hands is the solution if you but have the Will to Action. The menace of militarism and preparedness will disappear when **you refuse to produce the implements of human slaughter.**

Thus, thus only can a labor anti-preparedness parade be made dignified, purposeful and fundamentally effective.

The Great Adventure

LUKE NORTH, editor of *Everyman*, is the father of the Great Adventure. Last year, when he first spoke to me about it, he pictured it a truly great social adventure: the spontaneous uprising of the people against monopoly and privilege, against landlordism and the holding of the Earth out of the use of the common people. An uprising that involves the breaking down of established tradition and precedent, the bold defiance of rule and regulation, the denial of the sanctity of legal possession and parchment lore. In truth, a Great Adventure.

I believe there is nothing more potent in the individual as well as in the collective life than the appeal of the Ideal. The urge of freedom, of independence, the joy of life, the social instinct, the love of family, of country, of humanity—these are the passions of Man. Wrongly directed, they make for murderous patriotism, persecution of unpopular ideas and social antagonisms. Properly directed, these very forces would rejuvenate the world and transmute this vale of hatred and tears into a world of sunshine and laughter.

But to be thus directed, our appeal to the people must be based upon the fundamental idealism of the human heart. An appeal that shall set the minds and emotions of man aflame with the fire of Liberty, of free Manhood, and in the quest of this great Social Grail be inspired by the joy of Daring, the hope of Achieving.

I know that my good friend Luke shares this view. But with full appreciation of the sincerity and devotion of the workers in the Great Adventure, I must frankly say that the methods employed are not designed to inspire either the joy of Daring or the hope of Achieving.

What matter the methods—I am told—so long as we accomplish the Great Adventure? And why—they further argue—should not all libertarians, rebels of every school and shade, for once unite upon this great object?

Indeed, there is too much enervating division among the radicals. Too much hairsplitting over philosophic differences, too many isms, too much narrow patriotism to one's particular church and creed. No one regrets this lack of unity and cooperation, this sad lack of understanding, more than I do. In fact, the chief purpose of THE BLAST is to get the rebels throughout the country in closer touch with each other, to develop a better mutual understanding among them, to crystallize the scattered revolutionary sentiment in some definite, active expression, regardless of theoretical differences and varying isms. THE BLAST is open to, and we are anxious to co-operate with, every and all revolutionary elements, irrespective of their program for the all-too-distant future. THE BLAST is an open revolutionary forum in the fullest sense.

But every intelligent man realizes that such co-operation can proceed only upon some common basis. There can be no unity of thought or action among people differing in their fundamental conceptions. Forced co-operation among such can lead only to confusion and disappointment, and is doomed to failure from the very beginning.

To be successful, to be even educationally worth while, illuminating, the Great Adventure and all similar projects must make it its first, perhaps even its exclusive purpose, to emancipate the people from their hoary prejudices and traditions. I don't care what our plans for the future, there will never be taken the first step toward the Dawn till we have undermined and destroyed the universal belief that "the other fellow" must be held down, forced to conform and to live by rule and regulation. In other words, the spook of authority walking in almost all of us must be driven out before we shall have at least that modicum of liberty without which social life is a dismal failure and curse.

To gather signatures for a petition to put the Great Adventure on the ballot, to direct men and women to the voting polls, be they Single Tax, Socialist, Labor, or what not—these are the cogs and wheels of present day society. They are there to keep the existing machinery of our social and political life going and intact. However you may manipulate that machinery, it is designed to serve but one purpose: to stupefy the mind, to weaken the will, to paralyze independent thought and action —in short, to kill the spirit and purpose in the endless meshes of the complex political machinery.

An appeal to the policeman for protection gives him added dignity and power, and makes him the more necessary. Playing politics, using the machinery of courts, of law and government, merely serves to strengthen these institutions, destroys the initiative and self-reliance of the individual, deludes the masses with the hope of reform through politicians, and perpetuates the belief in the authority and faith in the justice of our rulers and masters.

Not on that road lies the solution of any social problem. You will persuade the Lords of the Earth to get off their unused acres when you have induced the Captains of Industry to get off the back of Labor. Not till then. The Masters of Life will not allow you to manipulate their own game to their detriment. They will give you this and that political plaything as long as it does not endanger their seat in the saddle. But there will always be rider and ridden as long as we merely tinker with their relative position.

The monopoly of land is not the real issue. Nor, alone, the monopoly of the mechanical means of production and distribution. Our motto must be, Land and Machinery. Free land alone will solve absolutely nothing. Without free access to the means of production and distribution, the land is useless.

Neither can be had separately, or is to be gotten for the asking. It is pernicious activity to lead the people to believe so. It is this belief that is the cornerstone of man's slavery.

In the Camp of the Enemy

THE case of the Brothers Magon is in the hands of the jury as we go to press. Of course, Comrades Enrique and Ricardo have no faith in the justice of the courts. Old seasoned veterans of the Revolution, they are prepared again to seal their devotion to the great cause of free Mexico with their lives, if need be.

My personal impression in the court room strengthened my conviction that a revolutionist gains nothing by resorting to legal technicalities. It is equally naive in the political as in the judicial arena to hope to beat the masters at their own game.

Our Comrades Magon of course know it. But unfortunately their imperfect command of English made a personal, revolutionary defense by themselves impossible. However, they made the best of the situation on the stand, in spite of continuous interference by Prosecutor and Judge.

Whether doomed to prison or not, Enrique and Ricardo Flores Magon will continue to inspire the great Mexican struggle with their own lofty ideals and devoted courage.

The New Strike

THE striking longshoremen of San Francisco seem to have chosen effective methods to bring the ship owners to their senses. The million dollar fire on the water front is a good beginning. Repeated visitations of the "red cock" will impress the masters with the novel idea that the strikers are "on the job" even if they have quit work.

When the industrial slaves not merely lay down their tools but actually strike a blow in behalf of their interests, the bosses soon come to the conclusion that the "common good" demands a quick settlement. That is the history of every strike, small or big. If the toilers would apply this lesson on a larger scale, wage slavery would not survive very long.

Perhaps the near future has in store a strike of solidaric Labor, throughout the country, that shall initiate a more positive phase of the Labor struggle. A strike that shall no longer demand a few more crumbs off the table of the masters. Rather one that will make no demands whatever, but which will simply exclude the employer parasite from the scheme of things. Instead of leaving his work, for instance, the New Strike will take possession of factory, railroad, of mill, field and ship, and organize production and distribution on the basis of free exchange without bosses and without profits.

Then exploitation and poverty will disappear, and life be worth living.

To the People of San Francisco

Whereas, The police and press have continued to misrepresent the facts in connection with the killing of Sergeant Moriarity and thereby destroying the character of a great revolutionary soul by leading the public to believe our comrade, Vladimir Osokin (Philip Ward), a crook, a bandit or a counterfeiter, instead of what he, even in his dying hour, was not afraid to seal with his life blood in the words: "I am not a bandit, but an Anarchist Communist."

Whereas, We, his comrades, knowing his real character, his high ideals, his great soul in the cause of humanity, feel the necessity of sketching his character, life and beliefs as we knew and loved him.

Whereas, It is known to us that Vladimir Osokin (Philip Ward) was a Russian political exile, a man of brilliant learning in his own country, and one who withstood the tortures of the Siberian prisons of the Czar, and escaped to this country still imbued with the lofty principles for which he had suffered

persecution in Russia, namely: the education, the organization and the rebellion of the masses of Labor to free themselves from industrial slavery and poverty.

Whereas, It is known to us, his comrades, that he has been an active spirit all over this country in organizing and stimulating the spirit of resistance to oppressive industrial conditions generally, especially among his own people, the Russian workers.

And Whereas, It is known to the Russian working men of the Union Iron Works that he was the leading spirit in gaining solidarity among them, and that he wrote their manifestos and demands and was prominent in their councils in their recent strike for better working conditions.

And Whereas, It is known, and the police do now know, that our comrade, Valdimir Osokin (Philip Ward), was sent on an errand from the lunch stand near the Union Iron Works, where he worked, to the car barns near by to change a $5.00

gold piece into small change, necessary at the lunch stand, and that further, owing to the early morning hour and his inability to speak or explain himself in English, the car barn employes became excited and took him either for a bandit or a counterfeiter. They summoned the police, who on arrival laid violent hands on our comrade, who not understanding what was the cause and probably believing that he was to be jailed for his strike activities, resisted such violence with the same means that would have been employed to subdue him, even knowing that such an act would cost his life.

Now, therefore, Be It Resolved, That this manifesto be published that a great revolutionary character shall not die unheard, unhonored and unsung.

THE VOLONTA ANARCHIST GROUP
UNION OF RUSSIAN WORKERS
FREEDOM GROUP
FEDERATIVE COMMITTEE OF THE
    RUSSIAN RADICAL ORGANIZATIONS
THE BLAST GROUP

Why Women Will Get the Vote
B. C. Federationist

MORE than 70,000 women are now employed at skilled and semi-skilled trades in Birmingham, England. Presumably this is but an instance of what is being brought about as one of the results of the war, not only in England but in all the rest of the war-cursed countries. The introduction of female labor into a large number of industries and at skilled occupations heretofore filled solely by male workers, affords grounds for much speculation as to what the status of the male worker is to be in industry after the war ends and matters are once more adjusted to a peace level. The question naturally arises, will the female workers quietly abandon their new-found employments and meekly revert to their former economic level in the productive process, or will they insist upon clinging to that which the fortunes of war have placed in their hands, regardless of the protests and demands of the erstwhile aristocrats and semi-aristocrats of the Labor world who find themselves thus displaced?

As a matter of further speculation it would be quite interesting to know just how the masculine job-chaser is going to act in the face of this increased competition that he may be called upon to meet. We note already that the Liverpool longshoremen have threatened to go out on strike unless the women who have invaded their ancient and honorable calling at the Leyland line docks in that city are discharged. This may possibly presage another war to follow close upon the heels of the present fratricidal holocaust that is rending Europe. A war between the sexes over the possession of jobs instead of a war between national bands of commercial brigands over "places in the sun," "the freedom of the seas," "the rights of small nations," for "civilization," for "kultur," for "freedom," for "democracy" and other things too numerous to mention, as well as "self defense," which is thrown in for good measure. That a sex war is more than apt to occur as a result of this opening of the door of opportunity to the so-called weaker sex, through the necessity arising from war conditions, has been already pointed out by at least one French observer. It is not readily seen how such a struggle can be well avoided, for it is scarcely possible that the female workers will abandon the economic advantage they may have gained, or the male workers relinquish that which they have so long held, without a struggle.

To anyone at all acquainted with the nature of the capitalist beast, the attitude of the employer of labor in such a controversy is a foregone conclusion. He will become as valiant and noisy a champion of woman's rights, espe-

cially the right to work where she will and for such wages as she may be forced to accept, as he now is of the rights of the male workers to do similar things for the peace of mind and repose of the soul of those who, by divine providence, have been duly appointed to "give them work," irrespective of sex, color, race or creed. Women having proven equally or more profitable, will not be dispensed with by the employers of labor because of the pitiful wailings or noisy threats of male job-seekers who may feel aggrieved thereat. After having fought for their respective countries, and saved them for their masters, those who are either lucky or unlucky enough to return to civil life will face conditions infinitely worse than anything they even dreamed of before. The breaking down of the last remaining barriers that have thus far prevented the complete sacrifice of woman upon the altar of profit in the competitive shambles of the capitalist wage mart, by her swift and complete introduction into the skilled and semi-skilled trades, will augment and emphasize the sacrificial agony that Labor has suffered since the first slave was sweated in order that a sweet savor might arise unto the nostrils of his master.

The noisy advocates of "votes for women" may rest assured that their pet hobby will go through with flying colors as soon as the war is ended. Industrially emancipated woman must needs be armed with political power in order to withstand such assaults as might be directed against her by those masculine workers who might feel exceedingly sore because of her having invaded those industrial precincts previously held sacred to themselves. The master class will see that she gets the franchise. There is little doubt of that. And with her franchise she will become a bulwark of defense to everything that is conservative in political and industrial life. The political activities of woman in those localities where she has already received the franchise leads inevitably to that conclusion.

Hoist the Flag of Betterment
Copy of Letter Sent to Edward Swann, District Attorney, New York

SIR: As a lover of children, as a believer in the right of every child to health, happiness and opportunity, I address myself to you with reference to the recent arrest of Emma Goldman in New York City on a charge of disseminating information relating to methods of birth control. I happen to be a personal friend of Emma Goldman, but that fact is not guiding me to protest in the present connection. I consider, and reason supports me, that the issue of birth control is larger than any individual, any sect or any antiquated conviction based on indifference to the welfare of the child itself.

You happen to represent one little district—a very little district if measured by the broad conception of human relationships, human worth and human possibilities. New York, even though unnecessarily crowded to the point of suffocation, weighs only a modicum in the world's scale of action, discernment and accomplishment.

But even so, you represent the venomous clutch of a backward society which in the main thinks only of delivering blows and not at all of the effect of the bruises. In your capacity of district attorney you are in the fullest sense the agent of the present and serve as changing passion dictates to carry out the fiats of unawakened conscience. Nevertheless, I think you will admit that you are supposed to represent the intelligent minority as well as the dumb, cloven-brained, unthinking majority. Did I not believe this to be the fact, I would not bother to address you.

You may not know it, Mr. District Attorney, but birth control is not new. It has been practised successfully for a very great number of years. In proof of this contention it is only necessary to cite the numerous couples of means who have either a few children or none. Incidentally, I may say to you that I was a professional nurse for many years, and I know it to be a fact that the use of preventives even among the bourgeois class is general.

Now and then through carelessness these secret defiers of lawful decorum find it necessary to resort to an abortion, but statistics will bear me out when I say that there is an over-supply of practitioners at all times able and willing to put an end to unwelcome human life—providing the elastic fee for such services is forthcoming; and all this notwithstanding the fact that law is supposed to prevent the commission of abortions. All of which bears only on the cases of those who have the price. It does not touch the poor who, alas, have to pay dearly in added burdens for their lack of knowledge.

Now if a woman in comfortable circumstances desires children, that is her right, her just due, her privilege; but the case of the poor, ignorant, over-taxed mother is entirely another matter. Who are you or who am I that we should impose trials on another merely because we happen to cling to an outworn notion that woman's body is neither more nor less than a receptacle for the whims of chance? What manner of effrontery is it that dares appropriate the term intelligence to itself and at the same time sentence womankind to a compulsory service which she can't either in justice to herself or her offspring bear?

I answer you that such an infliction is the product of a mouldy conception that too long has had the say over innocent victims borne into life without their sanction. I say to you that our world is blood soaked this day because the hand of willful ignorance, superstition and unseeing prejudice guides the destinies of men—the same hand that would still force woman to conceive children on a basis of indifference to their welfare. I say to you furthermore that only insanity will insist on over-working an exhausted product, and that even if the bearer, in the case of children, be conditioned, what sort of an intellect would deliberately will our future generation a bequest of indigence, frailty and want of opportunity? I do not have to tell you the poor receive such a portion. You can look about you anywhere and see that they do.

It is the children of the poor I speak for—the sickly, ill-nourished, stunted dupes of a callous-visioned pseudo-civilization. In behalf of the child, of any and every child, I tell you that you do wrong if you lend your energies toward the prosecution of any individual who shall stand fearlessly for lifting the curtain which shuts out light, knowledge and life from the great submerged human mass. You do yourself a greater injustice than you could possibly do any torch-bearer of enlightenment if you knowingly, willfully aid the powers of night to stem the approach of a better day.

Knowledge is what is needed—free, frank, open knowledge which shall be no man's secret, but the possession of all men and women who need and desire it. Whether the information relates to birth control or any other vital theme, any and all knowledge which will benefit mankind should be made accessible without hindrance to the human race.

Not for Emma Goldman do I speak to you, but for the children who are to come after both her and you. Not every man is given an opportunity to help hoist the flag of betterment, but in this case a really great one is given you. You have the chance to show that you are a man of appreciation, of sympathy, of discernment; that you would not willingly inflict misery on dumb defenseless souls; that if your voice is to be heard, it will be heard in defense of little children, not against them.

I am going to hope that you will hear what I have said to you. It is a long cry, a lasting cry—one that touches the fiber of well-being for all of us to the uttermost depths of thought and feeling. In the end this sphere will be a fit habitation for the sons and daughters of men, I hope; but meantime individuals can accelerate progress by standing for it. *You* can assist by lending your aid to a cause which is worthy of any man's support. I am, sir, sincerely yours,   REBEKAH E. RANEY

"The Pest and Other Plays"

"THE PEST, and Other One-Act Plays," by Emanuel Julius, is now ready for distribution. In "The Pest" the writer pokes fun at American novelists. This play contains a criticism of American literary art in a form that is most attractive. His second play, "Slumming," is frankly a Socialist's opinions on present-day conditions. The third, "Adolescence," hits puritanical intolerance. The plays may be obtained by writing direct to Emanuel Julius, Box 125, Girard, Kans. Enclose ten cents.

YOUR laws do not prevent robbery; they cause it. They first make the thieves and then they hang them. Everywhere in this country of yours I see idle landlords living on the toil of helpless tenants, the idle few enriched, the hard-working many becoming paupers, and so thieving for their bread. In fact, the whole social system seems to be a conspiracy of the rich against the poor, its whole legal system a device for sanctioning that conspiracy. * * * The ownership of private persons in land and proprietary claims must be abolished and exiled; till that is done, poverty and wretchedness and crime are inevitable.   —Sir Thomas More

Notice to Readers of The Alarm

1605 Milwaukee Avenue,
Chicago, Ill., June 1, 1916.

Comrades:

The postoffice officials have notified us that all past issues of the ALARM are unmailable. As we have no intention of changing the policy of the paper, we will not be able to send it out as heretofore. But we are determined to continue the publication and to get same out to the subscribers and to reach the workers of this country with our propaganda.

As our expenses will be more than doubled, we must ask your financial aid. Send us a donation and help us to carry on the propaganda against ignorance, poverty and oppression. Order bundles of fifty copies or more for distribution every month. We will ship by express.

Yours for freedom,
THE INTERNATIONAL PROPAGANDA GROUP OF CHICAGO

HELPFUL PROTEST FUND

John Snyer, Passaic, N. J., $1.00; Jennie Arnott, $2.00; Group II Risveglio, Ybor City, Fla., $2.50; S. Applefield, Baltimore, Md., 50c; J. H. Grigsby, Louisville, Ky., $1.00; S. O. Bishop, Baton Rouge, La., $1.00; Francis Donnelly, $1.00; E. Trusciewiecz, Los Angeles, $1.00; E. O'Hare, Steubenville, Ohio, $1.00; I. H. Benedict, Montpelier, Vt., 30c; Chas. Tucci, 50c; S. Ossovsky, $1.50; Jos. Rothberg, Albany, N. Y., $2.50; O. Werner, Ocean Park, Cal., $2.00; Per M. Charnick, Chicago, $12.00; J. L. Barker, Santa Barbara, Cal., $1.00; A. Iglesias and M. Pereira, Carmel, Cal., $1.00 each; Seattle Comrades, per S. Cohen, $7.00; A. Inglis, Ann Arbor, Mich., $1.00; C. Boecklin, Congers, N. Y., $1.00; R. A. Morehouse, Edmonds, Wash., 55c; Martin Larson, Garretson, S. D., $5.00; Joe Basone, Roslyn, Wash., $1.00; H. D. Brown, Los Angeles, $1.00.

Eight   THE BLAST

Our Mail Bag

SAN FRANCISCO FRIENDS. Received per S. $15.10 for David Caplan. As I am to be in Los Angeles by the time this issue is out, I will turn the amount over to D. C. in person, if possible.

EDITOR BRAUEREI ARBEITER ZEITUNG, Cleveland. If you had read your exchanges more carefully, you would not have credited the Allentown *Labor Herald* with the article on "Prohibition: A Crime and a Menace," which you republished in your issue of May 13. The *Labor Herald* copied the article from THE BLAST of April 1. You are perfectly welcome, though. I do not believe in copyrights, least of all in ideas. Crediting is also a nuisance. If you see a good thing in THE BLAST, cop it, friend, cop it.

INDUSTRIAL WORKER AND OTHER LABOR PAPERS. The suppression of the radical press is the greatest menace to *every* revolutionary propaganda. It is not a question of our differing tactics or ideas. It is fundamental for all of us. It is both criminal and petty to ignore in your columns the recent suppression of several radical papers. THE BLAST is still excommunicated by the Post Office. For full details see our issue of May 1.

H. SCHORR, St. Louis. $1.00 for tickets and the previous $2.00 received. Too bad you are leaving. We need such good workers in St. Louis, but I know that you'll be on the job, no matter where the storm of life may land you. Will supply the missing copies as soon as you send permanent address.

MR. AND MRS. STERRETT, WASHINGTON, D. C. I regret that in No. 12 of THE BLAST your *quotation* from Margaret Sanger's paper reading, "The Post Office was supposed to be, etc. (till end of paragraph), appeared without extra quotation marks. Purely an oversight. No harm done, I hope.

PREMIUM

If you like THE BLAST, help us get subscribers. In appreciation of your efforts we will present you with a copy of PRISON MEMOIRS OF AN ANARCHIST for every 6 yearly subscriptions.

Los Angeles, Attention

A Series of Lectures by

EMMA GOLDMAN

Just Out of the New York Workhouse, Where She Spent 15 Days for Advocating Birth Control

At Burbank Hall
542 S. Main Street

Sunday, June 11th, 8 P. M.
"Anarchism and Human Nature—Do They Harmonize?"

Monday, June 12th, 8 P. M.
"The Family—Its Enslaving Effect Upon Parents and Children."

Tuesday, June 13th, 8 P. M.
"Art and Revolution: The Irish Uprising."

Wednesday, June 14th, 8 P. M.
"Preparedness, the Road to Universal Slaughter."

Thursday, June 15th, 8 P. M.
"Friedrich Nietzsche and the German Kaiser."

Saturday, June 17th, 8 P. M.
"The Right of the Child Not to Be Born."

Sunday, June 18th, 8 P. M.
"The Philosophy of Atheism."

ADMISSION, 25 CENTS

San Francisco Headquarters for Radical Literature of All Kinds
New or Old

McDevitt's Book Omnorium

1346 Fillmore—Ellis
2079 Sutter—Fillmore

Books Rented at 5c a Week
All Sorts   No Censorship

TANYA MISHKIN

College Graduated Midwife

Expert Massage, Electric Treatment, Sulphur Baths Skillfully and Scientifically Administered - - -

1316 Buchanan St., San Francisco
PHONE WEST 1985

VOL. 1   SAN FRANCISCO, JULY 1, 1916   **No. 15**

YOU AND I CANNOT LIVE IN THE SAME LAND

Freedom Only to Be Conquered

PROF. J. B. BURY has written for the Home University Library series, Henry Holt & Company, publishers, a condensed "History of the Freedom of Thought." He arraigns the Church as the chief offender. Not just the Roman Catholic Church. From its larger place in history it naturally has the larger share of the undesirable record. But he shows that the Church in power was always the foe of Free Thought, be the Church Roman Catholic, Greek Catholic or Protestant; because of the alliance of Church and State much of the political tyranny against Free Thought rests with the Church also. He points out that Freedom of Thought is useless without Freedom of Speech. The author seems to think that in England at least Freedom of Speech exists. We doubt it. We doubt if ever speech will be free to harmfully assail those in power or the conventional ignorances and idols of society. A few "cranks" may be permitted to air themselves, so long as they are harmless; but let the agitators once begin to foreshadow a revolution, and Free Speech will end quickly. In this country it does not exist, even to the degree it does in England. There is scarcely a city where a man must not get leave in advance to address the populace in the open places of the city and he must show what he intends to say. If agreeable to the authorities, yes. If contrary, no. Such Free Speech has always existed. A Soap Box Orator may harangue a crowd and block all traffic on "Old Glory" Soap or Patent Medicines, or for the Democratic or Republican parties, or for the soul's salvation. These are all harmless delusions. But let your Soap Box Orator speak on I. W. W., Socialism, Anarchism or other subject not expressly a crime on the books, yet obnoxious to the government (city, state or national) and see how quickly he will be hustled to jail and clubbed for "Obstructing the Streets," "Using Profane and Obscene Language," or some other trumped-up charge.

At Portland, Oregon, Emma Goldman was not long ago notified by the Mayor's secretary, a Mr. Warren, through the Chief of Police, that "she would not be permitted to speak *on any subject whatever.*" That, too, in a hall hired for her lectures. The City Attorney advised a modification of this ukase, but the practical effect was the same. She was arrested when she began to speak on the Russian Dramatists and her meeting was broken up. The pretext for this was that at a meeting a few evenings before some circulars had been distributed. She was held in excessive bail, five hundred dollars (it was by this time nine o'clock at night) and promptly fined next day two hundred and fifty dollars. But on appeal the whole case was contemptuously thrown out of court with a scoring of the police methods. Such results on appeal are, however, rare. Usually the fine is set just below the appealable amount, or the court says we cannot on appeal try the facts, "Whether the street was obstructed or not, etc." So paper constitutional guarantees of Free Speech are just paper, nothing more. There is no such thing as true Free Speech, or true freedom of the press in the United States. Within the last two months the Federal government suppressed the following rebel voices: *Revolt*, of New York; *The Alarm*, of Chicago; THE BLAST, of San Francisco; *Regeneracion*, of Los Angeles, and the New York Spanish publication, *Voluntad*. And yet people speak of our "constitutionally guaranteed" freedom of speech and of the press!

True freedom secures to the advocate of unpopular and "dangerous theories" the same right to speak and print them as if they were popular theories approved by the Puritans or the Plutocracy. The truth is, freedom for each generation exists in the blood of the people and if it be not there, written constitutions cannot establish it. The people of this country are satisfied. A few are satisfied to rule and exploit the masses, and the masses are as yet satisfied to be ruled and exploited. The many still place the old Jew myths above science. The ignorance and superstitions of the Jews of some four or five thousand years ago or more are the "Word of God" and man's aspiring to the throne of Reason is blasphemy. Man's aspiring to be his own sovereign is rebellion.

THE BLAST will put up what fight it can for freedom, while it survives; but it does not expect any substantial backing, because the oppressed are indifferent. If the oppressed don't care, who should?

More Suppression

Washington, June 6, 1916.

Mr. Alexander Berkman, Publisher, THE BLAST, Box 661, San Francisco, California.

Sir:

You are hereby notified that, in accordance with the Act of Congress approved March 3, 1901 (ch. 851, 31 Stat. L., 1107), you will be granted a hearing at the office of the Third Assistant Postmaster-General, Washington, D. C., at 2 p. m., on Tuesday, June 27, 1916, to show cause why the authorization of admission of THE BLAST to the second class of mail matter under the Act of March 3, 1879 (ch. 180, sec. 14, 1 Supp., 246), should not be revoked, upon the following ground:

The publication is not a "newspaper or other periodical publication" within the meaning of the law, Act of March 3, 1879, governing second-class mail matter and, furthermore, it is not regularly issued at stated intervals as a newspaper or other periodical publication within the meaning of the law. Moreover, it is in conflict with the provisions of the law embodied in section 480, Postal Laws and Regulations.

Your appearance at the hearing may be in person or by representative. In any event, your answer must be in writing. It should be submitted on or before June 27, 1916, and will be given the same consideration as though you appeared in person or by representative. Respectfully,   A. M. KELLY,
Third Assistant Postmaster-General.

Third Assistant Postmaster-General: June 21, 1916.

In reply to your communication of the 6th inst. (C. D. No. 172,588), I want to inform you that it is impossible for me to be personally present at the hearing at your office on the 27th, nor do I care to have a representative there. I hereby present my reasons why the admission of THE BLAST to the second class of mail matter should not be revoked.

My chief reason is that such revocation would be tantamount to the actual suppression of THE BLAST, and nothing short of a crime against the freedom of the press.

You are an employe of the Federal Government. Your salary is drawn from funds supplied by the taxpayers. You are supposed to *serve* the people in connection with their postal facilities. But the tragedy of your situation—as that of all other employes of the government—is that, instead of being the servant of the public, you—by virtue of your office—automatically become a cog of the governmental machinery, wherein your integrity as a man, an independent and thinking being, becomes subservient to the ends of government, whatever those ends may happen to be in a given case.

In the present case your communication to me is prompted by the attempt of the government to commit one of the greatest crimes against the people whom you are sworn to serve: The suppression of free press. Personally, you probably realize that all progress depends on the liberty of expression, and that the unpopular voice should be respected. As part of the governmental machinery, however, you yourself, whatever your views and feelings in the matter, are made the very instrument of the suppression of free press, though you are specially paid by the people to *further* the means of their inter-communication.

Concerning the points specified in your form letter of the 6th inst., let me inform you that THE BLAST *is* a newspaper, if by the term is meant a paper publishing news and information in the field of its particular choice. Your statement that THE BLAST "is not regularly issued at stated intervals" is entirely without foundation. Your assumption is probably due to the fact that copies of THE BLAST do not regularly reach the Post-office. But that is the fault of the Postoffice, not mine, since the postal authorities of San Francisco, on orders from Washington, have refused to accept copies of THE BLAST for transmission. Nevertheless, THE BLAST is published regularly, at stated intervals, and regularly supplied to our agents throughout the country, by express, as you will see from the enclosed issues of the paper.

THE BLAST was first issued as a *weekly* publication on January 15, 1916, and second-class mail matter applied for and granted. Then THE BLAST was changed from a weekly to a semi-monthly publication. Your office was informed accordingly, whereupon you revoked the second-class mail of the *weekly* BLAST and granted second-class mail to the *semi-monthly* BLAST. At all times since its inception, THE BLAST has appeared regularly, at stated intervals, first as a weekly, then as a semi-monthly.

Thus you will see that there is absolutely no reason why the second-class mail of THE BLAST should be revoked. If it is done, nevertheless, it will be because some one in Washington is determined to *suppress* the unpopular voice of THE BLAST. Personally, I do not care what the government will do in this case. I know that government means oppression and tyranny. But for *your* sake, I hope that you will refuse to be a willess cog in this machinery of suppression.

(Signed) ALEXANDER BERKMAN,
Editor THE BLAST, San Francisco.

Do You Want This?

This is not art, not "description"; it is the thing itself. Has any one seen anything more vivid, more ingenuously brutal, than this private letter from a wounded British soldier to a friend in Chicago, and printed, with the latter's permission, by *The Public?*

"I am all in. I am in a hospital in England. I am sorry to say I am deaf and dumb through shock and wounds. I have been on the armored cars during the last five months. I was a motorcycle dispatch rider and armored car driver. I was driving a 60-horsepower armored car. I could not drive my car through the dead bodies fast enough. The bodies of horses and men were so thick that it was impossible to get through. All at once a 50-pound shell hit my armored car and blew us up in the air. When they got me from underneath the wrecked car I was deaf and dumb, with my ribs crushed and spine hurt. That was a month ago. The three other men that fired the Maxim guns inside the car were blown to bits. It was an awful sight on the battlefield. Sometimes I would open wide my car and drive into a regiment of Germans at about fifty miles an hour. The car weighs four tons with three Maxim guns, three men besides myself and ten thousand rounds of bullets inside. And when I would take a mad drive through a regiment I could kill about 50 or 100 every time. After making a dash for it, my wheels and radiator would be full of blood and legs and arms when I got back to the base. Then I would have to get all flesh and bones from my wheels. It has nearly made my hair white. I am tired of killing people. It is on my nerves. If you had seen me this summer up to the eyes in blood! One might as well be in hell as in a charge. We had to stand face to face and batter each other's brains out. I have had my bayonet through fellows' bodies. I have been so weak that I could hardly pull it out again. When you are like that you don't care what becomes of you. I

only wish I were with you now. The battlefield is like Hell. The sky is lit up all night by torch lights and shells. We have fist fights and bayonet fights. We are killing one another any way we can. I am so weak now I cannot write any more this time."

A Plea for Preparedness

ISSUED BY THE PACIFIC COAST BUSINESS MEN'S PREPAREDNESS LEAGUE

Adequate Troops Needed to Deal With Domestic Strife and to Suppress Probable Labor Uprisings

IN the general apprehension for greater Preparedness to cope with foreign nations it is believed that a necessity fully as grave and serious is being overlooked or at least greatly minimized; and that is the need for an adequate military establishment to act as a civil police force.

The "Post-Intelligencer" for May 22nd quoted ex-President Taft in his address before the League to Enforce Peace as saying "We need a police force at home." In fact Mr. Taft has heretofore affirmed the need for greater preparedness for riots and internal disturbances. Bulletins of Manufacturers and Employers' Associations in the East, notably in New Jersey, which has been the scene of so many acute labor disturbances, have urgently treated of this need, but they have been given scant hearing outside the councils of business men themselves.

In the hearings before the Industrial Relations Commission at Seattle, a representative business man, Mr. J. V. Patterson, addressing the labor members on the Commission with great courage stated, "We will fight you. We will rise with a counter revolution; we will certainly have the power. We will destroy you. Let us have no more class legislation, or we will have it repealed with bayonets; we will do it, no doubt about that."

Due to lack of sufficient militia, business men in the United States have frequently been placed under the undue burden of having to engage and pay for the services of men recruited privately and to have them commissioned as deputies by the civil authorities. In the nature of things these private forces are without efficient military training as at Youngstown, Ohio, in Pennsylvania and elsewhere. In the single month of October, in 1913, the meagre military forces of four separate states were required in the field against labor; in Calumet, Michigan, in Indianapolis and in Colorado and West Virginia.

Certainly no intelligent person can oppose "Preparedness" when he reflects upon what may happen in the event of a general strike of the two million railroad workers of the country to gain the eight-hour workday, and which is even now threatened. It must be remembered that the Federal troops were required to suppress the strike of the American Railway Union which was an effort in precisely the same direction, and under the leadership of Eugene V. Debs. That disturbance, it will not be forgotten, was largely local in character when now it would be widespread and in the nature of a general rebellion against the business and transportation interests of the whole country.

In view of these facts we urge all business men, whether affiliated with this league or not, to spare no effort to further the idea of preparedness; and it is doubly important that all employers take advantage of this opportune time to solicit personally their loyal and dependable employes to join the militia of their several states.

In this entire matter business men should be sensible of the advantages to be had from military training in point of greater discipline and efficiency of the work people for their ordinary civil employment. Every employe returning from training camp or militia drill will forthwith show himself more obedient and faithful, and the trouble-maker will disappear.

PACIFIC COAST BUSINESS MEN'S PREPAREDNESS LEAGUE

Four   THE BLAST

THE BLAST

Revolutionary Labor Paper
Published every 1st and 15th of the month
569 Dolores St., San Francisco, Cal.

Mail Address, Box 661   Phone, Park 499

Alexander Berkman, Editor and Publisher
M. E. Fitzgerald, Associate Worker   Carl Newlander, Assistant

SUBSCRIPTION
$1.00 Yearly   60c Six Months   5c Copy
Bundle rates 2½c per copy in bundles of ten.
Entered as second-class matter at the postoffice at San Francisco,
Cal., January 14, 1916, under the Act of March 3, 1879.

Reflections

Re-election by Murder

WHY not speak as honestly and frankly of men in high places as of the street sweeper? If the latter kill a man because of greed or selfishness we call him a murderer. And if he send thousands of men to certain death, is he not a willful, cold-blooded monster?

This is what Woodrow Wilson is about to do. I cannot conceive of any more heinous crime than war with Mexico. The President has solemnly assured the country on numerous occasions that under no circumstances would there be any intervention in Mexico. Later on, however, armed forces were dispatched across the border to hunt Villa. Still the honest Woodrow kept telling us that we were at peace with Mexico, though American soldiers and Texas rangers were shooting every peon in sight. At the present moment a quarter of a million soldiers are held in readiness to invade our sister Republic.

There is no disguising the purpose of the administration. It is safe to say that if Roosevelt had not double crossed his Progressive flock, and had headed a third Presidential ticket, we would not now be on the verge of war with Mexico. The American troops, having vainly chased Villa for months, would gradually be withdrawn, and the people of Mexico freed from the sight of the deservedly hated American uniform. Not that Wall street has not all along been trying to force American intervention. But Wilson knew that the people of this country were not enthusiastic over such an undertaking for the benefit of the Hearsts, the Guggenheims and the rest of the land-grabbing canaille. And Wilson certainly keeps his ear to the ground.

But the flip-flop of Roosevelt changed the situation. Most of the Progressive political strength will now go to Hughes. That almost certainly means the defeat of Wilson in the coming Presidential election.

How to keep himself in the saddle? This is what s worrying Wilson. Of course, he had solemnly promised not to seek a second term. So did Roosevelt before him. But what are pre-election promises to a politician? The sole ambition of Wilson now is to be re-elected. His *only* chance is to embroil the United States in war—with some country. Mexico is revolution torn, weak and exhausted—it offers an easy mark, Wilson believes (though he may find her a tough customer before long). Besides, war with Mexico will secure for Wilson the support of Wall street. He will become a war President, and his re-election is sure; it will give him this, the strongest appeal to the people: Don't swap horses while crossing a stream

Thus we must be forced into war with Mexico and thousands of lives sacrificed to the ambition of Wilson for re-election.

What would we call the street sweeper if he murdered a man for a selfish purpose? And if he caused thousands to be slaughtered to further personal ambition?

A murderer, an inhuman monster.

Cowardice on Parade

IT IS an open secret that great numbers of those that marched in the Preparedness parades in the various cities were forced to do so by the fear of losing their job. In many cases employes were actually ordered to march on threat of being discharged for refusal. In the light of these facts, the number of paraders can by no means be taken to indicate popular approval of Preparedness.

It is sad, however, to contemplate to what extent American manhood and womanhood has degenerated. There was a time when the average American prided himself on his independence and sovereignty. Outside of the shop or factory he felt himself as good as the next man. Economically dependent, he was at least the master of his ideas and thoughts. Away from his place of work, his home was his castle and he its sovereign.

Today the average American does not dare call his soul his own. He is afraid to voice his innermost thought or feeling, for fear of "getting in bad." He marches in Preparedness parades because he is afraid to lose a half-day's pay. With thousands of others he helps to swell the number of paraders for fear of losing his job.

It is this submissiveness, this acquiescence that strengthens the hand of the enemy and lends him courage to ever greater invasion. This servile spirit is undermining the last bulwarks of our life. Obedience, submission, has become the keynote of our existence.

There are thousands, perhaps hundreds of thousands, of men and women in this country who have seen through the meshes of our social fabric and recognized it, in the words of Ibsen, as machine made. Thousands whose understanding and experience have unmasked to them our life as a network of hypocrisy, sham and lies. Thousands that are filled with hatred of tyranny and exploitation, and whose very souls are sick of the composite lie called modern life. Thousands, aye, millions passionately opposed to child slavery, the mutilation of women in factories, the slow murder of men in the mills. Hundreds of thousands are opposed to murder in uniform, to the slaughter on battle field or picket line, to the crime and disease rampant in sweatshop and tenement. Thousands and thousands are sick of the false values that dominate our lives from cradle to grave, poisoning the sunshine and joy of our being.

And yet—where are they? Most of them marching in the parade of false values, keeping step to the drum beats of sham gods, while their hearts are bleeding with the misery and cowardice of it all.

O for the spark of courage to ignite the smoldering tinder of discontent that shall burn away the tinsel of seeming necessity and fire mankind with the elemental passion to life and joy!

Armor Plate Patriots

THE greatest American patriot is the Armor Plate Ring. It is this Ring which is the prime mover back of the militarist campaign, with its newspaper publicity, forced parades and presidential Preparedness issues. The Ring consists of the Midvale, Carnegie and Bethlehem companies. It is strenuously opposing the plan to build a government owned armor plate plant. Its president, Chas. M. Schwab, is now publishing paid bulletins in the Eastern press for the purpose of impressing it upon the people that "there is no occasion to waste $11,000,000 in building a government armor plant."

Why does the Armor Plate Ring so passionately object to a government owned armor plant?

Here is the reason.

During the last twenty years, the Federal government has bought from the Ring 233,339 tons of armor, paying for it an average of $439 a ton, or a total of $102,504,292, besides millions for other war materials. The average estimate of government officials for armor plate manufactured in a government plant, including all overhead charges, is $250 a ton, without blowholes.

No wonder Schwab & Co. think that it is "unfair" to deprive them of their armor plate monopoly. No wonder also that Schwab and his confreres are the founders and supporters of the Navy League that demands more armor-plated warships for Uncle Sam.

In our estimation it is immaterial whether the armor plate for American murder machines is made by a private monopoly, a government monopoly or in a competitive market. At best, it is a difference of mere dollars. The more important issue involved is, shall we invest in more murder machines? In this the government, the Armor Plate Ring, the powder trust and the whole brood of munition manufacturers are at one. It is merely a question of who shall reap the graft.

The Opportunity of Labor

THE San Francisco Labor Council at a recent meeting decided with a large majority against Preparedness. The splendid arguments given at the session by some of the labor representatives prove that the more intelligent workers already discern the menace of militarism back of the soft words of the Pacific Coast Defense League. The latter organization, represented in the Council by Andrew Gallagher, Supervisor and alleged labor man, was scored as a branch of the Navy League, the mouthpiece of Rockefeller, Morgan and Schwab.

The Council, representing numerous labor bodies of San Francisco, is to be congratulated on its intelligent and manly stand. The case of Labor vs. Preparedness was put splendidly by Scharrenberg, Ernst and Schulberg, with the result that the Council officially went on record as opposed to Preparedness. There is no doubt that this action will encourage thousands of workers throughout the country to take a similar stand.

There are indications that labor bodies in various industrial centers are about to register a like attitude. We suggest that the San Francisco Labor Council immediately organize a country-wide Anti-Preparedness campaign, soliciting the co-operation of local and central labor bodies in the United States and Canada, and thus crystallize and co-ordinate the only real force that can adequately cope with the menace created and subsidized by Morgan & Co.

Hail to the Magons!

WE LIVE in a civilization in which the noblest and best of men are looked upon as criminals. We admire and glorify the reversal to the primitive, the Hun man that cold-bloodedly orders large masses of men to certain death—and then boasts of his infamy. We shower him with praise and emoluments, pin medals on his breast, and proclaim him a great hero.

But the man of the higher type is scorned and condemned. He who looks upon all men as brothers, to be loved and helped instead of murdered; he in whose heart and mind is reflected the pain and sorrow of mankind and whose sensitive psychology intensifies to him the injustice and brutality suffered by his fellow-men—he is calumnied, misunderstood and persecuted.

Such men are Ricardo and Enrique Flores Magon. They are the scorned of the world, the "criminals" of today, whom tomorrow will acclaim as the pioneers of a better life.

The brute man sits in judgment over them and dooms them to prison life, there to expiate their love of fellow-men. Ricardo and Enrique have been sentenced to one and three years, respectively, and fined $1000 each. Could injustice be greater, more crying to heaven? The Beast of Greed sits enthroned on human corpses and leers at the effort to dislodge it from its vampire seat. Leers and victimizes every one within the reach of its octopus tentacles, and poisons the minds of men to call the Jungle Beast blessed and take up arms in its defense. And those who cry out against the monstrous crime, those who sacrifice life and liberty to shake off the nightmare of man—for them the prison and the scaffold.

Thus the Brothers Magon are immured behind iron bars, and the spirit of manhood crushed. And the tool of the Beast, sitting in judgment, pronounces solemn sentence: "The duty of the State is to protect itself against the disturbers of its security. The Magons are criminals, their crime equal to treason."

Aye, treason against the bloodthirsty Moloch that lives on the flesh and blood of widows and children. Treason against the State, the destroyer of man, the enemy of life. May this treason grow and multiply, and disturbers of the security of State arise in even greater numbers from the persecuted spirit of the Magons, till the arch-fiend, the State, is no more; till the very memory of Judge Trippett and his lackeys is lost in oblivion, and the Magons, traitors to the State, are hailed as the emancipators of man.

The Birth Control Fight

THE latest development in the Birth Control campaign in New York City is the arrest of Bolton Hall, of the Free Speech League, and Mrs. Ida Rauh Eastman, author and sculptress, wife of Max Eastman, editor of *The Masses*. Both Mr. Hall and Mrs. Eastman are charged with circulating pamphlets on contraception at a meeting held in Union Square, New York City, May 20th, to protest against the imprisonment of Dr. Ben L. Reitman, who is serving a sentence of sixty days for a similar "crime." The list of victims of this antiquated law and disgusting injustice now stands: Margaret Sanger, William Sanger, Emma Goldman, Ben Reitman, Ida Rauh Eastman, Bolton Hall and Joseph Macario of San Francisco. Mrs. Rose Pastor Stokes has *dared* the police to arrest her, but she is still at liberty. Leonard Abbott is as yet unarrested, and there are others. But no man knoweth what a day may bring forth.

Nor is the fight limited to New York. In Portland, Oregon, three men were arrested at a recent meeting of Margaret Sanger for circulating printed information on Birth Control. This movement has assumed national proportions, and now it is a question of whether the people shall have access to the knowledge they demand or whether the authorities will continue to execute a law that has generally fallen into disrepute. The end is not hard to foresee. In this case, as in numerous others, history will repeat itself. The law will be ignored and defied with increasing frequency till general sentiment will compel its repeal. What is a crime today will be an accepted and approved fact tomorrow. Meanwhile the Moloch of Law will demand its human sacrifices—the martyrs that strew the road of progress.

Law has ever been the enemy of human welfare.

The Sacred Rag

BOUCK WHITE, the pastor of the Church of the Social Revolution, and author of "The Call of the Carpenter," is in prison in New York for having circulated a cartoon in which the American flag was represented as stamped with the dollar mark. When White's term expires he will be tried for having "destroyed and desecrated" an American flag. In this second trial he will have nine comrades. The case grows out of an international ceremony held the night before White's trial. On that occasion the flags of nine countries, including that of the U. S. A., were burned in a melting pot from which was then drawn the international banner of blood red.

There may have been a time when the American flag stood for freedom of conscience and political justice, though even that is doubtful. Today the flag stands only for exploitation and militarism. It is the emblem of prostituted justice and greedy capitalism. It waves proudly over the tents of Ludlow, where women and children of striking miners are burned alive by hired gunmen protected by the American flag. It is the symbol of the subtlest enslavement in the name of democracy and of the most intense exploitation of labor that the world has ever seen. The very fact that men are sent to prison for "desecrating" a rag proves that there is no freedom of conscience under that flag.

No decent man or woman can respect the symbol of such tyranny.

Anent the Cloakmakers' Strike
Alexander Berkman

FOR over two months the Cloakmakers' Union of New York has been involved in a life-and-death struggle with the Manufacturers' Protective Association. The Union is virtually fighting for its very existence: the right of the workers to maintain the closed shop principle and to collectively bargain for the terms of their employment.

In strikes of this character the employers make a strong bid for public sympathy on the ground that the closed shop principle is anti-libertarian; that it curtails the freedom of the "independent" worker to choose his own master and conditions. Sad to say, the public is often duped by this argument.

It is misleading to speak in the indefinable terms of "right" and "wrong," especially in matters of a socio-economic character. It cannot be denied that the scab has as much "right" to work and live as the union striker. Similarly has the snake the "sacred right" to life and liberty. But we crush the snake, on the ground of *our* equally sacred right to live.

Life, the struggle for existence, is not a matter of right or wrong. It is time to emancipate ourselves from these metaphysical, meaningless concepts. Much fruitless discussion of "the rights of Labor," equal justice," violent methods and similar problems would be obviated, once we realize the actual character of the struggle. Nature knows neither right nor wrong. It knows only forces—harmonious or antagonistic, as the case may be. Was the storm "right" in devastating the forest? Was the lightning "wrong" in destroying that beautiful young tree? Or the sunshine and rain "right and moral" in coaxing forth new life from the debris of the dead?

No less meaningless are ethical concepts applied to the hungry stomach. That is why our ideas of "right" and "justice," with their bastard brood of "legality," "crime," and punishment are a most vicious perversion of the very essence of life and struggle for existence.

Progress consists in the inter-play of man's destructive and constructive tendencies; the elemental tendencies developed by—and in their turn furthering—the struggle for existence. In order to survive, man had to eliminate or destroy every factor inimical to his wellbeing. The beasts of the forest are no more where man's foot has trod. He also had to protect himself against inimical or dangerous forces of nature—lightning, storm, cold and the like. The need of such protection against a *common* danger developed co-operation and solidarity among men. It called into action his *constructive* tendencies and enabled him to protect himself against forces he could not eliminate or destroy.

The constructive and destructive tendencies of man were *not* antagonistic. In fact, both were expressions of the identical instinct of self-preservation; both served a common purpose.

With the growing security of man, as against inimical environment or natural forces, the demands upon his destructive activity are decreasing, with the corresponding increase of opportunity to apply himself constructively.

The social struggle is characterized by the same tendencies: the destructive and constructive activities of man. *Destructive* toward forces and conditions inimical to our growth and life; *constructive* toward circumstances and elements that further our purposes.

The class struggle—the fight of Labor against Capital—is founded on the very same conditions. It is inherent in the individual struggle for existence and in the *modus operandi* of our social and economic arrangements. A sane society, by eliminating individual and class antagonisms, would further and strengthen the constructive instinct of man and thus develop ever increasing co-operation and solidarity. Society as at present constituted, with its artifically created and multiplied antagonisms, cultivates the destructive tendencies of man.

Conditions of wage slavery have forced upon the workers destructive activity toward everything inimical to their wellbeing and improvement. On the other hand, the same conditions are calling into being greater constructive effort on the basis of a common interest. Hence the growing solidarity of Labor, in the degree that the toilers realize their community of interest. Thus in the Labor struggle are reflected and manifest the very tendencies that have characterized the whole march of man's development:

1. Destruction activity toward inimical environment and antagonistic forces.
2. Constructive, solidaric co-operation with elements and factors of harmonious, common interest.

Capitalism has forced upon the workers the necessity of combined action among themselves, as against those inimical to their interests. The individual worker is absolutely helpless in the face of the strongly organized employers. As the latter are constructive within the sphere of their own interest and destructive toward Labor, so also the workers must practice similar activities within the area of *their* interests. Hence Labor's growing solidarity on the basis of common interest. Hence also the necessity of eliminating every obstacle in Labor's path, the destruction of every factor inimical to the maintenance and improvement of Labor. Therefore the bitter struggle between striker and scab. Therefore also the vital need of the closed shop. It is made imperative, hence justified, by the character of the Labor struggle.

The cloakmakers of New York are fighting one of the battles of humanity, of progress. At the cost of much suffering and privation they are heroically maintaining the principle of wonderful solidarity among the thousands directly involved in the struggle, and firmly presenting a determined front against the forces that threaten to destroy them.

Upon the victory of the cloakmakers depends to a considerable degree the resultant economic and social wellbeing of great masses in the East. It is one of the important battles in the universal war of the masses against the classes that will ultimately result in the destruction of social class divisions and thus abolish the great economic strife. Then—then only—will the human energy now forced to be destructive be released for constructive purposes and a tremendous impetus added to man's constructive, harmonious efforts toward Life and Progress.

The State is the only institution that compels a man to kill his fellowmen. In the name of law and order.

* * *

LAW is the most narrowing and the most degrading of all professions. All human law is a system of fossilized injustice, and the habitual study of it only demoralizes. There is not enough of thought or principle in our whole system of law to occupy a man of intellect for an hour; all the rest is mere chicanery and injustice.
—H. F. Durant

In the Words of Shaw

THE main reason why I do not make our British voters happy in M. Saintyves' fashion is that I do not want to make them happy. I want to make them howl, to drive them to rend their hearts and not their garments; to see them heap ashes on their silly heads whilst they confess in the dust, with humble and contrite hearts, that, though they may buy victory with their blood and iron, they deserve defeat and even extermination, and have no plea to offer against that doom except that the Germans deserve no less. For just consider how I must feel about it. I read in the *Times* Lord Curzon's demand for the suppression of the Derby on the ground that it is unbecoming to have "junketings" in the face of bereavements and wounds and death. I asked Lord Curzon whether he supposes that there has been a single Derby run during his lifetime, or a single junketing of any description, that has not been held in the teeth of the most abominable socially preventable evils, including child mortality, compulsory prostitution, artificially produced vice disease, degradation, suffering, squalor, fraud, violence, famine, battle, murder and sudden death. Mr. Sidney Webb offers to put an end to British unemployment and destitution, with their infinite loss and demoralization, for a paltry couple of million pounds. Sir Horace Plunkett offers to quadruple the produce of the Irish soil, and thereby avert the land and labor war that is hanging over Ireland, at a cost of three thousand pounds a year for technical education in agriculture. They might as well ask for the sun and the stars. No mother sends her son to live for England. No father shakes his son's hand and says: "I wish I were young enough to stand beside you in the fight for a decent country to live in." Yet, for this senseless, suicidal slaughter of civilization in Flanders and Poland, this illusory hatred, this monstrous fruit of selfish, lazy apathy, soothed by huge doses of falsehood, we are putting down thousands of millions of pounds eagerly; and the mothers and fathers are sending their sons to kill and die, to maim and be maimed, because none of them took as much thought and care for the welfare of Europe as for the shininess of their boots. And now that we are waked up at last, our first step is to cut off all the little grants-in-aid that a few struggling reformers have managed to procure for our social needs, and to sweep them into the till of the armament contractor. This is what it costs to make a Briton serious. We are more callous than Tartars or Hottentots. With them, a few dozen heads chopped off and piled in the middle of the street, and a few girls buried alive under the door post of the king, produce public seriousness enough for a whole reign. But we must have thirty thousand men in the flower of their youth bayoneted and smashed and shattered and pierced and blinded and deafened with inconceivable violence every morning for months before we can feel really fine and thrill with admiration of ourselves. Even then, our notion of rising to the occasion is to applaud the gentlemen who write to the papers calling on me to cease frivoling and flatter them.

Indecent Exposure
R. S.

THERE is no more instructive spectacle than that of a marionette which has been performing for the edification of the curious, suddenly turning turtle and falling clean off the hinge of artifice which has been supporting it. Even if you have known the thing wasn't real, there is still a shock in seeing what appears to have vigor and motion come to a sudden halt.

This time it isn't a tramp who has executed the stunt unspeakable; it isn't a poor, old, tattered, bug-bonneted derelict. The act wasn't committed in a park, or in an alleyway, or in a vacant lot, or on a crowded street-car platform. It was done by *wire*, in the sight of the interested and indifferent, to the tune of words embellished with that well-known signature—"T. R."—the very same person who has told us what honor is; who has defined "virtue" till little remains of it but the "chew"; who has warned us that the only test of character is to stand up when the fuse begins to sizzle; and that the man who wouldn't fight — if by accident tobacco juice flew in his eye — is an earthworm, a mollycoddle and a meaningless mockery.

All these things have been told to us by our most famous animal killer, the human Blowout, of Oyster Bay. He has spoken in such terms that even children knew what he meant; and it is a safe wager that many a poor lad, who wasn't equipped with a yellow suit and a pop-gun, has blubbered his envious soul away in some dark corner of disappointment.

This man not only made word pictures of what it meant to be brave, but he showed himself in moving pictures, seated on a dead lion, musket in hand, with not another person in sight — not even the camera man; showed us himself coming out of the South American jungle with an army of black men carrying spears (and his luggage), ready at a moment's notice to fell even a tree that threatened to fall in the Intrepid One's way.

Of course, people admired such an exhibition of personal pluck. Hadn't he all the earmarks of a Leader? Hadn't he autographed his acts with such touches of valor as no seeing person could resist? Here was a man to liberate the multitude, a really great man, who would swing his club in the very eye teeth of oppressive rule.

Then there was a Convention, and yearning groups of hand-clapping Concurrers shook the air in their impatience to help place this personage on the public platter. There was never a question in the minds of one of these overwrought proponents but that their idol would stand right up in the middle of the square and battle till the last enemy lay stark in his path.

But did the redoubtable one answer the call? Did he? He did, but not in line with Expectations, hidden in the breasts of his votaries.

This Leading Actor, this Clown of Climaxes (who carried dishes fastened to a tray), when expected to stand by his following, did two things — two Other things:

First, as soon as he espied that Whiskers were the thing to win the Ringmaster's notice, he suggested that that pillar of plutocratic propriety, Henry Cabot Lodge, be given place. Failing in this suggestion, he sent a telegram to his own flock, which in substance, read:

"Count me out. The man with the whip didn't come to my ring; and I can't make this horse go unless I hear that old familiar crack."

The Fearless One! Theodore, the Weakling Smasher! Teddy, who presented more bones to the Smithsonian Institute than any other living skeleton gatherer! He, the Brave One, has done this thing!

Thus fall the rubber Gods, who can persuade four million people to sign a ballot and never feel a puncture!

Mr. Smoot, Mr. Penrose, Mr. Barnes and Chauncey — dear, old "Conventional" Chauncey, et al.: There's one thing about your crew: They stand for something, and it isn't a conundrum. What you are is written in the very air that evaporates. Your color is bad. You are purple to the roots. Still, at that (politically), I don't know but what you are to be preferred to the Reformation Syndicate which topples in a heap when one of its members loses his footing.

It's pretty hard to choose between rummies, but if we must, the writer prefers the brand that shows its stripes and gives a marksman a chance to do something with his gun.

Eight   THE BLAST

Young Folks

"TELL me a story, papa."
"What shall I tell you?"
"About the porcupine."
"Suppose I tell you a new one, about Noah and the Ark?"
"Noah?"
"Yes."
"Who was Noah?"
"I'll tell you about it."
"All right, tell about Noah."

Settles himself comfortably in his father's lap and listens.

"Once upon a time a long time ago, all the people on the earth were so bad that the Lord decided to destroy all of them but Noah."
"Why, what did they do?"
"Oh, they were bad."
"Well, what did they do bad?"
"They did all kinds of bad things."
"Like the East Bottoms boys?"
"Yes, and worse."
"Did the policemen come after them?"
"Yes."
"And did they take away the policemen's clubs?"
"Yes, and a lot of other bad things. Keep still now and let me tell you the story."
"Did they take away the policemen's stars?"
"Yes, and so the Lord——"
"Did the policemen put them in the jail house?"
"Yes, yes; you keep quiet now and I'll tell you all about it. And so the Lord said he would send a big rain and drown all the people but Noah and his family."

Boy jerks upward into sitting position and asks earnestly:
"Drown them?"
"Yes, drown them."
"In the river?"
"No, not in the river, drown them with a big rain."
"Pour water on 'em?"
"No, no; the big rain came down for forty days and forty nights and the water rose until it covered the earth."
"And floated this house away?"
"No, not this house. This house wasn't built then."
"Well, when is it going to do it?"
"It did do it a long, long time ago. The Lord told Noah to build a big ship and take his family in there and two of every animal on the earth. And he did, two elephants, two lions, two tigers——"
"And two bears?"
"Yes, two bears, and——"
"And two mousies?"
"Yes, and two——"
"And did the bears eat the mousies?"
"No, no."
"Well, why didn't they?"
"Noah put them in different rooms."
"Oh, papa, where did you hear that story?"
"I read it in the Bible. Now lie still and listen or I won't tell it. And Noah put all the animals in it and then the Lord sent the big rain and the water came up and came up, and covered all the earth and drowned all the people except Noah and his family."
"All the babies, too?"
"Yes, everybody."
"The little babies?"
"Yes."
"And their mammas?"
"Yes."
"The Lord's a bad man, isn't he, papa?"
"No, no, child, the Lord is the good man up in the sky. Don't you know? You pray to him every night. Now listen.

And so it rained and the water came up until it floated Noah's ark away."
"Floated it away?"
"Yes."
"Did it break in two?"
"No, it just floated on the water."
"And was Noah in it?"
"Yes."
"Why didn't all the people get in?"
"Noah wouldn't let them."
"Noah was a mean man, wasn't he?"
"No, he was a good man."
"No, sir, he was mean, and the Lord was mean, too. Didn't he drown the little babies and their mammas?"
"Well, I'll tell you what I'll do."
"What?"
"You lie still and I'll tell you about the porcupine."—Ex.

INTERNATIONAL PICNIC

OF

"THE BLAST"

TUESDAY JULY 4

1916

BEGINNING AT 10 A. M.

Address by ALEXANDER BERKMAN

MILLET'S PARK COLMA

Tickets, 25c

Take any car and transfer to Cemetery or San Mateo Cars

VALUABLE GATE AND GAME PRIZES

NOTICE
INTERNATIONAL Meeting every Thursday, 8 p. m., at clubrooms of Group Volontá, 1602 Stockton street, San Francisco. Radicals of all shades invited.

GROUP Louise Michel meets at the same place every Friday, 8 p. m. A club of Radical Women of every nationality.

PROCEEDS from Social and Dance given June 11th by Group Volontá and BLAST for the Magon Fund ($12.00) turned over to the International Workers' Defense League, Los Angeles.

VOL. 1   SAN FRANCISCO, JULY 15, 1916   No. 16

THE REAL PURPOSE OF PREPAREDNESS

Come, Workers, Let Us Take Counsel Together

THERE is not the least doubt that the Powers That Be fully realize that there is a strong anti-militarist sentiment among the people of the country. The Lords of finance and industry, of commerce and government know that something must be done to cure that evil. And they are doing it. Are you watching the methods used by the Masters of Life to gain their ends—ends that can be gained only by strangling the last vestige of liberty and compelling abject obedience to the supreme will of the plutocracy? You ought to watch them, for they are fraught with direct consequences to you, to every man, woman and child; aye, even to the coming generations.

The ruling banditti know that primarily it is the revolutionary elements that oppose their schemes of Preparedness and War. Therefore their first step is the summary and wholesale suppression of the opposition papers. Within a few weeks the Postal arm of Preparedness seized the following publications, depriving them of the second-class mail or declaring them entirely unmailable: THE BLAST; the "Revolt" of New York; the "Alarm" of Chicago; "Régeneracion" of Los Angeles; "Voluntad" (Spanish) of New York; "L'Allarme" (Italian) of Chicago, and "Volne Listy" (Bohemian) of New York.

The revolutionary press being the most potent disseminator of solidarity and intelligent resistance to oppression, its elimination is the first step to capitalist Preparedness.

Closely following it comes a bill submitted to Congress, authorizing the Postoffice to virtually suppress every publication unfavorable to the rulers, and vesting the Postmaster General with arbitary power more unlimited than that possessed by the military censor of Russia.

The next step is to silence the advocates of undesirable ideas. Ricardo and Enrique Flores Magon, Emma Goldman and Ben Reitman, Margaret and William Sanger, Elizabeth Gurley Flynn and Joe Ettor, Bolton Hall, Ida Rauh, Jessie Ashley and numerous others are arrested, some of them railroaded to prison, others awaiting trial.

With most of the revolutionary papers silenced, and some of the most active protestants out of the way, the field is clear for further activity on a bigger scale. It is now the turn of the larger bodies of social discontent.

Who is handicapping the triumphant march of Preparedness for Profit? Who dare doubt the benevolence of militarism and retard the chariot of capitalism?

The Labor Unions. Away with them!

Throughout the country organized capital is now grappling in a life and death struggle with organized labor. The unorganized do not count. They are no menace to the plutocracy. On the contrary. The disorganization of Labor is the strongest bulwark of the employers. Lacking unity and solidarity, the unorganized toilers are powerless to present a solid front against their exploiters. True, now and then even the unorganized, goaded by misery and starvation, may rebel and in a passionate moment avenge a ten-millionth part of their wrongs. But these sudden spurts of rebellion are sporadic and momentary, their flames quickly subdued and held in control by the iron fist of the Masters' Law.

But the organized forces of Labor—they are a constant and ever increasing menace to the employing class. To be sure, there is much division and internal strife among the unions, and the bosses take the best possible advantage of it to pit industry against industry, craft against craft, creeds and nationalities against each other. Yet, after all, large bodies of workers ARE organized. They are gradually learning the lesson of solidarity that promises to weld all workers in tremendous national and international units of Labor on the common foundation of ONE cause and ONE enemy.

Here is the great menace. The organizations of the toilers must be disrupted, by fair means or foul, discord must be sown and encouraged among them, antagonisms of religion, race and color must be cultivated to keep strife alive, and all must be imbued with a common ideal alien to their own interests and welfare but "dear to our hearts." Aye, Patriotism, Preparedness!

And if all this fail, or any obstacles are placed in our way by disgruntled Labor, then down with the unions. We proclaim the great American gospel of the Open Shop.

The Open Shop has now become the slogan of the plutocracy. The unions must be destroyed at all cost. It will then be an easy matter to deal with the individual toiler, the "independent American worker" absolutely powerless to face or fight the giant of organized capital. The strength of organized workers destroyed, objectionable Labor bodies wiped off the map, Preparedness, Militarism, capitalist Law-and-Order can march to ultimate triumph over a people patriotically submissive and efficiently obedient for the greater glory of Mammon.

Throughout the country a bitter struggle is being waged by the workers to maintain the right of organization. Practically every industry is now involved in a fight for the life of their unions. Everywhere the bosses claim the inalienable right to accumulate millions by paying starvation wages in the open shop.

In New York, 60,000 cloakmakers are battling for their very existence. The coal miners in several states are fighting the same fight. More than 400,000 members of the four great railroad brotherhoods are now taking a referendum vote for the right to assert their manhood. In the Tennessee copper fields, in the dangerous Fluorspar mines of Southern Illinois, on the iron ranges of Minnesota, on the harvest acres, on the water fronts of the Atlantic and the Pacific—from coast to coast the great industrial war is raging.

Bread and Life! cry the hosts of Labor.

Preparedness, more Guns! replies the Beast of Capital.

Police, armed thugs, the militia and the army rush to the rescue of threatened Profits.

In vain this struggle of the workers, in vain the great sacrifices, the bloodshed, the misery heroically suffered. These sporadic upheavals, these rebellious uprisings of isolated Labor units may stimulate the spirit of resistance and train the toilers for further greater combat. As such they are good, splendid. But they are powerless to achieve any real improvement for Labor. All these strikes, drawn out for weeks and often months, become tests of endurance in which capital is always the winner. The workers are finally starved and beaten into submission.

The time has come for a GENERAL STRIKE. This, this alone holds out victory for Labor. A general, nation-wide strike, at one stroke paralyzing every wheel of industry, demonstrating the power and fundamentality of Labor.

Come, workers of every craft and industry, producers of all the wealth of the world, organized or unorganized, let us take counsel together. The revolutionists of every shade stand ready to help you. Come, let us talk it over.

Let us invite our fellow workers of Mexico and of South America (Europe is busy) and let us talk matters over in a Pan-American Labor Conference. Let us talk over the fundamental demand of ALL Labor and of all fair-minded men and women throughout the world: LAND and LIBERTY.

Never fear, we shall find ways and means of accomplishing our aim, once we get together on the common basis of THE EARTH AND ITS PRODUCTS TO THE PRODUCERS.

ALEXANDER BERKMAN

For the People

James Jeffrey Roche

WE are the hewers and delvers who toil for another's gain,
The common clods and the rabble, stunted of brow and
brain,
What do we want, the gleaners, of the harvest we have reaped?
What do we want, the neuters, of the honey we have heaped?

We want the drones to be driven away from our golden hoard;
We want to share in the harvest; we want to sit at the board;
We want what sword or suffrage has never yet won for man,
The fruits of his toil, God-promised, when the curse of toil began.

Ye have tried the sword and scepter, the cross and the sacred word,
In all the years, and the kingdom is not yet here of the Lord.
Is it useless, all our waiting? Are they fruitless, all our prayers?
Has the wheat, while men were sleeping, been oversowed with
tares?

What gain is it to the people that a God laid down his life,
If, twenty centuries after, His world be a world of strife?
If the serried ranks be facing each other with ruthless eyes
And steel in their hands, what profits a Savior's sacrifice?

Ye have tried, and failed to rule us; in vain to direct have tried,
Not wholly the fault of the ruler; not utterly blind the guide.

Mayhap there needs not a ruler; mayhap we can find the way,
At least ye have ruled to ruin; at least ye have led astray.

What matter if king or consul or president holds the rein
If crime and poverty ever be links in the bondman's chain?
What careth the burden-bearer that Liberty packed his load,
If Hunger presseth behind him with a sharp and ready goad?

There's a serf whose chains are of paper; there's a king with
parchment crown;
There are robber knights and brigands in factory, field and town,
But the vassal pays his tribute to a lord of wage and rent;
And the baron's toil is Shylock's, with a flesh-and-blood per cent.

The seamstress bends to her labor all night in a narrow room;
The child, defrauded of childhood, tiptoes all day at the loom;
The soul must starve; for the body can barely on husks be fed;
And the loaded dice of a gambler settle the price of bread.

Ye have shorn and bound the Samson and robbed him of learn-
ing's light;
But his sluggish brain is moving; his sinews have all their might.
Look well to your gates of Gaza, your privilege, pride and caste!
The Giant is blind and thinking, and his locks are growing fast.

Preparedness—For What?

Ed. Gammons

IT IS full time that we endeavored to analyze the Preparedness agitation, and show the people what is really
behind this flag-waving sound and fury. Any intelligent
workingman can enumerate enough reasons in five minutes
to pull aside the curtain and disclose the skeleton in the
cupboard. So in the space allotted me I shall follow some
aspects which perhaps have not occurred to many, but which
seem very logical to me. The idea of *defense*, in view of the
difficulties attending the transportation of large bodies of
troops, as shown in the European war, is childish and absurd. Furthermore, John Jones does not buy an arsenal
because Bill Smith next door loses both legs and an arm.

Our masters are boosting Preparedness for many reasons. Five of the principal are:

1. Industrial discontent. The report of the Federal
Commission on Industrial Relations. the thousand strikes of
the past few months, peremptory deportations of labor leaders—for instance, Joe Ettor and Gurley Flynn—the suppression of THE BLAST, *Revolt, Alarm, Regeneracion*, etc.—
all this is eloquent of the industrial unrest and the fearful-
ness of our kings of industry.

2. Commercial mastery of South and Central America.
Wall Street watered at the mouth at sight of the commercial
melon of the South when the European war began. The
Latins distrust "Confidence Sam." so Sam must fight off
European traders via the Monroe Policy and force his commerce upon his Latin brothers in the same Christian spirit
with which England forced her opium upon China. The
republics of the South remember Roosevelt's rape of Columbia and will not kiss that gentleman's foot except under
duress.

3. The conquest of Mexico. This will require an enormous army, both to conquer Mexico and overawe the re-
mainder of the Latin republics. It seems certain that Mexico is marked out for exploitation on a huge scale, and that
it will have in the near future its Ludlows. Triangle Factories and McNamaras.

4. Protection of the Morgan interests. Many careful
observers are of the opinion that some of the European nations may repudiate their war debts. In this contingency it
would be eminently desirable to have a Roosevelt in the
White House and a large army and navy to collect his
master's debts.

5. To aid in the exploitation of the world by the newly
formed International Trust. This new combine, jointly financed by Morgan and Rockefeller, aims at the exploitation
of everyone and every country. Its ends are as indefinite as
those of the old South Sea Bubble. It has every force behind
it: church, bayonet, watered stock and an unlimited crop of
suckers.

Preachers, money magnates and labor fakers are equally anxious to convert the country into an armed camp. Even
the vaudevillian preacher cannot get a decent audience nowadays. They have abolished hell in many sects, introduced
whistling beauties and "movies"—without result. The
"hoochee-koochee" will soon be tried with perhaps better results. The financial powers are scared sick by the growing
unrest of the day, and welcome war, as did Russia, England
and Italy. So we are to march away to war shoulder to
shoulder with Linderfeldt of the Colorado militia. who
bravely crushed Louis Tika's skull from behind at Ludlow
("I broke the stock of my rifle on his skull." Linderfeldt
swore, smilingly, after): with the cowardly thugs who bayoneted and shot the women and children of Lawrence, Ludlow and West Virginia: with all the medley of traitors and
spies who aid the exploiters. How damnably impossible!
The rising tide of industrial unionism continues to menace
the livelihood of the Gompers gang. It is slowly permeating
the A. F. of L. It caused paunchy Sam to emit a mournful wail in Washington the other day to the effect that
wages increase in the same proportion as the cost of living.
Common sense brands this statement an obvious lie. Even
the Government statistics show that there is a glaring dis-
proportion. Two years ago a Government statistician gave

data showing that wages increased 11 per cent in a given period, whilst the cost of living increased 35 per cent. So every parasitic influence is lined up: cleric, labor mis-leader and Theodore of spiked-club fame. Never in the history of American politics have the vampire interests stood so solidly together upon the common platform of Preparedness for slaughter and profit. This desperate militaristic boom is the crescendo of American capitalism and is, perhaps, the prelude to the toppling over of the unwieldy system.

Everything seems arranged to put the thing over, and only an incessant, persistent propaganda can save the workers from the peril of militarism. Under the infallible leadership of that "horny-handed son of toil" and A. F. of L. leader, Andy Gallagher of San Francisco, and the "gallant" degenerate bourgeoisie of Portland and Long Beach, with the band blaring "My Dollar, 'Tis of Thee," the "Blocks" of the Pacific Coast are ready to march on—to disaster and disease. If the test of conscription does come, and an effort be made to array our comrades against one another, let us hope that in that crucial hour we will have our Liebknechts, Ginnells and Connollys. Let us emulate the Irish rebels. Let our effective protests, physical and moral, bear silent testimony that there were some proletarians who fought their common enemy at home rather than be shipped like a lot of cattle to a foreign battlefield to help butcher men of their own class, of similar exploitation and similar suffering.

The Creed of the Cave Man
J. W. W.

WE are constantly being told that war is the supreme test which proves whether or not a nation is fit to survive. That out of it come those types which alone are fitted to continue the work of procreating and perpetuating the human race. It is the doctrine of Might is Right. It is the application to human kind of the principle which governs the animal life of the jungle. Now whichever view a person may hold, it will at least be conceded by all that the first requisite for strong and healthy children is strong and healthy parents. So if war produces strong and healthy men, it will justify itself so far as that part is concerned.

But does war make strong and healthy men? Just at present we are able to look at this matter from a very practical standpoint. If a man wishes to go to the war and offers himself as a recruit, his enthusiasm for the fight is only a secondary consideration in deciding the question of whether or not he will be accepted. The first thing required is perfect physical fitness. His wind and limb must be sound, his eyesight keen, and in every bodily respect he must be the kind of man who, from an eugenic point of view, is physically fit to perpetuate his kind. The weedy, the wilted, and the weakly are not accepted. The result is that if the war is of the magnitude of the present one, thousands of physically fit men are killed, and thousands more are broken and maimed so as to be unsuitable types afterwards for the work of reproduction.

The plain object and result of war is to kill healthy men. It does not seek the survival of the fittest, but their annihilation. That is perhaps even more true in these days than in Roman times. The bodily strength of the individual had more to do with victory then than it does today. Men were killed by the strength of men. Today they are killed by the perfection of applied mechanics. It took a strong man to carry a heavy shield and armour and wield a battle-ax. But it does not require a Goliath to work a Maxim gun, which will kill more men in ten minutes than a man could kill with an ax in ten weeks.

So that instead of modern warfare preserving the fittest from death by reason of their superior strength, it

slaughters them under conditions where their strength cannot be used for their protection. As war is carried on now it does not, therefore, eliminate the unfit types. On the contrary, it insures their survival by keeping them out of the conflict. And to them, along with the fit types who do not go to war, the work of reproducing human kind is left. That means that the proportion of unfits in the community is greater than before. Looking at it from a purely utilitarian standpoint, that is the real result of war, despite all the specious arguments and sophistry put forth by the "blood and iron" school. They are the pests of the earth, hovering like vultures wherever peaceful men and women are striving to purge the race of the cave man. In peace they produce nothing. In war they destroy everything. They are the arch-parasites of the age.

Stupidity+Profit=Preparedness

PEOPLE who stand on the lowest rung of the ladder—partly as a result of being stupefied by a patriotic pseudo-religious education and partly for the sake of personal advantages—cede their freedom and sense of human dignity at the bidding of those who stand above them and offer them material advantages. In the same way—in consequence of stupefaction and chiefly for the sake of advantages—those who are a little higher up the ladder cede their freedom and manly dignity, and the same thing repeats itself with those standing yet higher, and so on to the topmost rung—to those who, or to him who, standing at the apex of the social cone, have nothing more to obtain: for whom the only motives of action are love of power and vanity, and who are generally so perverted and stupefied by the power of life and death which they hold over their fellow-men, and by the consequent servility and flattery of those who surround them, that, without ceasing to do evil, they feel quite assured that they are benefactors to the human race. It is the people who sacrifice their dignity as men for material profit that produce these men who cannot act otherwise than as they do, and with whom it is useless to be angry for their stupid and wicked actions. To kill such men is like whipping children whom one has first spoilt. That nations should not be oppressed, and that there should be none of these useless wars, and that man may not be indignant with those who seem to cause these evils, and may not kill them —it seems that only a very small thing is necessary. It is necessary that men should understand things as they are, should call them by their right names, and should know that an army is an instrument for killing, and that the enrolment and management of an army—the very things which kings, emperors and presidents occupy themselves with so self-confidently—is a preparation for murder. If only each king, emperor and president understood that his work of directing armies is not an honorable and important duty, as his flatterers persuade him it is, but a bad and shameful act of preparation for murder—and if each private individual understood that the payment of taxes wherewith to hire and equip soldiers, and, above all, army service itself, are not matters of indifference, but are bad and shameful actions by which he not only permits but participates in murder — then this power of emperors, kings and presidents, which now arouses our indignation, and which causes them to be murdered, would disappear of itself. * * * The crowd is so hypnotized that they see what is going on before their eyes but do not understand its meaning. They see what constant care kings, emperors and presidents devote to their disciplined armies; they see the reviews, parades and manoeuvres the rulers hold, about which they boast to one another; and the people crowd to see their own brothers, brightly dressed up in fools' clothes, turned into machines to the sound of drum and trumpet, all, at the shout of one man, making one and the same movement at one and the same moment; but they do not understand what it all means. Yet the meaning of this drilling is very clear and simple; it is nothing but a preparation for killing.—**Tolstoy**

THE BLAST

Revolutionary Labor Paper
Published every 1st and 15th of the month
569 Dolores St., San Francisco, Cal.

Mail Address, Box 661   Phone, Park 499

Alexander Berkman, Editor and Publisher
M. E. Fitzgerald, Associate Worker   Carl Newlander, Assistant

SUBSCRIPTION
$1.00 Yearly   60c Six Months   5c Copy

Bundle rates 2½c per copy in bundles of ten.
Entered as second-class matter at the postoffice at San Francisco,
Cal., January 14, 1916, under the Act of March 3, 1879.

Reflections

Industrial Mobilization

THE real purpose of Preparedness is daily becoming clearer. The spokesmen of Big Business are growing bolder and letting the cat out of the bag. What they really aim at now is compulsory military training and compulsory military service. Their plan involves not only military but industrial Preparedness. That means no less than industrial mobilization. It means placing in the hands of the Federal government, on call, the whole power of the industrial life of the country, actually turning every industry to war purposes, converting every ploughshare into an instrument of slaughter, if so ordered by our rulers.

Labor does not seem to fully realize the peril of this movement. In its practical application it means the destruction of the whole Labor movement. It means, as the Cincinnati (O.) *Post* frankly puts it, "the organization of our industries for immediate and effective use in case of war."

The scheme is aptly characterized by Howard E. Coffin, Chairman of the Committee on Industrial Preparedness:

"There are three distinct initial steps. The first is to find out what American industry can actually produce in munitions of war. The second is to apply that knowledge in a practical way, which will put the plants of this country into the service of the Government, behind the army and navy. The third step is to form such an organization of skilled labor as *will not get off the job when war comes.*"

In other words, to force the disaffected workers of a given industry into submission, to paralyze their unions and make strikes impossible.

What is going to be the answer of Labor? Is it not time for the workers to prepare against this Preparedness of the Masters?

Militaristic Capitalism

THERE is also another object back of industrial mobilization. The Committee on Industrial Preparedness is requesting the business men and manufacturers of the country to supply detailed data and a complete report of every industrial plant. The Committee is taking pains to assure the people that the returns will be treated as absolutely confidential. "No one but the men actually in charge of the material collected," says the Boston *Daily Advertiser*, one of the spokesmen of the Committee, "will ever know what the report on any individual industrial establishment has been; the data will be in the hands of well-known experts for tabulation, classification and report, and the standing of those men precludes any chance that this information will ever 'leak.'"

Considering that numerous bureaus for this work have already been created, with an army of chiefs, statisticians, clerks, typists, etc., it can readily be seen how "absolutely confidential" the reports will be. The whole scheme plays well into the hands of the big combinations of capital which seek to destroy independent competitors. The latter will be committing suicide by supplying the confidential information to the Committee on Industrial Pre-

paredness, which is merely doing the dirty work for the big monopolists.

Thus Big Business is seeking to kill two birds with one stroke: to make a shortcut to eliminating competition and thereby create a few universal trusts; and, on the other hand, to reduce Labor to absolute submission by abolishing strikes and destroying the organizations of the workers.

Industrial Preparedness is indeed "a tremendous undertaking," as some capitalist editors boast of it. It is an undertaking to reduce the people of America to abject slavery beneath the heel of a gigantic combination of militaristic capitalism.

Smouldering Fires

THE British government, true to its tradition of ruthless extermination of the weaker, has laid a heavy hand on Ireland. The best and bravest sons of Erin have been executed and slaughtered. Now Roger Casement is sentenced to death. He, like his comrades Pearce, Connolly, Sheehy-Skeffington, et al., must pay with his life for the failure of the revolution.

In governmental ethics, failure is the greatest crime. High purpose and noble motive do not count.

If Washington had failed, his life would have been forfeited to England.

What a superficial world that measures value by such a criterion! Failure is the initial step of all success. Only the weak are discouraged and paralyzed by failure. By it the strong grow stronger.

The cause of freedom draws strength from failure. Ireland will not be daunted. The fires of rebellion are not extinguished in its suffering millions. Soon they will burst into flames again with new vigor and more determined purpose, in the clearer consciousness that true freedom and independence for the people of Ireland can be found only in the emancipation of the oppressed masses of every country.

The Vampires of Misery

HIGH dignitaries of the Roman Catholic Church, aided by Irish Labor men, are collecting funds for the sufferers of the Irish revolution. Of course, the Church is very eager to aid the widows and orphans of the rebels murdered by the British government, and incidentally to show to the world the "good works" of the holy Church.

But where was this tender-hearted Church and its benevolent high priests when the Irish revolution was being stifled in the blood of the best and noblest children of Ireland? Did the Vatican or any Prince of the Church make a protest against the slaughter of Pearce, of Connolly and their comrades? By no means. The Pope was the first to condemn the revolutionists and thus justify and encourage the wholesale murders by the British government. Now the Catholic clergy is asking for funds to support the widows and orphans the Church has helped to make.

O ye generation of vampires and hypocrites!

But what have self-respecting revolutionary Labor men in common with this brood? To work hand and hand with these official representatives of the Church means to support this curse and to perpetuate this blackest menace to liberty and progress.

No money on earth can bring back to life the thousands and millions of victims slaughtered by the greed and tyranny of Great Britain, in Ireland, India, Egypt and in England itself. There is not enough money anywhere to support the widows and orphans that government and capitalism are constantly making in the military and industrial trenches of the "civilized" world.

Ireland needs funds, but not for the widows and orphans of the murdered revolutionists. Much more does it need money for arms and ammunition to enable the surviving rebels to resist the increased brutality and oppression by King and Landlord.

But more than all that, it needs the solidarity of the workers in England as well as in Ireland to make common cause against the common enemy of the exploited and disinherited in every land and every country.

An Inspiring Example

THE stand of Carl Liebknecht, of Germany, against the continuance of the war, is highly significant. An act of physical bravery is ennobling. A deed of moral courage is an inspiration. Liebknecht, daring to be true to his ideals in the face of a powerful government and the still more powerful public war-madness, is a great inspiration. Moreover, back of Liebknecht is an intelligent minority in Germany of which he is merely the emphatic spokesman. In every warring country of Europe there are these intelligent minorities, opposed to the slaughter of their fellow men and courageous enough to act up to their beliefs. If all the revolutionary elements of Europe had the sincerity and courage of Liebknecht, there would have been no war. As it is, in every country there are numerous rebels killed and imprisoned because of their opposition to human slaughter. At this very moment our Comrade Guy A. Aldred, editor of the London *Spur*, his co-workers Henry Sara, Allan McDougall, and numerous others, are tortured in the "black houses" of English prisons because of their loyalty to their ideals. The new English Military Service Act excuses from service men having conscientious objections to murder. In spite of it, our anti-militarist comrades are forced into the army or navy and, if objecting, subjected to imprisonment, degradation and torture.

But the example of these valiant protestants is compelling the respect of thinking men and women, and rousing the people to the true character of militarism and government.

May the workers of this country not fail to learn the lesson. Militarism and conscription are about to be foisted on the people of the United States. This country is to be turned into an armed camp, like England, Russia and Germany. Only the immediate active opposition of the workers can save us from the fate of Europe. On this most fundamental issue all revolutionists, rebels, radicals of every shade can and must immediately get together, and in co-operation with the more intelligent element of Labor, help to crystallize and organize the scattered anti-militarist sentiment of this country and rear an effective barrier against the powers of tyranny and greed.

War on Labor

THE Chamber of Commerce of San Francisco has declared open war on organized Labor.

At a mass meeting of its members in one of the local hotels they organized a Law and Order Committee, to establish once for all the principle of the open shop on the Coast. A fund of $1,000,000 is to be raised to exterminate the unions.

Similar action has also been taken by the Chamber of Commerce of Portland. Other cities are to follow the noble example.

After the first flush of indignation, "calmer judgment" prevailed within me, and I decided that, in the last analysis, the war declaration of the Chamber of Commerce is to be welcomed. What's the use of the old hypocrisy, anyway? Why mislead the workers by pretending belief in the harmony of Labor and Capital? The interests of employer and employee are antagonistic, irreconcilable. Why prate of "getting together" between the sheep and the wolf? Each side is working in its own interest. The boss is to be blamed no more than the worker. But it is well for both to know that there is war between them; not as individuals, of course, but as members of two classes of opposing interest, aim and aspiration.

But this declaration of war does not create the condition of war. That has always been there—the war of the classes. But it is well to have the veil of sham and pretended friendship torn off, and the social condition exposed in all its vile nakedness.

It is tragic that there should be strife and war among human beings who, after all, are brothers. But there can be no brotherhood between the master and the slave. Brotherhood is possible only among equals. If you hold the sources of life in your closed fist and I must beg for a chance to exist, you are the master of my life. The time will surely come when all men will have an equal opportunity to live and enjoy. Then we shall be brothers.

To bring that time about, it is necessary to eliminate masters as well as slaves. That can be done only by abolishing the conditions which make them. That is what we are trying to do.

The organization of the workers, the development of their understanding and solidarity, of their initiative and co-operation in a common cause—these are the first steps toward the abolition of existing conditions of wage slavery, oppression and strife.

But the Masters of Life, the Tsars of industry and commerce, declare war upon us. They will not have the workers organize. They will not have them learn the lesson of co-operation and brotherhood. They demand abject submission and threaten us with war.

Well, then, if it is war, be the blood on the head of those who force it upon the workers. It is up to the toilers to defend their organizations, their families, their welfare; aye, their very lives.

What is Organized Labor of San Francisco, of the Coast, going to do?

The Hope of the Longshoremen

THE strike on the water front is too long drawn out. Strikes, to be successful, must be quick and sharp. The longer such a struggle lasts, the less chance for the workers to win: their funds are exhausted, the enthusiasm of the men wanes, their families begin to feel the pinch of hunger. The men grow pessimistic and are ready to return to work under almost any conditions.

This applies to every strike. Even unions with big treasuries are quickly exhausted. You can't match dollar for dollar with the Steel Trust, the Merchants and Manufacturers' Association, the Cloak Manufacturers, the Standard Oil, or other similar plutocratic organizations. The whole capitalist class, practically speaking, comes to the rescue of even the unorganized employer involved in a labor struggle; in fact, he is aided by the whole power of government, with its police, courts and soldiery.

But who comes to the aid of a body of workers defending themselves against the greed of the boss? Only their union; often not even their own international organization. That's why Labor generally loses in these skirmishes—for the lack of solidarity.

The striking longshoremen have repeated the serious mistake of many other strikes: they signed up with the bosses who are not members of the Waterfront Employers' Union and permitted part of their men to go back to work. Thus they defeated the very purpose of their strike: to cause a complete tie-up.

Now the Employers' Union demands the unconditional surrender of the strikers. The only reply the workers of the Coast can give to this demand, coupled as it is with the war ultimatum of the San Francisco Chamber of Commerce, is *immediately to declare a General Strike*.

That alone can save the day and turn the now almost certain defeat of the longshoremen into a decisive victory.

The Cossack Regime

THE terribly underpaid and mistreated iron miners on the ranges of Northern Minnesota have at last rebelled against the Steel Trust and several independent mining companies. Members of the I. W. W. and other revolutionists have loyally come to their support, fighting shoulder to shoulder with the miners and encouraging them in their struggle for more tolerable conditions.

Wm. D. Haywood, General Secretary of the I. W. W., has issued an urgent appeal for help, from which we quote:

"The iron miners are mustering. Twenty thousand have left the mines and pits. The steam shovels are idle. The drills are silent. The miners are on strike in the following camps: Hibbing, 4,000; Chisholm, 2,800; Virginia, 2,500; Buhl, 1,400; Eveleth, 1,600; Gilbert, 900; Biwabik, 600; Aurora, 900; Kinney, 800; and other small camps.

"The demands are $2.75 a day for top men. For miners, dry places, $3.00; for miners, wet places, $3.50. The eight-hour day.

Bi-monthly pay days. Abolition of contract labor. To be paid at once when discharged or leaving work.

"It is the Iron Miners who are making these demands. Men who are doing hard, hazardous work. They take their lives into their hands every time they go down into the mines or pits. They are the men who produce the ore that is converted into iron and steel to make the machinery of the world. Without these men civilization could not exist.

"These barehanded Iron Miners, driven to desperation, have declared industrial war against the United States Steel Corporation. The Masters of Bread are fighting with their usual weapons—gunmen, detectives, courts and the press.

"We are united, but must have help. This is your fight. You must raise money for food, clothing, shelter and organization work. Send funds to WM. D. HAYWOOD, Room 307, 164 W. Washington St., Chicago, Illinois."

The Steel Trust is resorting to the most drastic methods. Four of the miners have been murdered in cold blood by the hired thugs, and the most active men of the strike have been thrown in jail, among them Carlo Tresca, James Gilday, Sam Scarlet. Joseph Schmidt and others. George E. Andreytchine, one of our most energetic and devoted comrades, was arrested for leading a procession of miners to their place of meeting. Shortly after being put in jail he was hurriedly ordered deported by the local immigration inspector, Brown McDonald, of Duluth, Minn.

We have received the following communication from Andreytchine, dated July 8th, Duluth, Minn., and mailed in an official envelope marked U. S. Department of Labor, Immigration Service:

My dear Comrade Berkman:

Last greeting from this land of sorrow, misery and inhuman suffering. The Federal authorities want to deport me to Europe on account of my being an Anarchist and my activities among the striking miners on the Mesaba Iron Range. This is a frame-up of the vile Steel Trust, and as I was an undesirable to it, it is trying to get rid of me. I am not alarmed a damn bit by the barking of this dog, but want you to make good propaganda of my case. If possible make protests in meetings of workers, radical groups, or the way you find best.

You will hear soon from Europe from me.

Hoping that you will do something to stir up the spirit of rebellion among the oppressed in this valley of sorrows, I am

Yours for the cause of suffering humanity,
GEORGE E. ANDREYTCHINE.

Shall these Cossack methods of the American government go unchallenged?

The Magons Bailed

OUR FRIENDS will be glad to learn that at last we succeeded in getting our valiant Comrades Ricardo and Enrique Flores Magon out on bail.

Put under $8000 bonds, the Federal government demanded twice that amount in real estate. It was very difficult to secure in Los Angeles unencumbered property worth $16,000. But good friends came to the rescue and the necessary bail was finally put up. Even then the Federal District Attorney tried his utmost to keep our comrades in jail. Every imaginable obstacle was put in our way by the authorities, but persistence won and the Brothers Magon are now out of their cells, breathing fresh air and enjoying the sunshine and breeze of Lake Silver—a beautiful spot on the outskirts of Los Angeles, where dwells the community of our Mexican comrades.

The Magon case has been appealed. Ricardo and Enrique have no more faith than myself in the justice of "superior" courts. But as both are in poor health, the respite will benefit them. Possibly also the intense feeling against Mexicans manifested at present in the South may lose some of its bitterness in the meantime. At any rate, our comrades will have a chance to recuperate before they must go to prison again.

The Call of the Blast

IT GIVES us pleasure to inform our readers that THE BLAST Picnic, held on July 4th, was a great success—morally. It was truly an international gathering, such as can be found only on the Coast: men, women and children of practically every country on the face of the globe fraternized in a truly international spirit.

On the occasion of the picnic we gave away the premium of Nietzsche's Complete Works, which was "gathered in" by No. 1775A, held by E. Barabino, a young Italian comrade of Oakland, Cal., member of the Circolo Studii Sociali L'Aurora of that city.

In this connection we want to confide to you, friends, a little information that will surely gladden the heart of every well-wisher of THE BLAST. You all know what difficulties a revolutionary publication has to face; what obstacles especially THE BLAST had to overcome, what with the postal suppression, exclusion from the mails and so forth. And yet, in spite of it all, our paper has paid its way. It is going to live and grow in strength. We have decided to double our circulation and to that end it is necessary that each reader make it his business to secure several subscriptions for THE BLAST.

To work, then. There has never been a time when a paper like THE BLAST was needed more than now. Do you agree with us? Then it is up to you.

Those who subscribed only for six months should send in their renewal at once, so as not to miss any issues.

A Word to "Blame" Fools

DID you ever blame the Munitions Makers because we have war?

Did you ever blame the "trusts" because things are high?

Did you ever blame the "rulers" because abuse exists in the different countries?

Did you ever blame "judges" because they send poor devils "over," and order the rope collar for not a few?

Did you ever denounce a newspaper for obviously unfair procedure—and yet keep on taking the paper yourself?

Did you ever blame the "government" for invading your rights of free speech and free press—for suppressing some paper you liked, such as THE BLAST, for instance?

Well, if you only blamed "them," you made a mistake—you should have included someone else.

Stop blaming things—DO something!

In the case of THE BLAST, get subscribers. Explain to your friends that here is a paper which really does offer something apart from the hackneyed. That here is a really courageous voice which will give unpopular truth a hearing, if only it is allowed to do so.

Tell your friends that such men as Charles Erskine Scott Wood and Robert Minor contribute to THE BLAST. It is you who really have something to offer—you need not be ashamed of your mission.

And you will find doing such a thing as this a thousand-fold more profitable than blaming Shadows.

THE BLAST is going to live if you refuse to be a party to its assassination.

THE BLASTERS.

The Strange Mr. X.

Emanuel Julius

I DON'T remember just how I first came to know him. I think, however, that he dropped into my apartment one Sunday afternoon while I was entertaining a group of friends. Who brought him, I cannot say. It may be that he came with Harry, or Frank, or Charlie, but I think he came alone. Instead of introducing himself to us, this stranger succeeded in getting all of us to tell him our names. One asked for his, but he politely evaded.

He had a soft voice that always struck a responsive chord in me; it was slow, clear—well, I may as well quote Frank and say that it impressed one as being "Christ-like," a voice that made you feel as though you were right close to the man. There was a suggestion of pathos in it.

When he stood with his back to the window, the sunlight playing on his huge crop of brown hair, he gave one the notion that he was wearing a halo. The mysterious Mr. X.—so we soon named him—had a brown beard that took on a golden hue when he stood in the light. He wore one of those soft hats that may be crumpled into a ball. Most of the time he kept it in the pocket of his loose, black coat.

The strange Mr. X. soon convinced us (without effort on his part) that he had a keen sense of appreciation and that his taste in art was faultless. He had a beautiful philosophy that pervaded his opinions, thoughts, and actions. His code of ethics seemed to out-Christian Christianity. He made me think of Manson in Charles Rann Kennedy's "The Servant in the House": there was that sense of spiritual calm about his personality, a majestic serenity. * * * *

I GREW to like him immensely. After an hour with him one felt as though he had taken a soul-bath. I remember how Frank—who worked with me on the *New York Star*—once swatted a fly while in the presence of my friend. Mr. X. actually winced, so intensely did he feel the suffering of that creature. "Life is precious," he almost sighed.

Once, while we were walking, a pick-pocket attempted to rob my friend; but, caught in the act, the booty-seeker loosened his grip on the bills, letting them fall to the ground. Instead of calling a policeman, my friend leaned over, picked up the money and handed it to the thief. "You must need it or you wouldn't try to steal it," he said.

I learned — purely through accident — that Mr. X. had been married. Without going into detail, he told me how his wife —a beautiful woman—had decided that her love should go to another. Despite his great love for her, he calmly stepped aside, giving his full permission to what many may have considered an escapade. "She felt that I wasn't good enough for her," was his amazing statement, amazing because he was looked upon as the soul of goodness.

While we were walking again some days later, we were approached by a beggar who implored help. What did my friend do but empty a handful of coins from one of his pockets. * * * *

THE CITY editor had given me an assignment that I did not relish. I left the office and hurried to the Grand Central Station, where I took a train for Ossining, where Sing Sing is located.

On the train I met my friend. He seemed very sad and downcast. Learning that he was going to Sing Sing, I felt as though here was a Christ entering the temple to drive forth the money-changers.

We were both going to an execution. The State was going to take a human life. "Life is precious"—those were the words I recalled as I looked at my friend. He had said this when a fly had been crushed. How intense his feelings must be when it is a human being who is to be placed in an electric chair by grim men determined to burn the life out of him!

* * * *

WE LEFT the station, my friend allowing me to lead the way. It was while we were walking along the road that I noticed him draw back suddenly. I soon learned the reason: he had almost stepped upon an ant. In this he reminded me of the *Good Man* in Victor Hugo's story. Mr. X., like the character in the novel, almost sprained his ankle rather than destroy precious life!

I soon began to wonder why he was going to Sing Sing. Was it to voice a great protest against the taking of a human life? Was it to call attention to an evil? Was it to point the way to love and brotherhood?

These questions I asked myself as we walked that road. Imagine my indescribable astonishment when I later realized that my friend, the mysterious Mr. X., was the State Executioner.

EMMA GOLDMAN

In San Francisco, at
Fillmore Street Averill Hall
1861 Fillmore Street
Between Sutter and Bush Streets

SUNDAY, JULY 16, 8:00 P. M.
"Anarchism and Human Nature — Do They Harmonize?"
TUESDAY, JULY 18, 8:00 P. M.
"The Family—Its Enslaving Effect upon Parents and Children"
WEDNESDAY, JULY 19, 8:00 P. M.
"Art for Life"
THURSDAY, JULY 20, 8:00 P. M.
"Preparedness, the Road to Universal Slaughter"
FRIDAY, JULY 21, 8:00 P. M.
"Friedrich Nietzsche and the German Kaiser"
SATURDAY, JULY 22, 8:00 P. M.
"The Educational and Sexual Mutilation of the Child"
(The Gary System Discussed)
SUNDAY, JULY 23, 8:00 P. M.
"The Philosophy of Atheism"
(The lecture delivered before the Congress of Religious Philosophies held at San Francisco during the Exposition)
Questions and Discussion at All Lectures

Admission, 25 Cents

VOL. 1   SAN FRANCISCO, AUGUST 15, 1916   No. 17

WORSHIPING THE GOD OF DYNAMITE

Worshiping the God of Dynamite

MILITARISM is the worship of the mailed fist, of force and violence, of wholesale slaughter by powder, lead and dynamite.

The tragedy of July 22d, when a bomb or infernal machine was exploded with fatal results during the Preparedness parade, is to be traced directly to the murder psychology developed by the military preparedness agitation. That agitation is imbuing the minds of the people with national and racial antagonisms, with thoughts of hatred, violence and slaughter. If you persist in charging the social atmosphere with the spirit of violence and murder, you may expect sooner or later to reap the inevitable results.

The advocates of militarism are creating this spirit. What are Preparedness parades for but to pave the way for wholesale murder? You may disguise it with the cloak of patriotism and national defense, but whatever its uniform, Preparedness means preparation to kill, to kill on a large scale.

To try to connect the Anarchists, the I. W. W., the Labor elements or the participants in the Peace meeting with the bomb tragedy is stupid. The act was obviously the work of an individual who evidently sought to express his opposition to Preparedness for Slaughter by using the ammunition of Preparedness. Terrible as the tragedy is, it is merely a foretaste in miniature of what the people may expect, multiplied a million times, from the Preparedness insanity. It should serve as a lesson of the real meaning and menace of Preparedness and of the spirit it is already generating among the people.

It is also possible that the bomb was meant as an answer to the Chamber of Commerce to its declaration of war on organized Labor of San Francisco. In any event it is clear that oppression and threats from above, and preparation for military and industrial slaughter, inevitably lead to bitter resentment and violent opposition below.

Force, violence and murder are the keynote of our whole civilization. We may get hysterical over the bomb tragedy, rage and rave over it, and condemn this and condemn that. But we will not prevent the recurrence of such acts unless we seek and. find the underlying CAUSES. Creating special detective bureaus, offering greed-exciting rewards, or thundering anathemas by pulpit and press will not do the least to solve the question. All that only serves to confuse the minds of the people, to arouse cupidity and to create new opportunities for graft and oppression.

If the people of San Francisco really want to prevent the recurrence of such acts of violence, let them realize that as long as the workers are exploited and robbed of their product, we will have poverty and unemployment, desperation, wars and crime of every kind. Abolish the conditions that foster privileged monopoly on the back of Labor and you will do away with the strife and antagonism of our life, with crime and war, with Preparedness parades and the spirit of violence bred by them.

Planning Another 11th of November

ON THE afternoon of July 22d, while the Preparedness parade was in progress, a bomb exploded on Steuart street, San Francisco. The explosion cost the lives of nine persons who were in the immediate vicinity.

As usual, in such cases, the local authorities immediately raised the cry of "Anarchist." The pulpit and the yellow press began inciting the populace to mob violence, and the Hearst papers openly advocated the immediate extermination of every radical and progressive element in San Francisco, aye, in the whole country.

It must be said to the lasting credit of the people of San Francisco that they refused to be moved by the homicidal hysteria of Hearst and his press prostitutes. Rave as he may in his blood-dripping editorials, the public remained calm and reasonable, awaiting the result of three separate investigations, instituted by the Federal authorities, the Post Office and the police.

It appears that hundreds of letters and postal cards had been mailed to prominent citizens as well as to local newspapers, *warning* them that an act of violence was to be executed against the Preparedness parade. Incredible as it may sound, none of the papers or the leaders of the parade—all of whom had been warned days and weeks before the parade, according to the testimony of the police and postal authorities,—permitted the people to get the least hint of the planned catastrophe.

Thornwell Mullally, grand marshal of the parade, has since admitted that he himself received similar warnings, and yet he cruelly and apparently wilfully led the paraders to what might have been certain death.

Why? Why were the public not warned by those who had been warned? That is the question that is burning in the hearts of the people. It is especially vital to those who have lost friends and relatives in the explosion.

Why were the people of San Francisco not warned? Why were they blindly led to slaughter?

And what has become of the Federal and police investigations of the numerous letters of warning sent through the post office? Why is not the writer, or writers, apprehended? *Why has the search for them been abandoned?*

The people of San Francisco want to know. They demand an answer.

* * * *

Several weeks previous to the Preparedness parade, during the strike of the Longshoremen, the San Francisco Chamber of Commerce issued a public ultimatum declaring war on organized Labor. At the mass meeting of Big Business, held under the auspices of the Chamber of Commerce, the employers threw down the gauntlet to Labor. The chairman of the meeting was Frederick J. Koster, president of the Chamber of Commerce, and the keynote of the assembly was struck by Captain Robert Dollar, of the Ship Owners' Association, when he said that "the only way to settle the strike is to send several ambulance loads of strikers to the hospital."

This sentiment was vociferously applauded by the assembly of over 1000 respectable, *law-abiding* business men. Nor did this mass meeting merely talk. It acted. It acted as it talked. A Law and Order committee of 100 was elected with F. J. Koster as chairman and Captain Dollar as one of its most efficient members. A fund of $1,000,000 was pledged *to fight the unions* and to turn the strongly organized city of San Francisco into an open-shop town like Los Angeles.

This Law and Order committee of 100, the Vigilante body of employers, has since taken charge of the city. It represents less than one-tenth of the citizenship, but it is in practical control of the District Attorney's office and of the police, and is dictating the policy of the local press. It is crowding the police courts with its members when union men are arrested for picketing. Its attorneys are at the side of the public prosecutor for the purpose of influencing the judges and railroading the strikers to prison.

It is this Law and Order committee that is now bossing the city of San Francisco. The Vigilantes have usurped the administrative and executive power of the city government. Mayor Rolph and Police Chief White have been virtually stripped of authority, and the Chamber of Commerce has constituted itself investigator, prosecutor, and judge of the situation.

*   *   *   *

What are the Vigilantes of Big Business doing?

In pursuit of the scheme to kill the unions of San Francisco and make it an open-shop scab town, they have determined to terrorize organized Labor in the persons of its best-known radical representatives. At first they tried to victimize the speakers at the Peace meeting, held in protest against Preparedness a few days before the parade. They maliciously charged them with responsibility for the tragedy. This failing, they instituted a man-hunt after the prominent Anarchists that happened to be in the city at the time. They raided the office of THE BLAST, attempted to incite mobs against the lectures of Emma Goldman, and tried to suppress all street meetings. All this falling flat, they decided to exploit the bomb tragedy to further their warfare against unionism. The order went out to arrest those known as the most energetic and uncompromising Labor men.

Who are the best hated men by the bosses of San Francisco?

Edward D. Nolan and **Tom Mooney.** Forthwith both of them were arrested, thrown into prison, tortured with the third degree, and held incommunicado as in the darkest days of the Spanish Inquisition.

Ed Nolan, an idealist and active union man, is one of the most beautiful personalities in the American Labor movement. For years he has been recognized as one of the most intelligent and absolutely incorruptible Labor men, and as such he is beloved by the rank and file of the workers of San Francisco. He had just returned from the Machinists' convention in Baltimore, to which he was a delegate, when he was arrested.

Tom Mooney is a rare type of devoted and energetic worker, cordially hated by every corrupt Labor politician, but respected and admired by the intelligent element of the toilers. He is a member of the Moulders' Union, a former delegate to the Labor Council, and a man who has been active in every important struggle of the workers of San Francisco for almost a decade. As the authorized organizer of the International Carmen's Union, Mooney recently tried to organize the motormen and conductors of the United Railroads Company of San Francisco. A strike of the platform men, attempted on July 14th, failed to come to a head, and the United Railroads immediately marked Mooney for their victim. As a matter of fact, the U. R. R. had several weeks previously put up bulletins at the car barns denouncing Mooney as a dynamiter and warning their men to have nothing to do with him, on pain of immediate discharge. By a rather peculiar "coincidence" the U. R. R. denounced Mooney as a dynamiter one day *previous* to the blowing up of some supply towers of the company.

Briefly, the bosses have many old grudges against Tom Mooney for his activity in former strikes. Thus they did their utmost to railroad him to the penitentiary several years before, during the gas works strike, but after three trials Mooney was exonerated and acquitted by a jury.

It was in connection with this attempted railroading of Mooney that the authorities succeeded in sending **Warren K. Billings** to prison, the man who is now charged, together with

Mooney, with having been a principal in the bomb affair. Billings was formerly president of the Shoe Workers' Union, and he has always claimed that he was sent to prison on a police frame-up.

Among the others indicted for murder in this connection are **Israel Weinberg**, one of the directors of the Jitney Bus Union, which organization has long been a sharp thorn in the side of the U. R. R., and **Mrs. Rena Hermann Mooney**, wife of Tom Mooney, an artist and music teacher.

There were also arrested Julius Kastner, an Austrian; Tom Ryan, a picket of the Restaurant Workers, and Mrs. Belle Lavin, all of them finally discharged as perfectly innocent, after having been subjected to vile indignities, brutally sweated and held incommunicado for over a week.

*   *   *   *

Those who know Nolan, Mooney, Weinberg and Billings are absolutely certain that they are perfectly innocent of any connection with the bomb explosion. The unions to which these men belong have already signified their full confidence in them, and the Labor Council has voiced the firm conviction that our imprisoned friends have been picked as the victims of the bosses.

The whole Labor movement of San Francisco knows that in the persons of Nolan, Mooney, Weinberg and Billings the employers seek to terrorize organized Labor. It is the openly avowed purpose of the Chamber of Big Business to paralyze and destroy the whole Labor movement on the Coast. The arrest and indictment on the charge of murder of Nolan, Mooney et al. is but the masters' entering wedge, with the ultimate purpose of exterminating unionism in San Francisco and enthroning the ruthless will of Big Business.

The workers know what this means. The Chamber of Commerce is resorting to drastic, desperate methods. It is the opening chapter of their promised relentless warfare on Labor.

THE BLAST is the voice of the awakening toilers. It will fight to the last ditch this heinous murder conspiracy of Capital. The enemy is athirst for blood: it is planning to transplant to San Francisco the gallows of 1887 when five of Labor's best and truest friends were strangled to death in Chicago. We feel that the workers of America will not permit a repetition of that five-fold judicial murder. It is the solemn duty of every lover of liberty and friend of Labor to hasten to the rescue. Action is necessary—quick action—immediate, to prevent the planned diabolic outrage. Agitation and funds are needed at once. Publicity is necessary to enlighten the people about the bloody vengeance Capital is scheming. No stone must be left unturned to expose the vile conspiracy of the bosses and to tear Labor's prisoners of war from the rapacious maw of the bloodthirsty masters.

THE BLAST hereby pledges its unconditional support to these victims of the Law and Order canaille. All threats and intimidation notwithstanding, we are determined to devote our time, ability and energy to save these brave soldiers in the war of humanity from the doom already spoken against them by the enemies of Labor, of Progress, of Humanity. We solemnly appeal to every fair-minded and liberty-loving man and woman to respond to the call and to respond ere it is too late. Now is the time to demonstrate, once for all, that we of the awakened social consciousness will not tolerate a repetition of the hellish crime of the 11th of November, 1887.

THE BLAST will gladly accept contributions for the defense.

THE BLAST

Revolutionary Labor Paper
Published every 1st and 15th of the month
569 Dolores St., San Francisco, Cal.
Mail Address, Box 661   Phone, Park 499

Alexander Berkman, Editor and Publisher
M. E. Fitzgerald, Associate Worker   Carl Newlander, Assistant

SUBSCRIPTION
$1.00 Yearly   60c Six Months   5c Copy
Bundle rates 2½c per copy in bundles of ten.

Violence and Anarchism
Alexander Berkman

IT IS growing rather monotonous to hear the cry of "Anarchist conspiracy" raised whenever and wherever there happens an "unlawful" shot or bomb explosion.

Let us consider the matter dispassionately. Is violence specifically Anarchistic? Is the taking of human life such a very unusual occurrence among "civilized" peoples? Is our whole social existence anything but an uninterrupted series of murder, assassination, mutilation? All our honored institutions are rooted in the very spirit of murder. Do we build warships for educational purposes? Is the army a Sunday school? Our police, jails and penitentiaries—what purpose do they serve but to suppress, kill and maim? Is the gallows the symbol of our brotherhood, the electric chair the proof of our humanitarianism?

"All these things are necessary evils," we are told by the self-satisfied. True, they are necessary; necessary to preserve society *as it is*. But has it ever occurred to the "good citizen" whether it is really necessary to preserve things as they are? Is it indeed worth while?

Organized society can have but one *raison d'etre;* namely, the greatest good of its members. Let us examine, then, whether society, as at present constituted, can be justly said to fulfill its mission.

No life, individual or collective, is possible without the means of subsistence. The social members supplying these means are, consequently, the life-givers of the community. And who are they? The question answers itself automatically: the producers of the country's wealth are the conservators of its life. All members and classes of society should equally benefit by the fact of our combined effort as a society. But if, for any reason, distinctions are to be made, the producing class, the real backbone of the social body, should have the preference.

In other words, the workers are the ones who should enjoy the greatest benefits arising from social organization. That is the true mission of human society. Does the latter accomplish it? Does it come anywhere near accomplishment?

By no means. The producers are the very ones on whose shoulders rests the whole burden of our social evils. They are the disinherited, the submerged. The products of their toil are the property of some one else; the land and machinery, without which no production is possible, are not owned by them; as a result, they are forced to sell their labor for whatever pittance the employers condescend to give. Hence poverty, starvation, and widespread misery among the very class which, as the sole producer, has the best claim to enjoy the blessings of organized social life.

To support, defend and perpetuate these unjust and terrible conditions it is necessary to have police, prisons, laws and government. For the disinherited are not content to forever starve in the midst of plenty, and the exploited are beginning to cry out against their cruel bondage.

These cries, these signs of rebellious dissatisfaction must be stifled. That is the mission of law and government: to preserve things as they are; to secure to the rich their stolen wealth; to strangle the voice of popular discontent.

Such is the social life of "civilized" countries. A life of misery and degradation, of economic exploitation, governmental suppression, legal brutality and judicial murder. Sham, injustice and tyranny are the synonyms of organized society. Shall we preserve it as it is? Is it necessary and desirable? Is it even possible?

*   *   *   *

"But you can't regenerate society by violence, by a bomb," the well-meaning people argue.

Indeed, full well we know we cannot. Be fair; give ear. Do not confound the philosophy of a better, freer and happier life with an *act resulting from the very evils which that philosophy seeks to abolish.*

Anarchism is the science of social order, as opposed to existing disorder; of brotherhood, as against present Ishmaelitism; of individual liberty and well-being, as opposed to legal oppression, robbery and universal misery.

This condition of social regeneration cannot be achieved by the will or act of any man or party. The enlightenment of the workers regarding the evils of wage slavery, the awakening of the public conscience to a clearer understanding of liberty and justice—these are the forces which will abolish all forms of bondage, political, economical and social, replacing present institutions by free co-operation and the solidarity of communal effort.

"But the bomb?" cry the judges in and out of court. The bomb is the echo of your cannon, trained upon our starving brothers; it is the cry of the murdered striker; 'tis the voice of hungry women and children; the shriek of the maimed and torn in your industrial slaughter houses; it is the dull thud of the policeman's club upon a defenseless head; 'tis the shadow of the crisis, the rumbling of suppressed earthquake—it is Desperation's lightning out of an atmosphere of degradation and misery that king, president and plutocrat have heaped upon humanity. *The bomb is the ghost of your past crimes.*

You may foam and legislate, arrest, imprison and deport. You may still further tighten the thumb-screws of persecution, erect more gallows, and build electric chairs. Pitiful fools! Thus was Christ crucified as a disturber of "Caesar's peace." Did Golgotha suppress his teaching? Have the unspeakable tortures of the Inquisition eradicated free thought? Did Louis XVI save his crown—or his head—by *lettre de cachet?* Has the cause of the Abolitionists been defeated by the judicial murder of John Brown?

"Our graves will speak louder than the voices you strangle!" In spite of all the strenuous governmental, capitalistic and journalistic efforts to misrepresent and suppress Anarchists and Anarchism—because of those efforts—the people will yet learn the truth.

Valuation of Life
R. M.

AFTER the Sepoy Rebellion in India, the British military authorities discovered a peculiar condition among the English troops. The common soldier's mind had undergone terrible days of fighting and nights of slaughter until human life meant little to him any longer. For a typical instance, one soldier asked another, "Got a light, Joe?" "Go to hell, you blighter," was the reply. Whereupon the man who needed a light ripped the stomach of the other man open with a knife. Cases of that kind became so frequent after the Sepoy Rebellion that the army authorities had to take special measures to separate the soldiers from their small arms. Just the dwelling upon the idea of slaughter wears away a man's valuation of human life and promotes in his mind morbid tendencies to destroy.

I had an example of the same thing myself recently when I crossed the sea en route to Europe as a war correspondent. Everybody on the ship was talking war, weapons, killing. In war time the soldiers particularly idealize the bayonet. They call it "Rosalie" and sing songs to it as their "cold steel sweetheart." Morning, noon and night, this wild hubbub of war-talk went on, until one man went crazy and imagined that it was his duty to kill somebody. He tried to throw me into the sea. With a fight I saved myself, but his enthusiasm was too great to be thwarted, so with a wild laugh he threw himself into the sea and was drowned.

There are some of us to whom the idea of killing is repellant. I, for one, don't like guns, knives, bayonets, dynamite, guncotton and artillery. I hate such things because I hate the thing they are made for—killing.

We who dislike killing don't believe in it, and don't believe in getting prepared to kill—we who think that gun-toting, bomb-making, cannon-making and bloodthirstiness make the lowest ideal that man can stoop to—we are called anti-militarists. Since we do not like those things, we naturally express our dislike of the idealization of militarism. We have said frankly, honestly and openly that we do not believe in spilling blood.

But others have a love for military things, for guns, ammunition. They have been carrying on a campaign for many months, crying to the whole world: "Arm! Prepare! Be skilled in killing! Let us know how to kill better than any other people can!"

With all our hearts and heads we believe that that sort of talk is wrong, is injurious to the character of men and boys and women. We believe that it lowers the standards of every person who hears such a thing, lessens their respect for human life, human progress and decency. We believe that it nurtures all that is morbid in the human brain, all the traits that go back to the jungle from which the human race has progressed. And yet, when a cataclysm comes, when in the midst of a demonstration of the military ideal, some person uses an explosive (the very munition of war that is being idealized) thereby killing innocent sightseers and paraders who were probably forced to march by employers—those very persons who have trained morbid minds to violence, will blame *us* for the occurrence!

To those of you who are in the habit of thinking, who do not blindly take whatever rot you may see in the papers for the solemn truth, we ask—do you not think it possible that the long months of ranting by "preparationists," interventionists and explosive manufacturers may have had the effect of driving an over-susceptible brain to using the very munition for which they preach?

Down With the Anarchists!

WE must get rid of the Anarchists! They are a menace to society. Does not Hearst say so? Do not the M. & M. and the gentlemen of the Chamber of Commerce, who have also declared war on Labor, assure us that the Anarchists are dangerous and that they are responsible for all our troubles? Does not every skinner of Labor and every grafting politician shout against the Anarchists? Isn't that enough to prove that the Anarchists are dangerous?

But why are all the money bags and their hirelings so unanimous in condemning the Anarchists? Generally they disagree on many questions and they bitterly fight each other in their business and social life. But on TWO questions they are always in accord.

What are those two questions that all the capitalists and profit mongers are always in perfect agreement on? They are these:

Smash the Labor Unions!

Hang the Anarchists!

WHY? Because the Labor Unions are cutting the bosses' profits by constantly demanding higher wages. And the Anarchists want to abolish the boss altogether.

Now, what is the matter with the Anarchists? What do you really know about them, except the lies and misrepresentations of their enemies—who are also the enemies of the workers and opposed to every advancement of Labor? If you stop to think of it, you really know nothing of the Anarchists and their teachings. Your masters and their press have taken good care that you shouldn't learn the truth about them. Why? Because as long as they can keep you busy shouting against the Anarchists, they are safe in their saddle on the backs of the people.

That's the whole secret.

What do the Anarchists really want? When you know that, you will be able to decide for yourself whether the Anarchists are your enemies or your friends.

The Anarchists say that it is not necessary to have murder and crime, poverty and corruption in the world. They say that we are cursed with these evils because a handful of people have monopolized the earth and all the wealth of the country. But who produces that wealth? Who builds the railroads, who digs the coal, who works in the fields and factories? You can answer that question for yourself. It is the toilers who do all the work and who produce all that we have in the world.

The Anarchists say: The products of Labor should belong to the producers. The industries should be carried on to minister to the needs of the people instead of for profit, as at present. Abolishing monopoly in land and in the sources of production, and making the opportunity for production accessible to all, would do away with capitalism and introduce free and equal distribution. That, in turn, would do away with laws and government, as there would be no need for them, government serving only to conserve the institutions of today and to protect the masters in their exploitation of the people. It would abolish war and crime, because the incentive to either would be lacking. It would be a society of real freedom, without coercion or violence, based on the voluntary communal arrangement of "To each according to his needs; from each according to his ability."

That is what the Anarchists teach. Suppose they are all wrong. Are you going to prove it by hanging them? If they are wrong, the people will not accept

A Raid and a Visit

AT LAST! A squad of detectives of the newly created bomb bureau came down upon the office of THE BLAST. A raid, b'gosh!

It happened a whole week after the bomb explosion. Why did they give us so much time to "prepare"? "For ways and tricks peculiar, etc." Stupidity alone does not exhaust the explanation. Of course the police knew that we had nothing to do with the explosion. Cool and gentle as we are, we never explode. The guardians knew there was no cause for a raid. But having spent much precious time without securing the least clue to the perpetrator of the bomb, *something* had to be done. A special police bomb bureau had been created. Well, the bureau had to show that it was on the job.

The raid on THE BLAST was therefore an afterthought. It was led by Assistant District Attorney Cunha and three other "detectives," among them Swanson, formerly the local chief of the Pinkerton agency. We say "detectives" in quotation marks: the degree of intelligence the raiders showed convinced us that they couldn't detect the trail of an elephant on a muddy cowpath. They actually asked me whether I had explosives in the house! Of course I had. I thought Cunha's face blanched perceptibly when I held out to him a .38-calibre revolver, with the remark: "It's loaded and it's liable to explode." "This isn't what we want," he said rather petulantly, giving back the gun to me. But when I returned to the room a few minutes later I noticed that he had very cautiously removed the bullets from the revolver. Safety first!

I had another kind of explosive in the house which I strongly recommended to the visitors. It was mental dynamite in the form of copies of THE BLAST, Anarchist pamphlets and books. But the raiders didn't seem to care much for that kind of awakener. After a vain search for bombs, lasting four hours, they depaprted, their ideas, and therefore there can be no danger from them. But, if they are right, it would be good for us to find it out. In any case it is a question of learning what these Anarchists really want. Let the people hear them.

But how about violence? you say. Don't the Anarchists preach and practice violence and murder?

They don't. On the contrary, the Anarchists hold life as the most sacred thing. That's why they want to change the present order of things where everyone's hand is against his brother, and where war, wholesale slaughter in the pursuit of the dollar, bloodshed in the field, factory and workshop is the order of the day. The poverty, misery and bitter industrial warfare, the crimes, suicides and murder committed every day of the year in this country will convince any man of intelligence that in present society we have plenty of Law, but mighty little order or peace.

Anarchism means OPPOSITION to violence, by whomever committed, even if it be by the government. The government has no more right to murder than the individual. Anarchism is therefore opposition to violence as well as to government forcibly imposed on man.

The Anarchists value human life. In fact, no one values it more. Why, then, are the Anarchists always blamed for every act of violence? Because your rulers and exploiters want to keep you prejudiced against the Anarchists, so you will never find out what the Anarchists really want, and the masters will remain safe in their monopoly of life.

Now, what are facts about violence? Crimes of every kind happen every day. Are the Anarchists responsible for them? Or is it not rather misery and desperation that drive people to commit such acts? Does a millionaire go out on the street and knock you down with a gaspipe to rob you of a few dollars? O, no: He builds a factory and robs his workers in a way that is much safer, more profitable and within the law.

Who, then, commits acts of violence? The desperate man, of course. He to whom no other resort seems open. Violence is committed by all kinds of people. Such violence is mostly for the purpose of theft or robbery. But there are also cases where it is done for social reasons. Such impersonal acts of violence have, from time immemorial, been the reply of goaded and desperate classes, and goaded and desperate individuals, to wrongs from their fellow-men, which they felt to be intolerable. Such acts are the violent RECOIL from violence, whether aggressive or repressive; they are the last desperate struggle of outraged and exasperated human nature for breathing space and life. And their CAUSE LIES NOT IN ANY SPECIAL CONVICTION, BUT IN HUMAN NATURE ITSELF. The whole course of history, political and social, is strewn with evidence of this fact. To go no further, take the Revolutionists of Russia, the Fenians and Sinn Feiners of Ireland, the Republicans of Italy. Were those people Anarchists? No. Did they all hold the same political opinions? No. But all were driven by desperate circumstances into this terrible form of revolt.

Anarchists, as well as others, have sometimes committed acts of violence. Do you hold the Republican Party responsible for every act committed by a Republican? Or the Democratic Party, or the Presbyterian or Methodist Church responsible for acts of individual members? It would be stupid to do so.

Under miserable conditions of life, any vision of the possibility of better things makes the present misery more intolerable, and spurs those who suffer to the most energetic struggles to improve their lot, and if these struggles only immediately result in sharper misery, the outcome is sheer desperation. In our present society, for instance, an exploited wage worker, who catches a glimpse of what work and life might and ought to be, finds the toilsome routine and the squalor of his existence almost intolerable; and even when he has the resolution and courage to continue steadily working his best, and waiting until new ideas have so permeated society as to pave the way for better times, the mere fact that he has such ideas and tries to spread them brings him into difficulties with his employers. How many thousands of rebel workers, of Socialists, of Industrialists and Syndicalists, but above all of Anarchists, have lost work and even the chance of work, solely on the ground of their opinions? It is only the specially gifted craftsman who, if he be a zealous propagandist, can hope to retain permanent employment. And what happens to a man with his brain working actively with a ferment of new ideas, with a vision before his eyes of a new hope dawning for toiling and agonizing men, with the knowledge that his suffering and that of his fellows in misery is not caused by the cruelty of fate, but by the injustice of other human beings—what happens to such a man when he sees those dear to him starving, when he himself is starved? Some natures in such a plight, and those by no means the least social or the least sensitive, will become violent, and will even feel that their violence is social and not anti-social, that in striking when and how they can, they are striking, not for themselves, but for human nature, outraged and despoiled in their persons and in those of their fellow sufferers. And

obviously dissatisfied. I knew they wouldn't be happy til they found what they were looking for, but I don't believe in coddling people.

They appropriated, however, copies of our California subscription list, shockingly surprised to find that there were so many Anarchists in the otherwise happy and peaceful Golden State.

A few days later Miss Fitzgerald and myself were "invited" by the chief to visit headquarters. There we were forced to waste five perfectly good hours in answering fool questions. I found the "superior" officials of the District Attorney's office and of the Detective Bureau of a much inferior intelligence than similar officials in other cities. Not a single one of my half dozen inquisitors, including Assistant District Attorney James Brennan, showed the faintest understanding of social problems or of modern movements. I was glad of the opportunity to explain the philosophy of Anarchism to the assembled representatives of government. "There is no reason why even they should not learn something," I thought. But I soon gave up the attempt as hopeless when Detective Swanson, considered the most intelligent of the crew, met one of my arguments with this profound parry: "It's nonsense to say the land is monopolized. If you got enough money you can buy any piece of land you want."

The keynote of their intelligence and decency was finally struck by Assistant District Attorney Brennan (an aspirant for a Senator's toga) when he repeatedly shouted at me, "Every Anarchist is a criminal. We'll hang you all, every one of you!"

The same gentleman tried to intimidate and cajole, in turn, my associate worker, Miss Fitzgerald. He very discreetly inquired whether we hang our underwear on the same clothesline, and in the next breath wondered why "such a nice sweet lady with such a good Irish name" could have anything in common with the terrible Anarchists. He thundered maledictions on my unprotected head and assured her that I am the worst criminal in the country, intimately associated with every crook.

In her calm, well-poised manner Miss Fitzgerald replied that she was proud to be connected with the Anarchists; but she has been wondering ever since what had been my association with the District Attorney's office.

But for a quick presto change artist Mr. Brennan beats the champion vaudeville performers. When we were "invited" to his office the next day, I hardly knew him. His manner had completely changed. A bully the previous day, he was now the acme of Chesterfieldianism. Will Mr. Berkman please be seated? Will Mr. Berkman be good enough to answer a question or two? etc.

I was wondering what ruse was being

are we, who ourselves are not in this horrible predicament, to stand by and coldly condemn these piteous victims of the Furies and Fates? Are we to decry as miscreants these human beings who act with heroic self-devotion, often sacrificing their lives in protest, where less social and less energetic natures would lie down and grovel in abject submission to injustice and wrong? Are we to join the ignorant and brutal outcry which stigmatizes such men as monsters of wickedness, gratuitously running amuck in a harmonious and innocently peaceful society? NO! We hate murder with a hatred that may seem absurdly exaggerated to apologists for war, industrial slaughter and Ludlow massacres, to callous acquiescers in governmental and plutocratic violence, but we decline in such cases of homicide as those of which we are treating, to be guilty of the cruel injustice of flinging the whole responsibility of the deed upon the immediate perpetrator. The guilt of these homicides lies upon every man and woman who, intentionally or by cold indifference, helps to keep up social conditions that drive human beings to despair. The man who flings his whole life into the attempt, often at the cost of his own life, to protest against the wrongs of his fellow-men, is a saint compared to the active and passive upholders of cruelty and injustice, even if his protest destroy other lives besides his own. Let him who is without sin in society cast the first stone at such a one.

THE BLAST GROUP
GROUP FREEDOM
ITALIAN ANARCHIST GROUP VOLONTA
UNION OF RUSSIAN WORKERS

Per $\begin{cases} \text{ALEXANDER BERKMAN} \\ \text{EMMA GOLDMAN} \end{cases}$

Some Direct Questions for the District Attorney

In these columns Questions will be asked and Truths will be told that no other local paper dares to breathe. These columns are open to the public.

Question 1. What has become of Mrs. William Hinckley Taylor, who led the Women's Division of the Preparedness parade? She repeatedly declared that a note of warning had been handed to her by a small swarthy man just before the explosion. Where is that note? Why is the District Attorney's office silent about it? Who wrote that note? And where is that swarthy man? He is not among those under arrest.

Question 2. Mr. Prendergast, a veteran of the Spanish War, was among those knocked down by the force of the explosion. He has informed the authorities that he saw the man who placed the suitcase on the sidewalk and that he saw the bomb explode. He was positive that it was not Billings nor anyone else under arrest. Where is Mr. Prendergast? *Why has he suddenly disappeared from his home in Oakland?* Was he spirited away because his testimony would exonerate the men chosen as victims?

Question 3. Estelle Smith, identifier in chief of the prosecution, at first claimed that she saw a tall man with a drooping mustache in company with a short stout woman wearing thick glasses. Why has she changed her mind since she has talked with the police? Why did she subsequently identify Tom Mooney and his wife as the couple she saw, considering that neither of them answers to her original description?

Question 4. What has become of the scores of plug-uglies imported to break the Longshoremen's strike? Why have they so suddenly disappeared from the city, now that the Culinary Workers' strike is on, immediately after the explosion?

Question 5. Why were Mrs. Belle Lavin and T. Ryan arrested as dynamiters, kept 48 hours without food, water or sleep, and then discharged without even being booked on the police blotter? Are prisoners being tortured to secure confessions?

Question 6. Why are absolutely false rumors circulated from headquarters that each bomb prisoner has "confessed"? Are you trying the bomb case in the newspapers, and is the evidence of the prosecution so flimsy that the public mind must be poisoned with such lies in order to secure a conviction?

Question 7. Why are radicals gratuitously insulted in your office, Mr. District Attorney? Why was a prominent labor man invited by your assistant Cunha the other evening only to be abused and physically attacked by the "superior" official, who was evidently under the influence of liquor? Have you placed the bomb "investigation" in the hands of irresponsible rummies and drunken bullies?

Question 8. Does your office represent the taxpayers, or the U. R. R. and Mr. Koster of the Law and Order Committee? Why are you so busy picking up the intelligent foreign workers and Anarchists and turning them over to the immigration authorities, only to have them locked up for a week and then released without even an apology for your blundering stupidity?

concocted in that atavistic brain when Mr. Brennan naively volunteered the explanation for his changed attitude. "Mr. Berkman, I had dinner yesterday with Professor ——— of the University at Berkeley. We discussed you and your book. He thinks very highly of you."

I pitied him. But I was glad that he had decency enough not to offer to shake hands when I left. It saved him the experience of Assistant District Attorney Cunha, THE BLAST raider, whose proffered hand I had refused to touch.

On the Firing Line

COMRADES Cesare Veglio, Louis Aubert, and Julien Potter, arrested for distributing the leaflet, "Down With the Anarchists!" were quickly "tried" in Judge Sullivan's court and sentenced to 90 days in jail.

But the prosecution reckoned without the host. Friends of the arrested immediately blocked the judicial farce. An appeal was filed, bail secured, and now our good comrades are all watching proceedings from the outside instead of from behind the bars.

Our friend Jacob Lizzul, arrested for the same terrible crime, demanded a jury trial and is now also out on bail. It is well for the authorities to know that we emphatically refuse to be railroaded to prison or to be otherwise victimized.

The case of T. Sidorin, "picked up" because he is a "Rooshan," has just been decided by the immigration officials. Sidorin has been in this country over four years, and cannot be deported. But the dirty work continues. Released by the Federal authorities, he is now held on the charge of "disturbing the peace" by having in his hand a copy of our leaflet. He is out on bail.

A SIMILAR attempt to punish and terrorize the workers by hanging or imprisoning its most active and devoted friends is now being made in Minnesota in connection with the strike of the iron miners. Carlo Tresca and several other brave spirits are held on charges of murder committed by the Hessians of the Steel Trust. We will deal at greater length with the Minnesota situation, and with the other great strikes now convulsing the country, in our next issue. For the present it is appropriate to point out that the great lesson for the workers to learn is *solidarity*. Labor will have no real strength till the man with the pick is the full brother of the man at the throttle.

WE have printed 50,000 copies of the circular, "Down With the Anarchists!" It is a clear, enlightening document. Be sure to give some copies to your acquaintances and neighbors. The circular can be had free through THE BLAST. Contributions to help defray cost of printing and mailing will not be refused.

THE police and detective bureaus have assured us that they mean to kill THE BLAST. "Why, your cartoons alone are enough to incite to riot!" they told us.

But THE BLAST is *not* going to be killed. Not without a hard fight, anyhow. We have printed an extra large issue this time. If you want to help save the lives of Nolan, Mooney, Weinberg and Billings—the selected victims of the enemy—then help spread the paper. Order bundle copies. Get subscribers. Talk alone will not do. Get busy. Help swell the War Fund of THE BLAST.

THIS is a special issue of THE BLAST in the interest of the Labor men that Big Business wants to hang in San Francisco. The case is of utmost importance. A repetition of the judicial murders of 1887 must be prevented at all cost. Labor and radical papers are welcome to reprint the material published in THE BLAST.

A War Fund for The Blast

THE BLAST has been marked by the police for destruction. It is a sharp thorn in the flesh of the Law and Order reactionists. Their avowed purpose is to strangle every voice raised in protest against official outrage and injustice.

But we are determined to keep THE BLAST going. Never before was this paper as vitally needed as now. With the local press in complete control of the reaction, none daring to utter a free and fearless word, THE BLAST must live and keep up the fight. It is the only revolutionary voice on the Coast raised in behalf of our imprisoned comrades whom the masters have picked as victims of their revenge on Labor.

The enemy is prepared to kill THE BLAST. We are determined to continue its revolutionary propaganda. Nay, more: THE BLAST will bend every effort and marshal its increasing influence to expose and nip the conspiracy to hang our imprisoned friends. The enemy shall not gloat over new scaffolds erected for the most intelligent and devoted rebels of California Labor.

THE BLAST must have a War Fund of $1000.00. It must have it NOW, at once. A good friend has already contributed $100.00, and Emma Goldman $25.00. Who will be the next to respond?

ALEXANDER BERKMAN

Justice

David Leigh

IF Justice means:

The right to employ force to torture individuals in order to fasten guilt upon them;

If it means the right to invade one's privacy and carry off any material belongings which may happen to appeal to the fancy of the intruder;

If it means the right of the law's minions to sequester men and women *without warrant* and subject them to persistent discomfiture and the humiliation of enforced helplessness;

If it means the right of "officials" to not only harass imprisoned individuals with unjustifiable intrusions, but also to deny them their simplest needs, even to a cup of cold water;

If it means the utter abridgement of the right of accused persons to either see or consult with counsel;

If it means that merely on Suspicion men and women can be indicted, can be all but *hanged* before so much as a scintilla of evidence has been adduced against them;

If it means the right of uniformed bullies to jeer at and intimidate relatives and friends of accused persons;

If it means that the governing section of a community can decree the lengths and ends to which this thing called "justice" shall go, without regard to a single right of individuals—

Then I, for one, here and now declare myself for the OPPOSITE of "justice"—by whatever name it shall be called.

Vol. I   SAN FRANCISCO, SEPTEMBER 1, 1916   No. 18

Nine and Five Make Fourteen

Robert Minor

ON JULY 22nd last, the anti-union employers of San Francisco led twenty-two thousand of their employees down Market Street, to show the world their submissiveness and how many could be mustered to the call for militarism. The diminutive size of the procession registered a great victory for Labor. Labor was satisfied, and completely done with the affair before the day of march.

But somewhere in the city there lived a man or men who were not satisfied—who had probably been caught in the whirlwind of the theory of violence preached by the blood-and-iron militarists, and had brooded themselves into the frame of mind of those who believe in killing. This had its logical result. A bomb was exploded and spectators were killed. Six died immediately—then it grew to seven, eight; now nine are dead.

More are to die. The whole affair had been one of stupid, blind blundering. First the parade; then the hundreds of warnings were not heeded with precautions; the slaughter of persons who were not even in the parade, if that made any difference to the perpetrator, and now —FIVE MORE ARE TO DIE—five who also had nothing to do with the affair. Stupidity again; stupidity on the part of that big, blind herd, the people.

For the affair is in the hands now as before of fools and worse. A Government is supposed to have the running down of such things. But the Government has vacated, and a private organization has taken the management over.

The five new victims of this tragedy are to be Edward D. Nolan, Thomas Mooney, Israel Weinberg, Warren K. Billings and Mrs. Mooney, and the private organization that is to take their lives is the Chamber of Commerce of San Francisco, careful guardian of Calhoun's leavings, the United Railways. The Chamber of Commerce rules San Francisco now, and every column of every newspaper of the town. And the five victims they have picked are each a personal enemy of United Railways, because of their union activities.

There is evidence against these men, charged with murder—but evidence of what sort? In events of such justified excitement, thousands of different sorts of "evidence"—of any sort you may want—can be found in the rumors and growing imaginations of a terror-stricken crowd. By forming a set theory and sticking to it, building it up on what plastic-minded witnesses may be induced to contribute—and by carefully excluding all testimony that may show that your damnable pet theory is false (even eye-witnesses have in this case been discarded for circumstantial evidence)—thus you may prove anything you may want.

And what does the Chamber of Commerce want to prove in this case? That five conspicuous enemies of the Chamber of Commerce are guilty of murder!

I have been working on this case now for three weeks. In that time I have seen the most brutal and cowardly conduct on the part of newspapers and "public" men that my twelve years of newspaper experience have witnessed. I have been told on best authority that many of the men engaged in the prosecution's work do not believe in the guilt of these defendants. A newspaper man engaged on the case sought me secretly to say, "I am writing every day, under orders, in a tone calculated to hang those men, and they are innocent."

The prosecution, under the absolute control of the men who are trying to drive labor unions out of existence, has assaulted one witness, according to the press, because he testified to having seen in the act of placing the bomb someone who was not the labor union man they wanted to convict. Ugly stories come to us constantly of the vicious scramble of ex-Pinkertons for $21,000 reward that will be paid to them for hanging— well, just anybody that they can "get."

The public has been bludgeoned into believing in the guilt of the defendants before they are tried, by newspapers whose representatives stated point-blank that they print nothing of which the Chamber of Commerce's Law and Order Committee does not approve.

What do you want, People—fourteen victims instead of nine? Do you want innocent men, or the guilty?

Is Organized Labor going to stand by and let their own brothers go to death as murderers, at the hands of the very men who are this minute engaged in an open attempt to destroy all hope of labor unions?

Should not these men at least have a fair representation in court? Does anybody think they'll get it at the hands of their enemies, men to whom labor activity is in itself a crime? (As shown by their attempt to make peaceful picketing a prison offense.)

Come to the rescue of your Brothers, Union Men, and all who believe in making this a decenter world for working men! Give generously to the defense of these people. They are not bomb throwers, but innocent victims.

Send money, and much of it, QUICK, to the INTERNATIONAL WORKERS' DEFENSE LEAGUE, Robert Minor, Treasurer, 210 Russ Building, 235 Montgomery Street, San Francisco.

The San Francisco Conspiracy

IT IS becoming more apparent every day that the prosecution in the bomb case has determined to fasten the crime on the union men under arrest: Edward D. Nolan, Thomas J. Mooney, Warren K. Billings, Israel Weinberg, and Mrs. Rena Hermann Mooney. All have been indicted for murder.

Some one must be punished, the police argue. The accused labor men are as good victims as any one. Moreover, the United Railways wants **them** punished. As a detective prominent in the prosecution said to us: "We don't know if they are guilty, but we can get a jury of twelve men to convict them."

The attitude of the prosecution has been all along that it is not interested in looking up clews that do not point to the arrested as the guilty. An eye-witness who reported to the District Attorney that he saw the man who placed the bomb-containing suitcase on the sidewalk, was thrown out of the prosecutor's office, because the description of the man he saw didn't fit any of the arrested.

It is simply a case of "We'll convict the men we have." The people of San Francisco have really nothing to say about it. The prosecution of the bomb case is managed by a private organization, the United Railways, with the aid of another private organization, the Law and Order Committee of the Chamber of Commerce. When the cases come to trial, and the Clerk of the Court calls out in a confident voice, "The People of San Francisco versus Billings, Mooney et al.," he will be uttering a black lie. It will be the United Railways versus certain active labor men of San Francisco. It is significant that the chief detective on this case is a man who has for years been in the employ of the United Railways. A week before the bomb explosion this detective approached Weinberg and offered him the $5,000 reward of the United Railways for evidence in connection with the blowing up of some power towers of the company. Weinberg told the sleuth that he knew nothing of the matter, and the detective became abusive and angry. He returned a few days later, got into Weinberg's jitney, ordering him to drive to a certain place, and again insisted that Weinberg help him earn the $5,000 reward. Weinberg had nothing to tell, and finally the detective left him, with the threat: "You won't talk, eh? We'll fix you for it."

A few days later this detective caused the arrest of Weinberg in connection with the bomb case.

Similar tactics were used, before the bomb explosion, on the other men subsequently arrested.

When the cases come to trial, the people of the country will be astounded at the heinous character of the conspiracy of the United Railroads to railroad innocent men to the gallows.

Who are these four men? Every one of them is a prominent labor man who has been active in organization, strike and picket work against the United Railways, the Pacific Gas and Electric Company and similar concerns that dominate the political and commercial life of San Francisco. Edward Nolan, for instance, has within recent years secured four advantageous wage agreements in this district. The auto machinists' agreement nets the members of Nolan's union over $1,000 per week. Is it surprising that he is considered "dangerous" by the bosses? And Tom Mooney but recently incurred the hatred of the United Railways by trying to organize the street-car men and attempting a strike on the United lines. Three years ago the Pacific Gas and Electric Company sought to railroad Mooney to prison on a charge that was so palpably a frame-up that even an unsympathetic farmer jury finally acquitted him. The same interests succeeded, however, in sending Billings to prison because of his activities in the gas strike, and now the prosecution is planning to convict the indicted labor men solely on their previous record as effective organizers and strike leaders—the worst crime in the eyes of the Law and Order broadcloth mob that will sit in judgment on our arrested comrades.

Let no friend of Labor lull himself into self-satisfied inaction with the hope that these men will get a "fair trial," and that their absolute innocence guarantees an acquittal. The stage is set for conviction. You might as well expect decency in a brothel as to hope for justice at the hands of the ex-Pinkertons and Burns bloodhounds in the District Attorney's office, all mad with the scent of the $21,000 reward. District Attorney Fickert is notoriously the creature of the United Railways, and Chief of Police White did not change employers when he left his position with the Pacific Gas and Electric Company to become the head of the Police Department of San Francisco.

Under these circumstances one must be blind to see any chance for a "fair trial" for the accused labor men. Their jurors are to be selected from a panel of business men who will be scrutinized by the Law and Order Committee of the Chamber of Commerce. The very Chamber that has gathered a fund of a million dollars for the express purpose of establishing the open shop in San Francisco. The Chamber whose intent and spirit toward the unions has been publicly and unrebukedly characterized by one of its prominent members, Captain Robert Dollar: "The best way to deal with the strikers is to send ambulance loads of them to the hospital."

Do you expect a fair trial and justice from this crew?

No wonder District Attorney Fickert has so brazenly declared in public print that "we already have the hemp stretched around their necks."

There are persistent rumors about the District Attorney's office that it has been definitely decided by the "higher ups" that the principal two defendants are to be sent to the gallows and the rest railroaded to long prison sentences. A "prominent member" of the prosecution is to be rewarded with a high State position, and the $21,000 blood money is to be divided among the two chief witnesses of the prosecution and two police officials, one of them a United Railways detective.

* * *

This conspiracy to eliminate the best labor men of San Francisco is the prelude to a bitter campaign to exterminate the unions. "This is a fine opportunity for the open shop," said a prominent member of the Chamber of Commerce upon hearing of the bomb explosion. For years it has been the ambition of Big Business in San Francisco to non-unionize the city. They began an open-shop campaign before the Exposition, but, fearing failure and financial disaster, they formed a temporary truce with labor, according to which union hours were guaranteed on condition that no strikes take place during the Exposition. Thus Big Business cunningly made sure of the uninterrupted flow of shekels, but no sooner were the Exposition gates closed and the last dollar clinked in the coffers of the gentlemen of Commerce, than the fight on the unions was renewed with redoubled vigor.

The Preparedness Parade was to demonstrate the power of the open-shop campaign. They sought to whip every employee into line, but the unions took a stand against organized slaughter, and the advertised 150,000 paraders failed to materialize. A scanty 22,000 business men, society ladies and unorganized workers marched through the streets. The parade was a fiasco, and the Chamber of Commerce was raving mad. They seized on the bomb explosion as a timely opportunity to avenge their failure and to strike a telling blow for the open shop. Forthwith were arrested the most active men of the local labor movement. Clews leading in other directions have been ignored by the prosecution, and every effort is made by the District Attorney's office to discourage any investigation that does not point toward the arrested men. The double purpose is to do away with the best and most active labor men of this city and at the same time terrorize the organized workers into submission to the will of the masters.

The case of Nolan, Mooney et al. is thus really a fight for the open shop. And the workers of San Francisco are beginning to realize it. There are ugly rumors of secret conferences between the Mayor, Chief of Police and certain labor leaders. However that may be, it is a fact that the high labor moguls of San Francisco have not had a word to say concerning the arrest and the evident conspiracy to hang their brother workers. Even the official organ of the Building Trades, *Organized Labor*, has not published a line about the matter. It has ignored the whole thing as if an attempt to hang five workers is of no concern to a labor paper. Later on we may have occasion to expose, in detail and with data, the rotten politics back of this conspiracy of silence. Meanwhile it is enough to point out this fact to brand *Organized Labor* as a cowardly crew of traitors to the cause of the workers.

Fortunately the rank and file of the local unions are awakening to the character of their officials. They have taken steps to force the two official labor papers to speak up in defense of their brothers. The Machinists' Union voted $1,000 for the defense of Ed Nolan and other unions are taking similar action. The Chamber of Commerce has succeeded in terrifying some labor leaders and has formed a cabala with some others. But it has not been able to frighten the whole union element. The International Workers' Defense League has taken charge of the defense of our arrested comrades and numerous labor bodies have already sent their representatives there. Among them are: Plumbers, Riggers and Stevedores, District Council of Painters, Bakery and Confectionery Workers No. 24, Waiters No. 30, Cooks No. 44, Machinists No. 68, Automobile and Carriage Painters No. 1073, Stable Employees No. 404, Workmen's Circle No. 114, Workmen's Circle No. 511, Ladies' Tailors, Ladies' Garment Workers, Laundry Workers, and the District Council of Carpenters.

The Secretary of the League is Henry Hagelstein; Treasurer, Robert Minor, 210 Russ Building, 235 Montgomery street, San Francisco.

But these cases are not of mere local importance. Our own efforts will not be sufficient to defeat the conspiracy of Big Business. The case is of country-wide significance. It will require a national campaign of agitation to prevent the terrible crime planned by the masters of San Francisco. Time is short. The prosecution is rushing the cases to court, hoping to take advantage of the prejudiced state of the public mind. The first trial, that of Warren K. Billings, has been set for September 11. Every rebel and liberty lover is called upon to help stir the social consciousness of the country, to prevent the repetition of the judicial murders of the 11th of November, 1887.

All Together!

THE Chamber of Commerce announces that whoever differs from Koster, its new president, is a law-breaker. We hasten to go on record, here and now, that we beg to differ. San Francisco must be full of law-breakers. But few are Kosher.

Among the law-breakers are also the waiters of the city who are out on strike. The restaurant bosses do not believe in the strikers picketing their places. The Chamber has therefore declared picketing criminal. Subservient judges have issued injunctions against the pickets, postponing hearings for two weeks, during which time—the bosses hope—the strike will be broken.

Indeed, the fight for the open shop is in full blast. San Francisco is to follow Los Angeles by making peaceful picketing a crime. I don't see how the waiters can win their demands, in face of the combined forces of their bosses, the Chamber, and the courts—unless they quickly induce the bakers and the teamsters to refuse supplies to the struck places. What business have brother union men to scab on the waiters, anyhow?

Yesterday the longshoremen, today the waiters, tomorrow the machinists, day after the teamsters. Why not all strike *at the same time?* Why lose separately, when you can win together?

Vindicating Justice
A. B.

THE machinery of the law is for the purpose of dealing out even-handed Justice. The District Attorney is the legal representative of the people, his sole duty to serve the ends of justice. He is not to be only the prosecutor of the guilty; he is, also and equally, the defender of the innocent. He is not merely to secure conviction, right or wrong; on the contrary, he is to guard the scales of Justice with an ever jealous eye that will neither permit the guilty to escape nor the innocent to suffer.

That is the theory.

In practice, the District Attorney is the relentless prosecutor of every one indicted of a crime; innocent and guilty alike are his victims, and all his efforts are bent to secure a conviction, once you are unfortunate enough to fall into the net.

The process is simplicity itself. None is exempt from its fatal operation. You may be absolutely innocent, yet any policeman or detective may arrest you; you may be charged with any crime, and kept incommunicado at the pleasure of the police. In the course of time your case is submitted to the grand jury. You are not entitled to be represented by an attorney before that body, or to have witnesses in your defense. Nor need the police submit any actual evidence against you. The mere request of the District Attorney is sufficient to secure an indictment.

Now you are an indicted murderer, and the press trumpets the fact to the world. The public, stirred by the crime, is eager for details and news, and hungry for a victim. The newspapers do not permit that hunger to go unsatisfied. In glaring type they proclaim "John Johnson indicted for murder." The most innocent detail of your life is dissected with the single view of proving you capable of the crime charged against you. Detectives and reporters vie with each other in developing their "theories," and facts are distorted to fasten the crime upon you. "Extree! Extree!" shout the newsboys. "The murderer's caught." The public mind, excited and incited, readily absorbs the insistent suggestion of your guilt. You are tried in the press and convicted long before you are brought to trial.

At last you face the judge and jury. Your very presence in the dock, accused of a heinous crime, speaks against you. "He wouldn't be here, charged with this crime," argues the average mind, "if he were quite innocent." The suspicion of guilt is against you, from the very beginning. The very atmosphere and surroundings of the court-room point an accusing finger at you. "Where is he? Where?" whispers the pink-and-white young lady in the front seat. "There, there's the wretch!" replies the matron at her side.

Then begins the selection of the jury. The invisible monster of "public opinion" is at your side, at every turn glaring at you with a thousand accusing, reproachful, condemning and revengeful eyes, till your very soul sickens within you. "See how guilty looks!" you hear them say around you. You blush and pale with shame and anger, and you look guiltier still.

You hear the public prosecutor thunder imprecations upon your head. As in a mental mist you wonder in what dim past you might have been guilty of all the terrible crimes charged against you. The prosecutor grows more vehement. You are a monster unfit to associate with human beings. His passion sways even you, and you wonder if you are really fit to live. In the eyes of the jury you already read your doom.

You are worn and wearied by the long strain. Your only wish is that it were over quickly. It is almost a relief to hear the solemn words of the foreman: "Guilty as indicted."

"He'll hang!" says a rough voice near by. "It's coming to him, the brute!" replies another.

Justice is vindicated.

THE BLAST

Revolutionary Labor Paper
Published every 1st and 15th of the month
569 Dolores St., San Francisco, Cal.
Mail Address, Box 661   Phone, Park 499

Alexander Berkman, Editor and Publisher
M. E. Fitzgerald, Associate Worker   Carl Newlander, Assistant

SUBSCRIPTION
$1.00 Yearly   60c Six Months   5c Copy
Bundle rates 2½c per copy in bundles of ten.

Reflections

The Anarchist Pioneers

IT IS necessary and timely just now to point out some facts that certain folks are trying hard to forget. One of them is the origin of the eight-hour movement in this country. We want to remind our good friends who are always busy "proving" that Anarchism has nothing to do with Labor, that it was the Anarchists who initiated the eight-hour agitation, and that its first victories were literally bought with the blood of our Chicago comrades of 1887. It was Parsons, Spies and their co-workers who were most active in the great labor organization of those days—the Knights of Labor—in behalf of the shorter workday. It was they who inspired and organized the movement. The vicious and the stupid misrepresented and reviled them then, as they do us now. But history has indelibly engraved on the pages of Time the names of the Chicago Anarchists as the pioneers and martyrs of the eight-hour movement.

Eternal Vigilance

IN A recent issue of *Solidarity*, my good friend Joe Ettor pays me this well-deserved compliment: "Alexander Berkman's BLAST is a vigorous, well-edited and well-printed paper, written in good, literary English, and very readable."

Thanks, Joe.

But Ettor is more successful in his appreciation of a good paper than in his criticism of a social philosophy. Here he treads on dangerous ground. He quotes extracts from my articles on the "Great Adventure" and "Anent the Cloakmakers' Strike," and toils hard to prove that "economic determinism destroys Anarchism when it gives rise to the class struggle."

Well, the class struggle is here and has been for some little time, and so has economic determinism—and Joe still has to write long articles to prove Anarchism dead. There's something wrong with your logic, Joe.

Ettor is much worried about Anarchism not being consonant with unionism. Sure not, Joe. As long as unionism means the suppression of the individual, it is not Anarchism. Strong-arm unionism may be forced on the workers by the character of the class struggle. That is an argument against capitalism, not against Anarchism. Anarchism demands the freedom of the individual from invasion. To the extent that labor and other organizations—society itself—develop to the point where the individual enjoys greater and ever greater liberty, to that extent they are approaching Anarchism.

It's very simple, Joe. Do you get the point? If not, ask our comrades, the Anarchists, who are the most active members of the I. W. W.

Evoluting Labor Day

IT WAS a wise legislator who said that the best way to emasculate an idea is to enact it into a law. That's what happened to Labor Day. Originally it was fraught with significance: it was meant as a gesture of defiance to the legalized form of robbery known as wage slavery. The hosts of Labor, dropping their tools to march in the streets, were thus to demonstrate their conscious strength and their preparation for the coming life-and-death struggle for well-being and liberty.

The idea was revolutionary, dangerous. Forthwith it was incorporated into law: the bosses gave the workers kind permission to march, and Labor Day was castrated into obedient respectability.

And now behold the legal evolution of the idea: Archbishop Hanna has been invited by the labor leaders to preside over the Labor Day exercises in San Francisco!

An Urgent Call

IF I had time, I would collect data of the killed, wounded and imprisoned in connection with labor struggles. They would shed a very illuminating light on the real scope and character of the class war. The list of Toil's martyrdom is growing fast and faster. Merely to name those who are at this very moment imprisoned for their labor activities, would require all our space. There is not a prison in any industrial city of this country but holds some of our comrades. To name but a few:

Rangel and Cline—Serving life terms in Texas.

Ford and Suhr—Imprisoned for life in Folsom, Cal.

J. B. McNamara—Life prisoner in San Quentin, Cal.

J. J. McNamara—Fifteen years in San Quentin, Cal.

Mathew A. Schmidt—Sentenced to life; case appealed.

David Caplan—In jail in Los Angeles; awaiting retrial.

Ricardo and Enrique Flores Magon—Sentenced to one and three years, respectively; appeal pending.

Van K. Allison — Railroaded in Boston to three years for saying that a poor woman has some rights over her own body; appealed.

Carlo Tresca and ten others—In jail in Duluth, Minn., charged with murder in connection with the Mesaba iron miners' strike.

Fred H. Merrick—Three and one-half years
Rudolph Blum—Ten months
Geo. Zaber—One year
H. H. Detweiler—One year
Anna Goldenberg—One year
A. E. Weston—Nine months
Stephen Tipsick—Six months
Mike Essick—Six months

Recently sentenced to prison in Pittsburgh, Pa., in connection with strikes at the plants of the United States Steel Corporation.

Edward D. Nolan
Thomas J. Mooney
Warren K. Billings
Israel Weinberg
Rena Hermann Mooney

Victims of the open-shop fight in San Francisco, indicted on eight charges of murder.

Some of the cases are to be tried, others to be appealed. All of them demand our financial support. The number of our prisoners of war is increasing daily, and neither the radical nor the labor movement is in a position to finance them. And even with the best support, almost every such case terminates in the penitentiary.

Incidentally, it is well to notice that most of these cases resulted from the struggle against the Steel Trust and its subsidiaries.

It is the tactics of organized capital to weaken and beat down the workers by railroading their best men to prison. This method has the double advantage of discouraging active effort for improvement by eliminating the most energetic, and draining the treasury of the workers.

It is a hopeless struggle on the part of labor. If financial endurance is to be the test, the U. S. Steel Corporation will win every throw. It is high time that those who mean well with labor should realize the ineffectiveness of such methods. The war between labor and capital is a bitter fact; the tragedy of it is that labor doesn't do any real fighting beyond feeble attempts at measuring financial strength with the bosses. Where the workers take matters into their own hands and use their economic power, all the finances of the enemy become useless. Vide the railroad men.

New methods, new tactics must be initiated, and this especially applies to dealing with cases of Labor's prisoners of war. In a recent issue of THE BLAST, I suggested the necessity of a Pan-American Congress of the workers. Every day makes such a conference more urgent. Especially now, when legislative prohibition of strikes looms up as a menacing possibility, the situation imperatively calls for the action suggested.

Carranza a New Diaz

LAST year, at a luncheon tendered him in this city, Lincoln Steffens gave an entertaining talk on Mexico. He spoke very highly of Carranza and predicted great things of him. Knowing Steffens well, I was inclined to doubt his judgment. I have a faint recollection that he told me that Jack Reed did not agree with his estimate of the First Chief. I said I hoped so.

Was Max Eastman, in an unguarded moment, inoculated by Steffens with his optimism—an optimism which, unfortunately, brought dire results to others? I regret to see the *Masses*, usually so keen and wide awake, taken in by a certain Martinez, a Carranza hireling, who contributes an article in its September issue on "The Mexican Labor Movement."

The wily First Chief has been mouthing radical phrases as a bait to the workers and to dupe such radicals as Steffens. But surely the editorial gods of the *Masses* must have been napping when they permitted its pages to carry such stuff as this, italicized even:

"Under Carranza the workers are not only encouraged to organize, but their organization is part of his plan for the new State which he is trying to create."

And again:

"We believe that Venustiano Carranza will lead the oppressed of Mexico and especially the working class into the true liberty."

Now let Carranza himself speak. After declaring martial law in Mexico City, to terminate the strike of the General Confederation of Syndicates, Carranza promulgated, on August 1st, the following decree:

"In consideration of," etc. (references to recent strikes in Mexico City), "I have seen fit to decree:

"Article I. The death penalty shall be meted out to the disturbers of public order, as provided by the law of January 25, 1862, and hereby amplified—

"First: To those who incite to the suspension of work in the factories or enterprises destined to give public service or who propagate it; to those who preside over meetings in which suspension of work is proposed, discussed or approved; to those who defend and sustain it; to those who approve or subscribe to it; to those who attend such meetings or do not leave them as soon as they know their object; and to those who try to make it effective once a strike has been declared.

"Second: To those who, on account of the suspension of work in the factories, mentioned enterprises or any other place, take advantage of the occasioned disorder to aggravate it or aid in the spoiling or destruction of the property or enterprises to which the strikers belong, or try to induce others to join the strike, and those who with the same object provoke public disorders, be it against public functionaries or civilians, or use force on the person or property of any citizen, or to those who appropriate, destroy or deteriorate public or private property; and

"Third: To those who by threats or force prevent other persons from executing services in the enterprises against which the suspension of work has been declared."

Thus Venustiano Carranza is "leading the workers of Mexico into the true liberty"!

The Real Railroad Power

THE hand of anxiety is gripping the country. High finance, scornful of everything except its own power, is trembling on the brink. Kings of industry and Lords of commerce, bankers and manufacturers—all, all are living in terrible suspense. The calm tenor of even the White House is disturbed. The President of these great United States is almost ill with sleepless worry; the multitudinous cares of State are forgotten; whole days and feverish nights are spent in conferences, and matters weightier than national defense are heatedly discussed through the long hours. The Solons of the Nation are deeply perturbed: their toilsome labors done, they were about to return to their loved ones when they were informed that a special session of Congress may be called at any moment. The country is facing a great disaster!

What has so stirred the high and mighty? What has so disarranged the wheels of our national life? The threat of a strike! The workers of just **one** industry are about to quit work. Behold the general bewilderment, the hysteria of helplessness, nation-wide! Where is thy vaunted power, O State! Where your boasted might, O ye pretended masters of life!

A mere handful of the "common people," greasy, sooty toilers—one half of one per cent of the country's population—have set the whole Nation by the ears. The railroad employees are threatening to strike!

Never before in the history of this country has Labor so convincingly demonstrated its power. Never has the meaning of solidarity found such striking application in the practical affairs of life. They did not quit work, they did not yet even begin their strike. The mere possibility has put such fear into the hearts of the haughty magnates—the combined ten score and more railroad systems of the country—as no legislation or other clap-trap ever came near doing.

It is unnecessary to discuss at this late hour the merits of the controversy. What are the demands of the railroad employees? It is of no moment. The demands of the workers are always just; nay, their demands never approximate their due. For the present the four railway brotherhoods ask only for an eight-hour day, with extra pay for overtime. A very modest demand, when it is considered that not a single passenger or ounce of freight can be moved without their effort, that they have had no wage increase in twenty years, and that the railroads have enjoyed unprecedented prosperity. Modest indeed are the demands of the men. The present situation may teach them that they can operate the railroads without the necessity of the railroad presidents' hogging the lion's share of profits, earning big dividends on watered stock and enriching idlers and speculators. They may learn the novel lesson that they—the railroad workers—are the railroads, and that the coupon clippers are a useless and harmful incubus. Then they will simply eliminate these obstacles and parasites, and take charge of the railroads and operate them for the benefit of the people of the country.

That time is not yet, though it may come sooner than some are inclined to believe. No one was taken more unawares by the French Revolution than the learned folk who, on the very eve of the uprising, ridiculed such a possibility. But to return to the present. The membership of the four railway brotherhoods had voted to demand better conditions, backing up their demand by the decision to strike on all the 225 railroads of the country. It is this unanimity, this solidarity of purpose and action that has sent terror into the hearts of the great railroad managers. With all their millions and paper titles they haven't the power or ability to move a single wheel of the iron steed—unless the workers do so. And the workers refuse. What's to be done? "Let's arbitrate the matter," the magnates beg. But the railway workers have been cheated by arbitration once too often. They have learned that arbitration is the modern way of lulling discontent to sleep. Concede our demands, they say; we'll arbitrate at our leisure.

At this writing the conferences at the White House have achieved nothing definite. The railway heads are playing for time, but the leaders of the men are seeing through the dilly-dally tactics and are losing patience. The strike, voted upon by the men weeks ago, may be initiated any moment. No one seriously doubts that a strike would be quick and decisive. The railroad men have it in their power to paralyze not only the whole railway machinery of the country, but every other industry as well. You can't do business without means of transportation. Nor can factories be run without coal that cannot be gotten after the present supply runs short. Industry as well as commerce would come to a standstill, with the result that the railway magnates would be speedily forced to capitulate.

The public! you exclaim anxiously. Why should the innocent public be made to suffer? The public has no rights that strikers are morally bound to respect. Who is this innocent public, anyhow? In the first place, it is anything but innocent. The public is responsible for the miserable conditions under which we live. The public is you and I. And whether we be cruelly indifferent to injustice and abuse, or stupidly indolent and acquiescent, we are equally guilty. That part of the public which comprises the producers and other useful workers, as well as all well-wishers of labor, cannot but be benefited, materially and morally, by every advance of the toilers, by every successful strike. Any temporary inconvenience this part of the public may suffer—as from interrupted railway communication—they will suffer cheer-fully for the sake of the larger common cause.

The rest of the public, that part which is not in sympathy with the workers and the ultimate aspirations of Labor for emancipation from wage slavery, the public that is antagonistic or even actively opposed to the cause of the workers — fundamentally the cause of progress and of humanity—that public may well be damned.

The sympathies of every decent man and woman must, therefore, necessarily be with the railroad men. Public sentiment in their behalf will strengthen the hands of their leaders. Powerful influences are being exerted to discredit them in the eyes of the people. Every effort is made to weaken their manly attitude of conscious strength and faith in the justice of their cause. We hope that they will not waste any more time in silly conferences with hypocritical railway managers who are merely playing for time, or permit themselves to be misled by political wire pullers in the White House. Nor to be cowed by the empty threat of special legislation, the very efficacy of which primarily depends on their submission.

As we go to press, the strike is set for Labor Day. It is probable that the President and Congress may successfully maneuvre to avert a general cessation of transportation. But strike or no strike, the railroad men have demonstrated their economic power, and the lesson of solidaric unity and its fearful menace to the masters will not be lost on the workers of other industries.

On the Iron Range

AN ACT in the tragedy of Labor is being played in Minnesota, the like of which is to be found only in the history of the Ludlow massacres. It is a story of government prostituted to private interests, of an industrial despotism reared on monopoly, of gunmen and bloodshed.

A great strike is in progress on the Mesaba iron range, in Minnesota. The Oliver Iron Mining Company, an arm of the United States Steel Corporation, has precipitated there one of the most bitter, as it is one of the most spontaneous and unorganized, industrial revolts of recent history. It has done this by its policy of treating the men like serfs, denying them any voice, herding them with the aid of a permanent force of private police, and driving them at top speed by a vicious piece-rate system of payment that leaves the door wide open for favoritism, injustice, and the extortion of bribes by the petty bosses who assign favorable or unfavorable working places.

The strike started without organization of any sort, and spread almost instantaneously through the iron range before any outside labor organization had participated. The men were unorganized and out of touch with the labor movement. According to George P. West, the investigator of the Industrial Relations Committee, the men do not even ask for the recognition of any union. Their demands are:

1. An eight-hour day.

2. A minimum wage of $3.00 in the underground mines, and $3.50 in the same but in wet places, and $2.75 on the surface for eight hours' labor.

3. Abolishment of the contract labor system.

4. Pay-day twice a month.

Laborers in the open pit surface workings are now paid $2.60 for a ten-hour day. In the underground workings, where the majority of the miners are employed, the miners work an eight-hour day and are paid on piece-rate basis, designed to speed the men up. Rates per car of ore mined are changed every week, resulting in driving the men at top speed and placing them in competition with each other.

The whole governmental power of Minnesota is being used in a relentless effort to crush out the strike of the 15,000 iron miners on the range. Governor Burnquist, Sheriff John R. Meining of Duluth, County Prosecutor Green, and the Duluth chief of police are bending every effort to support the steel companies against the strikers. According to the sheriff's own statement, more than 1,000 men have been deputized and armed with carbines, revolvers and riot sticks. Clothed by the sheriff with the State authority, they have been placed in tyrannical control of a district comprising at least 100 square miles and 75,000 population. The slums of Duluth and other cities have been combed to recruit this army of gunmen.

These company gunmen lost no time in doing their work. Their violence became the terror of the range. Supported by the deputy sheriffs, they arrested the strikers by the hundreds, beat them up unmercifully, turned some of them over to the Federal Government for deportation (among them George Andreytchine, a civil engineer and a fine type of young idealist), and threw scores of others into jail on trumped-up charges. Picketing was absolutely forbidden, peaceful meetings broken up, and Finnish Socialists were thrown out of their own halls and not permitted to hold any gatherings.

Every effort was made by the company to break the backbone of the strike and force the miners to return to work. This failing, more drastic methods were resorted to. A notorious character named Dick Dillon, a gunman in the employ of one of the companies, stormed into the home of a striker at Biwabik without knocking, armed with a revolver, and followed by three deputy sheriffs. This invasion of a workingman's home, the facts of which are admitted, was undertaken ostensibly to serve a warrant for the illegal sale of liquor. Surrounded by his wife, children and several miners, who boarded with him, the miner hotly resented the intrusion of the company guard, and a fight ensued, in which one deputy sheriff and a peddler friendly to the miners were killed, and a mine guard shot twice through the thigh. The miner and four of his friends were arrested, taken to Duluth and jailed for first-degree murder. A coroner's jury refused to return a verdict fixing responsibility.

Within a few hours of this outrage on the part of the company guard and the subsequent tragedy, some organizers for the I. W. W., stationed at distant points on the range, were arrested without warrants, refused a hearing, placed on a special train, taken to Duluth, seventy miles distant, and lodged in the county jail, charged with murder in the first degree. Among the arrested are: Our old friend and comrade Carlo Tresca, Frank Little, Sam Scarlett, Joe Schmidt, Joseph Gilday, Leo Stark, and others. Every effort is being made to convict them and send them to the gallows by County Prosecutor Greene of Duluth, on whose order Sheriff Meining arrested them.

In spite of all this terrorism, the miners stand firm. In fact, they have extended the strike to the Cuyuna range, where the companies get the high-grade ores to be mixed with the low. The strikers are making a noble fight against tremendous odds. They are doing their share in the great struggle of Labor. It is up to you to help. In Minnesota, as in San Francisco, the masters are planning to railroad to the gallows the best friends of the workers. Will Labor turn its back on the chosen victims?

Send funds to Wm. D. Haywood, Room 307, 164 W. Washington street, Chicago, Ill.

Undertones
By The Ear

(Among criminals, the Pinkerton Detective Agency is known as the Eye. The author of this is to be known as the Ear.—Editor.)

SAN FRANCISCO'S proverbial grey fog covered the city. A fine mist had dampened everything and everyone.

The Hall of Justice, a gloomy pile of stone, erected after the fire of 1906, massive and ugly on the exterior, presented a cheerless overheated interior. The marble floors were stained with tobacco juice and the walls and ceilings were dirty and smeared. It seemed very appropriate that this should be so, to one who knew the city of San Francisco with all its attractiveness, lovableness, romanticism, rottenness and evil.

It was nine o'clock in the morning. The faithful servants of the people and the friends of the workingman had not arrived to take up the business of the day. This business consisted mostly of prosecuting jitney drivers, "fixing" criminal cases, protecting the interests of the United Railroads, the Pacific Gas and Electric Company and the Catholic Church.

The Visitor wandered around the deserted corridors and began to draw comparisons between the theory and practice of government.

Then throbbing and pulsating through closed doors and above faraway footfalls, there came the sound of a violin. To the Visitor, whose ear was untrained, it seemed as if a master hand held the bow. The music rose and fell above the ugly noises of a public building just beginning to wake up. First it was happy and told of joy and love. Then it reminded the Visitor, whose ear was untrained, of the business of life, with its seeming tragedies and sorrows, ideals smashed and desires and ambitions unfulfilled. The music trailed off in a long drawn wail, as if the sorrow of life was too much for a human soul to bear.

The Visitor stood dreaming. A detective passed. The Visitor asked him who was playing the violin.

"Oh, that's one of the dynamiters," came the careless answer; "Mrs. Rena Mooney. She comes up for trial on a murder charge today."

The Strange Case of John Seiler

ANOTHER Daniel has come to judgment. He is William Herron, attorney for the Chamber of Commerce. He says that the term prostitute is not obscene."

During the case of the striker, Thos. Ryan, however, who was accused of using this word in reference to a female cashier of a scab restaurant, the word prostitute was perhaps the most horrible thing in the dictionary. Ryan secured a fifteen day sentence in the County Jail from Judge John J. Sullivan for the alleged use of the word.

For something like thirty minutes, Mr. Herron and Police Judge Matthew Brady gravely considered the meaning of the word. It had so many angles, ramifications and meanings that the case under consideration was put over for one week.

John Seiler is captain of the strike-breaking waiters in Tait's Cafe. The other night he poked his head out of the restaurant entrance and saw Mrs. Minnie Thomas, Waiters' Union picket.

"You Barbary Coast hooker," he called. Seiler said he used the word hasher, but it was proved that he said hooker. He was arrested on complaint of the Waiters' Union.

After a learned discussion "hooker" was admitted to mean prostitute. But upon the word prostitute the shining lights of the bar and bench were stumped.

The habitues of the crowded police court hung breathlessly upon the next words of the latest exponent of Law and Order, William Herron.

"Admitted," said Herron, slowly and weightily, "that the word prostitute, applied to the average person, might cause indignation upon the part of the person so addressed, Your Honor, but it is not obscene. In this charge of Disturbing the Public Peace, Your Honor, the statute does not once mention the word obscene."

And so the case was put over.

Outside, one newspaper man was heard to remark to another:

"I'll bet a dollar that Brady hasn't guts enough to send that man to jail as in the case of Ryan."

A War Fund for the Blast

THE BLAST is a sharp thorn in the flesh of the Law and Order reactionists. Their avowed purpose is to strangle every voice raised in protest against official outrage and injustice.

With the Chamber of Commerce in complete control of the local press, none daring to utter a free and fearless word, THE BLAST must live and keep up the fight. It is the only voice on the Coast raised in behalf of our imprisoned comrades whom the masters have picked as victims of their revenge on Labor.

The enemy is prepared to kill THE BLAST. We are determined to continue its revolutionary propaganda. Nay, more: THE BLAST will bend every effort and marshal its increasing influence to defeat the conspiracy to hang our imprisoned friends. The enemy shall not gloat over new scaffolds erected for the most intelligent and devoted rebels of California Labor.

THE BLAST must have a war fund of $1,000. Respond quickly.
ALEXANDER BERKMAN

Vol. I   SAN FRANCISCO, SEPTEMBER 15, 1916.   No. 19

Greater Love Hath No Man Than This, That a Man Lay Down His Life for His Friends

The Billings Trial

THE TRIAL of Warren K. Billings is now on. The case is progressing more quickly than is usual in trials of this character. Five days proved sufficient to select a jury and to submit almost all of the evidence of the prosecution. The defense, it is understood, will also require but little time to present its side. It is very likely that a verdict will be reached within another week.

Seldom has a trial of such grave character consumed so little time. Murder cases usually drag out for months and months. The trial of Mathew Schmidt, for instance, lasted over three months. David Caplan's trial almost as long. But the reason for the celerity with which the present case is carried on is simple. Rarely has an accusation of this character been so preposterous, rarely has the prosecution evidence been so flimsy as in the case of the United Railroads against Billings, Mooney et al.

I say "the case of the United Railroads" advisedly. For as the trial unfolds in the court room, from day to day, it becomes evident even to the most narrow-minded partisan of the prosecution that it is not the State that is prosecuting Warren K. Billings, as responsible for the Preparedness Parade explosion, nor even the Police Department of San Francisco, but clearly and unmistakably the real prosecutor is the United Railroads, in the person of one Martin Swanson.

And who is this man Swanson?

The daily press has assiduously sought to throw the mantle of mystery over the elusive Swanson. But in reality there is no mystery whatever about him. Swanson is just a plain detective. Very plain. Though a former Pinkerton, he is not of the old type plug-ugly whose very name has become synonymous with irresponsible brutality. Nor yet is Swanson the modern dime-novel sleuth that so delights the hearts of our incipient presidents. No, Swanson is just a common every-day detective. Every detective tries to be an actor off the boards. If he leans to heavy melodrama, he becomes a Pinkerton man; if he inclines to the lighter vaudeville, he joins the Burns staff; if his tendencies are in the line of realism, his ideal is Sherlock Holmes. But Swanson is a bad actor—which is here not meant figuratively but literally. His manner too obviously betrays a conscious, even a self-conscious, imitation of Conan Doyle's super-sleuth. Among that element of the local underworld whose intelligence is below the average, Swanson is considered "clever." I have no doubt he is, by comparison. Nor am I prepared to contradict a friend's statement to the effect that Swanson is "the most intelligent man in the District Attorney's office." It is probably quite true—which is not so much a testimonial to Swanson's intelligence as proof of the lack of it on the part of those that elected and chose the incumbents of the District Attorney's office.

This pen picture of Swanson can be completed by the story of my first meeting with him.

The door bell of THE BLAST office rang, and the editor—who was just then also filling the no less important position of janitor—answered the call. A stockily built man, above average size, his rather heavy face lightened by a pair of not unpleasant blue eyes, entered. I did not expect any visitors, and this man was a total stranger. I glanced at his face, then at his feet, suspiciously large. "What can I do for you?" I asked; "I see you are from the District Attorney's office." The man scowled. It was Swanson.

This "identification" of Swanson is necessary to understand the character of, and the proceedings at, the trial of Billings.

The evidence of the prosecution is now all in, and it is clear that it has entirely failed to establish its case. In fact, it has no case at all. The identification of Billings was the most preposterous ever attempted in a criminal court. A few hysterical women had him dressed in half a dozen different suits, all at the same time. No connection whatever has been shown, much less proven, between the accused and the bomb explosion.

It has not even been established whether it was dynamite or nitroglycerine, a bomb or infernal machine, or some other fatal contrivance that caused the deaths on Steuart Street. Indeed, the prosecution failed to prove anything except that an explosion took place on July 22d. And even regarding the circumstances and character of that explosion the District Attorney's witnesses were so hopelessly mixed that an out-of-town visitor in the courtroom might have been led to doubt the very fact of the explosion.

The essential features of the Billings trial may be summarized as follows:

Who shadowed Billings for weeks previous to the bomb explosion?

Swanson.

Who offered Billings a bribe of $5,000.00 to implicate Tom Mooney in the blowing up of the high-power towers of the United Railroads?

Swanson.

Who offered a similar reward to Israel Weinberg for the same purpose?

Swanson.

Who was the first to suggest that the most active labor men of San Francisco be accused of the bomb explosion?

Swanson.

Who arrested Billings?

Swanson.

Who helped to arrest and search the apartments of the other labor prisoners?

Swanson.

Who helped to raid the offices of THE BLAST?

Swanson.

Who grilled the editor and associate editor of THE BLAST?

Swanson.

Who helped to sweat the arrested labor men?

Swanson.

Who is always at the side of the official prosecutors, Fickert and Brennan?

Swanson.

Who threatened Israel Weinberg to "fix him", when—a week before the explosion—Weinberg refused to bear false witness in connection with the U. R. R. tower explosions?

Swanson.

Who made the statement, before the trial, to the effect that Billings is to be railroaded, and that after that it will be easy to convict all the other defendants?

Swanson.

Who stated that he will "get" Alexander Berkman and the rest of THE BLAST staff?

Swanson.

Who is the leading spirit in the specially created Detective Bomb Bureau?

Swanson.

Whose hand is so plainly seen behind the prosecution?

Swanson.

It's Swanson all through, the private detective of the Pacific Gas & Electric Company, who has also done yeoman service for the United Railroads. It is all Swanson, who, according to his own admission, is the "head detective of the Public Utilities Protective Bureau, an organization formed by the Pacific Gas & Electric Company, The Pacific Telephone & Telegraph Company, the Sierra and San Francisco Power Company, the Western States Gas and Electric Company, and the Northern Electric Railroad." The same Swanson who, according to the eleventh hour admission of District Attorney Fickert, is an officer of his staff.

*   *   *   *   *   *   *   *

Two main features characterize the trial of Billings. I have already described the first: the dominant business interests of

San Francisco directing the prosecution of Billings et al. through their private detective whose mouthpiece is the office of the District Attorney.

The second feature is even more significant. The keynote of the prosecution all through the trial has been, in the words of Assistant District Attorney Brennan: "This case is similar to the 'Spies Case' "—meaning the case of the Chicago Anarchists. We have a precedent, Brennan argued over and over again, in the conviction and hanging of the Chicago Anarchists for a "general conspiracy."

Intoxicated by his imagination run amuck, Brennan invoked the ghost of the "Haymarket Riot" to witness the parallel of the case of Billings with that of the Chicago men. He examined every talesman regarding his affiliations with Anarchists and Anarchism. "Have you been at any time, or are you now, connected with any organization of Anarchy?" "Have you ever been, or are you now, a subscriber for, or a reader of, the publication known as THE BLAST?" These were the insistent questions propounded to every prospective juror. The prosecution was evidently preparing to charge the accused with a "general conspiracy" to upset the whole social system. Billings, Brennan vociferated, was "in the business of going around dynamiting people," and he had repeatedly "terrorized property" (sic!). In 1913, Billings and Tom Mooney "entered a conspiracy to dynamite and terrorize persons and corporations entertaining notions and beliefs contrary to their ideas of social order and conditions." Here Brennan—who looks as if he might have successfully sat for that celebrated painting, "The Bull in a China Shop"—threw out his chest, justly feeling himself the legitimate descendant of the long mute and forever inglorious Grinnell of Chicago infamy. (State prosecutor against the Chicago Anarchists.)

It was too much even for the Court. Judge Dunne very properly ruled out the vague and indefinite "general conspiracy," remarking dryly: "Surely you are not seriously trying to prove a general conspiracy against the whole world." But this was just what Brennan was aiming at. That was the charge against the Chicago Anarchists, he contended, and the Court informed him that the Chicago labor men were "convicted and hanged for conspiring against the police."

That old parrot-cry of "Anarchist conspiracy" again! Almost thirty years have passed since the executions of 1887. The great Chicago trial has become a matter of history. Scores of books and innumerable magazine articles and essays have been written on the subject. We radicals thought ourselves justified in assuming that intelligent men of the present generation are familiar with the real facts of that great tragedy—the greatest tragedy in the annals of American labor. At the very least it could be expected that members of the legal profession should be cognizant of the long since established fact that the gallows of 1887 witnessed the blackest and most heinous judicial crime ever committed in an allegedly civilized and Christian country. Every school boy should know by this time that the Chicago Anarchists were *murdered*, cold-bloodedly murdered, by the mob in broadcloth and velvet, the Citizens' Alliance and their hirelings of the press and police, after they had bitterly prejudiced and ferociously inflamed the public mind. They were strangled to death for their love of liberty and devotion to the oppressed, and their foul murder has been crying to Heaven for now over a quarter of a century.

It was appalling to witness the crassest ignorance of this greatest criminal case of America masquerading in the court room in the guise of legal precedent. Neither judge nor prosecution seemed to have the least conception of the real facts of that historic case. And I have since realized that their ignorance in this matter reflects a similar condition of mind on the part of the public.

No decent man or woman can lay claim to intelligence if he persist in remaining ignorant of the most tragic event in the history of America—the terrible tragedy that cost the lives of seven of the noblest and best of mankind.

The following extract from the official review of the Chicago Anarchists' case (in 1893) by J. P. Altgeld, then Governor of the State of Illinois, will convince the impartial reader that never in all human ken was there a more infamous travesty on justice.

Gov. Altgeld's Reasons for Pardoning Fielden, Neebe and Schwab

ON THE night of May 4, 1886, a public meeting was held on Haymarket Square in Chicago; there were from 800 to 1,000 people present, nearly all being laboring men. There had been trouble, growing out of the effort to introduce an eight-hour day, resulting in some collisions with the police, in one of which several laboring people were killed, and this meeting was called as a protest against alleged police brutality.

The meeting was orderly and was attended by the mayor, who remained until the crowd began to disperse, and then went away. As soon as Capt. John Bonfield, of the police department, learned that the mayor had gone, he took a detachment of police and hurried to the meeting for the purpose of dispersing the few that remained, and as the police approached the place of meeting a bomb was thrown by some unknown person, which exploded and wounded many and killed several policemen, among the latter being one Mathias Degan. A number of people were arrested, and after a time August Spies, Albert R. Parsons, Louis Lingg, Michael Schwab, Samuel Fielden, George Engel, Adolph Fischer and Oscar Neebe were indicted for the murder of Mathias Degan. The prosecution could not discover who had thrown the bomb and could not bring the really guilty man to justice, and, as some of the men indicted were not at the Haymarket meeting and had nothing to do with it, the prosecution was forced to proceed on the theory that the men indicted were guilty of murder because it was claimed they had at various times in the past uttered and printed incendiary and seditious language, practically advising the killing of policemen, of Pinkerton men and others acting in the capacity, and that they were therefore responsible for the murder of Mathias Degan. The public was greatly excited, and after a prolonged trial all the defendants were found guilty; Oscar Neebe was sentenced to fifteen years' imprisonment and all of the other defendants were sentenced to be hanged. The case was carried to the Supreme Court and was there affirmed in the fall of 1887. Soon thereafter Lingg committed suicide. The sentence of Fielden and Schwab was commuted to imprisonment for life, and Parsons, Fischer, Engel and Spies were hanged, and the petitioners now ask to have Neebe, Fielden and Schwab set at liberty. * * *

The record of the trial shows that the jury in this case was not drawn in the manner that juries usually are drawn; that is, instead of having a number of names drawn out of a box that contained many hundred names, as the law contemplates shall be done in order to insure a fair jury and give neither side the advantage, the trial judge appointed one Henry L. Ryce as a special bailiff to go out and summon such men as he (Ryce) might select to act as jurors. While this practice has been sustained in cases in which it did not appear that either side had been prejudiced thereby, it is always a dangerous practice, for it gives the bailiff absolute power to select a jury that will be favorable to one side or the other. * * * The twelve jurors whom the defendants were finally forced to accept, after the challenges were exhausted, were of the same general character as the others, and a number of them stated candidly that they were so prejudiced that they could not try the case fairly, but each, when examined by the court, was finally induced to say that he believed he could try the case fairly upon the evidence that was produced in court alone. * * *

Upon the whole, therefore, considering the facts brought to light since the trial, as well as the record of the trial and the answers of the jurors as given therein, it is clearly shown that Ryce was appointed special bailiff at the suggestion of the State's attorney, and that he did summon a prejudiced jury which he believed would hang the defendants; and further, that the fact that Ryce was summoning only that kind of men was brought to the attention of the court before the panel was full, and it was asked to stop it, but refused to pay any attention to the matter, but permitted Ryce to go on, and then forced the defendants to go to trial before this jury.

While no collusion is proven between the judge and the State's attorney, it is clearly shown that after the verdict and while a motion for a new trial was pending, a charge was filed in court that Ryce had packed the jury, and that the attorney for the State got Mr. Favor to refuse to make an affidavit bearing on this point, which the defendants could use, and then the court refused to take any notice of it unless the affidavit was obtained, although it was informed that Mr. Favor would not make an affidavit, but stood ready to come into court and make a full statement if the court desired him to do so.

These facts alone would call for executive interference, especially as Mr. Favor's affidavit was not before the Supreme Court at the time it considered the case. * * *

No matter what the defendants were charged with, they were entitled to a fair trial, and no greater danger could possibly threaten our institutions than to have the courts of justice run wild or give way to popular clamor; and when the trial judge in this case ruled that a relative of one of the men who was killed was a competent juror, and this after the man had candidly stated that he was deeply prejudiced, and that his relationship caused him to feel more strongly than he otherwise might; and when, in scores of instances, he ruled that men who candidly declared that they believed the defendants to be guilty, that this was a deep conviction and would influence their verdict, and that it would require strong evidence to convince them that the defendants were innocent; when in all these instances the trial judge ruled that these men were competent jurors, simply because they had, under adroit manipulation, been led to say that they believed they could try the case fairly on the evidence, then the proceedings lost all semblance of a fair trial.

The State has never discovered who it was that threw the bomb which killed the policemen, and the *evidence does not show any connection whatever between the defendants and the man who did throw it.* The trial judge, in overruling the motion for a new hearing, and again, recently in a magazine article, used this language:

"The conviction has not gone on the ground that they did have actually any personal participation in the particular act which caused the death of Degan, but the conviction proceeds upon the ground that they had generally, by speech and print, advised large classes of the people, not particular individuals, but large classes, to commit murder, and had left the commission, the time and place and when, to the individual will and whim and caprice, or whatever it may be, of each individual man who listened to their advice, and that in consequence of that advice, in pursuance of that advice, and influenced by that advice, somebody not known did throw the bomb that caused Degan's death. Now, if this is not a correct principle of the law, then the defendants of course are entitled to a new trial. This case is without a precedent; there is no example in the law books of a case of this sort."

The judge certainly told the truth when he stated that this case was without a precedent, and that no example could be found in the law books to sustain the law as above laid down. For, in all the centuries during which government has been maintained among men, and crime has been punished, no judge in a civilized country has ever laid down such a rule before. The petitioners claim that it was laid down in this case simply because the prosecution, not having discovered the real criminal, would otherwise not have been able to convict anybody; that this course was then taken to appease the fury of the public, and that the judgment was allowed to stand for the same reason. I will not discuss this. But taking the law as above laid down, it was necessary under it to prove, and that beyond a reasonable doubt, that the person committing the violent deed had at least heard or read the advice given to the masses, for until he either heard or read it he did not receive it, and if he did not receive it, he did not commit the violent act in pursuance of that advice; and it is here that the case for the State fails; with all his apparent eagerness to force conviction in court, and his efforts in defending his course since the trial, the judge, speaking on this point in his magazine article, makes this statement: "It is probably true that Rudolph Schnaubelt threw the bomb," which statement is merely a surmise and is all that is known about it, and is certainly not sufficient to convict eight men on. In fact, until the State proves from whose hands the bomb came, it is impossible to show any connection between the man who threw it and these defendants. * * *

Again, it is shown here that the bomb was, in all probability, thrown by some one seeking personal revenge; that a course had been pursued by the authorities which would naturally cause this; that for a number of years prior to the Haymarket affair there had been labor troubles, and in several cases a number of laboring people, guilty of no offense, had been shot down in cold blood by Pinkerton men, and none of the murderers were brought to justice. The evidence taken at coroners' inquests and presented here, shows that in at least two cases men were fired on and killed when they were running away, and there was consequently no occasion to shoot, yet nobody was punished, that in Chicago there had been a number of strikes in which some of the police not only took sides against the men, but without any authority of law invaded and broke up peaceable meetings, and in scores of cases brutally clubbed people who were guilty of no offense whatever. * * *

It is shown that various attempts were made to bring to justice the men who wore the uniform of the law while violating it, but all to no avail; that the laboring people found the prisons always open to receive them, but the courts of justice were practically closed to them; that the prosecuting officers vied with each other in hunting them down, but were deaf to their appeals; that in the spring of 1886 there were more labor disturbances in the city, and particularly at the McCormick factory; that under the leadership of Capt. Bonfield the brutalities of the previous year were even exceeded. Some affidavits and other evidence are offered on this point, which I cannot give for want of space. It appears that this was the year of the eight-hour agitation, and efforts were made to secure an eight-hour day about May 1st, and that a number of laboring men standing, not on the street, but on a vacant lot, were quietly discussing the situation in regard to the movement, when suddenly a large body of police, under orders from Bonfield, charged on them and began to club them; that some of the men, angered at the unprovoked assault, at first resisted, but were soon dispersed; that some of the police fired on the men while they were running and wounded a large number who were already 100 feet or more away and were running as fast as they could; that at least four of the number so shot down died; that this was wanton and unprovoked murder, but there was not even so much as an investigation.

While some men may tamely submit to being clubbed and seeing their brothers shot down, there are some who will resent it, and will nurture a spirit of hatred and seek revenge for themselves, and the occurrences that preceded the Haymarket tragedy indicate that the bomb was thrown by some one who, instead of acting on the advice of anybody, was simply seeking personal revenge for having been clubbed, and that Capt. Bonfield is the man who is really responsible for the death of the police officers.

It is also shown that the character of the Haymarket meeting sustains this view. The evidence shows there were only 800 or 1,000 people present, and that it was a peaceable and orderly meeting; that the mayor of the city was present and saw nothing out of the way, and that he remained until the crowd began to disperse, the meeting being practically over, and the crowd engaged in dispersing when he left; that had the police remained away for twenty minutes more there would have been nobody left there, but as soon as Bonfield had learned that the mayor had left, he could not resist the temptation to have some more people clubbed, and went up with a detachment of police to disperse the meeting; and that on the appearance of the police the bomb was thrown by some unknown person, and several innocent and faithful officers, who were simply obeying an uncalled-for order of their superior, were killed. All of these facts tend to show the improbability of the theory of the prosecution that the bomb was thrown as a result of a conspiracy on the part of the defendants to commit murder; if the theory of the prosecution were correct, there would have been many more bombs thrown; and the fact that only one was thrown shows that it was an act of personal revenge.

It is further shown here that much of the evidence given at the trial was a pure fabrication; that some of the prominent police officials, in their zeal, not only terrorized ignorant men by throwing them into prison and threatening them with torture if they refused to swear to anything desired, but that they offered money and employment to those who would consent to do this. Further, that they deliberately planned to have fictitious conspiracies formed in order that they might get the glory of discovering them. * * *

I will simply say in conclusion, on this branch of the case, that the facts tend to show that the bomb was thrown as an act of personal revenge, and that the prosecution has never discovered who threw it, and the evidence utterly fails to show that the man who did throw it ever heard or read a word coming from the defendants; consequently it fails to show that he acted on any advice given by them. And if he did not act on or hear any advice coming from the defendants, either in speeches or through the press, then there was no case against them, even under the law as laid down by Judge Gary. * * *

The appeal of the petitioners is therefore granted and the unconditional release of Neebe, Fielden and Schwab hereby ordered.

JOHN P. ALTGELD.

THE BLAST

Revolutionary Labor Paper
Published every 1st and 15th of the month
569 Dolores St., San Francisco, Cal.

Mail Address, Box 661   Phone, Park 499

Alexander Berkman, Editor and Publisher
M. E. Fitzgerald, Associate Worker   Carl Newlander, Assistant

SUBSCRIPTION
$1.00 Yearly   60c Six Months   5c Copy
Bundle rates 2½c per copy in bundles of ten.

Reflections

THE BIG mass meeting in Dreamland Rink, on the eve of the trial of Warren K. Billings, was a significant and timely expression of the attitude of the workers of San Francisco in the cases of the labor men accused of the "dynamite conspiracy." No intelligent man in that vast audience could fail to realize that there is indeed a sinister conspiracy under way. But the labor defendants are not of the conspirators. These latter are to be sought in other quarters. The mask was torn from the face of the prosecution and the ugly cabala exposed to public gaze when Bob Minor, in a voice solemn and impressive, declared:

"I want Mr. Fickert's servants here tonight to repeat this to him: a man can be murdered as easily and more safely with a legal rope than with a bomb. And, Mr. Fickert, whether it be dishonesty or whether it be stupidity, try to understand that these men are not to be and cannot be lynched."

1886 and 1916! It was in 1886 that seven men were condemned to death for having initiated the eight-hour movement. The Citizens' Association of Chicago, composed of Board of Trade men, bankers and other open shop advocates, had raised a big fund to kill the demand for the shorter day and stifle the voices of its chief spokesmen, the Chicago Anarchists. They contributed $100,000 to *reward the jurors* that sent our comrades to the gallows.

Now, thirty years later, an attempt is made to repeat the heinous performance. In the year of the Lord 1916, the Chamber of Commerce of San Francisco has raised a million-dollar fund to exterminate organized labor and turn San Francisco into an open shop city. Now again a conspiracy is being hatched to crucify the most active labor elements.

But in vain! 1886 is past, and with it have gone the conditions that permitted our noble comrades to be sacrificed on the altar of greed and corruption. As Bob Minor so well said, in 1916 the labor prisoners "are not to be and cannot be lynched." The country, the workers, have made some progress since the perpetration of that blackest crime in the annals of American history, the judicial murders of 1887.

* * *

FOUR days before the great eight-hour strike of 1886, and only one week before the Haymarket tragedy, the New York *Times,* organ of the railroads and banks, said editorially:
"The strike question is, of course, the dominant one, and is disagreeable in a variety of ways. A short and easy way to settle it is urged in some quarters, which is to *indict for conspiracy* every man who strikes, and summarily lock him up. This method would undoubtedly strike a wholesome terror into the hearts of the working classes. Another way suggested is to pick up the leaders and *make such an example of them* as would scare others into submission."—N. Y. *Times,* April 25, 1886.

Other expressions were:
"The best policy would be to *drive workingmen into open mutiny* against the law."—N. Y. *Tribune,* April 25, 1886.
"Give them the rifle diet and see how they like that kind of bread."—Tom Scott, President of the Pennsylvania Railroad.
"The simplest plan probably, when one is not a member of the Humane Society, is to put arsenic in the supplies of food furnished the unemployed."—Chicago *Tribune.*

Thus the press in the days of the Haymarket. Would any newspaper *today* dare express such sentiments? I doubt it.
We *have* advanced. The Chicago Anarchists were hanged because they were Anarchists. They were not charged with the throwing of the Haymarket bomb, nor even with any knowledge concerning it. They were condemned because they were social heretics, and because they served labor faithfully and initiated the eight-hour movement.

Today, in 1916, thanks to the efforts of the martyred Chicago Anarchists and other friends of labor—today the President of the United States *begs* the workers to accept the eight-hour day.

The world do move.

SELDOM have the workers been so openly and brazenly tricked as were the New York car men in the settlement of their strike of a few weeks ago. Taken by surprise and being unprepared, the Interborough agreed to recognize the union, and the men returned to work on the solemn promise that their other grievances would be discussed by a conference of the representatives of the Company with those of the Amalgamated Association of Street and Electrical Railway Employees. Should these be unable to come to a settlement, the matter was to be submitted to arbitration.

But no sooner did the men return to work than the Company began to eliminate the active union men. It organized a "union" of its own, forced its men to sign individual contracts not to strike for three years, and then refused to deal with the Amalgamated.

When these developments became public, even some of the most conservative papers of New York branded the proceedings as perfidious. A general strike of all rapid transit workers of New York is now on, and it is to be hoped that the Amalgamated will profit by the example of the Railroad Brotherhoods. It is not to the point, in this connection, what the new Congressional eight-hour law may or may not do for the men. Its significance lies in the demonstrated power of solidaric labor to force an issue and to bring the industrial magnates, as well as the government, to their knees.

* * *

OF COURSE, no one doubts the sincerity of the Chamber of Commerce in its widely advertised stand for "law and order." We have been informed on reliable authority that Koster and his gentlemen of Commerce also "have a heart" and that their hearts are bleeding for the widows and orphans of the bomb tragedy. We do not doubt it. Have they not asked the public to raise thousands of dollars for the bereaved families? They have even made personal contributions.

Only *one* family seems to have escaped the humanitarian notice of Koster & Co. No tears were shed by the Commercial Chamber for the widow of Olson and her five orphans so cruelly robbed of husband, father and supporter. No fund has been raised, and not a penny contributed by Koster & Co. for *this* bereaved family. Is it possible they were overlooked in the general scramble to get press notices for the Chamber of Commerce?

We feel confident that it is only necessary to call the attention of the gentlemen of the Chamber to this sad case, to secure their immediate interest and support. For surely no one will be so mean as to believe that Widow Olson and her fatherless children were so pitilessly neglected by Mr. Koster only because Olson, the longshoreman, happened to be killed by Homer Waters, the negro ex-convict employed by Koster's Law and Order Committee as a gunman during the recent Longshoremen's strike.

Waters shot and killed Olson in cold blood. Surely the Law and Order Committee would thoroughly investigate the matter, if they were informed about the case. Surely they would take drastic measures to have the unprovoked murder punished!

Yes, they already have. One of the ablest and most expensive criminal lawyers of San Francisco, R. Porter Ashe, was retained by the Law and Order Committee to—prosecute the murderer, as they prosecute the culinary pickets, for instance? Oh, no. The Chamber hired Ashe to defend the murderous gunman. The least experienced assistant of the District Attorney's office was selected to prosecute the case and—strange to say—Waters, though convicted by the jury, is to be turned loose on probation. While in jail he was receiving a weekly check of $12.00.

The moral of the story is: The murderer of strikers earns the support of the Chamber of Commerce.

* * *

I WAS not in the city at the time, but I understand that Thornwell Mullaly, grand marshal of the Preparedness Parade, had been involved in the graft prosecutions against Calhoun, of the U. R. R., and that his name was connected with the mysterious blowing up of the home of one of the witnesses against the grafters.

A friend, noticing Mullaly in the District Attorney's office, asked me the other day: "Is Mullaly in the case as a suspect or as an expert on explosives?"

* * *

IF THERE ever was a time in this country when the people really believed in a free press and the freedom of assembly, it must have been in the dim and hoary past. Today only a few "cranks," and that mostly "foreigners," take any stock in Thomas Jefferson's, "Eternal vigilance is the price of liberty."

An orderly meeting is broken up by the police in San Francisco and nine of the participants arrested, but the occurrence hardly attracts the notice of the "good citizen." He is absorbed in swallowing the political clap-trap dished out to him by his bosses, never for a moment suspecting that the suppression of free assembly is a greater blow at his well-being than the loss of even the biggest strike. For the strangling of free expression is the most sinister step toward political and economic despotism.

As in San Francisco, so everywhere throughout this glorious land of liberty. In Boston, Van K. Allison is sentenced to three years' jail for giving a visitor at his office scientific information on birth control. In New York Ida Rauh, Bolton Hall and Jessie Ashley are under indictment for distributing necessary knowledge on the vital sex problem, though Mr. Hall had no part in the distribution, merely acting as chairman of the meeting where the "terrible crime" was committed.

Talk about liberty, when any stupid of a judge may give an order, at will, to raid any one's home or office and confiscate any book, pamphlet or picture that some filthy-minded Comstock or other pathologically sexed member of the Mudfog Association for Clothing the Naked Truth may consider "immoral." Thus a certain Sumner, undoubtedly a psychopatic degenerate and pupil of Comstock, raids the office of the *Masses*, confiscating every volume of "The Sexual Question," by Forel. Professor Forel, whose work is scientific and conservative, "immoral"!

From the suppression of the revolutionary press to the confiscation of works of art and science is but a step. Having submitted the one, we have exposed ourselves to the other. It is time to call a halt.

* * *

THE LOCAL newspapers failed to take note of an interesting incident at the Dreamland Rink mass meeting. Mr. Wm. A. Spooner, Secretary of the Labor Council of Alameda County, was the first speaker. He had talked but a few minutes when he remarked: "Ladies and gentlemen, I realize that there are several detectives distributed through the audience——"

Mr. Spooner did not get time to finish the sentence. There was a sudden commotion in the front rows of the audience: some one had taken a fit! Great excitement prevailed. People began to shout, some rushed to the front, and a panic seemed imminent.

But Mr. Spooner was equal to the occasion. "If it is an honest fit," he remarked, "I wish him good luck."

The audience "got" it. There was a roar that shook the rafters, and the threatened panic was over.

The detectives left in disgust.

Remember the Iron Range Strikers!

Fellow Workers and Friends!

Let us be brief and concise:

15,000 workers have been on strike on the Mesaba Range since the beginning of June.

100,000 men, women and children cut off from their regular livelihood.

Civil Government is suspended in Northeastern Minnesota. Steel Trust rule by gunmen about 1500 strong. Police, Courts, Press, Pulpit and Political machinery at the command of the Steel Trust. Hundreds of miners, wives of miners, their daughters and children jailed.

Four strikers, one striker's wife with a nursing babe, accused of first degree murder to cover up crimes of gunmen.

Five labor organizers held as participators in the murder under charge carrying life imprisonment.

Eight hundred families voluntarily starving themselves awaiting your action!

That is briefly, the situation on the Mesaba Range in Minnesota.

Fellow workers, who like ourselves are on the outside of this terror-stricken district, the Minnesota Miners are putting it up to us.

They have tackled the greatest enemy of labor in this country, they have staked their all, they have staked their breadless and homeless women and children.

The jails of the Range are right now resounding with the songs of freedom, sung by strikers, strikers' wives and strikers' children who have no other refuge.

It seems they are determined to conquer or die.

By their own power they cannot conquer. They are looking up to us with the confidence of children to their protectors, as men will do in the hour of need. They have nothing left but their undaunted spirit, which bids them to hold out and save this Verdun of the class war in America.

If we do not hasten to their aid they will perish, and we shall by our own negligence have destroyed this outpost of labor which occupies the most difficult ground on the whole industrial battlefield.

If we leave them in the lurch they shall go back to work some day perhaps, broken in spirit, and with hope extinguished in their hearts. They shall probably thereafter keep their peace, knowing they are standing alone in the world and have no help to expect.

If we help them to victory we shall have shot to pieces the fortress of oppression thrown up by the arrogant Steel Trust against Labor.

If we help them to win we shall at the same time liberate the ten fellow workers in the shadow of a living death.

Are we going to let these ten men and women be destroyed for being true to us, true to our common cause? NO!

We, the Committee of Defense, claim to know the workers of this country enough to have the right to call out to those men and women:

"Hold out a little while longer. Do not give in. It takes time for us to act but we are coming to your aid. Hold out a while longer."

Are you going to back us up? Yes, we know you are.

The miners of Minnesota need your financial aid and your moral aid. They need money to keep the destitute alive and hopeful, they need your peremptory command to their oppressors to desist on penalty of your tying up the industries of the whole country.

"Invest" the spare cash you have as an organization and as individuals in supporting them. We know it is not much, but if we all help out at once our mites will swell into a mighty flood that will accomplish wonders. This appeal is being sent to every labor organization in this country.

Let us surprise these unknown brave men and women by showing them that they have devout friends in every village of this country. Raise money by the usual methods if you have none on hand. As for moral aid, the Defense Committee implores you to send resolutions expressing your sentiments and your wishes to the Governor of the State of Minnesota, at St. Paul, Minn., and to the Sheriff of St. Louis Co., Duluth, Minn.

ACT, but act quickly. Call a special meeting if necessary and arrange mass-meetings to protest.

An injury to one is an injury to all. One for all and all for one.

It is your own fate you are deciding, it is your own destiny you are shaping when you help your brothers and fellow-workers now striking on the Mesaba Range.

Fraternally yours,

IVA SHUSTER,
Secretary.

Please send all money to JOHN SEPPANEN, treasurer of the strike committee, Box 372, Virginia, Minn., or to Pietro Allegro, the treasurer of the Defense Committee, 226 Lafayette Street, New York, N. Y., or through any other channel, just so you are sure the money gets to the strikers.

A Last Call to Radicals

THE INTERNATIONAL Workers' Defense League of Los Angeles is nearing the end of its work against the efforts of the capitalist class to suppress free speech and free press.

October 1st the appeal of the Magon brothers will be reviewed by the court. The decision of that court will determine the future of the radical press of this country—*your press.* A flimsy excuse will be all that is necessary to still its voice.

The persons of the Magon brothers do not interest the League or its members. Composed of all shades of radical belief, a large portion of the League members are at variance with the Magons and their propaganda, but these members realize that something greater than the Magons or their propaganda is at stake and have gone into the fight heart and soul.

The League was formed for defense and not for propaganda work, so that today it may be defending an Anarchist, tomorrow a Socialist and the day after an Industrialist. Your turn may come next.

What have you done in the fight! What can you do?

Listen! Five hundred dollars must be raised by October 1st to win the Magon brothers' appeal. Defeat means death to the radical press.

Get your local paper to publish this call and start a subscription list in their paper.

Go to your local and read this to the members.

If you do not belong to a local go to every radical or semi-radical meeting you can reach and *ask for five hundred dollars.* You may not get it all in one place, but get all you can. Get up a social, dance or mass meeting.

Secure a list of radical names or others whom you think will give money, mail the names to this office and we will mail them copies of the appeal.

INTERNATIONAL WORKERS' DEFENSE LEAGUE
231 Douglas Building, Los Angeles, California.

THE BLAST   Seven

The Open Shop

"WHAT is all this talk in the papers about the open shop?" asked Mr. Hennessey.

"Why, don't ye know?" said Mr. Dooley. "Really, I'm surprised at yer ignorance, Hinnissey. Whut is th' open shop? Sure, 'tis a shop where they kape th' dore open t' accommodate th' consthant sthream of min comin' in t' take jobs cheaper thin th' min whut 'as th' jobs. 'Tis like this, Hinnissey —suppose wan of these freebarn Amerycan citizens is wurkin' in an open shop for th' princely wages of wan large iron dollar a day of tin hours. Along comes another freebarn son-of-a-gun an' he sez t' th' boss: 'I think I could handle th' job for ninety cints.' 'Sure,' sez th boss, an' the wan-dollar man gets the merry jinglin' can, an' goes out into th' crool wurld t' exercise his inalienable roights as a freebarn Amerycan citizen and scab on some other poor divil. An' so it goes on, Hinnissey. An' who gets th' benefit? Thrue, it saves th' boss money, but he don't care no more for money than he does for his roight eye. It's all principle wid him. He hates t' see min robbed of their indipendence. They must have their indipendence, regahrdliss of inything ilse."

"But," said Hennessey, "these open shop min ye minshun say they are fer th' unions, if properly conducted."

"Shure," said Mr. Dooley, "if properly conducted. An' there ye are. An' how wud they have thim conducted? No sthrikes, no scales, hardly iny wages, an' damn few mimbers."

History Repeats Itself

JOHN P. FREY.

EVEN in the matter of disputes over the question of the union or non-union shop, history repeats itself. In the records of the city of Exeter, England, there is found reference to a bitter struggle by the Taylor's Gild during the years 1475-6-7, in its effort to bring about a thorough organization and force all tailors to pay dues to the gild, on the one hand, and the non-union, or non-gild tailors, supported apparently by the city authorities, on the other. We are informed in the most unique language that the members of the gild attacked the non-members and destroyed their shops in "modo querrino arriate, ve et armis, videlicet jactis, doblettis of defense, swerdis, bokelers, glayves, and staves, in domo," and that at other times they were armed with "arsubus, glayvis, baculis, et daggariis." In fact, the belligerent tailors seem to have used every weapon except scissors and pressing irons upon their opponents.

The record would make it appear that the non-gild tailors were good citizens and independent workmen and a credit to the city, while the union or gild tailors were a bad and desperate lot; but the story is told by the city authorities who were fighting the gild and endeavoring to put it out of business.

They did succeed in "putting it out of business," just as has been done to modern trade unions, only to discover that the motives and principles which prompt workmen to organize are more powerful than the mere edict of a court that they shall disband.

The gild-hating city fathers prepared a strong case, and armed with affidavits, presented it before the king at London. The king, Edward IV, sided with the Exeter authorities and issued a decree disbanding the Taylor's Gild. Two of the king's commissioners, John Fortesque and John Courtney, went to Exeter and officially decreed that the gild was no more. Afterwards, as we are told, jubilantly drinking wine with the mayor, John Denys, in the house of Matthew Tubbe, at the expense of the town, to the amount of viii d.

This celebration, however, was premature, for the union tailors refused to surrender their organization, and at last the city fathers compromised their attitude, and the gild not only held its own, but remained in existence some 400 years; in fact, long after it had lost its original character and had become an employers' organization in the modern sense of the term.

The experience of the Exeter tailors in the fifteenth century was similar to that of some other gilds, and our trade unions have had to contend with similar antagonism of the authorities, on many occasions, having been declared illegal organizations, yet the final story has been the same, the wage earners' organizations have not only remained in existence, but have become stronger.

⚏ ⚏ ⚏

THE UNITED RAILWAYS has decreed that the jitney bus must get off Market street. Accordingly it was ruled off by special city ordinance. Of course there's plenty of room on the main thoroughfare of San Francisco for limousines with bejeweled and bepainted political ladies, but none for a jitney carrying half a dozen workers to their places of employment. How dare they rob the U. R. of their nickels!

The *Bulletin*, which masquerades as a "liberal" paper, has sided with the corporations against the poor man's auto. It has followed the same profitable and easy line in the bosses' conspiracy against the men indicted in the bomb case. Fremont Older, the professed radical, has shut up like an oyster. He dare not say a word in behalf of decency and fairness. How well the poet expressed it: "The coward dies a thousand deaths."

⚏ ⚏ ⚏

DEFENSE FUND SAN FRANCISCO LABOR PRISONERS
Collected by Emma Goldman and Alexander Berkman
Collected at E. G. San Francisco lectures:

J. Lizzul	$ 10.00
Miss Buckbee	5.00
A. Feinberg	2.00
T. Mishkin	1.00
Sophia Rosenthal	2.00
Schwab	1.00
S. Rosenthal	5.00
A friend	1.00
A. Engel	2.00
M. Leon	1.00
B. Goldblatt	1.00
J. Thorsen	1.00
Esther Bercovitz	5.00
J. L. Wright	5.00
Bessie Kimmelman	5.00
A friend	1.00
A friend	1.00
Mrs. Rose	.50
Pierson	2.00
J. Nielsen	2.00
Anna Lawson	2.00
A friend	2.30
Collected by A. Berkman at Oakland Picnic.	17.20
A friend	25.00
Dr. Rose Fritz	5.00
Miss A. B.	200.00
Chas. Fisher, per Rosenthal	5.00
G. Barazzone and friends, West Frankfort, Ill.	1.50
H. G. Hanlon, Hood, Calif.	3.00
Mary and Stephen Furch	10.00
A. Bers, San Francisco	2.00
Joseph D'Angelo, Wilmington, Del.	1.00
M. E. Fitzgerald	5.00
Loan from friend, per A. B.	1000.00
M. K. Serailian, S. F.	5.00
A friend	2.50
A friend	2.00
Emma Goldman, in Seattle and Portland	18.65
	$1360.65

Turned over to the defense by Alexander Berkman:

Per E. B. M.	$ 100.00
Per Robert Minor, Treasurer	200.00
Per Robert Minor, Treasurer	1000.00
To prisoners per R. M.	25.00
To Ada Nolan	11.00
Per Robert Minor, Treasurer	24.65
	$1360.65

September 15, 1916.   ALEXANDER BERKMAN.

An Italian Restaurant

W. L. George

THEY sat at a marble-topped table, flooded with light by incandescent gas. In the glare the waiters seemed blacker, smaller and more stunted than by the light of day. Their faces were pallid, with a touch of green: their hair and moustaches were almost blue black. Their energy was that of automata. Victoria looked at them, melting with pity.

"There's life for you," said Farwell, interpreting her look. "Sixteen hours' work a day in an atmosphere of stale food. For meals, plate scourings. For sleep and time to get to it, eight hours. For living, the rest of the day."

"It's awful, awful," said Victoria. "They might as well be dead."

"They will be soon," said Farwell, "but what does that matter? There are plenty of waiters. In the shadow of the olive groves tonight in far-off Calabria, at the base of the vine-clad hills, couples are walking hand in hand, with passion flashing in their eyes. Brown peasant boys are clasping to their breasts young girls with dark hair, white teeth, red lips, hearts that beat and quiver with ecstasy. They tell a tale of love and hope. So we shall not be short of waiters."

⊠　⊠　⊠

SPACE in THE BLAST is too limited to publish even a small part of the many letters of appreciation and encouragement we receive from our readers. By request of our comrades in Cleveland, Ohio, we reproduce the following

Resolution

WE, the Anarchist Group of Cleveland, Ohio, want to express to you our admiration for your brave fight against injustice and oppression, and your stand in behalf of the arrested labor men, and we want to assure you of our moral and financial support in your struggle against the outrageous despotism of official and unofficial Vigilante scoundrels.

We are with you, now and ever, and we will fight with you.

Hoping that other labor and radical organizations will take similar action, we remain with revolutionary greeting,

THE ANARCHIST GROUP OF CLEVELAND
Per Jack Myers, Secretary.

P. S.—We enclose M. O. for $13.75, of which sum $4.35 was contributed by the Union of Russian Workers, and the balance collected at the gathering of our Group.

J. M.

⊠　⊠　⊠

THE CYCLOPS OF CULTURE. Whoever has seen those furrowed basins, which once contained glaciers, will hardly deem it possible that a time will come when the same spot will be a valley of woods and meadows and streams. It is the same in the history of mankind; the wildest forces break the way, destructively at first, but their activity was nevertheless necessary in order that later on a milder civilization might build up its house. These terrible energies—that which is called Evil—are the cyclopic architects and roadmakers of humanity.
—*Nietzsche*

PUBLICATIONS RECEIVED

OSCAR WILDE: HIS LIFE AND CONFESSIONS, by Frank Harris. Published in 2 vol mes, by the author, 3 Washington Square, New York.
THE NEXT STEP IN DEMOCRACY, by R. W. Sellars, Ph. D. Macmillan Co., New York; $1.50.
JUSTICE IN WAR TIME, by Bertrand Russell. The Open Court Publishing Co., Chicago; $1.00.
THE CRY FOR JUSTICE. An Anthology of the Literature of Social Protest. Edited by Upton Sinclair. Introduction by Jack London. The John C. Winston Co., Philadelphia; $2.00.
MURDER, by David Greenberg. $1.50.
NEUTRALITY, by S. Ivor Stephen. Neutrality Press, Chicago; 50 cents.
ECONOMICS OF LIBERTY, by John Beverley Robinson.
A CHRISTMAS CANTATA, by Charles Erskine Scott Wood, Portland, Ore.
THE POET IN THE DESERT, by Charles Erskine Scott Wood, Portland, Ore.
THE PEST AND OTHER ONE-ACT PLAYS, by Emanuel Julius, Box 125, Girard, Kansas.
SHAMBLES, by Henry T. Schnittkind, Ph. D. Ferrer Colony, Stelton, N. J.
THE BROOK KERITH, a Syrian Story by George Moore. Macmillan, New York; $1.50.
THE JEW TO JESUS, AND OTHER POEMS, by Florence Kiper Frank. Mitchell Kennerly, New York; $1.00.
SOCIALISM IN AMERICA, by John Macy. Doubleday, Page & Co., New York; $1.00.
THE TRADE UNION WOMAN, by Alice Henry. D. Appleton & Co., New York. $1.50.
MARTYRS OR CRIMINALS? by Theodore Schroeder, Cos Cob, Conn.
LIBERTY THROUGH IMPERSONAL SERVICE, by Theodore Schroeder.
WHAT THE CATHOLIC CHURCH HAS DONE TO MEXICO, by Dr. A. Paganel, Mexico, D. F.
A FEW FACTS ABOUT BRITISH RULE IN INDIA. The Hindustan Gadar, San Francisco, Cal.
INDIA'S "LOYALTY" TO ENGLAND. The Indian National Party.
THE METHODS OF THE INDIAN POLICE IN THE TWENTIETH CENTURY. The Hindustan Gadar, San Francisco, Cal.

⊠　⊠　⊠

A War Fund for the Blast

THE BLAST is a sharp thorn in the flesh of the Law and Order reactionists. Their avowed purpose is to strangle every voice raised in protest against official outrage and injustice.

With the Chamber of Commerce in complete control of the local press, none daring to utter a free and fearless word, THE BLAST must live and keep up the fight. It is the only voice on the Coast raised in behalf of our imprisoned comrades whom the masters have picked as victims of their revenge on Labor. The enemy is prepared to kill THE BLAST. We are determined to continue its revolutionary propaganda. Nay, more: THE BLAST will bend every effort and marshal its increasing influence to defeat the conspiracy to hang our imprisoned friends. The enemy shall not gloat over new scaffolds erected for the most intelligent and devoted rebels of California Labor.

THE BLAST must have a war fund of $1,000. Respond quickly.
ALEXANDER BERKMAN

Vol. I   SAN FRANCISCO, OCTOBER 15, 1916.   No. 20

"AS GOD IS MY JUDGE, I SEEN HIM"
—Star Witness in the Billings Trial

THE BILLINGS VERDICT

THERE is no justice in heaven or on earth. That is my final conviction. Where *is* that just Providence we hear so much about? Where the sense of justice of the Almighty, or of any one else, when a human being, utterly innocent, can be convicted and doomed to a living death for the rest of his natural life? Where, where is Justice?

Billings has been convicted. Convicted in spite of his proven innocence. For it is literally true that in the Billings trial the prosecution not only failed to make out its case, but the defense actually *proved* the innocence of Billings, proved that, even according to the State's testimony, it was a physical impossibility for Billings to have been at the place of the explosion.

And yet Billings was convicted. Was there ever a more crying injustice? No, not since the days of the Chicago Anarchists foully murdered by blind rage and bitter prejudice. Indeed, the San Francisco case is even more heinous in its cold-blooded bestiality. For history can at least explain, if not palliate, the judicial murders of 1887 by a temporary mental aberration of the people, a virtual insanity of fear and hatred resulting from the bitter class feeling in the tremendous labor struggles of those days.

No such excuse can be given in the Billings case. The people of San Francisco were deeply stirred by the Preparedness parade explosion, but they did not lose their heads. The tragedy filled them with grief, but they scorned the infamy of lynch law suggested by the Hearsts and their vile ilk. They refused to sanction a debauch of blood-drunk vengeance. They would not turn murderers, deeply as they mourned their loss. They waited patiently for the authorities to apprehend the guilty. They wouldn't shed innocent blood.

What little hysteria the yellow press, which thrives on it, was able to arouse or stimulate, had all died out long before the Billings trial began. The city had resumed its normal life, the people followed their accustomed pursuits, and even in the courtroom nothing disturbed the even tenor of the usual legal proceedings, save the occasional Holy Jumper antics of the public prosecutors.

There was nothing in the atmosphere in or out of the courtroom, nor anything beneath the surface of the life of San Francisco, to indicate unusual interest in the trial. The Preparedness parade, nay, its very object, was all but forgotten. The bomb passed into history and the great bulk of the citizenship evinced no particular interest in the trial, because it was generally felt that the police had failed to find a clew to the real perpetrators of the explosion, and that the criminal proceedings against Billings, et al., were a somewhat ungraceful mode of covering up the inefficiency of the District Attorney's office rather than a serious attempt to fasten the crime on the accused. It was therefore generally felt that the arrested labor men were mere police scapegoats, and that there was no case against them. And when the public prosecutor insisted on charging Billings, et al., with a "conspiracy to dynamite people holding different social views" and was sarcastically sat upon by Judge Dunne, who demanded actual evidence instead of "vague charges of a general conspiracy against the whole world," the public was convinced that the District Attorney was merely trying to save his official face.

But when the actual trial of the "bomb plot" began, and the prosecution introduced its witnesses, it quickly became apparent that there was indeed a plot, a deep, sinister plot—not a *bomb* plot, however, but a plot to clear the District Attorney's office of the charge of inefficiency and at the same time stifle the voices of certain men who had become a thorn in the flesh of the enemies of Labor.

* * *

Like the scenes of some absorbing drama, the "conspiracy" was being unfolded on the stage of the dingy court-room. Within the railing, on reserved seats, sat the main actors of this intense human play: Warren K. Billings, the first of the accused to be tried; District Attorney Chas. Fickert and his assistants, Brennan and Cunha; the attorneys for the defense, McNutt, Lomasney and Lawlor; and on the box-like bench, to the left of Superior Judge Dunne, the twelve men, "good and true," all retired business men, well known to the District Attorney for their loyal service in similar capacity on numerous previous occasions. The jurors, whose combined age was more than equal to five centuries, listened with varying degrees of attention to the straggling stream of witnesses—witnesses for the prosecution who testified under oath, so help me God, that Billings was in **three different places at the same time**, dressed in as many different suits of clothes. According to these witnesses, Billings was—between 1:50 to 2 p. m. on the fateful day of July 22d—on the corner of Steuart and Market streets, the place of the explosion, with a heavy suitcase, variously and positively identified as black, yellowish, and as a small grip; Billings was, *at the same time*, on the roof of 721 Market street, over a mile from the scene of explosion, and he was also, *at the very same moment*, talking to Policeman Earle Moore in front of 721 Market street, and also having a long conversation with Estelle Smith in the dental office of her employer.

The prosecution's identification of Billings was no less positive and sure than the establishment of his whereabouts. Estelle Smith, chief witness for the State, identified him by a "peculiar scar on his forehead," her certainty remaining unshaken even after it was proven that the only scar or rash Billings ever had was—on his knee. Nor could Miss Smith be swerved from her faithfulness to obligation when it was established that her mother, Mrs. Kidwell, had been promised by the prosecution a pardon for Mr. Kidwell, her husband, serving time in Folsom penitentiary for forgery, and that Miss Smith's uncle is imprisoned in San Quentin for murder. She protested that the reward of $17,000 offered for "the conviction of *anyone* for the outrage of July 22d," had no temptation for her whatever, though her salary as attendant at a dental office was insufficient for her mode of dressing.

Equally protesting and confident was the other star witness of the prosecution, a certain McDonald, a man about town and notorious dope fiend, who, according to his own testimony, "as in a dream saw the suitcase placed on the sidewalk." Confronted by several witnesses who swore that he boasted of being well paid for his testimony, McDonald admitted that his hotel expenses were being paid by the police to "protect" him against the defense.

Quite as devoid of any hope of reward were a number of other State witnesses, mostly police and detectives, whose testimony impressed every one as told with the facility bred of practice, and who unanimously agreed that they were incapable of being mistaken or telling a lie.

Subtly woven through the State testimony could be traced the fine handiwork of Private Detective Swanson, confidential representative of the Pacific Gas & Electric Co., the United Railroads, chief detective of the Public Utilities Bureau, etc. It was Swanson, looming large in the background of the District Attorney's office; Swanson offering a bribe of $5,000 to Billings and Weinberg, in turn, *a week before the bomb explosion*, to implicate Mooney in the blowing up of some power towers of the United Railroads corporation; Swanson, through Brennan, promising $15,000 to one of the attorneys for the defense for double-crossing Billings and Mooney; Swanson threatening friends of the accused labor men with dire punishment for refusing to bear false witness against them It was always Swanson, the Private Detective, hovering about the court, prompting the District Attorney at the trial, smiling encouragement at the State witnesses, gliding in and out of the court room, and nodding familiarly to the jurors in the corridor during recess.

All this in full view of the big audience attracted by the sensational trial. But unseen by the casual observer, unseen even—unfortunately—by the attorneys for the defense, there loomed behind the scenes a grim figure, silent and commanding, whose invisible presence was yet palpably manifest to every one of social intelligence: a figure whose heavy breath surcharged the atmosphere with an ominous sense of a stealthily waged class war, pregnant with mysterious hints of hidden forces, of whispered threats—"Chamber of Commerce"—"Open Shop"—"Labor and Capital"—"Law and Order Committee."

* * *

At last came the turn of the defense. Witness after witness exposed the false network of the State's accusation against Billings. Reputable citizens, professional and business men, Grand Army veterans, participants in the Preparedness parade and members of patriotic organizations—total strangers to the accused—completely disproved the testimony of the prosecution. They tore its evidence to shreds. The defense produced the man who had spoken to Officer Moore and whom the latter mistook for Billings. A youth on the roof of 721 Market street, resembling Billings, was proven to have been mistaken for the accused prisoner. It was a patient at the dental office who had held the conversation with Estelle Smith, attributed by her to Billings. Billings had no suitcase on that day, nor had he ever visited the place where Miss Smith was employed. Eye-witnesses, supported by photographic evidence, proved the accused to have been far from the scene of the explosion and in no way connected with it. Billings stood completely exonerated.

The prosecution was shaken to its very foundation. It did not dare ask for the death penalty. It ignored the evidence and wrapped itself in the folds of the flag. "Gentlemen of the Jury," implored Assistant District Attorney Brennan in his closing speech, "you must convict this boy to wash off the stain put on our flag. We do not ask for his life. We want to give him a chance to tell on the real men back of this conspiracy against our civilization."

The crowded court room held its breath as the jurors slowly filed in. They had been out three hours, two of which were spent at luncheon—at an open-shop place. The fate of a fellow human was in their hands, but long deliberation—it was felt on every hand—was unnecessary. The case of the defense was too clear for doubt.

"We find the defendant, Warren K. Billings, guilty of murder in the first degree, as charged."

Dead silence. The voice of the foreman of the jury died away, like a hollow echo, and a pall of darkness seemed to settle over the court room. The audience sat silent, motionless, as if stunned by a sudden blow. Then, as with a common instinct, all eyes turned on Billings. The youth stood with lips twitching, blank astonishment in his eyes, gazing mutely at the jurors.

It was only an instant—and then the Judge recovered himself. The jury was dismissed.

Like shadows, pale and silent, the people faded from the court room.

* * *

MEN and WOMEN of America, children of liberty and justice-loving sires, will you suffer such judicial assassination of innocent men?

How and Why Billings Was Convicted

CONTRADICTORY TESTIMONY OF STATE WITNESSSES

JOHN McDONALD:

It must have been eight or ten minutes to two when I first discovered him (Billings) * * at the corner (Steuart and Market streets) * * MOONEY was with him.

JOHN CROWLEY:

I am positive sure it was 1:55 * * Billings at Steuart and Mission streets * * It was not MOONEY at all.

ESTELLE SMITH:

After Mayor Rolph passed in the parade (nine minutes to two) * * Billings coming down from the roof of 721 Market street.

According to the evidence of the prosecution, therefore, Billings was at Steuart and Market streets, Steuart and Mission, and at 721 Market (a mile away), all at the same time.

HOW THEY "IDENTIFIED" BILLINGS

STATE Witness Policeman EARLE MOORE (motorman for the U. R. R. during car strike):

I tooted the horn several times, and I could not get the driver. Finally the party walked out who I later identified as Mr. Billings, walked out to the sidewalk * * I says, "Who is the driver of the car?" He turns around * * looks towards 721 Market street, and he says, "I don't know; he will be here in a minute."

DEFENSE Witness THOMAS DODGE:

He (Policeman Moore) says, "Is this your machine?" I says, "No, the owner of the machine has gone into the building there" (illustrating).

STATE Witness Mrs. NELLIE EDEAU:

I first saw Mr. Billings * * on the roof of 721 Market street * * talking to somebody down in the street. * * I am positive it was about 1:30 to 1:25.

DEFENSE Witness AL DE CACCIA:

About 1:30 * * I was on the roof of 721 Market street. * * I made sounds and gave directions to one of the boys in the store how to get up there.

DEFENSE Attorney MAXWELL McNUTT points out to the jury strong resemblance between BILLINGS and DE CACCIA.

Several witnesses corroborate DE CACCIA to the effect that it was he, DE CACCIA, and not BILLINGS, who was on the roof of 721 Market street, shouting down to them in the street directions how to reach the roof.

WHY THEY WANT TO "GET" BILLINGS, MOONEY, ET AL.

MRS. HAMMERBERG:

I told you (Mr. Brennan) at the time you and Mr. Swanson came up, the day that you told me you had to get somebody or they were going to get you. Q. Who said that? A. You (Mr. Brennan). Q. Where? A. In my house. Q. It was not in the office of the police department? A. It was in my house. Q. Who was present at the time I made that statement? A. Mr. Swanson and Mr. Hammerberg.

C. L. LOGAN:

McDonald * * said the Chief patted him on the back and said, "MAC, if you stick to this story, you can go back to Baltimore or Detroit on the cushions * * with a nice piece of change in your pockets." He told me that on the corner of Fourth and Natoma, near Fourth, in front of the Eagle House; also in Third and Natoma, and in front of the Peniel Mission, a few nights after.

COLONEL REQUA, of the Salvation Army:

Q. * * * You said to McDonald that "if he will testify and these men are convicted, that he will probably receive a large portion of the reward" to which he replied, "Yes, the Chief told me that I would go back to Baltimore on the cushions with plenty of change in my pockets."
A. That is correct. * * * he said he was going to get three dollars a day. * * * he said he was having a good time and he was going to the theatre right after.

FRED HARRIS:

McDonald said he had a good thing now. I said, "How is that?" He says, "I am a star witness in the bomb case, and when the trial is over, I will be able to go back East on the cushions and have money left."

FRANK SUMNEY:

Q. * * * Did you have with John McDonald, in substance, the following conversation: Sumney: "It's pretty bad about the bomb explosion, isn't it, Mac?" McDonald: "Yes, it seems to me like in a dream. I saw a man walk out and set down a suitcase; then I looked in the saloon to see the time and walked half way up the block when the explosion went off."
A. Yes, sir.
Q. * * * did McDonald say to you, "When those fellows go over the road and I get my divvy, back to the East for me?"
A. He did.
Q. * * * in Healy's barber shop, you cut McDonald's hair, did McDonald and you have the following conversation: McDonald: "I am getting paid for my work." Sumney: "Who pays you?" McDonald: "I think it comes off the State." Sumney: "Do you have to wait to get it until the end of the trial?" McDonald: "No, I am getting three dollars a day right along and I won't have to wait until the trial is over."
A. Yes.

Mrs. Allie Kidwell, MOTHER OF ESTELLE SMITH, was promised by the prosecution a pardon for her husband now in Folsom penitentiary. Admitted by District Attorney Fickert and Assistant District Attorney Brennan.

$17,000
is to be paid for the conviction of
A N Y O N E
for the outrage of July 22.

Affidavits by Eye-Witnesses to the Bomb Explosion Suppressed by the Prosecution

WILLIAM H. TAYLOR:

* * I went in the saloon on the 22nd day of July, 1916, and the saloon was crowded, I having entered from the Steuart street side. I just got inside the door and turned around and came out again when a man about five feet seven or eight, with a mustache, kind of sallow complexion, was not putting the suitcase down on the sidewalk but was shoving it against the building. * * Then I heard the bomb go off. * * The man who moved the suitcase above described was positively not WARREN K. BILLINGS. * * A sergeant of police stepped up to me and said, "Did you see the man place that suitcase there?" I said "I did." * * I was never taken by the police or anybody to see Warren K. Billings. * * Capt. Matheson then put me in charge of Officer Desmond, who took me down to the Stockton boat. * * I remained in Stockton three weeks, more or less. * * About ten days ago I returned from Stockton to San Francisco and have been here ever since. I reported to Capt. Matheson on my return and he said, "If we want you we will call you," and the same statement was made to me by Officer Desmond. I never was, however, called as a witness. * * I am absolutely positive that the defendant above named is not the man who moved the suitcase, and I did not see him in that neighborhood at all on July 22, 1916.

ELMER E. KIMBERLIN:

* * stood on Steuart street near Market within two feet of the spot at which an explosion occurred that day. * * that at 1:30 p. m. saw a man * * set suitcase down on the sidewalk within two feet from where affiant was standing; * * That the man who had set the suitcase as aforesaid was approximately five feet ten inches in height, weighed 170 pounds * * That during the course of the trial of Warren K. Billings, this affiant saw the said Warren K. Billings in the Hall of Justice; that affiant on said 22nd day of July, 1916, did not see the said WARREN K. BILLINGS at or about the scene of the explosion at all. * * That the watch of said affiant still remains at 2:08 as stopped on said 22nd day of July by said explosion or the missiles hitting the body of said affiant.

W. C. KERCHE:

* * I saw a man with a valise climb through the light-well and onto the roof of 721 Market street about one o'clock on the day of the parade. I also saw him go down the same way about half an hour later. He was * * fully five inches taller than BILLINGS. I so told Brennan when I saw Billings at the Richmond jail. Louis Rominger was with me at the time. He also agreed with me that the man he helped to the roof was five inches taller than Billings. That same day I asked Rominger to go with me to warn Estelle Smith to be careful about her identification. He refused and said, "They will be sore at me if I don't identify BILLINGS."

Chronological Sidelights on the Bomb Cases

May, 1916—Thomas J. Mooney, member of Molders' Union and formerly delegate to the San Francisco Labor Council, is quietly working among the street car employees of the United Railroads Company, with a view to organizing them. His services are given free. He is assisted in his efforts by the officers of the Carmen's Union, with the full knowledge and approval of W. D. Mahon, international president of the Amalgamated Association of Street and Electric Railway Employees of America.

June 9th—A circular letter is sent to every employee of the United Railroads, urging them to organize for their own protection and to secure improved working conditions and better wages. The letter, addressed to the "Slaves of the U. R. R.," compares conditions of the unorganized U. R. R. employees with those enjoyed by the employees of the Municipal Railroad, all of whom are union men. Letter is signed "The Carmen's Union."

June 10th, about 10 A. M.—The U. R. R. posts the following notice in all its car barns and workshops:

NOTICE TO EMPLOYEES

"This is to inform you that one T. J. Mooney, a molder by trade, but at present unemployed, who was arrested and confined in the jail at Martinez as a dynamiter, for his activities during the Pacific Gas & Electric Company strike in 1913, is at present endeavoring to enroll some of our employees in the Carmen's Union. It is needless to advise you that the company is thoroughly familiar with his every move, and takes this occasion to notify you that any man found to be affiliated with Mooney, or any union, will be promptly discharged.
(Signed) "UNITED RAILROADS OF SAN FRANCISCO."

June 10th, evening—Mass meeting of street carmen preparatory to calling a strike of the conductors and motormen on the U. R. R. Thomas J. Mooney one of the speakers.

June 13th—Newspapers report dynamiting of the U. R. R. power towers in the San Bruno Mountains. Dynamiting supposed to have occurred on June 10th, but news of it unaccountably withheld three days.

June 25th—U. R. R. advertises in the newspapers a reward of $5,000 for the arrest and conviction of the dynamiters. Circular letter offering similar reward sent broadcast. U. R. R. detectives visit every automobile owner, jitney driver, Municipal carman and men connected with Tom Mooney in the organization of the platform men.

July 14th—Attempt at a street car strike on the U. R. R. lines. Cars blocked on Market street. Police arrest about a dozen persons, among them Mrs. Mooney, on the charge of distributing strike circulars, blocking traffic, disturbing the peace, etc.

July 15th, July 16th, July 17th, July 18th, July 19th, July 20th—Tom Mooney daily in the police court (Hall of Justice) attending the hearings of the arrested. Engages counsel and secures bail. Is pointed out in the Hall of Justice as the man responsible for the attempted street car strike and is constantly under the gaze of police officers. Last case disposed of July 20th.

July 17th—Israel Weinberg, jitney driver, approached by Martin Swanson, Pacific Gas & Electric detective, with an offer of $5,000 reward for information about the San Bruno dynamiting. He is told by Swanson that real evidence is not necessary. "Circumstantial evidence against Mooney would do, as he has been charged with using high explosives." Weinberg tells Swanson that he knows nothing about the matter. Swanson leaves jitney driver in great anger.

July 17th—Swanson approaches Billings and offers him a job at the garage of the Pacific Gas & Electrical Co. Gives him application blank (later found in Billings' room after his arrest).

July 19th—Swanson again offers Weinberg. $5,000 to incriminate Mooney. Weinberg assures the detective that he knows nothing of the dynamiting, and Swanson replies: "You won't talk, eh? We'll make you talk."

July 19th—Swanson makes similar offer to Arthur Silkwood, electrical worker, member of Union No. 151. Silkwood approached three times. When he said he knew nothing of the dynamiting of the San Bruno towers, Swanson threatened that he would have him discharged from the Pacific Gas & Electrical Co., where Silkwood was employed. Silkwood told Swanson that he was trying to make an honest living for his wife and children, and that if Swanson made his family suffer, he—Silkwood —would make him suffer for it.

July 19th—Swanson introduces Billings to John Britton, President of the P. G. & E. Co., and to Mr. Cantrell, general manager of the properties of the P. G. & E. Co. Takes Billings to the garage for a job. Garage manager absent, apparently purposely. Swanson shows Billings a copy of the $5,000 reward circular. Tells Billings that such a bright fellow as he could do a lot with $5,000. Advises him to go to New York and begin life anew. Assures him of the reward and protection if he will give information to connect Tom Mooney with the dynamiting of the towers in the San Bruno Mountains. Billings informs him that he knows nothing about the dynamiting of the towers, and Swanson replies: "You don't have to have real evidence to convict Mooney. All we need is a little circumstantial evidence, as he has twice before been accused of having explosives in his possession. It would be easy to convict Mooney."

July 21st—Mooney shadowed by detectives. Busy preparing report (filing bills, receipts, etc.) for the International President of the Amalgamated Association of Street & Electric Railway Employees of America (W. D. Mahon, President).

July 22nd—Bomb explosion at Steuart and Market streets.

PUZZLE QUESTION:

HOW COULD MOONEY GET TIME TO ORGANIZE A BOMB PLOT?

United Labor of Chicago Pledges Aid

THE Chicago Federation of Labor, at its session on October 1st, passed the following resolutions:

Whereas, I. Weinberg of the Jitney Bus Operators' Union, Tom Mooney of the Molders, Ed. Nolan of the Machinists, Warren K. Billings, past president of the Shoe Workers, and Mrs. Rena Mooney are charged with preparedness parade dynamiting, and

Whereas, Warren K. Billings has already been convicted, though the San Francisco press report of the trial proves his innocence, and

Whereas, The opponents of labor never leave a stone unturned to divide and destroy us one by one, and

Whereas, The San Francisco Building Trades, two central bodies of Alameda County, California, thirty-five San Francisco local unions, and the Painters' District Council No. 14, Chicago, have resolved to extend their full support to these members in their fight for liberty and justice, be it

Resolved, That the Chicago Federation of Labor join in and become part of the bulwark between these members of Organized Labor and the San Francisco Chamber of Commerce.

J. A. JONES,
Local No. 147, Painters and Decorators.

We, your committee on resolutions, recommend the adoption of this resolution.

(Signed): JAMES MAGUIRE,
J. H. BRENNAN,
C. A. PENSE,
Committee.

Concurred in.

Dave Caplan

PENNED up in Los Angeles County Jail for nearly two years, after one undecisive trial, our friend and comrade Dave Caplan is being made a shuttlecock in the scramble for the office of District Attorney. The cost of railroading our Los Angeles comrades comes high, and an agitation started by the Earl papers against the extravagance of the city and county officials led towards making this special M. & M. sport a political issue. District Attorney Woolwine, "holier-than-thou" reformer and the subservient lickspittle of "Giniral" Otis, spent $150,000 on the trials of Caplan and Schmidt. All his friends got in on the good thing and an avalanche of prosperity hit the degenerate curs and plug-uglies of the M. & M. underworld of California. The Los Angeles Defense League had all the data at hand, published items of glaring extravagance in the daily press causing endless discussions in the taxpayers' associations. Otis and his "Man Friday" Tommie Woolwine were immediately put on the defensive and kept busy explaining the reckless and unnecessary expenditures incurred in gouging their victims. Three out of four opponents of Woolwine in the primary pledged themselves to drop the Caplan case, but Tommie kept up the parrot-cry of "Loranorder." His masters spent barrels of money trying to elect him in the primary, but failed by a narrow margin. His opponent in the November election, W. T. Helms, is supported by the Earl papers, which have advocated dropping all cases and indictments arising out of the *Times* explosion. The chances favor Woolwine's re-election.

Caplan's retrial starts on October 16th. He is unafraid, conscious of his innocence and confident of a full vindication IF enough funds are supplied to bring indispensable witnesses to Los Angeles. Dave Caplan, heroic soul and faithful comrade, must not be forgotten. Too many of our comrades are rotting in the state and federal prisons of America—Caplan must not be abandoned to such a fate.

There are many demands on rebel pockets, but some contributions MUST BE SENT to Luke North, of "Everyman," 232 Douglas Building, Los Angeles, so that Dave Caplan, that loyal comrade and soldier of the great social war, shall not be handicapped in this battle for his life.

—J. D.

A Prediction and Observations With Some Facts

By the Ear

(Among criminals, the Pinkerton Detective Agency is known as The Eye. Our special correspondent is to be known as The Ear.—Editor.)

THE NEXT sheriff of St. Louis County, Minnesota, will be R. D. McKercher, at present Duluth's chief of police. The reason for the change will be because of Sheriff John R. Meining's fear of the striking iron miners on the Mesaba Range. He did as much for the Steel Trust as his cowardice would let him, and then threats of gun-play frightened him. McKercher, on the other hand, is a man owned by the Duluth *News-Tribune*, a Steel Trust organ, and is not a coward.

There is a temporary truce now in the war against labor waged by the iron mining companies on the Mesaba Range, where three-fifths of the iron mined in the United States comes from. The miners work on a piece-rate basis and they want a standard wage of three dollars a day. Reasonable, isn't it? They also want an eight-hour day. That is also reasonable, isn't it? Yet the Steel Trust, through the Oliver Iron Mining Company, has said no. They say, "We will give you night schools with the curriculum that we shall supervise. We shall take you poor ignorant foreigners and teach you how to be good American citizens and support the preparedness movement. But we will not give you three dollars a day and we will not give you an eight-hour day. And we will rid you of the curse of the I. W. W., from which you are now suffering." Of course they don't actually say that in so many words, but that is their attitude. In fact, the Oliver Mining Company has in its files a complete plan for the "night school Americanization of its foreign employees."

The principal "Range town," as they call it in Minnesota, is Hibbing. There is a labor mayor there—Victor L. Power. He played square with the I. W. W. and with the striking miners.

On Sunday, September 10th, the *News-Tribune* published a front page article purporting to be extracts from the report of the Minnesota *State Examiner*, showing that Power, while mayor of Hibbing, had grafted and "used public moneys for purposes other than Hibbing's," that he had built miles of macadamized roadways which were unnecessary, and divers other things.

Peculiar coincidence, isn't it, that of all the papers in the State of Minnesota, the Duluth *News-Tribune*, admittedly a Steel Trust organ which is universally hated, should publish an article which tended to incriminate the mayor of a mining town who had been friendly to labor?

Carlo Tresca, Joe Schmidt, Sam Scarlett, four strikers and a woman, are now being held in Duluth for the alleged murder of James Myron, a deputy sheriff, who tried to help the Steel Trust with too much zeal. A legal battle is now being waged by Attorney John A. Keyes for the accused. He tried to have the Virginia Grand Jury indictments quashed, but was unsuccessful. The trials are scheduled to begin the first week in December, in Duluth. That city, benefiting as it does by the shipment of ore from the Mesaba Range to the steel plant, is almost solidly pro-capital.

That's the Minnesota situation at present. What will develop in the future, no one knows except Steel Trust officials and the owner of the *News-Tribune*. They might fasten the graft charge on Mayor Victor L. Power of Hibbing. They might convict Tresca and the others, innocent though they are. But there are plenty of Ears to hear of it and plenty of Voices to tell of it, and if all work in unison, none of these things may happen. In the meantime the miners have gone back to work, but it looks as if the State of Minnesota may prove a second Colorado in the near future.

The Need of The Hour

SOME of our radical exchanges suggest that a national General Strike be called, if necessary, to free Carlo Tresca, Joe Schmidt, Sam Scarlett, and the five Mesaba Range strikers now in jail at Duluth, Minnesota, charged with responsibility for the murders committed by the plug-uglies of the Steel Trust. Government in this country, so far as the workers are concerned, has developed into a new system: the rule of thugs decorated with the badge of a deputy sheriff. Well fed, fully armed and totally irresponsible, they carry on a reign of terror, supported by the police and militia. If an occasional worker resist this Cossack régime, the leaders of the strikers are arrested, charged with inciting riot and murder, and are held responsible as principals.

This is the ordinary procedure, not only in Minnesota, but in Wheatland, Ludlow, Lawrence, Paterson—in fact, in every strike region. It is certainly about time for labor to take measures to put a stop to such an outrageous state of affairs. I have no doubt that a General Strike would accomplish the desired result. It would also open the doors of every jail holding prisoners of the labor war.

But the question is, How? How induce conservative trade unions to join such a movement? The attempt in New York has failed. The General Strike proved a fizzle—and that by no means because of reactionary leadership. On the contrary, it was the rank and file that refused to listen to the call of the General Strike. Workers bred in the atmosphere of narrow craft unionism and trained in the "sanctity of contract," cannot be expected suddenly to develop the spirit of solidarity and class consciousness which is the necessary foundation of a General Strike. Much, much work will have to be done before we can hope to reach that stage in the American labor movement. **Solidarity must be our slogan and the keynote of all our labor activities.**

The Truth Forbidden

THE police authorities of San Francisco can hardly be blamed for stifling every free expression of opinion: they can't afford to have the truth told. Least of all in the Billings case. They have therefore muzzled free speech. Any one daring to assert his right to an opinion and to express it, is dealt with summarily. Thus nine of our Italian comrades, members of the I. W. W. and of the Anarchist Group Volonta, were arrested, one after another, when they attempted to discuss in public the Billings verdict. They demanded a jury trial and were quickly railroaded to prison and sentenced to terms varying from ten days to three months. A protest meeting in a hall and another in behalf of the bomb prisoners, were also suppressed by the police.

The press has totally ignored this crime against the most elemental rights of man. And yet the condemned are, in a fundamental sense, martyrs of liberty. Their names are worth remembering: M. Bombino, M. Centrone, G. Chiara, G. Cirio, L. Di Bari, A. Botti, L. Parenti, G. Tori and G. Scali.

Another young Italian, M. Civello, was sentenced to pay $100 fine, or serve 100 days, for exposing in the window of his business place the picture of a nun in the arms of a priest. Police Judge J. Sullivan thought, in his purity, that the picture was "obscene." He was too drunk to grasp the lawyer's explanation that the picture was an illustration of the attitude of France when that country legislated against the Catholic Church. The popular French *bon mot* of the day, "Go, priest, and take your nun with you," was aptly featured in the picture that fell under the ban of the stupid Police Judge.

Much Ado About Nothing

B. C. Federationist

A CAPITALIST court, the supreme court of Massachusetts, it seems recently rendered a decision to the effect that, "the right to work is property * * * It is as much property as the more obvious forms of goods and merchandise, stocks and bonds." This remarkable pronouncement has caused a most absurd and violent flutter of excitement throughout that dovecote of simplicity known as the Labor world. Laborious efforts are put forth from various quarters to point out to an anxious world the utter absurdity of such a decision, and these efforts are launched with just as much earnestness and zeal as could possibly be the case if it made an iota of difference to the working class whether such decision was, or was not, correct. Among the numerous yappers against the iniquity of this terrible court decision we notice a certain capitalist senator, one Robert M. LaFollette of Wisconsin. This worthy yaps something as follows: "Thus the highest court of one of the thirteen original states holds that labor is property. * * * The right to work is the right to live. * * * Labor cannot be property. The only way to possess labor is to possess men. That means slavery." So much for that republican yapper.

If the so-called Labor world has one pre-eminently distinguishing characteristic, it is that of always sitting up and yapping in unison with any yapper who attunes his yapping so as to pleasingly titillate the heartstrings of Labor, provided the aforesaid yapper belongs to the class that is made up of the political and economic enemies of labor. If one of their own class yaps, the workers will take no notice, but let some capitalist pirate, politician, professor, preacher, press-writer or other paid hireling of the ruling class, yap a few high-sounding phrases of pretended sympathy with the aspirations of labor, and every simp in the labor camp will fall at his feet in worship and lugubriously howl in approbation of his apparent heartbeats of sympathy with the masses. Anything that comes from the spokesman of the ruling class is taken by the Labor world as the law and the gospel, provided it be dished up in windy phrase suitably tinctured with sob stuff and sweet-scented sympathy for "the toiling masses."

It does not matter in the least what any capitalist court may decide in regard to the property status of the worker, the fact stares all who care to see, in the face, that the working class is all there is or ever was to property, in the sense that property is something that can and does bring to its owner an income or revenue, because of his property. There is nothing on top of this earth that can, or does, bring to the owner a revenue outside of his own labor, except the labor of others. No man or class can command the labor of others so as to appropriate the revenue resulting from the expenditure of their labor, unless he or they absolutely own them, body, soul and breeches. That ought to be plain enough for any one to understand, even a thick-headed labor leader who is given to parroting the sympathetic

THE BLAST   **Seven**

mouthings of capitalist tinhorn politicians and thimble-riggers. Of course, "labor cannot be property unless men are property," and it is true that, "that means slavery." That is exactly what exists under the capitalist regime. The working class is the property of the capitalists. That is the property from which they draw their billion of profit. Where is the fatheaded fool that is simple enough to fancy they get it from any other source? Wherever he may be found, let him be assured that the portals of the home for the feeble-minded are yawning for him. And yet the Labor press is loaded with the senseless mouthings of the LaFollettes and other windbags, over these court decisions and such ruling class rubbish, instead of carrying some message of real meaning and value to the enslaved millions that constitute the rank and file of the Labor army. A little more exercise of common sense and less ado about nothing, might help a little towards raising the Labor movement above the level of that dull mediocrity that blindly accepts the dangerous lip service of capitalist politicians and time-servers as its guide and its hope. If Labor is to be worthy of emblazoning upon its banner, "Labor Omnia Vincit," the workers must first conquer their own ignorance of their class and its position in present day society, and then go forth like men and conquer their freedom from the stigma of slavery and property.

What Do Wilson and Hughes Crowds Mean When They Talk About Liberty?

HORACE TRAUBEL

I don't know. Do you?

Everybody uses all the nice catch words. They're handy. They serve the immediate purpose of ignorance or hypocrisy.

Everybody says we must be honest. But very few people tell us how to be honest.

When you say you believe in liberty I want to know what you mean by liberty.

When you say you believe in justice I want to know what you call justice.

Some of the ugliest characters use the most beautiful phrases. And some of the most beautiful characters use the ugliest phrases.

Wilson is constantly saying he believes in liberty and honesty. But how can a man who upholds the capitalist system believe in either? For capitalism is the negation of both.

They believe in liberty by believing in everything that exists. And they believe in liberty by denying everything that's prophesied.

If you want to know what Wilson means by liberty ask him what he means by economic justice. Hughes and Wilson get all the established institutions under their feet and say: Upon this rock we stand.

It's as if a man put out the sun and said: I believe in light.

It's as if you shut your eyes and said you believe in seeing. As if you closed your ears and said: I believe in hearing. It's as if you tied your two legs together and said you believed in walking.

You gag a man and say you believe in human speech. You say you believe everybody has a right to an equal life. And then you make it impossible for them to get a living. You say every road should be wide open to everybody. Yet you choke every road with obstructions.

That's the liberty you talk about. For that's the only sort of liberty you leave to us.

After you've got all the liberty you want there's very little liberty left for anybody else.

Every man believes in liberty for himself. But few men believe in liberty for all.

You believe in the liberty of one to grab. I believe in the liberty of all to serve.

When a man who believes in profit says he believes in liberty it seems like a man who starves you to death saying he believes in food.

Wilson talks very vehemently about the liberty of Americans in other countries, but is very mild when he talks about the liberty of Americans in the United States. He says nothing about the liberty of negroes in Texas. He says nothing about the liberty of white women and children in Colorado. He says nothing about the liberty of the shirtwaist workers in New York. He gives us a heap big dissertation on liberty in general. But when it comes to liberty in particular he shuts up.

Wilson has a neat little expedient. He gets rid of questions that he's not ready for by calling them state, not national, questions. When he was governor of New Jersey he used to get rid of the annoying problems by calling them national, not state, questions.

What I want these men to do is to come down off their high horses and tell us just what they mean. We know what they say. But it's an unsolvable puzzle to know what they mean.

Liberty is that thing which helps you to live. You have much liberty if you live more. You have little liberty if you live less. A man might have all the liberty there is. But if he hasn't a living his liberty is a mockery.

What I want to know from our scribblers and chatterers is what they mean by liberty, justice, Americanism and fraternity. They roll these words off their tongues unctuously as if they didn't need to be explained.

The average American fools himself and is fooled by these oily phrases of our political masters.

We wrestle with the curse of words. We are tangled in the damnation of phrases. The orators cry: "God knows we're lovers of liberty." God may know. But I know I don't know.

You love to toy with the syllables of promise. You dangle them temptingly before our deceived vision. But in the perdition of your deeds you violate the paradise of your speech.

※ ※ ※

DEFENSE FUND SAN FRANCISCO LABOR PRISONERS
Per Alexander Berkman and Emma Goldman

Total collected to September 15th		$1,360.65
John Beverley Robinson, Douglas, Mich.	$ 10.00	
A. V. Stevens, San Francisco	1.00	
I. Blair, New York City	1.00	
Van K. Allison, Boston, Mass.	5.00	
Anarchist Red Cross, per A. Winocur, Dorcester, Mass.	2.50	
Francis Donnelly, Catesby, Okla.	2.00	
Albert and Edith Matheo, New York	3.00	
I. Bertason, Seattle	2.00	
Anarchist Group, Cleveland, Ohio, per Jack Myers	9.80	
K. Zomer, Denver, Colo.	5.00	
I. Cline, Salt Lake City	2.50	
Emma Goldman, collection at Denver lectures	22.00	
F. Rascher, St. Louis, Mo.	.50	
Ben L. Reitman, collection at street meeting, Chicago	4.00	
A Friend, per Emma Goldman	5.00	
Union of Russian Workers, Pittsburg	8.60	
Mrs. J. E. Baker, Portland, Oregon	1.00	
Louis Peck, New York City	1.00	
Joe Soyez, Los Angeles, Cal.	1.00	
Ernest Schleifer, Business Agent International Ass'n Machinists, No. 60, Detroit, Mich.	5.00	
W. S. Van Valkenburgh, Scotia, N. Y., subscription list No. 235, per Emma Goldman	4.50	
Samuel Hartman, New York, subscription list No. 148	4.75	
		101.15
		$1,461.80
Previously turned over to the Defense by Alexander Berkman		$1,360.65
To prisoners	$ 34.00	
Per Robert Minor, Treasurer	67.15	
		101.15

Oct. 15—Total amount turned over to the Defense....$1,461.80

Eight   THE BLAST

TO OUR FRIENDS AND COMRADES,

By whose generous co-operation we are enabled to keep up The Blast in spite of the greatest difficulties, we want to express our deepest appreciation. The defense of the accused labor men in San Francisco, and other work, is keeping us so busy that we cannot spare the time necessary for correspondence. We hope that our friends will bear with us.

The various organizations that have sent us letters and resolutions of sympathy have given us great encouragement in our work. We regret that space in The Blast at present precludes the publication of those resolutions.

THE BLASTERS.

BLAST WAR FUND

Nel M. Moyer, Garwin, Iowa, $1; Albert Steinhauser, Minneapolis, $2; G. A. Burri, Cleveland, $5; Carl Gleaser, Kansas City, $1; Charles Weil, Seattle, $1; Joseph D'Angelo, Delaware, $1; Carl Larson, Utah, $2; R. R. Sharma, $3; John Baff, Cleveland, $1.50; Van Cleave, $5; Russian Group, Cleveland, $8.30; Elizabeth Breese, Oregon, $2; A Friend, $50; Charles Wright, Chicago, 25 cents; Arthur Gow, Montana, $1; Robert Ladig, $1; Wade Stewart, $1; G. E. Nukel, $1; Manuel Pereira, $2; Clement Anastanoff, Portland, per subscription list, $15; A. Marietta, Sacramento, $10; Morris Becker, New York, per subscription list, $10.70; Laduska, Alhambra, $1; E. Levin, $6; H. J. Van Huzen, $1; Miss A. Kisluik, New York, $4; Nick Picirillo, Ohio, $1; Rose Stern, New York, $2; Petr Armanini, Ringo, Kansas, $10; Paul Kutchan, West Virginia, $5; Charles Campanaggi, New York, $2; M. Maselli, $1; Benjamin Axelrod, $2; Mary Giordanengo, $1; Hans Tall, subscription list, $8; E. B. Partain, Illinois, $1; Del Veccy, $1; L. E. Hall, $1; Josephine Lack, $1; Henry Wiedel, $1; P. Kuprin, Detroit, $5; Union of Russian Workers, Pittsburg, $12.80; E. Petersen, Kansas City, subscription list, $6.25; Workmen's Circle, Kansas City, $1; T. H. Houghton, $1; Joe Russo, Sacramento, $1; S. Amper, Chicago, 50 cents; J. Wridnan, Chicago, $1; J. L., San Francisco, $2; J. Iorio, $2; L. Caesar, Oakland, $1; Agnes Inglis, Ann Arbor, $1; Basara, $4; Russian Workers, Philadelphia, collection, $15.75; A Friend, Denver, $1; Joseph Rothberg, Albany, subscription list, $8; Van Valkenburg, $1; Tom Bell, Arizona, $5; H. Armand, Arizona, collection, $16; A, Friend, $1; James Hallbeck, $5; Union Russian Workers, per Jack Myers, $4.35; Sam Jetcoff, Detroit, $1; John Grigsby, Louisville, Ky., $1; Dorothy Alden, $10; A Friend, $1; Anarchist Red Cross, Boston, $1; K. Zomer, $5; collected by Rhoda Smith, Cleveland, $5.25; F. Belmas, Detroit, $5; Joe Bertino, subscription list, $5; A Friend, $1; contributions per David Shuffer, Lynn, Mass., $21; Mrs. E. Bond, Oregon, $1; Esta Milstein collection, New York, $3.70; Frances Donneley, $1; Edith and Albert Matheo, New York, $2; M. E., $1; Daniel Kiefer, Cincinnati, $5; I. Bertoni, Seattle, $1; Paul Herzog, New York, $10; D. J. Zimmerman, subscription list, $3.10; Roger Baldwin, St. Louis, $1; Alex Nelson, St. Louis, $2; W. H. Johnson, Kansas City, $5; S. Matta, Utah, 50 cents; J. M. Garrick, Los Angeles, 50 cents; subscription list, per Minna Lowensohn, New York, $30.40; Dora Pines, Brooklyn, N. Y., subscription list, $15.55; James L. Wright, $5; Henry Maroni, $2; Egisti Bertozzi, $1; Karl Herlitz, $1; Pauline Sperry, Maine, $1; subscription list, per Esther Lieb, Philadelphia, $14; Workmen's Circle, Toronto, Canada, per D. Levy, 50 cents; subscription list, per Sam Castagna, Chicago, $13.85; Workmen's Circle, New York, per A. Shipman, $3; contributions, per Cronaca Sovversiva, $28.50; John Chukan, Kenosha, $1; Hester Gibson, $8; Morris Becker, New York, $1; John Buchie, subscription list, $2.50; subscription list, per Benjamin Axelrod, Massachusetts, $11; Arbeiter Ring, No. 266, per I. Epstein, St. Paul, 50 cents; subscription list per Nick Picirillo, Steubenville, Ohio, $6.25; subscription list, per Benjamin Gordon, Detroit, Michigan, $11.35; subscription list, per Tony Williams, Buffalo, $3.75; Russian Labor Group, Brockton, Mass., per M. Antonovich, $2.50; W. Shepps, Dover, N. J., $2; Union of Russian Workers, Pittsburg, Pa., $5.25; S. Solomon, N. Y., $1; A. Westrup, $1; Wichita, Kansas, per J. Kabeinell, $2.50; Joe Soyez, Los Angeles, $1; S. Kirsh, 60 cents; John M. Paige, Maine, $1; Mrs. J. E. Baker, Portland, $1; Fritz Holm, Seattle, Wash., $1; Peter Prestianini, New York, $1; Sam Cohen, Seattle, $10; Charles Tambrello, Cardiff, per subscription list, $13.25.

IT GIVES me a good deal of pleasure to publish the note below from my friend Joe Ettor. I am glad that he was not guilty of the foolish "criticism" of Anarchism and Anarchists in a recent issue of *Solidarity*.

Virginia, Minn., Sept. 15, 1916.
Fellow Worker:
I notice in THE BLAST of September 1st an editorial in which you credit me with an article in *Solidarity* commenting on your paper.
You are among many that make the mistake to believe that "J. E." means Joe Ettor. That is a mistake. I never write under my initials. I always use my full name and the "J. E." of *Solidarity* is some one else.
Hoping that you will make this correction, with well wishes and salutations, I am,

Sincerely yours,
JOS. J. ETTOR.

Social and Dance

Given by

Radical Branch No. 511, W. C.

at

Fillmore St. Averill Hall,

1861 Fillmore St.

For the Benefit of

INTERNATIONAL WORKERS' DEFENSE LEAGUE

Sunday Eve., Oct. 22, 1916

Union Music   Admission 25c

You Should Read These Booklets Full of Information and a Real Inspiration

---

Gov. John P. Altgeld's

REASONS FOR PARDONING THE ANARCHISTS

And His Masterly Review of the Haymarket Riot

Lucy E. Parsons, Publisher, Chicago

30c Postpaid

Also

The Famous Speeches of the Chicago Anarchists

35c Postpaid

To Be Had Through THE BLAST

Vol. I   SAN FRANCISCO, NOVEMBER 1, 1916.   No. 21

THE NATIONAL DILEMMA: Whiskers or No Whiskers

1907——"Law and Order" in San Francisco——1916

THERE is probably no record of any important criminal case where a verdict of guilty was returned on the evidence of such a degenerate melee of underworld scum as in the Billings case, first of the bomb cases to be tried. It can only be explained by the damning fact that the same grasping, degenerate influences control the District Attorney's office in San Francisco today as in 1907 in the famous "Graft Trials."

"Behind the expert lawyers of the trolley magnates," wrote the S. F. *Call* of September 26, 1907, referring to the trial of Tirey L. Ford, street railway chief counsel, "troops a motley train of gun-fighters, professional plug-uglies, decoys, disreputable 'detectives,' thugs, women of the half-world, and the wolfish pack of gutter journalism. It must be indeed a hard case that needs such bolstering."

Writing of one of these trials (Calhoun's), Franklin Hichborn says in his book, "The System," page 434: "There followed one of the most extraordinary scenes ever recorded of a court of justice. The defendant's attorneys, the District Attorney, and even the prisoner at the bar openly and contemptuously defied the judge (Judge Wm. P. Lawlor) on the bench."

The District Attorney referred to is Charles M. Fickert, the same Fickert who in 1916 outrages justice by endeavoring to hang five labor people because the unionism of San Francisco still successfully resists the onslaughts of the Chamber of Commerce. Those who cowered before the outraged citizenry of 1907 have now usurped the courts, and through professional jurors and police-controlled witnesses, they hope to strangle Billings and his co-defendants. The attempted assassination, in 1907, of Francis Heney and the dynamiting of Supervisor Gallagher's home in Oakland (a witness against the United Railroads), are duplicated by the killing of the pickets, Tom Olson and Lewis Morey today, the convenient bomb explosion to discredit unionism and the penning up for slaughter of five innocent labor people.

The eloquent description by the *Call* of the Calhoun-Ford-Mullally following of 1907, quoted above, applies precisely to the personnel of the witnesses and the hidden wire-pullers of the cases now on trial here. The sewers of the underworld were grappled for human ghouls, without a vestige of honor or shame, all under the thumb-screws of the police, to swear "to order" so that four working men and one woman could be crucified on the Chamber of Commerce cross of greed.

Let us examine the prosecution forces—one by one:

1. **District Attorney Charles M. Fickert.** Lickspittle of the Calhoun-Mullally United Railroad gang, whom he refused to prosecute on his assumption of office in 1907, and who now demands Tom Mooney's life because he tried to organize the employees of this same United Railroads.

2. **Martin Swanson,** chief detective of the Pacific Gas & Electric Co., and other public utilities, including the United Railroads, who, prior to the explosion was offering a $5,000 bribe to anyone who would help to "job" Mooney. Both Billings and Weinberg were made—and refused—his offer.

3. **Estelle Smith,** "star witness," charged with the murder of Irene Smith in Los Angeles on April 2, 1913. Frequently arrested in "red-light" raids in the same city. James L. Murphy, her uncle, in San Quentin Penitentiary for murder. D. J. Kidwell, her stepfather, in Folsom Penitentiary for forgery.

Affidavit of Miss Suzanne Dean, social worker of Fullerton, Orange County, California, states:

"I know Mrs. Estelle Smith and frequently saw, read to and conversed with her (then Estelle Moore) in Los Angeles County Jail during the summer of 1913. She was then charged with complicity in the murder of Irene Smith at 1066 North Hill Street, Los Angeles, on or about April 2, 1913. Prior to this date Estelle Smith was reputed to have lived with a man named Bohanon. I have information and believe that Bohanon became infatuated with Irene Smith; that in a quarrel engendered by this fact Irene Smith was killed; and that there were present at the killing Estelle Smith, Bohanon, James L. Murphy, uncle of Estelle Smith, and the victim. Murphy was convicted of the murder and is now serving twelve years at San Quentin. After being released Estelle Smith lived in the underworld of the city of Los Angeles, and was frequently arraigned in the police courts of said city on charges of prostitution. During my acquaintance with Estelle Smith I became well informed of her general reputation in the jail and city of Los Angeles. Said reputation for truth and veracity was very bad, and she was generally reputed to be utterly depraved and beyond the reach of any good influence."

4. **Chief of Police David White.** Former employee of the Pacific Gas & Electric Co.

5 and 6. **Lieut. Duncan Matheson and Sergt. Charles Goff.** Heads of Police Traffic Squad, controlled by the United Railroads in their fight against the Jitney Bus Union, of which Israel Weinberg, one of the defendants, is a prominent member.

7. **Detective Steve Bunner,** "star witness" in frame-up of Dowdall in 1906. Dowdall was sentenced to fifty years' imprisonment as the result of a police plot. His innocence was established after long years of imprisonment, which broke down his health.

8. **John McDonald,** drug user. Operated on three times on account of his addiction to drugs. Graduated from a five-cent waterfront coffee house to a $3 a day police jackal. Related that Chief of Police White told him, "Stick to your story, Mac, and you'll go back to Baltimore on the cushions with plenty of change in your pockets." Said he saw Billings place the bomb "as in a dream."

9. **John Crowley.** Sneak thief and frequenter of Barbary Coast saloons where soldiers pick up other male perverts for unspeakable orgies. On probation for watch-stealing when District Attorney Fickert used him in the Billings case.

10. **Mrs. Kidwell,** mother of Estelle Smith. Billed as star witness, too, but withdrawn when the defense published a letter written by her, showing a deal with the District Attorney whereby her forger husband was to be paroled in exchange for her testimony.

11. **Earl R. Moore.** Traffic policeman and former United Railroads strikebreaker.

12. **Rominger.** Ex-private detective of Spokane.—Shades of Wm. Burns!

Such are the pillars of "law and order" in San Francisco today. Would you convict a dog on the testimony of such people?

Yet they hold the lives of five unionists in the hollows of their hands. Are they to be hurled into eternity on the gibberings and perjuries of loathsome degenerates of the Smith and Crowley type? Do your part in frustrating this contemplated series of legal murders by holding meetings, distributing and displaying literature and sending funds—at once—to Robert Minor, Treasurer, 210 Russ Building, San Francisco.

Press Committee,

INTERNATIONAL WORKERS' DEFENSE LEAGUE,

San Francisco.

In Bayonne

Mary Heaton Vorse

CHIEF of Police M. F. Rielly of Bayonne will tell you that Bayonne is quiet, and Director of Public Safety Wilson will say that the situation is well in hand. While I was listening to these reassuring statements, the groups of people on the street corners grew larger; there was a little apprehensive flutter in the crowd. Every face was turned in one direction. Two motorcycle officers appeared. Around the corner came Captain Edward Griffen in a pale gray suit, with a checked hat. He held a rifle tenderly in his arms. After him followed four detectives, also with rifles. Behind them marched thirty-six deputies, dressed in their new uniforms and swinging their new, pale-yellow riot clubs. After them, more armed and ununiformed detectives. Then came the patrol wagon, and in it were huddled three haggard, boyish-looking prisoners. After them were fifty deputized firemen.

The miserable little prisoners were being brought to judgment for carrying concealed weapons. After the firemen again came more detectives. One of them, Robert Russell, pointed his gun suggestively at the crowd and cried:

"Get along there! Get along down the street!"

He ran up to the dark little huddled group at the corner and pointed the gun at them, at which the women shrank back, frightened. The procession swung along, and one began to realize why it was that quiet was regained in Bayonne.

Meantime the crowd at the street corner had been lined up in two rows by two officers, who searched them rapidly for concealed weapons.

"Sometimes," the commissioner of public safety explained, "they follow their friends up, and we don't want any more trouble."

So, after three days of warfare, Bayonne is quiet, but it is an unnatural quiet. For fear and suspense are in the air. Every one is afraid of every one else. The people outside of the strike district are terribly afraid of the strikers—how afraid is measured by the exclamation of a young woman of whom we asked the way to the strike district.

"Oh!" she cried. "You mustn't go down there—you'll surely get shot."

Even the reporters, when you ask where the strike headquarters are, exclaim:

"Keep as far away from there as you can. You'll get all the news you want at Police Headquarters, where you'll be sent."

So after a short time in Bayonne, you realize the feeling of disquiet has deepened, and you realize that you are in a terrorized city, and that fear is in the very air that you breathe.

After the accounts of riot and bloodshed, after the warnings one has received concerning the violent character of the strikers, it was very strange to go through the silent, desolate streets. Life, temporarily, seems to have stopped. There seems to be some strange and mournful holiday—the saloons are closed, on each corner stands a dark group of strikers talking to one another in low tones. All up the street are more little groups of strikers. On the side streets women and children mingle with the men. On Broadway and the avenues E and F, the storm centres of the strike district, there are few women to be seen. And everywhere, wherever you go, you find the same atmosphere of fear and suspense.

The people are ready to scurry to their houses when the deputized police and the detectives with shotguns and rifles march imposingly past. They run to their houses and there they hide. For men and women have been shot while standing in their windows. Any one standing in a window is suspected of being a sniper, so the police shoot first, to keep from being shot themselves. But you can't be long in Bayonne or talk much with the men and women on the streets without feeling that the police have been very clever about shooting first. This deputized force of police includes not only the fire companies, but the city officials; inspectors of all kinds have been put into uniforms and have been called upon to perform the perilous duty of policing a town filled with 10,000 unorganized strikers.

It is no wonder that they, too, are afraid and that they turn uneasy faces toward the side streets as they pass them, fearing stray shots from back alleys or housetops. Up to this time, however, only about fifteen persons have been arrested for carrying concealed weapons, although all last night the town was patrolled and every passer-by searched and scores of homes have been invaded in the hunt for concealed weapons.

So, though the streets are quiet, every one is on the defensive; every one seems to be waiting apprehensively for something to happen. The strike district from the Hook to Avenue C is full of these groups of anxious people. Something strange is in the air. Calamity seems to threaten. The quiet is not the quiet of Sunday, but rather of a witch's Sabbath.

In three days the strike has seen a bloody harvest; there have been three deaths and a hospital full of wounded. Several are said to be dying; the number of minor wounds is not known, but after each conflict with the police many men have been seen limping away.

Severe beatings of the strikers are usual. There have been besides thirty or forty arrests, the wrecking of saloons—now by the police for the alleged breaking of the ordinance against selling drink, and now by the strikers.

Last night Mydosh's Hall, where the strikers were holding a meeting, was raided. Many arrests followed, seven men were said to have been wounded, and the hall was closed. The right of free speech and of assembly have been temporarily denied to the strikers. These extreme measures were considered necessary by the authorities for the preserving of order. The strikers' point of view is different.

The mournful little groups of huddled people seem glad to talk to you, especially the women, and their talk is about one thing—and that is shooting. In broken English one old Polish woman explained to us:

"Why should they at the windows shoot? You must go and hide when you go to your house. You must not go near your window—no! The men will shoot—and maybe you die, like that Sophie Torach down the street. That Sophie Torach, she should get married this Saturday, but she stands at the window and the police walk by, and a bullet comes through her head—and she is dead!"

Wherever you go, in whatever group you find yourself, the story is repeated with a ghastly and unvarying monotony. One story is of a woman with a child in her arms who has been hit; in another street an old man has been hit; in another place yet, they'll tell how a neighbor dodged just in time to escape being struck, and they will point to a hole in the window. One sees many suggestive bullet holes as one walks up and down the strike district.

* * * *

This strike came suddenly, but it is said that discontent has been growing for a long time and that the company has for a long time been expecting trouble. The strikers are asking for an increase of 30 per cent. for those who make under $2 and of 10 per cent. for those who make $3. They contend that they can't live as well now on what they make as they could a few years ago when wages were less. Other industries in Bayonne have shorter hours and pay higher wages. And the wives of these better paid workers have made the women of the Standard Oil employees discontented.

"We should like to dress our children just as well as those others do," they tell you.

The personality of George W. Hennessy, superintendent of the Standard Oil, is said to have helped to create the general atmosphere of discontent by his methods. Since the walkout he is said to have refused to listen to any of the representatives of the strikers. And, finally, the recent publication of the Standard Oil Company's profits for the year brought the crisis, and the men, unorganized and without leaders, struck.

As to why the conflict has been so bitter, there have been many contributory factors. It is asserted that the strikers have been blamed for the actions of toughs and gangsters. In fact, all of the disorderly element has seized upon this time as an excuse to make trouble; and the strikers have been naturally blamed for everything that has occurred, and have suffered accordingly.

The strikers, while they are silent and subdued, are both resolute and bitter—bitter toward the police for what they consider unjustifiable severity. They repeat over and over again:

"They had no right to shoot at our windows; they had no right to shoot at crowds where there were women."

They are bitter against the company that will not give them a fair hearing; and it is the opinion of the strikers' attorney, J. H. Dougherty, that had the strikers' representatives been received by Mr. Hennessy the trouble might have been averted. They are also bitter against the press, which they feel has not tried to find out their side, which has magnified their violence and overlooked the violence of the police. They have offered to co-operate with the director of public safety in keeping order and to patrol their own streets. And this offer has been refused, and at present they cannot congregate to discuss their affairs. Early next week Mr. Dougherty is going to New York with the strike representatives to present their demands at John D. Rockefeller's main office. He looks forward hopefully to settling the difficulties in this way.

The Everlasting District Attorney
R. M.

WHILE District Attorney Fickert was in Los Angeles to do some repairing to his frame-up in the case of Tom Mooney, he gave in an interview the following:

"In San Francisco we are up against a shrewd, clever gang of radicals, and they are taxing the ingenuity and resources of all our legal authorities to cope with them. Some of the best brains in the country are arraigned on the side of crime and violence and it behooves law-abiding people to exercise the most stringent methods to cope with them."

Don't you know, Mr. Fickert, that the best brains and hearts of all lands have ever been arraigned on the side of social change? And that the "district attorneys" of all ages have ever crushed and maimed and killed the best of the race? Don't you know that Torquemada in cruel medieval Spain—but you probably don't know anything about that, "not being an educated man," as your assistant, Mr. Brennan, might say—. But to get down to something that you *have* heard of, don't you know that Jesus was murdered by a "district attorney" of his day in a court of law—and that he was perfectly "legally" executed?

Don't you know that your counterpart—stupid, brutish and corrupt in alliance with property interests—has ALWAYS expressed the lowest in the race, against which all the hopes and the dreams and the brightness of the world have had to struggle?

Yes, the best brains of the whole world are arraigned on the side of what district attorneys consider "crime and violence." They cannot help being. The mind of every great figure in the world's history has led him on to a dream that in the end clashed with your kind, Fickert, and made him a "convict." Socrates, Michelangelo, Giordano Bruno, Jesus, Emerson, Thoreau, John Brown, Martin Luther and Christopher Columbus—all were *convicts*, Fickert, at the hands of your kind.

And George Washington and Thomas Jefferson were "wanted by the district attorney" of their day in this America, and it was because they escaped the clutches of "the law" that that flag exists which you now wave before your juries—asking them to murder an innocent boy.

Is Wilson Different?
A. B.

THE political situation just now presents a rather peculiar phenomenon. Organized labor is mostly for Wilson—Sammie Gompers is stumping for him—and even some Socialists have publicly endorsed Woodrow.

It is peculiar, in view of the very pertinent fact that Wilson is totally inimical to every basic principle of union labor. He is not only opposed to the closed shop, but to the eight-hour idea as well. At least he was, before he made his début into politics, and there is nothing to show that he has experienced a change of heart in the White House. As President of Princeton University, Wilson said in the course of a baccalaureate address:

"You know what the usual standard of the employee is in our day. It is to give as little as he may for his wages. Labor is standardized by the trades union, and this is the standard to which it is made to conform. In some trades and handicrafts no one is suffered to do more than the least skillful of his fellows can do within the hours allowed to a day's labor, and no one can work out of hours at all or volunteer anything beyond the minimum.

"I need not point out how economically disastrous such a regulation of labor is. It is so unprofitable to the employer that in some trades it will presently not be worth his while to attempt anything at all. He had better stop altogether than to operate at an inevitable and invariable loss. The labor of America is rapidly becoming unprofitable under its present regulation by those who have determined to reduce it to a minimum. Our economic supremacy may be lost because the country grows more and more full of unprofitable servants."

Thus Wilson, as college president, "dissertationed" on the open shop. He looked on the producers of the country's wealth as servants, and his only thought was how to make them more profitable to the employer. The tendency of unionism to standardize labor and thus protect the weakest member (theoretically, at least) Wilson considered disastrous (to whom, I wonder).

There is no record that Wilson has changed his attitude in this matter. Of course, it is one of the prerogatives of politicians to tailor their "deepest convictions" according to the exigencies of politics. But there is no reason to assume that the change from Princeton to Washington involved a change in Wilson's attitude toward organized labor, except as election needs might prompt. Why, then, is union labor in favor of Wilson? Is it merely a choice of the lesser evil, as between Hughes and Wilson? If so, let us say so frankly.

"But the eight-hour law!" some one exclaims. "Does it not prove Wilson's change of attitude?"

Decidedly not. In the first place, it does not give anybody an eight-hour day who has been working more than eight hours. Any railroad trainman will tell you that. The so-called eight-hour law is not an eight-hour law at all. It is a wage increase measure: it gives ten hours' pay for eight hours' work, and over-time pay at the same rate for the hours in excess of eight. Incidentally, this 25 per cent wage increase applies only to the highest paid railroad employees. The lesser paid employees, who need an increase more, are not benefited by this law. Moreover, it is very questionable whether this much-made-of labor legislation will remain on the statute books very long. Several railroads have already announced that they will ignore the law. They feel assured, they say, that the Supreme Courts of their respective states will nullify the law on constitutional grounds. And the railroad magnates surely ought to know what their Supreme Courts will do for them.

Aside from that, however, the passage of the so-called eight-hour law does not prove in the least that Wilson has changed his Princeton attitude. The threat of a general railroad strike forced him to some action. To allow the strike to have been disastrous to Business, and Business is the Most Supreme Deity of our life. Wilson knew that he must prevent such a disaster, at any cost. He had no alternative but to do what he did, his own convictions notwithstanding. He did what Weakness always does in time of stress: Pass a law! No doubt he knew it to be a very opportune casting of bread on the political waters. Many suckers would bite, Wilson figured. Labor did. And even some Socialists.

Even some Socialists! Surely they know that, superficial personal idiosyncracies discounted, there is no essential difference between Wilson and Hughes. Both stand for capitalism and wage slavery. Both serve Mammon, for all their humanitarian and nationalistic bunk. If Wilson "kept us out of war," it is only because the Big Interests find it more profitable to do business with the warring nations than to engage in the actual slaughter. Let it not be forgotten that it was President Wilson who signed bills appropriating hundreds of millions for military purposes. It was Wilson again who approved the law authorizing the President to draft citizens into the army, thus practically establishing conscription in this country It is President Wilson's Postmaster General who has strangled more labor and radical publications than any former administration.

Wilson more progressive? Credulous stupidity!

* * *

Let politicians play at politics. It is too indecent a game for honest men and women. And the sooner the workers concentrate their attention on the real issue—the fight for a greater share of the product of their labor—the fight in the shop, factory and mill—the nearer they will come to the actual solution of their problem.

THE BLAST

Revolutionary Labor Paper

Published every 1st and 15th of the month
569 Dolores St., San Francisco, Cal.
Mail Address, Box 661   Phone, Park 499

Alexander Berkman, Editor and Publisher
M. E. Fitzgerald, Associate Worker   Carl Newlander, Assistant

SUBSCRIPTION
$1.00 Yearly   60c Six Months   5c Copy
Bundle rates 2½c per copy in bundles of ten.

Entered as second-class matter at the postoffice at San Francisco,
Cal., January 14, 1916, under the Act of March 3, 1879.

Reflections

The Quadrennial Show

TIME was when a presidential election thrilled the hearts of men with torchlight processions, roaring brass bands and similar demonstrations dear to the spectacular-minded. Today the election of a president is a much duller affair. Enthusiasm is gone: it is as if the people felt that the country won't go to the dogs, after all, no matter who the next president is. Likely as not, the people are right. They have experienced quite a variety of presidents, even within the present generation, and still things are about as they always have been: monopoly is still monopoly, the cost of living is continuing its upward flight, the independent farmer is becoming a tenant, the workers strike, are shot down, their spokesmen are sent to prison or to the gallows, and the jolly Mammon dance goes merrily on.

Some day the children of man will grow up: they'll tire of the national Punch and Judy show called presidential elections. They will grow to understand that free men need no governors; that sane men need not tolerate slavery; that the idle are vampires on the industrious; that life is to live and enjoy, not to rob or be robbed. Then they will laugh at their blindness, and rulers and elections be a thing of the past.

* * * *

THAT Hughes is a rank reactionist is not denied even by his best friends. It is sufficient to recall to mind his record in the Danbury Hatters' case. He is anti-labor to the core of him. Some women are campaigning for him, admittedly only to spite Wilson, feminine-like. However, it must be said to the credit of the woman suffragists that the intelligent among them have no faith in the vote at all. They admit—generally privately—that politics is too rotten to hold out any hope of betterment for humanity. These women consider suffrage valuable only as a movement, one that will prove educational by interesting women in the larger issues outside of their narrow home sphere.

Be that as it may, there is no one in the camp of Hughes except the big grafters and some women who know better.

* * * *

San Francisco Bomb Case

THE people outside California do not seem to realize in the least the great importance of the so-called bomb trials in San Francisco. That is due chiefly to the conspiracy of silence on the part of the conservative press. Also to a great extent to the fact that the International Workers' Defense League, in charge of the cases, is not blessed with funds sufficient to flood the country with information regarding these cases, as should be done.

And yet, since the days of 1887 there has been no occasion fraught with such meaning to Labor. The situation in San Francisco is briefly this: the fight of the Big Crooks for the open shop had reached a point where the workers had to be terrorized into submission. The old tactics are therefore resorted to: Nolan, Mooney and his wife, Weinberg and Billings—of the most active and intelligent labor element on the Coast—are arrested and accused of murder. The $1,000,000 slush fund of the Chamber of Commerce and the powers of the District Attorney's office are used to corral prostitutes, crooks and drug fiends, manufacture evidence for the prosecution and intimidate witnesses for the defense. A professional jury obediently grants the demand of the prosecution and declares Billings guilty of placing the bomb on Steuart and Market Streets, in spite of absolute proof to the contrary. The road is now paved for the conviction of the other accused labor men.

Innocence does not count. For the dice are loaded against us, every time. And let me assure our readers most emphatically: if ever there was a case where the accused were absolutely innocent, it is these men charged with participation in the explosion on July 22d.

San Francisco is run by one of the most corrupt political gangs of the country—which is saying a good deal. The dominant power in that gang is the United Railroads, whose creature, Fickert, is the District Attorney of the city and county of San Francisco. The United Railroads is the real prosecutor in the case of Mooney, Nolan, et al. It was within the domain of the United Railroads that Mooney recently attempted to organize the men and call them out on strike.

The bosses of San Francisco are planning to hang some of the arrested labor men. If this hellish scheme is permitted to materialize, a crime second only to the judicial murders of 1887 will have been committed. There is no power in San Francisco to call a halt to this fiendish plot. For the workers here are partly terrorized, partly unconscious of the real significance of the planned outrage. It will have to be outside pressure, the voice of the country at large, that shall prevent the repetition of the Chicago murders.

The conscience of the country must be aroused. To work, friends! From New York to San Francisco the cry must be raised: Our brothers shall not be sacrificed to the greed and murder lust of Capital!

* * * *

Mesaba Range Victims

THE strikers on the Mesaba range have returned to work, but their struggle is not at an end. They have learned the lesson of organization and the potency of solidaric effort. A strike of this character is never lost, whatever its immediate result. It is valuable preparation for a bigger, more decisive struggle.

Meanwhile the victims of the Steel Trust in the Minnesota jails must not be forgotten. Carlo Tresca, Joe Schmidt, Sam Scarlett and their companions are the objects of a deliberate frame-up by the agents of the Steel Trust. They are accused of being participants and accessories to the murder of a deputy sheriff who, as a matter of fact, was shot in a row provoked by the deputies and in which all the shooting was done by themselves. But the hyena of greed is thirsting for vengeance: the bosses of the Range will do everything in their power to doom our friends to a living death.

Let us be warned in time, then: not to rely on the fictitious "justice" of the courts, nor on the mere fact of the innocence of the accused. But to understand that safety lies only in solidarity of our efforts, and to make the masters of the Iron Range feel the passion of our understanding.

* * * *

Their Silence Speaks

THE 11th of November, 1887, finds a striking parallel in the present situation on the Coast. Now in San Francisco, as then in Chicago, the Overlords are trying to strangle the aspirations of the workers with the rope or the jail. But whatever the momentary success of the enemies of Labor, the hands of time cannot be held back. And time means progress.

1887-1916! In 1887 our Chicago comrades were murdered for their advocacy of the eight-hour day; in 1916 the President of these United States begs the railroad workers to accept the shorter workday. Surely the Chicago Anarchists never hoped for a more significant vindication in the eyes of history.

In view of the local situation it is most appropriate that the revolutionary groups of San Francisco have arranged a mass meeting in commemoration of the martyrdom of 1887, the international gathering to take place Sunday, November 12th, 8 p. m., at Carpenters' Hall, 112 Valencia Street.

ENRIQUE FLORES MAGON, our beloved Mexican comrade, who has for years fought so valiantly in behalf of Land and Liberty, and who is even now under a Federal prison sentence for his unyielding devotion to the cause of Liberty, has promised his presence at this meeting. He will speak in English and in Spanish.

Our friends and readers in San Francisco and vicinity will take advantage of the opportunity for a general reunion of all rebels.

NOTICE

By request of the International Workers' Defense League of San Francisco, Alexander Berkman has gone to New York to work in behalf of Nolan, Mooney, Weinberg, Billings and Mrs. Mooney. It is hardly necessary for us to urge our comrades and friendly organizations to co-operate with him to their utmost ability in his important mission.

THE BLAST will continue publication as before, as the editor will contribute articles while in the East. Personal mail for A. B. should be addressed: 20 East 125th St., New York City.

After the War—What?

W. T. SHORE

AFTER the war, peace. For whom? For the workers? Before the war there was no peace, after the war there will be no peace for those who are employed by others. The wage earner's life is a continual warfare with adverse circumstances. He is born to work, to live for work, not to work for his livelihood. His struggle for existence ends with either the grave or a pitiable old-age pension. He fights for life. Note the difference between the treatment meted out to him and that given to the soldier; the difference between the man who fights for himself and the man who fights for others. The soldier is a hero, well deserving of his country; well fed, well clothed, well housed—comparatively; a pension when his service is done, which enables him to undersell his fellows in the labor market; his wife and family well looked after when he is away fighting; sung by poets and praised by politicians—a hero! But the worker, upon whom the well-being of the country depends in times of peace and of war—no security of livelihood for him, no pension, no clothes or shelter or food provided, no care for his wife and kiddies; not a hero by any means; just a rough, coarse, drinking, stupid man-machine, to be cast aside when worn out or when times are bad for the employer. Times are always bad for the employed. Who would not be a soldier?

But there is no call to be troubled. After the war there will be peace and plenty. There never have been such times as there will be then. Everybody will be happy; trade will flourish—and, then—what for the worker? It is always dangerous to prophesy, because one never knows for certain what will happen. But, occasionally, one can be quite sure what will not happen. When peace comes, the capitalist will not have turned from a wolf into a lamb. As far as concerns his attitude towards the men who make his money for him, there will be no change; he will take as much and give as little as possible. Then the workers will think of the days of war as of days of promises made which it was never intended to keep. There will be plenty of reasons found for not keeping those promises of peace on earth and goodwill between employer and employed. Those promises will be broken because the workers do not use the power that is theirs in order to insist on their being fulfilled. There lies the tragedy of it all! The workers have the power to do what they will, and to take what they desire—but the enemy cleverly leads the workers to dissipate their power in wrong directions and in futile efforts.

In early days the employer feared the trade unions; now he uses them as a subtle and powerful weapon. The law allows them, Parliament patronizes them; Lloyd George uses them as State-aided charitable societies; their leaders are bespattered with praise, and shackled by pleasant berths until they become the blind leading the blind. For the worker there is no peace, and will be no peace until he wages relentless and ruthless war upon his only enemy—capitalism. The worker can exist without the capitalist; the latter cannot exist without the former. When will the workers grasp that fact? When will they realize that they must win if only they will fight and have no parley with the enemy, and be content with no half-measures? That is the thing to make them understand and act on. There is no halfway house to economic freedom.

There are a great many idols which must be toppled off their pedestals, their altars overturned, and their priests destroyed. This idol, for example: There is no need for work to be done for any profit-making. The one right aim of work is to provide the necessaries and seemly luxuries of life; no more. Work to live, not live to work. When that fact is grasped by the workers, then—what? Then the beginning of a better day.—*London Freedom*.

◊ ◊ ◊

THE measure of a master is his success in bringing all men round to his opinion twenty years later.

—*Ralph Waldo Emerson*

Militarism at Home

HERE is a table based upon the official reports of the leading governments in which is given the appropriations of each for army and navy purposes for the year ending June 30, 1914:

	Army.	Navy.	Total.
Great Britain	$224,300,000	$237,530,459	$461,830,459
Germany	183,090,000	136,858,301	319,948,301
France	191,431,580	90,164,625	281,596,205
Russia	317,800,000	117,508,657	435,308,657
Italy	82,928,000	49,550,147	132,478,147
Austro-Hungary	47,571,755	35,975,338	83,547,193
Japan	49,000,000	48,105,152	97,105,150

(For year beginning July 1, 1917):

United States	346,418,000	315,000,000	661,418,000

◊ ◊ ◊

Revolt

ALDEN WARD

RED flames across a countryside,
　Red battle lines across the world,
　Red death, red hell, red heritage—
These battle flags are NEVER furled!

Red greed, red hate o'er all the earth,
　Red misery for all mankind,
Red lust, red shame, red dividends,
　Red madness burnt in ev'ry mind.

Red monarchs clad in scarlet power,
　Red armies in a red assault;
These are the things unloosed 'mongst men,
　Which breed and breed more RED REVOLT!

◊ ◊ ◊

David Caplan in Supreme Need

THE situation of David Caplan is desperate.

Unless financial aid is sent to him quickly this comrade is going to be sacrificed.

It was earnestly hoped that sufficient money could be secured without making this appeal to you, but the preliminaries of his second trial have used up all the money which has come for him from all sources.

Caplan went to trial Monday, October 23rd, with absolutely not one cent on hand.

We know of the many demands upon you for the defense of other comrades, but even so, we know you are not willing that David Caplan, after two weary years in the Los Angeles county jail, shall be railroaded to prison for life or to the gallows, to gratify the spleen of the enemies of labor.

There is no case against Caplan, as was proven by five jurymen in his former trial voting first to last for his acquittal. But the enemies of labor have not abated one jot of their prejudice and their determination to convict him.

The Caplan trial having been made an issue in the present local political campaign will also spur the present District Attorney to do his utmost for conviction.

LOS ANGELES COUNTY HAS JUST APPROPRIATED $10,000 TO CONVICT CAPLAN, AND CAPLAN HAS NO MONEY.

Whatever you do for him you must do quickly. His friends in Los Angeles are doing all they can, but without financial aid from outside his defense cannot be cared for.

Send money at once to Katherine L. Schmidt, P. O. Box 935, Los Angeles, Cal.

Sketches From Life

LOVERS of sincere expression in the field of literary art will rejoice to learn that Emanuel Julius has just published a collection of fifty of his best short stories and sketches under the winning title, "The Color of Life."

Some of the stories are infinitely tragic and pathetic, revealing the poignant heartaches and the deep emotions of the stricken and unfortunate who represent life's darkest color and who are seldom selected as subjects for the polite pens of the purse-writers. Other stories are prophetic with the promise of human nature, portraying the finer emotions of men and women and the deep, inherent longing of humanity for the light of liberty and knowledge; this is life's brightest color—what life will be when life is what it ought to be. Then there are satirical sketches that probe under the glittering surface of the sheltered and shallow lives of parasites and reveal the reality underneath; sketches that mercilessly smash with the gentle fist of ridicule the dishonest pretensions of "our best people."

One of the sketches in "The Color of Life," ("Mr. Blackstone's Peace Editorial" is the title of this particular sketch)—exposes the hypocrisy of a spurious peace advocate and the unimportance of an important man. There is a war sketch, too, which shows how the divine instinct of love triumphs over the base passion of murder in the heart of a soldier—and how this soldier's surrender to sentiment brought him punishment and death.

Emanuel Julius has viewed closely and intimately life in its varied phases; his writings are drawn from a wide and active experience which has made him a keen observer and a sympathetic interpreter of the mingled tragedy and comedy of our common humanity. Julius dips his pen into the heart of life and draws it forth colored with the crimson current of red-blooded realism. He is an artist who conscientiously devotes his art to picturing life in its true color.

A copy of "The Color of Life" will be mailed to your address upon the receipt of 50 cents by the author, Emanuel Julius, Box 125, Girard, Kansas.

Do you realize the Importance of a FEARLESS PRESS ?

Subscribe and get others to subscribe for

THE BLAST

$1.00 the Year

569 Dolores St., San Francisco

Defense Funds San Francisco Labor Prisoners

Per Alexander Berkman

Total collected to October 15th....$1,461.80	
A Friend ....$ 2.00	
H. G. Hanlon, Hood, Cal, 5.00	
Collection per R. Edelstein, Cleveland............ 9.30	
George Edwards, San Diego, Cal. 2.00	
Collection per M. Rypacek, Cleveland.......... 10.00	
Collection per Lillian Kisluik, Washington, D. C. 20.75	
Glaser .... .75	
Collections per Sarah Dudnik and Toby Robboy, Cleveland 8.35	
Collection per Peter Armanini Ringo, Kan..... 30.00	
Monia Semenoff, Oakland, Cal.................. 3.00	
Anna Levy, Philadelphia 1.00	
Anarchist International Committee, per Frank Mandese, New York City 25.00	
Pauline Sperry, Northampton, Mass. 5.00	122.15
	$1,583.95
Previously turned over to the Defense by Alexander Berkman $1,461.80	
To W. K. Billings.......$ 2.50	
Per Robert Minor, Treas. 119.65	122.15
Nov. 1st—Total amount turned over to the Defense $1,583.95	

You Should Read These Booklets Full of Information and a Real Inspiration

---

Gov. John P. Altgeld's REASONS FOR PARDONING THE ANARCHISTS

And His Masterly Review of the Haymarket Riot

Lucy E. Parsons, Publisher, Chicago

30c Postpaid

Also

The Famous Speeches of the Chicago Anarchists

35c Postpaid

To Be Had Through THE BLAST

Eight   THE BLAST

Chicago Anarchists Executed
for Advocating 8 Hour Day **1887 - 1916** *8 HOUR LAW PASSED BY CONGRESS*

International Mass Meeting

IN COMMEMORATION OF THE 29TH ANNIVERSARY OF THE
MARTYRDOM OF THE CHICAGO ANARCHISTS
ON THE 11TH NOVEMBER, 1887

August Vincenz Theodor Spies.

George Engel

A R Parsons

Adolph Fischer

Louis Lingg.

SPEAKERS:

Enrique Flores Magon
Celebrated Mexican Revolutionist
of Los Angeles
Editor of REGENERACION

Robert Minor
Famous War Correspondent
and Cartoonist

Alexander Berkman
Editor of THE BLAST

Wm. McDevitt
Socialist Lecturer

SPEAKERS:

B. Nikolayeff
Noted Russian Exile
In Russian

J. Shaffer
In Yiddish

ALSO

Luigi Galleani
Well-Known Orator and Editor
of CRONACA SOVVERSIVA
(Lynn, Mass.)
If He Can Reach the Coast in Time
In Italian

S. SHULBERG
Chairman

CARPENTERS' HALL
112 Valencia Street

Sunday, Nov. 12th,

8 P. M. SHARP

Auspices Radical Br. Workmen's Circle No. 511, with the Co-Operation
of the Federated Revolutionary Groups of San Francisco

Admission 10c

Vol. I   SAN FRANCISCO, DECEMBER 1, 1916.   No. 22

"Don't you think that if we can keep the names of the private detectives out of this and make the public believe that the regular authorities worked up the case, we can hang Billings and then get Tom Mooney, the man we want?"——Words of Martin Swanson, detective for the Public Utilities Protective Bureau.

Rusty Justice

THE "professional jury system" is a thing of the past in San Francisco. A lawyer resorted to direct action —and the whole thing vanished in smoke. Attorney Edwin V. McKenzie had fought a couple of hard battles for a client, getting only hung juries, and was going to trial the third time, when he found himself confronted by the same jury panel by the use of which the innocent Billings was sent to a living death. This was too much. McKenzie "blew up." The lawyer became human and took that most effective of all human actions, the direct action of simply refusing to take his client to trial before the famous "Billings butchers." He might have "made a motion" or "filed a writ" or otherwise taken a polite lawyer's way of dodging things, but he didn't. The lawyer refused to respect the pretense that the court house corridor vagrants were a jury, and was sentenced to jail himself—**but wiped the professional jury system off the books by his direct action.** For the whole city is aroused.

The public sees a mountain one atom at a time. It sees now, in San Francisco, the tiny truth that the professional juryman is a ghoul. Perhaps later some big human being, by a like direct defiance, may make the public see that a judge, too, is a ghoul—every judge. And the breaking light may illuminate more of the scene: not only jury and judge, but jailor and lawyer may show in all their ghastly significance, till men will understand that the whole machine of State is one vast crime that but fathers the little crimes. It will be a bright day when man ceases to believe in the beast-god, Punishment, and his church, The State.

But, to come back to earth.

It is a very little favor to ask the public intelligence, to request them to understand that the *hired witness* system is a crime unspeakable. Perhaps the minds of the San Francisco public could be induced to go that little step further, now that they have aroused to the professional juror.

A few years from now, people will listen in amazement to the statement that witnesses were actually allowed to appear in court and swear against a defendant's life when the witness had a **money interest** in shaping his testimony to convict the defendant. The mere statement of it ought to be enough to convince an intelligent reader of its wrong. But if more is needed, a glance at how the thing worked out in the Billings case, should close the argument. Not one disinterested or reputable person gave a word of testimony against Billings. Not one of the important witnesses but has been caught red-handed as a police "stool" with a criminal record ranging from watch-stealing to murder indictment, and *hired for the occasion* to testify against the defendants. No reflection is meant upon the few decent persons who testified to trivial matters.

such as weather conditions on the fateful day, but a reflection *is* meant against the district attorney who paraded a few credible persons through the trial for the purpose of putting a decent admixture into his jumble of opium-fiends, sneak-thieves and red-light professionals.

The point is that it is openly, publicly a custom to **hire witnesses.** Nobody even denies it: offers of large sums of money are published in blazing headlines, money to be paid for the conviction of *anyone* for a crime.

Does anybody contend that an honest man needs to be *paid* for telling the truth? On the other hand, would you be willing to take a chance on having $17,000 offered to anybody in this big city who would be willing to take your life by falsely swearing in court, with full protection and praise for doing it?

Detectives are going around hawking such "business offerings for perjurers."

Charles Organ, a man convicted three times of forgery, was recently added to the string of state's witnesses against Mooney, taking the place of Mrs. Kidwell, who lost her job as witness by writing an indiscreet letter telling of the price she was to get for her testimony. Organ was said to have been given $500 by Tom Mooney to "blow up the Liberty Bell." (There is no use to laugh: such stuff goes in this case, for it is used on the side of Capital against Labor men.) Charles Organ says he wrote several letters denying the story, but the letters were stolen by some officer of the law. Organ finally got a communication out to an attorney for Billings and gave the following statement:

"When I was arrested in Los Angeles two detectives came to me and asked if I knew Mooney. I said 'no.' They said, 'Oh, yes, you do: he's the preparedness parade bomb man.' Then they dictated the Liberty Bell story—how Mooney had given me $500 to blow up the relic, how I had got scared, dumped explosives out of a suitcase at the beach and left the suitcase in Market street, filled with bricks. The detectives told me they'd see I got off light on the check charge if I stuck to the bell story, and they said I'd get a piece of the $17,000 rewards in the bomb case. In San Francisco I refused to identify Mooney. I'd never seen him. They brought him out alone, and detectives prompted me, but I wouldn't identify him."

So proceeds the heart-breaking farce. These witnesses have been brought to the light of day, and are discredited. But who knows what other poison is being brewed for Mooney in the dark? "Hyena" Fickert is king of the kingdom of thugs and can produce a new one for every one unmasked. What new perjury is the Chamber of Commerce gold buying for the Mooney trial?

People of San Francisco, do you really think you ought to let witnesses be openly, publicly *hired?*

Is there a judge in San Francisco who will keep his court a little above the level of the house in which Estelle Smith was arrested in Los Angeles, by refusing to let *hired witnesses* hold sway?

Professional Jurors

A STORM of popular indignation against the "professional jury" is on in San Francisco. The rank injustice of the conviction of Billings, by a professional jury of retired business men, on the direct plea of their master's voice. made by Assistant District Attorney Brennan. that they bring in such a verdict as would allow the State to uncover the real criminals was "the straw that broke the camel's back."

There has been an abundance of wind turned loose on the subject of the "Jury." most of which is very tame and lady-like as befits the average citizen's regard for his own liberties. Everybody "passes the buck." first to the dear "System." then to the judges. then to the politicians, and then back to the people.

Let us have courage and lay it where it belongs, on the State, the government, the police power.

The trouble with citizens today is that they bow down and worship everything that spells "John Law." The right of the Writ of Habeas Corpus has never been so disregarded as it is today. Blood has flowed freely in Everett, Washington, to preserve the right of free speech, and this, mind you, in our day.

How weak and namby-pamby sound the modern mouthings about the "trial by jury" when compared with the thoughts expressed by the famous American Jurist Lysander Spooner in his great legal work. "Trial by Jury." in the 1840's. Listen to him and take heart!

"The trial by jury is a trial by the country—that is. by the people—as distinguished from a trial by the government.

"The object of this trial by the country. or by the people, in preference to a trial by the government. is to guard against every species of oppression by the government. In order to effect this end it is indispensable that the people. or the country, judge of and determine their own liberties against the government, instead of the government's judging of and determining its own powers over the people. How is it possible that juries can do anything to protect the liberties of the people against the government, if they are not allowed to determine what those liberties are?

"To secure this right of the people to judge of their own liberties against the government, the jurors must be taken from the body of the people, by lot, or by some process that precludes any previous knowledge, choice, or selection of them. on the part of the government. This is done to prevent the government's packing a jury with a view to maintain its own laws and accomplish its own purposes."

The voice of Authority is ever growing louder and bolder and all over our land their new cry is an echo of the old one. "the dead to the dung heap. the living to the scaffold."

The watchword of all classes of people in this. our day of "Laws," should be: "Resist aggression and preserve *all* our liberties and demand *more* liberties."

Art and Revolt
Sadakichi Hartmann

EVERY true artist is a revolutionist by instinct, by special endowments. by necessity. His talents. no matter in what direction they may exert and propagate themselves. are always exceptional. This in itself constitutes revolt. as the public bent on enjoyment without study or meditation. will accept willingly and cheerfully only the conventional and traditional in exchange for monetary recompense.

Then there are domestic relations. Comparatively few artists have escaped excommunication from their own parental hearth and ancestry. and if they are foolish enough to attempt to choose a playmate and build a family tree of their own, in most cases they share the fate of Socrates or the inmates of a deaf-mute asylum. The domestic revolt of carrying the latch key in one's pocket at all hours of the night is as bitter as the fight for the Ideal when the larder is empty and the children in need of underwear.

Of course Genius. dark. gaunt figure sharply silhouetted against the grey background of imbecility and greed. stalks on. Every step is one of conquest and disdain.

The artist who lives, survives, and "does" is entrenched most of his life: he takes part in many skirmishes.

carries the torn flag of beauty and liberty through the firing lines to summits far beyond the fighting crowds.

Rubens with his wonderful virility and technical dexterity, expressing an outburst of joy in living, unparalleled in the history of art except in Titian or Franz Hals. did more to deliver humanity from the clutches and throes of feudalism, and the despotism of Pope and Emperor than all the reformatory aspirations of advanced thought, which in the Renaissance, as well as today. was always of a tentative and dilettante character.

The revolt of artists may be on strictly esthetic lines. it may be even strictly technical, but as long as art is the reflection of the higher aspirations of the "play-instinct" in life in its finest expression. each accomplishment in the domain of art means an activity towards a finer equilibrium a more just balancing of the scales. a separation of finer thoughts and emotions from the every day sediments of dirt, ignorance and selfishness. And any superior energy. expression of ability. even aspirations towards the same mean revolt. Revolt that hates the commonplace, that attacks the unjust. that batters down the dungeon gates of prejudice and arrogance. and tries to make this short span of life saner. more tolerable, more independent and beautiful.

THE BLAST

Revolutionary Labor Paper

Published every 1st and 15th of the month
569 Dolores St., San Francisco, Cal.

Mail Address, Box 661   Phone, Park 499

Alexander Berkman, Editor and Publisher
M. E. Fitzgerald, Associate Worker   Carl Newlander, Assistant

SUBSCRIPTION
$1.00 Yearly   60c Six Months   5c Copy
Bundle rates 2½c per copy in bundles of ten.

Reflections

The Battle Line

IN an enormous arc from New York, through the Iron Range of Minnesota, touching with a scarlet stain the city of Everett, Washington, through San Francisco to Los Angeles—stretches the fighting trench of the war of Labor.

The battle line of France, "from Switzerland to the Sea," is not so important as this, nor will the war endure so long.

In New York, a peculiarly fortunate stupidity on the part of one Shonts, head of the traction corporations, has resulted in throwing the labor situation on subway, elevated and surface lines into startling clarity. The brazen greed of the corporations, and particularly their willingness to lie and betray, has caused Labor to rouse in New York as it seldom roused before. There has been serious talk of a general strike, or what is better, a "Social General Strike"—in the great city! It does not matter very much in the long run, just how the laurels of victory fall in the day's fighting—but it does matter very much that this Idea has been brought out in mountain prominence. The persistent propaganda of the direct action agitator put the seed in the soil, and the soil had to grow it in the very nature of things. There is now a bigger idea of "The Strike" for Labor to think upon, and a bigger fright for the New York brand of aristocracy to tremble under.

* * *

IT seems as though there were a monster God of Evil hovering above this land of ours, so shaping things as to bring all of Labor's battles at one time and to make it impossible to do aught but surrender. The resources of conscious strugglers against tyranny are taxed to the limit just now. "Money! Money! Money!" comes the cry from everywhere.

Perhaps it is not a god of evil, after all, but rather a good one, that bids fair to make it impossible to fight as we have, in sordid channels of Capitalism, with nauseating truckling to the courts we don't respect through lawyers whose profession we despise. Possibly it will drive us yet to nobler defiance and less hypocrisy.

Mesaba Iron Range

THE billionaires who give stock shares as dinner-party favors in New York are crushing with their long, sinewy arm of hirelings, the life of Labor in the Mesaba Iron Range in far-off Minnesota. The struggle is a bitter one there, and the lives of Carlo Tresca and seven others are demanded by the steel magnates who wax rich with the sales of a million murder machines for Europe—and who charge Tresca and his comrades with *killing a man*. The man was killed by a gunman in the employ of the steel trust, and most of the eight defendants were fifty miles away at the time, but—are you fool enough to think that justice has anything to do with courts?

To anyone who knows Sam Scarlett, Joe Schmidt and Carlo Tresca, this is a fight to stir the deepest anger of the soul, and those arrested with them must be built of the same timber, for it is always the *best* that are chosen for slaughter.

Do everything in your power for these men.

Everett, Washington

DID you ever hear of the party of 3,000 Southern gentlemen who lynched a disgraceful mob of one negro man and his wife? What is a mob, anyway? A mob is *the other side*. When the newspapers speak of a mob, they mean a group of persons whom the newspaper's owners consider enemies. A group of their friends will pass by the name of "Chamber of Commerce," or, at worst, "vigilantes," even though they go through the exact motions of a mob.

The newspapers announced that "a mob of I. W. W.'s" had been shot to pieces by a "posse of citizens" of Everett, Wash. What was the truth of it?

The I. W. W.'s were coming into the town on their own business, peaceably to be conducted. Some of them had been there before and found the dark streets infested with gentle business men with guns and slung-shots in their pockets, and

had gotten beaten up. So, on their return, they corrected a former oversight by putting a box of guns on the ferryboat for their protection.

They were right. A thug, or a sheriff (according to your point of view), met the ferry at the head of a multitude armed to the teeth. The chief of the gang announced their intention of assaulting the ferryboat load of men, women and children, and drew his gun.

The I. W. W.'s protected themselves as best they could, but were outnumbered five to one, inadequately armed and held in the middle of the river on the boat as a perfect target; so the tragedy of seven deaths in their ranks is offset by only two in the ranks of the mob.

Now, of course, comes the masquerade under the title of a trial for crime. What a pity it is that every splendid human act of revolt against wrong should have to wind up in a stuffy den of hypocrisy! Some day it will be different. The soldiers in the European armies at least get honor and credit for their courage, along with their imprisonment or death. The soldier of the greater cause—Human Progress—gets but dishonor for his greater courage.

Los Angeles, California

DAVID CAPLAN has a chance to win his case in Los Angeles. If he loses, it will probably be because he has not had the few paltry dollars necessary to marshal a defense. The city of Otis is concentrating profuse yellow gold to crush this penniless worker. All of the old machinery is working against him. A picturesque light is thrown upon the methods of courts by an old professional juryman. The pathetic fellow confided to a stranger in the courthouse corridor that he had been outrageously deprived of a job on the Caplan jury. He did not know that his confidant was a friend of Caplan.

Friends are asked to do anything they can for the Caplan defense. A few dollars sent to Katherine Schmidt, room 201 Labor Temple, Los Angeles, California, may mean the difference of freedom or conviction.

San Francisco, California

THE battle at San Francisco centers now about Tom Mooney. The case is postponed to January 4th. We must use that time, however, working as we never worked before.

It is amusing to see the dignity of the San Francisco police department exemplified by a middle-aged officer in uniform actually making faces like a child at a passerby, whom he recognized as active in the defense of Billings. So intense is the desire of the whole army of gunmen in and out of uniform to land their prey that large numbers of them infest the corridors of the court to heckle and threaten friends of the defense, in the hope of forcing an opportunity for arrests. Two policemen, upon Mooney's recent appearance in the court, approached a friend of Mooney's in the corridor, and after asking numerous impudent and insulting questions, informed him that they would "arrest him if they ever found him anywhere he didn't belong."

There are some people who think that peace is kept by policemen.

An Army of 100,000

RESPONDING to the call for labor loyalty, the tremendous body of New York workers, the United Hebrew Trades, is to hold a mass meeting in Carnegie Hall, New York City, Saturday night, December 2nd, in the interest of the defense of the Mooneys, Weinberg, Nolan and Billings, framed up on dynamite charges by the San Francisco labor haters.

Frank P. Walsh, Max Eastman, Emma Goldman, Max Pine (Secretary United Hebrew Trades), Arturo Giovannitti and Alexander Berkman will speak. A splendid meeting it will certainly be, for a richer subject or a better group of nationally famous speakers could not be found in America.

The United Hebrew Trades is going to give its financial support to the defense of the San Francisco labor men. This means a wonderful addition to the strength of the battle line. That a lawyer of national fame is giving his services purely for the sake of Justice, surely furnishes an inspiring example to Labor throughout the nation.

In years to come, the San Francisco cases will serve as a landmark of history. All men will then know that the cause was a good one. It is to blot out forever the stain on America that was left by the Haymarket executions—to stop the brutal license of hanging labor agitators on fantastic conspiracy pretenses.

Those labor unions who now come to the fore will be on the roll of honor. The Chicago Labor Council and the United Hebrew Trades will stand high on that roll as bodies eager to do their part though many hundreds of miles distant from the scene.

Two Hundred and Twenty-five Dollars

HAVE you ever been in prison? Have you ever spent your every twenty-four hours of your every day for years in the iron-bound sea of cruelty called "jail"? And that for merely speaking the simple truth from an honest heart?

That is the fate that awaits the Magon Brothers, *for the lack of* $225.

Enrique Flores Magon and Ricardo Magon are needed outside. Upon them has fallen the hardest task of keeping the real light of liberty burning in Mexico. Enrique told me not long ago, "It used to be that the work depended on us; but now there are others trained to do it and it does not matter much if we go to prison."

This is one of the few things about which I am sure Enrique Magon is mistaken.

By the use of $500 an appeal can be taken from that machine of injustice, the lower court. The higher court is another machine of injustice, but the point is that long, long months or years will be taken in the appeal, and meantime Ricardo and Enrique will be working, working for Land and Liberty for the Mexican people.

Two hundred and seventy-five dollars has been obtained. Two hundred and twenty-five dollars more MUST BE HAD QUICK. After December first, it would be too late.

Bourke Cockran

HUMAN nature is bigger than any theory that the brain can conceive. It is well that this is so—else all wisdom would have been written long ago and brains would have nothing more to do but memorize.

A big human heart has stepped from the beaten path. Bourke Cockran, greatest member of the New York bar, brilliant orator and fighter for Ireland's independence, is coming to San Francisco to battle for the Mooneys, Nolan, Weinberg, Billings and—simple justice. The papers say that he is doing it without compensation, though one of them hesitates to believe such a thing possible. It *is* an "unheard-of" thing, but unheard of things happen. Bourke Cockran is certainly coming. As he is reported to be a millionaire, accustomed to fees of many thousands of dollars for any case he would touch—and as these defendants are workingmen unable to scrape together more than a few hundred dollars—how could it be otherwise than true that he is coming without pay? Dust off your theories! Human nature is at work.

Let all get in and support this big man who is doing a big thing. Let's stop this lynching in San Francisco of four men and a woman on the pretense of a crime of which they know nothing. We know that the real reason for their prosecution is their labor agitation, to some of the tactics of which some people objected—but it is *not* that affair on Market street for which they are being prosecuted.

We all make mistakes that we must correct. Let ALL of Labor get behind those four men and one woman now, and fight out any difference of tactics when the hideous farce of a prosecution is ended.

A Frame-Up

THAT there could exist a man so vile as to plot to send another to prison for a dirty little reward, is too repulsive a thought for some minds to accept. We in the labor struggle often meet with that difficulty—people can't believe that such baseness is common. It *is* pretty bad, and yet, not only is it done every day in every city in the world, as a matter of the petty routine of the police courts, but we state that it is a common, universal custom to HANG men for a money reward. This happens year in, year out in the silent, secret caverns that underlie society. Unseen, not understood by even those who participate in it (for what rat knows that he lives but in a hole?), the life of the under-city seethes. Nearly the whole of the drama is concealed from view by the conventions of court and newspaper and by the stupid tendency to believe nothing that comes from another source. So the mock men stalk and mock women drift through unreal life, shallow-pated through long restriction of vision—and beneath all the superficialities lies the brutal actuality, putrid for lack of sunlight.

An old man was sent to prison the other day for placing odor-bombs in non-union restaurants. Now it is discovered that an odor-bomb was placed in the old man's pocket by the very detective who "found" it on him later. R. Porter Ashe, respectable attorney for the Chamber of Commerce, is indignant. That a detective should thus "frame up" an innocent old man for the

$500 reward offered by the Chamber of Commerce, is outrageous, and the poor victim shall be freed at once.

Now, R. Porter Ashe, we want to tell you something and we want you to listen to it carefully. That old man is not being freed because he is innocent. Is he? If it had been a union waiter that was framed up, would *he* get off? Think about this carefully.

Now we will tell you the real reason why the old man is let off. It is because he is a *remittance man* from England. That is, he belongs to the shabby petty aristocracy and is not a workingman. That is the reason; don't pretend that it isn't. Besides, it saves the Chamber of Commerce the $500 reward, which there is no use to spend if you can't "get" a labor man.

Detective Patterson can't put one over on the Chamber of Commerce. If he had just caught a member of the Cooks and Waiters' Union, it wouldn't have been a frame-up, and he would have gotten his reward, and no questions asked. AND YOU KNOW IT, Mr. R. Porter Ashe.

Do you remember the time the frame-up was thwarted in Stockton, when a labor man got his gun first and held up the employers' thug that came to kill him, and the confession of Emerson that dynamite was to be "found" in the possession of union leaders?

Let us suppose for a moment that you are sincere about it, Mr. Ashe. You have caught your detective Patterson. *Now look up your detective Swanson; scrutinize him a bit.*

Some "frame-ups" are for six months, and some are for Death on the gallows.

The Potency of Ideals

Enrique Flores Magon met and talked to a small group of writers and social workers the other evening in San Francisco. He told them in his simple, gracious way the facts about the Mexican situation. He pictured for them feelingly the future of the Mexican Anarchist Communists plan, already partly attained. The impressive silence following was broken by a Wilson-suffragist-wail—"A beautiful dream—but *so* impractical." And by an editor's sigh: "There is no hope for the human race."

But there *is* hope for the human race when we have men like the Brothers Magon—men who risk their lives for their ideals.

Ideals are a potent factor in the progress of humanity. The love of freedom, the passion for independence and well-being are inherent tendencies. To stimulate these into active operation is not "impractical." Men and women fight for ideals with greater enthusiasm and abandon than for their bread and butter. It is up to us, the intelligent rebels, to imbue humanity with new ideals, worthy to fight and die for, more worthy to live for: the ideal of Brotherhood versus hate, of Solidarity versus slaughter, of well-being in freedom versus misery in chains.

Defense Fund San Francisco Labor Prisoners

Per Alexander Berkman

Total collected to November 1st	$1,583.95
Subscription List, per S. Sharpman, Boston, Mass.	$ 5.45
Anarchist Group, New York City, per Frank Mandese	75.00
Subscription List, per Pauline Wolpert, Los Angeles, California	13.35
Cronaca Sovversiva, per M. Centrone, San Francisco	54.11
I. W. W., Brawley, California, per J. S. Furey	1.00
Per J. Kabcinell, Wichita, Kansas	20.50
Paul Jurk, San Francisco	1.00
Per Lucy Robins, Chicago	113.66
	284.07
	$1,868.02
Previously turned over to the Defense by Alexander Berkman	$1,583.95
To Prisoners	$ 25.00
Per Robert Minor, Treasurer	259.07
	284.07
	$1,868.02

Nov. 22d—Total amount turned over to the Defense.

Carranza's Doom

Enrique Flores Magon

CARRANZA'S present position could not be more untenable. At Vera Cruz he succeeded in fooling into his ranks thousands of workers by his promises of social, political and economic emancipation. With his *regime*, the Social Revolution was to begin. The toilers went gladly to lay down their lives in the battlefield to place this Messiah into power, but once in power the rank politician forgot all his promises.

As soon as he found himself securely in the presidential chair as the *de facto* government, backed by Wall Street, Carranza thought himself strong enough to subdue and drown in blood the aspirations of the Mexican people to emancipate themselves, and began to persecute the very men that had helped him climb into power. His persecutions reached their climax with the decree of August 1, 1916, by which the workers were given the death penalty for daring to strike. Over forty workers have already been shot down.

Such brutalities, aggravated by decrees of the death penalty for slight offenses and petty larceny, have taken the bandage from the eyes of the workers. They are no longer blinded by the farcical radicalism of Carranza. They realize now the *real* Carranza, and such knowledge has created a strong reaction against this tyrant. Hence, the perilous position of the so-called First Chief, who now finds himself surrounded by a wall of bayonets.

On the north, Francisco Villa has succeeded in getting the upper hand, mainly in the State of Chihuahua, and parts of Durango. Coahuila and Zacatecas. and as Villa has now taken the policy of expropriation and giving to the poor, the latter flock to his banner in large numbers.

In the southern State of Oaxaca and the central one of Mexico, Felix Diaz, the nephew of the old tyrant, Porfirio Diaz. is growing stronger. Young Diaz represents the old Diaz nefarious "Cientifico" party. and is backed by the millions of the exiled bourgeoisie and clergy. who provide the means to give arms to the thousands of workers who are deceived by his false promises of delivering the land to the people of Mexico.

In eleven southern and central States. covering an area equal to about one-fifth of the Republic, and inhabited by some three million people, Zapata. with his Agrarians and the Anarchist members of the Mexican Liberal Party. both working in conjunction. have succeeded in repulsing the Carranza soldiers and in obtaining a strong foothold. Their strength is due to the fact that in these regions the land, houses, tools, machinery, and all means of production and transportation are now the property of the people, and they are fighting to retain what they have forced from the hands of the masters. This movement of combined Agrarians and Anarchist Communists is spreading to other States of the center, east and west of Mexico.

Added to these already formidable antagonists of the Carranza *regime*—Villa. Diaz. Agrarians and Liberals— there is another not less important factor in this struggle: the independent "guerrillas." These "guerrillas," called

by the capitalist press "bands of bandits," are mainly real revolutionists, and are effective in keeping aflame the fire of the revolution, and holding in constant nervous strain all the new tyrants that try to climb into power. Thousands of these guerrillas, divided into small armies of two to three hundred men. roam over the country, constantly harassing the Carranza soldiers. Even his own men are deserting this tyrant to enlist in the different other factions or to become independent "guerrillas." Thus we find that Carranza's doom is unavoidable, and a matter of short duration, despite the staunch support of the moneyed interests in the United States.

The Mexican people are learning through long and cruel experience that freedom is never handed down from those on the higher steps of the social ladder. They have already learned that government is not instituted to protect the weak against the rapacity and tyranny of the strong. They have learned, too, that through peaceful means the emancipation of the proletariat shall never be accomplished. Through long centuries of brutal oppression and rank exploitation, they have learned the valuable lesson that the only way open to the workers to free themselves from the chattel slavery to which Authority. Capital and Church have subjected them. is to meet the violence of those above with the violence of those below, and that the guns of the master class must be answered by the guns of the slaves.

That is why Carranza's doom is at hand; that is why the Mexican people, determined to free the Land, have kept up for six long years the wonderful struggle known as the Mexican Revolution, despite the efforts of Wall Street; and that is why they shall finally reach their goal of implanting in the so-called Mexican Republic a New Social Order wherein all human beings. regardless of sex. race or color, shall be free, equal and brothers.

☒ ☒ ☒

TO PUNISH a man because we infer from the nature of some doctrine which he holds. or from the conduct of other persons who hold the same doctrines with him, that he will commit a crime, is *persecution*. and is, in every case, foolish and wicked.

—*Macaulay*. in
CONSTITUTIONAL HISTORY OF ENGLAND

Report of Social and Dance Given by Chicago Radicals

Workers' Institute Hall Given Free of Charge
Donations for refreshments to Lucy Robins as follows: Mrs. Sara Fox, $5; Lucy Robins, $1; I. Bloom, $1; Liebman, $1; Schoolman, $1; Anna Livshitz, $1; L. Percifal, $1; A. Nedos, 50c; I. Jaffe, 50c; M. Touler, 50c; Feifer, 50c; Musener, 50c; Morphas, 25c; Mrs. B. Schiff, $2; B. Slader, $1; Sivin, $1; Getler, $1; Reitman, $1; A. Tobinson, $1; S. Peck, $1; Agursky, 50c; Davidson, $1; Goldberg, 50c; A. Sigel, 50c; Marsol, 25c; Flora Finkler, $1; C. V. Cook, $1; Hyman, $1; Fein, $1; Sisman, $1; C. Weisberg, $1; Wolcott, $1; Shulman, $1; J. Burystein, 50c; Joe Goldman, $1; Slotkin, 50c; Shorr, 25c; J. Fishman, $1; Sopacov, 50c; Chessky, 50c.   Total refreshments
donations ....$ 36.75
Collected through Workers' Institute....................   6.80
Profit from Social 170.11

                                                                              $213.66

To "Freie Arbeiter Stimme" for David Caplan's Defense...$ 100.00
To THE BLAST for San Francisco Defense League............ 113.66

                                                                              $213.66

War: The Triumph of Barbarism
Guy de Maupassant

AT the mere mention of the word war I am seized with a sense of bewilderment, as though I heard of witchcraft, of the inquisition, of some far distant thing, ended long ago, abominable and monstrous, against all natural law.

When we talk of cannibals, we proudly smile and proclaim our superiority over those savages. Which are the savages, the true savages? Those who fight to eat the vanquished or those who fight to kill, only to kill?

The gallant little soldiers running about over there are as surely doomed to death as the flocks of sheep driven along the road by the butcher. They will fall on some plain, with their heads split open by sabre cuts or their chests riddled by bullets, and yet they are young men, who might work, produce something, be useful. Their fathers are old and poverty-stricken, their mothers, who during twenty years have loved them, adored them as only mothers can adore, may perchance hear in six months or a year that the son, the child, the big fellow, reared with so much care, at such an expense and with so much love, has been cast in a hole like a dead dog, after having been ripped open by a bullet and trampled, crushed, mangled by the rush of cavalry charges. Why have they killed her boy, her beautiful boy, her sole hope, her pride, her life? She cannot understand. Yes, indeed, why?

War! fighting! slaughtering! butchering men! And to think that now, in our own century, with all our civilization, with the expansion of science and the height of philosophy to which the human race is supposed to have attained, we should have schools in which we teach the art of killing, of killing from a distance, to perfection, numbers of people at the same time; poor devils, innocent men, fathers of families, men of untarnished reputation. The most astounding thing is that the people do not rise up against the governing power. What difference is there then between monarchies and republics? And what is more astounding still, why does society not rise up bodily in rebellion at the word "war"?

Ah! We shall ever continue to live borne down by the old and odious customs, the criminal prejudices, the ferocious ideas of our barbarous forefathers, for we are but animals, and we shall remain animals, led only by instinct, and that nothing will ever change.

Should we not have spurned any other than Victor Hugo, who should have launched forth the grand cry of deliverance and truth?

"Today might is called violence, and is beginning to be condemned; war is arraigned. Civilization, at the demand of all humanity, directs an inquiry and indicts the great criminal brief against conquerors and generals. The nations are beginning to understand that the aggrandizement of a crime can in no way lessen it: if to murder a great many does not create any extenuating circumstance, if robbery is a disgrace, invasion cannot be a glory. Ah! Let us proclaim the peremptory truth, let us dishonor war."

Idle anger, poetic indignation! War is more venerated than ever.

A clever artist in such matters, a slaughtering genius, Monsieur de Moltke, replied one day to some peace delegates in the following extraordinary words:

"War is holy and of divine institution; it is one of the sacred laws of nature; it keeps alive in men all the great and noble sentiments, honor, disinterestedness, virtue, courage; in one word, it prevents them from falling into the most hideous materialism."

Therefore to collect a herd of hundreds of thousands of men, to march day and night without respite, to think of nothing, study nothing, learn nothing, read nothing, be of no earthly use to any one, rot with dirt, lie down in mire, live like brutes in a continual besotment, pillage towns, burn villages, ruin nations; then meeting another similar agglomeration of human flesh, rush upon it, shed lakes of blood, cover plains with pounded flesh mingled with muddy and bloody earth; pile up heaps of slain; have arms and legs blown off, brains scattered without benefit to any one, and perish at the corner of some field while your old parents, your wife and children are dying of hunger; this is what is called not falling into the most hideous materialism!

Warriors are the scourge of the earth. We struggle against nature and ignorance, against obstacles of all kinds, in order to lessen the hardships of our miserable existence. Men, benefactors, scholars wear out their lives toiling, seeking what may help, what may solace their brethren. Eager in their useful work, they pile up discovery on discovery, enlarging the human mind, extending science, adding something each day to the stock of human knowledge, to the welfare, the comfort, the strength of their country.

War is declared. In six months the generals have destroyed the efforts of twenty years' patience and genius. And this is what is called not falling into the most hideous materialism.

We have seen war. We have seen men maddened and gone back to their brute estate, killing for mere pleasure, killing out of terror, out of bravado, from sheer ostentation. Then, when right no longer exists, when all notion of justice has disappeared, we have seen ruthlessly shot down innocent beings who, picked up along the road, had become objects of suspicion simply because they were afraid. We have seen dogs as they lay chained up at their master's gate killed in order to try a new revolver; we have seen cows riddled with bullets as they lay in the fields, without reason, only to fire off guns, just for fun.

And this is what is called not falling into the most hideous materialism. To invade a country, to kill the man who defends his home on the plea that he wears a smock and has no forage cap on his head, to burn down the houses of the poor creatures who are without bread, to break, to steal furniture, drink the wine found in the cellars, violate the women found in the streets, consume thousands of francs' worth of powder and leave behind misery and cholera.

This is what is called not falling into the most hideous materialism.

What have they ever done to show their intelligence, these valiant warriors? Nothing. What have they invented? Guns and cannons. That is all.

The inventor of the wheelbarrow, has he not done more for humanity by the simple and practical idea of fitting a wheel between two poles than the inventor of modern fortifications?

What remains of Greece? Books and marbles. Is she great by what she conquered or by what she produced? Was it the invasion of the Persians that prevented her from falling into the most hideous materialism? Was it the invasion of the barbarians that saved Rome and regenerated her?

Did Napoleon the First continue the great intellectual movement begun by the philosophers at the end of the last century?

Well, yes, since governments assume the right of death over the people, there is nothing astonishing in the people sometimes assuming the right of death over governments.

They defend themselves. They are right.

Reflections of An Old Agitator
Wendell Phillips

THE difficulty of the present day and with us is, we are bullied by institutions. A man gets up in the pulpit or sits on the bench, and we allow ourselves to be bullied by the judge or the clergyman, when, if he stood side by side with us on the brick pavement as an individual, his ideas would not have disturbed our clear thoughts an hour.

Stand on the pedestal of your own individual independence. Summon those institutions before you, and judge them.

Eight   THE BLAST

Our Funny Column

Wouldn't it be funny to see the great corporations arm their army of workmen, train them as a military force and issue ammunition to them? Why don't they? Why organize a Militia in which Labor has no part?

Honest, whom had the men in the trenches better be fighting? Each other? Or each turn round and fight their masters—or, rather, the system which makes masters? Wonder if those who are left will see it.

If only Labor had great warehouses of food and clothing, they would be stronger in conflicts with Capital. But they have. Every warehouse is filled by Labor. And the earth is theirs, if only they would unite to a man.

Isn't it funny, this aristocracy of Labor?

Labor will have no real strength till the man with the pick is the full brother of the man at the throttle.

There is only one lesson for Labor to learn—not Politics, but Solidarity.

A Crackerjack Pamphlet

Just Issued by the B. C. Federationist of Vancouver, British Columbia

"The Genesis and Evolution of Slavery," written and compiled by E. T. Kingsley and R. Parm Pettipiece, Vancouver, B. C., is the name of a pamphlet just off the press of the B. C. Federationist, the only Labor paper west of Winnipeg which has survived war conditions in Canada. This little booklet of 64 pages contains a wealth of information regarding the economic basis of capitalist society and the position occupied by the working class within it. It clears up much that has long confused, not only the workers themselves, but many others who have given thought to the vexations and anomalies of modern civilization. It is invaluable to every student of social phenomena and especially to every member of the working class. In lots of less than 100 copies, per copy, 10 cents, postpaid. In lots of 100 or more, at 5 cents per copy. Address: The B. C. Federationist, Labor Temple, Vancouver, B. C.

Do you realize the Importance of a

FEARLESS PRESS ?

Subscribe and get others to subscribe for

THE BLAST

$1.00 the Year

569 Dolores St., San Francisco

Grand Entertainment

GIVEN BY

YOUNG PEOPLE'S SOCIAL CLUB

AT 1256 MARKET STREET

SAN FRANCISCO

Saturday, November 25, 1916

8:00 P. M.

AVERILL HALL

For the Benefit of Carlo Tresca, Sam Scarlett, Joseph Schmidt and Others
Imprisoned by the Steel Trust in Minnesota

New York Readers Take Notice

International Concert and Ball given by the Group of Aid of the Anarchist Movement, for the benefit of THE BLAST, Carlo Tresca and the five comrades arrested in San Francisco. At Casino Hall, 85 East Fourth St., Saturday, December 9th. Tickets, 20c; hat checks, 10c.

You Should Read These Booklets Full of Information and a Real Inspiration

Gov. John P. Altgeld's REASONS FOR PARDONING THE ANARCHISTS

And His Masterly Review of the Haymarket Riot

Lucy E. Parsons, Publisher, Chicago

30c Postpaid

Also

The Famous Speeches of the Chicago Anarchists

35c Postpaid

To Be Had Through THE BLAST

OUR BOOK SHOP
569 Dolores St., San Francisco

By PETER KROPOTKIN   postage
The Great French Revolution, 1789-1793, reduced from $2.25 to ....$1.50   .20
Mutual Aid .... 1.00   .15
Memoirs of a Revolutionist.... 2.00   .20
Conquest of Bread............... .50   .05
Fields, Factories and Workshops .... .50   .05
Modern Science and Anarchism .... .25
Anarchist Communism .... .05
War and Capitalism .... .05
An Appeal to the Young......... .05
The State .... .05

By EMMA GOLDMAN   postage
Anarchism and Other Essays (with Biography) ......$1.00   .10
Social Significance of the Modern Drama .... 1.00   .15
Anarchism and What it Really Stands For .... .10
Syndicalism .... .05
Patriotism .... .05
Marriage and Love............... .10
Victims of Morality and Failure of Christianity .... .10
The Philosophy of Atheism and The Failure of Christianity .... .10
Mother Earth, Anarchist Monthly, 10c a copy............$1.00 a year
Bound Volumes .... 2.00   .15
PRISON MEMOIRS OF AN ANARCHIST, By Alexander Berkman ....$1.25   .15
SELECTED WORKS OF VOLTAIRINE de CLEYRE....... 1.00   .15
ANARCHISM, By Dr. Paul Eltzbacher .... 1.50   .15
   A clear-cut, impartial analysis of the various Anarchist theories by a scientific investigator.
LIBERTY and the GREAT LIBERTARIANS ...... 1.00   .15
   Compiled by Charles T. Sprading. The first anthology on liberty. An indispensable book.
THE FRUITS OF CULTURE, by Leo Tolstoi $0.25
THE EGO AND HIS OWN, by Max Stirner ....$0.75   .15
FREE SPEECH FOR RADICALS, by Theodore Schroeder .... .25
SPEECHES OF THE CHICAGO ANARCHISTS............ .30   .10
SYNDICALISM AND THE CO-OPERATIVE COMMONWEALTH, by Pataud and Pouget .... .50   .10
SONGS OF LOVE AND REBELLION, by Covington Hall .... .50
                                      Price
The Anarchist Revolution, by George Barrett .... .05
The Last War, by George Barrett...... .05
Anarchy, by Andre Girard............ .05
What Every Girl Should Know, by Margaret Sanger .... .50
What Every Mother Should Know, by Margaret Sanger .... .50
The God Pest, by John Most. Published in No. 18 of The Crucible, Agnostic Weekly .... .05
THE LITTLE REVIEW, Margaret Anderson, Editor (Chicago). A bold literary iconoclast ....15c a copy
EVERYMAN, monthly by Luke North (Los Angeles)............10c a copy

Vol. I   SAN FRANCISCO, DECEMBER 15, 1916.   No. 23

Peace and—REVOLUTION

The Great Hope
Robert Minor

THE German Government offers peace. The proposal echoes about the world with strange reception. Solemn "statesmen" in London pedantically utter the things that "one ought to say, you know"—things cheaply claiming victory. In the thin, piping voice of weakness. English aristocracy shrieks, "No! We will fight to complete victory."

But British Tommy rots in trenches, before iron walls of Germany that have stood almost undented for two years and are expected, so French soldiers told me, to stand another year. The British and the French have an iron wall, too, that cannot be broken. The two armies in Western Europe are literally living in underground fortified cities, within range of the human voice. Both sides are practically invulnerable.

So, what will a British refusal of Peace mean? It will mean **explaining to Tommy!**

Maybe they can fool the English soldier a little longer: from talking with them. I should say that if anybody can be fooled forever, it is the English soldier. But even they must have learned something in this war.

Belgium and Northern France are to be vacated, according to the German offer. A part of Alsace-Lorraine is probably a trading concession which they will later offer.

What would a French refusal of peace mean? It will mean **explaining to the French** *poilu!*

I heard a French soldier out in the fighting country sing "*l' Internationale.*" I saw a French soldier stand about the streets of Paris, iron hat on his head, mud of the trenches still on his boots, a loaf of bread and a greasy sausage strapped to his faded uniform—on seven-day vacation after a year and a half of fighting, with not a street car fare, not the price of a cup of coffee, as he wistfully watched the gaiety of the bourgeois. Not a chance even to sit down, except in a park in the rain!

There is no excuse that can be given to either the English or the French soldiers for a continuation of the carnage. I believe that peace will be made.

A strange but enlightening fact of this war has been that in the hour of the greatest need of brains, the two leading allied countries had to put their war business into the hands of "radicals." Not real radicals, of course, but men of that class who dally with radical tendencies, with brains to understand but not the hearts to act.

England has just gone into the hands of the little Welsh lawyer, Lloyd George, who has been telling the English working cattle all his life to rise in modest and peaceful revolt.

The men who are running France today—the only men in France who had brains enough to run a big war and were willing to do it—were until recently counted as dangerous "reds." Some of them have spent their lives preaching direct-action Socialism, and now wear the hypocritical broadcloth with ill-grace.

The war is being run by anti-militarists.

Such are the most powerful of the "statesmen" who will be called upon to answer the German peace proposal. It is they who, if the offer is refused, **will have to explain to Tommy and the** *poilu*. And these have been preaching rebellion to the men before they went into the trenches.

Gustave Hervé, one of the most influential and widely read editors in these war times in Paris, said to French Labor at the beginning of the war, "Go to war; it can't be helped. But after victory—**keep your rifles!**"

If Peace is not made, let us hope that the undeceived common soldier will about face with his bayonet and his anger upon the parasites for whom he has been fighting, and strew them about the fields of his home land in the same ungainly heaps of bodies with which his own flesh has fertilized the foreign war-fields.

If Peace **is** made, let us hope that the common soldier will ram down the throats of those same "red" politicians some of their eloquent phraseology of the past, and will insist upon a Peace on the lines of the destruction of old capitalist exploitation.

Of course, the common man will not know what to ask for other than immediate bread-and-butter things, and he won't understand what he is heading into—but he may in spite of his blindness turn up something.

For instance, there is the war debt. It will be about one hundred billion dollars (a hundred times the amount of indemnity fixed by Bismarck upon France for the purpose of ruining her). Let us hope the amount is even higher than this, the amount that the rulers will try to squeeze out of the sweat of the workers at the end of the war. For, if the working class will only **refuse to pay** that will be the greatest hope for the world. Money owed to the money-lending class by the working class as a result of the working class having fought for the money-lending class! When in Paris, I heard rumblings of the sentiment: "We can't receive back the lives of our dead brothers; let not the money lenders receive back their damned money!"

The *poilu* will come back from the trenches with a knowledge of guns.

It is the Great Hope. It will mean a short, sharp clash of steel on steel, a little torn broadcloth and bloody silk—and perhaps—Liberty!

This is not my theory alone: it's the theory of some of the biggest financial and political powers in America. They are getting ready for it.

That's what President Wilson's "International League to Enforce Peace" is for. You see, a good bit of that hundred billion is "owed" to Morgan & Co., and other American financiers down to a caliber small and numerous enough to create a war-loan sentiment throughout America.

When Europe went murdering for profit, Peace was none of our business.

If Europe seeks Liberty through revolution, **we** will be expected to "enforce peace" and Morgan's claims.

Let us have Peace now. But then, quickly, the Revolution, and no interference from the "Land of Liberty" on the excuse of **preserving Peace.**

Fighting to a Finish
Horace Traubel

WE ARE told that we must fight the war to a finish. What is that finish? The finisher might get finished in the process. If diplomats could fight diplomats to a finish. Or kaisers kaisers. Or munition people munition people. If Georges could fight Williams to a finish. If Nicholases could fight Poincaires to a finish. If the vitriolic German priests could fight the vitriolic English priesthood to a finish. If we could set the board and have those who want to fight fight others who want to fight to a finish. If all the pamphleteers, if all the so-much-a-worders, could be induced to fight pamphleteers and so-much-a-worders to a finish. Then I'd say yes. I wouldn't choose even that. But I'd not stand in the way. But when you propose that the German people should fight the English people to a finish. When you propose that any people should fight any people to a finish. Then I say no. If all the peoples of all the earth could fight all the swells of all the earth to a finish—all the rulers and robbers: then I'd not stand in the way. But short of that I can't see the right kind of a finish. But when the will of the people is known the will of their exploiters will crumple. When the time comes that the people might fight the anti people to a finish then it won't be necessary to fight. The weapons will have changed. The big guns are only necessary to the weak. They are not necessary to the strong. Carrying a gun is a cowardice. Using a gun is surrender. Some say we want no more war. That's right. We don't. But there's a lot more we don't want. And that lot more may be preliminary. * * * War don't cause war. Secret diplomacy is bad enough. Any diplomacy is too bad. But there's a secret something else back of all that by whose forefinger the moves of the game are made. Will any settlement short of that settle anything? There are good people who see nothing. And there are others who see everything but are bad. Is the war to be settled for the people? Or are they to settle it for themselves? We hear of leagues of democratic control. Will they be permitted to control anything? Carpenter says that even now at this very minute when the war's at its hottest our masters may be arranging a truce in their cabinets. And if they are. If they do. We know what sort of a truce it'll be. The people will be left out again. Yet the people are meekly apologetic in peace. How can we expect them to suddenly become conscious of themselves in war? They may be stirred up. They may wake. If they do, look out. Some heads'll go off. The great will become the small. Reputations will give way to character. Leaders will become servants. The road toward peace is over the ruins of systems. You can't remove little dribbles of ephemera and expect the millennium. I'm not afraid to say that I want peace at any price. And then I'm not afraid to say that I want justice at any price to go along with it.—The Conservator.

Popular Movements; Rent Strikes and Boycotts, vs. H. C. of L.
Elias Sang

IN ALL ages popular and democratic movements have endured the gibes and sneers of the aristocrats.

Beware, ye masters of the bread! The mob from out this same populace rent the Bastille from turret to foundation stone, and from the wreck rose a republic. The Tories in 1776 dug their own graves, and literally, too, as many Mexican Land Barons have recently taken to the homely shovel before shuffling off this mortal coil.

Once the mask is off, the mob will remember all the nice modern methods of extortion and starvation. They will not forget that you smug commission man dumped potatoes and fruits overboard to rot when they had no work and were hungry; and you, dear Landlord, drove them from sheltering roofs, nor yet will they forget the arrogance of the police nor the hypocrisy of the church. The mob has never yet in history risen which failed to pay its respects to fat merchants and landlords and their flunkeys.

All real radicals should not only join, but organize and foment any popular movement to reduce rent or boycott merchants or certain products that menace the standard of living.

To hell with the Efficiency Food Specialists and their alfalfa meal menus. Let the Diet Squads and the rest of the parasites eat the liver and tripe for a change. The working public has been on a diet since history began and does not need any lessons from these cheap fakers.

A great popular movement should be started in San Francisco and other big cities to cut rent in half. Demand a cut and refuse to either pay more or move. Organize a great exodus for the coming spring and summer, a big tent city on the sand dunes. Desert the rabbit warren flats and tenements for six months anyhow!

Organize neighborhood clubs and buy staples wholesale. Boycotting any article that can be reached, even for a few days, helps. A little experiment here and there will show the most effective way.

Don't weep any crocodile tears over some green grocer losing a few dollars; pity yourself and the mob first.

Draw all your small savings out of the banks and put them in the U. S. Postal Savings banks. You of San Francisco boycott the Big Department Stores and Market Street merchants and let 'em know it. They drove off the workingman's jitney—make them feel you have a good memory.

Get the women interested heart and soul and use the gang spirit of the children, too. Remember the Apprentices in Lyons made the Silk Weavers.

Do you remember Carlyle's French Revolution? "A puff of smoke here, a burst of flame in the east, a shot rings out in the night and Paris is in Revolt!"

Radicals should take up the Parisian Club or Group of Ten idea, and be the yeast in this great popular ferment.

THE BLAST

Revolutionary Labor Paper

Published every 1st and 15th of the month
569 Dolores St., San Francisco, Cal.

Mail Address, Box 661   Phone, Park 499

Alexander Berkman, Editor and Publisher
M. E. Fitzgerald, Associate Worker   Carl Newlander, Assistant

SUBSCRIPTION
$1.00 Yearly   60c Six Months   5c Copy
Bundle rates 2½c per copy in bundles of ten.

To Our Friends

I HAVE met many people in the East that read THE BLAST, and almost every one voiced admiration for the paper and the fight it is making. I take this opportunity to express the appreciation of THE BLAST staff to our friends and readers. I wish our friends could realize what a brave struggle my co-workers on the paper are making, especially now that they are deprived of my active efforts in behalf of THE BLAST.

I am giving my time and services exclusively to aid the four splendid men and the woman in the San Francisco jail. My services are given entirely free, and thus I find myself forced, so to speak, to rob Peter to pay Paul.

But THE BLAST is dear to me. I hope you, friends and readers, will make it your personal concern to keep THE BLAST blasting. We are short of ammunition. While the good Christians are manufacturing the machinery of slaughter in these Christmas days, will not you, heretics and infidels, show your un-Christian spirit by aiding the work that will ultimately bring peace on earth and well-being for everyone?

Place a half dozen of your friends on THE BLAST subscription list. You cannot give them a more sensible Christmas gift.

ALEXANDER BERKMAN

* * * *

Reflections

Baltimore Convention

ONE of the most encouraging events that happened at the Baltimore Convention of the American Federation of Labor was the appearance at the convention of the chiefs of the Railway Brotherhoods. Their speeches as well as the attitude of the delegates to the convention are a hopeful indication that the Brotherhoods, as well as the delegates of the A. F. of L., are beginning to realize that labor fights are not the exclusive interest of the particular industry involved. It is beginning to be understood even by the most conservative unionists that there is, properly speaking, no such thing as an individual fight on the part of one craft or industry under the present industrial situation. And especially in view of the tremendous combinations of capital, no single labor organization, however big, powerful or rich, can hope to win a big fight against combined capital. And Capital is always combined, in the face of threatening Labor. It is therefore very encouraging to note that the powerful Railroad Brotherhoods realize that they alone cannot wage a successful struggle against the railroads, back of whom is practically the whole financial strength of Wall street. As soon as this necessary understanding permeates the great body of the American Federation of Labor we shall have the beginning of a really vital and ultimately successful labor movement in this country.

Still Waiting

WE WERE waiting to see what Labor was going to get from Wilson. Four labor organizers—Frank Ladvinka, James Aates, Hiram Stephens, and Fanny Sullens—imprisoned for activity in the coal strike of 1914 in West Virginia, have been given their liberty by President Wilson.

After a Nation of a hundred million inhabitants has groaned and bustled about to elect a man president, it is probably not too mean to say that bigger results than the release of four prisoners ought to be expected by the element that elected their man.

So, we call attention to the fact that in nearly every jail in America, from coast to coast, there are rotting today labor men. They are prisoners of war—the Labor war, and if this Wilson election is a Labor victory, let's have the immediate release of all the Labor prisoners of war.

There's Carlo Tresca, with his comrades in the Steel Trust's dungeon in Minnesota; there are the McNamara brothers in the Otis Bastille; there are Schmidt and Caplan facing the same fate; there are the hundred or so jailed in the prison of the Lumber Trust, at Everett, Washington; here in San Francisco are the five enemies of the United Railroads in the shadow of the gallows for a crime of which they are ignorant—to say nothing of the thousands throughout the land who are just as important, though unknown.

When these thousands march out to their freedom, then we will say that Mr. President Wilson has made a small start toward an appearance of being "Labor's President."

But where is Labor's dignity? Are you going to be satisfied with four men out of jail and a rickety eight-hour law?

WHERE is the Socialist vote?
The Socialist vote this year is of such quantity that it has been little talked of in the Socialist press. The choice of the turtle-blooded Benson, in place of the "usual" candidate, the fiery, lovable 'Gene Debs, is not enough to account for it.

We know that a great spiritual force tries to express itself in the Socialist party, and we respect that spiritual force and will not taunt it in its hour of depression. But we believe that spiritual force to be misguided, and as friends with somewhat similar aims to those of the real dreamers of dreams in the Socialist party, we try to point out bluntly the naked truth of that error.

The Socialist Party makes one tremendous fundamental mistake; **It believes in indirection.**

It sees the wealth of Nature and Labor on one side, and a musty governmental hall on the other, and it thinks that the way to appease its hunger is to go toward—the governmental hall!

Socialists, you should let this thought go through your mind: **Possibly, after all, the trades unionists were right in expecting as much from a democratic representative as from a Socialist representative.**

We doubt if one iota more would have been gotten from the middle-class-minded Benson as president, than from Wilson.

"But it's not individuals—"

Yes, it is. The individuals whom the French Socialists called their "representatives," remained individuals, and shot the Socialists in strikes. And our own dear Meyer London has already bowed the knee in the American congress.

A Democratic politician is as good as a Socialist politician, possibly better, for he can be elected.

Workers, you are governed in the shop, not in the statehouse. **Free yourselves in the shop.**

Art Criticism

WE learn from the columns of the San Francisco *Chronicle* that a certain painting was carefully studied and decided to be unworthy of exhibition, by—ah—*two detectives!* This was printed as a sober news item.

As long as such imbecility, assininity—holy smoke!—what can we say?—as long as such things can be done, and as long as a little ninny of a reporter will write of such a thing as though it were the most natural affair in the world—there is no such thing as art in the land. Are there some persons who wonder why poor, foolish America has no art?

When the morbid-souled Puritans landed on Plymouth Rock, it was a leper colony—so far as concerned Art, or Morals, or Happiness. That leprosy traveled as upon the wind, blighting all it touched, till the great artistic impulse inherent in this land of romance died.

The microbe of Puritanism goes further, it is true, than America; it was already showing in France before the war (and French art had decayed accordingly); it had slightly touched Germany; and, as for England, well—that's where it came from in the first place. But the pity of it is most visible in this America, whose giant miles deserve a giant art.

The slimy, killjoy serpent of Puritanism lies in monster coils over this land, poisoning the air, poisoning play, deadening imagination.

When a woman, "past the age or condition where she can attract love or inspire joy," wishes to amuse her wealthy self, or when a political hypocrite wishes to prove his virtue—he or she resorts to Puritanism. A recent example is found in the case of a bourgeois woman, who, feeling the freedom of the suffrage air and wanting to rid herself of energy that should have been expended in dishwashing or plowing, started a movement to censor moving picture shows.

And a stupid ox of a policeman is placed upon the throne—to be king of Art! Thus America's art becomes an insipid thing—silly piffle suited to the brain of—*a policeman!*

R. M.

NATION-WIDE CONSPIRACY
AGAINST MRS. EDEAU'S CHICKENS

President of American Federation of Labor and Canadian Labor Leaders Probably Involved in Desperate Plot Against Respectable Oakland Fowls — Detective Martin Swanson Going Over to Look for Fingerprints on Chickens' Legs.

SAN FRANCISCO, December 15th.—A stupendous upheaval was caused in District Attorney Chas. M. Fickert's office when it was announced that molders' clay, Epsom salts, or some other high explosive of the type found in Ed Nolan's cellar and Tom Mooney's vest pocket, had been fed to the innocent fowls of Mrs. Sadie Edeau, one of the witnesses against Tom Mooney.

Mrs. Edeau was busy plotting out a modest $17,000 poultry yard, to be paid for when the blood-money for hanging Tom and Rena Mooney was available. The domestic plans were rudely disturbed by a wild anarchist plot, carefully arranged with the cunning known only to the superior brains of evil persons, to give the pip or death to Mrs. Edeau's beloved chickens.

Detective Hand, known throughout the Pacific Coast for his handsome face and gallant bearing, now has the position of guarding the lives and honor of Mrs. Edeau's hens. The responsibility doubtless weighs heavily upon his young shoulders, but no one who has ever seen him try to bully a witness in the courthouse corridor will doubt that every feather on the hens' heads will be safe in his care.

The peculiar perversity of desperate Mooney in blowing up Liberty bells and Plymouth Rock hens will yet be curbed, even if the citizens of the Barbary Coast have to form a permanent Witnesses' Association to that end.

Frame-Up System

A SPLENDID booklet, entitled "THE FRAME-UP SYSTEM; Story of the San Francisco Bomb," by Robert Minor, has been published by the International Workers' Defense League. It is one of the most remarkable exposures ever condensed into sixteen pages—the story of the dark intrigue by which the United Railroads intends to hang its Labor enemies. A story of gunmen, the scum of the legal profession, private corporation detectives—all working by the falsification of photographs, terrorizing of witnesses and hiring of petty criminals—to do the will of their corporation masters.

This is not merely an exposé of the Mooney-Billings-Nolan-Weinberg case. It is an exposé of a National institution, truly called "THE FRAME-UP SYSTEM." There exists in these United States an organized method of sending men to prison or the gallows for crimes of which they know nothing. This system is as dangerous and unscrupulous as any Blackhand Society or Mafia, and by it any man may be railroaded to his doom if he has enemies powerful enough to set its sinister machinery to work. It is right that all members of Unions should know of this in all its details.

The pamphlets are sold for ten cents a copy (bundles of 20 for $1.00), and are worth many times the amount. They are handsomely illustrated by photographs that prove conclusively that the labor defendants had nothing to do with the preparedness parade explosion. These photos make it not even a question of opinion, but a certainty that the men are innocent.

One of the photographs was so important that the District Attorney had to suppress it and turn over to the defense, on court order, a falsified copy, in order to convict Billings.

You'd better get the booklet; there's nothing like it for intense interest.

Address the International Workers' Defense League, 210 Russ Building, San Francisco, or THE BLAST office.

The Voice of Labor
(Correspondence from New York)

THE great Carnegie Hall meeting, on December 2d, held under the auspices of the United Hebrew Trades in behalf of our five arrested San Francisco friends, was a most imposing occasion. The beautiful hall was profusely decorated with the flags and banners of the numerous labor organizations participating and an atmosphere of responsive solidarity pervaded the great gathering. The speeches delivered by Max Eastman, Chairman of the meeting; Patrick Quinlan, but several days previously released from the Trenton penitentiary; Max Pine, Secretary of the United Hebrew Trades; Alexander Berkman, Arturo Giovannitti, and Emma Goldman, clearly set forth the conspiracy of the Chamber of Commerce of San Francisco to railroad to the gallows four men and the wife of one of them, who had given the best years of their lives to the cause of labor. For the first time since the arrest of our San Francisco friends, were the wider circles of labor in New York made familiar with the great struggle now being waged in San Francisco. The publicity thus gained is but the first step toward developing the nation-wide campaign in behalf of our labor prisoners initiated by the United Hebrew Trades.

Several telegrams reached the Carnegie Hall meeting, among them words of greeting and cheer from the Defense League, and individuals in Springfield, Mass., Kansas City, Topeka and other places. For lack of space we can produce but one:

Kansas City, Mo., Dec. 2, 1916.

It is with most profound regret that I am compelled to advise you that I can not be present at the meeting tonight. A rigorous investigation of the so-called San Francisco Bomb cases makes it apparent that unless the conscience of the nation is aroused another outrage is to be committed in the name of the law. The exploiters of Labor on the Pacific Coast, taking advantage of the abominable nature of the crime committed, have seized upon five of Labor's best and purest for sacrifice. The fact that Tom and Rena Mooney, Billings, Weinberg and Nolan are absolutely innocent may furnish them no protection. A vicious and obsolete jury system; a corrupt press, and millions of dollars in the hands of conscienceless men are the agencies aiming at their destruction; the labor movement of America which swung the Colorado prison doors outward for John Lawson a few months ago with a united and enthusiastic spirit can prevent this tragedy. I am indulging the hope that your meeting will be a tremendous success and that your action, financial and otherwise, will inspire hope in the hearts and courage in the souls of your imprisoned sister and brothers.

FRANK P. WALSH.

Not only morally, but financially as well, the Carnegie Hall gathering proved a most successful affairs. The great expense of the meeting (the rent alone amounting to $400.00) was more than covered by the sale of tickets. The collection totaled $500.00, which sum was immediately wired to San Francisco, together with telegraphic greeting of the meeting to the prisoners. A special wire was sent by the women of the gathering to Mrs. Rena Mooney.

And now for a systematic campaign of nation-wide proportions. The United Hebrew Trades has called a conference of all its allied labor bodies, Workmen's Circle branches, Jewish national bodies and progressive groups and organizations. It is urged that similar action be taken in other places, to multiply the sources of moral and financial support, and to swell and crystallize the voice of active protest throughout the country so effectively as to throw wide open the prison gates holding the brave soldiers of Labor's war.

⊻ ⊻ ⊻

WHOEVER produces anything by weary labor, does not need a revelation from heaven to teach him that he has a right to the thing produced.

—*Robert G. Ingersoll*

The Full Story of the Battle of Everett
Charles Ashleigh

THE lumber interests were afraid of the propaganda of the I. W. W. in Everett, Washington. There was a shingle-weavers' strike going on and the I. W. W. meetings served to stiffen the strikers' resistance. Also the meetings were creating a spirit of discontent among the other slaves of the Lumber Emperors; and this might mean less profit for these good gentlemen. Therefore, the speaking must be stopped.

Thereupon followed a series of arrests, beatings and deportations. The "respectable and prosperous" members of the Commercial Club organized a Vigilance Committee, disguised with handkerchiefs about their faces and armed with guns and saps.

James Rowan was arrested on the streets of Everett while reading from the box a portion of the Report of the Federal Commission on Industrial Relations. "You can't pull that sort of stuff here in Everett," remarked the sapient representative of the peace. Messrs. Frank P. Walsh and Basil Manly ought therefore to be arrested on a charge of writing pernicious and seditious matter, and the Federal Government prosecuted for the circulation thereof, according to this worthy's judgment!

Rowan was driven out along the county road and then released. As he was walking on, he was entrapped by a party of Vigilantes who had been waiting in ambush. His clothes were removed and he was then severely beaten until his back was a mass of welts, wounds and bruises. This, in the holy name of Law!

Fellow Workers Feinberg and Roberts were consigned, on another occasion, to the tender mercies of these law-loving thugs and were so badly beaten that they became unconscious.

On Monday, October 30th, forty-one men went to Everett from Seattle to hold a meeting. They were met on their arrival at the dock by a number of gunmen with automobiles and were driven out to the woods on the outskirts of town. There, they were met by a further contingent of the upholders of our country's integrity. The men were forced to run the gauntlet, under a shower of blows and amidst a hail of choice profanity. Several were knocked unconscious. Some assert that their money was taken from them by these "legal" gentlemen who, in the bosoms of their families or in their places of worship, are doubtless pillars of all the virtues. Some wounded men were dragged forcibly across the cattle-guards of the car track, so that the guards were found to be clotted with blood the next day. Visitors to the scene of this valiant exhibition of honorable citizenship described afterwards the tracks in the sand where the stupefied men had dragged themselves along, on their hands and knees, to a place of shelter. Also torn clothing and bloodstained hats were found.

The more liberal of Everett's citizens were highly indignant at this brutality and manifested great sympathy with the cause of Free Speech. Therefore, it was decided to try to hold yet one more meeting, this time in broad daylight and on a Sunday, when it was thought the publicity of the affair would prevent a repetition of the previous outrages.

But the rule of the thugs was stronger than had been reckoned. The trap was set for the slaughter of these brave workingmen. The gunmen were strategically placed in commanding positions on the docks. Barricades were erected so that the pillars of society might, in comfort and safety, enjoy the Lord's Day by sniping workingmen.

When the "Verona" landed with 250 workingmen on board, she was met by the Sheriff with his posse ranged behind him. In adjacent warehouses, and on another pier and a tug on the other side of the boat, were more civic enthusiasts well supplied with high-power rifles.

Before a man had a chance to land, the fusillade started. The volley from the dock swept the unprotected decks. Men began to drop, dead and wounded. It is an open question whether there was any return fire from the boat. The other posse, on the tug and the other pier were facing their accomplices on the further dock, with only the low-lying boat between. The fire swept the boat and also may have done destruction among their own men; they were in a good position to slaughter their own friends as well as the hapless workers on the steamer. Even Prosecuting Attorney Helsell is reported to have said that he estimated the number of guns among the steamer's passengers as from 18 to 25. About twenty revolvers against a small army with high-power rifles!

Eyewitnesses assert that several men toppled over the low rail of the boat. Their bodies will now have been washed out into the Sound so that the full tale of the destruction wrought by the murderers of Everett will never be told. Five workingmen were killed in this massacre and thirty-one wounded. Of the deputies, two died and a dozen were hurt. The steamer put about and returned to Seattle. On the way she passed the "Calista" with thirty-five free speech fighters aboard. The captain of the "Verona" hailed the "Calista" and told her to return to Seattle. This she did.

On returning to Seattle the men aboard the two boats were arrested. For several days the three hundred men were kept in jail while a weeding-out process went on. The prosecution gave out that they were looking for "ringleaders." Therefore, the crime they were guilty of was not murder, but being active in the Labor Movement!

The selective process is now ended, with the result that there are now nearly a hundred men in jail in Everett, **charged with murder!** And the Lumber Trust intends to get them! The thirty-five men on the "Calista" are still in jail in Seattle and are to be charged with unlawful assembly. Three women who were suspected with being sympathetic with the Free Speech fight were taken from a jitney bus on their way from Everett to Seattle and arrested. Two are out on bonds and the third, Edith Fernette, is still in jail charged with assault and "intent" to commit all sorts of crimes. The prosecution has not spared itself any time or trouble in tacking fearsome charges on to anyone suspected of sympathy with the Labor Movement. Men have been picked up on the streets of Everett, because they had overalls on, and jailed. In jail they have been subjected to various forms of torture.

The tale of the crimes of Everett against organized labor would fill a volume. Johnson, an active member of the Longshoremen's Union, was held several weeks in jail there, incommunicado. He is reported to have been beaten daily with a rubber hose.

The men in jail in Everett have recently gone on a hunger strike owing to the inefficiency of the food. They are fed mush at 8 a. m. and beans, or shadow stew, at 4:30 p. m. This is all they get. Two of the men are now suffering the tortures of the Black Hole, according to the Everett *Tribune*, a capitalist daily.

And these men in jail, facing a murder charge because of their heroic fidelity to the cause of Labor, are awaiting a message from their class brothers on the outside. Our five murdered fellow workers have died in OUR cause—the cause of the workers. Shall these other men go to the living death of the penitentiary because of their loyalty? They are all active rebels, therefore the bosses want to see them behind bars. But we, the workers, want them with us. We need all the active class-conscious workers we can get. We are not going to let the masters shut up these men for years to break their spirits and ruin their bodies.

We can free these men if you will help! We need publicity and we need a good defense. This all costs money. The money can only come from one source: the working class. It is up to you!

All funds should be sent to Herbert Mahler, Secretary-Treasurer, Everett Prisoners' Defense Committee, Box 1878, Seattle, Wash.

WORKERS, REMEMBER EVERETT'S BLOODY SUNDAY!

(Protests do not help much, but at least they show the bosses that our men are not friendless. Send them to Governor Lister, Olympia, Wash., and to President Wilson.)

A Note From the Steel Trust's Prison

County Jail, Duluth, Minn., Dec. 7, 1916.

MY DEAR F—:
The rose enclosed in your letter brought to memory the wonderful time I had while in California. It helps much to receive a flower in this cold, black, iron cell. The autumn season is exceptionally beautiful here—no snow—and the sun shines brightly. But its rays never reach the bleak and dirty little corridors where, two by two, we prisoners go for a short walk. I am feeling fine. My only wish is to be free again to fight in the battle line for Labor. It is not the severity of the jail that has power over me; oh, no! It is this compulsory inaction—the power over which we hope to win. To win because freedom means more chance to fight. And if the verdict of "guilty" means the command for the masses to arise and deliver the attack, the final attack on the master class—then let the verdict come. Oh, all of you, who have the privilege of being at liberty, do not rest. Fight, fight, fight!

I am glad for the publicity matter you sent me regarding the San Francisco cases. It makes the blood boil in my veins and I am thinking of those brave, courageous boys all the time.

Our case goes to trial on the 18th inst. I am more of a spectator and less of an actor in this judicial comedy.

Love to you and all our friends.   CARLO TRESCA

Wilson's Victory and Labor's Lesson
Harry Kelly

AS a choice between two groups of politicians, I confess a feeling of satisfaction when the most reactionary one is defeated. Had it been possible for both to lose that would have been a still greater joy, but as that was too much to ask, we are trying to extract as much satisfaction out of the election as possible.

It is my belief that Wilson is more sincerely liberal in his views on social subjects than Hughes, but it requires an optimism I do not possess to call his election a victory for liberalism.

But as the dust of the campaign settles, we trust it will not blind the eyes of the working men and women to certain fundamental facts. Under the administration of the liberal and scholarly Wilson we have had Ludlow, Mesaba, San Francisco, Bayonne and a score of other places, and now Everett, Washington. While we do not pretend that he is responsible for them, we do not intend that they shall be forgotten when others enumerate the advantages of his tenure of office.

Paper after paper has been suppressed by the post-office, refusing them transmission through the mails, until free press has become a myth and a joke, yet we have not heard that President Wilson has objected or in any way tried to curtail the ever growing perniciousness of his Postmaster General and his subordinates in these matters.

Much credit has been given President Wilson for the eight-hour law recently passed by Congress and the Senate when the Railway Brotherhoods held them by the throat, and also for his declaration that the moral sense of society was in favor of an eight-hour day. To talk about the moral sense of society expressing itself in favor of an eight-hour day is pure balderdash. That immense section of our population engaged in agricultural pursuits is not interested in an eight-hour day, and it is also questionable whether the few who may have an opinion on it, are even in favor of it. The majority of our working class are still scabs at heart

and while willing to profit by an eight-hour day are not prepared to work for it and have little or no ethical feeling about it. Wilson never discovered this moral sense of society until the railway workers were powerful enough to dislocate a large part of the railway system of the country, and it is giving credit where none is due to ascribe sympathy for organized labor because of this law. The law was put on the statute books by the organized power of the Railway Brotherhoods and no one else, and its benefits—if any—will come through **their power to enforce its provision.**

This victory of the railway workers is of far greater importance to labor than any presidential election in this country since the foundation of the republic. Labor will get under the coming administration exactly what it got under Wilson, Taft, Roosevelt, McKinley, Cleveland, or any other predecessors. Labor had its Lawrence and Paterson under Taft; its Ludlow, Bayonne, and Everett under Wilson. Its papers were suppressed and its advocates shot, beaten and imprisoned under them all and the difference has been almost indistinguishable.

The one thing that will alleviate the condition of the workers and finally emancipate them from slavery is an awakened social consciousness, a spirit of solidarity and a belief in their own power to grapple with and finally subdue this "hideous monster with the bloody lips," as Galsworthy calls it. Economic emancipation will come when men desire better things and are willing to share them with others. If these desires are accompanied by a feeling that each individual can play a part in the struggle for emancipation, the labor movement will go forward by leaps and bounds. If men will only believe in themselves, we shall soon smile at the modesty of the railway men's demands in the year of our Lord, 1916. Meanwhile, don't depend upon Wilson's liberalism, but remember: **"He who would be free, himself must strike the blow."**

A Birth-Control Meditation
Sara Bard Field

EMMA GOLDMAN was given fifteen days and Ben Reitman sixty days, for trying to improve the race. I am not surprised. Socrates was given a cup of hemlock; Jesus a cross; Savonarola a burning stake; the Japanese Socialists and the late Irish rebels a bullet through the heart — each of whom was trying, also, to improve the race in his own way and according to his own idea.

There has never been one move on the part of the individual to make a radical improvement in the condition of man, that man, in the form of organized Society, has not promptly rejected and punished the originator of the idea. Of course, if a man confine his improvement of conditions to better sewerage, improved lighting, cancer cures and sanitary housing, he is allowed to go on his way in peace. He may even make a useful invention and possibly win honors, so long as his invention can be capitalized and swept into the money-making flood. These inventions, cures and methods are all things. Matter is easy to deal with.

But to invent a new idea, to propose a reformation in thinking, in social and economic relations—swing wide the prison doors, get the hangman's noose ready for the offender. For such ideas are thought. Mind is difficult to deal with.

It is only for the man who makes a better mouse trap that the world wears a beaten track to his door to do him honor. The man who invents a better thought may also have a beaten track worn to his door, but it will be worn by the feet of a mob who come to annihilate him.

* * *

Emma Goldman and Margaret Sanger are soon to be tried again for birth control propaganda. Their courage ought to be a challenge to all of us who believe in birth control. Feminism is merely a movement of women to gain full possession of their own souls and bodies. Birth control is a woman's declaration of right as to the use to which her body shall be put. There ought not to be a thinking woman in the land who would refuse aid to this birth-control movement.

An Invitation, Please!

NEARLY A YEAR! Who would have believed it possible?

The timid were quite sure such a thing could never be. Not on the Coast, anyhow. It had never been done before, so—why be a fool and attempt the impossible.

True, the difficulties were great, and there has been no lack of trouble and worry. Chicken-hearted printers, fearful of what their respectable customers would say; sly underhand wire-pulling by grafters, high and low; bitter opposition by Mother Grundies in silk skirts and overalls; stupid censorship and arbitrary deprivation of second class rights; police-terrorized newsdealers, open persecution and hidden malice—but notwithstanding, THE BLAST will soon celebrate its first birthday.

If the youngster hasn't visited you quite regularly—well, he will acquire steadier habits as he grows in age, though—I hope—not in "discretion." But anyhow, he is anxious for your invitation for 1917. He hopes to come to your home next year. He'll do so joyfully, eagerly. He is awaiting your invitation, at $1.00 per.

THE BLASTERS

▨ ▨ ▨

Young Folks

DEAR UNCLE ALECK:

What has become of the "Young Folks"? I wanted to ask some questions but I thought I could not unless my name was Tom, but I guess Tom died of being too bright. Hoping you can answer my question, your loving little friend,

LEEDIA

(Dear Leedia: Ask your questions. "Uncle Aleck" is in New York, but is never too busy to answer you.—M. E. F.)

A Jack London Memorial Meeting

will be held at
Scottish Rite Auditorium
Wednesday Evening, Dec. 20th

Speakers
Frank Stone Hamilton
George Sterling, California Poet
Upton Sinclair, Novelist

The object of the meeting is the establishment of a Jack London Institute, which will include a Modern School for children, a Radical Library and classes in the Sciences for workers. All those interested in this plan, please communicate with L. S. Carasso, 52 Page street, San Francisco, Secretary of the Jack London Memorial Association.

FIRST AMERICAN EDITION
God and the State

A brilliant parallel of the relation between the deity of the State and the God idea, by

MICHAEL BAKUNIN

"The idea of God implies the abdication of human reason * * * and necessarily ends in the enslavement of mankind, in theory and practice."

96 PAGES, WITH PORTRAIT AND A PREFACE

By

ELISÉE RECLUS

Paper Cover, 50c

Vol. I   SAN FRANCISCO, JANUARY 1, 1917.   No. 24

INTOLERANCE

Social Revolution

DURING the recent raid on THE BLAST office, Assistant District Attorney Cunha and his detectives asked questions on the teachings of Anarchism. One of them said sneeringly: "When do you expect this Social Revolution? When is it coming?"

We reprint excerpts from an article written by Alexander Berkman about two years ago for *Mother Earth*. It may be possible to enlighten even the San Francisco District Attorney and his assistants. The article is as follows:

I SUPPOSE that in the life of every revolutionist there is a period—as there was in my life—when the words "Social Revolution" charmed forth the vision of a great upheaval, beginning perhaps in some little incident of rebellion, unexpected and sudden, and as suddenly sweeping the country—aye, the whole world—with the fire of a tremendous revolutionary uprising destined to end, after a short period of transition, in the triumph of Communist Anarchism.

But Time tempers the impatience of Youth with the clarified perception of experience and understanding. Slowly, but imperatively, life forces us to learn to conceive of the Social Revolution as something less cataclysmic and mechanical, something more definite and humanly real.

Not over night, nor from over the mountains, Messiah-like, comes revolution, much less the Social Revolution. If the latter means a complete and lasting social change, a fundamental reorganization of life based on the revaluation of popular ideas and conceptions, then it necessitates the gradual—primarily individual—substitution of new values for old ones. Human institutions are founded upon generally accepted, and therefore dominant, ideas. To uproot the former it is necessary to revolutionize the concepts underlying them. That is the most vital work within the daily evolutionary process of society. Its accelerated pulse-beats, called revolutions, are merely the mileposts indicating the distance covered; they measure individual growth within social progress; they materialize the conscious striving toward enlarged individual self-ownership, increased economic opportunity, and greater social liberty.

Many and various are the streams that pour into life's ocean, constantly agitating the apparently even flow of its waters. But never can this or that particular storm of itself force life into new channels. Rather, I take it, do the various disturbing elements—however different in tendency or often even antagonistic in purpose—conspire to agitate the lazy currents of human thought, awakening discontent and discussion, breaking down old traditions and dead men's barriers, and ultimately crystallizing into broader conceptions and higher aspirations, interpreted into action.

If the above be true, how vital then and significant is the propaganda of Anarchism, which seeks no illusory temporary advantage or the fickle acclaim of the unawakened. Rather does it labor to vitalize the self-consciousness of the social units and groups, to revolutionize understanding and stimulate emotion, to inspire the daring that translates ideals into reality and thus serves to undermine the accepted, the static and ossified. To rouse humanity to continuously greater self-consciousness—the first step toward self-ownership and assertion—is the purpose of Anarchist propaganda.

What it is accomplishing can be doubted only by the wilfully blind. In every phase of human activity the Anarchic spirit, the conscious breaking of old fetters and constant striving for greater liberty, is manifesting itself in no uncertain manner. In art and science, in literature and the drama, in education and the rearing of children, in the family and the attitude of woman—everywhere there is going on a progressive breaking of ikons a bold and determined seeking of new paths. Post-impressionism in art and literature, futurism in painting and philosophy, humanism in science, the rebellion of woman, the increasing menace of the disinherited, awakening to the dignity of man and the power of labor—what are all these but manifestations of the Anarchist spirit, the creation of new human and social values?

* * *

Here and there, it is true, the breath of reaction casts poisonous blackness athwart the path of light. It blinds the vision of man, and tortures him with the madness of the past. He loses his way, and gropes in the darkness; he mistakes friend for foe, and drenches the earth with the blood of his brothers. And all seems dark, and men lose hope.

Carnage walks the earth. The stench fills the air; it grows overpowering. It disgusts and revolts. . . . The mind staggers at the ghastly sight; hearts pant for breath and air, and then—the black clouds break, strong rays pierce the dark, and the cry of sobered hearts and minds beats back the foul madness and stamps the bloody fetich into the graveyard of the past.

Out of its ashes rise a clearer perception and a strengthened will—the will to be, to grow, to assert. The old lies dead, destroyed. No power can wake it into life again. The debris is cleared away, and the newer vision turns from the blackened old paths and casts about for a broader, freer road. The dynamic genius of liberty accelerates the pulse of humanity and vitalizes its firmer step.

ANARCHISM—The philosophy of a new social order based on liberty unrestricted by man made law; the theory that all forms of government rest on violence, and are therefore wrong and harmful, as well as unnecessary.

ANARCHY—Absence of government; disbelief in, and disregard of, invasion and authority based on coercion and force; a condition of society regulated by voluntary agreement instead of government.

DIRECT ACTION—Conscious individual or collective effort to protest against, or remedy, social conditions through the systematic assertion of the economic power of the workers.

ANARCHIST COMMUNISM—Voluntary economic co-operation of all towards the needs of each. A social arrangement based on the principle: To each according to his needs; from each according to his ability.

The Daylight Burglary

MARTIN SWANSON, private detective for the United Railroads and the Pacific Gas & Electric Company, with Assistant District Attorney Ed. Cunha and Detectives Draper Hand and Mike Burke, raided our office just as we were about to go to the printer with this issue.

The corporation detective rang the door-bell at about 10 o'clock Saturday morning, quickly stepped in and took charge. Cunha assisted Swanson in prying into bureau drawers and reading personal correspondence.

Cunha asked to see our card index file of subscribers. In clearing a place for him at my work table, I picked up a few letters, some of that morning's mail. Cunha asked: "What's that?" I told him they were personal letters and they did not concern the District Attorney's office. He said to his detectives: "Get them!" Immediately Hand and Burke grabbed my hands and the "desperate struggle" took place, as we see by the morning's papers. None of the four well-armed men was hurt. But they took my letters.

Three hours rummaging through the house, prying open bureau drawers, reading personal letters and taking mailing lists, manuscripts and cartoons, resulted in nothing more serious than delaying this issue of the paper.

The real reason of the raid was to introduce some shivery music into the "anarchist" melodrama that District Attorney Fickert is presenting to the public in the newspapers and staging in Judge Griffin's court.

While watching the activities of my visitors, I couldn't help a feeling of pity creeping into my heart. I said to Cunha: "How can a man like you engage in such dirty work? As a boy or young man, you must have had a spark of decency in you." To his credit, he blushed. Then stammered: "If I don't do it, someone else will. Life is short; it doesn't matter much after all." Yes," I said, "life IS short, but that's all the more reason why one should be on the side of right and decency."

Just think of Phadraig Pearse, Jim Connelly, Tom Clarke and the other gallant Irish rebels who made the world ring with their brave fight for liberty in the streets of Dublin, last Easter week! Then stand up the Mike Burkes, the Brennans and the Cunhas for comparison. What a pitiful spectacle! "Life is short, and if I don't do it, someone else will."

Dear BLAST, you have had a stormy year—but it has been a glorious one! You must live to carry on the fight for Truth.

M. Eleanor Fitzgerald.

THE BLAST needs funds if it is to have a second birthday. We haven't money enough to pay this week's printing bill. Won't you renew your subscription at once?

Let us hear from all lovers of liberty and justice.

Among the annoyances occasioned by the "daylight burglary" on our office, is the necessity to omit:

An article on the affair of Everett, Washington. (They need and deserve your help.)

An article on the release of Carlo Tresca, Sam Scarlett, Joe Schmidt and others, in the labor struggle in Minnesota. (A compromise was made in which the only concession by Labor was a one-year sentence for each of the three strikers. The "Haymarket" precedent was abandoned.)

The story of the slugging by the police of an investigator for the San Francisco Labor defendants, by two uniformed policemen in the city prison. This was done in vengeance for his having turned up the police-kidnaping of a witness.

THE BLAST

Revolutionary Labor Paper
Published every 1st and 15th of the month
569 Dolores St., San Francisco, Cal.
Mail Address, Box 661   Phone, Park 499
Alexander Berkman, Editor and Publisher
M. E. Fitzgerald, Associate Worker   Carl Newlander, Assistant
SUBSCRIPTION
$1.00 Yearly   60c Six Months   5c Copy
Bundle rates 2½c per copy in bundles of ten.

Comments

Trial of Tom Mooney

THE little courtroom crowded with prospective jurymen, the district attorney's staff bustling about, giving orders with woeful lack of grammar, to bull-necked plainclothes men, the crowd of sympathizers waiting outside, shoved back and forth by policemen, one little bright oasis of intelligence in the room—in the prisoners' dock, where Tom Mooney, Ed Nolan, Warren Billings, Israel Weinberg and Rena Mooney sit.

The atmosphere is much improved by the arrival of the defense counsel. The judge enters. His rather intellectual face and good English also improve the feeling of the room. The trial has started.

"Have you read any anarchistic or socialistic papers?" is almost the first question put to a proposed juror. With that, it started. The conventional question became: Are you an anarchist or socialist, or have you any sympathy for them?

The purpose of the silly raids on the office of THE BLAST became apparent. Mooney was to be, in spite of himself, made an anarchist. Once an anarchist, he was to be flaunted in the faces of the jury as a mysterious member of some unspeakable, unknown cult whose members ought to hang, one and all, without investigation. The break-down of the original case against Mooney, by the discovery of the astonishing frauds in the way of falsifying photographs, bull-dozing witnesses and hiring criminals, petty and grand, to supply lacking testimony, had left but one resort open to the prosecution—to hiss dread, mysterious words, such as "An-n-n-a-a-a-a-a-chist" at the jury, wave the flag and demand a lynching.

But the defense counsel happens not to be made up of cowards. After a dramatic but not grammatical question thundered by the little assistant prosecutor, Defense Attorney W. Bourke Cockran quietly asked the juryman, "What is the meaning of the term 'anarchist'?"

The courtroom was suddenly changed. Prosecutors looked about in surprise. What "new dope" was this—asking the meaning of a word? Police officials shifted in their seats impatiently and frowned. The spectators and jurymen sat up with interest. To actually care what a word means! The idea!

But, under the hands of Cockran and McNutt, the boat of reason kept its course. The big voice of Cockran halted every ambiguous term. To get at the true meaning of every mysterious term employed became the attitude of all men except the district attorney's staff, who floundered beyond their depth, but bent on confusing the issue. For poor little Cunha, assistant prosecutor, it was as though the miracle of Babel had changed the language of the court to an unknown tongue. Fortunately the judge seems to be well enough read to know what is being talked about.

The trial has at this writing advanced no further than the tentative selection of a half dozen jurors.

Whether Mooney will win or lose—we don't know. That he will be proven innocent is certain. If, after being proven innocent, they slaughter him anyway, it will be the coldest blooded, most heartless murder ever perpetrated by the Frame-Up System.

It is almost maddening to see a monster machine, made up of hundreds of men, some of them thoughtlessly, others deliberately trying to murder five human beings with—perjury!

Dave Caplan

AFTER a mock trial in a court determined in advance to convict him, regardless of any foolish notions of "justice," Dave Caplan goes to prison for ten years. Caplan is an idealist, so, apparently, prison is where he belongs. It has long been an axiom that the only men or women of soul and heart in Russia were to be found in prisons. Very soon that will be the case in America. While the average man is blinded with the pretty phrases on "liberty" that decorate Fourth of July orations, quickly the industrial machine of our society shapes itself to maturity, displacing what liberties and ideals ever existed in America.

There is nothing wrong with the imprisoning or hanging of idealists, the crushing of Liberty, the stifling of thought; that is just as it should be—in a bourgeois society. Every sturdy heart should be broken, every liberty crushed in chains, every freedom of expression punished with black death—Nature made ugly—to fit the scheme of our social system—if you believe in that system.

The "Munitions Church"

AT the time of the American Civil War, several churches were split by the dividing line of "Dixie" into two hostile camps, one pro-slavery and one anti-slavery. The owners of the churches in the North were manufacturers who disliked the competition of slave labor and therefore listened to the abolition idealists. The owners of the churches of the South were slave holders. Thus we saw established the Slave Church. "Moral principles" were decided by which way the money came from that supported the churches.

Certain American protestant churches of the "munitions belt" are organizing a league to oppose the making of peace—"for the present," they say.

The most prosperous men in a district always control the churches in that district. The greatest prosperity of the Eastern manufacturing districts, where the anti-peace churchmen operate, comes from selling hell-machines to Europe.

So of course there is a great moral issue involved that may soon cause splits in several Protestant churches. We may expect the early establishment of the Munitions Church.

IT is interesting to note with what blithe ease our American philanthropists contribute millions, earned for them by the efforts of American workingmen, to some remote cause. Three million dollars raised in one night for the Jewish war sufferers with promises of millions more to come, and millions for desecrated Belgium! Starving Poland arouses their moneyed sympathy! Saccharine phrases drop with the gold into the coffers which when filled will be served with proper rites to bleeding peoples as unction for the wounds inflicted by their oppressors.

Pity is an expensive emotion. What are the millions contributed compared to the complacent bliss derived from a front-page account of these tearful sacrifices?

To attempt to interest our charitable Gods of Finance in a cause that is near to the hearts and minds of our own people would be as futile as it would be absurd. The only interest we can create for them is by startling their minds into a consciousness of the power and independence of our cause. They must be made to realize that if there is of necessity occasional submission to tyranny, there never can be subscription to it. We want none of their sympathy and less of their resources to help carry our burden. The glory of our fight and its grandeur lie in the fact that we wage it alone.   —S. C

A REQUEST

ANYONE having a copy of the first issue of THE BLAST is requested to mail it immediately to Alexander Berkman, 20 East 125th street, New York City.

The Offer of Peace

Robert Minor

THE rulers through whom the greatest harm is done to the world are probably those of Germany and Russia. But the champion ass of all royal houses of all the world usually sits upon the throne of England.

Sitting on a useless chair in a useless palace in London is a useless vagrant by the name of George Guelph, by title, King of England, Emperor of India. Nobody pays any attention to George; he is not consulted about anything of more importance than the cut of his waistcoat; yet it now devolves upon Mr. Guelph practically to voice the reply of half the world to the other half on the world's most important question—Peace. And King George's answer takes shape with many phrases such as "my armies," "my navy," and "my resolve" to fight on to victory, though he really never had an army, a navy, or a resolve, in his life. The words were probably dictated to him by the little Welsh lawyer, Lloyd George, and the poor "king" is not to be blamed for more than his willingness to hold the job of town crier for London financiers. The job is well paid. King George has to be an ass; he is not allowed any secondary function as is his cousin Wilhelm of Germany.

But when the foolish king of England gave his speech to parliament as the answer of England to the peace proposal, it was the voice of George's master, the British plunderbund,—the White Star Line, the Cunard Line and the great freight shipping companies of London, the aristocracy fat with the blood of India, and, head of all, the Bank of England. It was a voice which said in effect: "No, we will not allow the Hamburg-American Steamship Company to compete with our ships. We will not let German merchants carry their trade nearer to our exploited India. We insist that the common British man shall forever cripple this growing German manufacture, which threatens by competition to force a reorganization, on a more democratic basis, of the British social system."

But the speech comes from the king, for the sake of the impression that will be made on the biggest fools in the empire. Then another speech comes from Lloyd George, for the next biggest fools. It is full of hope-you-will-believe-me excuses for the blarneying of Tommy and the conscripted munition worker. Those who are neither the biggest fools nor the next biggest fools, can be shot, when they refuse to take the excuses and insist upon the acceptance of peace. They can be shot—**unless there are too many of them.**

The excuses given by English Commerce for refusing the offer of German Commerce to call the war off, are full of meaningless phrases, hitting at some mysterious "moral issue," which they are in duty bound to settle without thinking of self-interest. The "moral issue" of this war exists about as tangibly as the "moral issue" of the bloody wars of the Crusades—the issue of "finding the Holy Grail."

The cause of the war is but one—Commerce. The soldier and the sailor are precisely what the traveling salesman is, simply advance agents for merchants, except that they carry death instead of bargaining.

As for peace—the English, French and Russian captains of industry will settle that question on two points: First, whether the cost of continuation of fighting will not be too great to pay for getting rid of the German merchant marine and the German Turkish railway project; second, supposing it to be good policy to continue the war, whether it is safe to try to goad the common soldier on to more sacrifice with the shaky lies upon which they will have to depend since Germany has offered peace.

Just a little mutiny now, in the allied armies—just a little rebellion in the cities—and the Allies' answer to the peace proposal would be: "Yes."

The Passing of the "Tin Soldier"

Robert Minor (Former Corporal Company G, Texas Volunteer Guard)

Over a blistering streak of sandy dust—auto, driver, passengers and road itself seeming dizzy with the heat—we drove to Fort Bliss. The day before I had arrived in El Paso on the fast train from New York, to work as a correspondent in the war with Mexico, supposedly about to break.

As we approached a row of crazy-shaped hills whose crests seemed utterly "unreasonable," the cowpuncher-like chauffeur announced "This heah is Fo't Bliss."

"Bliss," indeed! Quickly traversing the artificial oasis of the officers' quarters, we came upon the camp of the National Guard. The first sight was a miserable boy, standing over a discarded axe, picking cactus thorns from his blistered fingers and sweating mud. Then a long row of piles of debris, miscellaneous second-hand merchandise which passed for "tents, uniforms, food and artillery," forlorn "kids" standing about wondering what to do with it all and funny looking officers wondering what to tell them to do with it. Further on was a row of shaky tents under which lay a surprising number of listless youths, overcome with the heat.

Approaching a friendly looking chap, I asked him, "Well, how's everything?" He looked at me a few minutes sadly before replying, "Oh, hell! I thought I was coming on a vacation."

It is no surprise to hear the semi-official announcement that the "National Guard is a failure"—**if you've ever been in it.** Men are supposed to enlist for the purpose of "serving their country." They don't. **Boys** enlist in the militia for the purpose **of playing.** It is true that they play most hideously, at times, shooting, killing their own flesh and blood in a strike. Most of them don't mean any harm; they have a phrase upon which to blame the blood they spill, such as "obeying officers" or "protecting property." But they are playing, whatever may be the consequences.

The complaint is made, by those who care, that there was hardly any increase in the number of enlistments when war threatened with Mexico. Of course not; the number of boys who want to play at toting a gun with a gang of other boys, with mechanical stride, swagger hats, the girls a-looking—that number does not increase much with a call from play to reality—to war.

Young men who really like to fight join the regular army.

In time of peace, they fight in saloons and alleys with each other and bartenders. In time of war they find their delight in killing with impunity. A little loafing about military camps in France and Italy as well as on the Mexican border has shown me that most men dislike killing, but that a few, everywhere, "like to fight." "Like to fight," means to enjoy taking a rifle and carefully shooting a bullet through the head of a fellow human being, or sticking a bayonet into his stomach, for that is exactly what fighting, in the military sense, is, and nothing else.

There are few who like to do this, human nature being too good for such work. Their number cannot be increased very easily—only by greater poverty with its abyss-created brutality, can the number of men who like to be soldiers be increased. If industrial conditions become worse, till the earning of an en-durable living in workshops or fields is too hard for the average youth, and he is driven in multitudes to a cynical parasitism—then there can be built a successful voluntary military force. Otherwise not.

In any case, the amateur volunteer—the militiaman—is not a soldier. I remember the blushes that came to us when a more sensible "kid" shouted at us, as the company swung by, "Tin soldiers!" Sub-consciously we all realized that we were only playing. The real "soldiers" of the company always drifted soon to the regular barracks.

Many thousands of boys went playing in the cactus thorns of Mexico. The whimper with which they return, teaches the masters of finance that, unless greater poverty comes soon to force men into barrack life, the common man must be conscripted to be a soldier.

The Destroyers of Idols

Elias Sang

A FEW short weeks ago the unskilled and migratory worker was an honest workingman—a farm hand, a timber jack, a construction worker; now winter is here and most of the pioneer work is halted, the crops are harvested, and he has drifted to the cities. From now on, as his stake dwindles away, he will be labeled "the unemployed," the vag, the bum, and you can hear the small townsman wail: "What you goin' to do? Women folks feed 'em. Can't shoot 'em. Law protects 'em. Hold him, sheriff, hold him!"

These men, a distinct product of the present, with all the cold materialism of the industrial regime which has grouped them, fear no God or man-made law. They respect no customs or moral codes. Their code is extra-legal, all their own. "Unemployment," the ever present horror of all stable groups, has no terrors for them; it is part of the game, for theirs is the Will to Live!

They love liberty and they exercise free speech; they fight for it; they are irrepressible. When in jail they proselyte and the majesty of the law is compelled to listen to "You'll Get Pie in the Sky When You Die," or the "Red Flag." Hardships of the job and on the road, a common misery, strengthen the tie that binds them, and strong, real friendships are formed which hold no sacrifice too great for the cause.

The "jungle" is their trysting place, the box-car their Pullman, when on the move. Through the constant change of jobs and the travel incident thereto, is imparted to them the last word in industrial development. They are ultra-modern—no old saws or moss-eaten catch words or theories of radical groups impress them.

The newspapers echoing their masters' cry, blazon forth: "I. W. W. Anarchists Capture Train" or "Many I. W. W.'s Killed in Attack on Everett, Free Speech the Issue." The press mirrors the thoughts and fears of those who cling to all things static, towards the disturber, the agitator, the propagandist, the direct actionist, for all these elements spell the terror of change.

This branch of labor, the migratory workers, has within it the materials of which revolutions are made. It has the double strength of active individual units co-ordinated with numbers or mass. It has the same strategic position in the labor field as raw materials, iron, coal, occupy in the industrial field of manufacture. The only organization able to get these men together and keep them together so far has been the Industrial Workers of the World. The 10th annual convention of that organization, just closed, was the most representative gathering of rank and file workers since the early days of the Knights of Labor. A decade of hard fought battles in the face of all social creeds of both capital and labor, entitles this organization to the respect of all real men.

Our Insane System

Charles Fourier.

THE present social order is a ridiculous mechanism, in which portions of the whole are in conflict and acting against the whole. We see each class in society desire, from interest, the misfortune of the other classes, placing in every way individual interest in opposition to public good. The lawyer wishes litigations and suits, particularly among the rich; the physician desires sickness. (The latter would be ruined if everybody died without disease, as would the former if all quarrels were settled by arbitration.) The soldier wants a war, which will carry off half his comrades and secure him promotion; the undertaker wants burials; monopolists and forestallers want famine, to double or treble the price of grain; the architect, the carpenter, the mason, want conflagrations, that will burn down a hundred houses to give activity to their branches of business.

Football Reasoning

David Leigh

THERE was once a little boy named Charley, a nice little boy, plump and round and full of spirit, just like all the other little boys that hobnobbed and went to school with Charley.

Charley grew up (or appeared to) and went to college, and learned all about football and kicked the insides out of any number of balls and at last found himself quite a figure, where kicks are reckoned as the high notch of attainment.

And about this time a city nearby was having quite a time trying to settle whether it was right for some people to be allowed to steal, under the guise of Public Benefit; and whether for the sake of the children that were growing up, it wouldn't be better to put an end to frock-coated theft and keep the public streets just as they were, for the benefit of the whole community.

And so they had an election—you know—the kind that all the people are supposed to take part in and don't—and after it was all over, a young man found himself elected; and his name, his first name, was Charley—the very same Charley who had kicked the ball of local fame right underneath where he was sitting.

And now Charley was big and still kicking, but no longer kicking balls. He was kicking, from the time he was selected to run for the office of Public Kicker, for a set of Little Men, who knew what it would mean to them to have a husky kicker on their side of the fence.

Into office Charley went, and he kicked with such vigor at all the indictments that were piled up against the Little Men who, with their money, had elected him, that like a rickety shelf of books, they all toppled down in one big heap; and, thereafter, the Little Men went out grinning to think what a fine kicker they had.

And nobody seemed to notice very much. It was all right. Who wants to fight all the time, anyway? And wasn't he a fine kicker, anyhow? What more could you ask?

And then, a good deal of time went by till one day the city in which Charley lived had a parade.

The parade was blown up. We don't know who did it. We only know who profited by it—the same Little Men who paid for Charley's election.

Many people were killed who had nothing to do with the parade.

An awful excitement then followed and some of the Little Men, whose money had helped to elect Charley, held a meeting and said they'd give money—the same kind of money that helped to elect Charley—to catch the fiendish persons who had done this horrible thing. And they did give money—not then, but they said they would—and just how much—oh, such a lot, thousands and thousands of dollars, enough to make a poor man get almost dizzy to think of such a staggering heap.

And then the hunt began to catch the brutal culprits—or maybe to avoid catching the brutal culprits. And everybody wondered how long it would take those who were hunting, because everybody felt it must be some Poor Person (or Persons) who had done this awful thing, and it doesn't usually take very long to catch them. Most any jail will show you that.

And after a few days, they did catch some poor people— four or five of them, whom the hunters said were bad men; and the woman with them—they said she was bad, too. And it looked as if they were bad for a minute, because the hunters said such awful things about these people, and you know how it is when you hear that everything about a man or a woman is bad; you almost begin to believe it.

It seems that these people they captured were what is called "labor" people—they all worked when they could get work— and some of them had been in trouble before, on suspicion of having done harm to property that didn't belong to them—some

property that belonged to the Little Men—the same Little Men whose money helped to elect Charley, and who were going to give more money—the same kind of money—to catch the cruel persons who had caused all this sorrow.

You see, there was quite a bitter feeling between these Little Men and the "labor" people, because so many of the "labor" people who worked all the time. didn't have anything at all, whereas the Little Men, who never did any real work, had so much they couldn't possibly use it; and some of the people that were captured had only a short time before that been trying to get more people to see what a one-sided way of living they stood for. Besides, the people who were arrested had friends, known as "anarchists," a set of people who didn't believe in stealing at all, and Charley, knowing how unpopular the "anarchists" were, and knowing that to even be identified with them was enough to convict anybody of anything, took this for his tack and set out to prove that the people his hunters had lassoed were in league with the "anarchists," and, therefore, fit only to be hanged with what he called "hemp"—meaning rope.

One of the Poor Persons caught was tried and convicted, though the evidence in his case showed that he had nothing whatever to do with the terrible affair.

Just before it came time to try the next one, Charley, who had once before gone to the house of the "anarchists" and carried away most of their letters and papers in the hope of getting something against them, sent his hunters out to try again and see if they couldn't get something that would prove that the Poor Persons he was holding were closely connected with the "anarchists."

And the hunters went and made what was called a "raid" and carried away everything they could unfasten with their hands, including a lot of pictures which showed why the Little Men are not loved by the "labor" people, mostly drawn by a young man who had been helping the Poor Persons to get free.

And then Charley, angry because he hadn't gotten anything, decided he'd kick for all he was worth in the public papers and see if that wouldn't help him to put the "hemp" around the necks of these Poor Persons who were about to be tried for their lives. You see, he thought a crowd in the city was just like a crowd in the football field, and he imagined they would cheer a kicker, no matter what he kicked or how he kicked it. That was Charley's mistake.

Like a gust of wind, he hurled the word "anarch," which he thought would sound worse than "anarchist" to those who read papers to see what other people think. He had the papers put it in great big type—that the "anarchs" were in sympathy with these Poor Persons he wanted to hang. He said he had letters to prove that the "anarchists" had raised money to try to help these Poor Persons to get off; not only that, but that a rich woman, a society woman, a woman belonging to the set of people in which his friends, the Little Men, traveled, had actually given of her wealth, her position, of her energy to help these dastardly Poor Persons. It was an arch kick he thought he was making and he never once realized that a great many people had already perceived that he didn't even have a ball in his hand.

Poor Charley! He shouldn't be blamed. What would you expect of a man who didn't know any more of life than to imagine that just because he kicked a great lot of accusations and insinuations and asseverations into the air about people who had the temerity to try to help Poor Persons—that that would prove the guilt of the Poor Persons and enable him to stretch his "hemp" around their necks, and so make permanent the fame which this celebrated kicker had once enjoyed.

That was the way the case stood when Charley came to try the second of the Poor Persons; and if you would be interested to hear what happened when Charley was asked to show the ball, I will tell you about it in the next issue.

Eight   THE BLAST

"THE PUBLIC"

There are few magazines or other periodicals that seem to be worth the paper on which they are printed. We are cursed with magazines, more magazines and then a few. To see a pile of them on the table, with the task ahead of looking through them, is tiring. To read the mouthings of a censored coward and wonder what the poor fellow would write if he dared, is a daily task of these times when "free press" is a joke.

But among a few exceptions is *The Public*. Its refreshing fairness lures us to its columns.

The Public has moved from Chicago to 122 East 37th street, New York. We hope this is a sign of increased strength. Hail to Honesty!

NEW PUBLICATIONS

As you know, the *Revolt* and the *Alarm* were suppressed by the federal authorities a few months ago. Here is our answer: *"The Social War"*—Organ of Revolutionary Outcasts—will make its appearance on the first of January. Hippolyte Havel will edit the new publication.

Subscription, fifty cents per year.
1605 Milwaukee Avenue, Chicago.

The Slate, a monthly magazine for teachers, promises to be free, frank and fearless—at whatever cost. We have not seen it as yet, but it has been announced to appear January 1st. Single copies, 15 cents; yearly subscription, $1.20. Address Jess Perlman, 4 Charles street, New York, N. Y. Success to your new venture, Jess.

ACCOUNT OF THE BAUERN BALL—
Given by S. F. International Committee, December 16, 1916:

Proceeds	$190.30
Expenses	153.40
Profit	$ 36.90

Divided equally between THE BLAST and Group Volonta.

Volume 2 Number 1

203|

The BLAST

Vol. II.   SAN FRANCISCO, JANUARY 15, 1917   No. 1

"But this I know, that every Law
  That men have made for Man,
      Since first Man took his brother's life,
    And the sad world began,
        But straws the wheat and saves the chaff
      With a most evil fan."

"Thou Shalt Kill," Says Cunha

Robert Minor

ASSISTANT DISTRICT ATTORNEY CUNHA addressed the jury in an opening statement of the case against Thomas J. Mooney. Cunha is an unimpressive man, small, pretty-faced and of childish style; his words faltered, became confused and had to be repeated time and again. But it was soon to be seen that he was attempting his best oratory, a harangue, a plea to twelve men to kill one man.

It was a plea for death, pure and simple, not a recital of fact, not a recital of anything near fact; nothing that he could prove, but a wild collection of all words and all loose statements that he could summon to his tongue's end to goad that jury on to a killing. It was a speech by a man who believes in killing, who wants death to be done; and so deep was his desire to goad the jury on to it, that *fact* took wing and flew from the room. Lies reigned supreme, for lies, not truth, goad men to kill; and crazy lies they were, almost unbelievably crazy. One would almost have to question his ears to credit that the statements made by Cunha were not a joke.

"Mooney was engaged in a plan, an uprising to create prejudice against the government. I am going to reveal to you his real inward purpose, his ulterior motive, not in good faith: his object was revolution. He published it in a paper. I am going to prove that Mooney did not believe in preparedness; I am going to show, over his own signature, that he said that preparedness should be thrown right back into the teeth of the preparedness advocates; that he said that preparedness would be death to revolution. I am going to prove that to you.

"Mooney was a member of a group of people who wanted to take direct possession of capital for the class that might be called 'those who work.' They were interested in a newspaper called THE BLAST, and this newspaper was published for the direct purpose of opposing American preparedness. I am going to show you that it was not merely incidental, that they deliberately started that paper to oppose preparedness and that they said that they would oppose preparedness, and they announced in that paper their purpose. I am going to prove to you, beyond a reasonable doubt, that their purpose was printed in that paper, and that it was to oppose preparedness, and they wanted to confiscate private property; and these people call themselves 'The Blasters.' When they started that newspaper, THE BLAST, they sent letters and announcements to radicals; they wanted to find the radical people in the community to send this paper to, and they made up their subscription lists of radical people in order to get radicals; and they believed in direct action, such as to burn up a million dollar wharf and assassinate the President. They advised violence to stop the parade, and they accused certain labor leaders. *The Labor Clarion* refused to exchange with them. We are going to prove that Billings carried a suitcase; that he carried a suitcase from 721 Market street to Steuart and Market streets, and Mooney met him down at Steuart and Market. Billings was one of those radicals that this gang of people got their paper to. We are going to prove by persons whose testimony can not be disputed, that Mooney met Billings at Steuart and Market streets.

"Mooney was in a conspiracy against labor unions, against the American Federation of Labor. His real inward purpose was to betray organized labor. Mooney hated the government and the labor unions and the church, that are helpful in keeping society organized as it is."

"Organized as it is"—the words carried me off to a revery. "Organized as it is"—"keeping society organized as it is." Why, little Cunha? Why? I thought of the streets outside of that courtroom, as those streets would be a few hours later—ragged, hopeless men, stinking saloons, right in front of that Hall of Justice the park that is called by its denizens "Prostitute Square," and within reach of little Cunha's voice, the Barbary Coast, little narrow streets, red-lighted doors, blazing forth the shame that is for sale—about all of which little Cunha knows and for which little Cunha is not to blame any more than you or I, except insofar as he strives to keep Society, the Big Barbary Coast, "organized as it is." Little Cunha and Big Fickert may soon start a "vice clean-up," goaded on as they are by a little preacher in this city. But that would still leave society "organized as it is"—the same poor women following as legitimate a trade as Cunha's (or rather as illegitimate), hard-driven, heart-broken women, baited, as throughout the centuries, by the little Cunhas (assumed to be without sin as they throw their stones). "Society" that robs and starves men into feeble attempts to live, called "crime," and then drags them into the courthouse facing "Prostitute Square," and that pays little Cunha to shout foolishly at them. "Organized as it is"—

But the prosecutor's voice rises for the flourish of his closing:

"Thomas J. Mooney, Alexander Berkman, E. B. Morton and Miss Fitzgerald, if you please, were connected with that conspiracy by their own writings in their own handwriting. And, gentlemen of the jury, when we prove all of this to you, we will ask you to return a verdict of murder in the first degree."

Possibly I do not do justice to Mr. Cunha's speech, but it is hard to remember words spoken without any particular sequence of thought. His sentences were unrelated, his statements wild invective rather than statements. When he finished I sat in astonishment—what was he going to introduce in the way of evidence? It was a relief to hear him admit that he relied upon such trash, but surely the man must not expect to hang a human being upon that jumble! I began to wonder what was going on inside of the small cranium of that small man; and memory took me back to Texas, to San Antonio, and I thought of one evening, in the very shadow of the old Alamo, I stood, at the age of twelve, talking to some other boys, when a shout broke the stillness of the night: "Nigger! Get a rope!" The five of us boys did not wait for more. "Nigger, nigger, nigger!" we yelled. "Get a rope! Get a rope!" We joined the stampede of rushing men and boys—big, burly, ox-faced men for all the world like Fickert, and stupid, irresponsible, pretty-faced boys for all the world like Cunha—running, panting, shouting, shrieking: "Get a rope! Nigger! Nigger!" Wildly the mob swirled down the plaza past the Alamo, trampling over grass and shrubbery, scaring horses, starting runaways, joined by ragamuffins, cowboys, merchants and children. The chase wound up at a saloon. A small dark figure ahead of us I saw duck through the door of "Jake's Place." The stampeding mob crashed through the door with such force that it could not stop itself before almost upsetting the bar. A whiskey bottle turned over and fell off with a crash. The bartender took it philosophically. "Nigger! Nigger! Get a rope!" Under such circumstances even whiskey was not precious.

"Nigger, nigger—get a rope!" But the "nigger" was gone. The mob had overlooked a side entrance out of which he had slipped. Everybody laughed. "He done got away," said a florid-faced gentleman. "Where'd he go?" "Have a drink." "Hell, we missed him." "Have a drink."

A few minutes of quiet, and then somebody asked: "What's he done?" "I don't know," said the florid-faced gentleman, "somethin'."

"What did the nigger do? Do you know?" "Say, Joe, what did the nigger do?" "I don't know. Harry said he done something." "Where's Harry?"

Harry was brought in. "What did the coon do?" "Who, the nigger? Oh, he done hit a fellow. Dep'ty sheriff asked him what he was doin', and he got flip, and the dep'ty grabbed him and the coon hit the dep'ty and hiked."

"Hell, he clean got away. He looked like one of them fresh niggers from the No'th."

But I was brought to with a start—the first witness was to be called; Cunha was speaking; his little eyes turned upon me whom he had accused of being in a plot here in California to kill the governor at a time when I had never even been in the State in my life. Cunha has never seen fit to apologize since then. Poor little Cunha!

His eyes were not the eyes of viciousness, precisely; something hopeless in them, something hopelessly shallow. Little, stupid eyes, that seemed to grope for some vague moral principle that he realized he could not easily understand. He looked so much like one of the young men that I saw in that mob; "Get a rope!" I could hear him say. "Get a rope! Labor Agitator! What if he didn't do it! He's an anarchist, rank anarchist! Get a rope!"

The first witness was called, Dr. David Stafford, autopsy physician who performed the autopsies on nine of the ten victims of the preparedness parade bomb. Dr. Stafford told the details of the wounds, of the mangled human flesh, of the death that was caused by that bomb. I can never get used to mangled flesh—to death. I have seen it by the trainload, by the battle-fieldful; I have carried it on stretchers, I have smelled it and lived through a night of crashing artillery-thunder with it; but I can't get used to it. And my heart ached as the doctor told the story of the men and women and children that were killed on July 22d. I asked myself why they were killed, and I could not answer the question. People were marching in a parade, they were expressing a belief just as they might have expressed the same belief by word of mouth or from the printing-press. They had a right to express that belief. The most sacred principle on earth is the right of free expression. I remember what Emma Goldman once said when a leading citizen of Chicago expressed the desire to lead a mob "to hang every anarchist to a lamp-post." Emma Goldman's reply was this: "I believe in free speech; I would shoulder a rifle to fight for the right of that man to express that idea."

I believe in the right of those who differ with me to express their opinions, and I believe that an assault upon a free expression by any man, no matter how vicious or stupid his thought may be, or whether made by word or by peaceful demonstration, is the most dangerous, the most criminal of all acts. I think that I truly express the anarchist's viewpoint in that matter.

But suddenly there is a stir in the courtroom; little Cunha is excited—"What did he say?" Dr. Stafford had ceased the routine recital and begun to answer questions in a more general way. Bourke Cockran raised an objection; more confusion; cross-examination, and then the words of truth rang out through the courtroom: "I believe the bomb exploded before it reached the sidewalk!"

The Frame-Up system was betrayed by a word of truth from the State's first witness! Black with anger, Cunha stumbled, hesitated, and sought to impeach his own witness—too late. Fickert flushed red and looked at the floor. The truth is out; the vile plot to destroy five human lives on the perjury of the underworld has been stripped naked.

That night the autopsy physician had a long interview with the district attorney. In the morning he was recalled to the stand to withdraw his testimony that the bomb must have been thrown. He'd "been talking to the district attorney since, and he didn't think he should have said what he did"—

But, never mind, Doctor, nothing you can do will change it; you first spoke the truth gathered from your scientific work on the bodies of the victims. Now you've "seen the district attorney," as you admit, and feel that it is your duty to help his theory in the hanging of Tom Mooney; we know how it is, when a man has an official position.

But the back of the Frame-Up is broken, and the truth from the mouth of the State's first witness cannot be erased.

The suitcase theory, built up probably from the psychology of the McNamara suitcase bomb trial, has always looked dishonest; probably it will soon be deserted and the cry "Get a rope! Get a rope! Labor agitator!" will die out in the light of truth.

Hymn of Courage
JAMES WALDO FAWCETT

I see old men grow tired and fall beside the path,
I see sweet youth bend in the storm, and take
The sheltered road beneath, and furl our flags,
And speak no more of that great day in which Revolt
Shall flame across the sullied skies, and strike
The shackles from the broken limbs of Man.

I see the roses fade in girlish cheeks, and eyes
Grow dull and dim that once were filled with fire,
And see the old, worn kings go marching proudly by
And masters bend the race unto their will, and take
The bread from children's mouths, and steal the love
From out the souls of brothers in the strife.

But I am not cast down; my heart still cries for peace,
My eyes still hold the glint of hate for tyrant power,
My lips still sing the rebel song, my hands still ache
To catch the fallen banner and go down in the wild host
Wrapped in its folds all crimson with our own glad blood
Shed in the deathless cause of Light at war with Night.

Come stand together, Brothers, for the fray;
Take up with me the broken sword of common wrath,
And with me climb the steely gates of fortressed shame
And plant the people's pennon on the crumbled tower
To speak to all the world of Right too long denied;
Come stand together, Brothers; dawn is here!

Importance of Agitation

Men blame us for the bitterness of our language and the personality of our attacks. It results from our position. The great mass of the people can never be made to stay and argue a long question. They must be made to feel it through the hides of their idols. Eternal vigilance is the price of liberty.

Power is ever stealing from the many to the few.

The manna of popular liberty must be gathered every day or it is rotten.

The hand entrusted with power becomes the necessary enemy of the people.

Only by uninterrupted agitation can a people be kept sufficiently awake to principle not to let liberty be smothered by material prosperity.

Every government is always growing corrupt. Every secretary of state is, by the very necessity of his position, an apostate. He is an enemy to the people, of necessity, because the moment he joins the government he gravitates against the popular agitation, which is the life of the republic.

The public that sinks to sleep, trusting to constitutions and machinery, politicians and statesmen, for the safety of its liberty, never will have any.   GARRISON

Preparedness

FRED WATSON

I HAVE been asked to say something about the condition of things in Great Britain during the war. I may have many things to say that will be of interest to the readers of THE BLAST, but before I say them I want to give expression to a thought that has hit me forcibly since coming to the United States. It is a word of warning that I wish to utter, which comes to me as the result of my experience during the war period in Europe:

Be prepared! That is the cry of the militarists in America just now. It is a fine phrase—for them. For they are keeping a watchful eye on the future, and do not intend to take any chances in the matter of war. Being the party that make the wars, they know that war "cometh in such an hour as ye think not," and one-half the victory is assured to the side being best prepared. They are therefore getting ready, and their cry should have a peculiar significance for us who are anti-militarists. Are we prepared? "Prepared for what?" you ask. Prepared for that day for which the militarist is so anxious to be ready. That day when, at the drop of the hat, the wise men who rule over us will declare that the people of such and such a country have sinned against the dignity of the United States. We will be called upon to defend our honor; forthwith "these vile traducers of our fair name are our enemies," and they must be annihilated. Then the parrot cries of the jingo press will resound through the country; war-fever will set in, usually level-headed people will become stricken with it, and the erstwhile anti-militarists will shoulder their guns and march away in "freedom's cause." To check this fever when once it has begun, is like trying to check a rick fire in a gale.

There is a decided anti-militarist propaganda going on at this moment; but what are its objects, or more precisely, its plans? Has it any plan of campaign besides denunciatory outbursts in speech and pamphlet? Are the anti-militarists getting as prepared as the militarists?

A few years ago in Great Britain the militarists started a great preparedness campaign. They shouted, "We must have a bigger navy, and the army must be made more efficient." They warned the country to be prepared for a war with Germany. This was years ago. The government pooh-poohed the idea—in public, but went silently along preparing. The navy was doubled, the army was reorganized, and other schemes were set on foot. The pacificist M. P.'s uttered protests, and the wise, wise workingman only shook his head and said that a European war in this twentieth century was incredible, impossible, and he went to sleep again. We all, more or less, regarded things in his light, and so our propaganda became, like so many of our activities, relegated to purely academic dissertations, with occasionally a little practical work. The anti-militarist section of the Socialist bureau made noble speeches and issued literature, declaring that the workers were becoming too closely knit to allow a war between two such peoples as the British and the Germans. As a platform utterance this sounded very well, but in actual fact it left out of consideration one or two things.

It omitted to take into consideration the fact that governments make war without consulting the people; that when war is in the air, the Iron Hand is specially weighted; and, what perhaps is the most important factor, the psychological effect of a sentimental battle cry, which will have an effect that miles of argument will fail to produce, winning over all but the most deeply dyed pacifists, a small minority.

Anti-militarist propaganda in Great Britain before August, 1914, was, if anything, more active than it is here, but what did it consist of? Leaflet distribution, occasional speeches, and so on. A dozen or more men went to jail for their activities, and were acclaimed heroes. The net result of their labors and

their sacrifices was practically nil.

When it became obvious that Great Britain would (as the result of secret diplomatic promises) become embroiled in the quarrel between Austria and Serbia, the jingo press got busy. They wasted no time in speculation as to what might happen. They knew. The country was flooded with patriotic appeals. The handy and effective excuse, an essential preliminary to war, was supplied by Germany, and the flood gates of sentimental gush were opened wide. The heart of "the man in the street" was touched, and he threw aside his preconceived notions and rushed to join the colors. Too late then to appeal to reason. One could only stand and stare, and hold tight on to oneself to prevent being carried along on the tide.

The government prevented any concerted demonstration or expression of opinion, by one or two subtle moves. The first of these was the Press Bureau, an institution set up by previous arrangement with the large newspapers, for the purpose of keeping a rigid censorship on all news. Before this grand inquisitor all news or articles had to be submitted, and any criticism of the government, or news not of a favorable kind, was deleted. Not only did the Press Bureau censor news, but they made it; and if they had needed a motto they could have done no better than inscribe upon their portals, "*Suppressio veri, suggestio falsi.*"

This was the first card to be played, and the second was the infamous Defense of the Realm act, which placed Great Britain under the control of the naval and military authorities. All individual freedom was promptly extinguished. This act gave unlimited power to the competent naval or military authority He could enter houses, private and business, without a warrant; could seize papers, etc., without a warrant; and could arrest without a warrant any person whom he suspected of making statements or issuing reports which were calculated to cause disaffection or alarm among His Majesty's subjects, or to prejudice recruiting. To put it in a nutshell, in plain English, he could do as he damn well pleased, and he did. No trial by jury and no assumption of innocence until found guilty. The rights of Magna Charta were swept away by this act, which passed through Parliament in less minutes than the miners' eight-hour bill took years.

These things may be old, stale news to you now, but they are worth bearing in mind. These quick and adroit moves of the government, which had been mapped out years before and pigeon-holed, took the wind out of the sails of the anti-militarists, and made well-nigh impossible any real action. It was too late for propaganda and in their short-sightedness no thought had been given to doing anything; they had only talked about it. A few courageous spirits tried to catch up with the lost opportunities but they were as voices crying in the wilderness, and where they were not promptly clapped into jail, their cries were overwhelmed in the din of the storm. The leaders who were so often heard at the congresses, what of them? With one or two exceptions they rushed to the side of the bosses and became recruiting sergeants, and those who did not were threatened by the government.

Too late, too late.

The anti-militarists of Europe failed to have any effect in the moment of crisis, because, unlike the bosses, they had not prepared. Their campaign had been one of saying things. The campaign of the bosses was doing things, and they won.

The bosses here are doing things, and they will win, unless we take a lesson from the European catastrophe and prepare to do something besides talk, to meet the not remote possibility of a war in which America will be one of the belligerents.

The militarists are prepared.

The anti-militarists are ——?

THE BLAST

Revolutionary Labor Paper
Published every 1st and 15th of the month
569 Dolores St., San Francisco, Cal.
Mail Address, Box 661   Phone, Park 499
Alexander Berkman, Editor and Publisher
M. E. Fitzgerald, Associate Worker   Carl Newlander, Assistant
SUBSCRIPTION
$1.00 Yearly   60c Six Months   5c Copy
Bundle rates 2½c per copy in bundles of ten.

Reflections

Political Fruit

WHAT is the use of talking of the rights of labor, of justice in the courts, of free speech and press, when the very foundation of it all is gradually but fatally being removed from our very feet? But a very short time and we shall find ourselves hemmed in by the bayonets of a legislative imperialism such as the world had never seen before.

To mention but one signifcant instance of the dominant tendency of these days, Congress is planning a law that will effectively terminate the right of strike. The experiment is first to be tried on the railroad men. If successful, it will soon be applied universally. And successful it will surely be. Why not? Has not the hand of the military in these United States already been powerfully strengthened with a view of coping with the "internal enemy?"

Compulsory arbitration and deprivation of the right to strike means nothing less than the complete subjugation of American labor to the will of our captains of industry. Aye, those to be forcibly subjugated can themselves be called upon—by the power vested in the President by recent legislation—to do the subjugating. An emergency draft, nothing less. Compulsory arbitration spells the practical extermination of effective unionism.

And labor? What is its answer? These new Congressional projects are not the concern of the railroad men only, though the contemplated law is directed against them—for the present. It involves all labor, and every progressive man and woman. Indeed, it forges new and more terrible chains for the coming generations. And where is the united voice of the working class and of every decent man and woman in this country to cry a halt, to put an end to the new tendencies that will promise to out-Russianize Russia in these free United States?

The "Scab Book"

A PECULIAR mockery, there is, in the issuance just now of the great Chamber of Commerce "Scab Book," branding San Francisco Labor with the charge of crimes of every sort, from that of trying to get a living to that of blowing up the preparedness parade. This "Scab Book" recites an amusingly foolish tale of all the strikes of recent times about the Bay Cities and winds up with a brutally foolish statement in regard to the preparedness parade bomb.

"It was the terrible culmination of San Francisco's long period of lawlessness, of intimidation, of coercion" (referring to the Longshoremen's strike, the Culinary Workers' strike, etc.). "It came at a time when the Law and Order Committee had been organized to correct the evils at the foundation of just such conditions as led to the bomb outrage * * *."

What will Labor say to that? Of course, it is not true that labor activities had anything to do with the assault on the preparedness parade. But the assault upon organized labor members, using the parade bomb affair, as related by hired perjurers, is connected with the labor struggle by the Chamber of Commerce which inspires the attack. If you doubted it before, Labor, read the Chamber of Commerce "Scab Book" and then get into the struggle to save your innocent brothers and your movement from destruction.

If you need further convincing, take notice of the fact that the prosecution tried to jam into the jury one detective and one strikebreaker gunman from the Automobile Machinists' strike in which Billings and Nolan were aligned on the side of Labor, at the wrong end of that strikebreaker's gun. Also note that the rising anger of Labor has already put the politician prosecutors in a nervous state, so that, after carefully eliminating all union workingmen from the actual jury, they made a grand stand play by graciously accepting for the thirteenth juror, who is extremely unlikely to serve, a perfectly good union electrician.

Latest News

SAN FRANCISCO papers just announce that Martin Swanson, erstwhile private detective for the Pacific Gas & Electric Company and the United Railroads (now said to be only on the public pay-roll), has been subpoenaed as a witness for the defense of Tom Mooney. The papers suggest that Swanson may be asked questions in regard to his alleged attempt to bribe witnesses in the cases of Billings and Mooney.

Simultaneously, *The News* announces that Traffic Officer Clarence Bormouth admits that a woman long sought as a witness had given him her address and told him a few minutes after the explosion that she had seen a bomb thrown. The policeman claims very conveniently to have lost the notebook in which he put her name and address. In full accord with the diabolical scheme to hang innocent men on perjured testimony, the prosecution is frantically trying to keep this witness from being discovered. It will be remembered that one other eye-witness was shipped out of the city by the police and several terrorized tô keep them from appearing in the Billings case. District Attorney Fickert admits that he saw and received information from the woman witness as to the thrown bomb a few minutes after the explosion and tries to explain his effort to keep her from being discovered by saying that she was hysterical and not to be credited.

Why not let the jury decide whether to believe this woman who got excited upon seeing ten persons slaughtered, or to believe your drug-victim convict witnesses, who boast of the blood money you hold before their eyes, Fickert?

Ye Blasters

IF IT be necessary to explain so obvious a thing to minds above the caliber of detectives' minds, be ye hereby informed that the honorable assistant district attorney of San Francisco lied in stating that he found in the office of THE BLAST evidence connecting us all with many plots, such as "killing President Wilson," "assassinating Governor Johnson," "blowing up the State of California and the Rocky Mountains," "blasting a hole in the bottom of the Pacific Ocean" to let the United States Navy sink through, and "betraying organized labor."

Did you know, dear Blasters, that the blasting that you were to do was **physical** blasting with unmetaphorical dynamite? So the "blast" from the prosecuting attorney informed us last week. And did you also know that the drawing of the words, "THE BLAST," used as this paper's title head, is a drawing of a dynamite explosion? We also received a "blast" to that effect and to the astonishment of the artist, in the court where Tom Mooney is being tried.

(It appears that we have been thus concealing our sinister plots on the printing press and through the mails. Of course you have noticed that we have tried to sell as few papers as possible on the newsstands and to subscribers in order to keep the secret.)

RICARDO FLORES MAGON is sick. There is danger of his death. Not because his illness is of too serious nature for medical science, but because there is not enough money to pay for the printing of his glorious paper of rebellion,

Regeneracion. and to pay for doctors, too. And if one or the other must die, it will be Ricardo, for Ricardo will not save himself at the expense of the work for which he has risked his life and repeatedly lost his liberty these many years. We hope that there is somewhere someone who can make a little sacrifice to secure the scientific treatment that will save the Kropotkin of Mexico.

DR. BEN REITMAN has been sentenced in Cleveland to serve six months in the workhouse and pay $1000 fine, for **"giving information."**

The particular kind of information does not matter—to tell the truth is a sin. Dr. Reitman's information was given on the subject of birth control hygiene. If he had given some vicious form of misinformation such as given by the myriad of charlatans that feed upon men's and women's ignorance, he'd not have been prosecuted. But it was proven in court that the printed matter that Reitman gave out told the truth—and so he feels the heavy hand of Law.

AGNES THEKLA FAIR is dead. Thekla was a genius in her own peculiar way. All genius has its peculiar ways. Thekla's way made her known as a "soapboxer." Thekla rarely had railroad fare, and yet Thekla could not be kept away from where trouble brewed for Labor. So Thekla was known to many as the "Hobo Agitator." Her life expressed itself in another way, also, for her genius soared at times above the routine of breakbeams, strikes and soapboxes and expressed itself in verse. Thekla Fair's poems are not built on the usual line. In fact, I have heard them described as "crazy," just as Whitman's were once described. In talking to an editor recently, he told me that he couldn't make up his mind whether Thekla's poems were utterly worthless or stupendously great. I saw the editor again a few days later and he said that they were probably "wild" but that he could not forget them—could not erase the picture they put into his mind—and that they had to be, must be published.

Thekla ran to meet death—a death as wild as the life she lived, on the rails beneath a flying train. A death that she preferred to the slow and stealthy death of tuberculosis, which reached its hand toward her.   R. M.

Wanted: A Blast

ARCH PERRIN

A BLAST is usually a prelude to action. Some of us hear the noon-day whistle and start for the dinner pail. The traffic cop blows a blast and the motors move. The sound of the siren tells the ship that there are rocks near by in the fog and she moves away.

Why not blow a blast that will compel brain action?

Why not blow a blast to remove prejudice and allow clear thinking?

*   *   *

We hear the roars of destruction in Europe. The triumph of civilization means the mangling and maiming and murder of the best of Europe's sons. We see the culmination of frenzied preparedness. Are we to prepare for the same catastrophic climax? Blow a blast, somebody, that will startle us into thinking!

*   *   *

Our prisons are full to overflowing, and the stream of incoming convicts steadily swells. The damnable system is all wrong, has proved itself rotten, and still we are content to go on in the same old way. The position of warden is still a political plum instead of a vocation. Prison guards are still using loaded clubs instead of intelligence and understanding. No man is even taught a trade by which he can earn an honest living in the world outside the prison walls. Think that over!

Blow a blast that will force clear thinking! Let us forget catchwords, abolish old prejudices, destroy false sentimentality and do the thing most needed.

Birthday Greetings

New York, January 8, 1917.

Dear Blast:

GREETINGS and congratulations. What an eventful year you have just closed, and how wonderful that you have survived it all!

Every rebel who, like you, has launched out upon the path to undermine the citadel of Mammon has met with difficulties and hardships. They, like you, have had a thorny, up-hill road to travel. But none can boast to have crowded so much in so young a life as yours.

Think of having been suppressed by a mighty government of a hundred million people! To have been raided twice by the tools of the Chamber of Commerce and the United Railroads Company! To turn the peaceful sleep of the Law and Order Committee into a veritable nightmare; to harass the innocent dream of the prosecuting attorney! Think of having been the one lusty voice on the Coast to ring out powerfully against the vile and cruel conspiracy of Mammon's forces! At the same time to have brought cheer and hope to the victims of that conspiracy! Think of having brought together the bravest elements among labor from Coast to Coast to a realization of the dangers threatening the workers through this wide land!

What an achievement for *one year!* Verily, dear BLAST, you have good reason to rejoice and to begin your new year with justified pride and deep self-assurance.

Good luck, then, on your new journey. May it be more eventful than even the first year. May you grow ever stronger, ever more defiant, ever more powerful.

EMMA GOLDMAN

New York, January 5, 1917.

THE latest outrage of the authorities in raiding the offices of THE BLAST only serves to emphasize the very useful work that the paper is doing on the Pacific Coast.

It seems almost a miracle that THE BLAST has been able to survive for an entire year and to celebrate the anniversary of its founding. I know only too well the terribly difficult conditions under which it has been published, and I cannot recall that any other revolutionary Labor paper in the West has been able to live so long.

I have read every issue of THE BLAST since it was started, and I have always read it with interest. It has been a monument to the militant spirit of Alexander Berkman.

I know that Comrade Berkman does not want any bouquets, but I cannot refrain from expressing my admiration for his wonderful spirit. He has been almost alone in San Francisco. He has had to face the odium created by the bomb thrown at the preparedness parade last summer. He has had to meet and repel attacks that would surely have crushed a weaker man. And he has been absolutely fearless and absolutely uncompromising throughout the entire year.

Long live THE BLAST, and long live Alexander Berkman!

LEONARD D. ABBOTT

ATTENTION!

THE work I came to do in New York in behalf of our friends imprisoned in San Francisco, is about completed.

I am planning to leave New York the first week of February, and I shall be glad to address mass meetings in the large industrial cities, on my way to the Coast.

Labor organizations, Workmen's Circle Branches, Groups or individuals who are interested and willing to arrange meetings to aid the San Francisco labor victims, please communicate with me at once.

ALEXANDER BERKMAN,
20 East 125th Street,
New York, N. Y.

Extract From a Letter

(By Anton Johannsen to a Friend)

THE city of Everett is, in a sense, the center of the great lumber industry, which is the organic industry of the Pacific Northwest. A man by the name of Hartley is one of the largest lumber financiers in Washington. He resides in Everett and was the candidate for the republican gubernatorial nomination last fall, declaring himself, publicly, openly and defiantly for the open shop and the destruction of the menace of unionism. He failed in the nomination, but spent about $100,000 in the campaign. Mr. Hartley was the leading factor in the lumber trust against any and all forms of union labor.

The shingle weavers had an organization in Everett—in fact, they are fairly well organized in this lumber industry, being highly skilled men. A strike was declared at Everett last July and during the course of this strike which was conducted very respectably, the members of the chamber of commerce of Everett organized a vigilante committee of two hundred and fifty, took the law into their own hands and arbitrarily prohibited the shingle weavers from picketing the job, and when these men insisted upon the right to picket, they were treated with the most brutal form of violence by those so-called respectable bastard business men.

In one instance—called most forcibly to my attention—a young man 23 years old was arrested on suspicion that he was an I. W. W. because he wore overalls and had no steady job. The May of the city and two deputy sheriffs grabbed hold of this young man by the hair of the head and slammed his face violently against the iron floor of the jail until he was unconscious, after which they placed his fingers, one at a time, under the foot of an iron bedstead and then jumped on top of the bed until they literally crushed all his fingers. This extreme brutal conduct on the part of the business men of Everett fired the flame of hate and sowed the seed of revenge which, afterwards, culminated in the massacre of November 5, 1916.

On November 5, 1916, two hundred and thirty I. W. W.'s boarded a boat in Seattle and proceeded to Everett determined to hold a public meeting against the brutality of the chamber of commerce.

This boat was a regular passenger boat and on this particular trip carried about thirty-five passengers in addition to the I. W. W.'s. When the boat was about to land at Everett, they were met at the docks by the sheriff and a posse. The sheriff came to the edge of the water and demanded an interview with the leader. The I. W. W.'s on the boat in unison answered, "We are all leaders." After this the shooting began. It has not been ascertained who fired the first shot, each side claiming that the other did it.

A machine gun was planted on the wharf, but unfortunately, some well-aiming chump on the boat shot the only man that understood how to operate a machine gun, killing him instantly. What a shame that those brave business men that are so patriotic and generally in favor of war, were so helpless on this occasion, having only one man in their group that understood how to operate a machine gun!

This man was a former colonel in the army and he was the first one shot, perhaps this is part of the law of compensation, so ably set forth in (*) Emerson's "Essays."

The ex-sheriff of this county was also in the front to protect the robber class. He met the same fate as the colonel and was killed instantly. The present sheriff was formerly a member of the Shingle Weavers' Union, but after elected to office, became a bold and brutal defender of the privileged class.

Five I. W. W.'s on the boat were killed outright—all of them young men between the ages of 18 and 28—and some twenty odd were injured. The vigilantes had two men killed and twenty-five injured. Over two hundred I. W. W.'s were placed under arrest including the wounded. The dead ones, of course, were not put in jail.

The Mayor of Seattle, Mr. Gill, showed considerable courage and understanding. He issued a public statement charging that the business men of Everett were responsible for this unnecessary loss of life. He further stated that the chamber of commerce of Everett had taken the law into their own hands in a most disgraceful manner and used violence of a most abominable character in their mad endeavors to destroy the labor unions in Everett, Wash. You should have heard the members of the chamber of commerce of Seattle in their meeting denouncing Mayor Gill and demanding his recall, but Mayor Gill stood pat, telling them "to go to it." However, Labor is well organized in Seattle and has a splendid militant spirit. They backed up the Mayor with the result that the chamber of commerce put a quietus on the recall gossip.

The labor movement in Seattle is behind the I. W. W.'s in this defense, both morally and financially. A protest meeting was held November 19th, filling the largest hall in Seattle with an overflow meeting on the street.

Of course the "wobblies" came to this public meeting with their red song books singing "Onward Christian Soldiers." It was a splendid meeting and aroused a great deal of interest and enthusiasm in behalf of the men in jail.

One of the men on the boat by the name of Carlson was shot twelve times. He was a man of exceptional physique and has recovered. Carlson has entered suit for $100,000 against the city of Everett and a suit for a like amount against the chamber of commerce. Carlson is a republican in politics and has never been a member of any labor union. He should be able to make it rather warm for these lumber kings in Everett.

The jailors in Everett are certainly having their troubles with these eighty-four prisoners who seem very little concerned at the serious charges of murder filed against them. They are in the main, young men, ranging from the age of 18 to 45. Most of them have been working in the harvest fields. All of them have great faith in the coming social revolution and so they are singing their songs in the jail.

One of the first things they did was to inaugurate a hunger strike against the bad food. When the jailer brought the mush up to them one morning, they threw it right back into his "mush" and plastered it all over the prison bars. They made so damn much noise that the people on the street protested and they could not be quieted until their food demands had been gratified.

The first two weeks, the attorneys were not permitted to see the defendants, but I presume this was a little too raw even for the judges on the bench and so this rule was abrogated by judicial mandate.

Colonel Wood was up here to investigate the case and to give advice as to the best means of defense, etc. Fred Moore has been here for some time gathering the physical facts for preparation in the case. It is an excellent case in my opinion and I am certain will bring out, in a very clear manner, the hypocrisy and murder spirit of the business element in Everett, Wash.

A Story Labor Won't Forget

ON Bloody Sunday, November 5th, when the deputies of Everett shot down workingmen in cold blood, a call was issued for the local unit of the naval militia to muster. A lad, Ted Kenedy, a member of the Everett division, refused to don his uniform and go to the armory in response to this call. His company assembled under arms without him, and he was marched to the county jail under an armed guard of a squad of his company.

Kennedy, who is only 18 years of age, said that he was not required to take part in civil strife and that he would have nothing to do with the coercing or shooting of workingmen. He went willingly to prison, although threatened with Court Martial and all sorts of dire punishment for his "unpatriotic" act, rather than be used as a tool for the lumber bosses in the denial of Free Speech to Labor. The militia authorities thought it better to hush the matter up—probable because, if noised around, it would set a bad example to other young militiamen—so that the boy was not punished after all. But the bravery of this lad will long be remembered by the workers of America. It takes quite a little courage to stand out against your "superior officers" and to be branded by the young men with whom you went to school and have associated all your life. All honor to young Kennedy and may the spirit that moved him grow apace among the youth of the country!

"I should like to see every I. W. W. hanged!"

Why? Because they believe in free speech? Because they don't admire the present labor situation? Because they take the Declaration of Independence seriously? Why do we always read in the daily papers of a "mob" of I. W. W.'s and a "posse" of citizens?

A. P.

---

*(EDITOR'S NOTE—Dear Mr. Fickert: The man referred to here was one Ralph Waldo Emerson, a notorious and desperate anarchist of the Boston water-front and ex-convict, who wrote wicked books very hard for policemen to understand.)

The Four

OUR population is made up of four distinct classes. Catalogued in the order of their numbers these are: Those Who Do Not Think, Those Who Think They Think, Those Who Think Wrong and Those Who Think.

The first-named class has converted the pastime of not thinking about anything into that king of national sports called Cheery Optimism, whose motto, "God's in His heaven; all's well with the world," is peculiarly well suited to mental ineptitude, as it is quite apparent to even the meanest intelligence that just now all is not well with the world. Some idea of the numerical strength of this class may be gleaned from the fact that all books, magazines, plays and ballads called "popular" are addressed directly to them.

Editors refer to them affectionately, and carefully "de-thought" their literature in deference to their taste. For serious reading they give them "American Girls Who Wear Coronets," "Christmas in Many Lands," and "The Toymakers of Nuremburg." The characters most favored in fiction by Those Who Do Not Think are the cowboy who proved to be an English earl and the benevolent washerwoman who does so much good that her readers can cry and feel generous without spending a single cent. To this class a happy ending is a delicious mental cud, to be chewed from the closing of the book until bedtime.

A censorious world gives but grudging credit to the theatrical manager, who alone has proved the innermost recesses of the empty American head. It is he who engages a composer of the rum-ti-tum school and eight librettists to prepare a musical comedy whose finest fruit is the song, "Ain't I the Daisy Little Peach?" a splendid syncopation to which—the management having interest in the song rights—the "Don't Thinks" are played out into the lobby. where the words-and-music panthers lurk for their prey.

In the higher strata of society are to be found those who having escaped the primal curse of labor as well as the heavier burden of thought, seek out the restaurant that supplies the worst food at the highest cost to an accompaniment of music that kills all attempts to think.

The sense of humor in this class is such that they have been hee-hawing ever since Bryan was convicted of the one sensible utterance of his life—that grape juice is a good summer drink.—*James L. Ford in "Life."*

Have you renewed your subscription?

DEFENSE FUNDS SAN FRANCISCO LABOR PRISONERS
Per Alexander Berkman

Total collected to Nov. 22d, '16....	$1,868.02
Union Russian Workers, Detroit..	1.50
Dr. M. Rasnick, Pittsburgh............	5.00
J. H. Long, Oakland, Cal............	1.00
Benj. Axelrod, Chicago...............	3.00
Circola di Studdi Sociale, Seattle per I. Bertson, Secy................	10.30
Col. per Peter Armanini, Kan......	28.00
Group Fraternidad, Boston..........	6.00
Bessie Kimmelman, Sub. List......	4.10
Gus Telsch, Home, Wash............	1.00
R. R. Sharma, Lindsay, Cal........	2.00
Col. by "Volne Listy," N. Y., per V. Rejsek............................	50.00
Col. Carnegie Hall meeting, per Alexander Berkman	500.00
Union Russian Workers, Detroit, per H. Tsalewich	2.00
L. Grikstas, Brooklyn..............	1.00
Painters' Union, Tampa, Fla......	5.00
J. D. Angelo, Pa..................	2.00
N. Y. Collections per Berkman....	150.00
U. M. W. A., No. 1523............	55.40
Group Luca Tenace, Miami, Ariz., per H. Armand	9.40
Collection per T. Ivanoff, Hamtrank, Mich.....................	12.36
Martin Larson, Garretson, S. D...	5.00
	$2,722.08
Previously to Defense League......	$1,868.02
A. B. wired to League.............	500.00
To Robert Minor, Dec. 28th........	205.40
To League, Jan. 8th, 1917........	125.30
To Robert Minor, Jan. 23d........	23.36
Jan. 23d, to Defense League.........	$2,722.08

THE BLAST SUSTAINING FUND
From Oct. 15th to Jan. 15th, 1917

R. J. Robinson, St. Louis, $1; Kisluick, Sub. List, $3.25; F. Pece, $3; C. Farnara, Hawthorne, Cal., $1; Social in Cleveland, per Jack Myers, $6.90; M. Morris, Montello, Mass., $1; Lincoln Steffens, $5; Marian Wharton, Ft. Scott, Kan., $5; Lucha Terra, Miami, Ariz., per H. Armand, $14.25; Mrs. Edelman, Los Angeles, $1; Grupo Anarquista, $2; Thomas C. Hawly, Lodi, Cal., 50c; Burnstein, Chicago, $3; M. Cipriani, Anaconda, Mont., $9.50; Cornelia Boecklin, N. Y., $1; John Clerc, Seattle, $1; Col. by Cronaca Sovverseva, $3.50; Fanny Lansky, per Sub. List, $4.90; L. Rosenberg, Sub. List, $12.90; A. A. Sienkiewitz, $5; Grupo Baricata, Iowa, $1; Baker, S. F., $1; John Baff, St. Louis, $1; Constantine Taraboi, Kan., $1; Pellegrini, Denver, $1; Chas. Campomaggi, New York, Sub. List, $3.25; Group Freiheit, Baltimore, $10; W. W. Cummings, Los Angeles, $1; D. Masino, Henrietta, Okla., $1.50; Lydia Gibson, $25; R. R. Sharma, $1; Constantine Tarboi, Kan., $2; The Group of Aid of Anarchist Movement Social, per Max Koldrun, N. Y., $22.50; Lucha Terra Group, Miami, Ariz., Sub. List, per H. Armand, $11.30; A Friend, $1; A Friend, S. F., $5; Dr. Rasnick, Pittsburgh, $10; D. T. I., $6; Martin Larson, S. D., $5; Florence Sully, $1; Prince Hopkins, $10; Nell Moyer, $3; J. Kabunell, Wichita, Kan., $3; F. Rascher, St. Louis, $2; John Meyers, Detriot, Mich., $1; Theo. Ivanoff, Mich., $2; O. Crook, Minneapolis, $2; per A. Beyer, St. Louis, $3.

The BLAST

Vol. II.　　　SAN FRANCISCO, FEBRUARY 15, 1917　　　No. 2

The Vice Clean-Up

"But what other work can I get to do?"
"Well, I hear they need new witnesses against Mooney."

In the Shadow of the Gallows
Robert Minor

A NERVOUS, pale-faced crowd of Tom Mooney's friends hastened back to the courtroom after a quick meal in coffee houses, whilst the jury was dining in charge of the bailiff and guarding the secret of Mooney's fate. The dimly lighted room was soon filled with faces full of question and of pallor, offset here and there by the cynical smiles of detectives.

A bailiff whose heart seems still to reside with him despite his profession, showed a visage upon which was written tragedy. "Where's the judge? There will be a verdict in ten minutes. Get the lawyers, quick!" The tensest hour I have ever known, filled by a thousand sobs from Rena Mooney's sister, trembling efforts of Annie Mooney to smile, and the low unconscious moaning of "Mother" Mooney, displaced the expected ten-minute wait.

The courtroom is different from its usual appearance at night. It seems puzzlingly unofficial. For one thing, an assistant district attorney's wife was not there, alaughing at a man's plea for his life.

Assistant Prosecutor Brennan came in waddling, contented, eager. He sat in a juryman's chair, miscellaneous attaches gathering around him. District Attorney Fickert entered grinning. Assistant District Attorney Cunha seated himself and called a giant plainclothes man, whom he carefully placed between himself and the defendant's friends. The big "bull" completely covered Cunha's little body from sight. By these signs, hope was given farewell. Rumors of the worst sort flew from whisperer to whisperer. We lied to "Mother" Mooney. Some one sent a new and conclusive word across the room.

The coarse, metallic laugh of Jim Brennan, lolling back in the juror's chair, broke the semi-quiet. Then we knew that Tom Mooney was slated to die. Cunha looked coyly from behind his big policeman, toward "Mother" Mooney who rocked back and forth in her place, moaning, moaning with her eyes closed.

The Judge was fetched.

The jury came in. William V. MacNevin, real estate man, held the verdict in his hand. He was foreman; I wondered why.

"We, the jury, find the defendant—find Thomas J. Mooney, the defendant in the above mentioned cau—where do I begin to read?—find the defendant guilty of murder in the first degree." His fumbling hands could hardly hold the shaking paper. Mr. MacNevin, real estate man, looked at the Judge, and the Judge didn't look very happy or triumphant; and then MacNevin looked at the crowd and changed his eyes quickly to the face of Cunha.

"Guilty?" I think every friend in the room asked himself, "guilty?" Isn't it possible that he said "not guilty?" Didn't we miss the word "not"?

Annie Mooney screamed. "Mother" Mooney's moaning changed to a shriek that seemed to come from a thousand mothers' hearts. Mrs. Weinberg arose, stood for a moment dumb, then fell without a sound upon the floor.

Above the confusion rose the bellow of Fickert: "Get 'em out o' here!" They dragged "Mother" Mooney out by the arms, and Annie and Mrs. Weinberg were carried out.

There was but one calm man in the room. It was Tom Mooney. Standing erect, he looked for a moment at William MacNevin, real estate man, and then Tom smiled and turned about. "Don't cry, Sis, it's all right. Don't cry, Mother." The handcuffs closed about his wrists and Tom disappeared through the door that leads to—

The "bulls" were driving the crowd out. The bulls were happy, triumphant. "Get them out of here," shouted Fickert, with clenched fists and a grin. Suddenly he found himself facing Rena Mooney's sister. She looked at him. Fickert turned away and for the moment stopped his grinning. The "bulls"

didn't even hesitate to lay hands upon the lawyers of the defense. It was their day, and they always have resented Mooney's having a defense.

The newspaper men stopped their interviewing of ex-jurymen for a moment while the wail of Annie Mooney echoed through the corridors and died out as she was carried through the door below.

"Puff!" of a flashlight; William V. MacNevin, real estate man, is having his picture taken, standing just right, as the newspaper photographer instructed him, with the paper in his hand upon which was written "We, the jury—" The last of them filed out. The courtroom was still, scraps of paper on the floor, an upset chair, and an overturned cuspidor, in the dim light.

The next day many compliments were given. We heard some of them about the saloons in Real Estate Row. "Good boy, Mac, you done your duty. We'll get you back on the Real Estate Board"! The remarks were addressed to William V. MacNevin, real estate man. Later Mr. MacNevin replied to a question (the question being unheard), "Well, I don't know as I will make as much money out of it, anyway, as I lost by serving on the jury."

So was Tom Mooney condemned to die, "hanged by the neck until dead."

The means used to this purpose have not been limited by anything but the bounds of the imagination of the tools of the "Frame-Up System." When once the "slimy mind of Private Detective Martin Swanson" decided upon this opportunity to destroy the enemies of Swanson's masters, there was nothing too vile to be used to that end. The heat from the fire of the bomb had hardly cooled from the concrete pavement before sledgehammer and crowbar were put to work to manufacture an artificial "scene of the explosion" to be photographed by the police as fake evidence. This happened within a few minutes of the time that Swanson was put to work on the case, and the place was in charge of the famous "Frame-Up Steve" Bunner when the sledgehammer work was done.

The Frame-Up System gets witnesses exactly as a stage manager recruits a stock company—by simply hiring them. It was with an offer of $5,000 that Swanson tried four times during the week preceding this explosion to get Arthur Silkwood, Billings and then Weinberg to sell Mooney into his hands for alleged streetcar strike activity. So were witnesses recruited with which to convict Billings for the bomb crime, as Billings had refused to sell Mooney; and thus also is to be kept Swanson's promise to revenge himself upon Weinberg for refusing to sell Mooney.

Seventeen thousand dollars were offered as a reward for evidence against "the perpetrators of the bomb crime." A beautiful collection of: one prostitute, her mother, one convict, one drug victim, one live-by-his-wits private detective out of a job, and two women of unenviable standing—was brought to the "Stock Company" to play the death play against Billings. Billings was duly convicted upon the words of this crew, although each contradicted the others, and it was proven that at least one of them was testifying for cash in hand. The criminal records of these persons were successfully concealed until after the conviction of Billings.

As soon as the characters of the State's witnesses against Billings were fully ascertained, several of them were dropped and a new set was procured for the trial of Mooney. On and on they go, with a new set of perjurers for each of the five victims.

Estelle Smith, once indicted for murder, arrested in a bawdy house in Los Angeles, and notoriously lacking in veracity, was discarded as a witness, after convicting Billings and then having her reputation uncovered. Her mother, Mrs. Allie Kidwell, was discharged from her witness job even before the Billings trial, because the defense found a letter written by her telling how she was to receive as a reward for her testimony the pardon of her husband in Folsom penitentiary. It is not known whether her brother, who is in San Quentin, was also to be released or not.

John Crowley, who served to convict Billings by swearing that he saw the boy, a block away from the scene of crime, refuse to take his hat off when the band played the "Star Spangled Banner"—John Crowley was dropped as a witness because the defense had turned up the fact that he was an ex-convict for having given the syphilis to a seventeen year old girl, and that he was out on parole from another conviction for stealing a watch at the time he testified.

Louis Rominger was fired from his job as a witness against Mooney because, since he testified in the Billings case, the defense had published its proof that he had first declared Billings not to be the man he had seen, and that later he changed his statements upon the importunity of an assistant district attorney and of his fellow witness and friend, Estelle Smith.

Mrs. Mellie Edeau and her daughter Sadie were not discharged from their positions as witnesses, but merely given new lines to speak upon the stage that is called the witness stand. Each one suddenly remembered a lot of new things, Sadie explaining that she had not at first told the detectives because they had called **"so near church time"** that she hadn't time enough to tell it all. Her mother, however, assured the court that she had **"told an elder of her church"** all about it, and that "she didn't want no blood money."

John McDonald, the star witness of the Billings case, was kept on the job for the hanging of Mooney. Before being allowed to "go east on the cushions with plenty of change in his pockets," as he had explained to his friends, however, John had to change his story in two respects. For the defense had discovered that the district attorney had defrauded them in the Billings case by the suppression of photographs of Tom Mooney on the roof of his home at the very moment that John, the cocaine-sniffer, saw him a mile and a quarter away at the scene of crime. The prosecution had been ordered to turn these photographs over to the defense, but they had served their case and convicted Billings by fading the photographs out until the time could not be discerned on the street clocks showing in the pictures. Before Mooney came to trial, the defense discovered that fraud and forced the police to allow the great hand-writing expert, Theodore Kytka, to make enlargements from the films. These enlargements showed that Mooney was on the roof of his home at two minutes to two o'clock, one minute past two, three minutes past two, and four minutes past two. So John McDonald changed his testimony in the Mooney case, blandly denying what he had said in the Billings trial and placing the time that he said he saw Mooney, at sixteen minutes earlier.

When the defense announced the deciphering of the time on the street clock as one minute past two, the prosecutors published the statement that they had a witness to swear that Mooney entered his home at two o'clock. And we don't doubt that this witness would have appeared on the stand, had not the prosecution discovered later that the defense had also made out the time on the other picture as 1:58. So the two o'clock witness was dropped.

John McDonald had sworn in the first trial that Mooney and Billings both left the scene by "crossing the street through the parade" on foot, going each in a different direction. The discovery of the aforesaid clocks, however, did not leave sufficient time for Mooney and his wife to travel from the crime scene to their home on foot, so this time John McDonald swore that he did not see them "cross the street through the parade," but lost sight of them on the near side of the street, together.

Thereupon appears Frank C. Oxman, "worthy of credence,"

as the district attorney shouted, because he was "worth a million dollars, a wealthy cattleman from Oregon." The story of Oxman is not fully known at present, but rumor has it that a prominent keeper of redlight cafes turned him over to Fickert to use as a witness to hang Mooney. We do know this much: that that cafe-keeper was in need of Fickert's favor at the time, for the Rev. Paul Smith's vice crusade was on. And the resort-keeper got the favor, too, for his resorts have not been closed, as have nearly all others.

"Frame-Up Steve" Bunner it was who went to Oregon after the cattleman-witness. That in itself was suspicious; but what can you prove? Oxman blandly took the stand and supplied EVERY MISSING LINK IN THE STATE'S CASE. He swore that he saw all four of the defendants (except Nolan, whom the prosecution wants to let out as sop to Labor Unions) at the scene of the crime. Perfection itself falls short of the testimony given by Oxman. He assured everyone that he was a "country gentleman," and that he loved his wife and was rich. Under cross-examination he pulled from his pocket a telegraph envelope on which was written the number of Israel Weinberg's jitney bus! He had even taken the number of the automobile, "thinking those fellows had stolen the suitcase." Hardly ever has so dramatic a scene been witnessed as that when Oxman pulled from his pocket this damning bit of "proof." Hope fled from the room and the vision of five bloody nooses took its place.

Tom Mooney was condemned to death upon the word of Frank C. Oxman. No matter that John McDonald had contradicted Oxman; no matter that Oxman lied in saying that Captain Matheson was not in uniform, and Captain Matheson said that he was; no matter that it was impossible for a jitney bus to go down Market street at the time that the parade was in motion, and in violation of every police regulation; and no matter that Tom Mooney was known to every policeman on the street, as the recent streetcar strike leader, and would have been stopped for that fact alone.

Nor did it matter that the defense proved by photographs and the evidence of a City Supervisor, a police chauffeur, a reporter for the *Oakland Tribune*, another for the *Chronicle*, and a newspaper photographer, that it was **they themselves** who went down Market street at that time seated in the automobile exactly as Oxman described the Mooney party. No matter that Supervisor Andrew J. Gallagher answered the description of "a fat-faced man" that Oxman gave of Mooney; Spangler, the *Tribune* reporter, being wonderfully like Billings and exactly his size; and the police chauffeur is amazingly like Weinberg! No matter that it was proven by photographs that no other automobile was at that corner, during any of the time mentioned by Oxman, except that official car driven by the police chauffeur! No matter anything, for the Chamber of Commerce jury, a business man's jury, wanted but an excuse to hang the "agitator."

Tom Mooney stands condemned to death on the word of Frank C. Oxman, who appeared to be drunk on the witness stand. It is a choice in San Francisco between the professional jury of hungry two-dollar-a-day graft-seekers and the jury chosen from the Chamber of Commerce and business element.

This is the Frame-Up System! By switching witnesses, putting on a new set as fast as the old are found out; by "planting" evidence! A retarding coil from a telephone switch-board was "planted" at the scene two days after the crime and offered as an exhibit of a "dry-cell battery!" Just as catalogs from the Hercules Power Co., "planted" in Mooney's studio when Martin Swanson searched it in Mooney's absence, were shown to the jury and then quickly withdrawn when Mr. Cockran made his attack upon the Swanson frame-up. Just as Oxman was aided to identify Mooney by being shown the number of his cell on the roster of prisoners, looked at Mooney locked alone in his cell, and then "identified" him by the **number of his cell.** In this same way the Edeau women, the Smith woman, the Kidwell woman, McDonald the cocaine-sniffer, and all the rest, "identified" all of the prisoners by having them pointed out to them, and even introduced to them by name so that they could identify them and earn the reward money.

Twenty-five witnesses and seven photographs proved that Mooney was not at the scene of the crime. But the jury believed Oxman, the "home-loving cattleman"; and Mooney was condemned to drop through the death trap at the end of a tarred rope.

And Fickert, the same prosecutor who had laughed in old "Mother" Mooney's face upon the death sentence of her son, took advantage of the blow of the conviction to announce in the next morning's papers that a tremendous conspiracy of "anarchistic criminals" all through the United States was soon to be proven and the anarchists rounded up and hanged. Frank C. Oxman had done his work well. The resort-keeper is running at full blast, and William V. MacNevin, real estate man, is to be given back his place on the Real Estate Board for his services as foreman of the jury.

Then suddenly the frame-up of the Oxman testimony was exposed!

Mrs. R. E. Le Posee, wife of a shoe clerk, happened to remember Frank C. Oxman. He had come into a drygoods store where Mrs. Le Posee worked in Portland, Oregon—had come in with a woman to buy a dress, and the woman had whispered to Mrs. Le Posee that she had a "live one," and to bring out something worth while. Later Mrs. Le Posee happened to be in a cafe in company with her husband and to have seen the "home-loving cattleman" makes signals to a female entertainer by holding up "five fingers twice."

The pitiful fact, the desperate situation in which a labor man is placed in trying to defend himself, is illustrated by the fear that Mrs. Le Posee had that her husband would lose his job if she dared to tell the truth. (See in this issue the letter of a policeman engaged in the frame-up, who cannot tell, because he would lose his job.) Mrs. Le Posee was in the court-room when Oxman testified. She had seen him a mile away at exactly the time that Oxman was supposed to be identifying the Mooney party at the scene of the crime. Mrs. Le Posee had a long, hard struggle with her conscience before she came forward, but her husband happened to have an honest employer who promised that Le Posee would not lose his job for his wife's telling the truth. And so it seems, and so we hope, that Tom Mooney's life is to be saved from the Frame-Up System by this new discovery.

But now we hear that the police are besieging the little woman in her home, threatening her there and threatening her husband at his place of employment.

Is there any depth to which they will not stoop? To hire witnesses, buy witnesses, trade red-light favors for the testimony of cafe drunks!

"It isn't your bloody noose about my neck that hurts," said Tom Mooney. "It's the knowledge that men can be so base."

So we hope for a new trial for Mooney. Surely Judge Griffin, who has had the courage to defy some of the most disreputable acts of the prosecution, will have the courage now to grant Tom Mooney another trial. And you, Labor, must keep your shoulder to the wheel, support this fight now, and we may yet win.

Tom Mooney says: "There is just one place to which we can look for any aid, and that is the united efforts of Organized Labor. John Lawson, one of the biggest labor men in Colorado, was headed for the gallows, as I now am, because he dared raise his voice in behalf of the toilers. He is a free man today and he owes that freedom to Organized Labor. That alone saved him, and that alone can help us."

Will You Be Man Enough to Come Forward?

ON June 27th, 1916, Jim Larkin addressed a meeting in the Dreamland Rink, San Francisco. At the close of the address, a group of enthusiastic persons gathered round shaking hands and voicing their opinion on the subject matter delivered. A number of cards, copies of papers and letters were given to the speaker, who without perusing them, packed them into his bag and adjourned with a few friends to the Hotel Fresno in Eddy street. Upon examining the various documents, etc., in the collection, Larkin came upon a writing, which conveyed a message warning the writer as a fellow countryman from associating with Tom Mooney and his brother. Speaking from memory, the writing ran as follows:

"As a fellow countryman and member of the Clan-na-Gael for some time, not at present in good standing financially, but still at heart a Fenian and understanding that you are engaged in working for Ireland and being still sound at heart though I am twenty years from the old sod, and above all as a Catholic, I want to warn you as to a conspiracy organized and paid for by the U. R. Company of this city. Though I myself am engaged with others from the office of Chief of Police, there are few of us have our hearts in the job. The worst element in the group are the private detectives employed by the United Railroads, though the private men of the Pacific Gas Company don't come far short in villainy with the others. We of the official element get our instructions direct from the office of the M. & M. Employers' Association. The Main Guy in the conspiracy is a prominent member of the K. C. Of course, he is only in that organization for his own purpose. This lad was working for Attorney Fickert in the election. He is also employed or was doing work for the British Consul watching supposed dynamiters. Two other detectives are conductors on the Municipal cars and there are over half a dozen working as conductors on the United Railway. I saw two of these fellows shaking hands with you on Sunday at the picnic. One of them was along with Mooney. Now, the arrangement is to get the two Mooneys by fair means or foul. They have already tried to buy over some of Mooney's associates, others they have threatened with imprisonment. A report has been made to them that you have come on here to work at organizing the employees of the United Railways. You are followed everywhere. Mind yourself, especially on the waterfront. A fight will be started wherever you are, you will be invited to speak to the striking Longshoremen. Don't accept. It is a frame-up. They want to frighten you out of the city. They fear your influence among the Irish, but they mean TO GET MOONEY. Now, I don't like Tom Mooney. Jack Mooney is a decent fellow and I want to see him saved. Still I would not like to see harm come to Tom, though he is given to blowing off his head. Therefore, warn Mooney and those who are with him. They are not frightened by Berkman; they know he has no influence among the Unions, but Mooney is the dangerous man and there are people in the Central Labor Council who want to see him go over the road, along with a fellow named Nolan, who has been out of the state for some time, and another, named Sheehan, a sailor. They boast they can get Johannsen whenever they care to. A certain shipping firm is especially interested in Nolan. There was a report that you were in the home of a man out of the checking department of the United Railways; this man speaks with a strong Scotch accent, and he is being watched. I was glad to shake you by the hand on Sunday and some day I hope to make myself known to you. For though I am engaged in this dirty business, Jim, I have to feed a wife and a number of children, two of whom are in the high school. When they are educated, I will give up this cursed job and become a man again. Again, I warn you: Keep away from the waterfront and tell Nolan not to go out by himself under any circumstances." Beanacht Lait, "One of the Clan."

Will the writer of the above letter show himself a man, now that the victim has been framed up for the gallows? Don't be afraid! Others have renounced the dirty work and lived. Won't you be a man?

PRISON MEMOIRS OF AN ANARCHIST
By Alexander Berkman

"This is the only book that I know which goes deeply into the corrupting, demoralizing psychology of prison life."

—Hutchins Hapgood.

512 pages, illustrated. $1.40 postpaid.

How a Fake Witness Was Unmasked

MRS. R. E. LE POSEE has gone through days of terror and nights of wakefulness, believing herself the possessor of knowledge upon which the life of one man, and perhaps more, might hang.

She attended the trial of Tom Mooney until the prosecution's case was complete, when she says she decided that the case against Mooney was so weak that the jury could not possibly convict.

She says she resolved to remain silent from fear that her husband would lose his job.

When Mrs. Le Posee discovered that the verdict had been "guilty," without recommendation for mercy, she went to the telephone to place her story before Attorney Maxwell McNutt.

"There was no answer at his office and I looked up the Mooneys' telephone in the book. I called there and they said the phone had been temporarily discontinued. I called up the Palace and asked for Mr. Cockran. They said he had gone. Then I decided that it was fate and I would keep out. I kept thinking perhaps Judge Griffin would not sentence him to hanging and I would wait until today and see. I don't know what I can do now. It is terrible. I don't want to be mixed up in it, but what am I to do?"

Mrs. Le Posee is the wife of a salesman with Sommer & Kauffman. With her husband and her little boy she came to San Francisco from Portland. According to her story, she and her husband and the child went to Market street to see the Preparedness parade, leaving the Mentone Hotel about 1:15.

"It was the boy's birthday. We had dinner and a birthday cake and ice cream. When we finished we started right away so we would be in plenty of time. We stopped near the clock near Haas' candy store.

"In the crowd a man stepped on my shoe. I had on new shoes, and I mentioned it to my husband. Being the wife of a shoeman, I suppose I am a little particular about my shoes.

"He told me they could not be fixed. When I looked up at the man I recognized him. I had a business transaction with him in Portland, but did not know his name. I was working in a store in Portland selling suits. A man and woman came in one day, and I remembered them specially because the whole transaction was so raw. The woman whispered to me. 'I've got a live one. Show me the best you've got in the house.' There was a dress with a pm on it. That means that you get a dollar extra for selling it. I showed her that. She asked the man if he wanted to come into the dressing-room and see it tried on and he followed her. I also saw him at other times in Portland.

"That night I told my husband that I had sold a pm and made an extra dollar and I told him about the 'live one.'

"After that we were down at a grill one night and I saw one of the entertainers making signs. I turned around and saw the 'live one' sitting at a table. Then he held up five fingers twice in succession and she nodded.

"'There's the live one,' I told my husband.

"The next time I saw him was that day of the parade in San Francisco, when he stepped on my foot. He stood there beside us and when the policemen came on horses and my little boy asked to be lifted up, he took him in his arms and held him up above the crowd. I had been holding him and my arms were tired.

"We stayed there until the flag came along and then we tried to get into Haas' to get something cold. He was still there when we left. This must have been fully 2 o'clock.

Sees Oxman on Stand

"When the Mooney trial started I went to court just to hear what was going on. One day I noticed that 'the live one' was sitting in a seat not far from me. It never occurred to me to think he was a witness because I had heard all witnesses ordered from the court and he was there listening to the testimony. When they put him on the stand I couldn't believe my eyes. He was Oxman. When I heard him tell about all those things happening which I knew were not true because he was standing right beside me all the time he said he was watching the automobile, I wanted to get right up in court and call him a liar.

"Then I thought about my husband's job and how we were trying to get along and that this might queer everything for us; so I decided to wait. Then I thought that of course nobody would believe his testimony because it seemed to me no man living could see all he said he saw in that much time.

"I told my husband about it, but he told me to keep out of things and keep my mouth shut. He wasn't sympathetic, so I didn't say any more about it. I couldn't keep still, for I was so excited, so I told Mr. Klein, who lives in the Mentone, and Mr. Bowering, the manager."

"I didn't want to come into it. I saw some of those other women in court and I saw how the District Attorney got them all mixed up. I didn't know what to do. Finally I stayed away from court because it got me so upset.

"I wish I could keep out now. I don't want to get into the papers. I have my little boy and we are just getting a start. I have to keep him with my mother now most of the time so we can get along and I hate to have anything come up. I don't see what I can do, but I can't keep silent any more.

"I didn't want my husband to lose his job. I knew the Mooneys were with Labor and I thought maybe it might hurt him if I said anything on that side."

Mrs. Le Posee told her story in her room at the Mentone Hotel. Coffee was bubbling in a small percolator on the table and she was waiting for her husband to return for luncheon.

She agreed to see a reporter only after her husband had telephoned to her. Word of the situation got to *The Bulletin* office from a guest in the hotel who had become aware of the situation.

The Bulletin discovered first that a man by the name of Le Posee was employed at Sommer & Kauffman's. They sent for Mr. Sommer, who heard the story and sent for Le Posee. Mr. Sommer assured Le Posee that his position would not be jeopardized in the slightest by any truth which he and his wife might tell.

Even then Le Posee seemed to fear the consequences of revealing anything tending to discredit the testimony offered in the Mooney case.

He telephoned his wife at Mr. Sommer's suggestion and over the telephone she reiterated her statement that Oxman was the man to whom she had sold clothes in Portland and that he stood near them during the entire time that he claims to have been on lower Market street.

Her husband seems not to have known that she had talked to others. When he arrived at the hotel he said:

"Why didn't you tell me you had told these other men?"

"Because you were not sympathetic. You wanted me to keep still. I had to talk to someone," she said.

While Mrs. Le Posee talked to a reporter, Attorney Maxwell McNutt and Attorney J. G. Lawlor, having heard the story from one of the men to whom she told it, arrived and interviewed her preparatory to taking her affidavit.

Why I Don't Come to America
Bernard Shaw

"**M**Y anxiety lest I should disappoint America sometimes starts a train of thought which ends in my wondering whether America ever feels at all anxious as to whether it might disappoint me. If Americans knew anything about America, they would exclude all visitors until they had put their house in order. But I never yet met an American who had any notion of the institutions of his native land beyond a general and mostly erroneous idea that they are glorious.

"They do not know the risks they are asking me to run when they invite me to cross the Atlantic. They do not know that I should not be allowed to land if I told the truth about my political and religious convictions, or perhaps they never heard of any one telling the truth about such matters. They do not know that opinions on marriage and the population question would expose me to several years' imprisonment. They do not know that I quite frequently take railway journeys with ladies to whom I am not married (an abandoned practice common in Europe), and that for this I might in America end my days in a felon's cell.

"They do not know that in many states the purchase of a smart tie or the accidental protrusion from my pocket of an attractively colored handkerchief (and, until the war cut us off from German dyes, my ties and handkerchiefs were the stupefaction of London) would consign me to the penitentiary, if a policeman detected a lady in the act of admiring them.

"But I know all these things, and a good many more of the same sort, and they naturally make me nervous. If President Wilson will give me a safe conduct, insuring my return from the lines of American morality, I shall be much more likely to trust myself to the eagle's beak."

THE BLAST

Revolutionary Labor Paper
Published every 1st and 15th of the month
569 Dolores St., San Francisco, Cal.
Mail Address, Box 661   Phone, Park 499
Alexander Berkman, Editor and Publisher
M. E. Fitzgerald, Associate Worker   Carl Newlander, Assistant

SUBSCRIPTION
$1.00 Yearly   60c Six Months   5c Copy
Bundle rates 2½c per copy in bundles of ten.

203

Comments

Dishonorable "Honor"

COUNT VON BERNSTORFF, representing his imperial majesty, Wilhelm II, has been handed his passports. The people of the United States should never have had any representative of the tyrant Kaiser in their midst. But the severing of diplomatic relations is supposed to forecast war.

The war, so far as actual participation is concerned, will necessarily be a farce.

But the real horror of this impending declaration is the psychological change to be expected here at home. Every murder lust will have license, every Rooseveltian cave-man liar can spit blood in public and be acclaimed a hero; every expression of calmness, of breadth of mind, of decent brotherly love, will be branded as treason. It may even go so far as the hanging or imprisonment of every fine-spirited man and woman in the country. It will be an era of the skull-chewing and gut-spilling in life and literature. That will be the saddest part of it all.

And when it is over (which we hope will be in a very few months) the capitalist class of this country will find itself in the saddle with a standing army of a million or more to keep labor totally shackled for the industrial depression after the war.

What will Class Conscious Labor do? We have scorned European labor for its craven part. Will we do better?

The Battle With the Lumber Kings

ALL our readers should be familiar by this time with the story of the labor war centering about Everett, Washington. THE BLAST has become almost a local paper in recent times by the very necessity of the terrible struggle now going on in San Francisco. But we should not overlook the fact that a fight bigger in the number of lives envolved, if narrower in scope, is being fiercely waged in the Great Northwest. It is a combat which we cannot afford to neglect. Seventy-four men of the boldest type of working class warriors have their lives at stake! And the issue is a clear one, unbefogged by any suspicion of undeservedness.

Seventy-four defenses, even though they be without much truckling to lawyers, will cost an immense sum of money. That money must be forthcoming. Labor must respond.

It is a splendid opportunity for American Labor to show any backbone which it may possess. What a pity that Labor does not free such prisoners by means of its infallible weapon—the General Strike!—but since Labor will not use that weapon, let Labor come forth with full support of a legal defense.

Direct Action

THREE years ago a frail little woman decided to overthrow a great injustice or give her life in the attempt. Margaret Sanger took up the struggle to stop the reign of ignorance in matters so vital to the mothers of the poor as sex hygiene, especially "birth control." The law is deaf and blind. The monster of Intolerance set itself to crush her. But Margaret Sanger didn't mind being crushed, thrust herself into danger, defied the savage law of ignorance. And the blind beast saw.

Many individuals have in turn fought this fight. Emma

Goldman, Ben Reitman, Ida Rauh, Jessie Ashley, Bolton Hall, and Mrs. Sanger's sister, Ethel Byrne, have each received the heavy blow of the blind beast. But there is a limit to the blindness of even the public, and at last it has quailed before the choice of crushing a sincere woman willing to be crushed, and turning in its path.

So the machinery of the State of New York is creaking and groaning to find a way to avoid sending Margaret Sanger to jail to starve to death on hunger strike. It seems that the law will be repealed by the greatest of all legislatures: Direct Action.

All Hail—The Irish Worker

Jim Larkin has just issued the third number of *The Irish Worker*. In it the Irish radical movement finds a worthy champion and a reflection of the gallant spirits who last Easter week "had not the strength to wait, but only strength to die." Too long the splendid spirit of progressive Ireland has been exploited by Irish ward-heelers and soul-grinding Irish employers of the Ryan and Crimmins type. In his arduous task of dispelling the fog of economic ignorance from the ranks of the Irish workers here, the redoubtable Irish fighter deserves the co-operation of every radical in America. *The Irish Worker* is a well printed illustrated weekly of twenty-four pages, and is published at 1046 North Franklin street, Chicago. Its subscription rates are $2 a year; six months, $1. The Blasters congratulate Comrade Larkin on his enterprise and assure him of their loyal support. Faugh-a-Ballagh!

India and Ireland

THOSE Anglomaniacs who are rapturously applauding the imminence of war with Germany and our government's consequent alliance with England, "the protector and guiding star of small nations," should be handed a copy of that excellent illustrated pamphlet, *India Against Britain*, written and published by Ram Chandra, editor of the *Hindustan Gadar*, San Francisco.

In the world's history England's government ranks as the most arbitrary despot of colonial powers. Before the development of machinery, England was a comparatively happy country and its sturdy yeomanry was eulogized in song and story. With industrial growth grew its monopolists—with its overproduction grew its necessity for more and more markets and with its accumulation of territory grew its total disregard of the rights and liberties of smaller nations. In most of its wars of aggrandizement, its most potent weapon has been the machine gun.

In India, the British government's favorite weapon was artificial famine. Next was its stimulation of caste differences. I well remember being told at Irish firesides how, during the dark days of the Irish Famine of '41, the Sultan of Turkey was desirous of sending a ship-load of food to the starving Irish. The British Ambassador vetoed it at once. "Why, your Royal Highness," he urged, "the humane English people and their Queen shall never allow the Irish Race to perish whilst there is a loaf of bread in Britain." But whilst Merrie England ate its roast beef, the Irish died by the roadside eating grass.

In like manner India has been depopulated, whilst English rulers waxed fat on the country's wealth. India has been taxed to death and its people have been goaded to the point where honorable death has been preferable to the abject slavery imposed by Christian Britain.

India's story is the story of Ireland, the story of Egypt, the story of Persia, the story of every country Britain's parasites ever coveted. The crocodile tears that bourgeois Britain sheds for Belgium deceive no one. She encouraged the Belgians to resist the all-conquering Teutons and all the help she gave them was two thousand marines, headed by the innocuous "Winnie" Churchill, to defend Antwerp—a hopeless task.

The Indians have given a new crop of martyrs to the sacred cause of liberty and their blood has not been shed in vain.

The spirit of revolt is at large in India and its terribly perse-cuted people are preparing for a final battle against the invaders who have starved and exploited them so long. Their problem is exceedingly well set forth in Ram Chandra's publications, *India Against Britain*, 15c; *British Rule in India*, by W. J. Bryan, 5c; *Tyranny of Indian Police*, 5c.   ED GAMMONS

Society's Wives Go to Church
Pauline Smith

SOCIETY guards carefully its favorite myth, monogamy. Every man is supposed to have a wife—and nearly every man does, either a whole wife or else a part interest in one. Wives are bought in this rotten society. A supposedly first-class wife, fit for permanent use by a select gentleman, commands the price of being fed, clothed and named, with her owner's name, for life.

Then a second-class wife, good for a year's use or so by a young gentleman not wishing as yet to invest in permanent property, is paid with enough to live upon while being used, and a little consolation fund upon being discarded.

But the third-class wives—there's the rub!—the wives who are fit but for a half hour's use. These wives are purchased by poor young men who can only afford a half-hour of them, and by such rich young men as have third-class taste.

As the poor buys its coal by the bucket, so the average starveling "hall-room boy" buys his "wife" by the hour. 'Tis the best he can do.

He who can afford it gets himself a wife exclusively for his own use—just as those who can afford it have a bathroom for their exclusive use. The poor young man of the average sort whose family shares a bathroom with five other families—this young man usually, "until he gets his start," meets the sex urge by sharing a wife with twenty or forty other men with whom he is not even acquainted. One might say, they "club together," forty men sharing one wife—and her price. My God, what a filthy thing you are, Society! When I was a small girl I used to pass by the cottage of a dark-haired "public" wife. There were often a dozen men lined up at her door waiting their turns.

This is Society's third-class "wife." Society is ashamed of her and tries to make believe that there don't exist any second-and third-class wives, but only the first-class kind, kept "ex-clusively for one's own use." Whenever Society's third-class wife indiscreetly shows her face to daylight, Society shudders and pulls its clothes about itself, if it has them on at the time, and advises the poor lady to go seek God.

*   *   *   *   *

SUDDENLY three hundred of Society's third-class wives went to church the other day, in San Francisco, looking for God.

God wasn't in. Only a little preacher, a little peevish preacher who had made the mistake of talking too loudly about the third-class wives proposing half hour marriages at the door of the house of God. The third-class wives waked up, if God didn't, and three hundred of them came to church.

Church is the last place on earth that Society wants its so-called prostitutes to come—Church is the place for male prostitutes—not female.

But Society's bluff was called. The hypocritical invitation to "come to God" was accepted. Society's half-hour wives stormed the church and demanded to know whether the little minister's religion stopped at the door of the religious house.

This is probably the most dramatic scene ever brought to light in America—a thing more likely to happen in a Latin country than in stodgy Anglo-Saxon parts. The respectable city was stirred to its depths. Glaring headlines flashed the astonishing fact that three hundred "prostitutes" went to the Reverend Paul Smith's church to see him. The poor little preacher didn't know what to do, for what preacher ever does? He didn't want to associate with them and he didn't want to refuse to associate with them. The hell of it was that there were too many to send away in a patrol wagon without making the public take notice, so the poor trembling man of God took Society's wives into the church and tried to talk to them. The trouble is he tried to talk **down** to them and suddenly one of them asked him "What are you going to do with us when you have thrown us out onto the street? How are we to make a living?" "Will your respectable ladies see that we can have jobs with which to make a living?" "Why don't you drive us into the sea?" "Is there any place in this city where we can get a chance to live by working?" "What do you know about us, anyway?"

The Reverend Paul Smith asked, "How many of you would take a job at $8 a week?" The answer was a derisive and bitter laugh. Then Society's wife began to **talk down** to little Paul Smith and told him some things that he never knew before, and which he doesn't know even now.

Stumped beyond his ability to extricate himself, little Smith admitted that it was the "saddest day of his life," and he didn't recover his equilibrium and Pharisaical gall until the women were beyond the "door of God" and the power to answer the preacher. Whereupon the ecclesiastical gentleman used the news-papers, which would refuse (with the exception of *The Bulletin*) the third-class wives a chance to reply. He published an accusation (apparently false) that Mrs. Gamble, chief mouth-piece for the women, is a "vicious exploiter who had stolen $180 entrusted to her care by a girl." Then the little preacher continued his interrupted career of mental prostitution, content with having worsted the physical prostitute.

The details are of no consequence, but the event itself has been one of the most valuable for enlightenment, the most wonderful, the most wholesome as a reaction to hypocrisy, that has been seen in America in years.

The Barbary Coast is quieter now; a "vice clean-up" has staged itself, and "Vice" is holding a mask before its face till the play is over. But the event is written indelibly in history. "Society's wife" came to God, and God wasn't in.

The Straight Road

THEY got y', kid, they got y'—just like I said they would.
    You tried to walk the narrow path,
    You tried, and got an awful laugh;
And laughs are all y' did get, kid—they got y' good!

They never knew the little kid—the kid I used to know;
    The little bare-legged girl back home,
    The little kid that played alone—
They don't know half the things I know, kid, ain't it so?

They got y', kid, they got y'—you know they got y' right;
    They waited till they saw y' limp,
    Then introduced y' to the pimp—
Ah, you were down then, kid, and couldn't fight!

I guess y' know what some don't know, and others know damn
        well—
    That sweatshops don't grow angels' wings,
    That workin' girls is easy things,
And poverty's the straightest road t' Hell!   —Paul Hanna

Eight   THE BLAST

Another Radical College!

ALL schools of radical thought in San Francisco have found, at last, a comfortable, rallying centre and at the same time an opportunity to educate the public and the youth of the city to a better understanding of the big problems confronting our civilization. The new centre is the *Jack London Memorial Library and School of Social Science*, 1256 Market street.

Its primary aim is to complete the incomplete education given in our State colleges on questions of sociology and government.

Its faculty is composed of people of wide attainment who are recognized as leaders of progressive aims and thought.

Amongst them are Emil Liess, economist and educator; Emil Kern, President of the San Francisco Radical Club; Max Bedacht, editor of *Vorwaerts;* Ethel Cotton, of the Ethel Cotton School of Dramatic Art and Expression; Professor Leo Wax, of the Department of Bionomics and Biology at Harvard and Stanford; Cameron King, noted Socialist Lecturer and attorney, and William McDevitt, Election Commissioner.

The courses now open for instruction are Logic, Labor History, Evolution, European and American History, Voice Culture and Public Speaking, Universal Literature and Scientific Socialism. There is also a department for children.

No instruction fees are charged, and those capable and willing to help correct the social and economic fallacies of the masses are cordially invited to enroll themselves and their friends in these courses.

Six thousand volumes, representative of the best radical thought of the world, are free to the public at all times. In the splendid reading room may be found also all the current periodicals and radical literature. The founders plan to increase this splendid library to twenty thousand volumes before many moons have passed. Success attend their efforts!

I 'LL niver go down again to see sojers off to th' war. But ye'll see me at th' depot with a brass band whin th' men that causes wars starts f'r th' scene iv carnage.—Mr. Dooley.

Vol. II.   SAN FRANCISCO, MARCH 15, 1917   No. 3

THIS man subjected himself to imprisonment and probably to being shot or hanged under the new Espionage Bill

THE prisoner used language tending to discourage men from enlisting in the United States Army

IT is proven and indeed admitted that among his incendiary statements were—

THOU shalt not kill

and

PEACE on earth good will to men

Why Not Burn the Declaration of Independence?

Robert Minor

WE are plunging into war head-first. That is, Wall Street-first. There are probably not a thousand civilians in the United States outside of Wall Street (or a branch of it) who are in the least interested in having a war, or in the purposes of the impending entrance of this country into war. Yet we are headed straight for it. The reluctant majority of the body politic remains passive and dumb, scared stiff by the fetich of patriotism, while the head of the body politic, Wall Street, drags all into the turmoil.

In a moving picture show the other day we saw a photograph of Wall Street. Every inch of available space seemed to hold a flag. The owners of buildings everywhere are beginning to follow the lead of the owners of buildings in Wall Street, and the rest of the populace simply looks on and thereby discovers that it is patriotic, i. e., bloodthirsty. It is a wonderfully clear lesson. There is no reason for war except the Wall Street reason—that Wall Street backed the Allies and intends to see them win if it costs the life of the last American moujik.

With the principal news agencies owned or tampered with by Lord Northcliffe, the country has been saturated with the insolent royal English propaganda until it is a wonder that Wilson, with the Department of State and the Army and Navy heads, does not have a public burning of the Declaration of Independence on the Capitol steps.

Wilson has been swallowing "insults" from London fast enough to choke him. The English navy has demanded and received the privilege of controlling the United States mails without a whimper from Wilson. The shipping of American capitalists has been the plaything of the British, handled in any way that Britain saw fit, without even the trouble of an apology. When a few poor simple German-Americans made a noise about it, the insolent British government merely explained that it was "done in the interest of civilization."

Nothing counts but the war loans, and the war loans are bet upon the Allied side, so a hundred million Americans are slowly slipping into the abyss, dumb and paralyzed by their worship of symbols as silly as the sacred bull that was used to paralyze the minds of ancient Egypt. Wall Street drapes itself in the flag which means no more to it than forty cents' worth of bunting, and the rest of America slowly, stupidly is kicked into line behind the flag that is to it some strange narcotic. We saw a soldier in a saloon the other day singing in hectic drunkenness "The Grand Old Rag"; and the look of his blood-shot eye gave assurance that it meant to him blood. In blind duty, the common man, with a blank stare of stupidity, takes up the cry of "The Grand Old Rag."

In another moving picture show some marines were shown marching under arms; simultaneously a silly jingle was played that passes for sacred music in American patriotic circles; in other words, some patriotic air. To our surprise, only a few asses applauded upon seeing the uniforms and the guns and hearing the sacred jingle. A few minutes later the scene of the "Departure of Count Von Bernstorff" was flashed upon the screen and to our surprise many asses applauded! It was rather interesting to note that at a time when everyone expected war to break within a few hours, Count Von Bernstorff got more applause in conjunction with a silly German patriotic tune than the American marines did in conjunction with a silly American patriotic tune! And that right here in San Francisco! It is true that the Von Bernstorffian applause was followed by a few hisses, but immediately the applause doubled and the hisses were drowned out, and the aye and nay vote had gone to Von Bernstorff.

Of course, we have as much contempt for the Von Bernstorffian patriotism as we have for the Wall Street spawn. It's interesting, that's all, and may be a forecast of some hideous hell likely to break loose within the borders of America when Wall Street steers us the rest of the way into war. It may indicate that the asses will not all be of the same school of asininity; it may mean that the declaration of war will be followed by an insane orgy of killing right and left on the streets of American cities, lynching of men with German-sounding names in New York and San Francisco and the lynching of men with English-sounding names in Milwaukee and Cincinnati.

What fools men are! Always willing to give and take death for any cause on earth except Liberty and Justice.

OF course, the British asses in American skins are fast coming to the front; the gnashing of Theodore Roosevelt's teeth echoes across the continent as he rushes into the soul-depressing situation to hysterically inform "us" "how to win."

Then there is a particularly loathsome fellow in New York by the name of Whitman, who holds the job of governor of the State, which job he obtained over the corpses of those he sent to the electric chair as district attorney in various popular newspaper-led lynchings. This Governor Whitman evidently is close to the hypnotic smell of bunting in Wall Street, for he gave vent to one of the most amusing bits of stupidity of all. A certain prize-fighter by the name of Les Darcy was scheduled to fight in New York, and Whitman saw a chance to make a grand stand play. Whitman announced that Les Darcy would not be permitted to fight—why? **Because he was not doing his duty fighting in the British army!** A governor of the State of New York becomes a recruiting sergeant for the British army! How loathsome is the lack of even their own pretense of self-respect in such persons as governors! Yes, Governor Whitman denounced the prize-fighter thunderously in the London-owned New York papers—denounced the prize-fighter with the London-coined epithet, **"slacker."**

By these straws we know the wind; we know that the gold that is poured into American coffers for powder and shot and bombs and bayonets has corrupted the American governmental machine; we know that every square inch of honor has been bought by London, and we know that nothing on earth will save us from the impending tragedy unless a little rebellious spirit should appear in the lines of Labor—the faint hope that lingers, not because there is any chance of much spunk in Labor, but because a very little particle of it would go a damned long way.

THE prostitutes of State and college are busy paving the way for the American sheep to be sheep gracefully. A perfectly idiotic scrap of paper, the size of a man's hand, has been pounced upon by Woodrow Wilson. A letter written by an insignificant German, Zimmerman, is shoved into the faces of a hundred million Americans as an excuse for war. And the note means, if it is not a forgery—nothing at all.

A certain professor of the University of California let slip a few words the other day that are illuminating: **"The whole Balkan question is not worth the bones of one Berkeley boy."**

Balkan question? What has that to do with it? Professor, you should not let the cat out of the bag; remember, it is **"honor"** that is involved; remember, it is the submarines that sink a British ship containing two or three American pleasure-seekers and thirty thousand tons of ammunition that are the basis of this war. The Balkan situation? Oh, Professor, how can you be so stupid as to tell the truth at a time like this? You proceed to say, "The whole Balkan question is not worth the bones of one Berkeley boy, **but we must do our duty and not let anyone else do our fighting for us."** (Meaning precisely the opposite of what you say.)

The Balkan situation is simply this: An enormous cross-mark drawn upon the map of Europe, one line from Berlin down through Asia Miner, the other line from Central Russia to the Mediterranean Sea, would intersect at Constantinople. This **X** mark is the story of the Balkans. German manufacturers, being more or less shut off from the West by Great Britain, want to sell their goods in Asia Minor and build up markets eastward. The way to do that is to get a continuous railroad line from Germany to Bagdad.

The British don't want Germans to get direct rail connection with territory so close to India. The big, fat, dropsical British industrial system is too soft and slovenly for competition, and for German merchants to reach the border of India with their products would mean a hundred thousand British asses tumbling out of comfortable clubs and homes to earn a living instead of feasting upon bleeding India; therefore, Britain, controlled by the East Indian trading interests, is against a German railroad through the Balkans.

Now for the other line of the X, from Central Russia to the Mediterranean. This is the only hope of Russian commercial interests to ever attain a modern status and strength, for the northern sea-ports of Russia are bound in ice a part of the year and Russia must have a backward commercial system until she can get a warm-water outlet for wheat and her other products, unhampered by the tariff restrictions of an unfriendly power. Therefore, Russian interests are set on keeping Germany's line of communication broken so that Germany cannot obstruct Russia's other leg of the X.

That is what the war is about. When the Austrian government demanded that Servia permit Austrian police authorities to participate in running down the assassins of the Austrian archduke, the Austrian government really meant nothing more or less than to get a toe-hold in the management of Servia for the purpose of ultimately forcing railroad concessions for Austria

and Germany. They didn't give a damn for the killing of the archduke; it was the Berlin to Bagdad railroad for which Germany and Austria saw a chance of breaking a right of way through Servia, that caused the Austrian demands. The reason the Austrian demands were refused was simply that Russia saw its hopes of controlling warm-water ports going glimmering if Austria got a toe-hold in Servia; and because the fat English aristocracy saw its blood-sucking hold on the throat of India about to be broken.

NOW, why are the peace offers of Germany refused by the British?

Because Germany controls at the present time an almost complete right of way from Berlin to Bagdad, and if the war stopped at the present moment, the British East Indian interests would go to smash and have to be reorganized on a modern plane of small profits and sharp competition.

So London refuses peace and commands New York to start war upon Germany.

Wall Street is flaring, glittering with bunting. Since when did Wall Street become honorable? It means that you Americans are to go and dot the hills of France, and possibly the Balkans, with your graves, because Lord Northcliffe bought the New York newspaper interests and J. P. Morgan financed the Allied arsenal; and London commands that India must remain its prostrate victim if it cost the life of the last American moujik.

Poor Woodrow Wilson is nothing but the tin whistle through which the war blast blows. Wall Street blows the blast and you Americans are commanded to kill and to die.

Are you so paralyzed with stupid fetiches and rag-time songs about a "grand old rag" that you cannot refuse?

The Lynching

ALEXANDER BERKMAN

MOONEY convicted! What almost everyone believed impossible has actually happened. In spite of the self-contradictory evidence of the prosecution, in spite of the badly-jointed perjury of the State's important witnesses, in spite of the overwhelming proof of his innocence, Mooney has been convicted.

Are there still humans extant who believe that justice for workers is to be found in the courts? That the Fickerts, Swansons, Cunhas et al., have deliberately plotted to railroad innocent men to the gallows is now plain even to the lowest intelligence. Could the judge have been so blind as not to see it? If he was, he is not fit to be a judge, as indeed no one is fit to sit in judgment over others. "Judge not that ye be not judged."

But the judge could not be so blind. His charge to the jury proves that he was not. Indeed, his charge would have ordinarily acquitted any man not in the prisoners' dock as the representative of a cause, of a new ideal, of the best aspirations of Labor for ultimate emancipation. And here is where the root of the thing lies. Mooney and his co-defendants are not being tried for bombing, for murder or any other crime of such ordinary, common nature. No indeed! They are being tried for a far greater crime, more heinous than any on the court calendar— the crime of heresy.

They have propagated a new message, the freedom of man and the dignity of Labor. They have preached a new gospel, even like unto Christ. Like unto Christ, they are to be crucified. For no sin is greater in the eyes of the ruling class, no crime more unforgivable than the preachment of the brotherhood of Man and the solidarity of Labor.

Judge Griffin is a small man. He lacked the bigness of heart and mind to rise to the great opportunity that the perjured and prejudiced verdict offered him. Convinced as he must be of the innocence of Mooney—as his charge to the jury proves him to be—he lacked the probity and courage to refuse to accept the foul verdict. He could have graven his name large on the

tablets of history as an exceptional, wonderful phenomenon— a just judge. But he is not an Altgeld. He did not dare expose the frame-up that is thirsting for the blood of innocent men. He preferred to remain a judge, craven-hearted and conscience-stricken, rather than to immortalize his name at the cost of political preferment.

AND so Mooney must die to satisfy the vengeance of the Chamber of Commerce? And with him others of his co-defendants? Oh, Justice, thine eyes have been bandaged so long, thy sight, mind and heart have rotted away. It is sheer folly to look for the fair goddess, the Goddess of Fairness, in the temples built for the special worship of the blind bawd. No, never will there be found "Justice" for Workers. The Power of Labor alone holds the true scales. Its mighty hand alone can deal the workers fair play. In the last analysis it will not be the judge or jury that will pronounce the final verdict in this case. The awakened conscience of the people, of the great masses of workers of America, will speak the final verdict that will expose the Pilate crime of San Francisco to the undying execration of mankind and enshrine the names of its victims among the martyrs of Labor and the immortals of history.

Already the voice of Labor is being heard in protest against the heaven-crying outrage. The Labor Council of San Francisco and of other California cities, the Federation of Labor of Chicago, the Central Federated Union of New York, the United Hebrew Trades, and the Central Labor bodies of numerous other cities have unqualifiedly condemned Lynch Law against Labor in California. Every labor and labor-friendly organization must at once go on record in behalf of Mooney and his co-defendants. A mass-movement must be organized to sweep the country from the Pacific to the Atlantic in a storm of protest that shall terminate the masters' conspiracy to legally murder these labor men. In this alone there is hope for justice; in this alone lies the saving of our brothers and sister and the prevention of the repetition of the judicial murders of 1887.

THE BLAST

Revolutionary Labor Paper
Published every 1st and 15th of the month
569 Dolores St., San Francisco, Cal.

Mail Address, Box 661   Phone, Park 499

Alexander Berkman, Editor and Publisher
M. E. Fitzgerald, Associate Worker   Carl Newlander, Assistant

SUBSCRIPTION
$1.00 Yearly   60c Six Months   5c Copy
Bundle rates 2½c per copy in bundles of ten.

Reflections

Food Riots

FOOD everywhere, warehousefuls of it, carloads upon carloads—and nothing to eat for the poor. That is the present situation in New York as in other great cities of America.

Think of the spectacle! The richest city of the richest country in the world, in the most prosperous period of its existence, has thousands, hundreds of thousands of men, women and children actually starving for the necessaries of life—and forced to riot for bread.

Nor is it the unemployed who, because of lack of work, cannot secure their livelihood. Oh, no! Work is plentiful, and the husbands and brothers of the rioting women are toiling from early morn till late into the night. But their earnings cannot compete with the soaring prices of the necessaries of life. It is not the unemployed or "shiftless" that are starving. It is the wives and children of the "fortunate" employed that cannot afford to buy sufficient food. Lo, the triumph of capitalist civilization!

Back again we are in the darkest days of old Rome, when the helots massed in the street with the cry of despair, "Panem, panem!" ("Bread, bread!") The masters of Rome at least had the excuse that there was not enough food to go around. But what excuse have the Neros of today? The hostelries of the rich are stocked with viands of the choicest sort; the cold storage fortresses are bursting with food. Provisions by the trainloads are forbidden to be unloaded. Last fall, fish and fruit in large quantities were dumped into the rivers to create an artificial scarcity.

Speculation is the Lord God of our day. The city fathers, the legislators, State and National, stand helpless before the great King Mammon. No one claims that there is not enough food to go around. Food, good food, there is a-plenty, but the speculators keep it from the people! And the mayors and governors, the humanitarians and reformers know no better than to advise the starving to—eat rice! Forthwith the price of rice soars Zeppelinward. The idea of expropriating the murderous speculators, of returning to the people the food they themselves have produced, never occurs to these benefactors. What! To give back to the people the things they have been robbed of?—that would be "lawless," "criminal," sacrilege against the holiest of holies, Monopoly.

And so the good, patriotic, law-abiding people must starve in silence. The more daring cry for a crust of bread or a potato for their children, and are clubbed and arrested by the police for "rioting."

This is civilization in the blessed country of the free—home of the brave.

WHY should these people not be patriotic and shed their last drop of blood in defense of their country? What if they have to riot in their own land for an onion or a potato, or if they have not an inch of space they may call their own? The "honor" of the country must be protected at all cost, the honor of Wall Street and the right of speculators to coin millions out of the European slaughter.

Above all, one must be a patriot, must love and protect the country that starves him.

Flim-Flam

NOW it appears that Germany has been making "indecent proposals" to Mexico and Japan. Nothing less than a sinister plot to invade these United States. And President Wilson, it seems, knew of it all along, but refused to take the sovereign American citizen or even Congress into his confidence. He subtly saved the information to be sprung at a psychological moment, to stampede Congress into giving him the power of a dictator. Wily Woodrow, whom the pacifists and other well-meaning but weak-minded persons adored as the very personification of sincerity, straightforwardness and peace.

Not since the days of the Royalist Hamilton has this republic had such a shrewd politician at the helm as Wilson. Under his inspiration the democracy is being transformed into an armed camp—for the protection of the starving American masses against their native exploiters and blood-suckers? Oh, no! Rather for the safeguarding of the blood-dripping profits of the American munition hucksters abroad and the protection of the American employers against the ever-growing discontent of labor at home.

Workers, be on your guard. Militarism means your complete subjugation. It means industrial conscription and the paralysis of the whole labor movement. You have nothing to fear from the workers of other countries. They are similarly oppressed and exploited as you are. Your interests are common; your enemy is the same—the capitalist class that feeds on your toil. Your greatest, your only danger is from your enemy at home—the exploiters of labor.

EVERYONE likes to be thrilled and some liked to be humbugged. But in the present "foreign foe" scare there is nary a thrill. It is all pure humbug. The munition makers will be the only beneficiaries; the people will foot the bills; and labor will be industrially conscripted.

WITH a bluster, certain men are now stating that "Labor disputes that rent England and France a year ago will not be repeated in this country should the United States be plunged into war. Disputes between the government and labor held those countries back more than a year. It will not be that way in America. Labor will know what is expected of it and Labor will be ready for the call."

Why say this so loudly? Has anybody denied it? The reason for saying it seems to be the fear that it may not be true. Let us hope.

German Militarism

IN order to save us from German Militarism, the "Espionage Bill" comes to light. Under this law, if finally passed, any person who expresses an opinion that might discourage men from joining the army, may be taken out and shot. Russia is, it seems, the future ally of the United States, and the United States will try to go Russia one better on beastly military tyranny. Germany is bad enough; Russia is worse; and the United States, to save the world from the tyrannical German system, is to be more despotic in its laws and submit its citizens more rigorously to the bucolic whims of uniformed murderers than either Russia or Germany or any other place under the sun.

If you express your opinion that the politicians that rule the land might be sending us to slaughter for the benefit of the financial class, you are a traitor, a spy, a criminal to be shot immediately.

It is a good thing that laws are never enforced simply for being laws. Sometimes the law happens to be what the people will stand; then it is enforced. If it is not what the people will stand, it is not enforced. And everything that the people will stand is always enforced anyhow, so it doesn't make much difference what the law is.

The law is practically no more than an indication of what it is the intention of the powers-that-be to enforce, and a feeler thrown out to see what the multitude will stand. There are thousands of laws on the statute books that are not enforced and no public official, except in grand-stand speeches, makes any pretense of enforcing all of the laws. We constantly hear of some judge or police chief announcing that he intends, "after this," to enforce a certain law, "if," etc. The "if" always means if a strong element demands it.

The perfect abandon with which enemies of the financial powers have vengeance heaped upon them in violation of all law proves that a law is not needed for the enforcement of any desire of the powers. And the perfect immunity of any powerful person or interest from all law shows that any law is a joke unless the strongest power in the land demands its enforcement.

According to law, as doubtless it soon will stand, you can be taken out and shot for speaking sanely or decently on this most important subject—war. But, as a matter of fact, they can do nothing of the kind to you if you are strong enough—and brave enough. The espionage law is merely a bluff to scare timid pacifists from protest. If pacifists have the courage to defy it, this cowardly, tyrannical, beastly law will not dare to touch them.

A Woman Dares

CAPITALIST civilization is a monster bawdy-house. Everyone in it is expected to be a prostitute. And most particularly those who have positions in any governmental institution are supposed to hold their very souls subject to the demands of the bawdy trade.

The bawdy-house is now and then thrown into a hubbub by the refusal of some clean soul to prostitute itself.

Now particularly is the bawd trade booming as war time approaches. Everyone is expected to be a perfect prostitute, and the penalties are heavy.

A teacher in a Kansas City school has refused to prostitute her calling as a teacher—she has been really teaching; she has dared to speak the truth. Kansas City is turned upside down and the Navy Department has gone into action like the body of hysterical ninnies that a Navy Department should and must be. Pompous naval officers are running about, burning the telegraph wires, and Washington is groaning with anguish because a little woman teacher wrote upon a blackboard, in an obscure Kansas City school-room:

"Why enlist? You have nothing to gain and your life to lose. I refuse to kill my brother and hide my fists in the folds of any flag."

Miss Warneson's sin was merely that of advising against killing.

"I do not think these sentences are any more radical," said she to the president of the Board of Education, "than those enunciated by Christ when He said, 'Thou shalt not kill.' I don't think they are more radical than 'Peace on earth, good will toward men.'"

What "patriotism" really is has been thoroughly shown by the fact that Miss Warneson's teaching of "Thou shalt not kill" has been denounced as anti-patriotism. Indeed, "Thou shalt not kill" is the antithesis of patriotism.

How dare the little woman disturb the house of prostitution by shouting, while the customers are here, "Thou shalt not prostitute?"

Brave little woman! You have shown Americans what one individual can do. If you, a lone little school teacher, can turn the Navy Department upside down and cause a hubbub from Coast to Coast, what could not a thousand courageous individuals do?

The capitalist bawdy business requires absolute submission, and a few hundred brave spirits in evidence would stop this particular bawdy business of militarism now and save the land from the hell that is breaking.

SEND for a copy of Margaret Sanger's new magazine, *The Birth Control Review*, 104 Fifth avenue, New York City.

The Bought Lie

IF ever a common man had any cause to believe in the courts of law, the events of recent times in America should bring him flatly to the point of view that the purpose and effect of all court procedure is merely to put a blessing upon crime. In Everett, Washington, the crime of hanging or imprisoning seventy-four I. W. W. prisoners calls, of course, for a perjurer or two. A perjurer was sure to be forthcoming; we could have foretold that a half year in advance. He has come.

One Charles Auspos, alias Austin, has decided to take the thirty pieces of silver, or, in American money, five thousand dollars, and his liberty in exchange for swearing to what the employers want in the way of "testimony" against the other seventy-three prisoners.

Five thousand dollars! The regular price for perjury on the Pacific Coast. The same price that was offered Weinberg and Billings for the blood of Mooney in San Francisco.

Auspos seems to be a last resort, several others having been made the offer before he accepted. One of the I. W .W.'s by the name of McDowell was smuggled away to the little town of Mount Vernon, Washington, and offered the same $5,000 and a trip to Honolulu in consideration for perjury against his comrades. McDowell happened to be a decent man and will probably hang for it. The whole result of the attempt to bribe McDowell was merely the exposure of the dirty plot.

The trial of Thomas H. Tracy is commencing at the present time. The same old farce it will be, of course.

We wonder what the result would be if all of the seventy-three prisoners were to unite in one grand defiance and refusal to join in the court procedure. Nothing else seems to work in securing justice. Advice is cheap and we don't wish to impose it; but perhaps some day someone may try the logical attitude toward a contemptible institution and will find that his defiance will paralyze the institution through the appeal of courage to public opinion.

Another Gallows Stampede!

ISRAEL WEINBERG'S trial is set for March 26th. With the treasury of the Defense League exhausted, Weinberg has not even been able to arrange for attorneys. He was brought into court alone, March 13th, and he asked for time to get together attorney fees and hire a lawyer. The judge's response was merely to call to the bar a young attorney who had appeared for Weinberg in a small technical matter and demand that he defend Weinberg on the murder charge and that the trial proceed almost immediately. When the young attorney explained that Weinberg did not desire to be defended by him, the judge threatened the lawyer with jail and intimated that he would force Weinberg to go to trial with that attorney whether he wished or not.

A Huge Corporation and What It Stands For

The American International Corporation has been organized with a capital of fifty million dollars for over-seas trade and financing. It is financed and officered by Standard Oil and Morgan interests. It is the American expression of the big exploiting banks of England, Germany and France. The officers of this corporation are boldly insisting that this country must enter the fields which they have laid out for it, that the adverse decision of President Wilson in the Chinese five power loan must be abandoned and that America must stand back of these exploiting and investing interests in their over-seas activities.—Frederic C. Howe in *The Public*.

What is Freedom? It is obedience to Nature's laws, and to those laws only.—Laurie J. Quinby in *The Public*.

Full Story of Mooney Conviction

M. E. F.

FRESH from the press comes the second edition of the now famous pamphlet, *The Frame-Up System*, the story of the trials of Billings and Mooney. A splendid story it is, chock full of brand new news of live interest to everyone, whether having read the earlier edition or not. The first edition of sixteen pages was sold to the number of 50,000. This second edition has thirty-two pages and is twice as good, with an array of photographs that explain the most astonishing story of fraud that ever came out of a so-called criminal trial. It is expected to sell to the number of half a million or more, the first order having been placed for 100,000 copies.

At the blackest hour in the legal status of these historic cases, the dawn of public understanding seems about to break. For, if Mooney stands sentenced to death, nevertheless the truth is known to a few of those big souls who cannot be denied a hearing; therefore the truth is flying fast throughout the East, the West, the North and the South. W. Bourke Cockran has gone to the American people with his story. On March 14th he opened a campaign at Carnegie Hall, New York, under the auspices of the Central Federated Unions, with tremendous effect. On March 25th he will speak in Chicago under the auspices of the Chicago Federation of Labor, with every union man in Chicago summoned to attend.

So also is Frank P. Walsh under arms for the fight. It looks as though within a few weeks the whole tremendous body of American Labor will fully assert itself in active protest against this most cold-blooded judicial crime in American history.

The San Francisco Labor Council on February 16th took a worthy stand, passing by a heavy majority the following resolution which has since been passed by forty or fifty other Bay City Labor bodies:

Whereas, In the recent trial of Tom Mooney, a member in good standing in The International Molders' Union for the past fourteen years, he was convicted and is in imminent danger of being railroaded to the gallows on a trumped-up charge, and on the most brazen and contradictory testimony; and

Whereas, It has been proven that the testimony of Estelle Smith, Crowley and McDonald, used to convict Warren K. Billings, is a flat contradiction of the evidence of Oxman, used to convict Mooney; and

Whereas, Twenty-one alibi witnesses, numerous photographs and time clocks have established an unmistakable alibi; and

Whereas, The verdict is at total variance with the evidence produced, and is the result of the prosecution's past six months' activity in the public press in misrepresentations of facts and an appeal to the most severe prejudices of the public; therefore be it

Resolved, That we, The San Francisco Labor Council, affirm our belief in the innocence of Thomas J. Mooney and his co-defendants, and pledge them our aid in their efforts to secure justice; and be it further

Resolved, That a copy of these resolutions be forwarded to the labor and daily press.

Frank P. Walsh, in a letter to Mooney, says:

Kansas City, Mo., February 27, 1917.

Dear Friend Mooney—I have hesitated in answering your splendid letter of the 18th inst., so overwhelmed have I been with the thought that such a travesty upon justice could take place within the borders of our nation.

I agree with you that your case has become the concern of labor everywhere and that if there are those who have been unmindful of their duty toward you, that now, at least, they will be stimulated to the utmost endeavor to repair this frightful wrong.

It is certain that I have never before received a letter which made such a profound appeal to me as did yours, and I am lost in admiration for this expression of your brave and unquenchable spirit.

You may count upon me to do all in my power to present the facts in your case to the people of the United States, especially the world of labor. I agree with Mr. Cockran that your conviction may be the entering wedge to an awakening of the American people to the absolute necessity of reform in the administration of law. The greatest legal minds of this country, including the heads of great universities, high judicial officers, former presidents of the great bar associations of the country, and other leaders of thought, testified before the late Commission on Industrial Relations that the humble citizens, particularly the workers, were discriminated against in the courts of the country—a fearful arraignment, I would say, of our whole system of jurisprudence.

I cannot believe that your life is to be sacrificed, though I fully realize that in order to save it a strong, intelligent and well-directed appeal must be made to the nation. In my small way I have done all I could along this line.

You know that you have the deepest sympathy of my heart and I wish that you would extend the same to your good wife and your fellow sufferers. I hope that I may have something better and more definite to write to you further on.

As always,

Your sincere friend,

(Signed)   FRANK P. WALSH.

W. Bourke Cockran writes:

My Dear Mooney—I have reached the deliberate conclusion that the appalling Judicial Crime committed against you will never be allowed to reach the consummation which induced its perpetrators to plan it.

I think it can be shown clearly to all reasonable men that we are in the presence of another Dreyfus case, the only difference being that the object of the French perversion of legal procedure to the perpetration of the very crimes which courts are organized to prevent, was exclusion (by force and threats of force) of Jews from the Army; while the object of your prosecution for a crime repugnant to every element of your nature, is to drive laborers from organizing, by killing a man who has had the temerity to urge some of his fellows to form unions for their own protection.

If we can succeed in making this clear to the public mind, I have no doubt that the popular conscience of America will prove itself as capable and as eager to overrule the plans of the men who are conspiring to encompass the destruction of your life, as the conscience of France showed itself to defeat the men who, in adjudging Dreyfus guilty of treason, had succeeded in perverting to the destruction of Liberty and Character the very agencies organized to defend them.

Depressed as I was when met by a sense of utter helplessness to avert a calamity which threatens not merely your life, but the whole fabric of Civilization (for the whole purpose of Civilization is protection of life, which agencies of Civilization are here conspiring to destroy), I probably failed to appreciate the force of your suggestion when it was made yesterday.

But now I am convinced that the justice which appears to have fled from the California courts will be found to have taken refuge in the bosoms of the men and women who constitute the masses of our population, and their decision will be enforced against the officials who have foresworn their oaths to satisfy the malice and cupidity of corporation employers.

So be of good cheer. Your conviction may yet prove to be a source of such judicial reforms as will prevent forever the repetition of the conspiracy which has had you for its object; but which has not yet succeeded (and please God it never will succeed) in making you its victim.

Pray give my cordial regards to your companions in persecution, and also to the splendid woman whose devotion and self-renunciation have given me new and higher regard for our common humanity.

Yours faithfully,

(Signed)   W. BOURKE COCKRAN.

The Industrial Relations Committee, through George P. West, reports after careful examination from all sides:

Supported by the greatest financial interests in America, a powerful group of capitalists and employers in San Francisco has undertaken a campaign to crush trade unionism in the Pacific Coast metropolis. * * *

My investigation leaves not the slightest doubt that Mooney, Mrs. Mooney, Nolan, Billings and Weinberg are being prosecuted primarily because of their activity in conducting strikes and attempting to organize the unorganized. * * *

The district attorney of San Francisco, C. M. Fickert, was put into office by the United Railroads. He has the hearty endorsement and full confidence of the "Law and Order Committee" of the Chamber of Commerce.

This was expressed to me by Hugh Webster, the committee's Executive Secretary. * * *

Should Nolan, Mooneys, Billings and Weinberg be sent to the gallows for murder, there is not the slightest question that their conviction will be heralded throughout the United States as additional proof that organized Labor or the union shop can not be tolerated in a law-abiding community.

Eugene V. Debs, too, is in the battle and the whole Socialist Party seems on the verge of showing its best spirit in a whole-souled fight for justice.

From across the seas the Syndicalist Federation of Labor has sent a large donation to the defense from Amsterdam, Holland, and assures Tom Mooney and the boys that the organized labor movement of Holland is with them to the finish of the fight.

The date for the blackest crime in California history is set for May 17th. That is when Tom Mooney is booked to mount the scaffold and die for trying to organize the employees of the United Railroads.

To those perverted persons who glean their livelihood by making dead clay of what had been a brother man, we make the suggestion that the noose for Tom Mooney's neck be woven from the trolley ropes of the United Railroads.

But away with cynicism! **Tom Mooney must not be allowed to die.**

Send your orders for *The Frame-Up System* to International Workers' Defense League, 210 Russ Building, San Francisco.

Through the Baptism of Blood

Romain Rolland.

THE European thought of tomorrow is with the armies. The furious intellectuals in one camp and the other who insult one another do not represent it at all. The voice of the peoples who will return from the war, after having experienced the terrible reality, will send back into the silence of obscurity these men who have revealed themselves as unworthy to be spiritual guides of the human race. Amongst those who thus retire more than one St. Peter will then hear the cock crow, and will weep saying, "Lord, I have denied thee!" The destinies of humanity will rise superior to those of all the nations. Nothing will be able to prevent the re-forming of the bonds between the thought of the hostile nations. Whatever nation should stand aside would commit suicide. For by means of these bonds the tide of life is kept in motion. But they have never been completely broken, even at the height of the war. The war has even had the sad advantage of grouping together throughout the universe the minds who reject national hatred. It has tempered their strength, it has welded their wills into a solid block. Those are mistaken who think that the ideals of a free human fraternity are at present stifled! They are but silent under the gag of military (and civil) dictation which reigns throughout Europe. But the gag will fall, and they will burst forth with explosive force. I am agonized by the sufferings of millions of innocent victims, sacrificed today on the field of battle but I have no anxiety for the future unity of European society. It will be realized anew. The war of today is its baptism of blood.

Is the Horror of Bloodshed a Neurosis?

THE apologists for war with all its brutalities have found another indictment against the pacifists. They have made a discovery. They say that those who hate war simply suffer from a neurosis, the horror of bloodshed being a "well-known" minor nervous disease. Perhaps so. If horror of brutality and bloodshed is a neurosis, then I confess I am one of its victims,—and am rather proud of the fact. But may we remind the public that if the horror of bloodshed is a "well-known" neurosis, the love of bloodshed is a well-known perversion? May we remind the good editors and war apologists that lust-murder and sadism are phenomena well known to psychiatrists? May we also suggest the possibility of the truth of the assertion made by many students that *some* people go to war not out of patriotic motives, but out of sadistic impulses?

If those who hate, detest and abhor war are suffering from a neurosis, those who love and glorify and apotheosize war are suffering from one of the vilest of human perversions — sadism in its bloodiest, cruelest and most atavistic manifestations.

—WM. ROBINSON in *Critic and Guide*

What! Honest Senators!

Robert Minor

WE hesitate to make such a radical statement as that honesty can survive in a United States Senator, but nevertheless two or three Senators engaged in the filibuster against the law to make Wilson a dictator with power to make war at pleasure, have given suspicious signs of being honest.

We wouldn't go so far as to say that any great number of Senators could be honest; for instance, there's "Gum-shoe Bill" Stone of Missouri, who probably is on the side of decency because he represents a multitude of Missouri Germans, whose indecent prejudices paradoxically align them now against the war. But so elusive is the key to human character that honesty will creep up anywhere that we least expect it. There is so much strength and weakness mixed into every character that classifications are hard and even "Gum-shoe Bill" has for the past two years been astonishing those who thought they knew him, by his singularly decent and intelligent opposition to the Wall Street bomb-throwers—who throw shiploads of bombs across the Atlantic Ocean.

Senator La Follette has long been a strange sight of an apparently clean man who can remain clean through years spent in that Washington pig-sty, the Senate.

"The little group of twelve willful men" which is leading the fight in the Senate against leaving to the pleasure of one man the matter of plunging a hundred million Americans into war, are good to hear about, whatever their motives may be, hyphenated vote or what not.

Yes, and there's even an honest publisher it seems. Oswald Garrison Villard, publisher of the New York *Evening Post*, the only big New York paper that pretends to give sincere news, stated in plain English the point of view of his reactionary class. Mr. Villard said in a public speech: **"I have too much proof of people who give large checks to the preparedness and universal service movements on the ground that this will lead to the suppression of the coming social revolution, for me to have any doubt that that is one of the main factors behind the agitation."**

Eight   THE BLAST

DEFENSE FUND SAN FRANCISCO LABOR PRISONERS

Per Alexander Berkman.

Total collected to January 15......$2,722.08	
Grupo Anarquista, Boston, Mass..	5.00
Bessie Kimmelman, New York....	.50
R. N. Douglas, Postville, Iowa......	1.00
Hilda Kovner, Boston, Mass.........	3.75
Hjolmer Hakason, Waukeegan, Ill. (I. N. O. V.)......................	3.00
Mrs. E. A. Riley, Los Angeles, Cal.	2.50

$2,737.83

Previously to League.....................$2,722.08	
To Henry Hagelstein	3.75
To Robert Minor	12.00

March 15, to Defense League........$2,737.83

THE BLAST SUSTAINING FUND

From January 15 to March 15

W. H. Johnson, Dallas, Texas............	$5.00
T. H. Bell, Phoenix, Arizona............	5.00
Jennie Arnott, Palo Alto, Cal............	1.00
Group Light and Freedom, N. Y.......	5.00
Ellen Kennan, Denver, Colo..............	4.00
John Speis, Denver, Colo..................	4.00
Gertrude Nafe, Denver, Colo.............	1.00
Italian Group, Philadelphia, per *Cronaca Sovversiva*	5.00
M. Van Appeldoorn, Rochester, N.Y.	2.00
Circola Di Studi Sociali, Rosland, O.	3.60
Grupo Anarquista, Boston, Mass......	2.00
S. Rosenthal, Oakland, Cal................	2.00
Grupo Libertario, Iowa...................	2.00
Nathan Bassis, Philadelphia, per Sub. List	10.00
Group Bread and Freedom, Springfield, Mass....................................	12.00
John Chiara, Benicia, Cal.................	1.00
Rubin Edelstein, Philadelphia............	2.00

Total...............................$66.00

CONTRIBUTIONS RECEIVED FOR RICARDO MAGON

A. Hockstatter, New York.................$ .50	
Constantine Tarbol, Livingston, Ill....	7.00

Feb. 24, turned over to Magons........$7.50

WERE half the power that fills the world with terror,
Were half the wealth bestowed
on camp and courts,
Given to redeem the human mind from error,
There were no need of arsenals or forts.
—Henry Wadsworth Longfellow.

Do you realize the Importance of a

FEARLESS PRESS ?

Subscribe and get others to
subscribe for

THE BLAST

$1.00 the Year

569 Dolores St., San Francisco

Chicago Readers Take Notice !

W. Bourke Cockran

Ex-Senator, Famous Orator, who volunteered to defend Tom Mooney without fee in San Francisco, will address a mass meeting under the auspices of

The Chicago Federation of Labor

AT

Coliseum
March 25, 1917

Mr. Bourke Cockran will tell the real facts of the trial and conviction of Tom Mooney, organizer of the street car men in San Francisco, who has been condemned to die May 17th.

IF TOM MOONEY DIE
Then Three Million Union Men Will Know the Reason Why

JOHN G. LAWLOR
ATTORNEY AT LAW
Pacific Building, Market and Fourth Sts.
San Francisco

WAR AGAINST WAR

THE DAWN

A National Peace Magazine,
Edited by James Waldo Fawcett and Leigh Danen.
Published Every Saturday
At 63 Fifth Avenue, New York City.
10 cents the copy.

A SANE VOICE IN A MAD WORLD

Write for sample copy today.

Vol. II.　　　NEW YORK, MAY 1, 1917　　　No. 4

Why We Must Have An Army in France When the War Is Over

"Monsieur Morgan, I will pay back your dollars when my brothers' lives are repaid".

March and May

Alexander Berkman

MARCH, the revolutionary month of the proletariat, has again fulfilled its historic mission. A revolution, actually and potentially greater than any of the March days of 1848 and 1871, has been born in the Red Month of 1917.

The Russian Revolution has already accomplished much. It has justified all the sacrifices of the past fifty years. It has honored and hallowed the martyrdom of the number-less heroes and heroines in the fortress of the Petropavlovskaya and the Schluesselburg dungeons, in the frozen wilds of Siberia and the unspeakable hells of Katorga.

Only the first word has yet been spoken in the Dawn of Russia: only one leaf has been turned in the great book of the New Era. The Coming Days are passionate with promise.

After Red March, the bloom of May. The storm has broken and scattered the black clouds. It has purified the atmosphere. On its heels follows the bright sunshine, bringing balm to torn hearts, warming to new life and growth.

The womb of May holds re-birth and rejuvenation. Prophetic was the vision that chose the First of May for the gathering of the forces of the submerged. Its legions rise, stretch their formidable arms and sense their ac-cumulating power in the Springtime of Life.

March, the storm petrel of the revolution! May, the day of new hope and life! That their fruition may blos-som in Nineteen Hundred and Seventeen!

The echo of the Russian March storm is resounding through the breadth of Europe. More and more distinct grows the rumbling of universal Discontent. Its voice, though gagged and stifled, is heard above the thunder of contending cannon. The breath of May is in the air. The million-felt urge of Life and Liberty cannot be drowned in the sea of warm human blood. Aye, the red juice of Life has softened the soil; the flesh and bone of a million comrades has manured the earth. The Spirit of March is brooding over it.

The Sun of May is growing nearer, larger. The warm rays penetrate deeper and deeper. They melt the bitter-ness and hatred of brothers. Hearts are flooded with the joy of Spring and the Youth of Life. Out of the sea of comrades' blood rises the Red International. Out of the fresh graves steps forth the Brotherhood of Man, the Solidarity of the Submerged.

May, life-giver and liberator! Would that the coming of your days fulfill the passionate promise of the Red Month of March.

Repudiate the War Debts!

Robert Minor

WHAT is the first battle cry in this holy war for a sacred cause? Listen! Do you hear it?

"A Five Billion Dollar Loan!" "Unlimited Credit to the Allied Powers!"

Why is the first move, in this sacred war, a move of cash instead of men? Five billion dollars loaned by the government of the United States to the government of the allied powers! Why is this? What has gone before that calls now for this?

It means that the American generals of finance are sending us to go fetch back the money that they threw into the European War. And with a heavy per cent of profits. The war debt was getting too big. Morgan and the rest of Wall Street started financing the fight and got in so deep they couldn't stop. Their side did not win quick enough, and the debts kept mounting, hundreds of millions upon hundreds of millions, until the staggering total was dangerous. The American financiers couldn't stop the supply of money for fear the allies would have to quit and would never be able to repay what they had already gotten. It was more, more, more all the time, and a nervous feeling gripped Wall Street's heart that good money was being sent after bad. The Allies would win in the long run, but the strain was too much for sure-thing gamblers.

The talk has honeycombed the armies of Europe, of re-fusing to pay the war debt.

So the American government had to be gotten to back up the situation quickly. The American army and navy and public opinion had to be gotten where they would fight

for those war debts. It was indeed the honor of our coun— — *banks.* In fact, it meant everything. It meant the destruction of the United States—that is, the destruc-tion of the parasites of the United States.

So insults were carefully swallowed or ignored from the debtors of France and England, too desperate to be humbled, and excuses were quickly found for a war declar-ing against the government that didn't owe Wall Street anything.

Now the United States government has practically guar-anteed the redemption of Morgan's and of Wall Street's pawn tickets, and two million American boys are to be got-ten as quickly as possible to the fields of France to slaughter —the Germans?

Oh, no. To slaughter the French Syndicalists at the end of the war, when they throw Morgan's notes back in his teeth and say: "To hell with your dollars; I will pay them back when my dead brother's life is returned."

Don't worry, silly German patriots! The American army and navy won't hurt your Kaiser; they are going over to kill Frenchmen and restore order and war taxes at the end of the war. To destroy the new French revolution.

Don't imagine that Russia is the only land that will reap a revolution from this war.

Suppose, when the war ends, the people of Britain, France, Russia, Italy, Germany and Austria do actually agree that the war debt is too great to be paid. The very thought made the fat knees of Wall Street shake with fear. The idea began to circulate in New York banks: "Have the United

States represented at that peace conference! The war debts must not be repudiated."

Do not take the word of a radical paper for this. Here are the words of E. P. G. Harding, of the Federal Reserve Board, published on March 22d:

"As banker and creditor, the United States would have a place at the peace conference table, and be in a much better position to resist any proposed repudiation of debts, for it might as well be remembered that we will be forced to take up the cudgels for any of our citizens owning bonds that might be repudiated."

In other words, the army of from two to five million men now to be wheedled or conscripted into uniform in America is for the purpose of being present on the fields of France under arms for "the credit nation," while the diplomats gather around a table to discuss whether or not the war debts are to be paid!

Do not let anything deceive you. There were financial reasons behind every phase of this war from its beginning, and *that* is the financial reason for the declaration of war by American Wall Street.

ALL the institutions of man are thrown into the issue in the present world conflict which involves practically every square foot of the earth. Already the most tremendous autocracy the world has ever known has fallen to destruction in Russia. I do not doubt that more of them are about to fall. At least a million French soldiers are talking in their shelter trenches about destroying the insti-

tution of war debt—the enslavement of posterity to the war lords. And it will fall to the lot of *America* to perpetuate the slavery? Shame!

The destruction of the institution called the War Debt would mean more than the Russian Revolution. It would mean the smashing of tyranny, of brutality and poverty. The destruction of more war potentiality than any other thing that could be done. It would seal the doom of Imperialism—perhaps of Capitalism itself.

That is the weak point of the War Lords. It is the thing they tell you the least about. In that one spot you can mortally wound the giant of financial autocracy of the world.

You cannot stop the war now, but you can pull down the whole damnable structure of murder if enough of you would take up the sane, logical, unanswerable cry: REPUDIATE THE WAR DEBT!

Five million men have given their lives, never to be repaid. Seven million cripples have given their precious flesh and blood which can never, never be returned. So let the fathers of these dead men, their mothers and their children and the men who are maimed for life refuse to pay back the dirty dollars that have made the murderous war.

An active propaganda should be carried on in America, in Russia, in France, in Germany and in England: REPUDIATE THE WAR DEBT!

The Russian Revolution
Alexander Berkman

THE Russian Revolution is unquestionably the greatest event of modern times. Only Russians, or those familiar with Russia, its people and their character, can realize the full significance of the revolution. To non-Russians it may seem similar to the revolution in China or to the change of monarchial Portugal to a republic. The revolution in Russia means all that, but it means a great deal more. The spirit of the Social Revolution has long been gestating in that country. The present change may be the first step toward a fundamental reorganization, not only of political but of social and economic conditions as well.

I do not believe that the war or any of its developments, was a determining factor in bringing about the revolution. In fact, the war perhaps delayed the popular uprising. On the eve of the declaration of hostilities Russia was agitated by numerous local and several general strikes. The revolution was imminent then. But the declaration of war and the cry of "external enemy" served to check it. The general dissatisfaction with the government remained, however, though the first flush of patriotism suppressed its manifestation during the two years of the war. But the incompetency of Russian arms, the gigantic graft and the corruption becoming more and more apparent, added fuel to the fire of popular dissatisfaction. The masses, taxed to poverty even before the war, were now on the verge of starvation. They rioted for bread. Hunger created the revolution.

The liberal bourgeoisie, itself a victim of tyranny and

oppression by the autocracy, took advantage of the opportunity. It was the psychologic moment. Previous revolutions failed because of the opposition of the army. Now the latter joined hands with the revolutionists, and the revolution was an accomplished fact almost over night

In other countries, as in China and Portugal, the abolition of autocracy terminated the revolt. Not so in Russia. There the removal of the Czar is only the first step toward great revolutionary changes in the life and conditions of the people. The revolutionary propaganda of the last fifty years has kindled in the Russian toilers ideals and aspirations that will not be gratified with a mere political change. The people of China, unfamiliar with European conditions, believed that the overthrow of the old regime meant liberation, but today the great masses of the Chinese suffer the same exploitation, poverty and evils under the republic as under the monarchy. The Russian people, on the contrary, are familiar with Western conditions. They will not be duped into contentment by the mere change of governmental and political forms. Indeed, they are already demanding the fruit of their revolutionary effort. The peasant wants the land. He knows that he cannot live on Constitutions. The factory workers demand greater well-being. They know that altered political forms do not lessen the greed of the exploiters.

Herein lie the great hope and future of the Russian Revolution. The peasant, used to communal ownership of the land, will have no faith in his newly-won liberties unless the landlord is expropriated and the soil returned

Four   THE BLAST

to those who till it. The proletariat in mill and factory has already made demands for a four-hour day. Russia is having a revolution.

I have no fear of the Russian Revolution failing. Its success is assured. It is making substantial progress daily. The return of thousands of political exiles and revolutionists will accelerate its progress until it will finally find a fitting echo in the neighboring countries. Nor will it be the provisional government or any other authority that will benevolently "give the Russian people their rights." These rights will have to be fought for. Indeed, they are being fought for at this very moment by the constantly increasing revolutionary demands and by the actual expropriation of the land of the muzhik. In the very granting of the political amnesty, the hand of the provisional government was forced by the revolutionary element. The appointment of Kerensky, a Socialist, was itself a concession by the governmental bourgeoisie to the revolutionists whom it fears. The government is now seeking to delay the demands for fundamental changes in the social and economic life of the people by the weak excuse of "danger from the external enemy." The Rodziankos and the Miliukovs consider the revolution complete with their own elevation to power. Nothing is more sacred to them than the holy capitalist system and the exploitation of the toiler. But they will have to reckon with the Russian people and especially with the ultra revolutionary hosts. In these is the hope of the future of the revolution. These, the extreme social revolutionists and Anarchists, know that to continue the war means to strengthen the hands of the government and postpone fundamental changes, weaken the revolutionary element and assure the triumph of the bourgeoisie upon the backs of the people. A speedy peace, on the other hand, would concentrate all the energies of the populace upon their revolutionary demands; it would quickly reorganize the whole social and economic life in Russia and start the march of the people toward political liberty based on the motto: "The land to the peasant; the fruits of labor to the worker."

The dawn of this great Russian Day will soon illuminate the whole of Europe and possibly also America. The German proletariat, even now fermenting with revolt, would draw courage from the example of their neighbors. German autocracy and militarism will then receive their death blow instead of being supported—as now—because of foreign attacks. The revolution in Russia would thus cross the boundaries and march over the continent, bringing with it the downfall of war and tyranny everywhere and ushering in the birth of a really free and beautiful New World. May the revolutionists everywhere help speed that day.

THE BLAST

Revolutionary Labor Paper   :   :   Published when funds permit
20 East 125th Street, New York
Phone Harlem 6194

Alexander Berkman, Editor and Publisher
M. E. Fitzgerald, Associate Worker   Carl Newlander, Assistant

SUBSCRIPTION:
$1.00 Yearly   60c Six Months   5c A Copy
Bundle Rates 2½c per copy in bundles of ten.

Reflections

THE President and his military clique are certainly in a pickle. They have started a war, and no soldiers. No wonder they need conscription. Had there been the least enthusiasm in favor of war, this country could quickly raise millions of volunteers. It is pitiful, though very encouraging, to listen to the whining of the military and naval procurers: "Your country needs you! Your country wants you!" But few enlist.

Conscription is necessary only where the people are opposed to war and refuse to fight. That is why we are to have conscription in America. The encouraging factor in the situation is that the people evidently feel that they have nothing to fight Germany for. Else why don't they enlist, solicited as they are even by the fair militant ladies?

HOW "great" the enthusiasm for war is, can be judged by the proclamation issued by the mayor of Oakland, California, threatening every one with imprisonment who fails to display the Stars and Stripes at his business place or residence, and even ordering automobile owners to carry a flag. When American citizens must be threatened with prison to make them patriotic—Good Night Columbia!

We are a generous people: we are going to introduce democracy in Germany even if we have to deprive ourselves of the precious thing. The Professor in the White House will brook no opposition from Congress or the people to his plans for Prussian democratization. Like the Czar, he seems to think that Congress is only a Duma to ratify the wishes of the autocrat. But history often repeats itself.

I PITY, yet respect, the youth who enlists in the army or navy—the boy who, ignorant of the real cause and meaning of the war, is inspired by youthful idealism to sacrifice his life for his country. A great many, of course, are fired by the love of adventure, the hope of change from their humdrum daily existence, and the all-too-human desire of playing hero and feeling themselves such. Were it not for these tendencies in man, wars would be impossible. Splendid qualities exploited for base purposes.

To fight for a cause with full understanding of its meaning, with one's eyes open to consequences, requires unusual physical and moral courage. Such men and women are few. That is why social ideals enlist only the few. The more unpopular such a cause, the greater the courage of the men fighting under its banner. Wars do not require this courage. **The coward is a hero when there are enough of him.**

I can't respect, however, those who are deliberately

THE BLAST   Five

trying to induce thoughtless youth to offer up their lives on the altar of false gods. The militarist leaders, at least the more intelligent among them, know that America is not going to war for humanity or any other high ideals. They know, as does Wall Street, that we have declared war to secure the thousands of millions of dollars owed to American bankers by the Allies. They know that slaughtering the German soldier-worker is a war upon the German **people** and not against the Kaiser. The latter and his Junkertum could be abolished as easily as the revolutionists in Russia did away with the Czar and his ducal regime, if conditions in Germany itself and the attitude of the German people favored such action.

(And, by the way, the anti-Anarchist law of this country provides severe penalties for any conspiracy on American soil for the violent overthrow of the legally constituted authority in any country. Yet Wilson, according to his own proclamation, has formed a conspiracy to overthrow the legally constituted government of Germany, by force and violence.)

On the other hand, the entrance of this country into war gives the Kaiser a powerful argument to bolster up the weakening loyalty of his subjects. It has strengthened his claim that Germany is menaced by the whole world. The German people, inspired by the example of the Russian Revolution, might revolt against their militarist government were it not for the added danger to their country from America.

"I KNOW that you are starving," sayeth Lloyd George to his people, "but be patient awhile and give us more soldiers—or the Kaiser will get you."

"Cease now," sayeth the provisional government to the Russian Revolution; "you are only encouraging the Kaiser."

"Never mind long hours of work and small wages," sayeth Wilson and the munition manufacturers. "Now is no time to dicker. Sic the Kaiser."

I know that you are sick of this slaughter and on the verge of starvation," sayeth the Kaiser to his people, "but be good patriots and do not harass the government **now**: the whole world menaces your fatherland."

ON another page our readers will find the details of the exposure of the frame-up against Tom Mooney and his co-defendants in San Francisco. It is the most heinous conspiracy ever hatched to legally murder four men and a woman because of their labor activities. I have been crying for months up and down the country that if the people realized the whole truth of this terrible frame-up, they would rise up in arms against the Chamber of Commerce of San Francisco which has instigated and organized the conspiracy. Perhaps the Associated Press agrees with me. That is why it has entirely suppressed the facts of the frame-up which have now been bared by the press of San Francisco, notably by *The Bulletin*.

Of course it would not do for the capitalist papers to inform the people of this hellish attempt to strangle Mooney, Billings, Nolan, Weinberg and Rena Mooney. They might ask why they should sacrifice their lives to democratize Germany while a worse autocracy than the Kaiser's is murdering their brothers in their own country.

The frame-up has been exposed by documentary evidence that absolutely proves that Oxman, the chief witness of the prosecution, had given perjured testimony which resulted in the conviction of Tom Mooney and his sentence of death. The numerous telegrams and letters exchanged between Oxman, Assistant District Attorney Cunha and F. E. Rigall, a hotel man of Grayville, Illinois, and other matter now in the hands of the defense, prove that the authorities of San Francisco had deliberately manufactured evidence to hang the labor men. Their incentive was the big reward offered for the conviction of the defendants and the secret slush fund of the Chamber of Commerce at the disposal of Fickert and Cunha.

Oxman has been arrested on the charge of perjury and subornation of perjury. But Oxman, miserable creature that he is, is only a tool. The real murderers are Fickert and Cunha and the men above them—the respectable, patriotic gentlemen of the Merchant & Manufacturers Association and of the Chamber of Commerce who are calling upon us to defend their glorious country. It certainly needs defending. "The insult to the American flag must be avenged", to use their own language. We suggest to Wilson, the champion of the interests of humanity and of justice, that the American army be sent forthwith to California to protect the people against their autocratic enemies at home.

ED NOLAN, one of the victims of the frame-up and the most noble and beautiful character in the labor movement on the Coast, has been released on $250 bail. We understand that Judge Griffin, who sentenced Tom Mooney to death in spite of the evident perjury of the State witnesses, is now in favor of granting Mooney a new trial. The thing is preposterous. Judge Griffin is himself as guilty of murder as are Fickert, Cunha, Oxman and the gentlemen of the Chamber of Commerce of San Francisco. Tom Mooney was to be hanged on the 17th of this month. It is not their fault that evidence was discovered in the nick of time to upset their all but accomplished lynching. Instead of torturing Mooney and Billings with new trials, every one of the defendants should be immediately released and the prime movers in the frame-up sent to the first line of the trenches. They favor conscription and they should have it.

WE hope that the unmasking of the frame-up will have a good effect on the I. W. W. cases in Everett, Wash., as well as on the appeal of Mathew Schmidt and Dave Caplan in Los Angeles.

The same power, organized capital, is back of all of these prosecutions. The Lumber Trust in the State of Washington has determined to wipe out the I. W. W. boys because of their splendid work during the shingle weavers' strike. The encouraging feature of the cases now on trial in Seattle, Wash., is that the labor unions have come forward and some even are preparing for a general strike in case the boys are railroaded to prison. Instead of the I. W. W. boys being on trial for the Everett massacre, it should have been the sheriff and the broadcloth vigilantes of Everett, for they alone are responsible for the cold-blooded murder of the boys on the boat Verona.

THE national anthem stands for liberty. If you don't get up, I'll knock you down.

IF this issue of THE BLAST is suppressed in free America, we will move to Petrograd.

The Hangmen of the Law

Fremont Older

(Editor San Francisco Bulletin, April 20, 1917.)

THE perversion of justice as shown by the Oxman exposure raises an issue of the gravest public import. The public is entitled to know all the facts which led up to Mr. Fickert's public statement.

Last Wednesday night, *The Bulletin* published a special edition, in which it told of the Oxman letters to F. E. Rigall, of Grayville, Illinois. The next morning it gave a complete account of Oxman's attempt to induce Rigall to perjure himself to hang Mooney, with photographic reproductions of the letters. The letters later landed Oxman in jail and there has been no word of explanation of them made public.

Friday morning *The Bulletin* published the still undenied story of Inspector William H. Smith, of the Oakland police department, which overthrows the testimony of Mrs. Nellie Edeau.

Late Friday night, Mr. Cunha called me up at the Fairmont Hotel. He explained his failure to keep an appointment earlier in the day by saying that Fickert had returned and that he had been kept in conference with him. He then came to my room and we had a long conversation. Cunha said he had believed the defendants were guilty, but had had no desire to convict them on perjured testimony and said he would agree to procedure for their release.

Saturday morning, following the meeting at the Fairmont, Cunha met me at my office with O'Connor and McKenzie. At this meeting Cunha definitely agreed to a new trial for Mooney. He said that with Oxman on the stand Mooney would undoubtedly be acquitted. Upon his acquittal they would release Billings.

Sunday afternoon, Cunha met O'Connor and McKenzie and said Fickert had agreed to drop the remaining cases, to confess error in the case of Mooney and to get Mooney a new trial with Oxman on the stand. It was suggested that the three go to my home near Cupertino to visit me that afternoon. As they were about to leave in the automobile, a reporter for the *Chronicle* approached. Cunha said he was afraid of the *Chronicle* learning that he was on his way to confer with me, and did not take the trip. O'Connor and McKenzie came to my home and told me of this meeting, delivering Cunha's message regarding Fickert's agreement.

Monday morning I joined a conference with Cunha, McNutt, O'Connor, McKenzie and Charles Brennan in the office of Attorney Nate Coghlan. The arrangement for the release of the defendants was freely discussed. Cunha said he was ready to stand for the previous arrangement, and that Fickert had agreed. He was greatly distressed.

"I know I'm in the dump heap for the rest of my life," he said. "But if you think you're going to get me in jail you're mistaken."

I said:

"Cunha, I don't want to 'get' anybody. My position is just this: Here is the evidence that these men were the victims of a perjury conspiracy. All I want is to see that they get a square deal."

After continued discussion, Cunha said that before any final arrangements could be made, he and Fickert wanted to see Oxman.

It was agreed that they were to let us know when Oxman would be here, and that they should see him without attempting any arrangement which would prevent a full public investigation of the whole affair.

That afternoon, Captain Duncan Matheson and Lieutenant Charles Goff came voluntarily to *The Bulletin* office and asked to see me. We discussed the Oxman case. I raised the question about the conflicting testimony of John McDonald and Oxman. Captain Matheson drew a diagram of Steuart and Market streets. I recalled that McDonald had testified that after Billings had deposited the suit case Mooney met him, the two consulted their watches and then

Mooney walked diagonally through the parade in one direction and Billings in another. I stated that Oxman had testified that they both got into the automobile and drove toward Mission street.

McDonald had testified that Billings and Mooney had gone north, through the procession, and that Oxman had said they had taken the automobile south in Steuart street.

Lieutenant Goff said they could have gone through the procession and then returned to the machine.

"You're eating up time pretty fast," I said.

"You must remember that McDonald testified that the suitcase was planted at eight or ten minutes to two. You must get Mooney up on the Eilers building by one and a half minutes to two because he showed in a photograph at that time."

At this point in our conversation Captain Matheson looked at Goff and remarked:

"Charlie, it won't do. There is something wrong."

Goff agreed with him.

I then showed Captain Matheson an anonymous letter which I had received in which it was stated that Estelle Smith had said Oxman had offered her money to testify that she had seen Weinberg at 721 Market street.

"Yes," said Captain Matheson, "I know about that. Estelle Smith told me Oxman had offered her a 'sum in five figures' if she would give this testimony." * * *

Estelle Smith made an affidavit making this accusation against Oxman.

Oxman came to San Francisco Wednesday morning. Assistant District Attorney Tyrrell unsuccessfully opposed the issuance of a warrant for his arrest. That afternoon O'Connor said that Fickert, through his intermediary, Attorney Harry Stafford, had asked for a conference with me and with the defense attorneys. The conference was arranged to be held at the Olympic Club early that evening.

Fickert, Cunha, McKenzie, O'Connor, Stafford and I were present at this meeting. Fickert said that the Oxman letters had shown him that there was "something wrong about the whole business," and that he wanted to open it all up. * * *

There was a general discussion about the best means of dropping the cases and getting a new trial for Mooney.

I suggested that the best thing for Fickert to do would be to issue a statement to the papers, explaining, in effect, that the case against the bomb defendants had fallen. Fickert asked whether I thought it should be given to the morning papers. I said I had no objection. Then Stafford suggested that a short statement be given to the morning papers, and that *The Bulletin* be given a full and complete statement the next day. This was finally agreed upon.

O'Connor was insistent that there should be no secret grand jury investigation, and that the Oxman developments should come from his prosecution on the warrant on which he was arrested. Fickert definitely and finally agreed that he would not present the matter to the grand jury.

There was a general friendly discussion, and the agreement that there should be no grand jury probe was repeated. We all shook hands when we parted.

At about 2 o'clock the next morning, Assistant District Attorney Cotton called me up and said the grand jury had taken up the case on its own initiative.

The next morning I learned that, after midnight, Cotton had appeared before the grand jury and asked that Fickert be heard. This request was granted. Fickert appeared and asked that he be allowed to conduct an investigation of the Oxman matter before that body. He said he was familiar with all the facts and could manage it better on that account. The jurors refused to agree to this, but decided to ask the attorney-general to take up the case.

In yesterday's *Bulletin* the story of Fickert's betrayal of faith was told. He replied this morning with the implication that I had guilty knowledge of the bomb cases.

In my discussion with Cunha and Fickert, I did not, in any way, suggest that I was threatening them with unpleasant publicity.

I suggested to Fickert that a short, frank, simple statement from him to the public should be made, and it would go far toward removing the impression that was rapidly growing that he had guilty knowledge of Oxman's perjury.

I explicitly told Cunha, as I have stated, that under no circumstances did I wish to put anybody in jail. I entered into these negotiations with them because I believed a terrible injustice had been uncovered in the Oxman exposure. The actual guilt or innocence of the defendants was not in any way an issue. It is Mr. Fickert's duty to prosecute them to the full extent of his legitimate evidence. But it is not his duty to hang them on perjured testimony.

The District Attorney
Robert Minor

AN artistic little story in the April *Masses* is a study of the morbid degeneration of a lonesome old woman to a point of criminality. The daughter of a butcher, as a little girl she had watched the slaughter of cattle. The balance of her life was devoted to the handling of sick animals, all of which she would sooner or later find excuse "to put out of their misery." The story ends with a diabolically clever arrangement for the suffocation of a little boy. The sick brain of the mad woman, step by step, constructed its morbid philosophical justification of the deeds which grew more hideous at each step. The neighbors first held her to be within her rights "to put her animals out of their misery." But slowly they began to understand that the woman and her house were cruel and loathsome things. At the culmination of the diseased mind's havoc, a general conviction has seized the neighbors that something terrible is being done. The little boy's life is saved by his father rushing into the house and breaking open a casket, in which the living child is being smothered by the old woman, who croons her own invented mad formulae of justification.

Fiction is good only as it symbolizes the happenings of life. In reading this story, I could not help thinking that it symbolizes something that is now going on in San Francisco.

THERE is a miserable man. He started out some time ago "putting people out of their misery," crooning to himself and to the neighbors the formula of justification—that he is district attorney. He had a perfectly good justification at first—that is, according to the mental standards of the public—men must be punished for their misdeeds in order to protect society. Well, he started this way. Through each experience he crooned all the justifications he could think of, and heard himself echoed from the walls of the courtroom as "defender of the public peace, protector of women and children." But it was so easy, and there was so much applause from foolish little newspaper men that wanted stories from him, and from quite prominent business men whom he could serve without anybody objecting, that our district attorney went further and further along the line. After awhile, he found the field broadened and systematized, and everybody willing to help him, and he found favors at his disposal with which he could buy almost any help that he wanted. It became a principle with him "to put people out of their misery." It became his pride to succeed. Pride of a craftsman is a great thing. The hangman thinks of ropes, pulleys and fine triggers that work just right; he gets away from questions of ethics, to dwell upon which might make him a poorer hangman. A district attorney weds the art of getting a man to the hangman whenever a murder is done, and to have the approval of those who arbitrate the life in which he lives, whom he serves and who serve him. A successful district attorney is one who hangs and pleases. A successful policeman is one who supplies evidence that hangs. Not any other kind of evidence, but evidence that **hangs**. All policemen must be loyal to—the district attorney. They might be loyal to people, defendants, but——

So we find everything adapted to the district attorney "putting people out of their misery" right straight along as fast as he can. Especially at certain times, it is very easy indeed.

Last July our district attorney, Charles M. Fickert, arrested a Jew named Weinberg, and Tom Mooney, and several other people, after a crime had been committed. Fickert didn't know just who committed the crime, but he was helped a lot in the choice of persons to accuse. One very energetic man, named Swanson, of the type that is so active that it is easy to leave to them a great deal to do, helped Fickert. The crime was horrible and Fickert was district attorney and he must punish somebody for it. After these persons were arrested, the situation was rather reassuring, for nobody objected at all. The investigation was rather perplexing, and maybe nobody would ever be found to accuse of the crime except these fellows. The district attorney must get somebody; he **had** somebody and the newspaper reporters were always asking whether he was sure these were the men, and everybody seemed to think the district attorney was quite a capable and important man, and, well, **if nobody objected**—

Everybody said they were guilty very soon after Mr. Fickert did himself, and nobody seemed to care. Swanson was delighted to help Fickert, for he had just been trying to get Mooney for the United Railroad four days before, and the United Railroad thought Mooney might very likely be the man to have done it anyway. Everybody being willing to help along this **easy** line and nobody going off on the hard chase after unknown persons, of course Mooney and those fellows were finally agreed upon.

Policemen and detectives, assistant artists of conviction, were, of course, **discreet**. All evidence was properly attended to and photographs and other things that "the dynamiters" might use to cheat justice were discreetly hidden. Little things that were missing, that surely ought to have been there, were discreetly placed about the scene of the crime, and other things that would have been rather disconcerting to the punishment of "the dynamiters" were discreetly lost. No officer of the law would do anything that might help "a fellow that had done a thing like that." Policemen consulted the district attorney, of course, as they understood it was their duty, before they talked on the witness stand, just to "refresh their memories" and to be sure that everything was consistent.

In short, everybody strained a point and a lot of people each supplied a missing link just to help out the case. Then a lot of the original links dropped out of the chain and more missing links had to be supplied by a policeman forgetting something here or "finding" something there, or straining a point. And then when the chain was examined it showed that it was nearly all composed of links that had at first been missing and that somebody supplied by straining a point or forgetting or finding or having his memory refreshed. All the links that were real were little simple things such as going to a picnic or sending a friend a message, things which didn't have anything to do with the crime.

It wasn't very comfortable for its manufacturers to contemplate, that the chain of evidence which was to hang a man was composed of "missing links" supplied by straining points—things that have to be **remembered** so carefully. The district attorney went ahead and put one boy into the penitentiary for life; the chain having gotten a little shaky at the critical moment, he had to compromise with his jury and to send the boy to prison for life because the proof slipped out that he wasn't guilty. Instead of "putting him out of his misery." And then, hurriedly the "missing links" were overhauled and the weak ones mended and some new missing links were wrought in. Then the district attorney went ahead to hang Tom Mooney. He had started long ago, now, and the thing had to be gone through with. He braced up; this was the main case anyhow and "Tom Mooney was a bad fellow," and Fickert looked around uncomfortably and found that the neighbors didn't care much, only a few of them and they were just working people who are all noise and no action anyway.

Fickert went ahead, and talked loud, saying all of the things he could think of that justify district attorneys. He went into books and found phrases and things that great district attorneys had said, that sounded justifying and comforting.

Some of the things which had been discreetly lost turned up uncomfortably and some of the links of the chain were proven to have been just put there to serve the purpose and not to be honest, and it all looked rather bad, but Mr. Fickert managed to worry through with it somehow, and some of the gentlemen on the jury were sorry for him and helped him out, and earned a great deal of gratitude. It was well to be done with it.

TOM MOONEY is sitting in the death cell. The long, long chain of queer "facts' with which he was put there, are still being thought of. It would be so much more comfortable if they could be forgotten. All these things that have to be remembered so carefully—one wishes one didn't have to remember. They seem to make a long, hanging, greasy rope that dangles in the death cell over Mooney, but perhaps doesn't stay there, for maybe it wanders in the night and hangs over Fickert's bed when he is trying to sleep, and seems to talk, saying "don't forget, don't forget, remember each strand, each twist, each grimy knot and how they were made; there is danger that we fall apart; don't forget, don't forget!"

The worst of it is that the neighbors are beginning to talk. One wishes that they would think about the war or something and not worry about the hangman's ropes and pulleys and fine triggers that work just right when they are not interfered with. But the neighbors keep talking and talking. Those working people who have no action—

they keep talking and thinking there's something wrong and bandying about these "facts", these manufactured "missing links." And they prod the chain with their grimy fingers where the very weakest links are, and there is great danger.

Slowly they begin to understand that the man and his house are cruel and loathsome things. A general suspicion has seized the neighbors that something terrible is being done. And the man Fickert stands over the casket of Mooney, crooning all the formulae that he can think of and wondering unhappily whether the neighbors will understand and whether the thing will hold together until Mooney is dead. If it does not hold together——?

Do You Want THE BLAST?

THE BLAST has moved from San Francisco to New York. We feel that our work on the Coast, in connection with the cases of the imprisoned labor men, has been accomplished. It is safe now in San Francisco to expose the conspiracy. The Bulletin, a local daily, is doing that. THE BLAST reserves for itself the right of being where there is the greatest need and the greatest danger. Therefore we came to New York to devote most of our time and energy to anti-militaristic work.

At this moment of general war hysteria and patriotic drunkenness—at a moment when even some radicals and revolutionists have lost their bearings and are swayed hither and thither by the changing winds of popular excitement—we need a voice of sanity and strength, a voice that will speak aloud and unafraid the whispered longings of every thinking man and woman—a voice of peace with other nations—a voice of revolution of the proletariat against the Romanovs of Europe and America.

THE BLAST is needed. It has made a heroic struggle during its existence, and its path has been a thorny one. But it has fought the battle unflinchingly, and with your help it will continue. If you believe that the work we are doing is important, give us your aid. We are getting plenty of letters full of admiration for our stand and persistence. We appreciate them, but the printer refuses to credit them on our bill. If you want THE BLAST to continue, you must help us. It is absolutely necessary that you do so at once. NOW.

If your subscription is due, your immediate renewal will greatly assist our work. Subscribe for your friends and interest others in the paper. If you will secure three yearly subscriptions for THE BLAST, we will present you, as a token of our appreciation, with a copy of Alexander Berkman's Prison Memoirs of an Anarchist, or Voltairine de Cleyre's Selected Works, containing her biography.

Whatever you do, we must have funds immediately if THE BLAST is to continue.

Our new address is: 20 East 125th St., New York City.

ALEXANDER BERKMAN,
M. E. FITZGERALD.

ATTENTION!

The All-Nations Political Prisoners' Ball, held in New York on March 7th, for the benefit of the San Francisco Labor Defense, proved a very great success, morally and financially. The attendance was 4,700; net proceeds, $2,028.54.

Organizations and individuals who have not yet fully accounted for tickets, please do so at once. A detailed report of all receipts and expenditures will be published later.

For lack of space the report of various contributions must be postponed until the next issue.

Vol. II.   NEW YORK, JUNE 1, 1917   No. 5

YOUNG RUSSIA:—"What's the idea?"

YOUNG AMERICA:—"Democracy!"

YOUNG RUSSIA:—"Well, You know how I got mine."

To The Youth of America

TYRANNY must be opposed at the start.
Autocracy, once secure in the saddle, is difficult to dislodge.

If you believe that America is entering the war "to make democracy safe," then be a man and volunteer.

But if you know anything at all, then you should know that the cry of democracy is a lie and a snare for the unthinking. You should know that a republic is not synonymous with democracy, and that America has never been a real democracy, but that it is the vilest plutocracy on the face of the globe.

If you can see, hear, feel, and think, you should know that King Dollar rules the United States, and that the workers are robbed and exploited in this country to the heart's content of the masters.

If you are not deaf, dumb, and blind, then you know that the American bourgeois democracy and capitalistic civilization are the wost enemies of labor and progress, and that instead of protecting them, you should help to fight to destroy them.

If you know this, you must also know that the workers of America have no enemy in the toilers of other countries. Indeed, the workers of Germany suffer as much from their exploiters and rulers as do the masses of America.

You should know that the interests of Labor are identical in all countries. Their cause is international.

Then why should they slaughter each other?

The workers of Germany have been misled by their rulers into donning the uniform and turning murderers.

So have the workers of France, of Italy and England been misled.

But why should *you*, men of America, allow yourselves to be misled into murder or into being murdered?

If your blood must be shed, let it be in defense of your own interests, in the war of the workers against their despoilers, in the cause of real liberty and independence.

Registration

REGISTRATION is the first step of conscription.
The war shouters and their prostitute press, bent on snaring you into the army, tell you that registration has nothing to do with conscription.

They lie.

Without registration, conscription is impossible.

Conscription is the abdication of your rights as a citizen. Conscription is the cemetery where every vestige of your liberty is to be buried. Registration is its undertaker.

No man with red blood in his veins can be forced to fight against his will.

But you cannot successfully oppose conscription if you approve of, or submit to, registration.

Every beginning is hard. But if the government can induce you to register, it will have little difficulty in putting over conscription.

By registering you wilfully supply the government with the information it needs to make conscription effective.

Registration means placing in the hands of the authorities the despotic power of the machinery of passports which made darkest Russia what it was before the Revolution.

There are thousands, perhaps hundreds of thousands of young men in this country who have never voted and who have never paid taxes, and who, legally speaking, have no official existence. Their registration means nothing short of suicide, in a majority of cases.

Failure to register is punishable by imprisonment. Refusal to be conscripted may be punishable by death.

To register is to acknowledge the right of the government to conscript.

The consistent conscientious objector to human slaughter will neither register nor be conscripted.

Alexander Berkman.

War As a Test of Anti-Militarist Sincerity

Leonard D. Abbott

THE man whose convictions crumble at the first touch of reality can hardly be described as a man of principle.

The anti-militarist who surrenders his convictions in the face of war forfeits, by this surrender, his right to be called an anti-militarist. In the present crisis, the libertarian movement is being tested as by flames of fire. We are finding out who were in earnest in their radical protestations, and who were not. We are called upon to testify, each one of us, whether, when we said we were opposed to militarism, we meant what we said, or whether our words were mere sound and fury, signifying nothing.

This country is confronted by a program of complete militarization. President Wilson, after declaring two years ago that he was opposed to plans for turning America into an armed camp and for making our young men soldiers, has reversed himself and is vigorously prosecuting the very policy that he has hitherto denounced. The man who was re-elected to the Presidency on the ground that he "kept us out of war" is now leading us into war. We are entering, it seems, on a veritable debauch of patriotism and flag-worship. Enlistment posters on every boarding offend the eye. Recruiting stations are being established on every street corner. Soldiers swagger up and down our streets, or clatter by on horse-back with arms and accoutrements. America, which has boasted in the past that it was one of the

least military nations of the world, now bids fair to become one of the most military.

It took England two years to pass a conscription law. Australia still refuses to take its citizens by force and to ship them across the seas to be slaughtered in Europe. The issue is unsettled in Canada. But the United States, with indecent haste, put upon the statute books a law that is more drastic than even the European laws, and that gives the lie to our vaunted "liberty."

A movement has been started to send a replica of the Statue of Liberty in New York Harbor to Russia. Why not send the original statue, since we seem to be through with it?

Salesmen commissioned by the Government at Washington are going up and down the land asking us to buy "Liberty" Bonds. These ought to be called "Slavery" Bonds, for they are the outward and visible manifestation of our efforts to put this country under the yoke of a military despotism.

Hand in hand with the militarization of America goes, of course, the suppression of our civil liberties. The two have ever gone hand in hand. Censorship and the suppression of a free press are taken as a matter of course. Standards to safeguard labor, carefully built up through years, are swept aside. Public meetings are being broken up by the police. Socialist and radical club-rooms are being raided. Men and women are being arrested for no other reason than that they have the courage to reassert their allegiance to principles of liberty that hitherto have been regarded as American principles, but that now are being shamelessly trampled under foot.

We are told that these sacrifices are necessary in order to defeat Germany. We do not admit the necessity. There is less reason for the Socialists, Syndicalists and Anarchists of this country to go into war than there has been for the radical groups of any of the other countries now engaged in the war. We are not invaded. Germany is unwilling, even yet, to make formal declaration of war against the United States. The fact that American ships, carrying munitions of war, have been destroyed 4,000 miles away is no adequate reason for turning this country into an armed camp. The militarization of America is an evil that far outweighs, in its anti-libertarian effects, any good that may be accomplished by America's participation in the war.

In the efforts that are now being made to militarize this country, we can only assert, more emphatically than ever, our opposition to militarism and to everything that it stands for. We opposed this country's entry into the war, and we still oppose it. We are not interested in wars waged by capitalistic governments.

We oppose militarism, first of all, because we are internationalists. We give no allegiance to a country as a country. We join hands with our own kind in every country. Our loyalty is not to a locality, but to principles of freedom and justice and to the economic interest of the working class.

We oppose militarism, in the second place, because we are anti-Statist. We take our stand not with the military establishments of any existing capitalistic government, but with our own brothers of all nations in the fight for social revolution. If the revolutionary movement needs to use force, it ought to create its own army as the rebels in Ireland did last year. The working class recognizes only one enemy—the capitalist and exploiting class of the world.

The power of thought and the power of the working-class movement—these, as Bertrand Russell says in his last book, "Why Men Fight"—are the forces that shall finally rid the world of the curse of militarism.

The working-class, if it were class-conscious, could end war, *all* war, tomorrow. Without the consent of the working-class there could be no war. Munitions that slay men, food that sustains men, trains and ships that carry soldiers to the field of battle, are all produced and carried forward by working men. Some day, the working-class will be educated to the realization of their own interest and the interest of humanity. They will know the power of their strongest weapon, a non-military weapon, the General Strike. They will make common cause in all countries. In that moment war will end.

In the meantime, let us remember that no power on earth is stronger than the conscience of even one individual. No power on earth can make a man a soldier, or can make him fight, if he refuses to be a soldier and if he refuses to fight. The young man who with clean sincerity and idealism refuses to be conscripted is stronger than any and all the governments of the earth. He fights with spiritual weapons. He fights for the liberty not only of himself, but of all generations to come. And he will be vindicated, finally, in the eyes of the whole world.

Die Mutter—True Story

From "Short Rations." by Madeline Z. Doty.

THE sky was shining blue. The air was still. The warmth of summer brooded over the land. But no bird's song broke the stillness. No bees fluttered over flowers. The earth lay torn and bare. In deep brown furrows of the earth, hundreds of restless men lay or knelt or stood.

The land was vibrant with living silence. But now and then a gigantic smashing roar broke the tense stillness. Then in some spots the ground spit forth masses of dirt, a soldier's helmet, a tattered rag of uniform, and bits of a human body.

It was after such a blast that a great winged object came speeding from the north. It skimmed low over the trenches and dipped, and circled and paused above the English line. Like a great eagle it seemed about to rush to earth, snatch its prey, and then be off. But as it hung suspended, another whirring monster flew from the south. It winged its way above its rival, then, turning, plunged downward. The great cannons grew silent. The eyes of the pigmies in the trenches gazed skyward. A breathless tenseness gripped the earth. Only sun and sky shone on with no whisper of the mad fight of these two winged things.

For a few wild moments they rushed at one another. Then the bird with wings of white rose high, turned back, and plunged again upon the creature marked with huge, black crosses.

IT missed its prey, but there came a crackling sound. A puff of smoke, like a hot breath, burst from the bird of the iron crosses. It shuddered, dropped, turned, and fell head down. With sweeping curves the pursuer also came to earth. A lean young Englishman sprang from the whirring engine. His body quivered with excitement. He sped with running feet to the broken object lying on the ground. He knelt by the twisted mass. Beneath the splintered wood and iron he saw a boyish figure. It was still and motionless. He gently pulled the body out. A fair young German lay before him. A deep gash in the head showed where a blow had brought instant death. The body was straight and supple, the features clear-cut and clean. A boy's face with frank and fearless brow looked up at the young Englishman. The eyes held no malice. They were full of shocked surprise. The brown-haired lad felt the lifeless heart. A piece of cardboard met his fingers. He pulled it from the coat pocket. It was a picture—a picture of a woman—a woman with gray hair and kindly eyes—a mother whose face was lined with patient suffering. Scrawled beneath the portrait in boyish hand were the words, "Meine Mutter."

A SOB choked the young Englishman. Tenderly he gathered the lifeless form in his strong arms. Then he rose and walked unheeding across the open field of battle. But no angry bullets pelted after him. The men in the trenches saw and understood. Behind the lines the boy laid his burden down. Taking paper and pencil from his pocket and placing the little picture before him, he began to write.

When he had finished he placed the letter and portrait in a carefully directed envelope. Then walking hurriedly to his machine, he prepared for flight. Soon he was skimming low over the enemy trenches. Leaning out, he dropped his missile. The cannons roared, but no rifle was turned on the bright figure. Instinctively, men knew his deed was one of mercy. As the little paper fluttered downward it was picked up by eager soldier hands. A little cheer broke from a hundred throats. Willing messengers passed it to the rear. Speedily it went on its way.

Twenty-four hours later a mother with pale face and trembling hands fingered the white scrap of paper. Her unseeing eyes gazed out on a smiling landscape. Between green meadows in the warm summer sunshine lay the glittering Rhine. But she saw nothing. Her baby boy was dead. Memories of him flooded her. She felt again the warmth of the baby body as it clung to her's and the pull of the tiny hands at her breast. She saw him as a boy, his eager restlessness. She heard his running steps at the door and his cry of "mother." It was over. That bright spirit was still. The third and last son had been exacted.

HER fingers touched the letter in her lap. Her eyes fell on the penciled words. Slowly they took meaning. This boy who wrote: he'd seen the beauty of her son. He'd held the dear body in his arms. His heart was torn by anguish. What was it he said:

"It's your son. I know you can't forgive me, for I killed him. But I want you to know he didn't suffer. The end came quickly. He was very brave. He must also have been very good. He had your picture in his pocket. I am sending it back, though I should like to keep it. I suppose I am his enemy, yet I don't feel so at all. I'd give my life to have him back. I didn't think of him or you when I shot at his machine. He was an enemy spying out our men. I couldn't let him get back to tell his news. It meant death to our men. It was a plucky deed. We were covered up with brush. He had to come quite low to see us and he came bravely. He nearly escaped me. He handled his machine magnificently. I thought how I should like to fly with him. But he was the enemy and had to be destroyed. I fired. It was over in a second. Just a blow on the head as the machine crashed to earth. His face shows no suffering, only excitement. His eyes are bright and fearless. I know you must have loved him. My mother died when I was quite a little boy. But I know what she would have felt if I had been killed. War isn't fair to women. God! how I wish it were over. It is a nightmare. I feel if I just touched your boy, he'd wake and we'd be friends. I know his body must be dear to you. I will take care of it and mark his grave with a little cross. After the war you may want to take him home.

"For the first time, I'm almost glad my mother isn't living. She could not have borne what I have done. My own heart is heavy. I felt it was my duty. Yet now when I see your son lifeless before me and hold your picture in my hand, it all seems wrong. The world is dark. O Mother, be my mother just a little, too, and tell me what to do.—HUGH."

SLOWLY great tears rolled down the woman's cheeks. What was this monster that was smashing men? Her boy and this other, they were the same. No hate was in their hearts. They suffered—the whole world suffered. Her country went in hunger. The babies in the near-by cottages grew weak for want of milk. She mustn't tell that to the English lad. His heart would break. Why must such suffering be? Was she to blame? There was the English lad without a mother. She had not thought of him and others like him. Her home, her sons, her Fatherland, these had been sufficient. But each life hangs on every other. Motherhood is universal.

Suddenly she knew what to write, what she must say to that grief-stricken English boy. Quickly her hand penned the words:

"Dear Lad: There is nothing to forgive. I see you as you are—your troubled goodness. I feel you coming to me like a little boy astounded at having done ill when you meant well. You seem my son. I am glad your hands cared for my other boy. I had rather you than any other touched his earthly body. He was my youngest. I think you saw his fineness. I know the torture of your heart since you have slain him. To women brotherhood is a reality. For all men are our sons. That makes war a monster that brother must slay brother. Yet perhaps women more than men have been to blame for this world war. We did not think of the world's children, our children. The baby hands that clutched our breasts were so sweet, we forgot the hundred other baby hands stretched out to us. But the Earth does not forget, she mothers all. And now my heart aches with repentance. I long to take you in my arms and lay your head upon my breast to make you feel through me your kinship with all the earth. Help me, son, I need you. Spread the dream of oneness and love throughout the world. When the war is over come to me. I am waiting for you.—DEINE MUTTER."

War Dictionary

Alexander Berkman

ALLIES—The fairies of Democracy.

BARBARIANS—The other fellows.

CONGRESS—The valet of Woodrow the First.

CENSORSHIP—The rape of Free Speech.

CONSCRIPTION—Free men fighting against their will.

CIVILIZATION—In God We Trusts.

DEMOCRACY—The voice of the Gallery Gods.

FREE SPEECH—Say what you please, but keep your mouth shut.

HUNS—Loyal patriots from Central Europe.

HUMANITY—Treason to government.

JUSTICE—Successful target shooting.

LOYAL CITIZEN—Deaf, dumb and blind.

KAISER—A President's ambition.

LIBERTY LOAN—The bread line of the Unborn.

LIBERTY BOND—A bone from a bonehead.

SEDITION—The proof of Tyranny.

MILITARISM—Christianity in action.

PATRIOTISM—Hating your neighbor.

REGISTRATION—Funeral march of Liberty.

SLACKER—Jesus Christ.

TRENCHES—Digging your own grave.

UN-AMERICAN—Independent opinion.

UN-DEMOCRATIC—Ideals.

UNIFORM—Government strait-jacket.

VICTORY—Ten million dead.

WAR—The propaganda of Democracy.

* * *

WHICH is the braver? The man who falls in line with the great majority or he that faces the wrath of millions for conscience sake?

Do not confound us with the pacifists. We believe in fighting. Aye, we have been fighting all our lives—fighting injustice, oppression and tyranny. Almost single handed at that.

We are not pacifists. But we want to know what we are fighting for, and we refuse to fight for the enemies and the exploiters of humanity.

* * *

THE endurance of the inequalities of life by the poor is the marvel of human society.

—*James Anthony Froude*

DO not waste your time on Social Questions. What is the matter with the poor is Poverty, what is the matter with the Rich is Uselessness.

—*George Bernard Shaw*

THE BLAST

Revolutionary Labor Paper   :   :   Published when funds permit
20 East 125th Street, New York
Phone Harlem 6263

Alexander Berkman, Editor and Publisher
M. E. Fitzgerald, Associate Worker   Carl Newlander, Assistant

SUBSCRIPTION:
$1.00 Yearly   60c. Six Months   5c, A Copy
Bundle Rates 2½c per copy in bundles of ten.

Reflections

I DO not see how any thoughtful man could witness the spectacle of Congress in the past month or two without having his faith in representative government entirely destroyed. Legislation of the most vital and fundamental character has been passed without even the pretense of getting the consent of the people. Laws affecting the well-being of the nation, aye, the very lives of the citizens, have been put on the statute books without affording the voters an opportunity to voice their sentiments. More than that, representatives and senators have been forced to vote in favor of things in which they do not believe, and to which many of them are even opposed. In this manner war has been declared, and thus conscription and a score of other important laws have been passed, and no one had really anything to say about it except the President and the small clique of Congressional Wall Street heelers.

Talk about democracy! Never in the history of man has there been devised a more subtle snare to throttle the liberty and expression of the people. Behind the mask of American representative popular government, there hides a monster more autocratic and despotic than seen in Russia in the palmiest days of the Romanovs.

There is nothing more criminal than to delude the people with the promise of legislative panaceas. Politics is the game of the masters. The rules of the game are made by themselves, with or without the consent of the people, according as it serves the best interests of the rulers and always is the Law—the tool of oppression.

* * *

PACIFISTS and others claim that the American people do not want war. I do not know whether it is really true. To be sure, they were not consulted. It is also true that the citizens have refused to volunteer, which explains why we have conscription. Yet I do not know whether the people are really opposed to the war strongly enough to refuse to fight.

Wilson and the munition manufacturers cannot fight the war by themselves, nor would they if they could. It takes the mass of population to fight it. It takes, first of all, the labor element to make a war possible. It takes munitions and ships, and even heroes need food. All this neither Teddy nor Woodrow can supply. Labor alone can do it. And evidently Labor is doing it.

If the workers of even one vital industry in this country were honestly and determinedly opposed to war, a hundred proclamations of the President and all the ravings of Congress could not make it a reality. The coal mining industry, for instance. A general strike of the miners would quickly paralyze all the other industries. Neither railroads, factories, nor ships can be run without coal.

Radical leadership could have easily enlightened the toiling masses concerning the plutocratic character of the war. It could have roused the solidarity of Labor throughout the country into a mighty protest that would have shaken the Wilsons out of their military ambitions. It could have demonstrated the effectiveness of direct economic action and the power of united Labor.

But the misleaders of Labor, with Samuel Gompers at their head, have betrayed and sold the workers body and soul. For years they have been training the toilers to be patient with injustice, to be law-abiding in the face of oppression, to be submissive to tyranny and then proudly assert their sovereignty on the Fourth of July and bravely cast a piece of paper into a box on November And when the crisis came and the Wilsonites tried to feel the pulse of the people before plunging the country into war, it was Gompers & Co. that rushed to the rescue of the militarists and pledged the patriotic support of the deluded and exploited laboring masses.

But some day they may awaken—awaken as the people of Russia have, and then the Labor climbers and politicians will loose their throne together with the other uncrowned kings of America.

* * *

THE DREAD "Third Division" of the Russian police department, whose special mission it was to "unearth" or manufacture terrorist plots, is now fortunately defunct—in Russia.

But its spirit seems to have been resurrected in the Secret Service of the Federal government. Think of a Democracy having a secret police service, with almost unlimited power and practically irresponsible to any control by the people!

Back of every revolutionary activity in this country, the American "Third Division" is now "unearthing" dark conspiracies hatched with the aid of Prussian *thalers*. Recently they have arrested in San Francisco a well-known Hindu intellectual, Ram Chandra, and eleven of his comrades, who have for years been carrying on a peaceful agitation for the liberation of their countrymen from the strangle hold of the British government. The prisoners are held incommunicado in the black hole of Federal detective secrecy.

And now word reaches us from the Brothers Magon that three Mexican comrades, Raul Palma, Odilon Luna and Miguel Tari were arrested while addressing a gathering at the Mexican Plaza, the open-air public forum of Los Angeles. Our comrades were brutally beaten by the police and then turned over to the Federal authorities. Palma and Luna are charged with being Anarchists, and by telegraphic order from Washington they have been sentenced to be deported to Mexico, which means certain death for our comrades.

The American "Third Division" should be returned to Russia where they know how to treat such vermin.

* * *

DISCUSSING the Root commission, a humorous Russian said, "The Russians have such a primitive way of burial; Root should have taken along an American undertaker."

Figuratively, my friend undoubtedly voiced the sentiments of the Russian Revolutionists. Root is well-known and as thoroughly hated by the radicals of Russia as by those of his native country. It was certainly stupid on the part of Wilson to send to Russia a representative whose irrepressible reactionary character is well calculated to antagonize the Revolutionary elements of Russia. Stupid and yet fitting, for Root is the most class-conscious representative of the American plutocracy, whose interests he is to further in Russia.

In the same spirit the Washington authorities have refused to issue passports to the American Socialists who were to go as delegates to the Stockholm Convention. The action of the government is no doubt in the highest degree autocratic, yet I rather welcome it. It will serve to enlighten the Stockholm conferees how much more liberal are the monarchs of Europe than the autocrat of America. Most important of all, the Russian delegates will carry convincing proof to their people of the menace and snare of democratic "liberty" in America.

Wilson and Lansing may have unwittingly helped to clarify the true character of the American government to the people of Russia. It may help them to see through the *mirage* of representative government and strengthen them in the determination not to follow in false footsteps, to ignore precedent and to hew their own path in consonance with the instinctive communistic tendencies of the people and the Russian anarchic spirit of liberty and independence.

RUSSIAN exiles by the hundreds are returning from America to their native land. It saddens us to part with them, especially at this crucial moment when true revolutionists are so scarce and yet so badly needed in this benighted country. Yet we are glad that our friends are returning home. Russia is going through the pangs of a new birth. It needs the aid of clear-sighted men and women, of big, courageous souls, the chanteclers of the New Day. Heartily we bid them good speed, and may they energetically help the rebels of Russia to clear away the debris of the old, destroy all that is false and rotten, however democratic in appearance. The Revolution will have been in vain if it will permit old injustice and oppression to survive, though under high-sounding, pleasing "republican" mottoes of Justice, Equality and Fraternity. Away with all sham and pretense! Not a single limb of the thousand headed hydra of government and capitalism must remain intact if Russia is to be really free. No master, no exploiter—that is the only solution, the sole guarantee of liberty, peace and well-being.

* * *

NO FINER spirit of solidaric understanding has ever been shown by American labor than that evidenced by the total suspension of work by the toilers of Seattle, Wash., on May 1, in protest against the Mooney verdict. It lasted only 10 minutes, but it was a golden ten minutes that radiated the deepest understanding and finest comradeship.

It is very likely that this action, and the First of May street demonstration with the members of the Union of Russian workers carrying the red flag, had a good effect upon the trial of the I. W. W.'s in Seattle. At any rate, Tom Tracy, the first of the defendants to be tried, was acquitted and all the other prisoners released without bail.

A similar attitude on the part of the workers of San Francisco would soon open the prison gates to Mooney, Mrs. Mooney, Billings and Weinberg. California labor owes it to them, for it is the cowardly silence of the San Francisco unions that is primarily responsible for the conviction of Billings and Mooney. Had the unions from the very start made a protest against the palpable frame-up, the Fickerts and Swansons would have never dared to go as far as they did. The deliberate silence and in some cases the tacit approval of the District Attorney by the rotten politicians of the San Francisco unions, directly encouraged the fiendish plot of the prosecution.

Not even when Mooney was sentenced to death, on evidently perjured testimony, did the bigwigs of labor show the least interest. But when the whole frame-up was exposed so that even some capitalistic papers in the East became aroused over the attempted judicial murders of innocent workers, then at last the leaders of the S. F. Labor Council and of the Building Trades Council were forced to pale action. But they alone may now not be able to save Mooney and his co-defendants. The thing has gone too far. Though the entire frame-up is exposed, and the whole mur-

derous clique—the Chamber of Commerce and its hirelings Fickert, Cunha, Oxman, et al—are convicted of perjury and subornation of perjury—it does not matter. The beast is holding on to its prey, aye, tightening its clutches. Tom Mooney is still under sentence of death, with no new trial granted. Indeed, they have had the brazen effrontery to bring Mrs. Rena Mooney to trial!

It seems unbelievable, yet it is true. The very District Attorney who has been plotting in cold blood to commit judicial murder, is the official prosecutor of Rena Mooney! And the people of San Francisco actually permit this fiendish outrage, this Satan's play, to continue! It were better that not a soul had escaped from the earthquake and fire that destroyed the city in 1906!

There is no hope in San Francisco. If these labor martyrs are to be saved, the workers throughout the country will have to act, at once, and in no uncertain manner. The following telegram, just received from San Francisco, states the situation clearly:

Superior Court to-day held Oxman for trial, Chief Justice Angelotti said evidence of Oxman's guilt overwhelming. Special committee appointed by San Francisco Labor Council and Building Trade Council appeared in person before Att'y Gen. Webb, requesting answer on his disposition of Judge Griffin's request, confessing error in my case. Att'y General said that the records did not show error and it would be impossible to confess same. Powerful publicity, monster demonstrations absolutely necessary for successful outcome. California lynch law crowd fighting desperately to save themselves. This precludes a new trial unless the unforeseen happens.

Give these facts widest publicity.

TOM MOONEY.

The Shame of California
Robert Minor

THERE is not the slightest doubt that within ten years the entire press and public of America, however steeped in hate and prejudice against the class known as the "labor agitator," will admit that the prosecution of the Mooneys, Nolan, Weinberg and Billings in San Francisco was the most shameless crime of the century. For the record is indelible and so indisputable that even in this day of hot-headed controversy there is no one so brazen as to attempt a defensive explanation of the perjury conspiracy against the labor defendants. The trapped, branded and proven perjurers and suborners that have given San Francisco the name of a village of thugs will within a decade be universally referred to as the classis scoundrels of the city's history.

But why must we wait until the shame is made complete? Why must San Francisco in future years blush for the crime of hired public murder consummated, instead of merely to blush for the plot uncovered and stamped out? It is the fault of human cowardice.

Yes, the hanging of the labor prisoners proceeds without hesitation. Tom Mooney remains under the shadow of the gallows. His principal murderer-by-perjury has been as thoroughly shown up as ever man was. Two of the next most important of the witnesses of the State have confessed that they lied his life away.

Frank C. Oxman, the "honest cattleman from Oregon," has lost his appeal to the Supreme Court of California on writ of habeas corpus to escape prosecution for his letters offering to pay for perjury against Mooney. He is to be tried for the felony.

Mrs. Mellie Edeau and her daughter Sadie have been visited by attorneys for Mooney in company with Chief of

Police Peterson and Police Inspector Smith, of Oakland. Mrs. Edeau admitted to all of them that she had first reported seeing "two old men with a black suitcase—two very old, feeble men—at the corner of Steuart and Market street," and that she had called at the jail in San Francisco to see Mooney and Billings and reported positively that they were not the men she saw. When she later learned that Estelle Smith was going to win a large reward for saying Billings and Mooney were at 721 Market street, she changed her story. Asked why she did this, Mrs. Edeau first took a revolver and tried to shoot attorney O'Connor and then explained that "her soul told her Billings was guilty." "When I saw the brown eyes of my dear dead husband," said Mrs. Edeau, "I knew I must do it."

Yet, the prosecutor for the Chamber of Commerce does not ask that Mooney be given a new trial. Instead, he is now trying to hang Rena Mooney and has announced that FRANK C. OXMAN WILL BE USED AS A WITNESS AGAINST HER. Doubtless the Edeau woman will be used, also.

THE selection of jurors is now going on. The prosecutors are asking prospective jurymen "Are you prejudiced against giving the death penalty to a woman on circumstantial evidence?" Of course the jurors are not.

It is hard to predict just how the Chamber of Commerce will present its case. But, judging from the past, they will bring out a new corps of witnesses whose records and inducements have not been exposed. They have done this twice before.

The Chamber of Commerce of San Francisco is making anarchists faster than Alexander Berkman is. Labor at last has its eyes fastened upon the Pacific Coast crime. Labor will understand this case, and that is more important, Tom Mooney says, than to save their lives.

Never has there been so clear a lesson. There are a few who have learned. Tragedies of this kind bring out the qualities of men in places where they are least expected to understand. We all remember a man that was called "Governor Altgeld of Illinois," who, in 1893 was enrolled on the books of history as "Altgeld, the Man." There are signs of the making of one or two more Men in this California tragedy.

For, despite every power of vice, greed and vengeance, Franklin A. Griffin, the judge who sentenced Mooney to death, is now working his hardest to undo the wrong. A police judge, Mathew Brady, has also disobeyed orders from the Chamber of Commerce. He has held the honest perjurer from Oregon to answer for his crime against Mooney. Brady has resisted as fierce an onslaught as ever a man braved.

As a result of Brady's stand, insisting on holding Oxman in spite of the plea of the shameless prosecutor that he had no case against Oxman, his own perjury accomplice, even the Court of Appeal and the Supreme Court have had to verify the truth.

Attorney General Webb, however, refused at first to even answer a letter from the Labor Council asking why he does not immediately confess error and give Mooney a new trial. When waited upon by a committee from all the State and City Labor Organizations, the attorney general was evasive and points out that a technicality stands in the way of releasing Mooney from the death grip of the Frame-Up Ring. (RESPECT THE LAW, OH WORKERS!)

The attorney general, however, let a cat out of the bag in excusing himself for not answering the Labor Council letter. He explained that he is flooded with similar letters and telegrams from all over the United States in such volume that he cannot answer them. Labor organizations comprising millions in their membership have hounded him with the pertinent question.

If Tom Mooney hangs, Labor will know why. If Rena Mooney is convicted, Labor will know why. That is the important thing.

The Breaking of the Ice

WE are in Russia. The Neva is frozen. Heavy carriages roll upon its surface. They improvise a city. They lay out streets. They build houses. They buy. They sell. They laugh. They dance. They permit themselves anything. They even light fires on this water become granite. There is winter, there is ice, and they shall last forever. A gleam pale and wan spreads over the sky, and one would say that the sun is dead. But no, thou art not dead, oh Liberty! At an hour when they have most profoundly forgotten thee; at a moment when they least expect thee, thou shalt arise, dazzling sight! Thou shalt shoot thy bright and burning rays, thy heat, thy life, on all this mass of ice become hideous and dead. Do you hear that dull thud, that crackling, deep and dreadful? 'Tis the Neva tearing loose. You said it was granite. See, it splits like grass. 'Tis the breaking of the ice, I tell you. 'Tis the water alive, joyous and terrible. Progress recommences. 'Tis humanity again beginning its march. 'Tis the river which retakes its course, uproots, mangles, strikes together, crushes and drowns in its waves not only the empire of upstart Czar Nicholas, but all of the relics of ancient and modern despotism. That trestle work floating away? It is the throne. That other trestle? It is the scaffold. That old book, half sunk? It is the old code of capitalist laws and morals. That old rookery just sinking? It is a tenement house in which wage slaves lived. See these all pass by; passing by never more to return; and for this immense engulfing, for this supreme victory of life over death, what has been the power necessary? One of thy looks, O Sun! **One stroke of thy strong arm, O Labor!**

The Cry of the Nations
Edward Carpenter

LIKE a great cry these words today rise from the lips of the nations—"Never Again!" Never before certainly have such enormous masses of human beings been locked in deadly grip with each other over the earth, and never before, equally certainly, has their warfare been so horrible in its deliberate preparation, so hideous, so ghastly in its after effects, as today. The nations stand round paralyzed with disgust and despair, almost unable to articulate; and when they do find voice it is with the words above written. How are we to give effect to the cry? Must we not call upon the workers of all countries—those who are the least responsible for the inception of wars, and yet who suffer most by them, who bear the brunt of the wounds, the slaughter, the disease and the misery which are a necessary part of them—to rise up and forbid them for ever from the earth? Let us do so! For though few may follow and join with us today, yet tomorrow and every day in the future, and every year, as the mass-peoples come into their own, and to the knowledge of what they are and what they desire to be, those numbers will increase, till the cry itself

Eight   THE BLAST

is no longer a mere cry but an accomplished fact. It is a hopeful sign that not only among bewildered onlookers and outsiders but among the soldiers themselves (of the more civilized countries) this cry is being taken up. Who, indeed, should know better than they what they are talking about? The same words are on the lips at this moment of thousands of French and English and German and Russian soldiers, and in no faint-hearted or evasive sense, but with the conviction and indignation of experience. We may hope they will not be forgotten this time when the war is over.

. . . . I certainly would say—as indeed the peasant says in every land—"Let those who begin the quarrel do the fighting"; and let those who have to do the fighting and bear the brunt of it (including the women) decide whether there *shall* be fighting or not. To leave the dread arbitrament of war in the hands of private groups and cliques who, for their own ends and interests, are willing to see the widespread slaughter of their fellow countrymen and the ruin of innumerable homes, is hateful beyond words.

Army Recruiting Methods

Maxwell Bodenheim

ON ONE of the busiest street corners of New York stands an open-air army recruiting-station. As I passed by, a young corporal with a megaphone was screaming to a fairly-large crowd of jocund, carefully-dressed idlers, contented-faced, elaborately-covered women, stiff-eyed clerks, and shiny, heavily-cherubic business men.

I stopped to listen.

He raised up the flag beside him.

"All those who honor this emblem of united democracy —this emblem that has always been carried to glorious victory—take off your hats!"

Every man in the crowd instantly removed his hat. Even some of the women indecisively plucked at their fashionable hats, for a moment, and then reconsidered the matter.

The corporal made the usual impressive pause.

"Now" he shouted. "All those who honor our president for the courageous stand he has taken in defense of humanity and democracy, say aye!"

The crowd promptly shouted, in response.

Another theatrical pause from the corporal.

"Now! All those who are willing to shoulder a gun and support our president in his glorious stand—all those who are willing to serve in the United States Army, step forward!"

Nobody stepped forward. Ten seconds passed by—still nobody stepped forward. The hat-snatching and the shouting had been easy, and had stimulated the crowd to a pleasant sense of righteousness. But the command to join the army was like a dash of mountain-brook water. Everybody stood nervously, perplexedly.

It was the noon-hour, and their shops and offices were insidiously beckoning to them. Or, perhaps, it was shopping and theatre-matinees, to those who toiled not with their hands.

The change from high-sounding phrase to ugly reality gave these people the reaction of bewildered children. They must have obviously known what the climax of the corporal's talk would be, but they had expected an indirect appeal instead of a straight challenge. They squirmed about, miserably. They were all unconscious traitors—according to the strict law of the land they should all have been immediately

arrested. They all stood there, suddenly realizing how much they liked their peaceful lives. . .

The corporal went on, passing smoothly into a scourging of the Kaiser. I looked about me, and saw men sighing relievedly. Soon the crowd recovered its shattered composure, and settled down to eager listening and quick applause.

A militia lieutenant took the stand. He spoke of his wife and mother—how they had blessed him for giving up a lucrative position and joining his command. He spoke of the men who, he claimed, had rushed to the marriage license bureau when war was declared, and he smothered them with indignation. He blessed all women, and said that if the law permitted, an army of them could be raised in a week.

(This last statement awoke the men in the crowd to a sense of indulgent admiration, and they glanced approvingly at the smartly-gowned women beside them, while the women broadly smiled.)

He gave no serious, logical, patriotic argument, but seemed to place his entire dependence upon obvious sentimentality.

He talked for ten minutes. Then he suddenly pointed a finger at the crowd.

"You! You two men back there, what are you smiling about? If you think this is a show, get out of here! Take those grins off your faces!"

A seargent and two privates hurried at once through the crowd, to the two men.

The men frightenedly expostulated, and said that their smiles had been innocent.

The seargent would have no explanations.

"The lieutenant wouldn't a' spoken to you, if you had'nt had a nasty expression on your faces!" he thundered.

Has some new law been passed, making it treason to smile? And in what way can it be determined, at a distance, whether a smile is one of hearty approval, or humorous contempt?

These are interesting questions, and to me they seem difficult ones. But army officers find them very simple.

AK Press Titles

Books

AK Press Titles

ANONYMOUS . . . . *Test Card F*

CLASS WAR FEDERATION . . . . *Unfinished Business: The Politics of Class War*

DARK STAR COLLECTIVE . . . . *Beneath the Paving Stones: Situationists and the Beach, May 68*

DARK STAR COLLECTIVE . . . . *Quiet Rumours: An Anarcha-Feminist Reader*

HELLO . . . . *2/15: The Day The World Said NO To War*

CDs

THE EX. . . . . *1936: The Spanish Revolution*

MUMIA ABU JAMAL . . . . *175 Progress Drive*

MUMIA ABU JAMAL . . . . *All Things Censored Vol. 1*

MUMIA ABU JAMAL . . . . *Spoken Word*

FREEDOM ARCHIVES. . . . . *Chile: Promise of Freedom*

FREEDOM ARCHIVES. . . . . *Prisons on Fire: George Jackson, Attica & Black Liberation*

JUDI BARI . . . . *Who Bombed Judi Bari?*

JELLO BIAFRA. . . . . *Become the Media*

JELLO BIAFRA. . . . . *Beyond The Valley of the Gift Police*

JELLO BIAFRA. . . . . *High Priest of Harmful*

JELLO BIAFRA. . . . . *I Blow Minds For A Living*

JELLO BIAFRA. . . . . *If Evolution Is Outlawed*

JELLO BIAFRA. . . . . *Machine Gun In The Clown's Hand*

JELLO BIAFRA. . . . . *No More Cocoons*

NOAM CHOMSKY . . . . *American Addiction, An*

NOAM CHOMSKY . . . . *Case Studies in Hypocrisy*

NOAM CHOMSKY . . . . *Emerging Framework of World Power*

NOAM CHOMSKY . . . . *Free Market Fantasies*

NOAM CHOMSKY . . . . *Imperial Democracy, The*

NOAM CHOMSKY . . . . *New War On Terrorism: Fact And Fiction*

NOAM CHOMSKY . . . . *Propaganda and Control of the Public Mind*

NOAM CHOMSKY . . . . *Prospects for Democracy*

NOAM CHOMSKY & . . . . *For A Free Humanity: For Anarchy*
CHUMBAWAMBA

WARD CHURCHILL. . . . . *Doing Time: The Politics of Imprisonment*

WARD CHURCHILL. . . . . *In A Pig's Eye: Reflections on the Police State, Repression, and Native America*

WARD CHURCHILL. . . . . *Life in Occupied America*

WARD CHURCHILL. . . . . *Pacifism and Pathology in the American Left*

ALEXANDER COCKBURN . . . . *Beating the Devil: The Incendiary Rants of Alexander Cockburn*

ANGELA DAVIS. . . . . *Prison Industrial Complex, The*

NORMAN FINKELSTEIN . . . . *An Issue of Justice: Origins of the Israel/Palestine Conflict*

AK Press Titles

JAMES **KELMAN** . . . . *Seven Stories*
TOM **LEONARD** . . . . *Nora's Place and Other Poems 1965–99*
CASEY **NEILL** . . . . *Memory Against Forgetting*
CHRISTIAN **PARENTI** . . . . *Taking Liberties: Policing, Prisons and Surveillance in an Age of Crisis*
UTAH **PHILLIPS** . . . . *I've Got To know*
UTAH **PHILLIPS** . . . . *Starlight on the Rails: A Songbook*
DAVID **ROVICS** . . . . *Behind the Barricades: Best of David Rovics*
ARUNDHATI **ROY** . . . . *Come September*
ROBERT F. **WILLIAMS** . . . . *Self-Defense, Self-Respect & Self-Determination*
HOWARD **ZINN** . . . . *Artists In A Time of War*
HOWARD **ZINN** . . . . *Heroes and Martyrs: Emma Goldman, Sacco & Vanzetti, and the Revolutionary Struggle*
HOWARD **ZINN** . . . . *People's History of the United States: A Lecture at Reed College, A*
HOWARD **ZINN** . . . . *People's History Project*
HOWARD **ZINN** . . . . *Stories Hollywood Never Tells*
VARIOUS . . . . *Better Read Than Dead*
VARIOUS . . . . *Less Rock, More Talk*
VARIOUS . . . . *Mob Action Against the State: Collected Speeches from the Bay Area Anarchist Bookfair*
VARIOUS . . . . *Monkeywrenching the New World Order*
VARIOUS . . . . *Return of the Read Menace*

DVDs

NOAM **CHOMSKY** . . . . *Distorted Morality*
NOAM **CHOMSKY** . . . . *Imperial Grand Strategy*
ARUNDHATI **ROY** . . . . *Instant Mix Imperial Democracy*
HOWARD **ZINN** & . . . . *Readings from "Voices of a People's History of the United States"*
   ANTHONY **ARNOVE**